Edmund Martin Geldart

A Guide to modern Greek

Edmund Martin Geldart

A Guide to modern Greek

ISBN/EAN: 9783743331037

Manufactured in Europe, USA, Canada, Australia, Japa

Cover: Foto ©Lupo / pixelio.de

Manufactured and distributed by brebook publishing software (www.brebook.com)

Edmund Martin Geldart

A Guide to modern Greek

CONTENTS.

	PAGE
INTRODUCTION	v
PLAN OF THE WORK	xi

PART I.

ALPHABET, PRONUNCIATION, ETC.	1
TABLE OF CHANGES IN ARYAN LANGUAGES . . .	11
MR. SUSAMÁKIS' EVENING PARTY (analyzed and explained in fourteen lessons)	12

PART II.

A JOURNEY TO GREECE (Dialogues)	128

PART III.

A CLASSIFIED VOCABULARY	152

PART IV.

ACCIDENCE	212
SYNTAX	249
APPENDIX (Correspondence)	257

INTRODUCTION.

THE Modern Greek language is the direct descendant of the language of the Byzantine or Eastern Roman Empire (whence its name Romaic), as this was immediately developed from the Alexandrine Greek, or "common dialect," resulting from a blending and merging of all the various Greek dialects when the ascendency of the Macedonian king and conqueror, Alexander the Great, united the various tribes of Greece, and spread their language as the medium of intercommunication among the subjugated populations of his enormous empire. Although the political supremacy of Greece, even in its comparatively bastard Macedonian and Byzantine forms, in which, however, alone it can ever be said to have existed as a united and powerful nationality, has long been a thing of the past, the inherent vitality, and vigour, and self-recreating power of the Greek language have never waned, and in the present day Greek performs much the same office, as the language of the most thriving commercial race in the East, that it did in the days of Alexander's successors. The subjects of free Greece—two millions and a half of souls—are but a fraction of the Greek-speaking population of the East. In the days of Mezzofanti, at the beginning of this century, Greek was still commonly spoken among the remnants of the ancient Greek colonies on the coast of Calabria, part of the old *Magna Græcia* in Italy; and even in Sardinia, it is said, there are still Greek-speaking colonies. But however this may be, *Magna Græcia*, "Great Greece," is still outside the limits of "Little" or "Free Greece." In Bulgaria, in Albania (the ancient Macedonia and Epirus), in Thessaly (which was part of Ancient Greece), in all the islands east of Greece in the Mediterranean Sea, on the coasts as well as far inland in Asia Minor and in Egypt, in many parts of Palestine and Syria, indeed throughout the dominions of Turkey, Greek is the one language which is almost everywhere spoken and understood. A person with a competent knowledge of Modern Greek may travel nearly anywhere in the East without invoking the aid of that most terrible institution of modern tourism, the dragoman, who, by the way, is generally a Greek. This alone is a fact which has only to become duly known and appreciated in order to secure for Greek a foremost place among the modern languages which the ubiquitous English traveller is, or ought to be, anxious to acquire.

But it has another, and, if possible, a still stronger recommendation to our notice. Ten years ago I stated in my book "The Modern Greek Language in its relation to Ancient Greek" (published by the Clarendon Press, Oxford, in 1870), that "Modern Greek is nothing but Ancient Greek made easy." Constant study and converse with Greeks since that period have but served to confirm me in the opinion that that statement is literally correct. But if so, what follows? Why, that the study of Modern Greek is the true key to the mastery of the classical idiom. This view has been directly or indirectly advocated by some of the foremost educationalists in England. The late John Stuart Mill, in his Rectorial address to the students of the University of St. Andrew's, referring to the growing discontent that so much valuable time was wasted at our schools and universities in learning, or too often not learning, Latin and Greek— time which might otherwise be saved for the study of natural science and other essential branches of a liberal education—rightly vindicated the claims of the classics to a prominent place in higher education, not as against, but alongside of, the so-called modern subjects. Why, he pertinently asked, should not time be found for both? And he lays the fault of the dilemma, in which those are placed who in regard to these conflicting claims feel inclined to say in the words of the popular song—

> "How happy could I be with either,
> Were t'other dear charmer away!"

on the execrably bad system of teaching the classics which prevails amongst us, and which, after consuming four-fifths of the entire time at the disposal of a schoolboy in Latin and Greek, afterwards sends him out into the world not only unable for the most part to take up an easy classic, and read him for pleasure and for profit, but often imbued with a thorough disgust for classical literature. "Why," says Mill, "should not Latin and Greek be taught like any other language? Why should not a man learn the classics as he would learn his mother tongue?" Why, indeed, except perhaps for the obvious reason that it is only within the last few years that even modern languages have been taught on a rational system, or like our "mother tongue." Still, since the days of Pestalozzi and Fröbel, among all intelligent educationalists the belief has been gaining ground, that the only true method of teaching, both morally and intellectually, is to proceed from the known to the unknown, and not from the unknown to the known; that the learner should be dealt with not as a parrot, but as a human being; that, e. g. we should begin the study of history with the reign of Queen Victoria, and not with the creation of the world; and so on with other subjects.

In accordance with these principles it is well worth consideration whether the student of Latin ought not in England to begin with French, and thence proceed to the cognate and more archaic Romance dialects, as Portuguese, Spanish, Italian, Roumanian, and so on; thence to the older Norman and Provençal, and from them through the later Latin of the period of the decline to the Latin of the Augustan era. Else, to be consistent, why begin with Sallust rather than with Oscan and Umbrian, or the Salian hymns?

But as regards Greek the problem is immensely simplified. Ancient Greek has but one modern representative, which is spoken with comparatively insignificant variations throughout Turkey, Greece, and the Levant. Whoever is thoroughly conversant with Modern Greek will find no more difficulty in reading the Greek Fathers and the New Testament, than an Englishman of the nineteenth century finds in understanding Spenser. The passage from the New Testament or Septuagint to Xenophon is incomparably easier than that from Spenser to Chaucer; and from Xenophon to Thucydides, from Thucydides to the Tragedians, from them to Herodotus, and from Herodotus to Homer, is far more simple than would be the somewhat analogous transition in English from Chaucer to Piers Plowman, from Piers Plowman to Layamon and Ormin, from them to the Anglo-Saxon of King Alfred, and from the Saxon of King Alfred to the Gothic of Ulfilas.

Indeed, the change which has passed upon the Greek language since Homer's age is so very much slighter than that which English has undergone in the far shorter period intervening between the times of the Saxon kings and the present reign, that there are whole lines of Homer which would scarcely require the alteration of a word to convert them into idiomatic Modern Greek; for example, Il. A. 334 :—

$$\text{Χαίρετε, κήρυκες Διὸς ἄγγελοι ἠδὲ καὶ ἀνδρῶν}$$

where only the word ἠδὲ is not good Modern Greek, although χαίρετε means now rather "good-bye" than "hail," and ἄγγελοι rather "angels" than simply "messengers." In line 362 of the same book the question τέκνον τί κλαίεις; is good Modern Greek. Far less is the difference when we come to Plato, the first words of whose Republic: κατέβην χθὲς εἰς [τὸν] Πειραιᾶ μετὰ Γλαύκωνος τοῦ Ἀρίστωνος, with the single addition of the definite article, which need not have been omitted, might be heard any day in the streets of Athens in the year 1883.

Greek, then, is essentially a living language—the language, unchanged in its main features, of Aristotle, Xenophon, and Demosthenes—and there is no reason why it should not be taught as such. It is impossible to draw any such rigid line of demarcation between Modern and Ancient Greek, as between the language of ancient

Rome and the modern Latin or Romance languages, inasmuch as Greece never suffered that complete break-up of its grammar which befell the Latin language on the dissolution of the Roman Empire. When the scholar has become thoroughly familiar with the Modern Greek declension and conjugation, which for the most part are identical with the classical forms, so far as they go, it will be an easy step to add the dual number, the archaic conjugation in -$\mu\iota$, the perfect tense, and the extended use of case-endings and infinitive moods, almost all of which survive, or have been revived, in isolated phrases even in Modern Greek.

Perhaps in no department of classical learning will the benefit of Modern Greek be more apparent than with regard to accentuation. The rules of prosody are learnt at Eton, Rugby, Harrow, and all our great public schools; rules which are numerous and intricate enough in all conscience, but few and simple by comparison with their exceptions. And what is the result? After seven or eight years' hard study, scarcely the most eminent of living Greek scholars unacquainted with Modern Greek is able to write from memory a single sentence in Greek without the accents being at fault. Let a man be accustomed from the first never to pronounce a single Greek word without its appropriate accent, and he will never be in doubt how to write it, or "hardly ever;" the cases where he might hesitate between a circumflex and an acute being very soon mastered when not only the ear, but the eye and ear together are exercised by writing and reading aloud with due regard to the accent.

PLAN OF THE FOLLOWING WORK.

THE First Part, after discussing the alphabet and pronunciation, contains a story from common life, "Mr. Susamákis' Evening Party,"[1] which has been chosen as embodying in its narrative a fair illustration of the literary form of Modern Greek, while its dialogue represents the more colloquial vernacular. Each word and sentence as it comes is grammatically analyzed, repetition being for the most part avoided. When the student has worked diligently through this portion, he will find himself in possession of the main features of Modern Greek accidence and syntax, not learned by rote, as is usually the case, but gathered by actual experience. In the earlier lessons a transliteration is interlined, to facilitate pronunciation; this is dispensed with later on. The idiomatic translation also given with the earlier lessons is dropped when the student may be presumed to have gained an insight into the general structure of the language. At the end of each lesson an exercise, based on the principle of "ringing the changes" on the words and phrases occurring in previous lessons, is added.

In addition to the grammatical analysis, considerable space is allotted to the indication of the philological affinities of each word as it occurs, wherever these are so apparent as to be placed beyond the field of mere conjecture. The comparisons are confined as far as possible to English and those languages with which the average student may be expected to have some

[1] The Greek text of the above is taken from Dr. Daniel Sanders' "Neugriechische Grammatik," founded on Messrs. Vincent and Dickson's "Handbook to Modern Greek." The author is Angelos Vláchos.

acquaintance. Apart from the interest attaching to such investigations, it is believed they will form a most valuable "memoria technica." It is always easier to remember two things than one, provided there is any rational link of association between them. In this part of the work I have followed (when in doubt) that sound and cautious philologist, Georg Curtius, in his "Grundzüge der griechischen Etymologie," 3rd ed., Leipzig, 1869. In order that the reader may see on what principle such comparisons are founded, and may know beforehand what sounds to expect as the representatives of the Greek in the various cognate languages, I have appended a table showing the regular changes which the sounds of words undergo in passing from one language to another of the Aryan family of speech.

Part II. consists of dialogues, to which I have attempted to supply a continuous chain of interest by supposing them to take place on a journey to Greece. In order to relieve the strain which a lengthened perusal of dialogues sometimes occasions, I have shifted the Greek and English respectively from right to left and from left to right, without notice.

Part III. consists of a classified vocabulary, borrowed in the main from the excellent Modern Greek Grammar of Antonios Jeannarakis ("Neugriechische Grammatik nebst Lehrbuch der neugriechischen Volkssprache und einem methodischen Wörteranhang, von Antonios Jeannarakis," Hannover, Hahn'sche Buchhandlung, 1877).

Part IV. is an attempt to summarize in a simple form what the student will by the time he has worked through Parts I. to III. actually have learned by practice. This part will be published in a separate form among the series of "Simplified Grammars" commenced by the late lamented Professor E. H. Palmer, and published by Messrs. Trübner. His own Simplified Grammars of Hindoostanee, Persian, and Arabic have been of invaluable use to me as models in the preparation of this portion of the work.

A GUIDE TO MODERN GREEK.

PART I.

The Alphabet.

§ **1.** The Greek alphabet of to-day consists of the following letters, the names of which, to be pronounced as far as possible in English fashion, we have given under each character :—

A α	B β ϐ	Γ γ	Δ δ	E ϵ
Ah'lfah.	Vee'tah.	Ghah'mah.	Dheh'ltah.	Eh'pseelon.
Z ζ	H η	Θ θ ϑ	I ι	K κ
Zee'tah.	Ee'tah.	Thee'tah.	Eeaw'tah.	Kah'pah.
Λ λ	M μ	N ν	Ξ ξ	O o
Lah'mvdhah.	Mee.	Nee.	Ksee.	Aw'meekron.
Π π	P ρ	Σ σ ς	T τ	Υ υ
Pee.	Raw.	See'ghmah.	Tahv.	Ee'pseelon.
Φ φ	X χ	Ψ ψ	Ω ω	
Fee.	Khee.	Psee.	Awmeh'ghah.	

The letter Ϝ (*ϐαῦ, vahv*), pronounced as β, is only used in ancient (pre-classical) Greek words.

§ 2. Of these letters, α, ε, η, ι, ο, υ, ω, are vowels (φωνήεντα, *faunee'ehnda*), while the rest are consonants (σύμφωνα, *see'mfawnah*); and two of the vowels, ι and υ, have, in certain positions, a consonantal or quasi-consonantal value.

Vowels.

§ 3. A sounds always as the English interjection *ah!* by which syllable we shall always represent it.

E is like the sound of the English interjection *eh!* but rather broader, with a slight inclination to the sound of *a* in *that*. We shall represent it by *eh*. The nearest approximation in English to the exact sound is that of *a* in *care*. Our sound *ai* or *ay* in *day*, *chaise*, &c., has an *ee* sound at the end, which must be specially avoided in pronouncing ε.

H, I, and Y are phonetically equivalent, though etymologically distinct; they all sound like *ee* in *see*, and we shall represent them accordingly.

O and Ω are also indistinguishable in sound. Originally ω was a long or double *o*. At present, when either stands last in a syllable, it has a tendency to be sounded somewhat longer than when followed in the same syllable by a consonant; and this applies more or less to all the vowels. O and ω both sound like *oa* in *broad*, *o* in *lord*, or *aw* in *saw*. We shall represent them uniformly by *aw*.

Diphthongs.

§ 4. Although etymologically diphthong means "doublesound" (Greek, δίφθογγος, *dhee'fthawngawss*), most of the diphthongs at present, as already in the age of Greek grammarians of the Roman period, stand for a single vowel sound, while a few represent a vowel sound followed by that of a consonant. They are as follows:—

Αι sounded as ε in Greek, represented like that letter by *eh* in English.

Ει
Οι } all sounded as ι or η; represented by *ee*.
Υι

Ου sounds like *oo* in *mood*, and will be represented accordingly.

Αυ sounds as *ahv*, except before θ, κ, ξ, π, σ, τ, φ, χ, ψ, when it sounds as *ahf*.

Ευ sounds, under the same conditions as the foregoing, *ehv* and *ehf* respectively.

Ηυ as *eev* or *eef*, according to circumstances.

Besides the diphthongs proper, there are three so-called improper diphthongs (δίφθογγοι καταχρηστικαί, *dhee'fthawngee kahtahkhreesteekeh'*), viz. ᾳ, ῃ, ῳ, in which the letter ι (*eeaw'tah*) is simply written under the vowel in question, but not pronounced.

CONSONANTS.

§ 5. These are divided into simple and compound.

The simple consonants are classified in two ways; first, according to the organs by which they are pronounced, as—

(*a*) Lip-letters: β, π, φ, μ.
(*b*) Tongue-letters: δ, ζ, τ, θ, ν, λ, ρ, σ.
(*c*) Gutturals: γ, κ, χ.

Secondly, according to their qualities, as—

(*a*) Liquids: λ, μ, ν, ρ.
(*b*) Sibilants: ζ, σ.
(*c*) Spirants: either (α) sharp, as φ, χ, θ, or (β) soft, as β, γ, δ.
(*d*) Hard Explodents (*tenues*): as π, κ, τ.

The true *medials* or soft explodents are only heard when π, κ, and τ are found in combination with μ and ν.

The compound or double consonants are:—

ψ, which stands for βσ, πσ, or φσ; and
ξ, which stands for γσ, κσ, or χσ.

With regard to the pronunciation of the consonants the reader should observe—

Β sounds as *v* in English.

Γ sounds as a rule like German *g* in *Tag, lag*, i. e. it is the guttural spirant, just as β is the labial. We shall represent it by *gh*.

Before the vowels ε, η, and ι, or their equivalents among the diphthongs, however, γ has the sound of *y* in *year*; while γγ sounds as *ng* in the words *anger, longer, stronger, linger*, &c., never as the mere guttural *n* in *singer, ringer*, &c. This direction will be of little use to North Country people, as they constantly confound these perfectly distinct sounds. A further modification of the sound of γ occurs when γγ is followed by ι, η, ε, or their equivalents; in this case the sound of the last γ is slightly palatalized, and may be best described as halfway between *g* and *j*. We shall represent it by an upright letter, to distinguish it from the surrounding italics, or *vice versâ*; thus ἄγγιστρον, ah'ng*geestrawn*, 'a hook;' ἀγγεῖον, ah*nggee'awn*, 'a vessel.'

Δ sounds as the English *th* in *then, thither, this, that*, and all the pronouns and pronominal adverbs in which it occurs. We shall represent it by *dh*.

Ζ is the English *z*, and will be so represented.

Θ is the English *th* in *thin, thorough, thousand*, &c. We shall represent it by *th*.

Κ is the English *k*, save before the vowels ε, η, ι, and their equivalents, where it has a slightly palatal sound inclining to *ch* in *church*, but stopping a good way short of it, except in the Cretan and some other dialects, where it is completely transformed into the English *ch*, like the Italian *c* in similar circumstances. We shall represent this modification, as in the case of γ, by an upright letter in the midst of italics, as καιρός, k*ehraw'ss*, 'time;' Κύριος, k*ee'reeawss*, 'Mr.,' 'Lord.' Besides this it is to be noted that γκ is phonetically equivalent in all respects to γγ.

Λ is the English *l*, but before ι, η, υ, &c., it sounds almost as *ly*, i. e. *ll* in Spanish, *lh* in Portuguese. We shall represent it by an upright letter in the midst of italics, and *vice versâ*; e. g. λύσω, *lee'ssaw*, 'I may loose.'

M is equivalent to English *m*. It cannot stand as the last letter in a word.

N is like *n* in English, but subject to the same modification as λ under like conditions. This will be indicated in our transliteration in the same manner, e. g. νῦν, *neen*, 'now.'

Ξ is pronounced as English *x* in *six*, except when preceded by ν, written γ, in which case it is sounded *gz*, or like *x* in *example*; e. g. ξένος, *xeh'nawss*, 'a stranger,' 'guest;' but σφιγξὶν, *sfeengzee'n*, 'to sphinxes.'

Π is sounded as *p* in English, except when preceded by μ, when it sounds as *b*; e. g. παρά, *pahrah'*, 'by,' 'than;' but ἔμπορος, *eh'mbawrawss*, 'a merchant.'

P is equivalent to English *r* in *embarrass*, but is never pronounced smooth as in *hard*, *bar*.

Σ is always sounded sharp, as the English *s* at the beginning of a word, except when followed by μ, in which case it has the sound of *z*; e. g. σῶος, *saw'awss*, 'safe;' but Σμύρνα, *Zmee'rnah*, 'Smyrna.'

T sounds as the English *t*, except when preceded by ν, in which case it is pronounced as *d*; e. g. τόνος, *taw'nawss*, 'tone;' but ἔντονος, *eh'ndawnawss*, intense.

Φ is the English *f*.

X is sounded as the German *ch* in *Bach*, or the Scotch *ch* in *loch*, except before ε, ι, or their equivalents, when it is pronounced as German *ch* in *ich*, &c. We shall represent the first sound by *kh*, and the second by kh, or *vice versâ*; e. g. τάχα, *tah'khah*, 'perhaps;' but ταχύς, *tah*khee'ss, 'swift.'

Ψ is sounded *ps*, except when preceded by μ, in which case it is pronounced as *bz*; e.g. ψυχή, *pseekhee'*, 'soul;' but ἔμψυχος, *eh'mbzeekhawss*, 'animate.'

OTHER SIGNS.
BREATHING.

§ 6. Every vowel or diphthong at the beginning of a word is marked by a sign called a breathing (πνεῦμα, *pneh'vmah*). This breathing is either smooth (ψιλή, *pseelee'*) or rough (δασεῖα, *dhahssee'ah*)—sub. προσῳδία, *prawssawdhee'ah*, accentual sign. The smooth breathing is written as a comma over the vowel, the rough as an inverted comma; thus ᾠδή, *awdhee'*, 'a song;' ὁδός, *awdhaw'ss*, 'a way.' As in most of the modern languages of Southern Europe, the rough breathing is no longer heard, but only written. Its presence, however, in cultivated usage is recognized in case a consonant liable to aspiration immediately precedes; such consonants are π, τ, and κ. Thus ἀπὸ ὅλων, *ahpaw-aw'lawn*, becomes, by elision of the o, ἀφ' ὅλων, *ahfaw'lawn*; κατὰ ὅλον, *kahtah-aw'loo*—καθόλον, *kahthaw'loo*; οὐχ οὕτως, *oukh oo'tawss*, stands for οὐκ οὕτως.

The rough breathing is frequently, though not always, written over the ρ at the beginning of a word, as ῥόδον or ρόδον, *raw'-dhawn*, 'a rose.' In the case of two ρ's coming together in one word, either the aspirate is omitted altogether, or the first ρ has the smooth, the second the rough breathing, as θάρρος or θάῤῥος, *thah'rawss*, 'courage.'

In the case of initial diphthongs the breathing is written over the second vowel; if it stands over the first, the two vowels are heard separately; e.g. αὐλός, *ahvlaw'ss*, 'a flute;' but ἄυλος, *ah'-eelawss*, 'immaterial.'

THE ACCENTS.

§ 7. With the exception of the following words:—ὁ, ἡ (*aw*, *ee*), 'the,' masculine and feminine nominative singular; οἱ, αἱ (*ee*, *eh*), 'the,' masculine and feminine nominative plural; εἰ (ee), 'if;' ὡς (awss), 'as;' οὐ, οὐκ, and οὐχ (oo, ook, ookh), 'not;' ἐκ and ἐξ, 'out of'—all words in Greek are accented.

The accents are three in kind:—

(a) The acute, ὀξεῖα (awksee'ah), which indicates that the syllable so marked has the principal stress—a stress which is given much as in English, but usually with a more distinct elevation of tone.

(b) The grave, βαρεῖα (vahree'ah), which indicates that the syllable has a more decided stress than any unaccented syllable, yet less than one which has the acute accent.

(c) The circumflex, περισπωμένη (pehreespawmeh'nee), in practice no longer distinguishable from the acute, though in theory and origin it is compounded of the acute and the grave. It was held by the ancient Greek grammarians that every unaccented syllable had in reality the grave accent; consequently a word like ἀγαπάει (ahghahpah'ee), 'he loves,' might be regarded as if written ἀγὰπάει. When ἀγαπάει was contracted to ἀγαπᾷ, the accents ′ ˋ were supposed to coalesce, and form a kind of musical wave or transition from a higher to a lower key. Hence arose the circumflex, first written ˆ, and afterwards in cursive manuscript rounded into ˜ or ˉ. It may be assumed that so long as the ι subscriptum was heard in ἀγαπᾷ, so long would the grave accent be heard; and then, when this was no longer audible, only the acute would be so.

The acute accent may stand over either of the two last syllables but one in a word, or on the last syllable when it comes at the end of a sentence or clause; or over a monosyllable interrogative, as τίς, τί.

The grave accent can only stand over the last syllable of a word, or over monosyllables, as τὸ μικρὸν πτηνὸν ᾄδει, 'the little bird sings.' At the end of a clause or sentence the grave becomes acute, as ᾄδει τὸ μικρὸν πτηνόν, or ᾄδει τὸ πτηνὸν τὸ μικρόν. In writing, the acute is frequently used throughout in place of the grave.

The circumflex accent from the nature of the case cannot stand farther back than the last syllable but one; otherwise we should have to assume before contraction the existence of an acute accent on the last syllable but three, which is inadmissible: thus such a form as ἤμεθα would presuppose ἐέμεθα, which is impossible. In the case of an accented diphthong, the accent like the breathing goes with the last vowel, and in case of an initial diphthong is written, if a grave or acute, *after*, if a circumflex, *over* the breathing; as αὕτη, αἷμα, αἴ, οἶνος, ποῦ, παῖ, αὗται. The relative position of the accent and breathing is the same in the case of the simple vowel, as ἄν, ἤν, ἦν, ἧς. In the case of initial capital vowels the accent and the breathing are written before the vowel, as Ἀθῆναι, Ἄδης, Ὦ; but when a whole word or sentence is printed, both accents and breathings are usually omitted.

Stops.

§ 8. These are the comma, κόμμα (*kaw'mah*) or ὑποστιγμή (*eepawsteeghmee'*), as in English.

Full stop, τελεία (*tehlee'ah*), as in English.

Semicolon, ἡμίκωλον (*eemee'kawlawn*), which serves the purposes both of the colon and semicolon in English; it is also called ἄνω στιγμή (*ah'naw steeghmee'*) or μέση στιγμή (*meh'ssee steeghmee'*), and consists of a dot placed at the top of the line, as ἡ ἐκδίκησις εἶναι γλυκεῖα· ἐν τούτοις ἡ συγχώρησις εἶναι γλυκυτέρα (*ee ehkdhee'keesseess ee'neh ghleekee'ah; ehndoo'tcess ee seengkhaw'reessness ee'neh ghleekeeteh'rah*), 'Revenge is sweet; notwithstanding, forgiveness is sweeter.'

The sign of interrogation is the English semicolon, e.g. τίς; 'who?'

Other Signs.

The apostrophe, ἡ ἀπόστροφος (*ee ahpaw'strawfawss*), does not differ in form or use from our own, as ὑπ' ἐμοῦ (*eep' ehmoo'*) for ὑπὸ ἐμοῦ (*eepaw-ehmoo'*) 'by me.'

§ 9. The coronis, ἡ κορωνίς (*ee kawrawnee'ss*), is really the smooth breathing written over a vowel which is no longer initial, simply because two words have coalesced into one, e. g. τοὐλάχιστον (*toolah'kheestawn*) for τὸ ἐλάχιστον (*taw-ehlah'kheestawn*), 'at least.'

The diæresis, or as it is more usually called, τὸ διαλυτικὸν (*taw-dheeahleeteekaw'n*), is sometimes used to distinguish two vowels separately pronounced from a diphthong, as καϋμένος (*kah-eemeh'nawss*), 'poor,' from καυμένος (*kahvmeh'nawss*), 'burnt.'

This sign is indispensable where the syllable has neither accent nor breathing, otherwise these are sufficient to prevent confusion, as we have seen above. It is, however, generally written even where superfluous.

The diastole or hypodiastole, διαστολὴ (*dheeahstawlee'*) or ὑποδιαστολὴ (*eepawdheeahstawlee'*), is simply a comma used not to indicate an appreciable pause, but to distinguish the relative pronoun ὅ,τι (*aw'-tee*) from the conjunction ὅτι (*aw'tee*).

N.B. The marking of every accent, and the fact that every syllable of which the sound has once been learnt, is always pronounced with uniform identity and distinctness wherever it may occur, renders the acquirement of a correct pronunciation of the language by the foreigner easier than that of any other European tongue.

We conclude this introductory chapter by a sample of the Greek alphabet as written, with a sentence in cursive characters, which will be found on the following page.

MODERN GREEK AS WRITTEN.

A a	I ι	P ρ
B β	K κ	Σ σ ς
Γ γ	Λ λ	T τ
Δ δ	M μ	Υ υ
E ε	N ν	Φ φ
Z ζ	Ξ ξ	X χ
H η	O ο	Ψ ψ
Θ θ	Π π	Ω ω

Ὁ Θεὸς ἔδωκε τοὺς πόνους τῆς ἁμαρτίας ὡς ἐπακολούθημα τῆς ἐν τῇ ἁμαρτίᾳ παραφροσύνης. Ἀλλ' ὁ ἄνθρωπος ὅλως εἶναι ἐλεύθερος νὰ ἐκλέξῃ μεταξὺ τοῦ κακοῦ καὶ τοῦ κακοῦ, ἁμαρτάνων, οἰκειοθελῶς ὑποβάλλει ἑαυτὸν ταῖς ποιναῖς.

Aryan Family of Speech.

PRIMITIVE INDO-GERMANIC IDEALLY RESTORED.	SANSCRIT.	ZEND.	GREEK.	ITALIAN.	TEUTONIC.		SCLAVONIAN.	LITHUANIAN.	ALBANIAN.
					GOTHIC.	OLD HIGH GERMAN.			
a	a	a	ŏ ε ο	a o o	a i u a i u	a i u o o	a e o ŏ	a e i o u	a e o ŏ[9]
ā	ā	ā	ā η ω	ā ō ō	ō ō	ā ō uo	ā o	a o o ŏ[9]	ā ō[9]
i	i	i	ĭ	i	i ai	i o	i i	i	i
ī	ī	ī	ī	ī	ei	ī	ī	y	i
u	u	u	ŭ	u	u	u	u	u	u[9]
ū	ū	ū	ū	ū	au	ū	u	ū	ū[9]
ai	ai	aē	αι οι	ai ōi ae oe	ai	ei	e[3] ěj	ěi	
āi	āi	āi	η	ī					
au	au	ao áu	αυ ου	au ou			ov[3] ój	aj	
āu	āu	áu	ω ηυ	au	au in	on ōin io	av	au	
k	k kh k' ç[1]	k kh c[2] ç	κ	o g (Umbr. ç)	h (g)	h (g)	k ó cs	k sz	k (h) k' g[3] (t)
g	g g'[3]	g ghj zh[3] z	γ	g	k	k (ch)	ź ž ż	g ż[4]	g c' k
gh	gh h	g gh j zh z	χ	h initial, g in mid.	g	g (k)	ğ ż ż	g ż[4]	h z ð
t	t th	t th	τ	t	th (d)	d	t	t	t
d	d	d dh	δ	d	t	t	d	d	ġ d
dh	dh	d dh	θ	{ Lat. Osc. & f in. d, b mid. Umbr. f. }	d	t	d	d	d
p	p ph	p f	π	p	f	f v (b)	p	p	p
bh	bh	b (w)	φ	{ Lat. Osc. & f. in. b mid. Umbr. f. }	b	b (p)	b	b	b (g) z t
n	n ñ	n ñ	ν	n	n	n	n	n	n n'[10]
ņ	n ṇ	n	μ	m	n	n	n	n	n
m	m	m	μ	m	m	m	m	m	m
r	r	r	ρ	r	r	r	r	r	r ĭ[11]
l	l	r	λ	l	l	l	l	l	l ľ'[10], y final
j	j	y	'initial	j	j	j	j	j	y
s	s sh	s ç sh h	σ, ς initial	s (r)	s (z)	s (r)	s ch[3]	s	s ş[5]
v	v	v	F	v	v	w	v	v	v

[1] k' = ch in church; ç = s palatal sometimes heard in the mouths of children who cannot pronounce our sh.
[2] c (Zend) = k' Sanscrit, and ç Slavonic, while Slav. c = German z pron. ts.
[3] g' = j in English and in Zend. The Albanian k' and g' respectively are similar.
[4] zh, ż = sound of s in pleasure; or French j; ž in Slav. and Albanian, and sz in Lithuanian = sh in English and Zend.

[5] ş = yes in year, and is similar to Lithuanian š.
[6] ô long, narrow, ay sound inclining to ee.
[7] f like ou in Soar.
[8] g as French e in le, de, &c.
[9] ŏ French o, German ü.
[10] l' and n' like Spanish ll and ñ respectively: i.e. liquid.
[11] ĭ rough r.

These various transliterations might easily be made more consistent, but only at the expense of disturbing existing usage.

ΠΡΩΤΟΝ ΜΑΘΗΜΑ.—First Lesson.
Praw'tawn   mah'theemah.

πρῶτον: neuter nominative of πρῶτο-, superlative degree of πρό, akin to English *fore*, of which *first* is also superlative. Hence πρῶτον = 'first.'

μάθημα: from root μαθ-, 'learn;' link-vowel η and noun ending -ματ-, the τ necessarily lost at the end. Hence μάθημα, 'a thing learnt,' 'a lesson.' μαθ- for μανθ-, is kin to English *mind*.

N.B.—τ cannot stand at end of a word.

Ἡ ἑσπερὶς τοῦ Κυρίου Σουσαμάκη.
Ee   ehspehree'ss   too   Keeree'oo   Soossahmah'kee.
The evening-party of-the   Mr.   Susamákis, or *Mr. Susamákis' evening-party.*

Ἡ: feminine nominative article, kin to English *she*, and standing for σή; cf. ἑξ for σέξ, 'six.'

ἑσπερὶς = ἑσπερίδ + ς (nominative ending), from root ἕσπερ- for Ϝέσπερ-, compare *vesper*, Latin, and stem-ending -ιδ. Hence ἑσπερίδ- = 'an even-ing,' i. e. an open evening.

τοῦ: shortened from τοῖο for τόσϳο,[1] possessive or genitive of το- (masculine and neuter stem) = *the*, with which it is cognate.

Κυρίου: for Κυρίοιο, Κυρίοσϳο, possessive or genitive of Κύριο-, 'lord,' 'master,' 'gentleman,' 'Mr.,' 'sir.'

Σουσαμάκη: possessive or genitive of Σουσουμάκη, proper name.

Οἰκογενειακαί σκηναί.
Eekawyehneeahkeh' skeench'.
Domestic   scenes.

οἰκογενειακαί: ι = plural nominative ending; a sign of feminine gender; κ makes adjective of οἰκογένεια, 'family,' formed of noun ending -εια, and roots οἰκο- for Ϝοῖκο-, Latin *vicus*

[1] The Greeks represent the consonantal value of ι by writing that letter inverted and circumflexed, thus, ϳ.

(*vico-s*), 'a dwelling,' and γεν-, English *kin*. Hence οἰκογενειακαί = 'belonging-to-house-kindred,' 'domestic.'

σκηναί: plural of σκηνη-, whence our *scene*, cognate with *sheen, shine*.

'Ο Κύριος Παρδαλὸς καὶ ἡ Κυρία Παρδαλοῦ εἶνε
Aw Kee'reeawss Pardhahlaw'ss keh ee Keeree'ah Pardhahloo' eeneh
The Mr. Pardalós and the Mrs. Pardalós are

προσκεκλημένοι τὸ ἑσπέρας εἰς συναναστροφήν.
prawskehkleemch'nee taw ehspeh'rahss eess seenahnahstrawfee'n.
invited the evening to a party.

ὁ: for ἰὸ, kin to German *je* in "je länger je lieber," nominative masculine definite article = 'the.'

Κύριος: nominative of Κύριο-.

Παρδαλὸς: nominative of Παρδαλὸ-, proper name.

καὶ, 'and,' kin to Latin *que*.

Κυρία, feminine of Κύριο-, accent drawn forward to ι because α is long, 'Mrs.,' 'lady.'

Παρδαλοῦ: for Παρδαλόη, feminine by ending η of Παρδαλό-.

εἶνε: for ἐντὶ, and that for ἐστὶ, from root ἐσ-, 'be,' cf. English *is*, and -ντι, personal ending = 'they.' It means both [he, she, or it] 'is' and [they] 'are.' Hence εἶνε = [they] 'are.'

προσκεκλημένοι: from πρὸς, 'to,' and κεκλημένοι, nominative masculine plural (by ending ι) of κεκλημένο-, perfect participle passive by reduplication and lengthening of vowel from root κλε-, also καλ-, κελ-, 'call;' not related to *call*, for κ must = h [2] English, but probably to *hal-* in *halloa!* *hol-* in *hollow, hulloo*, &c.

τὸ: neuter, also crude form of article το- = *the*, with which it is cognate.

ἑσπέρας: indeclinable neuter, from root ἑσπερ- for Ϝέσπερ-, kin to *vesper*, 'evening.' The case of τὸ ἑσπέρας is called in

[2] See table on page 11.

grammars the accusative of time; it means here '*for* the evening.'

εἰς, 'to,' preposition always with accusative case.

συναναστροφήν, accusative case of συναναστροφή, from root στρεφ-, 'turn,' whence, with changed vowel usual in forming nouns, στροφ-ή-, 'a turning' + σύν = 'together,' ἀνὰ, 'up,' 'about.' Hence συναναστροφή-, 'a turning about together,' the literal equivalent of 'conversation,' from Latin *con-*, 'together,' *versa-*, 'turn about' = 'conversazione' (Italian), i. e. company, party.

Exercise I.

Ὁ Κύριος Παρδαλὸς καὶ ἡ Κυρία εἶνε προσκεκλημένοι εἰς οἰκογενειακὴν συναναστροφήν. Ἡ ἑσπερὶς τοῦ Κυρίου Παρδαλοῦ. Τὸ ἑσπέρας εἶνε προσκεκλημένοι ὁ Κύριος καὶ ἡ Κυρία. Ἡ σκηνὴ εἶνε οἰκογενειακή.

In the evening [there] is a party. The domestic scene. The gentleman and the lady are invited. Mr. and Mrs. Pardalós are at the party for the evening.

ΔΕΥΤΕΡΟΝ ΜΑΘΗΜΑ.—Second Lesson.
Dheh'ftehrawn   mah'theemah.

δεύτερον: from δευ-, strengthened from δυ- in δύο, our *two* + τερον, neuter nominative of τερο-, comparative ending of adjectives. Hence δεύτερον = *two-er*, *twoth*, or *second*.

Ὁ Κύριος Σουσαμάκης ὑπάλληλος τοῦ γραφείου ὅπερ
Aw Kee'reeawss Soossahmah'kees eepahl'leelawss too ghrahfee'oo aw'pehr
[*The*] *Mr. Susamákis   clerk   of-the   office   which*

διευθύνει ὁ Κύριος Παρδαλὸς, ἐνυμφεύθη πρό τινων
dheeehfthee'nee aw Kee'reeawss Pardhahlaw'ss ehneemfeh'fthee prawteenawn
manages [the] Mr. Pardalos, had married before some

μηνῶν τῇ ἀγαθῇ συμπράξει τοῦ προϊσταμένου του,
meenwn'n tee ahghahthee' seembrah'ksee too praweestahmeh'noo-too,
months with the kind   help   of-the   principal of him,

πλουσίαν   νύμφην   ἐκ   Πατρῶν   ἔχουσαν   μὲν   ἕνα
ploossee'awn neem'feen   ehk   Pahtraw'n   eh'khoossahn   mehn   eh'nah
a rich   *bride*   *from* *Patras*   *having*   *indeed* *one*

ὀφθαλμὸν   ὀλιγώτερον   αὐτοῦ,   ἀλλ'   εἰς   ἀποζημίωσιν
awfthahlmaw'n awleeghaw'tehrawn ahftoo'   ahl' eess   ahpawzeemee'awseen
eye   *less*   *than-he,* *but*   *for*   *compensation*

τοῦ   ἐλλείποντος   ὀφθαλμοῦ,   δεκαπέντε   ἔτη   ἡλικίας
too   ehlee'pawndawss awfthahlmoo', dhehkahpeh'ndeh   eh'tee   eeleekee'ahss
of the *lacking*   *eye,*   *fifteen*   *years*   *of-age*

περισσότερα,   καὶ   εἰς   ἀποζημίωσιν   τῶν   περισσευόντων
pehreessaw'tehrah   keh   eess   ahpawzeemee'awsseen   tawn-behreeessehvaw'ndawn
more,   *and* *for* *compensation*   *of-the*   *excessive*

δεκαπέντε   ἐτῶν,   τριάκοντα   πέντε   χιλιάδας
dhehkahpeh'ndeh ehtaw'n,   treeah'kawndah   peh'ndeh   kheeleeah'dhahss
fifteen   *years,*   *thirty*   - *five*   *thousands*

δραχμῶν   προῖκα.
dhrahkhmaw'n   proe'kah.
of-drachms   *dowry.*

ὑπάλληλος: nominative masculine of ὑπάλληλο-, compounded of ὑπό, 'under,' for συπό, kin to Latin *sub*, and ἄλληλο-, a reduplicated form of ἄλλο- standing for ἄλ?ο, and kin to Latin *alio-*, our *el* in *else*, &c. = 'other.' Hence ἄλληλο- = 'one another,' ὑπάλληλο- = 'under one another,' 'subordinate,' 'clerk.' Similarly formed are κατ-άλληλο- (from κατά, 'according to,' and foregoing) = 'fit,' 'suitable,' and παράλληλο- (from παρά, 'beside,' &c.) = 'side by side with each other,' 'parallel.' Observe prepositions ending in α and ο, except πρό, lose these syllables in composition. Not so the ι of περί.

τοῦ: originally τόσ?ο, from root το- = *the* + σ?ο, genitive (masculine and neuter) ending = 'of the.'

γραφείου: genitive of γραφεῖο-, as τοῦ of το-. Observe change of accent. The theory of this is as follows:—Every syllable in Greek not having the acute accent ´, or high tone, is supposed to have the grave ῾, or low tone. γραφεῖο-, four syllables, contracts to γραφείο-, the ΄ and the ῾ combining to form ῀ or ῏, the circumflex. But γραφείου is contracted from γραφείοσιο, and as the acute cannot stand further back than the third syllable in Greek, it follows that in the old form of γραφείου it could not have fallen on the ε; hence the combination ει̇́ = εῖ could not arise. From this we get the general rule—first, that the circumflex can never stand further back than the second syllable; and, further, that in no case can it be followed by a contracted syllable. It may be followed by a long syllable not arising from contraction, e. g. πόλεως, ῥινόκερως.

γραφεῖο- is from root γραφ-, cognate with which, + an *s* lost in Greek, we have *scrib*-, Latin, *schreib*, German, and *shrive*, English (the priest writing down the confessions of the penitent) + ειο-, noun ending with local meaning. Hence γραφεῖο = 'writing-place,' 'office.'

ὅπερ: from ὅ, neuter (also root form) of relative pronoun (see above) + περ, intensive or emphatic particle, kin to *per*, Latin, *far*, English, in sense of 'very.' Hence ὅπερ = literally 'the very one which.'

διευθύνει: from διά for δϝιά, kin to δύο, also to *two*, *twice*, be-*tween*, a preposition here meaning 'in two [or more] directions ' + εὐθυν-, verbal stem from root εὐθύ-, 'straight' = 'straighten.' Hence διευθυν- = 'straighten in all directions,' 'control,' 'direct,' like Latin *di-rig-*, in *dirigere*. -ει = 3rd person singular, 'he,' 'she,' or 'it,' corresponding to English *s*. Hence διευθύνει = 'directs.'

ἐνυμφεύθη: ἐ-, sign of past time placed before every past tense; νυμφευ-, verbal stem from νύμφη, 'bride,' the suffix -ευ meaning 'be,' 'become '—hence νυμφευ- = 'become a bride;' -θη = 'he was' or 'was.' Hence ἐνυμφεύθη = '[he] was become a bride to,' i. e. a bride was given to him, or he married (transitive). With νύμφ-η are connected Latin *nubeo*, and the English derivative, *nuptials*.

πρό, kin to English -*fore*, *fore*-, &c. = 'before;' a preposition construed with genitive case.

τινων: stem τιν- for κϝιν-, kin to Latin *qui-s*, English *which*, &c. = 'some' + genitive plural ending -ων; accent thrown back upon πρό.

μηνῶν: stem μην-, kin to *month*, *moon*, &c. + same ending -ων.

τῇ: stem τη- (feminine form of definite article) + ι, sign of dative, now written underneath called ἰῶτα *subscriptum*, meaning 'by the' or 'with the.'

ἀγαθῇ, ending as in τῇ: stem ἀγαθ- means 'good' or 'kind,' by suffix -θ-, from root ἀγα-, which appears in ἄγαμαι, 'I admire,' ἄγαν, 'very.'

συμπράξει: ι as above, added to σύμπραξε-, modified from σύμπραξι-, from root πρακ-, 'do' + συμ- (as single word σὺν) = 'with,' old form ξὺν for κὺν, kin to Latin *cum*, *con*-, Italian and Spanish *con*, Portuguese *com* + noun ending -σι- = -*ing*. Hence σύμπρακ-σι-, written σύμπραξι- = 'a doing-with' or 'doing together,' 'co-operation,' 'aid,' 'help;' thus, τῇ ἀγαθῇ συμπράξει, 'with the kind aid.' The dative is here used in an instrumental sense. This phrase is a resuscitation of classical usage. The popular modern Greek would be μὲ τὴν ἀγαθὴν σύμπραξιν.

τοῦ, explained above, only here masculine, not neuter.

προϊσταμένου: πρό as above, only here in composition = 'fore,' 'before;' -ου ending as that of τοῦ, &c.; μεν-, participial suffix corresponding to English -*ing*, only that it is not primarily active and transitive, but, as here, passive, middle, or intransitive in meaning; ἰστα- for σιστα-, imperfect (reduplicated) stem from root στα-, kin to *sta-* in *stand*. Hence τοῦ προϊσταμένου = 'of the before-standing-one,' i. e. principal.

του: the grammatical form the same as τοῦ explained above, but in sense a modern relic of the old Homeric meaning of το-, which was not 'the' but 'he.' Hence του without the accent as enclitic, or with it as proclitic, means 'of him,' 'his.' τοῦ προϊσταμένου του, 'of *his* principal.'

πλουσίαν νύμφην: in both these words the ν is the sign of the objective or accusative case. Subtract it, and we get the stems πλουσία-, νύμφη-, respectively. νύμφη- as above; πλουσία-, feminine adjective formed by suffix σια-, from root πλου- for πλεο-, kin to *full*. Hence πλουσία = 'rich.'

ἐκ: before vowels ἐξ, kin to Latin *ex, e, ec* (in compounds), 'out of,' 'from.'

Πατρῶν: genitive plural, contracted from Πατράων (hence circumflex), from Πάτραι, of which the accusative plural Πάτρας, 'Patras,' from its frequent occurrence has become the name by which foreigners know the town.

ἔχουσαν: ν as above; ἔχουσα-, feminine participle imperfect active for ἔχοντσα, which cannot stand in Greek, from ἔχοντ-, participial stem + σα-, feminine suffix; -οντ- answers to our 'ing,' and is cognate with the German ending *-end* in *habend*, *liebend*, &c.; ἐχ- means 'have,' probably for σέχ-, and cognate with German *Sieg*, 'victory,' i. e. the holding out against, or successfully withstanding an enemy. Hence ἔχουσαν = 'having,' or more idiomatically, 'with.'

μὲν: a little word or particle hard to render, and seldom rendered in English. 'Indeed' is its nearest equivalent, but is too strong. The German *zwar* almost exactly answers in sense and use.

ἕνα: for ἕναν, which is likewise the popular form; ἑν- means 'one,' to which it may be related; -αν is accusative ending.

ὀφθαλμὸν: ν accusative ending; stem ὀφθαλμὸ-, 'eye,' from root ὀπ-, originally ὀκϝ-, 'see,' with which Latin *oculus* and German *Auge*, English *eye*, from Anglo-Saxon *eage*, are akin, + θαλμό-, a suffix of obscure derivation. The word is masculine.

ὀλιγώτερον: ending -ον as in ὀφθαλμὸν; ὀλιγώτερ-ο-, comparative of ὀλίγο-, which is made up of adjectival suffix -ο + root λιγ-, with prefix (merely phonetic, and in some dialects, notably in modern Romaic, wanting) ὀ-; λιγ- seems to stand for an original λικ-, with which are probably cognate, Low Dutch *leeg* or *laag*, and English *low*, perhaps also *least*.

αὐτοῦ: ending as in τοῦ, &c. ; αὐτὸ-, masculine personal pronoun, = 'he,' 'him,' &c.

ὀλιγώτερον αὐτοῦ, literally 'less of him,' i. e. less than he. Various prepositions or cases are used in different languages to express this relation. In Hebrew and the Semitic languages generally *min*, 'from,' is employed. In the north of England they say "better till him," i. e. better to him. We ourselves say "my elders," "my betters," where 'my' is possessive or genitive.

ἀλλ' = ἀλλὰ, the -α being cut off before the following vowel; ἀλλὰ for ἀλιά, cognate with *alius*, *alias*, &c., in Latin, and with ἄλλος for ἄλιος in Greek, means literally 'otherwise;' hence 'moreover,' 'but.'

εἰς, see above ; here equivalent to 'for' or 'as.'

ἀποζημίωσιν: ν as above ; σι as above in -πρακ-σι- ; ἀποζημίω-, with ο lengthened in derivation from ἀποζημιο-, verbal stem meaning 'to compensate,' 'indemnify;' from ἀπὸ, 'from,' and ζημία, old form δαμία, cognate with *damnum*, and *dem* in *indemnify*. Hence ἀποζημίωσι- = 'indemnification.'

ἐλλείποντος : -ος, genitive masculine ending ; -οντ- explained above, cf. ἔχουσα ; ἐλλείπ- for ἐνλείπ-, from ἐν, 'in,' and λειπ-, strengthened imperfect stem from root λιπ- for λικϝ-, kin to Latin *licv-*, root of *linquo*, &c. ; λικϝ- meaning 'leave' or 'fail.' Hence ἐλλιπ-, 'lack,' 'be wanting.' τοῦ ἐλλείποντος ὀφθαλμοῦ, 'of the lacking eye.'

δεκαπέντε: δέκα, kin to *decem*, Gothic *taihun*, German *zehn*, our *ten*; πέντε for πέμπε, German *fünf* for *fümf*, our *five* for *fife*, and that for *finf*. Hence δεκαπέντε = ten + five = 'fifteen.'

ἔτη: for ἔτεα, old form ϝέτεσα, from stem ϝέτεσ-, kin to Albanian ϝίτš, 'year,' Latin *vetus*, 'old;' α being neuter plural ending, here accusative after ἔχουσα.

c 2

ἡλικίας : ς, sign of genitive singular ; -ία-, substantive suffix, making noun of ἡλικ-, adjectival stem, meaning literally " how great ;" hence " how old ;" thus ἡλικία = '[a certain] age.'

περισσότερα : α as in ἔτεα ; -ότερ- as in ὀλιγώτερον ;[3] περισσ- (for περι-κ?-), formed from root περ-, kin to *fur-* in *further*, meaning 'abounding,' 'excessive.' Hence περισσότερα = 'more,' or 'more excessive.' Of the adjective περισσὐ- ἡ- ὀ-, there is another form, the later Attic περιττὀ-, κ.τ.λ. But περιττὀ- when used in Modern Greek means 'superfluous,' the old classical sense, whereas περισσότερο- is the only comparative form in use, and signifies simply 'more,' as already in the New Testament.

τῶν : genitive plural of τὀ-.

περισσευόντων : -ων as in τῶν, τινῶν, κ.τ.λ. ; -οντ- as explained above ; περισσευ-, verb from περισσ-, meaning ' to be in excess.' Hence τῶν περισσευόντων, 'the being-in-excess,' ' the excessive.'

ἐτῶν : for ἐτέων ; hence circumflex ; cf. Πατρῶν.

τριάκοντα : from τρια- = ' three ' (in composition), and -κοντα, an ending answering in sense to *-ty* in English. Hence τριάκοντα = ' thirty.'

χιλιάδας : ending -ας for ανς, accusative plural feminine ; -αδ-, substantive suffix used to form a collective noun from numeral χιλι- (ο- α- ο-) = ' thousand.' Hence ' *a* thousand.' χίλι- is probably connected with χιλὀ- 'straw,' Latin *hilo- hilum*, from the difficulty of counting straws in a stack.

δραχμῶν : ending as above ; for δραχμάων : stem δραχμά-, literally ' a handful ;' kin to δράσσομαι for δράκ?ομαι, ' I lay hold of ;' μα being verbal substantive suffix. The nominative singular is δραχμή. The Greek δραχμὴ, in modern as in ancient times, is about 8½d. of our money.

προῖκα : for προῖκαν, accusative singular of προῖκ- for πρόκ?-, ' dowry ;' probably kin to Latin *procus*, 'suitor,' *precor*, ' I pray,' German *fragen*, 'ask.'

[3] Observe, however, that in forming degrees of comparison, ο follows a long, ω a short vowel, in the preceding syllable.

Idiomatic English Translation of the above.

Mr. and Mrs. Pardalós are invited out for the evening. Mr. Susamákis, clerk at the office managed by Mr. Pardalós, had married, a few months before, a rich bride from Patras, with one eye less than himself, 'tis true, but as a set off to the eye that was wanting, with fifteen years' seniority, and as a set off to the fifteen extra years, with thirty-five thousand drachms of dowry.

Exercise II.

Mr. and Mrs. Susamákis are invited out for the evening. Mr. Pardalós had married a wife a few months before. He had married a wife with a dowry. He had married one eye less, but a dowry of thirty-five thousand drachms. Fifteen years' seniority are as an indemnity for one eye less.

Ὁ Κύριος Σουσαμάκης εἶνε ὑπάλληλος τοῦ Κυρίου Παρδαλοῦ. Ὁ Κύριος διευθύνει τὸ γραφεῖον. Τὸ γραφεῖον ὅπερ διευθύνει ὁ Κύριος Σουσαμάκης εἶνε τὸ γραφεῖον τοῦ Κυρίου Παρδαλοῦ. Ἡ Κυρία Παρδαλοῦ εἶνε προσκεκλημένη τὸ ἑσπέρας εἰς συναναστροφήν. Ἡ Κυρία ἔχει προῖκα τὴν ἡλικίαν. Ὁ Κύριος ἐνυμφεύθη πρό τινων μηνῶν νύμφην πλουσίαν μέν, ἀλλὰ ἔχουσαν ἕνα ὀφθαλμὸν ὀλιγώτερον, καὶ δεκαπέντε ἔτη περισσότερα αὐτοῦ.

ΤΡΙΤΟΝ ΜΑΘΗΜΑ.—Third Lesson.
Tree'tawn   mah'thoemah.

τρι-, kin to English *three*.

Ὁ ὄλβιος Σουσαμάκης ἐσυλλογίσθη τὸ κατ' ἀρχὰς εἰς
Aw aw'lveeawss Soossahmah'keess ehseelawyee'sthee taw kaht'arkhah'ss eess
The fortunate Susamakis thought at first in

πανηγυρισμὸν τοῦ σπουδαίου τούτου καὶ εὐτυχοῦς
pah«eeycerceezmaw'n too spoodheh'-oo tootoo keh ehfteekhoo'ss
celebration of the important this and happy

συμβεβηκότος τοῦ βίου του, νὰ δώσῃ χορὸν εἰς
seemvehveekaw'tawss too vee'oo too, nah dhaw'ssee khawraw'neess
event of the life of-him, that he-should-give a-ball to

τοὺς παρανυμφους τὴν αὐτὴν τῶν γάμων του ἑσπέραν·
tooss pahrahnee'mfooss teen ahftee'n' tawn ghah'mawn-too ehspeh'rahn
the   wedding-guests the   very   of-the marriage of-him evening;

εἶχε δὲ μάλιστα παρακαλέσει καὶ ὑπαξιωματικόν τινα
eekheh dheh mah'leestah pahrahkahleh'ssee keh eepahkseeawmahteekaw'n-deenah
he-had too   actually   begged   also a non-commissioned officer

φίλον του νὰ τῷ προμηθεύσῃ ἐκ τῆς στρατιωτικῆς
fee'lawn-doo nah taw prawmeetheh'fseee ehk teess strahteeawteekee'ss
friend-of-him that him he-should-procure from the   military

μουσικῆς ἐν φλάουτον, ἐν κλαρινέττον, καὶ ἐν τρομπόνι,
moosseekee'ss ehn flah'ootawn, ehn klahreeneh'tawn, keh ehn trawmbaw'nee
band   a   flute,   a   clarionette, and a trombone,

ἤτοι ἕνα πλαγίαυλον, ἕνα ὀξύαυλον, καὶ μίαν
ee'tee eh'nah plahyee'ahvlawn, eh'nah awksee'ahvlawn, keh mee'ahn
or-in-other-words a sideways-pipe, a shrill-pipe, and a

βαρυσάλπιγγα ὡς γράφουσι σήμερον οἱ νεοφώτιστοι
vahreessah'lpeengghah awss ghrah'foossee see'mehrawn ee neh-awfaw'teestee
heavy-trumpet   as   write   to-day the newly-enlightened

τῆς γλώσσης καθαρισταί, ὅπως τὸ ἐναρμόνιον αὐτῶν
teess ghlaw'sseess kahthahreesteh', aw'pawss taw ehnarmaw'neeawn ahftaw'n
of the language   purifiers, in-order-that the harmonious of-them,

μέλος πτερώσῃ τοὺς πόδας τῶν προσκεκλημένων.
meh'lawss ptehraw'ssee tooss paw'dhabss tawn prawskehkleemeh'nawn.
strain might-wing the feet of-the invited-ones.

ὄλβιος : ὄλβιο- + ς, sign of nominative. Probably for σόλβιος, cf. Latin *salvus*, whence "salvation," German *selig*, English *silly*, the old meaning of which was 'happy.'

ἐσυλλογίσθη: form as ἐνυμφεύθη (see above), from stem συλλογιδ, δ becoming σ before θ; συλλογιδ- is a verbal stem λογιδ- compounded with preposition συν (see above), formed of λόγο-, 'word,' 'ground,' or 'reason;' hence λογίζομαι for λογίδ:ομαι (the ? being added for imperfect tenses), 'I reason.' συλλογίζομαι, 'I reason with myself,' 'I think.' In older Greek, when the συν was still felt as a separate word, the augment ε was inserted between it and the verb, thus συνελογίσθη instead of ἐσυλλογίσθη.

κατ': for κατὰ before vowel, preposition construed with accusative in sense of 'at;' elsewhere with genitive it means 'against,' or 'down on to,' as κατ' ἀρχῶν, 'against principles,' κατὰ γῆς, 'down on to the earth.'

ἀρχὰς: stem ἀρχὰ- + ς for νς, accusative plural ending = 'beginnings.' Hence κατ' ἀρχὰς, 'at beginnings,' 'at first.' With this is cognate ἄρχω, 'I am first,' 'I rule;' Sanscrit arhâmi, Zend arey, 'deserve,' 'be noble,' whence the word Aryan, i. e. the noble or ruling race.

Observe the Greeks say τὸ κατ' ἀρχὰς, 'the at first,' instead of 'at the first.'

πανηγυρισμὸν: ν sign of accusative after εἰς (see above); πανηγυρισμὸ-, μὸ- = verbal substantive ending, making noun of verbal stem πανηγυριδ- (δ becoming σ before μ); πανηγυριδ- is also a substantive stem, and means 'fair,' 'merry-making,' from πᾶν (for πάντ) = 'all,' and ἠγυρ- or ἄγυρ-, bye-form of ἀγειρ-, root ἀγερ-, 'to gather.' Hence 'a gathering of all,' 'a general gathering.' From root ἀγερ- is formed also the noun ἀγορά, 'a market-place,' whence ἀγοράζω (ἀγοράδιω), 'I market,' 'I buy.'

σπουδαίου, genitive neuter of σπουδαῖο- (observe accent), from substantive stem σπουδὰ- + adjective suffix ιο- ια-. Σπουδά- means 'haste,' 'zeal,' 'earnest.' It stands for στουδά-, τ having become π through the influence of the vowel sound ου, which is a lip-vowel; and answers to the Latin studium, studeo, &c., whence our *study*.

εὐτυχοῖς: contracted from εὐτυχέος = adjective stem εὐτυχέ(σ) + ος, genitive ending, from εὐ, 'well,' and root τυχ-, 'to hit,' 'strike,' 'hap;' εὐ stands for ἐσὺ, Sanscrit su for asu, and is perhaps cognate to root as, Greek ἐς = 'be,' preserved in English *is*: according to Pope's view, "whatever is, is right."

συμβεβηκότος: for σὺν + βεβηκότ-, reduplicated participle perfect active, from root βα- for γα-, English *come* + genitive ending -ος. The insertion of κ is common but not invariable in the formation of perfects. The active perfect is a classical, not a vernacular, form. συμβα- meaning 'come together,' or 'go together;' hence 'happen,' τὸ συμβεβηκὸς means 'the happening,' 'the event.'

βίου: from βίο-, 'life,' cognate with Latin *vivus, vita*, &c.

νὰ: relic of ἵνα, conjunction, 'that.'

δώσῃ: δο-, lengthened in formation to δω-, 'give' + σ, sign of aorist or momentary tense, and ῃ, subjunctive third person ending = 'he may;' here = 'he should' or 'might,' but on account purely of the context, the subjunctive having no power in itself to distinguish past from present. This can only be done in the indicative by the prefix ἐ. -ῃ stands for -ητι, as in the present indicative -ει does for -ετι. The falling out of a consonant, especially σ or τ between two vowels, is a constant characteristic of Greek etymology. νὰ δώσῃ is the Modern Greek way of saying 'to give,' the use of the infinitive being extremely limited.

χορὸν: for ν see above; χορὸ-, probably originally the enclosed green where dances took place, kin to χόρ-τος, 'grass,' 'sward,' Latin *hortus*, English *garden* and *yard*.

τοὺς: for τὸνς = τὸ-, 'the' + νς, sign of accusative plural.

παρανύμφους: ending as above; παράνυμφο- (observe accent) from παρὰ, preposition meaning 'by,' 'along with,' and νύμφα-, 'bride.' Hence παράνυμφο-, 'bride-attendant,' 'wedding-guest.'

τὴν = τὴ-, 'the' (feminine) + ν, sign of accusative; cf. συναναστροφὴν, νύμφην.

αὐτὴν: ending as above; αὐτὴ-, feminine form of αὐτὸ-, explained above.

γάμων: ending as in τῶν, κ.τ.λ.; γάμο-, 'marriage;' cf. γαμβρὸς for γαμ-ρός, 'kinsman by marriage,' Latin *gener*, English *kin*, *kindred*.

ἑσπέραν = ἑσπέρα-, feminine form, from root ἕσπερ-, 'evening' (cf. neuter ἑσπέρας) + ν, sign of accusative, as above.

εἶχε: shortened from ἔεχε, in which ἔ = sign of past time, εχ- = 'have,' and ε signifies 'he.' Hence εἶχε = 'did have-he,' i.e. he had.

δὲ: adverbial conjunction; the English *too*, German *zu*, Dutch *te*, the two latter, however, differing in use.

μάλιστα: superlative of μάλα, 'much;' hence = 'very much,' 'actually,' 'indeed.' It is the commonest word for 'yes' in Modern Greek.

παρακαλέσει: παρακαλε-, from παρὰ and καλε-, explained above = 'call to one's side,' 'beg,' 'ask' + -σει, classical -σαι, ending of first aorist infinitive active; used in Modern Greek to form the compound pluperfect εἶχε παρακαλέσει, 'had asked.'

ὑπαξιωματικόν: from ὑπὸ for συπὸ, kin to Latin *sub*, 'under,' and ἀξιωματικὸ-, from ἀξίωμα, which is formed from verbal stem ἀξιο- (Modern Greek, ἀξιον-), 'to count worthy,' 'to claim,' 'to demand,' from ἄξιο-, 'worthy,' and this from root ἀγ-, 'to bring' + adjective suffix -σιο-, whence ἄγσιο- = ἄξιο-, 'to be brought,' 'worth taking.' Hence ἄξιο + ματ- with vowel lengthened in composition gives us ἀξιωματ-, 'a claim,' 'demand,' 'dignity,' 'office;' hence with adjective suffix ἀξιωματικὸ-, 'an officer,' ὑπαξιωματικὸ-, 'an under-officer,' 'a non-commissioned officer.'

τινα (cf. τινῶν above): for τιναν = τιν + αν (accusative ending) = 'some,' 'a;' used here, as elsewhere the numeral, for the indefinite article. Observe loss of accent thrown back on preceding word, of which the grave becomes acute.

φίλον = φίλο + ν, 'a friend;' perhaps kin to φυλὴ (from root φυ-, English *be*) = 'race,' 'kindred.'

τῷ: τό- + ι, dative = 'him,' 'for him.'

προμηθεύσῃ: ending, &c., as in δώσῃ ; προμηθευ-, from προμηθέ-, originally προμηθές-, 'thoughtful,' 'provident.' Hence προ-μηθεύω, 'I am thoughtful,' 'I provide,' 'procure.'

τῆς : τῇ + ς, genitive ending = 'of the,' feminine.

στρατιωτικῆς: ending as above ; κη-, adjectival suffix ; στρατιωτι- for στρατιώτη-, 'a soldier'—this from στρατιά-, 'an army.' Hence στρατιωτικό- ή- ό-, 'military.'

μουσικῆς: adjective used as substantive, formed similarly to above, from μοῦσα, 'a muse,' 'music ;' μοῦσα stands for μόν-σα, σα = feminine ending, as elsewhere ; μον- is kin to *mind*, *mental*, &c.

ἕν : neuter and crude form of numeral.

φλάουτον = φλάουτο (Italian *flauto*) + ν, neuter nominative, vocative or accusative ending ; so κλαρινέττον. τρομπόνι for τρομπόνιον, later form of τρομπόνιν. Hence, dropping ν, τρομπόνι, from Italian *trombone*.

πλαγίαυλον : from πλάγιο- = 'sideways,' and αὐλό-, 'a pipe' or 'flute.' This, like the following, is a manufactured Greek word employed by modern purists to supplant the foreign importation given above. Observe change of accent in composition.

ὀξύαυλον : as above, with ὀξύ- = 'shrill,' 'sharp.'

βαρυσάλπιγγα : βαρύ-, originally γαρύ-, kin to *gravis*, Latin, 'grave' + σάλπιγγ- + α(ν), accusative singular ending = 'trumpet.' The suffix -ιγγ- individualizes. The root σαλπ- for σϝαλπ- is probably kin to *swallow*, *schwalbe*.

γράφουσι : for γράφοντι, from γραφ-, 'write,' our *grave* in *engrave*, Latin *scrib-ere* ; also kin to 'scrub,' 'rub.' The *s* before the original Indo-Germanic *k* probably preserved it as *g* in the Teutonic languages, or as *c* in *scrub*, whereas in *rub* it has first become *h*, according to Grimm's law, and then disappeared. For the identity of *scrub* and *rub*, cf. German *schreiben* and *reiben*.

σήμερον (old form τήμερον): from ἡμερ-, root of ἡμέρα, 'day,' and τ-, root consonant of article, once demonstrative. Cf. τώρα for τῇ ὥρᾳ, 'now.'

οἱ : nominative plural masculine of ὁ-, 'the.'

νεοφώτιστοι : from νεο-, our *new*, and φωτιστοί, verbal adjective (observe accent) from φωτιζ-, formed (like λογιζ- above) from φῶτ for φάοτ, 'light,' formed in turn by substantival suffix or- from φα-, 'show,' 'declare;' cf. Latin *fama*, 'fame,' *fa-ri*, 'to speak,' &c.

γλώσσης = γλωσση, Ionic form of γλώσσα- for γλώκϳα, 'tongue.'

N.B.—These Ionic forms are retained only in genitive and dative. The nominative and accusative are γλῶσσα, γλῶσσαν.

καθαρισταὶ: from καθαριζ-, 'cleanse,' formed (as above) from καθαρὸ-, 'clean' + suffix τὰ- sign of agent + ι, sign of nominative plural.

ὅπως (originally ὅπωτ): old instrumental case used for adverb of stem ὅπο- (for ὅ-κϝο-), 'which' (cf. ὅπου, genitive in locative sense 'where,' &c.) = 'by which means,' 'how,' 'in order that.'

ἐναρμόνιον: compounded of ἐν, 'in,' and ἀρμονία-, 'harmony;' -μονία- being derivative suffix added to root ἀρ-, 'to fit,' being kin to our *ar* in *arm*, and also to *li* in *lid*, the German *Glied*, &c.

μέλος: nominative neuter of stem μέλεσ-, 'a strain;' means also 'a limb,' 'member,' and is perhaps a bye-form of μέρος, 'part.' Cf. Milton's "*linked* sweetness long drawn out." See p. 54.

πτερώσῃ: ending as in προμηθεύσῃ, κ.τ.λ.; πτερο-, formed (like ἀξιο-) from πτερὸ-, 'a wing.' Hence 'to wing,' 'to make fly.' πτερὸ- is kin to our *feather*, transposed for πετ-ρό-; root πετ- = 'fly.'

πόδας: for πόδανς, from πόδ-, our *foot*.

προσκεκλημένων: classical passive participle genitive plural, from προσκαλε-, explained above.

Idiomatic English Translation.

The lucky Susamúkis thought at first of giving a ball, in celebration of this happy event in his life, to the wedding guests, the very evening of his marriage; and he had even asked a non-commissioned officer of his acquaintance to procure for him from the military band, a flute, a clarionette, and a trombone, or, as our modern purists of to-day would write it, a side-pipe, a shrill-pipe, and a bass-trumpet; in order that their melodious strains might give wings to the feet of the guests.

Exercise III.

Mr. Susamákis thought how (ὅπως) he might give wings to the feet of the wedding guests, in celebration of this happy event in his life. The very evening of the wedding he invited a non-commissioned officer. The melodious strain is fortunate. The modern purists (of our language) write to-day.

Οἱ παράνυμφοι εἶνε προσκεκλημένοι αὐτὴν τὴν ἑσπέραν τῶν γάμων. Ὁ ὄλβιος Κύριος εἰς πανηγυρισμὸν τῶν γάμων του ἐσυλλογίσθη νὰ προμηθεύσῃ ἐναρμόνιον μέλος ἐκ τῆς στρατιωτικῆς μουσικῆς ὅπως πτερώσῃ τοὺς πόδας τῶν προσκεκλημένων παρανύμφων. Εἶχε φίλον τινα ὑπαξιωματικόν. Πλαγίαυλον, ὀξύαυλον καὶ βαρυσάλπιγγα γράφουσι σήμερον εἰς τὴν γλῶσσαν των ἡ νεοφώτιστοι καθαρισταὶ αὐτῆς.

ΤΕΤΑΡΤΟΝ ΜΑΘΗΜΑ.—Fourth Lesson.

τέταρτον : for κϝέτϝαρτον ; cf. Latin *quatuor*, 'four.'

Ἀλλ' εἶτα μετενόησε, σκεφθεὶς ὅτι δὲν ἦτο
Ab'l ee'tah mehtehnaw'eesseh, skehfthee'ss aw'tee dhehn ee'taw
But then he-changed-his-mind, considering that (it) not was

καλὸν νὰ παρατείνῃ τὸ μεταξὺ τῆς στέψεως καὶ
kahlaw'n nah pahrahtee'nee taw mehtahksee' teess steh'pseeawss keh
good that he-prolong the between the wedding and

τῆς ἀπομονώσεως αὐτοῦ χρονικὸν διάστημα καὶ
teess ahpawmawnaw'sseeawss ahftoo' khrawneekaw'n dheeah'steemah keh
the retirement of-him time's space and

ἀπεφάσισε νὰ ἀναβάλῃ εἰς προσφορώτερον καιρὸν τὸν
ahpehfah'sseessee nah ahnahvah'lee eess prawssfawraw'tchrawn kehraw'n tawn
resolved that he-defer to a more suitable season the

χορευτικὸν τῶν γάμων του πανηγυρισμόν.
khawrefteekaw'n tawn ghah'mawn-doo pahneeyeereezmaw'n.
dancing of-the marriage-of-him celebration.

εἶτα, 'afterwards,' 'then ;' kin to Latin *ita*.

μετενόησε = μετ' for μετὰ (Gothic *mith*, our *with*; cf. *we*, *wir*, and South German *mir*; kin to *mit* are probably *wieder* and *wider*, a kind of comparative of the preposition. The meaning in all languages fluctuates between 'with' and 'again' or 'against ;' cf. *withstand*, *widerstehen*. In Greek μετὰ in composition has the latter sense) + ε, sign of past time as above + νοε-, verbal stem from root νοϝ- for γνοϝ-, our *know* (whence νοῦ- for νοϝ-, 'mind') + σ, sign of aorist or instantaneous action + ε = 'he.' Hence μετενόησε = 'he changed his mind,' 'he repented ;' μετάνοια for μετάνοϝja, 'repentance,' the common New Testament words.

σκεφθεὶς : for σκεπθέντς = σκεπ-, transposed for σπεκ-, Latin *spec-*, as in *spectaculum*, *specula*, *spectrum*, *inspicio*, &c., German *spähen*, our *spy*, 'to look, see, regard, consider' + θεντ-, stem of passive aorist participle + ς, sign of masculine nominative agreeing with Σουσαμάκης understood. The passive is here used in a middle or deponent sense ; cf. German *sich umsehen*, 'to look about one,' and *circumspect*, which means 'looked about.' Hence σκεφθεὶς = 'having reflected' or 'reflecting.'

ὅτι : made up of two relative pronouns, ὅ, cf. ὅπερ above, and τι for κϝι[ν], cf. τινῶν above ; τι[ν] being neuter of τιν-. Here used to link clauses, i. e. as conjunction ; cf. similar use of English 'that,' French *que*, &c.

δέν : for οὐδέν, i. e. οὐδὲ ἕν, 'not even one,' hence 'nothing,' 'naught,' and so in Modern Greek 'not.'

ἦτο : for ἔεστο = ἐ + root ἐσ-, English *is*, see above, + το, sign of 3rd person singular in past imperfect tense of middle or passive verbs. Hence ἦτο = 'he was.'

καλὸν : neuter nominative of καλὸ-, masculine or neuter stem of root καλ-, kin to *hale*, English, meaning 'good,' 'fair,' &c.

παρατείνῃ : for παρατένσῃ (cf. προμηθεύσῃ, κ.τ.λ.), from παρὰ, 'along,' and τεν-, 'stretch,' kin to our *thin*. Hence νὰ παρατείνῃ, 'that he stretch,' or 'to extend.'

N.B.—σ after liquids is dropped, and the foregoing vowel lengthened by way of compensation.

μεταξὺ: for μεταξὺν = μετὰ + ξὺν (see above) = 'together-with,' 'among,' 'between.'

στέψεως: for στεπσεως, genitive after preposition of stem στέπ-σι-, literally 'crown-ing.' All words thus formed are feminine. στέπ-σι- is for στέφ-σι-, the root στεφ- itself however seems to have been modified from στεπ-, kin to Latin *stipare*, 'to crowd,' German *Stift*, *Stufe*, and *Stapfen*, our *step*. The original notion was that of fixing firmly down; hence in Greek στεφ- means 'crown,' στέφος, neuter, and στέφανος, masculine, 'a wreath' or 'crown,' and from the bridal wreath στέφω and στεφανόω (Modern στεφανόνω) mean 'to marry.'

ἀπομονώσεως: formed like στέψεως from ἀπομόνωσι-, from ἀπὸ + verbal stem μονο-, from stem μόνο-, 'alone.' Hence ἀπομόνωσις, 'sequestration,' 'withdrawal,' 'retirement.'

χρονικὸν: adjective neuter accusative, from stem χρόνο-, 'time;' probably kin to χορὸς in sense of limit (see above).

διάστημα: from διὰ for δϝιὰ, kin to *two*, *tween*, in the words *in two*, *between*, 'apart' + στη-, lengthened in derivation from στα- and μα(τ), substantive ending. Hence, 'what stands between,' 'the space.' χρονικὸν διάστημα, 'time-space,' or 'space of time.'

ἀπεφάσισε: formed like μετενόησε from ἀπὸ, 'off' or 'from,' and φασιδ-, from φάσι-, formed like στεψι-, κ.τ.λ, from root φα-, 'say.' Hence ἀποφασίζω, 'I say off,' i.e. make up my mind, decide.

νὰ ἀναβάλῃ: from ἀνὰ, 'up,' 'away,' 'off,' and βαλ-, 'put;' ending as in παρατείνῃ, κ.τ.λ. Hence νὰ ἀναβάλῃ, 'to put off,' 'defer.'

προσφορώτερον: formed like ὀλιγώτερον from πρόσφορο-, and that from πρὸς-, 'to,' and φορ- modified in nominal stems from φερ-, our *bear*, Latin *fer-*. Hence πρόσφορο-, 'fit to be brought to,' 'applicable,' 'suitable.'

καιρὸν (nominative, καιρὸς) = καιρὸ- + ν, 'season,' 'weather,' 'time.'

χορευτικὸν: χορευτικὸ- + ν; χορευτικὸ- formed like χρονικό κ.τ.λ., from χορεύ-, 'dance' (verb), from χορὸ-, 'a dance' or 'ball.'

Idiomatic Translation.

But afterwards he thought better of it, reflecting that it would not be well to prolong the interval between his wedding and his retirement, and he decided to put off to a more convenient season the celebration of his wedding by a ball.

Exercise IV.

Ὁ χορευτικὸς πανηγυρισμὸς τῶν γάμων δὲν ἦτο καλός. Ὁ καιρὸς δὲν ἦτο πρόσφορος εἰς τὸν χορευτικὸν πανηγυρισμόν. Τὸ χρονικὸν διάστημα μεταξὺ τῶν γάμων καὶ τοῦ χοροῦ ἦτο προσφυρώτερον. Δὲν εἶναι καλὸν νὰ ἀναβάλῃ ὁ Κύριος τὴν ἀπομόνωσίν του. Ἐσυλλογίσθη νὰ ἀναβάλῃ τὸν χορὸν, ἀλλ' εἶτα μετενόησε καὶ ἀπεφάσισε (decided on) τὸν χορευτικὸν πανηγυρισμὸν τῶν γάμων του, εἶχε δὲ μάλιστα προςκαλέσει τοὺς παρανύμφους.

It is not good to extend the interval of time. The season was suitable, but the celebration (nominative) was not. He decided to procure a military band, but afterwards he changed his mind, reflecting that it was not suitable to defer his retirement. He decided to give wings to the feet of the guests, and therefore he invited them (προσεκάλεσέ τους) to the celebration of his wedding by a dance. The time between his marriage and his retirement was less than (ἢ) he decided to be (Gr., that it was) suitable.

ΠΕΜΠΤΟΝ ΜΑΘΗΜΑ.—Fifth Lesson.

πέμπτον is precisely our *fifth*, for *fimfth*.

Οὕτω λοιπὸν μετά τινας μῆνας, ἡμέραν τινὰ πέμπτην
Oo'taw leepaw'n mehtah'-teenahss mee'nahss, eemeh'rahn-teenah peh'mbdeen
Thus then after some months, one-day fifth

32 A GUIDE TO MODERN GREEK.

τῆς ἑβδομάδος, ὡραῖα ἐπισκεπτήρια δίκην
teess ehvdhawmah'dhawss, awreh'-ah ehpeeskehptee'reeah dhee'keen
of-the week, beautiful cards in-the-form

μετριοφρόνων προσκλητηρίων διενεμήθησαν εἰς τοὺς
mehtreeawfraw'nawn prawsklecteeree'awn dhee-ehnehmee'theeasahn eess tooss
of-modest invitations were-distributed to the

γνωρίμους καὶ φίλους τοῦ Κυρίου Σουσαμάκη ὧν ἕν
ghnawree'mooss keh fee'looss too Keeree'oo Soossahmah'kee awn ehn
acquaintances and friends of-the Mr. Susamákis of-which one

ἔλαβε καὶ ὁ Κ. Παρδαλὸς ἔχον οὕτω—Ὁ Κύριος
eh'lahveh keh aw K. Pardhahlaw'ss eh'khawn oo'taw — Aw Kee'reeawss
received also the Mr. Pardalós, running thus — The Mr.

καὶ ἡ Κυρία Σουσαμάκη παρακαλοῦσι τὸν Κύριον καὶ
keh ee Keeree'ah Soosahmah'kee pahrahkahloo'ssee tawng-Gee'reeawn keh
and the Mrs. Susamákis beg the Mr. and

τὴν Κυρίαν Παρδαλοῦ νὰ λάβωσι τὴν καλοσύνην νὰ
teeng-Geeree'ahn Pardhahloo' nah lah'vawssee teeng-gahlawssee'neen nah
the Mrs. Pardalós that they-have the goodness that

πάρωσι τὸ τζάϊ εἰς τὴν οἰκίαν των τὴν Κυριακὴν,
pah'rawssee taw tsah'ee eess teen eekee'ahn-dawn teeng-Geereeahkee'n,
they-take the tea at the house of-them the Sunday

δέκα Νοεμβρίου εἰς τὰς ὀκτὼ τὸ ἑσπέρας.
dheh'kah Naw-ehmvree'oo eess tahss awktaw' taw ehepeh'rahss.
ten(th) of-November at the eight the evening.

οὕτω: before a vowel οὕτως, for οὕτωτ, old instrumental case, from demonstrative οὕτο-, 'this,' = 'thus.'

λοιπὸν: neuter accusative absolute of λοιπό-, verbal adjective, from root λιπ-, 'leave,' with which it is cognate. Hence λοιπὸν as adverb = 'what is left,' i. e. accordingly, therefore; first used in this sense by Polybius, afterwards in New Testament. Formerly οὖν for ὄντ, i. e. 'being,' was employed in this sense.

μετὰ: with accusative = 'after.' Observe accent.

τινὰς: for τινὰνς, accusative plural of stem τιν-. Loses accent when enclitic.

μῆνας: for μῆνανς; see above.

ἡμέραν = ἡμέρα, 'day' + ν; accusative of time.

τινὰ: for τινὰν, accusative, masculine, or feminine; here feminine.

πέμπτην: 'fifth,' here 'Thursday,' as explained by τῆς ἑβδομάδος = ἑβδομάδ-, + ος, genitive ending; from ἕβδομο-, 'seventh,' adjective of ἑπτὰ, 'seven,' for σεπτὰν, itself softened from ἑπτομο-; cf. Latin *septem, septimus*. ἑπτὰ(ν) is probably a bye-form of ἑπτὸν, i.e. σεπτὸν, verbal adjective from ἑπ- (σεπ-), 'to follow,' and this for σεκϝ-; ἑπτὰ meaning perhaps, originally, 'the following,' 'the next,' like *secundus* for *sequendus* in Latin: counting being in early times on the fingers, in which seven would be the second of the second series, as two was of the first. This is Professor Sayce's suggestion.

ὡραῖα: from ὥρα-, our *year*, Latin *hora* + ι, adjectival suffix + α, neuter plural ending. Hence ὡραῖα = 'seasonable,' 'fair,' 'beautiful.'

ἐπισκεπτήρια: from ἐπὶ, 'upon,' σκεπτ-, verbal adjective stem of σκεπ- (see above) + substantive suffix -ήρια, neuter plural nominative of -ήριο-, meaning the instrument with which a thing is done. Hence ἐπισκέπτομαι meaning 'I visit;' ἐπισκεπτήρια are 'visiting-cards.'

δίκην = δίκη, 'form,' 'fashion' + ν; accusative and as adverb, meaning 'in the form of'—as we say, 'the shape of,' without 'in.' δίκη also means 'a form of law,' 'justice,' 'trial,' &c.

μετριοφρόνων: genitive plural of μετριόφρον-, from μέτριο-, 'measured,' 'moderate,' and φρον-, 'thinking.' Hence μετριοφρόνων, 'modest.'

προσκλητηρίων: formed like ἐπισκεπτήρια from προσκλητ-, verbal adjective stem of root προσκλε- (κλα- καλ-); see above. Hence προσκλητήρια, 'cards of invitation.'

διενεμήθησαν: δι (for διὰ) + ε, sign of past + νεμη, lengthened

D

stem of root νεμ-, 'arrange,' 'assign' + θη- = d, sign of passive + σαν = 'they.' Hence διενεμήθησαν = '[they] were distributed.'

τούς : for τόνς.

γνωρίμους : for γνωρίμονς, accusative plural of γνώριμο- = stem γνωρ-, as in *gnarus*, *ignoro*, &c., from root γνοϝ-, *know* + -ιμο-, adjectival ending. Hence γνώριμο-, 'a knowable' or 'known one,' 'an acquaintance.' γνώριμοι, nominative of γνωρίμους (observe accent), 'acquaintances.'

φίλους : for φίλονς, from root φιλ-, 'dear,' whence also φιλέω, 'I love,' 'I kiss,' literally 'I am a friend of.'

ὦν : for ὅων, genitive plural of ὁ-, relative.

ἔλαβε = (ἐ + λαβ = 'take' + ε = 'he') = 'did-take-he' = '[he] took,' 'received.'

ἔχον : for ἔχοντ, literally 'having,' here 'running' or 'reading.'

παρακαλοῦσι : for παρακαλέοντι = stem παρακαλε- + οντι = 'they.'

λάβωσι : for λάβωντι = λάβ-, 'take' + ωντι, 'they may,' subjunctive. Observe λαβ- is aorist or instantaneous stem, viz. the simple root. The imperfect is λαμβαν-, putting in μ and adding αν; λαμβάνω, 'I take,' ἔλαβον or ἔλαβα (Modern), 'I took,' ἐλάμβανον (a), 'I was taking.'

καλοσύνην : from καλο- + -σύνη = -ness. Hence καλοσύνην, 'goodness.' The ending ν has been so often explained that we shall not mention it again, unless for some special reason.

πάρωσι = παρ + ωσι, explained above. παρ- is for ἐπαρ-, from ἐπί, 'up,' and ἀρ-, 'take.' Imperfect stem, παίρν-.

τζάι : the Chinese word, sometimes declined to the extent of a genitive, τοῦ τζαίου. An alternative is the more Greek-looking form τὸ τέιον, τοῦ τείου, from the French *thé*.

οἰκίαν : feminine formed from masculine stem οἰκο- for ϝοῖκο-, Latin *vico-* (nominative *vicus*), 'a house,' 'a dwelling.'

των : 'their,' 'of them ;' cf. του above.

Κυριακὴν: from Κυριακὀ- ἢ, adjective by suffix -κ- from Κύριο-, 'Lord.' Hence Κυριακὴ = (dies) dominicus or -a. Cf. Spanish *domingo*, French *dimanche*, &c.; 'the day of the Lord,' 'Sunday.'

δέκα: cardinal used for ordinal, explained above.
τὰς: i. e. ὥρας, 'hours.'
ὀκτώ: Latin *octo*, our *eight*.
τὸ ἑσπέρας: accusative of time.

Idiomatic Translation.

Accordingly, in a few months, one Thursday, some beautiful cards in the form of modest invitations were distributed among the friends and acquaintance of Mr. Susamákis, one of which was received by Mr. Pardalós, and ran as follows:—" Mr. and Mrs. Susamákis request the favour of Mr. and Mrs. Pardalós' company to tea on Sunday, the 10th of November, at eight o'clock in the evening.

Exercise V.

Οὕτω λοιπὸν διενεμήθησαν τὰ ἐπισκέπτηρια τοῦ Κυρίου Παρδαλοῦ. Ὁ Κύριος Παρδαλὸς ἦτο γνώριμος καὶ φίλος τοῦ Κυρίου Σουσαμάκη. Ἡ Κυρία ἔλαβε προσκλητήρια δίκην μετριοφρόνων ἀλλὰ ὡραίων ἐπισκεπτηρίων ἐχόντων οὕτω. Ὁ Κύριος καὶ ἡ Κυρία Παρδαλοῦ ἔχουσιν τὴν καλοσύνην νὰ πάρωσι τὸ τζάϊ εἰς τὴν οἰκίαν τῶν φίλων καὶ γνωρίμων των Κυρίου καὶ Κυρίας Σουσαμάκη. Τὴν πέμπτην, δέκα Νοεμβρίου εἰς τὰς ὀκτὼ τὸ ἑσπέρας οἱ γνώριμοι τοῦ Κυρίου ἐσυλλογίσθησαν νὰ πάρωσι τὸ τζάϊ εἰς τὴν οἰκίαν του.

The lady and gentleman are invited to take tea at the house of their friends and acquaintances. Beautiful visiting cards in the form of modest invitations were distributed on a Thursday. Thursday is the fifth of November and the fifth day of the week. After a few months and a few days he altered his mind and decided thus. Mr. Pardalós received some modest invitations in the form of visiting cards. Sunday is the first day (ἡ πρώτη ἡμέρα) of the week.

ΕΚΤΟΝ ΜΑΘΗΜΑ.—Sixth Lesson.

ἕκτον: for σέκτον, adjective, from ἐξ (ἕκ-ς), 'six.' The ς, though an integral part of the word, is lost in the process of composition in Greek. Cf., however, *sextus* in Latin.

N.B.—The interlinear transliteration is henceforth dispensed with.

Σημειωτέον ὅτι τὴν ἡμέραν ταύτην ἐξέλεξεν ἡ ἁβρὰ
To-be-noted that the day this chose the fine

πρόνοια τῆς Κυρίας Σουσαμάκη καθότι τὴν Κυριακὴν
foresight of-the Mrs. Susamákis forasmuch-as the Sunday

ἐκείνην συνέπιπτεν ἡ ἐπέτειος τῆς ἑορτῆς τοῦ νεαροῦ
that coincided the yearly of-the festival of-the youthful

τῆς συζύγου—ὁ Σουσαμάκης ἐκαλεῖτο Ὀρέστης—καὶ ἡ
of-her consort (the Susamákis was-called Orestes) and the

νεόνυμφος Πασιφάη ἐσκέφθη ὅτι προσφυέστατον ἦτο νὰ
new-wed Pasiphae reflected that most-fitting was-it that

πανηγυρισθῶσι διὰ τοῦ αὐτοῦ χοροῦ καὶ διὰ τοῦ αὐτοῦ
be-celebrated by the same ball and by the same

κυπέλλου τείου ὅ τε γάμος της καὶ ἡ ἑορτὴ τοῦ
cup of-tea both-the marriage of-her and the festival of-the

συμβίου της.
spouse of-her.

Σημειωτέον = σημειο-, verbal stem from σημεῖο-, and that from σημα(τ)-, verbal substantive from root ση- (not found) + suffix τε, meaning 'to be' + neuter ending ον = '[It is] to be remarked.'

ταύτην: feminine stem ταύτα- (η-), answering to masculine τοῦτο- = 'this.'

ἐξέλεξεν: for ἐξέλεγσεν = ἐξ, 'out' + ε, sign of past time + λεγ-, root = 'choose' + σ, sign of first aorist, instantaneous tense + ἐ(ν) (for ετ) = 'he,' 'she,' or 'it' (3rd person). Hence ἐξέλεξεν, ['she,' i. e. πρόνοια] 'chose.'

ἁβρὰ, nominative and stem (feminine), probably from root μαρ-, Indo-Germanic *mar-*, 'to grind,' 'powder,' and often bye-form of μαλ-, ἁβρὸ- ἁβρὰ being itself a bye-form of μωρὸ- μωρὰ; cf. vocative βρὲ for μωρέ, now a mere interjection. μωρὸς, originally 'fool,' means 'a boy' in Modern Greek, as ἅβρα in the Septuagint means 'a maiden.' The root idea seems to be that of softness, tenderness in the noun, softening, bruising in the verb. Cognate are probably *mill*, μῦλος; German *Mühle*, and *mahlen*, 'to grind;' our *meal*; Greek μάρ-ναμαι, 'I fight;' Modern Greek μαλόνω, 'I fight;' cf. the slang use of *mill*. Cognate is English *mild*, with suffix *d*; also Greek μαλ-ακὸς and μαλ-θακός. The change μρ- μλ- to βλ- βρ- in Greek is a constant phenomenon, while ἁ or ὁ, either aspirated or not, is a common phonetic prefix.

πρόνοια: for πρόγνοια (cf. ἄγνοια, 'ignorance,' and Modern Greek ἔγνοια for ἔννοια, i. e. ἐν-γνοια) = πρὸ, kin to *for, fore*, and γνοια- = γνο + ια, ια being feminine nominative stem. Hence πρόγνοια, πρόνοια, 'foreknowledge,' 'prudence' (*providentia*), 'foresight.'

καθότι: for κατ' ὅτι, i. e. κατὰ ὅτι. Though the rough breathing (‘) is not heard in Greek, classical tradition requires π, τ, κ to be changed to their corresponding aspirates when immediately followed by ‘. καθότι = literally 'according that' or 'according as.'

ἐκείνην: demonstrative pronoun, formed from demonstrative adverb ἐκεῖ, 'there,' by formative suffix ν- ο-, ν- η-.

συνέπιπτεν: συν, see above; ε as before; πιπτ-, reduplicated, imperfect, or frequentative stem (cf. *sist-*, ἵστα-, κ.τ.λ.) for πίπετ-, from root πετ-, Sanscrit *pat-*, 'to fly,' 'leap,' 'fall' [upon]. From same root are probably Latin *petere*, 'to seek,' our *find* (by nasalization); also πτερόν, English *feather*, &c.; -εν as above. Hence συνέπιπτεν, imperfect, 'coincided,' i. e. would coincide.

ἐπέτειος = ἐπέτειο + ς: masculine and feminine nominative; ἐπέτειο- = preposition ἐπ- for ἐπὶ + ἔτες-, 'year' + ιο, adjectival stem, masculine, feminine, neuter. Hence ἐπέτειος = 'on-the-year,' 'yearly.' The lost ϝ of ἔτος for ϝέτος appears as aspirate in the Modern Greek form ἐφέτος for ἐπέτος, 'this year,' i. e. in (the current) year; cf. "to-day" for "this day." ἡ ἐπέτειος [ἡμέρα] = 'the anniversary [day].'

νεαροῦ: from νεαρὸ-, from νέο-, 'young' + adjectival suffix ρο- = -ish. Hence νεαρὸ-, 'youngish,' 'youthful.'

συζύγου: from σὺν + ζυγὸ-, 'yoke,' whence adjective and substantive σύζυγο- (observe accent), 'yoke-fellow,' the Latin *conjug-* (nominative *conjux* for *conjugs*), 'consort,' 'husband,' 'wife;' masculine or feminine.

ἐκαλεῖτο + ἐ + καλέ- (see above) + ετο + 'he was;' contracted from ἐκαλέετο; hence '[he] was called.'

Ὀρέστης: from stem Ὀρέστα- (η-) + ς; literally, perhaps, 'a mountaineer:' ὄρες- = 'mountain' + τα- τη- = 'man who does, or has to do with,' like ending *eer*.

νεόνυμφο + ς: from νέο- and νυμφ-, see above; masculine or feminine; here feminine.

Πασιφάη, literally 'bright to all:' from πᾶσι for πάντ + σι, dative plural ending + φάη, kin to φάος for φάοτ-, φῶς for φωτ-, 'light.'

προσφυέστατον = πρὸς + φυ-, our *be* + ες-, adjectival suffix + τατο + ν = superlative suffix with neuter accusative (also nominative) ending. Hence προσφυέσ- = 'grown-to,' 'fit,' 'natural,' 'proper;' προφυέστατον, 'most fitting.'

ἐσκέφθη: formed like ἐσυλλογίσθη from root σκεπ-, see above.

πανηγυρισθῶσι: for πανηγυρισθῶντι = πανηγυριδ + θ, sign of aorist or instantaneous passive + ωντι, ending, 3rd person plural = 'they,' lengthened from indicative ending οντι; cf. -ῇ for -εῖ, above, &c.

διά: for δϝιά, 'through,' 'by means of;' see above. In this sense construed with genitive.

αὐτοῦ: after article = 'same;' before article, 'very,' or 'it self;' or in Modern Greek also 'this,' 'that;' e.g. διὰ αὐτοῦ τοῦ χοροῦ (δι' αὐτοῦ τοῦ χοροῦ), 'by the dance itself;' διὰ τοῦ αὐτοῦ χοροῦ, 'by the same dance.'

κυπέλλου: neuter (nominative κύπελλον), a diminutive from obsolete root κύπο- or κύπα-; in Modern Greek κοῦπα, 'a cup.'

ὅ τε: τε, bye-form of καὶ pronounced κὲ, but always enclitic like Latin *que* and Sanscrit *cha*. Hence ὅ τε, 'both the;' observe accent thrown back from τὲ to ὁ, which, else unaccented, has now the acute.

ἑορτή: for ἐ-Ϝορ-τ-ή, containing, perhaps, root *var*, our *ware*, 'to keep,' 'observe,' kin to Latin *vereor, reverentia*, &c. + nominal suffix τα- (τη-). Hence ἑορτή, 'a ceremony,' 'festival;' the ἐ seems like the ἁ in ἁβρά, merely phonetic; -τ- is noun suffix.

συμβίου = σὺν + βίου = genitive of σύμβιο-; βίο- for βίϜο-, pronoun ϜίϜο- or βίβο-, kin to Latin *vivo-, vivus, vivere*; cf. *vis* and βία, 'force.' Hence σύμβιο- = 'living with,' 'husband,' or 'wife;' masculine or feminine.

Idiomatic Translation.

We should observe that the fine foresight of Mrs. Susamákis had chosen this day, because on the Sunday in question the anniversary of her youthful husband's birthday also fell, and the newly-married Pasiphae reflected that it would be just the thing to celebrate, by means of the same ball and the same cup of tea, both her own marriage and the birthday of her spouse.

Exercise VI.

Ἡ Πασιφάη ἦτο νεόνυμφος σύζυγος τοῦ νεαροῦ Σουσαμάκη. Ἡ Κυριακὴ εἶνε προσφυεστάτη ἡμέρα πρὸς πανηγυρισμὸν τῶν γάμων. Συνέπιπτεν ἐκείνην τὴν ἡμέραν καὶ χορὸς καὶ γάμος. Ὅ τε Ὀρέστης καὶ ἡ Πασιφάη εἶνε νεόνυμφοι σύζυγοι. Ὁ Ὀρέστης ἦτο σύζυγος τῆς Πασιφάης. Ἡ Πασιφάη εἶνε σύμβιος τοῦ νεαροῦ Κυρίου. Ἡ ἐπέτειος ἑορτὴ συμφυέστατον νὰ πανηγυρισθῇ, καὶ οἱ νεόνυμφοι σύζυγοι είνε προσκεκλημένοι. Ὁ σύμβιος τῆς Πασιφάης ἐκαλεῖτο Ὀρέστης.

It is to be observed that Sunday is the anniversary of his birthday. His spouse and himself (αὐτὸς) were (ἦσαν) newly married. Is it suitable that the marriage and the anniversary of the birthday of that gentleman should be celebrated by the same dance and the same cup of tea? It is just the thing.

ΕΒΔΟΜΟΝ ΜΑΘΗΜΑ.—Seventh Lesson.

Οὕτω λοιπὸν τὴν ἑσπέραν τῆς Κυριακῆς διπλαῖ
Thus then the evening of-the Sunday twofold

συγχρόνως γίνονται ἑτοιμασίαι· ἑτοιμασίαι ὑποδοχῆς
simultaneously happen preparations; preparations of-reception

ἐν τῷ οἴκῳ τοῦ Σουσαμάκη, καὶ ἑτοιμασίαι ἐπισκέψεως
in the house of-the Susamákis, and preparations of-visit

ἐν τῷ οἴκῳ τοῦ Παρδαλοῦ. Ἂς μνημονεύσωμεν ἐν
in the house of-the Pardalós. Let us-observe in

παρόδῳ, καὶ πρὶν ἢ εἰσέλθωμεν εἰς τὰς οἰκίας τοῦ
passing, and before we-enter into the houses of-the

Ἀμφιτρύωνος καὶ τοῦ ξένου του, ὅτι τὴν προτεραίαν,
Amphitryon and of-the guest of-him, that the day-before,

τὸ ἑσπέρας, καθ' ἣν στιγμὴν ὁ Κύριος Παρδαλὸς
the evening, at what moment the Mr. Pardalós

ἡτοιμάζετο νὰ ἀναχωρήσῃ ἐκ τοῦ γραφείου, ἐπλησίασεν
was-preparing that he-depart out-of the office, approached

εἰς αὐτὸν δειλῶς ὁ Σουσαμάκης, καὶ περιελίσσων εἰς
to him timidly the Susamákis, and twisting-round in

τοὺς δακτύλους του τὴν ἅλυσιν τοῦ ὡρολογίου του, ἵνα
the fingers of-him the chain of-the watch of-him, that

διασκεδάσῃ πως τὴν δειλίαν αὐτοῦ, τῷ εἶπε, μειδιῶν
he-divert somewhat the timidity of-him, to-him said, smiling

γλυκερὸν μειδίαμα σεβασμοῦ καὶ ὑποταγῆς· — Λοιπὸν
a-dulcet smile of-respect and of-subjection:— Then

. . . θὰ σας ἔχωμεν αὔριον τὸ ἑσπέρας, Κύριε Διευθυντά;
shall you we-have to-morrow the evening, Mr. Director ?

Χωρὶς ἄλλο, Κύριε Σουσαμάκη . . . χωρὶς ἄλλο!
Without aught-else, Mr. Susamákis — without aught-else!

ἀπήντησεν ὁ Κύριος Παρδαλὸς ἀντιμειδιῶν καὶ ἐκεῖνος
replied the Mr. Pardalós back-smiling also he

μειδίαμα ὑπεροχῆς καὶ προστασίας.
a-smile of-superiority and patronage.

διπλαῖ: short for διπλόαι = δι-, 'two' (in composition) + πλο-, 'fold,' with first three letters of which it is identical + αι, ending of feminine plural.

ἑτοιμασίαι: ending as above; from ἑτοιμαδ- from ἕτοιμο-, 'ready' + αδ-, verbal suffix + σία-, feminine substantive suffix. Hence = 'a making ready.'

συγχρόνως: for συγχρόνωι (cf. οὕτως), old instrumental (adverbial) case of σύγχρονο-, from συν + χρόνο-, 'time ;' i. e. 'at one time,' or 'simultaneously.'

γίνονται: for γίγνονται, from γιγν-, imperfect stem doubled from γεν-, akin to kin + ονται = 'they,' middle or deponent and passive ending, 3rd person plural. We here exhibit all persons : γίγν-ομαι, I become ; γίγν-εσαι (classical, γίγν-ῃ or ει), thou, &c. ; γίγν-εται, he, she, it, &c. ; γιγν-όμεθα, we, &c. ; γίγν-εσθε, you, &c. ; γίγν-ονται, they, &c. (as above).

ὑποδοχῆς = ὑπὸ, 'under' + δοχὴ, 'a taking' + ς, genitive ending, from root δεχ-, 'take,' whence δέχομαι, &c., 'I take.' Thus ὑποδοχὴ = 'an undertaking,' 'taking up,' 'reception.' Cases as follows: Singular, ὑποδοχὴ -ὴν -ῆς -ῇ. Plural, ὑποδοχαὶ -ὰς -ῶν -αῖς.

The order of the cases here and elsewhere is as follows: Nominative, Vocative (only given separately when different from nominative), Accusative, Genitive, Dative.

οἶκο-: masculine form of οἰκία-, explained above. οἶκος, ε, ον, οἴκου, οἴκῳ· (observe accent), οἶκοι, οἴκους, οἴκων, οἴκοις.

ἐπισκέψεως: from stem ἐπισκεπ-, explained above + σεως, genitive ending of substantive suffix σι-. ἐπίσκεψις, ἐπίσκεψιν, ἐπισκέψεως, ἐπισκέψει. ἐπισκέψεις, ἐπισκέψεις, ἐπισκέψεων, ἐπισκέψεσι(ν).

Ἄς: shortened from ἄφες, i. e. ἀπ' for ἀπὸ + ἕς = ἕ, root meaning 'send' + ς, sign of 2nd person. Hence ἄφες, 'send thou forth,' 'let go,' 'let be,' 'suffer,' 'let.' Thus ἅς μνημονεύσωμεν, 'let us observe;' cf. in New Testament, ἄφες ἐκβάλω, 'let me cast out,' ἄφες ἴδωμεν, 'let's see,' &c.

μνημονεύσωμεν: aorist stem of μνημονευ- from μνήμον-, 'remembering,' 'mindful,' from root μνα- μνε- lengthened to μνη-, 'remind,' 'remember' + μον-, ending signifying 'man-doing,' 'agent.' Hence μνημονευ-, 'make mindful,' 'remind,' 'observe,' 'relate,' 'record' + ωμεν = 'we may.' Persons as follows: μνημονεύσω, μνημονεύσῃς, μνημονεύσῃ· μνημονεύσωμεν, μνημονεύσητε, μνημονεύσωσιν (vernacular, μνημονεύσουν).

παρόδῳ: from παρ' (παρὰ), 'by,' and ὁδὸ- for σοδὸ-, from root ἑδ- (σεδ-); perhaps kin to English *send*, Spanish *senda*, 'a path.' N.B.—The nasalization of a root, e. g. *send* for *sed*, is a very common phenomenon in all the Aryan languages. Hence πάροδος, 'a passing,' 'a going by;' observe accent, which in oxytone substantives compounded with prepositions goes back to last syllable but two. Cases with article: ἡ πάροδος, τὴν πάροδον, τῆς παρόδου, τῇ παρόδῳ· αἱ πάροδαι, τὰς παρόδους, τῶν παρόδων, ταῖς παρόδοις.

πρὶν: for πρὶμ, kin to *primus*, Latin, and to our *fore, first*, &c.

ἤ: connecting particle, link-word or conjunction, joining πρὶν with verb like our "that" in "before that." Generally, ἤ when alone means either 'or,'—ἤ ... ἤ, 'either ... or'—or 'than.'

εἰσέλθωμεν : second aorist, in construction like μνημονεύσωμεν. A second aorist means one formed from the simplest root of the verb, without the aid of σ or its substitutes; it is like a *strong* as opposed to a *weak* formation in German or English, only that it does not necessarily modify the vowel. There is a superstition in the mind of the learner, difficult to eradicate, that there is some difference of force between a first and second aorist. There is no more than between *digged* and *dug*. εἰσέλθωμεν = εἰς, 'into' + ἐλθ-, short for ἐλυθ-, 'come' or 'go' + ωμεν = 'we [may] go in,' 'enter' (subjunctive).

οἰκίας : for οἰκίανς, accusative plural of οἰκία-, explained above. οἰκία -αν -ας -ᾳ· -αι -ας -ῶν -αις.

Ἀμφιτρύων + ος, proper name. ἀμφὶ is a preposition = Latin *ambi* in *ambidexter*, &c., apparently compounded of the syllables ἀν- or ἀμ-; cf. ἀμφορά, 'a holder-round,' 'container,' 'vessel,' the German *um* in *umfassen*, &c. + φὶ = *by*, not found save as case-ending or in composition in Greek; τρύων (for τρύωνς), nominative, means really 'the borer.' The root τρυ-, with its variants τερ- τρα- τρο-, &c., is found in our *through*, *thorough*, *thrust*, *thread*, *thrums*, &c., always with suffixes, but the idea of piercing is present in all. Amphitryon was a character in Grecian mythology, and the allusion is here apparently to the wedding-feast which he gave at Thebes, when Zeus forestalled him in his marriage with Alkmene. It is about as inappropriate as forced classical allusions usually are. See Grote's "History of Greece," vol. i. p. 127. Ἀμφιτρύων, Ἀμφιτρύωνα, Ἀμφιτρύωνος, Ἀμφιτρύωνι· plural (scarcely found): Ἀμφιτρύωνες -τρύωνας -τρυώνων -τρύωσιν.

ξένου : genitive of ξένο-, 'stranger,' 'guest,' probably from preposition ἐξ, by means of an aorist ἐξένευσα through ἐκνευ-, ἐκνεϝ-, 'sail forth,' 'go,' being mistaken for that of a supposed ξενευ-, 'to be a ξένος.' ξένος, ξένε, ξένον, ξένου, ξένῳ· ξένοι, ξένους, ξένων, ξένοις.

προτεραίαν, i. e. ἡμέραν : from προτερο-, comparative of πρὸ (see above) + adjective suffix αι-ο, -α (masculine and feminine) = 'belonging to.' Strictly speaking, the adjective suffix is simply -ι- added to the feminine προτέρα [ἡμέρα].

καθ' ἥν: for κατὰ ἥν, see above; ἥν, relative feminine accusative. ὅς, ἥ, ὅ· ὅν, ἥν, ὅ· οὗ, ἧς, οὗ· ᾧ, ᾗ, ᾧ· οἵ, αἵ, ἅ· οὕς, ἅς, ἅ· ὧν, ὧν, ὧν· οἷς, αἷς, οἷς. The use of this relative belongs to literary style. In the vernacular, either the indeclinable ποῦ or ὅπου, in classical Greek meaning 'where'—cf. our *who*, and the German provincial *wo*—is employed, but never with prepositions; or else the compound ὁ ὁποῖος, ἡ ὁποία, τὸ ὁποῖον, which exactly answers in original sense to the French *lequel, laquelle*, Spanish *el cual, la cuale*, from Latin *illum qualem, illam qualem*.

στιγμὴν: στιγμὴ + ν = στιγ-, 'prick' + μη- (μα-), verbal substantive suffix. Hence στιγμὴ = 'point of time,' 'moment.' Cases as ὑποδοχή.

ἡτοιμάζετο: formed, like ἐ-καλέ-ετο above (ἐ + ἐ coalescing into ή), from ἐτοιμαδ-, see above. ἡτοιμαζόμην, ἡτοιμάζεσο (classical -ου), -ετο· -όμεθα -εσθε -οντο.

ἀναχωρήσῃ: cf. προμηθεύσῃ· = ἀναχωρε- + σῃ, with ε lengthened to η in composition. ἀναχωρήσω -ῃς -ῃ· -ωμεν -ητε -ωσι (-ουν). From ἀνά, 'up,' 'away;' χωρε-, 'move,' cognate with χώρα-, 'place.'

ἐπλησίασεν = ἐ + πλησιαδ + σεν for σετ; πλησιαδ- like ἐτοιμαδ-, from πλησίο-, 'near.' Hence ἐπλησίασα, 'I approached.' ἐπλησίασας, ἐπλησίασεν· ἐπλησιάσαμεν -άσατε -ασαν.

δειλῶς: for δειλῶτ from δειλό-, adjective of root δι-, 'to fear,' whence δεες- for διες- (nominative δέος), 'fear,' by addition of ending λό, δειλῶς standing for δεελῶς, kin to Latin *di* in *dirus*. The primary notion seems to be that of 'haste,' 'flight:' Sanscrit *dî-yá-mi*, 'I haste,' 'flee.' Hence also δῖνος, 'whirlpool,' 'eddy;' δίνω, δινέω, δινεύω, 'I whirl,' 'swing,' 'brandish;' δεινός, 'terrible,' active corresponding to δειλός.

περιελίσσων: for περιελίσσοντς from περί, 'round,' 'about' + ἐλίσσοντ + ς; ἐλίσσοντ- is for ἐλίκοντ-, imperfect participle stem from root ἑλικ-, whence ἕλιξ (ἕλικς), 'a snail;' ἑλικ- is lengthened by suffix -ικ from root ἑλ- for ϝελ-, kin to *volvo*, 'turn.' Imperfect participles are declined thus :—

ἑλίσσων (-οντς)	-ουσα (-οντσα)	-ον (-οντ)
-οντα	-ουσαν	-ον
-οντος	-ούσης	-οντος
-οντι	-ούσῃ	-οντι
-οντες	-ουσαι	-οντα
-οντας	-ούσας	-οντα
-όντων	-ουσῶν	-όντων
-ουσι(ν)	-ούσαις	-ουσι(ν).

τούς: for τόνς. We here give the article entire :—

ὁ ἡ τό,   τὸν τὴν τό,   τοῦ τῆς τοῦ,   τῷ τῇ τῷ.
οἱ αἱ τά,   τοὺς τὰς τά,   τῶν τῶν τῶν,   τοῖς ταῖς τοῖς.

δακτύλους: for δακτύλονς from δάκτυλο + ν + ς, from root δακ- (δικ-), kin to German *zeigen*, *zeihen*, 'point,' 'show,' 'inform,' 'accuse;' the word δάκτυλο- itself being kin to *digitus*, *zehe*, *toe*. δάκτυλος (vocative -ε), δάκτυλον, δακτύλου, δακτύλῳ· δάκτυλοι, δακτύλους, δακτύλων, δακτύλοις.

ἄλυσιν: from verbal stem ἁλυ-, enlarged from root ἁλ- ἁλ- ἐλ- from ϝελ-, 'to bind,' 'shut in ;' kin to Sanscrit *var*, German *wehren*, *Gewehr*; suffix -σι, as in στέψι-, ἐπίσκεψι-, κ.τ.λ. ἅλυσις, ἅλυσιν, ἁλύσεως, ἁλύσει· ἁλύσεις, ἁλύσεων, ἁλύσεσιν.

ὡρολογίου: from ὡρολόγιο- = ὡρα- (ὡρο- in composition) + λόγιο-, from root λογ-, 'to reckon.' Hence ὡρολόγιον, 'timepiece,' 'watch,' 'clock.' ὡρολόγιον -ίου -ίῳ· -ια -ίων -ίοις.

N.B.—Neuter nominative and accusative are always the same.

ἵνα: full form of να, and with fuller sense, 'in order to;' in vernacular, διὰ νά.

διασκεδάσῃ: for διασκεδάδ-σῃ = διά, 'about,' 'in different directions' + σκεδαδ-, 'scatter' + σῃ = 'he may.'

δειλίαν: noun from δειλό-, 'fearful.' Hence δειλία = 'cowardice,' 'timidity.'   δειλία -αν -ας -ᾳ, plural (scarcely found) δειλίαι -ας -ῶν -αις.

τῷ: proclitic pronoun personal = τὸ + ι dative.

μειδιῶν: for μειδιάοντς, imperfect participle of μειδια-, 'smile,' with which (cf. μειλίχιος, 'mild,' 'kind') it is probably kin. Cf. also δάκρυ-, 'tear,' and Latin *lacruma*, old form *dacruma*, also *lingua* for *dingua*. Many words in Greek now beginning with μ have lost a σ; cf. μήρινθος, σμήρινθος; σμικρὸς, μικρός.

μειδιῶν	-ῶσα	-ιῶν	-ῶντες	-ῶσαι	-ῶντα.
-ῶντα	-ῶσαν	-ῶν	-ῶντας	-ώσας	-ῶντα.
-ῶντος	-ώσης	-ῶντος	-ώντων	-ωσῶν	-ώντων.
-ῶντι	-ώσῃ	-ῶντι	-ῶσιν	-ώσαις	-ῶσιν.

N.B.—Observe accents.

γλυκερὸν: from γλυκὺ-, 'sweet' + suffix ρὸ + ν = 'sweetish,' 'dulcet.'

μειδίαμα = μειδια- + μα(τ), verbal substantive suffix, 'a smile.' μειδίαμα, μειδιάματος, μειδιάματι; μειδιάματα, μειδιαμάτων, μειδιάμασιν.

N.B.—Suffix ματ- is always neuter.

σεβασμοῦ: for σεβαδ-μοῦ from σεβαδ-, verbal stem + suffix -μοῦ, genitive of μό-.   σεβασμὸς -μὸν -μῷ -μοὶ -μοὺς -μῶν -μοῖς.

ὑποταγῆς: like ὑποδοχῆς, from ὑπὸ (συπὸ), 'under' + ταγ-, 'range,' 'order.'

θὰ: a particle used with subjunctive to form future tense. Compare Homeric κε, κεν.

ἔχωμεν: lengthened from ἔχομεν, indicative, to form subjunctive imperfect. Personal endings as aorist.

αὔριον: αὔριο + ν, from stem αὐ + suffix ριο; αυ- appears also in ἑώς, αὔως for ἀϝώς, 'dawn,' Latin *aurora* for *ausosa*, &c. The aspirate in Attic ἑώς seems a relic of the ϝ in ἐϝώς, ἀϝώς, and though the common form αὔριον has the smooth breathing, the rough appears in the Modern Greek μεθαύριον for μετὰ αὔριον, 'the day after to-morrow;' cf. ἔτος, ἐφέτος, above.

Κύριε: vocative of Κύριο- by modification of final vowel.

Διευθυντά: from διευθυν- (see above) + τα- = 'man who does,' 'agent.' Hence διευθυντά- (nominative -ής), 'director,' 'manager.'

N.B.—Διευθυντά is at once the stem and the vocative case.

χωρὶς: for χωρίδ-ς, 'without,' from stem χωριδ-, 'to divide.'

ἄλλο: for ἄλιο, Latin *aliud*, &c., our *el* in *else*; χωρὶς ἄλλο, literally 'without an alternative,' i. e. of course, certainly.

ἀπήντησεν: from ἀπὸ + αντα- + σεν (σετ); αντα- = 'reply,' 'retort,' and is verbal stem from root ἀντ-, 'back,' found in preposition ἀντί, German *ant* in *Antwort*, our *ans* in *answer* for *answord*.

ἀντιμειδιῶν = ἀντὶ, 'again' or 'back' + μειδιῶν, 'smiling.'

ὑπεροχῆς: for ὑπὲρ (συπὲρ), Latin *super*, Albanian *siper*, 'above,' and root ἐχ-, 'have.' Hence ὑπερέχω, 'I have the advantage,' 'am superior,' and substantive ὑπεροχὴ, 'a having the advantage,' 'superiority.' Cases as ὑποταγή.

προστασίας = πρὸ + στα + σία, substantive ending, + ς, sign of genitive. Hence προστασίας = 'of a standing before,' i. e. patronage.

Idiomatic Translation.

Accordingly, on the evening of Sunday, the tenth of November, a double set of preparations are going on at the same time: preparations for a reception in the house of Susamákis, and preparations for a visit in the house of Pardalós.

Let us mention, in passing, and before we enter the homes of our Amphitryon and his guest, that on the evening of the day before, at the moment that Mr. Pardalós was preparing to leave his office, Susamákis timidly approached him, and twirling the chain of his watch in his fingers, the better to divert his timidity, said to him, with a dulcet smile of veneration and subjection,—

"Then we shall see you to-morrow evening, sir?"

"Certainly, certainly, Mr. Susamákis," replied Mr. Pardalós, smiling in his turn a smile of superiority and patronage.

Exercise VII.

Ἡ προστασία τοῦ Κυρίου διευθυντοῦ ἦτο γλυκερὸν μειδίαμα. Τὸ μειδίαμα τοῦ ὑπαλλήλου ἦτο μειδίαμα σεβασμοῦ καὶ ὑποταγῆς. Θὰ ἀναχωρήσῃ αὔριον τὸ ἑσπέρας. Περιελίσσει τοὺς δακτύλους του εἰς τὴν ἅλυσιν τοῦ ὡρολογίου ἵνα διασκεδάσῃ πως τὴν δειλίαν του. Ὑποδοχὴ καὶ ἐπίσκεψις γίνονται συγχρόνως. Τὸ μειδίαμα τοῦ διευθυντοῦ διεσκέδασε τὴν δειλίαν τοῦ ὑπαλλήλου. *Ας μνημονεύσωμεν ἐν παρόδῳ τὰς διπλᾶς ἑτοιμασίας αἵτινες γίνονται συγχρόνως εἰς τὰς δύο οἰκίας τοῦ Ἀμφιτρύωνος καὶ τοῦ ξένου του.

Sunday is the tenth of November. Preparations for a reception and preparations for a visit take place simultaneously in the two houses. Let us mention that at the moment when Mr. Pardalós was preparing to leave the office, he smiled a dulcet smile of superiority and patronage, and his subordinate in his turn answered by a smile of veneration and subjection. We approached him smiling, in order to dispel his timidity. You will see us (have us) to-morrow evening. Will they leave the office at the same time? Certainly.

ΟΓΔΟΟΝ ΜΑΘΗΜΑ.—Eighth Lesson.

ὄγδοον: for ὀκτοϝον, Latin *octavus*; cf. ἕβδομον for ἕπτομον.

Θοδωρῆ.—Ὁρίστε, ἀφέντη.—Πήγαινε νὰ πιάσῃς ἕν
John!—Command, master. — Go that you-take a

ἁμάξι μετὰ μισὴν ὥραν!—Πές του νὰ περάσῃ καὶ ἀπὸ
carriage after a-half hour!— Tell him that he-pass also by

τῆς Λιζιὲ νὰ μοῦ πάρῃ ἕνα ζευγάρι γάντια
the [Madame] Lisié's that me he-get a pair gloves

ἑπτάμισυ ἀριθμό, ἄσπρα! ἐφώνησεν ἐκ τοῦ δωματίου
seven-and-a-half number, white! shouted from the room

της ἡ Κυρία Εὐφροσύνη. — Καλά . . . καὶ τώρα
of-her the Mrs. Euphrosyne. — Well . . . and now

ἐνθυμήθης νὰ πάρῃς γάντια, εὐλογημένη;—Τὸ
you-have-remembered that you-get gloves, blessed-one? — It
ἐλησμόνησα! τί θέλεις νὰ κάμω τώρα;—Μὴ
forgot-I! What will-you that I-do now? — No
χειρότερα! ἐψιθύρισεν ὁ σύζυγος καὶ διεβίβασε τὴν
worse! whispered the husband and passed-on the
παραγγελίαν εἰς τὸν ὑπηρέτην ὅστις ἀπήντησε μὲν
order to the servant who answered indeed
μεγαλοφώνως·—Πολὺ καλὰ, ἀφέντη, ἀμέσως. . . . Ἀλλ᾽
aloud: — Very well, sir, directly. . . . But
ἐψιθύρισεν ὅμως σιγὰ καὶ ἥκιστα εὐσεβάστως· Μὰ
whispered however softly and least respectfully: Nay
ἀφεντικά, ἀλήθεια, ποῦ ὄχι καλλίτερα. Μεσ᾽ς τῂ
my-master, truth, since not better. In-the-midst-of the
λάσπη καὶ ᾽ς τῂ βροχὴ τρέχα ν᾽ ἀγοράζῃς γάντια καὶ νὰ
mud and in the rain run that you-buy gloves and that
πιάῃς ἁμάξι! Ἀ! δὲν θὰ γείνω κ᾽ἐγὼ ἀφέντης καμμιὰ
you-get a-cab! Ah! not shall become I-too a-master some
φορά;
time?

Θοδωρῆ: for Θεοδωρῆ, vocative and stem. Θοδωρῆς, Θοδωρῆ, Θοδωρῆ[ν], Θοδωρῆ: dative not used, since the form is vernacular. It is a further extension of the proper name Θεόδωρο-, from Θεὺ-, 'God,' and δῶρο-, 'gift.' Hence Θεόδωρος, 'the gift of God,' Greek translation of Hebrew *Johannan*, 'John,' a common name for a servant.

Ὁρίστε: shortened from ὁρίσατε, imperative first aorist, 2nd person plural of ὁριδ- from ὄρο-, 'a boundary;' cf. λογιδ-, from λόγο. Hence ὁρίζω (i. e. ὁρίδ?ω) = 'I set bounds, 'ordain,' 'command.' Ὁρίστε is a very common expression in colloquial

E

Greek; addressed by a servant to his master it means, 'Yes, sir,' 'Here, sir,' &c.; among equals it answers to the French *plait-il?* and the German *wie beliebt?* Ὁρίστε ἐδώ or ἀπ' ἐδώ means 'This way please,' or 'Come this way;' Ὁρίστε by itself sometimes means simply 'Come!' 'Come in!' καλῶς ὡρίσατε, aorist indicative, is equivalent to καλῶς ἤλθατε, 'You are welcome' (well-come).

ἀφέντη: vocative and stem (observe how often these coincide). Cases: ἀφέντης, ἀφέντη(ν), ἀφέντη, ἀφέντη; no dative. This word is usually regarded as a corruption of αὐθέντης, shortened for αὐτοέντης, i. e. αὐτὸ-έντης = αὐτὸ-, 'self,' 'very' + ἔντης, 'doer' (only found in this combination), from root ἐ, Sanscrit *ja*, 'go;' in causative sense, as in ἵημι, 'I make to go,' 'send,' 'put in motion' + derivative or paragogic ν + -της = -er. αὐθέντης in classical Greek means 'the real doer.' Hence as euphemism, sometimes 'criminal,' sometimes 'suicide,' *felo de se*; once, perhaps, in Euripides, 'lord,' 'master,' a meaning confirmed by the Septuagint derivative αὐθεντία, 'authority,' and the adjective αὐθεντικός used by critics and grammarians, as opposed to ἀδέσποτος, 'masterless,' 'unowned.' Hence our *authentic*, and hence too the false spelling *author, authority*, which should have been *autor, autority*, being shortened from Latin *auctor, auctoritatem*, and having nothing whatever etymologically in common with αὐθέντης. It is, however, more than doubtful whether αὐθέντης would naturally contract to ἀφέντης in Modern Greek. αὐθέντης would be pronounced αὐτέντης (*ahftèh'ndeess*) in the vernacular, and as αὐτός becomes ἀτός, never ἀφός, so αὐθέντης (αὐτέντης) might become ἀτέντης, but scarcely ἀφέντης. It seems more rational to take ἀφέντης as coming straight from ἀπὸ + ἐ- = ἀφέ-, as in ἀφίημι, 'I send,' and meaning simply 'the sender,' a frequent character of the master of a slave. Perhaps, too, ἐφέντης, 'the commander' (cf. ἐφίεμαι, 'I command' (middle), from ἐπὶ + ἐ-), may have played a part in producing the bye-form of ἀφέντης, viz. ἐφέντης, whence the

Turkish title *Effendi*, which is simply the Greek stem ἐφέντη. Possibly these popular forms (not found in the language of literature) may have been confounded by scholiasts and annotators with αὐθέντης, and thus influenced its meaning and interpretation.

πήγαινε: a curious word with a curious history. ὑπάγω = ὑπὸ + ἄγω, literally 'I lead up,' Latin *subigo* for *subago*, is the common word in later Greek for 'I go.' 'I went' is ὑπῆγον, Hellenistic or more modern form ὑπῆγα, shortened to πῆγα. This is really an imperfect, but in verbs of going, from the nature of the case, the senses of aorist and imperfect are not so clearly marked off as in some other verbs. Moreover, the real aorist of ὑπάγω would be ὑπήγαγον, and reduplicated forms fell into general disfavour in later Greek. Especially would ὑπήγαγον be a long and awkward word for 'I went.' The shortened imperfect πῆγα was therefore accepted as an aorist, often with augment ἐπῆγα. The preposition ὑπὸ was consequently lost; παγ- was regarded as the root, lengthened in the aorist indicative to πηγ-. An imperfect stem, πηγαιν- or παγυιν-, was formed on the analogy of the modern forms μαθαίνω from μαθ-, παθαίνω from παθ-, κ.τ.λ. πήγαινε is therefore 2nd person imperfect imperative from modern root παγ-, 'to go,' of which the aorist subjunctive is πάγω, πάγῃς, πάγῃ· πάγωμεν, πάγητε, πάγουν (ωσι); colloquially, πάω, πᾷς, πᾷ (also πάῃς, πάῃ· πᾶμε, πᾶτε, πᾶσι, or πάουν).

πιάσῃς: 2nd person, 1st aorist, from stem πιάζ-, Doric form of πιέζ-, in classical Greek 'to squeeze,' 'nip,' in New Testament 'to catch,' in Modern Greek also 'to get,' 'take.'

ἁμάξι: for ἁμάξιν, i.e. ἁμάξιον, diminutive of ἄμαξα = ἅμα, kin to *same*, Latin *similis*, &c. + αξ-, the root element in ἄξον-, 'axle.' Hence ἄμαξα = 'with like axles,' 'a four-wheeled carriage' or 'cart,' as opposed to ἅρμα, 'a two-wheeled war-chariot.' ἄξων, kin to *axle*, is from root ἀγ + ς, and = 'that which should draw.'

μετὰ: with accusative = 'after;' elsewhere with genitive, 'with' (see above).

μισὴν, 'half,' adjective, as in German; μισὸς ἄνθρωπος, 'half a man;' μισὸν τέταρτον, 'half a quarter;' μισὴ ὥρα, 'half an hour' = *Ein halber Mann, ein halbes Viertel, eine halbe Stunde*. The full classical form is ἥμισυς (for σήμισυς), ἡμίσεια, ἥμισυ· ἥμισυν, ἡμίσειαν, ἥμισυ· ἡμίσους, ἡμισείας, ἡμίσους· ἡμίσει, ἡμισείᾳ, ἡμίσει. Plural: ἡμίσεις, ἡμίσειαι, ἡμίσεα (η)· ἡμίσεις, ἡμισείας, ἡμίσεα (η)· ἡμισέων, ἡμισειῶν, ἡμισέων· ἡμίσεσι(ν), ἡμισείαις, ἡμίσεσι(ν). In composition ἡμι-, Latin *semi*; in the vernacular, μισο-. Hence Modern Greek μισεύω, 'I divide,' 'I part,' 'depart.'

πές = stem πε-, 'say,' 'speak' + ς, sign of 2nd person singular. Hence πές = 'say,' 'tell;' cf. ἄφες, ἄς, 'let go,' 'let.' The stem π- is made pronounceable by the addition of paragogic ε to the letter π, which is a truncated form of ἐπ- for Ϝεπ-, in which the last letter has, probably through influence of lip-letter Ϝ, become labialized from κ. Hence Ϝεπ- is Greek form of root *vak*-, Latin *voc*- in *vox* (*vóc-s*), *vŏcare*, *equivŏcus*, &c.

του: for τῳ, genitive for dative; πές του, 'tell him.'

περάσῃ = stem περα- = 'pass' + σῃ, ending of 3rd person aorist subjunctive. Hence νὰ περάσῃ, 'that he pass,' i. e. call; πές του νὰ περάσῃ, 'tell him to call.'

ἀπό, literally 'off,' 'from,' here = 'at;' compare nautical use of 'off.' Thus, του, ἀπ' ἐδῶ, literally 'from here' = this 'way.'

νὰ μοῦ πάρῃ, 'to get me;' μοῦ for μοί; cf. του for τῳ above. πάρῃ for ἐπάρῃ, from ἐπὶ + ἄρῃ, present imperfect 1st person singular ἐπαίρω; but a similar fate to that of ὑπάγω, κ.τ.λ, has befallen this word, it being regarded as aorist of an imperfect πέρνω or παίρνω. The root ἀρ-, 'take,' 'lift,' seems to be shortened from ἀϜερ-, and that from ἀσϜερ-, which again would appear to have been lengthened by euphonic ἀ from σϜερ-, and point back to an Indo-Germanic root *svar*, in Sanscrit *sar*, of which the original meaning seems to have been that of 'swaying,' or 'hovering,' 'hanging.' Hence ἀείρω, αἴρω for ἀσϜέρϳω, 'I lift,' 'I raise;' σειρά for σϜειρά, 'a chain,' 'line,' 'row,' Latin *series*, &c.

ἕνα: for ἕν, formed from the metaplastic masculine nominative ἕνας by dropping the ς. A metaplastic form is a secondary grammatical formation. From the accusative nominative ἕνα(ν), root stem ἑν-, nominative masculine εἷς for ἕνς, genitive ἑνός, κ.τ.λ., a possible stem, ἕνα-, is unconsciously inferred, whence the nominative masculine ἕνας, neuter ἕνα. These formations are frequent in Modern Greek, but are not unknown to Ancient Greek and to Latin; in Sanscrit they are likewise common.

ζευγάρι: for ζευγάριν, i. e. ζευγάριον, diminutive of ζεῦγος, 'a pair,' genitive ζευγαριοῦ arising by rapidity of pronunciation from ζευγαρίου, plural ζευγάρια, ζευγαριῶν for ζευγαρίων. ζεῦγος is kin to ζυγὸ- (ς or ν, masculine or neuter), ευ being the regular strengthening of υ in Greek; cf. ἔφυγον, ἔφυγα, 'I fled, φεύγω, 'I fly.' ζυγό- is for ϳυγό-, Latin *jugo- jugum*, English *yoke*. Hence *jungo* in Latin, ζευγνύω, ζεύγνυμι in Greek, 'I join.'

γάντια: plural of γάντι, French *gant*, 'glove.' The fine Greek word is χειρόκτιον, χειρόκτια.

ἑπτάμισυ: for ἑπτὰ ἥμισυ, 'seven [and] a half.'

ἀριθμὸ: for ἀριθμὸν, accusative after πάρῃ, in apposition with γάντια; ἀριθμὸ- = root ἀρ-, 'to arrange' (whence Modern Greek ἀράδα, 'row,' 'turn,' ἅρμα(τ), 'a thing fitted,' 'a chariot,' *arma*, Latin, Modern Greek ἅρματα, 'arms,' *armus* and *arm*, &c.) + -ιθ-, formative suffix + μὸ-, substantive suffix, as often above. From the same root, Gothic *lithus* for *rithus*, the German *Glied* for *Gelied*, with prefix *ge*, and probably our *lithe* as adjective; also, with different suffix, *limb*: probably also our *lid* is kin to German *Lied*, *Gelied*, *Glied*; cf. *Augenlieder*, 'eyelids,' and also the use of numbers, "melodious numbers," with *Lied* in sense of "song." *Link* is a further formation from the same root, and reminds us in this connexion of Milton's lines,—

> "In notes, with many a winding bout
> Of linked sweetness long drawn out."—*L'Allegro*, 139.

Cf. μέλος above.

ἄσπρα: neuter plural accusative of ἄσπρο-, 'white,' the classical word for which is λευκό-; probably for ἄσπλο-, i. e. ἄ-σπιλο-, 'unspotted.'

ἐφώνησεν, 'called,' 'shouted,' from φωνά-, verb-stem and noun (nominative φωνή), 'voice ;' for form, cf. ἀπήντησεν above.

ἐκ: the Latin *ex*, also ἐξ before vowels, construed with genitive.

δωματίου: diminutive of δῶματ-, nominative δῶμα, 'a room,' 'chamber,' from root δεμ-, 'build,' German *zimmern* (verb), *Zimmer* (noun), our *timber*.

καλὰ: neuter plural, used adverbially.

τώρα: for τῇ ὥρᾳ, 'the hour,' 'now,' as the Scotch say "the day" for "to-day;" cf. Welsh *rwan* and *nawr* for *yr awr hon* and *yn awr*, 'the hour this,' i. e. this hour, and 'in hour,' respectively.

ἐνθυμήθης: ending as in ἐσυλλογίσθης (cf. ἐσυλλογίσθη above), from ἐνθυμε- = ἐν + θυμέ- for θυμὸ-, 'to have in one's mind' (θυμό-), 'to remember.' θυμός is kin to Latin *fumus*, 'smoke,' but in Greek has only the metaphoric sense of *mind, spirit, anger*; cf. our *fret* and *fume*; the old meaning peeps out, however, in θῦμα, 'sacrifice,' θυμιάματα, 'incense offerings,' θύμον and θύμος, 'thyme,' θύω, 'I sacrifice,' κ.τ.λ. Our *dust* and the German *dunst* are (with different endings) from the same root.

εὐλογημένη: feminine participle perfect passive of εὐλογέ- = εὐ, 'well' + λόγο-, word 'to bless.' Hence εὐλογημένη, 'blessed woman!' 'bless your heart!' Cf. Plato's use of δαιμόνιε.

ἐλησμόνησα: from λησμονέ- (λησμονέω, λησμονῶ, κ.τ.λ.), from λήσμον- (nominative λήσμων for λήσμονς) = ληθ-, lengthened from λαθ- + adjective suffix -μον-, = 'forgetful.' Hence λησμονῶ = 'I am forgetful,' 'I forget;' ἐλησμόνησα, 'I forgot;' root λαθ-, whence also Λήθη, 'the river of forgetfulness;' λανθάνω, 'I hide from,' 'escape;' ἔλαθον, 'I shunned;' kin to Latin *lateo*, 'I lie hid,' whence our *latent*.

θέλεις = θελ-, 'will,' kin to Sanscrit root *dhar*, 'begin,' 'undertake' + ending εις = 'wilt thou.'

κάμω = root καμ-, 'labour,' 'make,' 'do' + ending ω = 'I.' νὰ κάμω, 'that I do,' i. e. me to do. Imperfect stem, κάμν-.

μή: negative particle = 'not,' 'lest,' with subjunctive, imperative, and participles only—never with indicative, except in questions, e. g. μὴ or μήπως σᾶς ἐνοχλῶ; 'do I disturb you?'

χειρότερα: 'worse,' neuter plural for adverb, in classical Greek generally χείρονα from χείρον; kin to χείρ, 'hand,' Sanscrit *hárámi*, 'I seize,' *haranam*, 'hand,' Old Latin *hir* for *manus*, also *herus*, *hera*, 'master' and 'mistress.' Thus χείρον- seems to mean originally 'in the hands of;' hence 'inferior,' 'subordinate.' The expression μὴ χειρότερα seems to signify μὴ [κάμῃς] χειρότερα, 'do no worse than you have done,' i. e. you have done enough already.

ἐψιθύρισεν: from ψιθυρίζ- (ψιθυρίζω), a word formed from the sound.

διεβίβασε: διαβιβάζ- (διαβιβάζω) = δια + βιβάζ-, reduplicated for βαζ- from root βα-, originally γα-, our *come*, Sanscrit *gá*, *gíyámi*, transitive form of βαίνω for βάνῳω, = 'make go.' Hence διαβιβάζω, 'I pass through,' 'pass on,' a watchword or message.

ὑπηρέτην: from ὑπὸ + ἐρετ-, 'row,' literally 'an under-rower;' hence 'a servant,' 'waiter.'

ὅστις: double relative = 'the which,' or 'he who.'

ἀπήντησε: explained above.

μεγαλοφώνως (-ωτ): from μεγάλο- and φωνά-, 'with a loud voice.'

πολὺ: stem and neuter singular, kin to *full*, *voll*, *viel* (German) = 'very.'

καλὰ: neuter plural used as adverb = 'well.'

ὅμως: for ὅμωτ, old instrumental case of stem ὅμο- for σόμο-, kin to *same*. Hence = 'all the same,' 'however,' 'but;' with different accent, ὁμῶς, it means 'at the same time.' In Modern Greek, however, ὁμοῦ (genitive) is usually employed in this sense.

σιγὰ : adverb, for σϝιγὰ, probably softened from σϝικὰ, kin to German *Schweigen*.

ἥκιστα : neuter plural (cf. καλὰ), from stem ἥκιστο- α-, of which -ιστ- is superlative suffix, kin to -*est* in English, and ἥκ- probably stands for σηκ- σᾱκ-, kin to *sachte*, German, 'slight,' 'light,' 'soft.' ἥκιστα = 'slightest,' 'lightest,' 'least.'

εὐσεβάστως (εὐσεβάστωτ): adverb of εὐσέβαστο-, from εὐ, 'well' + σεβαστὸ- (observe accent), verbal adjective of σεβαζ- for σεβαδγ-, verbal stem from σέβας, 'honour,' 'worship,' 'respect.' Hence σεβαστὸ-, 'worshipped,' εὐσέβαστο-, 'worshipful,' 'respectful,' εὐσεβάστως, 'respectfully,' ἥκιστα εὐσεβάστως, 'anything but respectfully.'

μὰ : perhaps the Italian *mà* for *mai*, from Latin *magis*, a relic of the Venetian and Genoese occupations of Greece, but not without echo of Ancient Greek μὴν, Doric μὰν, 'nay,' 'but.'

ἀφεντικά : neuter plural vocative of adjective ἀφεντικὸ-, i. e. what belongs to a master, like the German *Herrschaft* for *Herr*, or the English "Your Lordship" for "Lord." It means simply 'Sir.'

ἀλήθεια : from ἀ = 'not' + ληθ-, lengthened from λαθ- (see above) + εσ = adjectival suffix + ια = noun suffix. Hence ἀλήθεια (for ἀλήθεσια) = 'what cannot be hid,' i. e. the truth, or, perhaps better, 'the unmistaken.' Here the noun is used as an interjectional adverb, "troth !"

ποῦ : literally 'where,' locative genitive of root πο- (κϝο-); cf. Latin *quâ*, *quô*, and our own *where*, which is genitive feminine of same root *who*-, Modern English *who* ; cf. German *wo*. Here used in sense of 'since,' 'so that.' ἀλήθεια, ποῦ ὄχι καλλίτερα, 'truth, so that nothing better,' i. e. true as true can be.

ὄχι : the classical οὐχὶ, compounded of οὐκ + ἰ, an old demonstrative particle = 'here;' cf. οὑτοσί, 'this here man' (classical). ὄχι = 'not,' 'no.'

καλλίτερα, 'better,' from καλό- 'good' + ending τερα, neuter plural of τερο-. The proper form would be καλώτερα, but the classical comparative was καλλίων, κ.τ.λ, where the λλ is probably due to the presence of suppressed ? ; cf. ἄλλος for ἄλϳος, and the Modern Greek καλλίτερος, κ.τ.λ, also written less correctly καλήτερος, may be due to a compromise between καλλίων and καλώτερος.

μεσ': for μέσα, neuter plural for adverb, from μέσο-, 'midst,' 'in the midst of.' Μέσο- for μέτιο-, kin to μετά.

's: for εἰς or ἐς, 'in ;' μεσ' ς = 'in the midst of,' literally 'midway in.'

λάσπη(ν) (cf. τὴ for τὴν): stem λάσπα-, 'mud.'

βροχὴ: stem βροχὰ-, 'rain,' verbal substantive from root βρεχ- βραχ-. Hence βρέχει, 'it rains,' ἔβρεξε, 'it rained,' θὰ βρέξῃ, 'it will rain.'

τρέχα, 'run,' imperative imperfect 2nd singular, as if from τρέχημι. The imperfect in regular and classical use is τρέχω, ἔτρεχον, imperative τρέχε, but in the vernacular we get τρέχα, 'run,' and the middle present participle τρεχάμενος, 'running ;' kin to Gothic *thragja*, 'I run.'

ν' ἀγοράζῃς: for νὰ ἀγοράζῃς from ἀγορὰ, 'market.' Hence ἀγοράζω = 'I buy.' ἀγορὰ in turn means 'an assembly,' 'a gathering,' being verbal substantive of root ἀγερ-, 'gather,' whence ἀγείρω, 'I gather ;' cf. πανήγυρις above.

γάντια, 'gloves,' the French *gants*. The Greek word is χειρόκτια or χειρίδες.

πιάνῃς: a bye-form of πιάζῃς, Doric and New Testament for πιέζῃς, of which the classical meaning is 'squeeze,' the later 'catch,' and the modern simply 'get' or 'take.'

Ἀ: the interjection 'Ah!'

δὲν: shortened from οὐδὲν, i. e. οὐδὲ ἕν, 'not even one,' 'nothing.' Hence simply 'not ;' cf. *non*, from *ne unum*, in Latin.

καμμιὰ: for κἂν (i. e. καὶ ἂν) μία(ν), 'even if one,' 'so much as one,' 'any,' 'some;' καμμιὰ φορά, 'some time or other,' 'one of these days.'

φορά: verbal substantive from φερ-, kin to *bear*, literally 'a bearing,' 'taking,' 'turn;' cf. *una vece*, Italian, *una vez*, Spanish, from Latin *unam vicem*, from root *vec-*, *veh-*, 'to bear,' 'carry.'

IDIOMATIC TRANSLATION.

"John!"

"Yes, sir!"

"Go and fetch a cab, to be here in half an hour."

"Tell him to call at Madame Lisié's, to get me a pair of gloves, number $7\frac{1}{2}$, white!" cried Mrs. Euphrosyne from her bedroom.

"All right! . . . and so now you have just remembered about getting gloves—bless you!"

"I forgot it! What would you have me do now?"

"I hope that's the worst!" whispered her consort, and passed the message to the servant, who replied aloud,—

"Very good, sir; directly!" but muttered to himself in anything but a respectful tone, "Ay! master! and no mistake, to send me running through the mud and rain to buy gloves and fetch a cab. I wonder whether I shall ever be a master myself."

EXERCISE VIII.

Ὁ Κύριος ἐφώνησε πρὸς τὸν ὑπερέτην· Πήγαινε νὰ πιάσῃς ἐν ἁμάξι καὶ ἕνα ζευγάρι γάντια.

"Ἀμέσως Κύριε," ἀπήντησεν ὁ ὑπηρέτης μειδιῶν μὲν γλυκερὸν μειδίαμα σεβασμοῦ καὶ ὑποταγῆς, ἀλλὰ ψιθυρίζων σιγὰ καὶ ἥκιστα εὐσεβάστως! Καλὰ καὶ τώρα ἐνθυμήθης νὰ μὲ στείλῃς νὰ ἀγοράσω γάντια καὶ νὰ πιάσω ἁμάξι! Τρέχα σὺ μεσ᾿ς τὴ λάσπη καὶ 'ς τὴ βροχὴ· καὶ ἂς γείνω ἐγὼ ἀφέντης κάμμιὰ φορά.

"John!" cried the lady; "tell the carriage to call in half an hour (say that the carriage call). Did you remember to get gloves?"

"I forgot it! What am I to do now?" the servant answered aloud; but whispered to himself, anything but respectfully, "Master, true enough!" and passing on the order (διαβιβάζων) to another servant, said, "Run in the mud and rain, bless you, to fetch a carriage, and buy gloves. You will be master, too, one of these fine days."

ΕΝΝΑΤΟΝ ΜΑΘΗΜΑ.—Ninth Lesson.

ἔννατο-: for ἐννέατο- = ἐννέα + το = 'nine' + 'th' = 'ninth.' The ἐ is a kind of taking breath before pronouncing the word, ε and ο being common prefixes in Greek, of which we have numberless instances. Thus ἐννέα stands for ἐνέƑα, and that for νέƑα[ν]; Sanscrit *navan*, Latin *novem*, Gothic *niun* for *nivun*, English *nine*.

Ὁ Κύριος Παρδαλὸς εἰσέρχεται εἰς τὸν κοιτῶνά του,
The Mr. Pardalós enters into the sleeping-room of-him,

καὶ προσπαθεῖ νὰ ἐνδυθῇ. Ἀλλὰ τοῦτο εἶναι ἀδύνατον,
and tries to get-dressed. But this is impossible,

καθότι ἡ εὔσωμος σύζυγός του ἔχει πλῆρες τὸ δωμάτιον
in that the well-bodied consort of-him has full the room

ἐσθήτων, μεσοφορίων, μανδυλίων, στηθοδέσμων, καὶ πάσης
of-clothes, petticoats, handkerchiefs, stays, and all

τῆς πολυμόρφου συσκευῆς τοῦ γυναικείου ἱματισμοῦ.
the multiform apparel of-the womanly attire.

Συνάγει λοιπὸν τὰ ἐνδύματά του, λαμβάνει ἓν μικρὸν
He-gathers therefore the clothes of-him, takes a little

κάτροπτρον καὶ ἓν κηρίον, καὶ ἀπέρχεται εἰς τὸ γραφεῖον
looking-glass and a candle, and departs into the office

του ὅπως συντελέσῃ ἐν αὐτῷ τὴν ἐνδυμασίαν του.
of-him that he-may-finish in it the dressing of-him.

Ἀλλὰ μετ' ὀλίγον ἐνθυμεῖται ὅτι εἶνε ἀξύριστος, καὶ ὅτι
But after a-little he remembers that he-is unshared, and that

πρέπει νὰ ξυρισθῇ πρὶν ν'ἀλλάξῃ. Μεταβαίνει καὶ πάλιν
it-behoves that he-share, ere he-change. He-moves yet again

εἰς τὸν κοιτῶνα, ἀνοιγοκλείει τὴν θύραν, διαμαρτυρομένης
into the sleeping-room, opens-and-shuts the door, protesting

τῆς Κυρίας Παρδαλοῦ, ὅτι θὰ τὴν κρυώσῃ καὶ ἐπιστρέφει
the Mrs. Pardalós, that he will her give-cold, and returns

κρατῶν τὸ ξυράφιόν του, καὶ τὰ λοιπὰ ἀπαιτούμενα.
holding the razor of him, and the other requirements.

Ἐνθυμεῖται τότε, ὅτι θέλει θερμὸν ὕδωρ, ἀλλὰ
He-remembers then that he-wants warm water, but

παρατηρῶν ὅτι ἡ ὥρα εἶναι προκεχωρημένη, καὶ δὲν
observing that the hour is advanced, and not

ὑπολείπεται καιρὸς ἵνα τὸ ὕδωρ θερμανθῇ, ἀρκεῖται εἰς
is-left time that the water warm, he-contents-him with

τὸ ψυχρὸν, καὶ ἄρχεται περιαλείφων μὲ σάπωνα τὴν
the cold, and begins smearing-over with soap the

σιαγόνα καὶ τὰς παρειάς του, λέγων καθ' ἑαυτόν—
chin and the cheeks of-him, saying to himself—

Θὰ μοῦ ἔλθῃ πάλιν καμμιὰ καταιβασιὰ εἰς τὰ
There-will me come again some going-down into my

δόντια ποῦ νὰ μὲ τρελλάνῃ· ἀλλὰ τί νὰ γείνῃ! Καὶ
teeth such as me will-madden; but what may-be-done! And

ἡτοιμάζετο νὰ φέρῃ τὸ ξυράφιον ἐπὶ τὴν παρειὰν
he-was-preparing to bring the razor against the cheek

αὐτοῦ, ὅτε ἠχεῖ καὶ πάλιν ὁ κώδων τῆς ἀνοιγομένης
of-him, when sounds yet again the bell of-the opening

θύρας.
door.

εἰσέρχεται = 'comes in,' from εἰς, 'in' + ἔρχεται, 'comes.'
ἔρχομαι, ἔρχεσαι, ἔρχεται· ἐρχόμεθα, ἔρχεσθε, ἔρχονται.

κοιτῶνα[ν]: stem κοιτῶν-, from κοίτα-, 'bed' + suffix -ῶν-, which has the force of 'a place for' or 'of ;' cf. δενδρεών, 'place for trees,' 'orchard,' γυναικεών, 'women's apartment,' and many others.

κοίτα- is formed by a modification of stem κει- = 'lie.' κεῖμαι, κεῖσαι, κεῖται· κείμεθα, κεῖσθε, κεῖνται + noun ending -τα-. Cf. ἔρχομαι above. From stem κει- are also derived: κοι-μά-ω, 'put to sleep ;' κῶμος, 'a banquet,' literally 'a lying down ;' κώμη, 'a village,' 'hamlet ;' the proper name Κύμη. Cognate are Latin qui-e-s, qui-esco, ci-vi-s ('a dweller'), our *home*, *-ham*, German *heim*, &c.

προσπαθεῖ: for προσπαθέει, from πρὸς, 'toward' + πάθες-, 'feeling,' 'passion.' Hence προσπαθέω, 'I direct my feelings (efforts) towards anything,' 'I endeavour,' 'attempt,' 'try.' προσπαθῶ -εῖς -εῖ· -οῦμεν -εῖτε -οῦσι (-οῦν -οῦνε).

ἐνδυθῇ = ἐν + δυ + θῇ, of which εν = 'on' or 'in ;' δυ = 'clothe ;' -θῇ is tense and personal ending, as frequently above = 'he may be.' Hence ἐνδυθῇ, 'he may be dressed' or 'dress himself.' ἐνδυθῶ -θῇς -θῇ· -θῶμεν -θῆτε -θῶσι (θοῦν -θοῦνε).

ἀδύνατον: ἀ = 'un-,' 'in- ;' δυνα = 'can ;' τον = adjective ending neuter nominative. From stem δυνα- we get δύναμαι -σαι -ται· -μεθα -σθε -νται, 'I can,' &c.

καθότι = κατὰ + ὅτι, 'forasmuch' + 'as.'

εὔσωμος = εὐ, 'well' + σωμο-, the essential part of σῶματ-, 'body' + ς, 'sign of nominative case. Compounds of this kind (cf. εὔμορφο-, 'beautiful,' from εὐ- and μορφὰ-, 'form') are the same for masculine and feminine. ὁ καὶ ἡ εὔσωμος, τὸ εὔσωμον· τὸν καὶ τὴν καὶ τὸ εὔσωμον· τοῦ καὶ τῆς εὐσώμου, τῷ καὶ τῇ εὐσώμῳ· οἱ καὶ αἱ εὔσωμοι, τὰ εὔσωμα· τοὺς καὶ τὰς εὐσώμους, τὰ εὔσωμα, τῶν εὐσώμων· τοῖς καὶ ταῖς εὐσώμοις. σώματ- for σάο-ματ-, 'that which is saved;' in Homer always a corpse saved in battle, the only thing saved when the hero is killed, a euphemism for a dead body, like λείψανον (λείπ-σα-νον), 'that which is left,' 'remains.' The root σάο-, σόο- appears in σώζω, 'I save,' and is kin to *sa-* in *sanus, sou* in *sound, su* in German *gesund*, &c.

πλῆρες: stem and neuter accusative, from root πλε-, 'fill' (see above) + adjectival suffix -ρες = 'full.'

ἐσθήτων: stem ἐσθῆτ + ων, genitive plural ending. ἐσθῆτ- from ἐς = εἰς, 'on,' 'on to' + θη = *do*, to which it is akin. Hence ἐςθη = 'do on,' 'don' + τ, suffix forming substantive stem ἐσθῆτ- = 'garment.' ἐσθής for ἐσθῆτς, ἐσθῆτα[ν], ἐσθῆτος, ἐσθῆτι· ἐσθῆτες -ῆτας -ήτων -ῆσιν (for ῆτσιν).

μεσοφορίων: from μεσο-, 'middle' or 'inside,' and φερ- (φορ-), 'wear;' kin to English *bear*, Latin *fero*, &c. + diminutive ending ιο-, in genitive plural ίων. Hence μεσοφορίων = 'of little things worn inside,' 'inside-wearing-lets,' i. e. petticoats.

μανδυλίων: diminutive of μάνδυς, a Persian word, our *mantle* = 'of handkerchiefs.'

στηθοδέσμων: from στηθο-, stem (in composition) of στῆθος, 'breast' + δέσμων (genitive plural of δέσμα, otherwise δέσματα), 'bindings,' 'tyings,' being substantive of δε-, as in δέω, δίνω, 'I tie;' kin to English *tie*. Hence στηθοδέσμων = 'breast-bindings,' 'stays.'

πάσης: for πάντσης = stem παντ + σ-η, feminine suffix + s, genitive ending. In παντ- the π is a labialized κ, the ground form being κϝαντ-, kin to Latin *quanto-*. The whole declension is as follows:—πᾶς (for πάντς), πᾶσα, πᾶν· πάντα[ν], πᾶσαν, πᾶν· παντός (observe accent, and cf. ἑνός above), πάσης, παντός· παντί, πάσῃ, παντί· πάντες, πᾶσαι, πάντα· πάντας, πάσας, πάντα· πάντων, πασῶν (shortened from πασάων), πᾶσι(ν), πάσαις, πᾶσι(ν). With reference to the straight and curved brackets here employed, be it remarked that πάνταν is a form etymologically postulated, but only found in vulgar Greek, whereas πᾶσιν is a recognized form always used before a vowel, as πᾶσιν ἀνθρώποις, 'to all men.'

πολυμόρφου: genitive singular feminine (cf. εὔσωμος above), compounded of πολὺ- and μορφὰ-, 'form,' 'shape.' Hence πολυμόρφου = 'multiform,' 'multifarious.'

συσκευῆς: compounded of συν and σκευὴ, 'equipment,' from root σκυ-, whence κύτος, with its bye-form σκῦτος; kin to Latin *scu-tum*, ob-*scu-ru-s*, *cu-ti-s*, our *hide*. For the occasional disappearance of σ, cf. μειδιῶν above.

γυναικείου: from stem γυναίκ- + adjectival suffix εἰο-. γυναίκ- is lengthened by suffix -κι- from stem γύνα, standing for γυνάκια-. γύνα- is kin to our *queen*, *quean*, &c., and to the word *kin* in English, root γεν- and *gen*- in Greek and Latin, and means 'the bearer,' 'mother.' γυναικεῖο- means 'womanly,' 'feminine,' 'female.'

συνάγει = συν-άγει, 'brings together,' ἄγει being kin to Latin *agit*.

ἐνδύματα: neuter plural accusative of ἐνδυματ- = ἔνδυ-, explained above + ματ-, substantival suffix; cf. μάθηματ-, κ.τ.λ. Hence ἐνδύματα = 'clothes.'

κάτροπτρον: from κατὰ, preposition = 'at' + root ὀπ- for ὀκϝ- (see above) + substantival suffix τρο-. Hence κάτοπτρον = 'a thing to look at,' 'a looking-glass.' A masculine adjective form, ὁ κατόπτριος (i. e. ὕαλος), is probably responsible for the popular word ὁ καθρέφτης through the stages κατόπτριος, κατόπτρις, κατρόπτις, κατρόφτης, καθρέφτης, the aspiration of the τ into θ being probably due to the proximity of the ρ, that of the π into φ to a regular law of vernacular pronunciation, πτ (and also φθ) becoming uniformly φτ in the mouth of the common people, while the changed vowel is probably a case of *Umlaut*, the ο becoming ε as a compromise or approximation to the final palatal vowel η or ι.

κηρίον = κηρ-, kin to Latin *cera*, 'wax' + ιο-ν, diminutive ending. Hence κηρίον = literally 'a waxling,' 'a taper,' 'a candle.' The vernacular form is κερί[ν]. Declension as follows, in writing and familiar speech respectively:—κηρίον, κηρίου, κηρίῳ· κηρία, κηρίων, κηρίοις. κερί, κεριοῦ· κεριὰ, κεριῶν. Observe the shifting of the accent in genitive through rapid pronunciation.

ἀπέρχεται, 'goes away ;' cf. εἰσέρχεται, 'goes in' (above).

ὅπως: for ὅπωτ, old instrumental form, relative stem ὅ-πο- for ὅ-κϝο-, where the ὁ seems to be the article in a petrified and indeclinable form; cf. *le-quel, el cuale*, &c., in French and Spanish. ὅπως means 'in order that,' 'in-a-way that' such and such a result may follow.

συντελέσῃ: ending -σῃ, as above. συντελε-: from συν + τελε-, 'to finish up,' 'complete,' τελε- being for τέλες- (nominative, τέλος), and probably kin to root τελ-, τλε, 'to bear,' 'carry.' τλῆναι, infinitive aorist, Latin *tuli* (perfect), Scotch *thole*, German *dul-den, Ge-dul-d*, &c. As we say the *bearing*, in sense of tendency, ultimate issue. Hence ὅπως συντελέσῃ = 'that he may accomplish.'

ἐνδυμασίαν: further formation from stem ἐνδυματ-, as explained above, by addition of substantival suffix ·ία-, standing therefore for ἐνδυματία, with sigmated τ = σ, as often in Greek ; ἐνδυμασία = 'clothing.'

μετ' ὀλίγον, 'after a little,' according to regular sense of μετὰ with accusative.

ἀξύριστος: from ἀ- = 'un-,' and ξυριστὸς, 'shaved,' with regular change of accent. ξυριστὸς from ξυρίζ-, from ξυρὸ-, 'razor,' and that from root ξυ-, ξε-, 'to shave.' The Sanscrit *kshuras*, 'razor,' seems to be cognate.

πρέπει, 'it behoves,' 'is right.' This seems akin to Latin *prope*, 'near,' *proprius*, 'proper,' &c., but the link in meaning is open to some doubt.

ξυρισθῇ: cf. ἐνδυθῇ.

πρὶν: conjunction = 'before,' for προῖον, πρόϊν (also πρῴην), comparative degree of πρό, as Latin *prius* for *proios*.

ἀλλάξῃ = ἀλλάγ-σῃ: from ἄλλο- (ἄλιο) + verbal suffix αγ-, perhaps = root ἀγ- in ἄγω, *ago*, 'to bring.' Hence ἀλλάγ- = 'bring-otherwise,' 'change.' ἀλλάξω for ἀλλάγςω, ἤλλαξα, ἀλλάξω, κ.τ.λ.

μεταβαίνει: μετα- = 'across,' βαίνει, 'he goes ;' kin to Latin *ven-it*, Albanian *vïen*; root βα- for γϝα-, our *co-me*. The Dutch *kwam*, 'came,' retains the labial *w* = F.

πάλιν: adverb = 'again.'

ἀνοιγοκλείει, 'opens and shuts :' made up of ἀνοιγ-, 'open,' and κλει-, 'shut,' a curious sort of compound, commoner in colloquial Modern Greek than in classical. κλείω is kin to Latin *clau-do*, German *schlie-ssen*, the original root being *sklu-*.

θύραν, 'door,' kin to same, also to Latin *for-es*, German *Thüre*, Albanian *derę*, Sanscrit *dvâr*, &c.

διαμαρτυρομένης, 'protesting' = διά, 'through,' 'thoroughly,' 'persistently' + μαρτυρομένης, 'witnessing,' from μάρτυρ-, 'witness' + ομένη-ς, middle participial imperfect ending, feminine genitive. This genitive is called absolute because its government is not obvious, that is, it depends, not on any particular word in the sentence, but on the sentence taken as a whole. In Latin, the ablative is used in this way ; in English, the nominative. μάρ-τυρ, of which -τυρ is ending, meaning 'agent' (genitive, μάρτυρος), comes from root μαρ-, *mar-*, 'to call to mind,' 'remind,' 'remember,' reduplicate in *memor, memoria*, 'memory,' found in μέρ-ι-μνα, 'care,' &c. οἱ διαμαρτυρόμενοι is the ecclesiastical term corresponding to our Protestants.

κρυώσῃ = verbal stem κρυο + σῃ ; κρυο- is found in adjective κρύο-, 'cold,' noun κρύες-, 'cold[ness],' derivative κρύ-σταλλον, κρού-σταλλον, 'ice ;' kin to Latin *cru* in *cru-or, cru-dus, cru-delis, cru-s-ta*, old Norse *hrí* in *hrí-m*, our *rime*, old High German *hrâo*, our *raw*.

ἐπι-στρέφει, 'turns about,' 're-turns.'

ξυράφιον: from ξυρὸ- (see above) + diminutive ending -άφιον, elsewhere also ύφιον, as χωράφιον, 'a little field;' ζωΰφιον, 'a little animal,' 'an insect.'

ἀπαιτούμενα = 'things asked,' 'requirements:' participle imperfect passive, from ἀπαιτε-, 'to ask (of)' = ἀπὸ + αἰτε-, 'ask.' ἀπαιτούμενα stands for ἀπαιτε-όμενα.

θερμὸν: from root θερ-, as in θέρος, 'summer,' kin to Latin *fur- for-* in *furnus, formidus* (cf. θύρα, *fores*), Sanscrit *gharmas*, 'glow,' Gothic *varmjau*, our *warm*, Lithuanian *žer-ě'-ti*, 'to 'glow,' Albanian *ziarm*, 'fire.' There can be little doubt of the kinship of these words, but the form assumed in the various languages by the first consonant is irregular, and hitherto unexplained. In θ for *gh* we have simple dentalization, but in the Sanscrit a *v* after *gh*, and in Gothic a *g* before *v*, seems to have been lost, while none of the other tongues seem to retain a trace of the *v*.

ὕδωρ: for ὕδορτ-, genitive ὕδατος for ὑδαρ-τ-ος, kin to *water*. The vernacular for θερμὸν ὕδωρ is ζεστὸ νερό: ζεστὸ- being verbal adjective from ζε-, 'boil;' νερὸ-, akin to νηρὸ-, 'liquid,' adjective from root νε-, 'flow,' or else popularly imagined in the aorist ἐνέρ(ρ)ευσε, 'it flowed in,' as ξηρὸ-, 'dry,' in the aorist ἐξέρ(ρ)ευσε, 'it flowed out,' from ἐν-ρέϜ- and ἐκ-ρέϜ- respectively; for, as the suffix -ευ- has elsewhere the force of 'to be' or 'become,' ἐξέρρευσε and ἐνέρρευσε (applied to water-courses) might seem to imply the presents ξερεύω = ξερός εἰμι, and νερεύω = νερός εἰμι respectively, the ε of ἐξ and ἐν being mistaken for the augment, and the true augment in the second syllable for part of the radical word.

παρατηρῶν (παρατηρέων), 'observing:' from παρὰ, 'by,' and τηρε-, 'keep' or 'watch.' παρατηρῶν -οῦσα -οῦν -οῦντα -οῦσαν -οῦν· -οῦντος -ούσης -οῦν· -οῦντι -ούσῃ -οῦντι· -οῦντες -οῦσαι -οῦντα· -οῦντας -ούσας -οῦντα· -ούντων -ουσῶν -ούντων· -οῦσι(ν) -ούσαις -οῦσι(ν).

προκεχωρημένη: perfect participle passive, feminine nominative, from προχωρε- = προ + χωρε-, 'go.' Hence προχωρε- = 'go forward,' 'advance.' χωρε- is itself a derivative from χώρα-, 'a place,' and means originally 'to take a place,' 'to take up,' 'hold,' e. g. τὸ ἀγγεῖον χωρεῖ δύο μέτρα, 'the vessel holds two measures.' χώρα, whence diminutive χωρίον, 'a farm,' is probably, as regards its first syllable χω-, kin to German *Gau*, as in Ammergau, &c., the English *gay* in Fotheringay, Gamlingay, Bungay, and other names of places.

ὑπολείπεται = ὑπὸ, 'under,' here 'behind,' as though 'at the bottom' + λείπεται, from λειπ- (root λιπ-), kin to *leave* + -εται = '[it] is.' Hence ὑπολείπεται = 'is left,' 'remains.'

θερμανθῇ = θερμὸ + αν (verbal suffix) + θῇ, ending as often above. Hence θερμανθῇ = 'may be warmed.' The verbal stem θερμαν- is in the imperfect, θερμαίν- for θερμάν-. Hence θερμαίνω, θερμαίνομαι· ἐθέρμαινον, ἐθερμαινόμην· ἐθέρμανα, ἐθερμάνθην, θερμανθῶ, κ.τ.λ.

ἀρκεῖται (ἀρκέ-εται): from root ἀλκ- ἀρκ-, literally 'to ward off;' Latin *arc-* in *arceo*. Hence, 'to secure oneself.' ἀρκοῦμαι, 'I am secure,' 'content,' 'I content myself.' Hence ἀρκετόν, 'enough.'

ψυχρὸ-ν, literally 'that which is blown upon' or 'spat upon:' from stem ψυχ-, 'to cool by blowing or spitting,' root φυ- for σπυ-, kin to *spi-* in *spit*. Hence ψυχή, 'the breath,' 'the soul.' Cf. ἄνεμο-ς, 'wind,' and *animu-s*, *anima*, 'mind' and 'soul' in Latin.

ἄρχεται: middle form of ἄρχει, 'he is the first,' 'he rules,' this form meaning 'he begins.'

περιαλείφων: from περὶ, 'about' + ἀλείφ-ων, 'smearing.'

σάπωνα[ν] = the Latin *saponem*.

σιαγόνα[ν]: nominative σιαγ-ὼν (for -ὸνς) -όνα -όνος -όνι· -όνες -όνας -όνων -όσι(ν).

παρειάς: from πάρος (πάρες), 'before' + noun suffix -ιὰ = παρεσιά, the 'frontage' of the head = 'the sides of the face,' 'the cheeks.'

ἑαυτὸν = ἐ for ἐν, old accusative pronoun + αὐτὸν = 'self.' Hence ἑαυτόν = 'himself.'

καταιβασιὰ = κατὰ, καταὶ, 'down' + βασιὰ (root βα + σιὰ), verbal substantive ending. Hence καταιβασιὰ = 'a going down,' i.e. a twinge of pain descending into the tooth; a thoroughly vernacular and most expressive word.

δόντια: for ὀ-δόντια, diminutive from ὀ-δόντ-, 'tooth,' Latin *dent-*, &c.

ποῦ νὰ μὲ τρελλάνῃ, 'such as to drive me mad,' literally 'such that it may,' &c. τρελλαν- from τρελλὸ-, 'mad' (cf. θερμαν- from θερμὸ-), supposed by some to be a corruption of the Ancient Greek τραυλὸ-, 'stammering,' as though for τρευλὸ-, τρεῦλό-.

γείνῃ: first aorist subjunctive, from root γεν-, cognate to *kin*. γίγνομαι, ἔγεινα, γείνω, κ.τ.λ. τὶ νὰ γείνῃ = 'what (is) to happen?' 'what's to be done?'

ἡτοιμάζετο: from ἕτοιμο-, 'ready,' ἑτοιμάζομαι, 'I get (myself) ready,' ἡτοιμάζετο, 'he was getting (himself) ready.' ἕ-τοιμο-, verbal adjective from root ἐ(ς), 'he,' *is*.

φέρῃ: kin to English *bear*, Latin *fero*, &c.

ἠχεῖ (ἠχέει): from ἦχο-, 'sound.'

Idiomatic Translation.

Mr. Pardalós enters his bedroom, and attempts to dress. But this is impossible, inasmuch as his corpulent spouse has the apartment full of dresses, petticoats, handkerchiefs, stays, and all the multifarious apparatus of female attire. He therefore gathers up his clothes, takes a small looking-glass and a candle, and withdraws to his office, to complete his toilet therein. But he soon remembers that he is unshaven, and that he must shave before he changes. Accordingly, he migrates a second time to the bedroom, opens and shuts the door, amid the protestations of Mrs. Pardalós that he will give her cold, and returns with his razor and the other requisites in his hands. Then he remembers that he wants hot water, but observing that the hour is advanced, he contents him with cold, and begins smearing over his chin and his cheeks with soap, saying to himself, "I shall have a fine twinge of toothache! but there's no help for it." And he prepared to bring the razor against his cheek, when once more the bell of the opening door resounds.

Exercise IX.

Δὲν εἶνε καιρὸς πρὸς θερμὸν ὕδωρ· ἡ ὥρα εἶνε προκεχωρημένη. Τί θὰ εἴπῃ (what means? *que veut dire?*) θερμὸν ὕδωρ; Ζεστὸ νερό. Εἰσέρχομαι εἰς τὸν κοιτῶνά μου κρατῶν τὸ κηρίον, τὸ ξυράφιον καὶ τὰ ἄλλα ἀπαιτούμενα πρὸς ἐνδυμασίαν. Προσπαθῶ νὰ ἐνδυθῶ ἀλλ' εἶνε ἀδύνατον, καθότι ἡ εὔσωμος σύζυγός μου ἔχει πλῆρες τὸ δωμάτιον πάσης τῆς πολυμόρφου συσκευῆς γυναικείου ἱματισμοῦ. Ὁ ἱματισμὸς τῶν γυναικῶν εἶναι κατ' ἀλήθειαν πολύμορφος, ἂν καὶ ὄχι εὔμορφος. Μετ' ὀλίγον ἐνθυμοῦμαι ὅτι δὲν ἔχω θερμὸν ὕδωρ νὰ ξυρισθῶ. Παρατηρῶ ὅτι τὸ νερὸ εἶνε κρύο καὶ ὅτι ἡ ὥρα εἶνε προ(κε)χωρημένη. Ἀλλὰ τί νὰ γείνῃ; Ἀρκοῦμαι λοιπὸν εἰς τὸ ψυχρόν, καθότι δὲν εἶνε καιρὸς ἵνα θερμανθῇ. Περιαλείφω μὲ σάπωνα τὴν σιαγόνα καὶ τὰς παρειάς. Μοῦ ἔρχεται καταιβασιὰ εἰς τὰ ὀδόντια, καὶ ψιθυρίζω ἥκιστα εὐσεβάστως " ἔχω γυναῖκα ποῦ νὰ μὲ τρελλάνῃ," καὶ τρελλαίνομαι κατ' ἀλήθειαν φέρων τὸ ξυράφιον ἐπὶ τὸ στῆθός μου.

It is impossible for me to enter my bedroom and to dress. Petticoats, stays, handkerchiefs, are requisites of multifarious female attire. The spouse of my friend is beautiful; but when he opens and shuts the door, she protests that he will give her cold. The hot water is not ready, but it is being got ready. No time is left me to complete my toilet. I must shave with cold water, and a twinge of toothache enough to drive me mad will attack me (come to me); but there's no help for it. The hour is advanced, and I am unshaved. I wish to shave before I change. I gather together the requisites for my toilet, and, holding the razor against my cheeks, migrate once more into my bedroom. The bell of the opening and shutting door rings enough to drive me mad.

ΔΕΚΑΤΟΝ ΜΑΘΗΜΑ.—Tenth Lesson.

Σὺ εἶσαι, Θοδωρῆ; φωνεῖ ὁ Παρδαλός, προβάλλων
You are (it), John?   calls the Pardalós, putting-forth

ὀλίγον τὴν σαπωνόφυρτον αὐτοῦ μορφὴν διὰ τῆς θύρας.
a-little the soap-smeared of-him face through the door.

—Ὄχι, ἀφέντη! ἀπαντᾷ κάτωθεν ἡ φωνὴ τῆς ὑπερετρίας,
— No,   sir!   replies from-below the voice of-the maid,

εἶνε ἕνας κύριος . . . θέλει κάτι νὰ σᾶς εἰπῇ.—Ἄς
it-is a gentleman . . . he-wants something that you he-tell.—Let

περάσῃ μίαν ἄλλην ὥραν, ἔχω ἐργασίαν.—Εἶνε ἀνάγκη
(him) pass an other hour, I-have business.—It-is need

νὰ σᾶς ἰδῇ τώρα, ἀπαντᾷ μετά τινα δευτερόλεπτα ἡ φωνὴ
that you he-see now, replies after some seconds the voice

τῆς ὑπηρετρίας.—Ἄλλο κακὸν! λέγει καθ' ἑαυτὸν ὁ ἀτυχὴς
of-the maid. — Another evil! says to himself the unlucky

Δημητράκης, καὶ μὴ δυνάμενος νὰ πράξῃ ἄλλως,
Little-Demetrius, and not being-able that he do else,

ἀπομάσσει ἐν τάχει τὸν σάπωνα ἀπὸ τῆς μορφῆς του,
wipes-off in speed the soap from the face of-him,

καὶ ἐξέρχεται τοῦ γραφείου τοῦ, ἐνῷ ὁ νυκτερινὸς
and comes-out of-the office of-him, while the nightly

ἐπισκέπτης ἀναβαίνει τὴν κλίμακα.—Ἡ Κυρία Τραχανᾶ,
visitor ascends the staircase.—The Mrs. Trachanás,

λέγει μειδιῶν ὁ νεωστὶ ἐλθών, σᾶς στέλλει τὸ κλειδὶ
says smiling the newly come, you sends the key

τοῦ θεωρείου δι' ἀπόψε, ἂν ἀγαπᾶτε.—Εὐχαριστοῦμεν
of-the stall for this-evening, if you-like. — We-thank

πολύ, παιδί μου, εὐχαριστοῦμεν, ἀπαντᾷ ὁ ταλαίπωρος
much, lad of-me, we-thank, answers the wretched

Παρδαλός, προσπαθῶν νὰ κολάσῃ τὸ ὀργίλον τῆς
Pardalós, endeavouring that he-restrain the wrathful(ness) of-the

μορφῆς του διὰ τυπικοῦ τινος μειδιάματος ... ἀλλὰ
face of-him by a carved sort-of smile ... but

εἴμεθα προσκεκλημένοι εἰς συναναστροφήν.—Ἆ, ἔτζι!
we-are invited to a-party. — Ah, so!

προσκυνῶ, καλὴν νύκτα σας.—Προσκυνήματα πολλά.
I-worship, good night to-you.—Worshippings many.

Καὶ εἰσέρχεται εἰς τὸ γραφεῖόν του γρυλλίζων ἐκ τοῦ
And he-enters into the office of-him grunting from the

θυμοῦ.—Διάλεξε καὶ αὐτὴ τὴν ἡμέραν καὶ τὴν ὥραν νὰ
passion.—She chose too this the day and the hour that

μᾶς στείλῃ τὸ θεωρεῖόν της.—Ποῖος ἦτον; φωνεῖ ἀπὸ
us she send the stall [key] of-her.— Who was-it? cries from

τοῦ κοιτῶνός της ἡ Κυρία Παρδαλοῦ.—Ἡ Κυρία
the bedroom of-her the Mrs. Pardalós. — The Mrs.

Τραχανᾶ ἐνθυμήθη νὰ μᾶς στείλῃ τὸ θεωρεῖόν της. —
Trachanás remembered that us she-send the stall [key] of-her.—

Ἐσπολλάτη της! ὅταν βρέχῃ μόνον καὶ χωνίζῃ μᾶς
To many years of-her! when it rains only and snows us

θυμᾶται! . . . μᾶς καθυποχρέωσε! — Μετ' ὀλίγας
she-remembers ... us deeply-she-obliged!—After few

δὲ στιγμὰς ἀνακράζει καὶ πάλιν, Κοντεύεις,
however minutes exclaims-she too again, Are-you-getting-on,

Δημητράκη; — Ποῦ νὰ κοντεύω, ἀδελφή! ἀκόμη δὲν
Little-Demetrius?—Where that I get-on, sister! yet not

ξυρίσθηκα. Ἔπειτα,δὲνβλέπω κϳ'ὅλα, καὶ κατακόπηκα.
shaved-am-I. Besides, not see-I even-at-all,and cut-to-pieces-am-I.

—Οὔ, καϋμένε! ἔλα 'δὼ, ποῦ ἔχει περισσότερον φῶς.
—Oh, poor-fellow! come here, where it-has   more   light.

—Αὐτοῦ; καὶ ποῦ νὰ σταθῶ; εἰς τὸν ἀέρα;—Ἔλα, ἔλα
—There? and where that I stand? in the air?— Come,come

τώρα, καὶ σοῦ κάμνω τόπον. Ἐγὼ ἐτελείωσα σχεδόν·
now, and you make - I room.   I have-finished almost.

μόνον τὴν τραχηλιά μου ἔχω νὰ βάλω.
Only the necklace of-me have-I that I-put-on.

προβάλλων = πρὸ, 'forth' + βάλλ-ων, 'putting:' βαλλ- for
βαλϳ-, stem of imperfect, from root βαλ- for γϝάλ-, German
quell- in Quelle, quellen, our well, well forth, &c.

σαπωνόφυρτον (cf. εὔσωμος above) = σαπωνο-, stem in composition of σάπον- + φύρ-, 'to knead,' 'smear,' 'puddle,' kin to
bar in barm, 'yeast,' German Bärme + το-ν = verbal adjectival
suffix + ending ν.

ὑπηρετρία-ς : feminine of ὑπηρέτη-ς, explained above.

κᾶτι : for κἂν (καὶ ἂν) τὶ, literally 'even if aught,' 'something.'

περάσῃ = περά + σῃ : περα, 'pass,' kin to our fare, imperfect
stem περνα-, whence περνάω, περνῶ, 'I pass,' &c.

ἐργασίαν : for ἐργαδ + σίαν, of which σί-α equals noun suffix,
ἐργαδ- = verbal stem forming imperfect stem ἐργαδϳ- (ἐργάδϳομαι),
ἐργάζομαι, κ.τ.λ. ; root ἐργ- for ϝεργ-, kin to work. Hence
ἐργασία = 'business.'

ἀνάγκη : ἀν-άγκ-η, literally 'up-string-ing,' from root αγκ-,
'curved,' whence ἀγκύλη, 'sling,' ὄγκινος, 'barb,' ὄγκος, 'bend,'
'bulk,' &c.

ἰδῇ (also ἴδῃ) : from root ϝιδ-, Latin vid- in video, kin to
English wot, wit, German wissen, witz.

δευτερόλεπτα : from δεύτερο-, 'second' + λεπτά, 'minutes,'

neuter plural of λεπτὸ-, 'fine,' 'minute.' Observe accent, as it is typical of all such compounds.

ἀτυχὴς: stem ἀτυχές-; degrees, ἀτυχέστερος, ἀτυχέστατος.

Δημητράκης: diminutive of Δημήτριο-, in which common Greek name that of the old goddess Δημήτηρ (Δημήτ(ε)ρ-) is preserved. The diminutive suffix -άκης is said by Sophocles to be of Slavonic origin, but it appears to be a modification of the same -ακ- which we had in γυναῖκα- for γυνάκϳα above. This does not hinder its being cognate to Slavonic -ak.

μὴ: negative particle, used instead of δὲν and ὄχι with subjunctives and participles, where, however, ὄχι (οὐχὶ or οὐ) is sometimes found, but in a different sense. μὴ δυνάμενος means 'since he was unable;' οὐ δυνάμενος would mean 'though he was unable.'

πράξῃ: for πράγ-σῃ or πράκ-σῃ, probably lengthened by κ from root πρα- (περα-), 'to further,' kin to *fur-* in same, *fare*, &c.; see above on περνῶ. Hence 'to do,' 'to accomplish.' In imperfect πράκϳω becomes πράσσω; tenses: ἔπραξα, πράξω, κ.τ.λ. From this root comes the common word πράγ-ματ- (πρᾶγμα), 'a thing.'

ἀπο-μάσσει, 'wipes off:' μάσσει for μάκϳει or μάχϳει. Hence μάγ-ειρος, 'a cook;' χειρό-μακ-τρον, 'a hand-wiper,' 'a towel,' κ.τ.λ.

τάχει: for τάχες-ι, 'in haste,' from τάχες- (τάχος), 'speed;' cognate are ταχύ-, 'swift,' τάχα, 'swiftly,' 'easily,' 'lightly,' 'perhaps.'

νυκτερινὸς (νυκτ-ερινός): in ending, as in root, kin to Latin *noct-urnus;* νυκτ-, kin to English *night*, Latin *noct-*, &c.; nominative νὺξ for νύκτς, as Latin *nox* for *nocts*.

ἐπισκέπ-της, 'visit-or;' see above on ἐπισκεπτήριον, κ.τ.λ.

κλίμακα [κλίμακαν]: stem κλίμακ- (nominative κλῖμαξ for κλίμακς). Like as this word looks to our *climb*, it has nothing to do with it, for English *c* or *k* implies Greek γ. Moreover, the Greek derivation is plain: κλίμακ- is from κλίμα[τ] (+ κ), whence *climate*; κλίμα(τ)- is verbal substantive from root κλι- in κλίνω, kin to Latin *clino*, *inclino*, our *lean* for *hlean*. The κλῖμαξ is that which is leant against the wall. Hence 'ladder,' 'staircase.'

νεωστὶ: strengthened by suffix τὶ, from νέως (νέωτ), instrumental adverb of νέο-, 'new.'

ἐλθών: second aorist, root ἐλθ- used with imperfect tenses of ἐρχ-, ἐλθὼν for ἐλθόντς, and declension accordingly.

στέλλει: for στέλῃει, root στελ- σταλ-; στέλλω, 'I send,' ἔστειλα for ἔστελ-σα, 'I sent,' ἐστάλην, 'I was sent,' also ἐστάλθην.

κλειδί (for κλειδίν, κλειδίον): diminutive of κλεῖδ- (nominative κλεῖς), from root κλει-, 'shut,' as above. κλεί-δ-, κλει-δί, 'the thing to shut with,' 'the key;' cf. German *schliessen*, *Schlüssel*.

θεωρείου (for θεωρείοσ͜ιο): stem θεωρεῖο- = θεα- θαϜ-, 'see' (θεά-ομαι, 'I see,' 'look,' 'behold') + -ρὸ- noun suffix, whence θεωρός [θαϜ-ρὸς], 'a seer,' θεωρέ-ω, 'I am a seer,' θεωρεῖον, 'a place for a seer,' 'a box at an opera or theatre.' Hence also θέα-τρο-ν, 'a place to see in,' 'a theatre.'

δι' = διά: with accusative means 'for.'

ἀπόψε: from ἀπὸ, 'from,' and ὀψὲ, 'late,' 'at evening.' Hence ἀπόψε, 'this evening,' 'to-night.' Observe how, in Greek and English, in words of this kind, the preposition sometimes supplies the place of a demonstrative pronoun. Cf. also ἐφ'έτος, 'this year.'

ἀγαπᾶτε: verbal stem ἀγαπα-, from noun ἀγάπα- (nominative ἀγάπη), 'love.' ἀγαπῶ, ἠγάπησα, ἀγαπήσω.

εὐχαριστοῦμεν (εὐχαριστέ-ομεν): verbal stem εὐχαριστέ-, from εὐ, 'well' + χαριστὸ-, verbal adjective, from χαριδ- (χαρίδ͜ιω, χαρίζω), 'to do a favour.' Hence εὐχάριστος = 'well-flavoured,' 'pleasant,' 'pleased;' εὐχαριστέω, 'I am pleased,' 'gratified,' 'I thank.' Hence, too, εὐχαριστοῦμαι, 'I am contented;' εὐχαριστημένος, 'delighted,' 'contented' (also ηὐχαριστημένος).

παιδί = παιδίν, παιδίον.

κολάσῃ = κολάδ + σῃ: κολαδ- = 'restrain,' 'prevent.' Hence

κολάζω, 'I restrain,' ἀκόλαστος (ἀκόλαδ-τος), 'incontinent,' ἀκολασία, 'incontinence.'

ὀργίλον: from ὀργά- + ἰλο-, adjectival suffix; ὀργά-, kin to Sanscrit *úrjâ* ('strength,' 'eagerness'), hence *wrath*; perhaps cognate also with Latin *urgeo*. Hence ὀργίλο-, 'wrathful,' τὸ ὀργίλον, 'the wrathful(ness).' This use of the neuter adjective should be noted, as it is common in Greek.

τυπικοῦ: τυπικὸ- from τύπο-, substantive of root τυπ-, 'to strike,' whence τύπ-τω, 'I strike;' Sanscrit *tup, tump*, our *thump*. From this root comes τύμπ-ανο-, 'a drum' (τὸ τύμπανον), whence our *tympanum*. Nothing to do with *tin pan*, as schoolboys fondly imagine.

ἔτζι: said to be a corruption of οὑτωσί = οὕτωτ, old instrumental + ί, demonstrative particle; not without influence of Italian *anzi* on the accentuation.

προσκυνῶ (προσκυνέω): from πρὸς, 'towards' + κυ-νέ-ω (νε = suffix of extension), 'I kiss.' Hence προσκυνῶ, 'I kiss towards' (as in Spanish *beso las manos*), 'I worship,' 'make my respects.'

καλὴν νύκτα σὰς, 'good night to you;' σας, enclitic accusative used for dative.

προσκυνήματ-α: verbal substantive from προσκυνε-.

γρυλλίζων (for γρυλλίδjων): formed from γρὺ, 'a grunt;' οὐδὲ γρύ, 'not a syllable,' 'not as much as a grunt'—a word made from the sound (onomatopoetic), like 'cuckoo,' κόκκυξ, &c.

διάλεξε: for διάλεγ-σε; διὰ, 'apart' + λεγ-, 'pick,' German *lesen* for *leksen*, Latin *leg-* in *lego*. Hence διαλέγω, 'I chose,' διέλεξε(ν), vernacular (ἐ)διάλεξε(ν), 'he,' 'she,' or 'it chose.'

αὐτὴ: for αὐτὴν, agreeing with τὴν ἡμέραν.

ποῖος: for κϝοῖος (κϝόσjος), adjective formed from genitive κϝοῖο, κϝόσjο of κϝο-, Latin *quo-* (cf. *cujus*), our *who* for *hwo*, literally 'of what kind?' Hence 'what manner of man?' 'who?'

ἦτον: imperfect middle 3rd singular of ἐς-, standing for ἔεστο, ἔετο with euphonic ν added by false analogy of words, like διέλεξε(ν), κ.τ.λ., where ν stands for τ, sign of 3rd person singular; cf. in classical Greek, λέγουσι(ν), κ.τ.λ. Persons: ἤμουν, ἦσο, ἦτο· ἤμεθα, ἦσθε, ἦσαν. Other forms: ἤμην, semi-classical, ἤμοινα, vernacular, ἦσοιν and ἦσουνε, ἤτανε· ἤμαστε, ἤσαστε, ἤτανε. The 3rd plural is from the active voice, as are all persons in the older classical Greek: ἦν, ἦς, ἦ, or ἦν· ἦμεν, ἦτε, ἦσαν.

'σπολλάτη της: for εἰς πολλὰ ἔτη της, an elliptical expression = 'εἰς πολλὰ ἔτη νὰ ζήσῃ' της, 'may she long live—to her' (genitive for dative), i.e. long life to her.

βρέχ: for Ϝρέχ- (cf. βροχὴ above), kin to Latin rigo for vrigo, German regen for wregen, our rain.

χιονίζῃ: for χιονίδι-ῃ from χιόν-, 'snow,' kin to hiem-s, Latin, which, with χεῖμα-τ- χειμόν-, 'winter,' is kin to Sanscrit hi-ma-s, 'snow,' Slavonic zima, Albanian dim̥e, 'winter,' Zend hima, also 'year,' as probably in Latin bimus, trimus, for bi-himus, tri-himus, &c. The Himalayas are the 'snowy mountains.' In Slavonic and Albanian the original gh has become dentalized, probably through the influence of the dental vowel i. In Sanscrit and Zend it has become h, as often in these languages.

καθυποχρέωσε: from κατὰ, 'downright,' ὑπὸ, 'under,' and χρέο(ς), 'debt.' Hence καθυποχρε-όνω, 'I put altogether under a debt;' καθυποχρέωσε, 'she has greatly obliged us,' as we say ironically, 'we are really very much obliged.'

θυμᾶται: vernacular for ἐνθυμεῖται. Colloquially, verbs in ε- are conjugated as if in α-; this is probably archaic, α- ε- ο- being originally mere variants of the same undefined vowel sound, and only specialized by custom in course of time.

στιγμὰ-ς: for στιγμὰ-ν-ς, from root στιγ- (στίζω (στίγϳω), 'I prick'), our 'stick,' literally 'a puncture' or 'point.' Hence 'a point of time,' 'moment.'

ἀνακράζει: literally 'cries up;' we say 'cries out.' κράζει = κράγϳει; root κραγ-.

κοντεύεις: from κοντὸ-, 'near,' probably nasalized from κοτὸ- or κατὸ-, adjectival stem answering to preposition κατὰ, 'at' or 'by;' suffix -ευ- means 'get' or 'be.' Hence κοντὸ-, 'near,' κοντεύ-, 'approach,' 'get on.'

ξυρίσθη-κα: for ἐξυρίσθην; the endings -κα -κας -κε' -καμεν -κατε -κασιν or -καν(ε) are used colloquially for the classical -ν -ς — -μεν -τε -σαν in this tense, on the analogy of ἔδωκα for ἔδων, ἔθηκα for ἔθην, &c. In the case of ἔβηκα for ἔβην the analogy is perfect. In classical Greek these endings are (regularly) added to *perfect* (reduplicated), not to aorist stems, e. g. βέβηκα, 'I have gone,' root βα-.

ἀδελφή: a familiar address to any woman (as ἀδελφὶ to any man), irrespective of real relationship. Cf. St. Paul: μὴ οὐκ ἔχομεν ἐξουσίαν ἀδελφὴν γυναῖκα περιάγειν; or, as it stands in the Modern Greek version: Μὴ δὲν ἔχομεν ἐξουσίαν νὰ συμπεριφέρωμεν ἀδελφὴν γυναῖκα; "Have we not power to lead about a sister as wife?" ἀδελφὸς, ἡ, 'brother,' 'sister,' kin to Sanscrit *sa-gharbh-jas*, i. e. of one womb; cf. δελφ-ίν, 'the belly-fish,' i. e. dolphin.

ἔπειτα = ἐπὶ, 'besides' + εἶτα (Latin *ita*), 'then,' the whole meaning 'moreover.'

κ᾽ὅλα = καὶ + ὅλα (neuter plural of ὅλο- for σόλϝο-, kin to *sol-* in Latin *sol-ido-*), literally 'even all (together),' 'already.' δὲν βλέπω κ᾽ ὅλα, 'Already I can't see,' i. e. I see no longer.

κατακόπηκα: for κατεκόπην, see above on ending -κα. κοπ- (also κοβ-) probably kin to our *hew*.

καϋμένε: apparently = classical κεκαυμένε, vernacular καυμένε, καμμένε, 'burnt,' from root καυ-, imperfect καίω, καύγω for κάϝϳω, but only in this sense when written with diæresis; kin to *ho-t*, German *hei-ss*.

ἔλα: aorist imperfect giving the stem which is found in classical Greek only in ἐλά-ω, ἤλασα, κ.τ.λ., of which the imperfect is ἐλαύ-νω for ἐλάϝ-νω, 'I march.' The same root also appears in classical future ἐλεύσομαι for ἐλάϝσομαι, 'I shall come.' ἔλα thus stands for ἔλαϝ or ἔλαυ.

δῶ: short for ἰδῶ, popularly supposed to be a transposition of ὧδε, but much more likely a form of ἰδοὺ, ἰδοῦ (ϝιδοῦ), 'see!'

'lo!' 'behold!' ἰδού is actually found in the sense of 'here,' or just passing into that sense, in Acts ii. 7: Οὐκ ἰδοὺ πάντες οὗτοί εἰσιν οἱ λαλοῦντες Γαλιλαῖοι; "Are not here all these who speak Galilæans?"

φῶς: for φῶτ, φωτός, φωτί· φῶτα, φωτῶν, φωσί.

στα-θῶ: literally 'be stood.' Hence 'stand.'

ἀέρα: stem ἀέρ-, probably 'the breather,' kin to ἄημι, 'I breathe.'

κάμνω = καμ + ν + ω, 'I do;' in classical Greek, 'I labour.' 'I am weary,' at most, 'I make.' Yet as make is the oldest meaning (Homeric), the modern is probably also of high antiquity, though not coming to the surface in literature.

τόπον: masculine (nominative τόπος).

ἐτελείωσα = ἐ + τελει + ω + σα: τέλειο- from τέλες-, 'end.' Hence for τέλεσjο- = 'that which has an end,' 'perfect,' whence τελειό(ν)ω, 'I finish.' Observe use of aorist ἐτελείωσα in sense of lost perfect τετελείωκα. The Greeks can also say ἔχω τελειώσει (for τελειῶσαι), infinitive aorist, if they desire to be explicit, or ἔχω (τε)τελειωμένον, but the latter only with nouns, transitively. ἔχω τελειωμένον τὸ ἔργον.

σχε-δὸν: adverb = root σχε- σέχ- (found in ἔσχον, aorist of ἔχω for σέχω, ἔ-σχη-κα, perfect, κ.τ.λ.) + adverbial ending -δόν; cf. βαθμη-δόν, 'by degrees,' &c. 'Having' or 'holding close to' anything is the notion which appears in σχεδόν, 'in a close manner,' 'nearly,' 'almost.'

τραχηλιά = τράχηλο + ιά: feminine suffix, 'a something for the neck;' τράχηλο-, kin to τρέχω, 'I run,' τρόχο-ς, 'a course,' τροχό-ς, 'a wheel,' kin to German drch-en, drechseln.

Idiomatic Translation.

"Is that you, John?" cries Pardalós, putting his lathered face a little way out of the door.

"No, sir," answers the voice of the maid from below. "It is a gentleman; he wishes to speak to you."

"More bother!" says our luckless Demetrius to himself, and having no alternative, hastily wipes the lather from his face, and issues from his office, while the nocturnal visitor ascends the staircase.

"Mrs. Trachanás," says the new-comer, smiling, "sends you the key of her box at the opera for to-night, if you like to go."

"Many thanks, my friend, many thanks; but we're invited out," replies the wretched Pardalós, trying to keep down the wrathful expression of his countenance under a forced smile.

"Oh, indeed! then I will take my leave. Good night to you."

"The same to you." And he enters his office, grunting with rage.

"Who was it?" cries Mrs. Pardalós from her bedroom.

"Mrs. Trachanás thought to send us the key of her box."

"Long life to her! It's only when it rains and snows she thinks of us! She is exceedingly obliging." But after a few moments she exclaims again,—

"Are you getting on, Demetrius dear?"

"Getting on! heart alive! I am not yet shaved. Besides, I can't see any longer, and have cut myself all to bits."

"Oh, dear! I'm so sorry! Come here, where there's more light."

"And where am I to stand—in the air?"

"Come, come, now, and I'll make room for you. I've nearly finished. I have only got my necklace to put on."

Exercise X.

Ποῖος ἦτον; σὺ εἶσαι Δημητράκη μου; Μάλιστα· ἐγὼ εἶμαι· καὶ ποῦ νὰ σταθῶ; Ἐδῶ νὰ σταθῇς! ἔλα καὶ σοῦ κάμνω τόπον· ἰδοὺ ἔχει περισσότερον φῶς. Ὁ ἀτυχὴς Δημητράκης προβάλλει ὀλίγον ἐκ τοῦ γραφείου τὴν σαπωνόφυρτον αὐτοῦ μορφὴν γρυλλίζων ἐκ τοῦ θυμοῦ. Ἄλλο κακόν! δὲν βλέπω κι' ὅλα καὶ κατακόπηκα, ἢ καὶ κατεκόπην ὡς γράφουσι σήμερον οἱ νεοφώτιστοι τῆς γλώσσης μας καθαρισταί. Ποίος ενθύμηθη να μας στείλη το κλειδί του θεωρείου δι' απόψε; Ή Κυρία Τραχανά, διότι βρέχει και χιονίζει, και μη δυναμένη να ύπάγη εις το θέατρον ενθυμείται ημάς.

'Σπολλάτη της· μας καθυποχρέωσε· είμεθα καθυποχρεωμένοι· ευχαριστούμεν πολύ και της στέλλομεν προσκυνήματα πολλά.

Παιδί μου μη προσπαθής να κολάσης το οργίλον της μορφής σου δια τυπικού μειδιάματος. Διατί διάλεξε και αυτή την ήμέραν και την ώραν να μας το στείλη; άς περάση μίαν άλλην ώραν· έχομεν έργασίαν τώρα και όχι μόνον τούτο άλλα είμεθα προσκεκλημένοι εις σιναναστροφήν. Πού είνε το κλειδί του γραφείου μου; Είνε ανάγκη να το έχω τώρα, να το λάβω αμέσως. Τι απαντάς; Δεν απαντώ τίποτε. διότι δεν έχω τίποτε ν' απαντήσω.

Ά έτζι! προσκυνώ, καλήν νύκτα σας.

Εξέρχομαι του κοιτώνος σαπωνόφυρτος και γρυλλίζων εκ του θυμού, και έτοιμος να σταθώ εις τον αέρα διότι δεν βλέπω άλλον τόπον, αλλά η υπηρετρία ανακράζει κάτωθεν μετ' ολίγας στιγμάς· Κοντεύετε κύριε; ένας κύριος είναι εδώ και θέλει, λέγει, κάτι να σας είπη. Πές του να περάση άλλην ώραν, και να μην αναβή την κλίμακα τώρα που ξυρίζομαι· άλλως θα ήνε ανάγκη να εξέλθω ημιξύριστος του κοιτώνος και θα μού έλθη πάλιν καμμιά καταιβασιά εις τα δόντια, διότι θα κρυωθώ.

It is necessary that (we must) call (pass) another time. The gentleman is engaged now, and is invited out. The nocturnal guest descends the ladder, endeavouring to conceal the angry expression of his face by means of a forced smile of respect and subjection. The wretched Pardalós, half-shaved, and grunting with rage, unable any longer to see, has cut himself to pieces ; and protruding his lathered visage through the opening door of the office, exclaims, " I must have more light. How am I to get on? Where am I to stand—in the air? I have no looking-glass and no candle, and the room is full of garments, petticoats, handkerchiefs, stays, and necklaces ?"

"Oh !" says his corpulent wife. " Come, poor fellow ! I

have nearly finished." I see that the hour is advanced. Don't try to bring the razor to bear upon your lathered cheek. It is not necessary. Let me wipe off quickly the soap from your face. Better to be half shaved than to (that you) cut yourself to pieces.

Long life to you! Here is (ἰδοὺ) the key of our box. We are invited to the theatre to-night, if we like. We have no business, so we will go. The new comer smiles a forced smile of patronage and superiority, but it is impossible for him (τοῦ εἶνε, κ.τ.λ.) to keep down the wrathful expression of his visage.

It rains and snows, and I shall have a twinge of toothache. Why should we choose this day and hour to go to the theatre? You have deeply obliged us, but we are only half shaved, and cannot come at present.

ΕΝΔΕΚΑΤΟΝ ΜΑΘΗΜΑ.—Eleventh Lesson.

Note.—As the learner is now presumably acquainted with the more constantly recurring peculiarities of Modern Greek idiom, the interlinear translation will be somewhat freer henceforth, and the free idiomatic translation will be as far as possible dispensed with.

Ὁ Παρδαλὸς πείθεται, συγκινούμενος ὑπὸ τῆς συζυγικῆς
   Pardalós obeys,   moved   by   the conjugal

μερίμνης τῆς Κυρίας Φρόσως, λαμβάνει πάλιν τὸ φῶς,
solicitude of   Mrs. Euphrosyne, takes   again the candle,

τὸ κάτοπτρον καὶ τὸ ξυράφιον, καὶ, ἡμιξύριστος, μεταβαίνει
the looking-glass and the razor, and, half-shaved, migrates

εἰς τὸν κοιτῶνα, ὅπου εὑρίσκει τὴν Εὐφροσύνην τοποθετημένην
into the bedroom, where he finds   Euphrosyne   located

πρὸ τοῦ κατόπτρου, μεταξὺ τεσσάρων κηρίων, καὶ
before the looking-glass, between   four   candles, and

καταγινομένην μετὰ πολλοῦ κόπου νὰ δέσῃ ὄπισθεν
exerting herself with much labour to tie from behind

τοῦ τραχήλου της μικρὰν ἐκ μέλανος βελούδου ταινίαν,
her neck a small black velvet ribbon,

ἀφ' ἧς κρέμαται ἐπὶ τοῦ ὑπερακμάζοντος στήθους
from which hangs upon her more than mature breast

τῆς χρυσοῦς λοβίσκος.—Καὶ ποῦ θέλεις νὰ σταθῶ τώρα;
a golden locket. — And where do you wish me to stand now?

ὑπολαμβάνει ὁ ταλαίπωρος Παρδαλός, μὴ βλέπων τόπον
interposes the wretched Pardalós, not seeing a space

κενὸν πρὸ τοῦ κατόπτρου.—Ἔλα, μὴ μουρμουρίζῃς,
vacant before the looking-glass.—Come, don't grumble,

ἀπαντᾷ μειλιχίως ἐλέγχουσα ἡ κυρία, περιπόρφυρος
answers gently reproaching the lady, all-red

ἐκ τοῦ ματαίου κόπου ὃν καταβάλλουσιν οἱ χονδροὶ
from the fruitless labour which expend her stout

αὐτῆς βραχίονες ἀνακαμπτόμενοι ὄπισθεν τῆς κεφαλῆς της.
arms bent back behind her head.

Δέσε μου μία στιγμὴ ἐδῶ αὐτὸ τὸ βελουδάκι, καὶ
Tie me a moment here this little (piece of) velvet, and

σοῦ ἀφίνω ὅλον τὸν τόπον ἐλεύθερον.—Ὁ Παρδαλὸς γίνεται
I (will) leave you all the space clear. — Pardalós becomes

κατ' ἀνάγκην πρὸς στιγμὴν καὶ θαλαμηπόλος τῆς συζύγου του,
perforce for a moment lady's-maid too of his wife,

ἥτις περατοῖ τέλος τὴν ἐνδυμασίαν αὐτῆς, καὶ καταπίπτει
who completes at length her toilette, and falls back

κάθιδρος καὶ ἀσθμαίνουσα ἐπὶ τοῦ ἀνακλίντρου, φυσῶσα
sweating and panting on the sofa, blowing

ὡς ἀτμομηχανὴ, καὶ ἀεριζομένη διὰ τοῦ μανδυλίου της,
like a steam-engine, and fanning herself with her handkerchief,

ἐνῷ ὁ σύζυγός της ξυρίζεται.—Ἀ, Δημητράκη . . . λέγει,
while her husband shaves. — Ah, Demetrius, dear! says she,

μόλις κατορθοῦσα νὰ ἀρθρώσῃ τὰς λέξεις, σὲ βεβαιόνω
scarce succeeding in articulating the words, I assure you

μεγάλο ἦτο τὸ χατῆρί σου ἀπόψε . . . νὰ ὑποφέρω ὅλον
great was your longing this evening . . . that I should suffer

αὐτὸν τὸν κόπον διὰ νὰ πάγω νὰ πιῶ τὸ τζάϊ τοῦ
all this trouble to go to drink the tea of

Σουσαμάκη σου. — Ἔννοια σου! Φρόσω μου,
your pet Susamákis.—Your fear! (i. e. never fear) my Phrosy,

ἀπαντᾷ ὁ Παρδαλός, πονηρῶς μειδιῶν, ἔννοια σου! καὶ
answers Pardalós, roguishly smiling, never fear! and

δὲν θὰ πιῇς μόνον τὸ τζάϊ σου ἀπόψε εἰς τοῦ Σουσαμάκη.
you won't drink only your tea to-night at Susamákis'.

Ὁ Ὀρέστης ξεύρει καὶ κάμνει τὰ πράγματα, καθὼς πρέπει.
Orestes knows how to do things (lit. knows and does) properly.

Θὰ μᾶς ἔχῃ καὶ σάντβιτζ καὶ κρασάκι καὶ φροῦτα.—
He will have for us also sandwich and wine and fruit. —

Ποῦ τὸ ξεύρεις; ὑπολαμβάνει ἠπιώτερον ἡ Κυρία Φρόσω,
How do you know it? interposes more gently Mrs. Phrosy,

ἥτις, λαίμαργος φύσει καὶ πολυφάγος, ἤρχιζε νὰ συγχωρῇ εἰς
who, greedy by nature and gluttonous, began to forgive to

τὸν Σουσαμάκην τὴν συναναστροφήν του χάριν τοῦ δείπνου του.
Susamákis his party for the sake of his supper.

—Τὸ ξεύρω, διότι τὸν εἶδα σήμερον τὸ πρωῒ εἰς τὴν
—I know it, because I saw him to-day in the morning at the

ἀγορὰν, καὶ   ἐψώνιζε.   — Αἴ, τότε κάπως
market, and he was making purchases.—Eh, then there's some

ὑποφέρεται, διότι μὰ τὴν ἀλήθειαν ... — Κρότος ἁμάξης,
enduring it, for in   truth ... — The sound of a carriage,

σταθείσης πρὸ τῆς θύρας τῆς οἰκίας, διέκοψεν αἴφνης
coming to a stand before the door of the house, interrupted suddenly

τὴν φράσιν τῆς Κυρίας Παρδαλοῦ.—Νά! ἀνεφώνησεν ὁ
the sentence of Mrs. Pardalús.—There! exclaimed the

μόλις τὴν στιγμὴν ἐκείνην τελειόνων τὸ ξύρισμά του
scarcely that moment   finishing his shaving

Δημητράκης. Τὸ ἁμάξι ἦλθε, κ' ἐγὼ εἶμαι ἀκόμη ἄνιπτος.
Demetrius. The carriage is come, and I am yet unwashed.

Καὶ σπογγισθεὶς ἐν τάχει, ἤρξατο ἀποδυόμενος.
And sponging himself quickly, he began undressing.

πείθ-εται = 'is persuaded,' hence 'obeys;' root πιθ- for φιθ-, kin to fid- in Latin fid-o, fid-us, fœd-us, &c., whence our confide, fidelity, &c.

συγκινούμενος = συγκινε-όμενος: from συν + κινε-, verbal stem from root κι-, kin to English hie, 'to move.' Hence συγκινούμενος = Latin commotus, 'moved,' 'touched.'

μερίμνης: stem μέριμνα-, of which -ιμνα is substantival suffix, cognate to participial ending -μενο- -μένα-; cf. δεξαμενή, 'a reservoir,' 'a receiver,' and participle aorist middle δεξαμένη from root δεχ-. μερ- is explained above.

ἡμιξύριστος = ἡμι-, 'half' (whence adjective ἥμισ-υ-ς, ἡμίσ-ει-α, ἥμισ-υ) + ξυριστό-ς, 'shaved.' Observe accent.

τοποθετημένην: from τοπο-, 'place' + θετό-, verbal adjective of θε-, 'set,' whence τοποθετε-, 'locate,' 'fix in place;' τοποθετημένην (perfect participle), 'located.'

μεταξὺ: double preposition for μετα + ξὺν, old form of σὺν, see above. Hence μεταξὺ = 'betwixt,' 'amongst.'

κατα-γινομένην, literally 'getting down,' 'getting deep' into anything. Hence = 'immersed,' 'buried,' 'absorbed' (in a task).

κόπου: genitive of κόπο- (after μετὰ in sense of 'with'), from root κοπ-, 'to cut,' 'wear,' 'tire.' Hence κόπο = 'toil,' 'trouble,' 'labour.'

δέ-ση: δε-, kin to English *tie*.

ὄπισθεν: from root ὀπ-, probably for σοπϝ-, σεπϝ- for σεκϝ-, Latin *sequ*- in *sequor*, &c. Hence ὀπ-ι-δ-, 'following,' 'visitation,' 'awe;' ὄπισθεν = ὄπιδ-θεν, 'from behind;' also κατ-όπιν, 'afterwards.'

μέλαν-ος, 'black:' kin to Latin *mal-us*, 'bad,' &c. μέλας [μέλανς], μέλαινα [μέλανϳα], μέλαν· μέλανα[ν], μέλαιναν [μέλανϳαν], μέλαν· μέλανος, μελαίνης, μέλανος· μέλανι, μελαίνῃ, μέλανι· μέλανες, μέλαιναι, μέλανα· μέλανας, μελαίνας, μέλανα· μέλασιν [-νσιν], μελαίναις, μέλασιν. μελάν-τερο-ς, 'blacker,' μελάν-τατος, 'blackest;' but in the vernacular, μελανώτερος, μελανώτατος, as also μέλανος, μελάνη, μέλανο(ν), in positive degree. Hence, also, ἡ μελάνη, 'the ink.'

βελούδου: a foreign word, the Italian *velutto*, nominative βελοῦδο(ν).

ταινίαν: seemingly for τεν-ία, certainly from root τεν- ταν-, strengthened from τε-, 'stretch,' τείνω (τένϳω), 'I stretch,' ἐτάν-θην or ἐτά-θην, 'I was stretched,' 'I stretched myself:' kin to our *thin*. Hence ταινία, 'a thin strip,' 'a thong,' 'a ribbon.'

ἀφ' ἧς: for ἀπὸ ἧς.

κρέμ-αται, 'hangs:' root κρεμ-, kin to Gothic *hram-jan*, 'to crucify,' German *Rahmen* (Old High German *Rama* for *Hrama*), 'a frame,' 'support.' Our *frame* may probably be explained like *fret*, from Gothic *fra-itan*, 'to *for-eat*,' 'to eat away,' as corruption of *for-rame*. Hence our noun *frame* would be derived from the verb 'to *for-rame*,' 'to *frame*.' From this root too, perhaps, are derived Latin *crem-or*, Italian *crema* (whence Greek κρέμα), German *Rahm*, 'cream,' i. e. what *hangs* or floats on the surface of the milk.

ὑπερακμάζοντος: from ὑπὲρ-, for συπὲρ, Latin *super*, 'over' + ἀκμάζ-οντ-ος, from verbal stem ἀκμαζ-, 'be ripe,' 'be at its prime,' from ἀκμά-, root ἀκ-, kin to our *edge* for *egg* + μά-, substantival suffix, whence ἀκμὴ = 'tip,' 'point,' 'summit.' As adverb, ἀκμὴν, 'at the point,' 'just now,' 'as yet;' in Modern Greek, ἀκόμην, ἀκόμη, ἀκόμα, in form probably influenced by the like-vowelled Italian *ancora*, i. e. *hanc-horam*, 'this hour.' Thus ὑπερακμάζω = 'I am past the prime.'

στῆθος: from root στα-, English *sta* in *stay*, *stand* + θ-ες-, substantival suffix. Hence στῆθος = 'chest,' as the most sturdy, steady, or stalwart part of the body.

χρυσοῦς: for χρυσέ-ος, adjective of χρυσό-, 'gold,' with which it is doubtless kin. χρυσό- standing for χρυτρό- by a frequent sibilation of τ, *l* in English for *r* as often, while *g* is the regular representative in Teutonic of χ. Metathesis has taken place in the English and German words, *gold* standing for *glod*, Sanscrit *hir-anam* for *ghir-anam*, Zend *zar-ana*, Slavonic *zla-to*. Cognate also are χλουνός, a Greek form mentioned by Hesychius, and the Phrygian γλουρ-ός, 'gold,' γλουρέα, 'golden.'

λοβίσκο-ς = λοβό, 'a lobe' + diminutive ending -ίσκο-ς. Hence 'a little lobe,' 'a locket.' λοβ-ό-ς is probably softened from λοπ-ό-ς, which is also found, and is kin to λεπίς (λεπ-ίδ-ς), 'a scale.'

ὑπο-λαμβάνει, 'takes up' the word. Hence 'continues,' or 'breaks in.'

ταλαί-πωρ-ο-ς: of this word, the first part means 'miserable,' and is kin to τάλαν- (nominative τάλας for τάλαν-ς), 'wretched;' while the second is kin to our *fare*. Hence ταλαίπωρος = 'a wretched-farer,' 'faring-wretchedly,' 'poor,' 'miserable. ταλαι- is cognate with the Old Greek root ταλ-, Latin *tul-* in *tuli*, German *dul-* in *dul-den*, Scotch *thole*, &c.

τόπο-: perhaps for στόπο-, and further formation of root στα-; cf. Sanscrit *stháp-áj-ámi*, 'I set,' 'place.'

μουρμουρίζῃς: a word formed from the sound; cf. *murmurare*

in Latin. Notice the tense with μὴ: μὴ μουρμουρίζῃς, 'don't murmur,' i. e. stop murmuring; μὴ μουρμουρίξῃς would mean 'do not murmur hereafter,' 'ever,' 'at any future time.' This use of the two subjunctive-imperative tenses with μὴ is very peculiar; it is quite invariable, and is common, like almost all tense usages, to classical and Modern Greek, only that in classical Greek the pure imperative form μὴ μουρμούριζε is used in the imperfect, and the subjunctive μὴ μουρμουρίσῃς (Doric μουρμουρίξῃς) only in the aorist; yet it seems to be ignored by every Western grammarian. The Rev. T. K. Arnold in his "Practical Introduction to Greek Composition," which, he informs us in the preface to the fourth edition (1841), was then used at nearly all our public schools, and has ever since maintained a considerable, and in many respects well-deserved reputation, gives on page 20 the following examples:—

"μὴ κλέπτε, 'do not steal' (forbids stealing generally).

"μὴ κλέψῃς, 'do not steal' (forbids stealing in a particular instance)."

Which is as precisely wrong as it could well be.

μὴ κλέπτε means 'do not steal' (as you are now doing).

μὴ κλέψῃς means 'steal not henceforth,' 'never steal at all.'

It is quite true that κλέπτε means 'steal' generally, 'be a thief by profession,' whereas κλέψον means 'steal a particular thing;' but in the case of prohibitions the point of view is changed, so that μὴ κλέπτε (Modern μὴ κλέπτῃς) means 'leave off stealing,' μὴ κλέψῃς, 'never steal.' So in the Lord's Prayer, μὴ εἰσενέγκῃς (aorist) ἡμᾶς εἰς πειρασμὸν (Modern μὴ φέρῃς, not φέρνῃς ἡμᾶς εἰς πειρασμὸν) = 'lead us not (at any time) into temptation;' but in Mark x. 14, "Ἄφετε (2nd aorist) τὰ παιδία ἔρχεσθαι πρός με, καὶ μὴ κωλύετε (imperfect) αὐτά;" in Modern Greek, "Ἀφήσατε (1st aorist) τὰ παιδία νὰ ἔρχωνται πρὸς ἐμὲ καὶ μὴ ἐμποδίζητε (imperfect) αὐτά," "Suffer the little children to come unto me, and forbid them not (as you now are doing).'

Observe how instinctively and accurately the Modern Greek version adheres to the tenses of the ancient.

μειλιχίως (μειλιχίωτ): adverb of μειλ-ίχ-ιο-, extension of μείλ-ιχ-ο, *mild*, with which it is cognate.

ἐλέγχουσα [ἐλέγχ-οντ-σα]: two etymologies of this word have been proposed, one connecting it as a nasalized form with ἐλαχ-ύ-, 'slight,' hence ἐλέγχ-ω = 'I slight;' another with Zend *eregh-ant*, 'bad,' the German *arg*, *ärgern*, &c.

περιπόρφυρος = περί, 'all over' + πόρφυρο- for πύρ-φορο-, *fire-bear*ing, with which it is kin. Hence περιπόρφυρος (ἡ καὶ ὁ), 'fiery-all-over,' 'all of a blaze.'

μάτα-ι-ου: from root μάτα-, as seen in adverb μάτη-ν, Doric μάτα-ν, 'vainly' + adjectival suffix ι-ο. Hence μάταιο- = 'vain,' 'idle,' 'ineffectual.'

κατα-βάλλουσι(ν) [for κατα-βάλλοντι], literally 'put down,' 'lay down,' 'invest,' 'spend.'

χονδρο-ί, 'coarse:' apparently a euphonic metathesis for χρονδό-, kin to Latin *granum*, *grandi-s*, and *granden-* ('hail'). N.B.—χόνδρο- or χονδρό- means, as a substantive, 'grain,' 'groats,' in classical Greek; and 'granular' or 'groat-like' is the only meaning given to the adjective in Liddell and Scott; but the analogy of the Latin *grandi-s* seems to imply that the common Modern Greek meaning belonged to the root before the separation of the Græco-Italic stock. Our own *groat* and *great* point back to a still earlier connexion. The connexion of meaning is probably to be sought in the contrast between *coarse* unground *grain* and fine (small) flour.

βραχίον-ες, 'arms:' the Latin *brac-i-a*. ὁ βραχίων means apparently 'the shorter,' i. e. upper arm, comparative of βραχύ-, 'short,' kin to Latin *brev-i-s* for *bregv-i-s*.

ἀνα-καμπτόμενοι, 'up-bending' or 'back-bending:' κάμπ-τ-ω, 'I bend,' κάμπ-τ-ομαι, 'I bend myself,' 'am bent,' root καμπ-, whence also κάμπη, 'a caterpillar,' from the ease with which it bends its body, especially in the case of the "Loopers" (*Geometrina*).

κεφαλῆ-ς: from κεφ + suffix -αλη-, the same word which, with another suffix, appears in Latin *caput*, Gothic *Haubith*, German *Haupt*, Dutch *hoofd*, Anglo-Saxon *heofd*, Old English *heved*, and Modern English *head*.

δέ-σε: in Old Greek δέσον, though Homer has φεῦξε for φεῦξον (for φεύγ-σε -σον, root φυγ-).

βελουδάκι: diminutive of βελοῦδο-, explained above.

ἐλεύθερον: ἐλεύθ-ερο- from stem ἐλευθ-, lengthened imperfect of ἐλυθ-, which we have in ἤλυθον, ἦλθον, 'I came;' so that ἐλεύθερο- means 'free to go,' -ερο- being adjectival suffix.

ἀφίνω: the modern form of ἀφίημι = ἀπὸ + ἵημι, 'I send forth.' The elements are ἀφ' for ἀπὸ + ἴ = 'send' + ν = sign of imperfect + ω = 'I.' Tenses: ἀφίνω, ἄφινα or -ον, ἀφῆκα or ἄφησα; infinitive ἀφίνειν (ἀφιέναι, classical); aorist ἀφήσει (ἀφῆναι).

θαλαμηπόλος: compound with changed vowel, from θάλαμο- = 'chamber,' and -πόλος, bye-form of -κόλος, 'care-taker,' kin to Latin *col-* in *agri-cola*, &c. Hence θαλαμηπόλος = 'chamberlain;' generally feminine = 'ladies' maid.'

περατοῖ (vernacular περατόνει): from περατὸ-, verbal adjective of περα- = 'accomplish,' 'go through,' kin to *fare* + personal ending -ει- = 'he,' 'she,' 'it.' Hence περατόει, περατοῖ, 'finishes,' 'completes.'

τέλος: accusative case used as adverb = '[at the] end,' 'at last.'

κατα-πίπτει, 'falls down:' πίπτει, imperfect stem by doubling from root πετ-, kin to *feath-* in *feather;* cf. πτερὸν above. Tenses: πίπτω, ἔπιπτον, ἔπεσα -ον, νὰ πέσω, κ.τ.λ.

κάθιδρος = κατ' + ἰδρο-ς: adjectival form (only found in compounds) of ἰδρῶτ-, nominative ἰδρὼς for σϝιδρώ(τ)s, of which the root-syllable σϝιδ- is our *sweat*.

ἀσθμαίνουσα (for ἀσθμάντ-οντ-σα): participle of verb formed from ἀσθ-ματ- for ἀστ-ματ-, from verbal adjective ἀστὸ-, from root α- for ϝα-, whence ἄ-ω, ἄ-η-μι for ϝά-ω, ϝά-η-μι, 'I breathe,'

Sanscrit *rá-mi*, 'I breathe,' Zend *vâ*, 'to blow,' Latin *re-nt-us*, 'a blowing,' the English *wind*, German *wehe*, 'blow,' *Wind*, 'wind.' The Greek ἄσθμα is adopted by us as the name of a well-known infirmity, asthma. Hence ἀσθμαίνουσα, 'panting.'

ἀνακλίντρου: substantive by suffix -τρο- of ἀνακλιν-, 'lean back,' κλιν- and *lean* being cognate; see above. Hence ἀνάκλιντρον (observe accent) = 'a place to lean back in,' 'an easy chair,' 'sofa.'

φυσῶσα: shortened from φυσά-ουσα (φυσά-οντ-σα), from φύ-σα, 'a blowing,' 'a bladder.' φυ- stands for σπυ-, the σ having first aspirated the π-, and then been lost; cf. Sanscrit *phu-t*, 'blowing,' Latin *spu-ma*, 'the froth blown off,' English *spue*, *spew*, also Latin *spi-r-are* for *spoi-s-are*.

ἀτμο-μηχανή, 'a steam-engine:' ἀ-τ-μὸ-ς, 'vapour,' 'breath,' from root α-, explained above + extension -τ- + verbal substantival suffix -μὸ-. Cf. Sanscrit *â-t-man*, 'breath,' 'soul,' 'self,' like Hebrew *nephesh*, Arabic *nafs*, which have the same meaning. μηχ-ανὴ, of which -ανὴ = substantival suffix -ανὰ- in nominative case, from root μηχ-, kin to Gothic and German *mag*, English *may*. Hence our *machine*, through Latinized form *machina*.

ἀεριζομένη (ἀερ-ιζ-ομέν-η): from ἀερ-, nominative ἀὴρ = ἀ-ερς, from root α-, 'breathe' + ερ-, our *er* in lead-*er*, read-*er*, &c., so that ἀὴρ is literally 'the breather;' hence 'wind' or 'air,' distinguished from αἰθ-ήρ, 'the blazer,' i. e. the starlit sky, as the lower part of the atmosphere, the region of winds, from the upper or region of lights. Hence ἀεριζομένη = 'fanning' or 'airing herself.'

ἐνῷ = ἐν ᾧ, 'in that' = 'while.'

κατ-ορθοῦσα: from ὀρθὸ-, 'straight,' comes ὀρθό-ω, 'I make straight,' κατορθόω (-όνω), 'I make straight down,' 'I send right home,' 'I succeed.'

μόλ-ις, 'scarcely,' 'hardly:' kin to μάλα and μάλισ-τα, 'very,' 'verily.'

νὰ ἀρθρώσῃ, 'to articulate:' from ἄρθρο-, ἄρ-θρο-, 'a link,' 'limb,' 'article.' Hence, also in grammar, τὸ ἄρθρον, 'the article;' likewise, ἄρθρον ἐφημερίδος, 'a newspaper article.' Etymology above.

λέξεις [λέγ-σ-ιν-ς], 'sayings,' 'words.'

βεβαι-ό-νω, 'make sure:' from βέβαιο-, 'sure,' 'what you can go by,' root βα- in βα-ί-νω, ἔ-βη-κα, ἔ-βη-ν, κ.τ.λ. Hence σὲ βεβαιόνω, 'I assure you.'

μεγάλο: the regular neuter, also stem of the word for great, Gothic *mikil-s*, English *mickle*. The classical forms are: μέγας [μέγαλ-ς], μεγάλ-η, μέγα[λ]· μέγα! μεγάλη! μέγα! μέγαν [μέγαλν], μεγάλ-ην, μέγα· μεγάλ-ου, μεγάλ-ης, μεγά-λου· μεγάλ-ῳ -ῃ -ῳ· μεγάλ-οι -αι -α· -ους -ας -α· -ων -ων -ων, -οις -αις -οις: whereas the vernacular are regular throughout: μεγάλος, μεγάλη, μεγάλο(ν)· μεγάλε! μεγάλη! μεγάλο! μεγάλο(ν), μεγάλη, μεγάλο(ν), κ.τ.λ.

χατῆρι(ν): for χα-τή-ρι-ον, substantive from χατε-, 'yawn,' 'long,' from verbal adjective χα-τό-, from root χα-, kin to our *ga*-pe and *yaw*-n, German *ga-ffen*, *gäh-nen*. Steps as follows: χα-, 'yawn,' χα-τὸ-, 'having yawned,' 'yawning,' χατέ-ω, 'I am yawning,' 'open-mouthed with eagerness,' χατ-ή-ρι-ον, 'eager open-mouthedness,' 'desire.'

ὑποφέρω: for συπο-φέρω, the Latin *suf-fero*, 'suffer.'

πῶ: arising by rapid speech from πί-ω, root πι-, Latin *bi* in *bibo*; reduplicated form of *po*, as in *potare*. πίνω, ἔπινα (-ον), ἔπια, or ἤπια, κ.τ.λ.

ἔννοια σου: properly ὄννοιά σου, literally 'your care!' i. e. what foolish anxiety! never fear! from ἐν + νοία, i. e. γνοία, 'knowing;' see above. N.B.—νοία is found in composition only; the simple word is νοῦς for γνό-ος.

Φρόσω: shortened for Εὐφροσύνη, a common Greek name, the goddess or muse of gaiety, from εὐ, 'well,' and φρόν-, 'thought,' 'mind' (as substantive φρεν-) + substantival suffix σύν-α (nominative -η). Hence εὐφροσύνη = 'glad-hearted-ness.' Forms like Φρόσω are declined: ἡ Φρόσω, τὴν Φρόσω(ν), τῆς Φρόσους or Φρόσως; dative not found.

πονηρῶς: adverb of πον-ηρό-, 'cunning,' 'wicked,' 'sharp;' originally 'laborious,' from πόνο-, 'labour,' root πεν-, whence πένομαι (classical), 'I labour,' πέν-η-(τ)s, 'a poor man,' πεν-ι-χρός, 'poor,' πενία, 'poverty,' πεῖνα for πέν-ja, 'hunger.' An initial σ has been lost, which we find in σπάνι-s, 'need,' also in our English words *spin, span*. Cf. use of German participle ge-*spannt*.

ξεύρει (for ἠξεύρει): from aorist ἐξεῦρον or ἤξευρον, 'I found out,' whence the popular instinct argued back to a supposed ἐξεύρω or ἠξεύρω, 'I know.' The real present imperfect of ἐξεῦρον is ἐξευρ-ίσκω, the force of -ισκ- being frequentative, as *-esc-* in Latin.

καθὼς = κατὰ ὡς, 'like as.'

θὰ μᾶς ἔχῃ, 'he will have for us:' accusative for dative, as in English 'he will give us.'

σάνδβιτζ: indeclinable, the English word *sandwich*. τζ is the nearest approximation to *ch*, and in some dialects is actually so pronounced. *Sandwiches* are so called from a Lord Sandwich, who originally introduced them at receptions. This fact should make us regard the word with something of awe and veneration, even in its Greek disguise.

κρασάκι: diminutive of κρασί(ον), 'wine,' from root κερα- (κερ-νά-ω, κερά-ν-νυμι), 'to mix.'

φροῦτα: the Italian *frutta*, Low Latin *fructa*, Latin *fructus*. The proper Greek for this is ὀπωρικά, literally "autumnals," from ὀπώρα, 'the after-season,' 'the autumn,' or, perhaps, 'the ripening season,' i. e. either from ὀπ-, 'after,' as in κατόπιν, or ἐπ- as in ἔψω [ἔπσω], 'roast,' 'ripen;' ἐπ- a bye-form of πεπ-; see below.

ποῦ τὸ ξεύρεις, 'Where do you know it?' i. e. How or whence do you know it?

ἠπιώτερον, more mildly, from ἤπιο-, mild.

λαίμαργος: for λαίμαλγος, from λαιμὸ-, 'throat,' and ἄλγος, 'pain.' Hence λαίμαργος = 'having an itching throat,' 'greedy.'

φύσει, 'by nature :' dative of φύ-σι-, 'be-ing,' 'growing,' 'nature.'

πολυφάγος : πολὺ = 'much,' -φάγος, 'eating.' φαγ- seems to be cognate to Sanscrit *bhag*, 'to distribute,' 'to receive one's share,' 'to share,' 'enjoy,' whence *bhaksh*, Sanscrit and Old Persian, 'enjoy,' 'consume.' Hence, too, apparently the Arabic and Turkish *bakshish*, borrowed, it would seem, from the Persian.

ἤρχιζε (ἐ-άρχιζε), 'began :' imperfect past of ἀρχιζ- from ἀρχά- (ἀρχή), 'beginning.'

συγχωρῇ (συγχωρέῃ): from σὺν, 'with,' and χώρα-, 'place' = 'find room for,' 'allow,' 'forgive.'

δεῖπνον, 'supper :' δεῖπνον = δέπ-ινον, from root δε-π- δα-π-. Cf. Sanscrit *dá-p-áj-ámi*, causative of *dá*, 'to distribute,' Latin *dap-s*, 'a meal ;' hence, too, Anglo-Saxon -*tiber*, -*tifer*, 'an offering,' 'victim,' and German *Un-ge-ziefer*, 'vermin,' literally 'what cannot be offered.'

πρωὶ : from προ-, 'the fore-part of the day,' 'the morning.'

ἐ-ψώ-ν-ιζ-ε : ψωνιζ- for ὀψωνιζ-, from ὄψο- (for πόψω, to avoid double π, from πεπ- for κϜεκϜ-, kin to Latin *coqu-o, quoquo*) = 'cookery,' 'food' + ὠνε- (ὠνέομαι), 'buy,' from ὦνο-ς, 'price ;' for Ϝόσνο-ς, Sanscrit *vasnas*, 'price,' Latin *vénum* for *ves-num*. Hence ὀψωνίζω, 'ψωνίζω, 'to buy eatables,' 'to get in provisions.'

κἄπως : for κἂν πως, i. e. καὶ ἄν πως, 'even if somehow,' i. e. more or less, if not much ; κἄπως ὑποφέρεται, 'there is some enduring it,' literally, 'it is in a manner endured.'

μὰ : this particle in Ancient Greek was generally used in negations, as οὔ, μὰ Δία ! 'No, by Jove !' its place being supplied in affirmations by νὴ (perhaps a bye-form of ναὶ, 'yes'), as νὴ τὸν Ἀπόλλωνα, 'Yea ! by Apollo.' In Modern Greek νὴ is obsolete, and μὰ is used in either case. It is probably a form of μὲ ('with'), from which με-τὰ is lengthened, just as κα-τὰ is from the particle κα, κε, or κεν.

κρότος, 'a noise,' especially of striking or rattling ; probably kin to κροίω for κρούσ-ω, Old High German *hruor-jan* for *hruos-jan*, Modern High German *rühren*, properly *rüren*.

σταθείσης for σταθέντ-σης: στα-θ-έντ- = root στα + θ, sign of passive aorist + -εντ- participial suffix. The whole declines: σταθείς (σταθέντς) σταθεῖσα σταθέν· σταθέντα -εῖσαν -έν· -έντος -είσης -έντος· -έντι -είσῃ -έντι· -έντες -εῖσαι -έντα· -έντων -εισῶν -έντων· -εῖσιν -είσαις -εῖσιν.

διέκοψεν = δι-έ-κοπ-σεν = διά, 'through' + ἐ, sign of past + κοπ, 'cut' + σ, sign of 1st aorist + ε(ν) for ετ, sign of 3rd person singular. Hence διέκοψεν or ἐδιάκοψεν, '(he) cut through,' 'interrupted.'

αἴφνης: for ἀπίνης, also with preposition ἐξ, ἐξαπίνης, ἐξαίφνης (vernacular ἔξαφνα), 'suddenly;' from same root comes αἰφνίδιος, 'sudden.' But probably in its turn ἀπίνης is for ἄπνη-ς; cf. καπινός for καπνός, 'smoke,' as also ἄφνω for ἄπνω, ἄπνεω, and the original meaning will have been *breathless, breathlessly*, from ἀ + πνέ-.

φρά-σι-ν, 'a saying,' 'sentence,' from root φραδ-, stands for φράδ-σι-ν. Hence φράζομαι for φράδιομαι, 'I say,' but in Homer always 'I show.' Probably kin to φαρδ-ύ-ς (for φραδύ-ς), our *broad*, German *breit*, the original meaning being 'to spread abroad,' German *ausbreiten*. φαρδύς is not found in Ancient Greek, but is certainly a genuine Greek word, as shown by the fact of the noun τὸ φάρδος, 'breadth,' as well as by the termination of the adjective -ύ-.

νά! an interjection, 'there!' probably the same with the second syllable of ἵ-να, which in Ancient Greek (with indicative) means *where*.

ἄ-νιπ-το-ς, 'un-wash-ed:' from root νιβ- for νιγ-, Sanscrit *nig'*, 'to wash,' whence νίζω for νίβιω or νίγιω, in the vernacular νίβγω, 'I wash.' This is another case of labialism, or the procession of a consonant from the throat to the teeth, which we meet with in βα- for γα-, English *come*, ἵππος for ἵκϝος, κ.τ.λ.

σπογγισθείς: for σπογγιδ-θείς, ending as in στα-θείς. σπογγιδ-

from σπόγγο-, *sponge*, Latin *fungu-s* for *sfung-o-s*, German *Schwamm*, English *swam*-p (cf. λογιδ- from λόγο-, above, &c.). σπογγίζομαι = 'I sponge myself' or 'am sponged,' σπογγίζω, 'I sponge.' Probably σφόγγο-ς was an older form.

ἤρξατο: elegantly for ἤρχισε, the old aorist middle of ἄρχομαι, 'I begin;' see above.

ἀποδυόμενος: also ἀπο-δυ-ν-όμενος, 'undressing,' from ἀπὸ, 'from' + δυ-, 'dress.' Hence ἀποδύ-ομαι = 'I doff,' 'undress.'

Exercise XI.

Ὁ Παρδαλὸς πειθόμενος ὑπὸ τῆς συζυγικῆς μερίμνης τῆς Κυρίας Φρόσους λαμβάνει πάλιν τὸ φῶς. Ἡ μέριμνα τῆς συζύγου του συγκινεῖ τὸν Παρδαλόν, καὶ οὗτος συγκινεῖται δι' αὐτῆς. Ἡ Εὐφροσύνη τοποθετεῖται πρὸ τοῦ κατόπτρου, καὶ εὑρίσκεται μεταξὺ τεσσάρων κηρίων. Καταγίνεται μετὰ πολλοῦ κόπου νὰ δέσῃ τὴν ταινίαν της ἐπὶ τοῦ ὑπερακμάζοντος στήθους της. Τὸ στῆθός της ὑπερακμάζει διότι ἔχει δεκαπέντε ἔτη ἡλικίας περισσότερα τοῦ συζύγου της. Ἡ ταινία της εἶνε ἐκ μέλανος βελούδου, ἀφ' οὗ κρέμαται λοβίσκος ὁ ὁποῖος εἶνε ἐκ χρυσοῦ. Δὲν βλέπω ποῦ νὰ σταθῶ, λέγει ὁ Παρδαλός. Ποῦ εἶνε τόπος κενός; Ἔλα καὶ σοῦ κάμνω τόπον· μὴ μουρμουρίζῃς. Ταῦτα λέγουσα ἡ κυρία μειλιχίως ἐλέγχει τὸν ἄνδρα της. Ἡ χονδροὶ αὐτῆς βραχίονες εἶνε περιπόρφυροι ἐκ τοῦ ματαίου κόπου ὃν καταβάλλει. Τέλος τὸ βελουδάκι ἐδέθη, καὶ ὁ τόπος ἀφίνεται κάπως ἐλεύθερος. Ἡ θαλαμηπόλος περατοῖ τὴν ἐνδυμασίαν τῆς κυρίας της, ἐνῷ ὁ σύζυγός της καταπίπτει κάθιδρος καὶ ἀσθμαίνων ἐπὶ ἀνακλίντρου. Ἡ ἀτμομηχανὴ φυσᾷ καὶ κάμνει κρότον πρὸ τῆς θύρας. Ὁ κύριος ἀερίζεται καὶ μόλις κατορθόνει νὰ ἀρθρώσῃ τὰς λέξεις του. Προσπαθεῖ νὰ γράψῃ ἄρθρον διὰ τὴν ἐφημερίδα ἀλλὰ ὁ κόπος του εἶνε μάταιος.

Μεγάλο τοῦ Δημητράκη μας ἦτο τὸ χατῆρι νὰ πάγῃ νὰ πίῃ τὸ τεῖον τοῦ ὑπαλλήλου του. Ὁ Ὀρέστης ἦτο εἰς τὴν ἀγορὰν· τὸν εἶδα καὶ ἐψώνιζε κρασάκι καὶ ὀπωρικά. Συγκινεῖται ἡ Φρόσω διὰ τῶν λέξεων τούτων καὶ γίνεται κάπως ἠπιωτέρα. Πολλοὶ ἄνθρωποι εἶνε λαίμαργοι φύσει καὶ πολυφάγοι, διὰ δεῖπνον μὰ τὴν ἀλήθειαν ὑποφέρουν πολύ. Κρότος ἀτμομηχανῆς καὶ πολλῶν ἀμαξῶν σταθεισῶν πρὸ τῆς θύρας διέκοψεν αἴφνης τὴν φράσιν τῆς μουρμουριζούσης γυναικός. Νά! ἐτελείωσε τὸ πρᾶγμα, ἀνεφώνησεν ὁ κύριος· ἄνιπτος καὶ ἡμιξύριστος πρέπει νὰ σπογγισθῶ ἐν τάχει.

A golden locket hangs from a velvet ribbon on the over-ripe bosom of the lady. Her arms, bent back behind her neck, endeavour in vain to tie the ribbon. The sound of a carriage pulling up before the door affects her with conjugal solicitude. "Are you getting on?" she exclaims to her husband.

"How should I be getting on?" he answers anything but mildly. "I am yet unwashed."

"Come, don't murmur," says his spouse, gently reproving him, and fanning herself with her handkerchief like a steam-engine. "Never mind, you will get wine and fruit where we are going, so there is some enduring it. You must forgive your clerk his company for the sake of his supper, like other naturally gluttonous and greedy men."

Just at that moment Demetrius finishes his shaving, and is sponging himself in haste, when the bell rings.

ΔΩΔΕΚΑΤΟΝ ΜΑΘΗΜΑ.—Twelfth Lesson.

Ἔχομεν ἀκόμη ὥραν, παρετήρησεν ἡ Κυρία, βλέπουσα
We have still time, observed the lady, looking

τὸ ὡρολόγιον. Εἶνε ὀκτὼ παρὰ τέταρτον. —
at the clock. It is eight short of a quarter (a quarter to eight).—

Ὁ Παρδαλὸς φορεῖ ἐν τάχει τὸν καθαρόν του χιτῶνα, καὶ
Pardalós puts on in haste his clean shirt, and

δένει ἤδη τὸν λαιμοδέτην του, ὅτε ἔξωθεν τῆς
is tying already his necktie, when from outside of the

θύρας ἀκούεται ἡ φωνὴ τῆς ὑπηρετρίας.—Ἀφέντη!—
door is heard the voice of the maid. — Sir!—

Καλὸ, καλό, ἆς σταθῇ λιγάκι, φωνάζει ἀφ᾽ ἑνὸς
Well, well, let him wait a bit, cries from one (side)

ὁ Δημητράκης, ἐνῷ ἡ σύζυγός του φωνάζει ἀφ᾽ ἑτέρου,
Demetrius, while his wife cries from (the) other,

Ἔφερε τὰ γάντια μου;—Δὲν ξεύρω, κυρία, θέλει
Has he brought my gloves? — I don't know, ma'am, he wants

νὰ εἴπῃ κἄτι τοῦ ἀφεντός.—Ὁ ἁμαξᾶς θέλει
to say something to master.—The cabman wants

νὰ μοῦ εἴπῃ κἄτι; Αὐτὸ θὰ εἶνε πάλιν ἀπὸ
to say something to me? That will be again of the

τἄγραφα. — Ὄχι, ἀφέντη, εἶνε ὁ Κύριος
unwritten (i. e. some new surprise)! — No, sir, it is Mr.

Ὀρέστης.—Ὁ Κύριος Ὀρέστης! ἀναφωνεῖ ἡ Φρόσω.
Orestes. — Mr. Orestes! exclaims Phrosy.

Περίεργον!—Λέγεις ν᾽ ἀργήσαμεν; ἐρωτᾷ ὁ Παρδαλός.
Curious! — Should you say we were late? asks Pardalós.

Τὸ ὡρόλογι μας θὰ πηγαίνει τρομερὰ 'πίσω! Ἂς ὁρίσῃ
Our clock must be going frightfully slow! Let him

'ς τὴ σάλα, καὶ τώρα ἔφθασα! προσθέτει,
take a seat in the parlour, and I'll be with him at once! he adds,

εἰς τὴν ὑπηρέτριαν ἀποτεινόμενος. Καὶ ταῦτα λέγων, φορεῖ
addressing himself to the servant. And thus saying, he puts

ἐν βίᾳ τὸν ἐπενδύτην του, καὶ εἰσέρχεται εἰς τὴν
on in haste his coat, and enters into the

αἴθουσαν, ὅπου ἀναμένει αὐτὸν δειλός, περίλυπος, καὶ
drawing-room, where awaits him timid, sad, and

καταβεβλημένον ἔχων τὸ ἦθος ὁ Κύριος Σουσαμάκης. Μᾶς
with downcast mien Mr. Susamákis. You

συγχωρεῖς ποῦ ἠργήσαμεν, φίλτατε Κύριε Σουσαμάκη,
excuse us for being late, dearest Mr. Susamákis,

λέγει ὁ Κύριος Παρδαλὸς, εἰσερχόμενος, καὶ τείνων
says Mr. Pardalós, entering, and stretching out

προστατευτικῶς τὴν χεῖρα πρὸς τὸν ὑπάλληλόν του, ἀλλὰ
patronizingly his hand to his clerk, but

τὸ ἁμάξι δὲν μᾶς ἦλθεν ἀκόμη, καὶ ... — Καλησπέρα
the carriage has not come for us yet, and ... — Good evening

σας, Κύριε Σουσαμάκη ὑπολαμβάνει, διακόπτουσα, ἡ Κυρία
to you, Mr. Susamákis breaks in, interrupting, Mrs.

Εὐφροσύνη εἰσερχομένη καὶ αὐτὴ θριαμβευτικῶς εἰς τὴν
Euphrosyne entering herself too triumphantly into the

αἴθουσαν, καὶ ἱσταμένη πλησίον τοῦ λαμπτῆρος,
drawing-room, and standing near the chandelier,

ὅπως σπινθηρίζωσι κάλλιον οἱ ἀδάμαι τές της. Πῶς
in order that her diamonds might sparkle better. How

εἶσθε; Ἡ Κυρία εἶνε καλά; Εἴμεθα ἕτοιμοι, βλέπετε.—
are you? Is Mrs. —— well? We are ready, you see.—

Εὐχαριστῶ, κυρία μου, ἀπαντᾷ μετὰ μεγάλης στενοχωρίας
Thank you, ma'am, answers with great embarrassment

ὁ πτωχὸς Ὀρέστης, προσποιούμενος ὅτι δὲν ἤκουσε τὸ
poor Orestes, pretending that he didn't hear the

τελευταῖον μέρος τῆς φράσεως. Ἐγὼ εἶμαι καλά, ἀλλὰ
last part of the sentence. I am well, but

ἡ Πασιφάη ...—Πῶς! τί τρέχει; κακοδιάθετος, ἴσως;
Pasiphae ...—Why! what's up? indisposed, perhaps?

—Δὲν εἶνε τίποτε! μὲ τὸν χορὸν περνᾷ, παρατηρεῖ
—It's nothing! with the dance it will pass away, observes

μετὰ πολλῆς στωμυλίας ἡ Κυρία Παρδαλοῦ. Ἔννοια σας!
with much volubility Mrs. Pardalós. Never fear!
κ᾿ ἐγὼ τὴν κάμνω καὶ χορεύει πολύ!
I'll make her dance well!

παρετήρησεν: from παρά, 'by' + τηρε-, 'watch,' 'keep.' Hence παρατηρε-, 'watch by,' 'observe,' παρετήρησεν = 'observed.'

ὡρολόγιον: from ὥρα-, Latin *hora*, 'hour,' and root λεγ-, 'to tell.' Hence ὡρολόγιον = 'time-teller,' 'clock,' 'watch.'

ὀκτὼ παρὰ τέταρτον = 'eight all but a quarter,' i. e. a quarter to eight. Observe idiom, and use of παρά with accusative. As from τεταρ + τον we get τέταρτον, 'a fourth,' 'quarter,' so from τρι + τον we get τρίτον, 'a third,' from πεμπ- (πεντε = πεμπε) we get πέμπτον, 'a fifth,' &c.

φορεῖ (φορέ-ει), 'puts on:' secondary formation from φερ-, 'bear,' 'wear;' also, as intransitive = 'wears.' καθαρὸ-ν, the German *heiter*, Latin *hilari-s* for *hidaris*; cf. Old Latin *dingua*, *dacruma*, for *lingua*, *lacruma*. The original meaning is that of the Greek, 'pure,' 'clean.'

χιτῶν-α (nominative χιτὼν for χιτώνς).

δέ-ν-ει: modern form with inserted ν of δέ-ει, *tie-s*. Cf. δύω, δύνω, both classical.

λαιμο-δέ-τη-ν = 'neck-tier.'

ἔξωθεν = ἔξω, 'out' + θεν, 'from' = 'from without;' cf. ἐκεῖ-θεν, 'there-from,' thence οὐρανό-θεν, 'from heaven.' δῆ-θεν, 'from now,' 'henceforth' (the probable primary sense) = 'forsooth,' 'to be sure, as pretended,' i. e. as no one would have suspected hitherto.

λιγάκι: diminutive of 'λίγο(ν), ὀλίγον, 'little,' i. e. a little bit.

φωνάζει (φωνάγ*ει*) = φωνά + ἄγ*ει*, 'he leads a voice,' 'prolongs a cry;' cf. Latin *vocem, carmen, ducere*, &c. N.B.—ζ stands sometimes for γ*ι*, sometimes for δ*ι*—the aorist shows which. Thus the aorist of γνωρίζω is γνωρίσω, ἐγνώρισα, κ.τ.λ., for γνωρίδ-σω, ἐγνώριδ-σα, whereas the aorist of φωνάζω is φωνάξω, ἐφώναξα. That this αγ- is really the same as in ἄγω, 'I bring,' seems likely when we consider that συνάγω, 'I gather,' is in the vernacular Modern Greek συνάζω, i. e. συνάγξω.

ἀφ' ἑνὸς: for ἀπὸ ἑνὸς (understand μέρους, 'side'); ἀφ' ἑτέρου for ἀπὸ ἑτέρου. ἑτερο- perhaps akin to *other*, in which case the ' is accidental.

ἔφερε: observe the aorist sense, the imperfects in the vernacular being φέρνει, ἔφερνε. In classical Greek ἔφερε would be regarded as imperfect, and the aorist is from another root ἐνεγκ-, ἤνεγκον, κ.τ.λ. In the phrase φέρ' εἰπέ, however, the aorist sense of φερ- appears.

ἀφεντός: as if from stem ἀφέντ-, of which nominative would be ἀφείς, instead of actual nominative ἀφέντ-η-ς. With exception of accent, ἀφεντός is identical in form with genitive of participle ἀφέντος (ἀφείς, ἀφεῖσα, ἀφέν), obsolete in vernacular Modern Greek.

ἁμαξ-ᾶ-ς: a common modern formation; cf. in classical Greek φαγ-ᾶ-ς, 'a glutton.' The elegant form is ἁμαξηλά-τη-ς, from ἅμαξα + ἐλα- ('drive') + της = *er*; cf. ἔλα above.

κἄτι: for καὶ + ἄν + τὶ = 'even if something.'

ἄγραφα, literally 'unwritten things,' 'secrets,' 'surprises.'

ἀφέντη: vocative of ἀφέντης by simply dropping s.

περίεργο-ν: from περί, 'about,' and ἔργο-, 'work.' Hence, as adjective, περίεργο- = 'what there is work about,' 'what is worthy of attention,' 'curious,' 'remarkable;' also in transitive sense, 'busy about anything,' 'curious,' 'inquisitive.'

λέγεις ν' ἀργήσαμεν: observe this use of νὰ with the indicative; it is equivalent, or at least analogous to the classical use of the optative in indirect (oblique) assertions. Its force is to imply that the statement (ἀργήσαμεν) is not that of the speaker, but that of the person addressed or referred to.

ἀργήσαμεν (classical, with augment, ἠργήσαμεν, see below) from ἀργε-, and that from adjective ἀργὸ- for ἀ-Ϝεργ-ὸ-, i. e. not-working, *un-working*, idle. Hence 'slow,' 'late.'

ἐρωτᾷ (for ἐρωτά-ει): apparently kin to ἔρωτ-, 'love,' 'desire,' 'appetite,' formed from verbal stem ἐρα- (ἐρά-ομαι), 'love,' as γελωτ-, 'laughter,' from γελα-, 'laugh,' by addition of substantival suffix -οτ-. From ἔρωτ- is then formed, by addition of -α-, the further verbal stem ἐρωτα-, 'to be in search for,' 'ask,' 'seek.'

θὰ πηγαίνει: observe use of θὰ with indicative. θὰ πηγαίνῃ would mean, 'will be going at some future time;' θὰ πηγαίνει means 'must now be going.' 'Will' is used in this sense in English, especially by Scotchmen and Northerners.

τρομερὰ: neuter plural of τρομερὸ-, used as adverb. τρομερὸ- = root τρομ- τρεμ- (τρέμ-ω, 'I tremble'), kin to Latin trem- in trem-o + adjectival suffix -ερό-.

πίσω: short for ὀπίσ-ω, 'behind,' old instrumental for ὀπίσωτ, from same root ὀπιδ- which we had in ὄπισθεν for ὀπιδ-θεν, ὀπίσω standing for ὀπίσϳω.

ἂς ὁρίσῃ: for ἄφες = ἀπὸ + ἒ + ς, old imperative of ἀφί-η-μι, Modern ἀφί-ν-ω, 'I send forth,' 'I permit,' 'allow,' "let,' and ὁρίσῃ for ὁρίδ-σ-ῃ, from ὅρο-, 'boundary,' 'limit,' 'term,' 'order,' 'condition' + verbal suffix -ιδ; cf. λογιζ-, κ.τ.λ. Hence ὁρίζω, 'I define,' 'order,' 'command.' ἂς ὁρίσῃ εἰς τὴ σάλα, literally 'let him command into the drawing-room' or 'parlour;' ὁρίσατε, short ὁρίστε, plaît-il? wie beliebt? 'What is your pleasure?' 'command,' i. e. What did you say; also 'Come!' 'This way, please,' &c.

σάλα(ν): the Italian word, French salle.

τώρα ἔφθασα, literally 'I am now arrived,' i. e. I will be with him directly: a graphic use of the aorist for the future. ἔ-φθα-σα (imperfect φθά-ν-ω), root φθα-. It would seem that φθα- is a corruption of ψα- (πσα-), and that a metathesis for σπα-, the same with spee- in speed, German spu-ten, Albanian špeit, 'quickly.' In classical Greek, φθάνω means 'overtake,' 'arrive first,' rather than simply 'arrive;' this sense is preserved in Modern Greek in the compound προφθάνω. φθάνει, in Modern

Greek, means also, 'it is enough,' 'it reaches;' προσθέτει (προσ-θέ-τ-ει), the modern form of προς-τί-θη-σι for προςτίθητι, 'he puts to,' 'he adds.'

ἀπο-τειν-όμενο-ς: for ἀπο-τεν-όμενο-ς, imperfect participle passive masculine nominative, from root τεν- ταν-, 'stretch,' 'direct' + preposition ἀπὸ- = 'away.' Hence ἀποτείνομαι = 'I direct myself,' 'address myself.'

βίᾳ (βία-ι): dative of βία-, 'force,' 'haste,' kin to vi- in Latin vis, vivo, vita, &c.; cf. the expression vis vivida vitæ. Hence also the masculine form βί-ο-ς, 'life.'

ἐπενδύτην: for ἐπι-ἐν-δύ-τη-ν, literally 'the over-dresser,' 'the coat.'

αἴθουσαν: the elegant classical for σάλαν = αἰθ-οντ-σα-ν, from root αἰθ-, 'burn;' cf. αἰθήρ above. Literally 'the burning-room,' 'the place where the fire burnt,' the central hall of the old Greek dwellings. αἰθ- kin to Latin aed- in aed-é-s, 'house,' 'dwelling-places,' plural; aestus for aed-tus, 'burning,' 'heat,' aestas [aestats], 'the burning season,' 'summer,' Anglo-Saxon ád for aid, 'a log,' Middle High German eiten, Modern High German heizen, so mispronounced for eizen, from supposed kinship to heiss, 'hot,' which, however, as we have seen, has quite a different etymology, being akin to Greek καίω, κ.τ.λ.

ἀνα-μένει = 'a-waits,' 'waits for;' μεν- kin to man- in Latin maneo, &c.

δειλὸς: for δε-ιλό-ς, from root δε-, 'fear,' whence also δέ-ος [δεες-], 'fright,' 'fear' (substantive), and δεινός, δε-ινό-ς, 'terrible,' 'fearful.' Observe active and passive meanings of the two suffixes -λὸ- and -νὸ- respectively.

περίλυπος, 'full of grief,' 'with grief all about one:' from περὶ and λύπα-, perhaps for ῥύπα-, kin to rup- in Latin ruptura, ru(m)po, the root idea being that of breaking.

καταβεβλημένον (κατα-βε-βλη-μένον): from κατα-βλα- καταβαλ-, 'cast down.' Hence 'downcast,' 'sorrowful.'

ἦθος: whence our ethics, 'manner,' 'mien,' of which a bye-form ἔθος has the sense of 'habit.' ἐθ- stands for σϝεθ-, and is apparently from the two elements, σϝε-, Latin *se* (cf. ἐ for σϝὲ in ἑ-αυτὸν, 'himself') + θε- = 'do,' 'put,' 'set.' Hence ἐθ[ε] = 'putting of one's self,' 'setting one's self.' Hence 'habituating;' cf. Latin *suus* and *suesco;* kin is German *Sitte*.

καταβεβλημένον ἔχων τὸ ἦθος = literally 'having the mien downcast;' in idiomatic English, '*with* downcast mien.' This is a very common use of ἔχων, and should be noted.

ποῦ, literally 'where,' here, 'that.'

ποῦ ἠργήσαμεν, literally 'that we are late,' or 'seeing we are late,' i. e. for being late. The Greeks lack anything analogous to our convenient verbal substantive in *-ing*. The nearest approach is the old infinitive in -ειν -αι -εσθαι -ῆναι (according to tense and mood), which, however, is not nearly so pliable, and is, moreover, confined to bookish style.

χεῖρα[ν]: for χέρια, nominative χείρ for χείρ-s, 'hand.' Probably kin to *gr-* in *grasp*, *grip*, *grab*, where we see one root with various suffixes.

θριαμβευτικῶς (-κῶτ): adverb of adjective θριαμβευ-τ-ικὸ-, formed by suffix -ικὸ- from verbal adjective θριαμβευ-τό- of θριαμβευ-, verb of noun θρίαμβο-, the Latin *triumpo- triumphu-*, a word of dark derivation, but most likely aspirated from τρίαμβος, τρι-ίαμβος, 'a triple throw (in wrestling).' ἴαμβος is explained by *Curtius* as substantive from nasalized root ἰαμβ- for ἰαβ-, which we have in ἰάπτω, 'to cast,' 'throw,' ἰαβ- being softened for ἰαπ-, and that labialized for ἰακ- (cf. ἵππος, κ.τ.λ.), kin to Latin *jac-* in *jacio*, *jaculum*, &c. ἴαμβος: the Iambic verse meant originally the coarse jest *flung* at the passer-by.

ἰσταμένη: present participle middle from root στα-, 'stand.' Hence ἴσταμαι, 'I stand,' ἵστασαι, 'thou standest;' other persons, ἵσταται, ἱστάμεθα, ἵστασθε, ἵστανται.

πλησίον: from root πελ- πλε- πλα-, lengthened also to πλαγ- πληγ- in πληγή, 'a blow,' πλήσσω for πλήγϳω, 'I strike,' ἐπλάγην,

'I was struck.' Hence πλησίον, literally 'abutting on,' 'striking against;' cf. German *anstossend*. Hence παραπλήσιος, 'resembling,' 'closely touching.'

λαμπ-τῆρ-ος, literally 'the shiner,' i. e. the lustre, chandelier; kin to Latin *limpidus*.

σπινθηρίζωσι : subjunctive after ὅπως, from σπινθηρ-ιζ-, verb of σπινθήρ- for σκιν-θήρ ; cf. Latin *scin-t-illa*, kin to our *shine*. σπινθήρ = 'sparkle,' 'ray,' σπινθηρίζω, 'I shed rays,' 'I sparkle,' 'glitter.'

ἀδάμ-αντες : noun with semi-participial characteristics, from ἀ + δαμ- = *untamable, untamed*, because the hardest mineral; used of various rocks as granite, *adamant*, but properly of the *diamond*, which, with its various kindred in Modern European languages, is a mere corruption of the Greek word.

στενο-χωρ-ία-ς, literally 'narrowness of room :' στενὸ-, 'narrow,' whence στένω, στενάζω, 'I groan ;' kin to German *stöhnen*.

πτω-χὸ-ς : probably for ψωχός (ψα-ο-χός) (cf. on φθάνω above), from root ψά-, 'to scrape ;' ψωχός, 'a man who has to scrape his platter,' 'a scraper,' 'a poor man.' It should, however, be borne in mind that πτωχός, the actual, is the older form, ψάω standing for πτάω.

προσποιούμενος, προς-ποιε-όμενος : from πρὸς, 'to' + ποιε-, 'make.' Hence προςποιοῦμαι, 'I make to myself,' 'I claim' or 'pretend.' Various etymologies have been suggested for the verbal stem ποιε-, but the simplest and most obvious is that it is from the pronominal root ποιο-, as in ποῖος, ὅποιος, &c., and means to 'make of a certain kind,' the derivative suffix -ε- having often in itself the force of 'make,' 'do.'

τελευταῖον : for τελευτά-ι-ον, from substantival stem τελευτά-, 'end' + adjectival suffix -ιο-. Hence τελευταῖον = 'last,' 'final.' τελευτά-, from verbal adjective τελευτὸ- (-ὰ- feminine), from verbal stem τελεϝ- or τελευ-, also τελε-, τελεσ-, 'to end' or 'finish,' substantive τέλες-, 'an end.'

μέρος (stem μέρες-), 'a part :' from root μερ-, 'to divide,' 'assign,' kin to Latin *mereo, mereor, meritum*. Hence, too, μοῖρα (μόρ?α), 'share,' 'fate,' 'appointed lot,' μόρος, 'doom,' 'destiny.'

τί τρέχει, literally 'what runs?' cf. German *was ist los?* i. e. what's loose? what's up? what's the matter? for which also the Greeks say, τί πρᾶγμα; 'what thing?'

κακοδιάθετος, literally 'ill-disposed,' i. e. indisposed, from root διαθε- (διὰ + θε-) (διατίθημι, διαθέτω); see above.

ἴσως [ἴσωτ], literally 'equally,' i. e. by an even chance; as likely as not, perhaps, from ἰσο- for Fίσfo-, Sanscrit *vishu*; root probably Fι- (vi-), 'to separate,' 'divide,' as in *di-vid-ere, vi-du-a, wi-dow*. Hence τὸ ἴσον, 'the fair share,' ἴσος, 'fair,' 'equal.'

τί-ποτε, 'anything-whatever,' 'anything at all:' ποτε, relative and interrogative of ὅτε, 'when.'

στωμυλίας: from στωμύλο-, literally 'mouthy,' from στώμα(τ-), 'mouth' (properly στόματ-), Sanscrit *çtaman*, perhaps kin to Gothic *stib-na*, German *Stimme*, 'voice.' Hence στωμυλ-ί-α, 'mouthiness,' 'volubility.'

τὴν κάμνω καὶ χορεύει, literally 'I make her and she dances,' i. e. I will make her to dance. Equally correct would be τὴν κάμνω νὰ χορεύσῃ (vernacular χορέψῃ). Observe familiar use of present for future.

Exercise XII.

Παρατηρῶ ὅτι δὲν εἶνε ἀργά, ἀλλὰ ὅτι ἔχομεν ἀκόμη ὥραν. Παρετήρησα ὅτι δὲν ἦτο ἀκόμη ἀργὰ ἀλλὰ ὅτι εἴχομεν ἀκόμη ὥραν. Βλέπω τὸ ὡρολόγι μου καὶ παρατηρῶ ὅτι πηγαίνει τρομερὰ ὀπίσω, ὥστε θὰ ἀργήσωμεν, ἂν μὴ περατώσωμεν ἐν τάχει τὴν ἐνδυμασίαν μας. Φορῶ ἐν βίᾳ τὸν ἐπενδύτην μου, καὶ δένω ἐν τάχει τὸν λαιμοδέτην ἀνακάμπτων τοὺς χονδρούς μου βραχίονας ὄπισθεν τοῦ τραχήλου. Ἠκούσθη αὐτὴν τὴν στιγμὴν ἡ φωνὴ τῆς ὑπηρετρίας λεγούσης, θέλω νὰ εἴπω κάτι τοῦ ἀφεντός. Τί θέλεις νὰ εἴπῃς; ὅτι σᾶς ἔφερα τὰ γάντια, ἢ μᾶλλον καθὼς λέγουν οἱ νεοφώτιστοι τῆς γλώσσης μας καθαρισταί, τὰ χειρόκτιά σας. Εἶνε τρεῖς (ὧραι) καὶ τέταρτον; Ὄχι· εἶνε τέσσαρες παρὰ τέταρτον. Ἂς σταθῶσιν λιγάκι οἱ νυκτερινοὶ ἐπισκέπται· ἔχω ἐργασίαν. Ἂς περάσουν ἄλλην ὥραν. Περίεργον! ἀναφωνεῖ ὁ ἀμαξᾶς. Ὁρίσατε εἰς τὴν αἴθουσαν, κύριοι, σᾶς παρακαλῶ. Λέγετε ν' ἀργήσαμεν; Διατί ἔχετε περίλυπον καὶ καταβεβλημένον τὸ ἦθος; τὰ ἤθη τῶν ἀνθρώπων εἶνε καθὼς τὰ ἔθη των. Μᾶς συγχωρεῖτε ποῦ ἔχομεν δειλὸν καὶ καταβεβλημένον τὸ ἦθος διότι ἠργήσαμεν τρομερά. Ὁ Κύριος εἰσέρχεται θριαμβευτικῶς εἰς τὴν αἴθουσαν καὶ ἀποτείνεται προστατευτικῶς εἰς τὸν ὑπάλληλόν του. Καλησπέρα σας, λέγει, βλέπετε ὅτι εἴμεθα ἕτοιμοι· ἀλλὰ τὸ ἀμάξι δὲν μᾶς ἔφθασεν ἀκόμη. Ἵσταμαι πλησίον τοῦ λαμπῆρος, καὶ ὁ λαμπτὴρ κάμνει να σπινθηρίζωσι κάλλιον οἱ ἀδάμαντες καὶ ὁ χρυσοῦς λοβίσκος μου. Προσποιοῦμαι ὅτι δὲν ἤκουσα τὸ πρῶτον μέρος τῆς φράσεως. Εἶσθε καλά; ὄχι· δυστυχῶς εἶμαι πολὺ κακοδιάθετος· νομίζω ὅμως ὅτι δὲν εἶνε τίποτε καὶ ὅτι μὲ τὸν χορὸν περνᾷ. Τί τρέχει λοιπόν; Δὲν ἠξεύρω, νομίζω ὅτι ἐκρύωσα. Ἔννοια σας· μὲ τὸ δεῖπνον καὶ τὴν συναναστροφὴν περνᾷ.

Why do you sponge yourself in haste? Because we are late. Why does the servant call from below? She wants to tell master something. She has not brought his gloves, but the carriage has come. Very well, let it wait a bit. We have still time. What is the matter? Some secret again? Curious! my watch must be going frightfully fast (ἐμπρός). It is quarter to five. Show the gentlemen into the drawing-room, and I will be with them directly. Who is waiting for me? A timid clerk with downcast mien. Stand near the light, that your diamonds may sparkle better. There is no need for you to pretend that you did not hear the last part of the sentence. Your volubility is great, but you will not persuade me (πείσητε) of that (περὶ τούτου); never fear! I excuse you for being late, but why did you not put on (ἐφορέσατε) your coat? I had no time; for while I was awaiting, with great embarrassment, my nocturnal visitor in the parlour, the bell of the opening door sounded, the maid shouted from one side, and my wife from the other, "Are you getting on, Demetrúkes?" and I had (ἦτο ἀνάγκη) to sponge myself hastily, and begin dressing. It is very curious that my clock goes slow; and that the maid has not brought my gloves. Do you think she can have forgotten them? Perhaps; for I observed that she had a timid, sorrowful, and downcast mien, so that I fancied (ἐφαντάσθην) what was the matter (imperfect).

ΔΕΚΑΤΟΝ ΤΡΙΤΟΝ ΜΑΘΗΜΑ.—THIRTEENTH LESSON.

Οὔ! ἐννοεῖται ὁ χορὸς εἶνε διὰ τὰς
Oh! of course (lit. "it is understood") dancing is for

κυρίας πανάκεια, — προςθέτει ἐν τέλει ὁ Κύριος
ladies a sovereign cure — adds at the end Mr.

Παρδαλὸς, μετ' αὐταρέσκου μειδιάματος, προφέρων βραδέως
Pardalós, with a self-satisfied smile, pronouncing slowly

τὴν τελευταίαν λέξιν, οἱονεὶ ἐναβρυνόμενος δι' αὐτὴν, καὶ
the last word, as if luxuriating in it, and

ἐπαναλαμβάνων εὐθὺς, ἔτι βραδύτερον — πα-νά-κει-α.—
repeating at once, still more slowly — a so-ve-reign cure.—

Ναὶ, ναὶ . . . ἀπαντᾷ δειλῶς ὁ Σουσαμάκης, καὶ προσπαθεῖ
Yes, yes . . . answers timidly Susamákis, and tries

νὰ μειδιάσῃ ἐπίσης. Πλὴν . . . δυστυχῶς . . . καὶ σταματᾷ,
to smile also. But . . . unfortunately . . . and he stops,

ὡς ἂν κατέλειπεν αὐτὸν ἡ δύναμις νὰ τελειώσῃ.
as if there had deserted him the power to finish.

Τίποτε σπουδαιότερον;—Ὤ! ἐπιφωνεῖ ὁ προϊστάμενος αὐτοῦ.
Anything (more) serious?—Oh! exclaims his principal.

Καὶ πῶς;—Δὲν ἠξεύρω, τῇ ἀληθείᾳ. Ἐκρύωσε φαίνεται,
How then?—I do not know, in truth. She has caught cold, it seems,

καὶ ἔχει τώρα ἀπὸ τὸ μεσημέρι ἕνα φοβερὸν πυρετόν.
and has now since mid-day a terrible fever.

Εἶνε εἰς τὸ κρεββάτι πρὸ τριῶν ὡρῶν, ὥστε—καὶ σταματᾷ
She's in bed these three hours, so that—and he stops

πάλιν, ἐλπίζων νὰ τὸν μαντεύσωσι τὸν δυστυχῆ.
again, hoping that they will guess him, poor fellow (i. e. his

Οὐδεὶς, ὅμως, θέλει νὰ τὸν μαντεύσῃ.
meaning). No one, however, will guess his meaning.

Ὁ Κύριος Παρδαλὸς καὶ ἡ Κυρία Παρδαλοῦ ἵστανται
Mr. Pardalós and Mrs. Pardalós stand

ἀπέναντί του ἄφωνοι, ὡς ἐρωτηματικὰ σημεῖα, ἐκεῖνος δὲ
opposite him dumb, like interrogatory signs, while

αἰσθάνεται ὅτι ἡ γλῶσσά του ἐκολλήθη ἐν τῷ λάρυγγί του.
he feels that his tongue has cloven in his throat.

Πλὴν, ὅπως δήποτε, διαλογίζεται, τὸ πρᾶγμα πρέπει
But, somehow or other, he thinks, the matter must

νὰ τελειώσῃ. Γίνεται λοιπὸν τολμηρότερος, καὶ κλείων
end. He grows therefore bolder, and shutting

τοὺς ὀφθαλμοὺς, ὡς οἱ δειλοὶ ἀσθενεῖς οἱ μέλλοντες νὰ
his eyes, like cowardly patients who are about to

καταπίωσι πικρὸν ἰατρικὸν, ἐπαναλαμβάνει· "Ὥστε εἶνε
swallow bitter medicine, he resumes: So that it is

ἀδύνατον ἀπόψε . . . νὰ λάβω τὴν τιμήν. . . . Δὲν
impossible this evening . . . for me to have the honour. . . . You

ἠξεύρετε πῶς λυποῦμαι, Κύριε Διευθυντά, σᾶς βεβαιόνω
don't know how grieved I am, Mr. Manager, I assure you

. . . μ' ἔρχεται νὰ σκάσω!—Ἄ, τίποτε! τίποτε!
. . . I am like to burst!—Ah, nothing! nothing!

ἀπαντᾷ ψυχρῶς ὁ Κύριος Παρδαλός· εὔχομαι νὰ ἦναι
answers   coldly   Mr.   Pardalós; I trust it may be

περαστικά. Ἡ Κυρία Παρδαλοῦ οὐδὲν
(only a) passing (ailment). Mrs.   Pardalós   says

λέγει· φυσᾷ μόνον καὶ ἀερίζεται μὲ τὸ μανδύλιόν της,
nothing; she only pants and fans herself with her handkerchief,

αἰσθάνεται δὲ ἀκατάμαχητον ὄρεξιν νὰ ἐξορύξῃ τοὺς
but she feels an invincible desire to gouge out the

ὀφθαλμοὺς τοῦ Κυρίου Σουσαμάκη, ὅστις, τέλος, ἀφ᾽ οὗ
eyes   of Mr. Susamákis, who, at last, after

μάτην προσεπάθησε νὰ προσθέσῃ μερικὰς λέξεις,
vainly   attempting   to   add   a few   words,

οὐδὲν ἄλλο εὗρε νὰ εἴπῃ, ἢ μόνον—Καλὴν νύκτα
found nothing else to say, save only — Good night

σας... Μᾶς συγχωρεῖτε, Κύριε Διευθυντὰ...
to you... You excuse us,   Mr.   Manager...

δὲν εἶνε ἔτσῃ; Οἱ δύο σύζυγοι ἔνευσαν ἐκ συμφώνου, ὡς
don't you? The couple nodded in concert, like

αὐτόματα, τὴν κεφαλήν, καὶ ὁ Σουσαμάκης ἀνεχώρησε. Μετὰ
automata, their head(s), and Susamákis departed. In

μικρὸν ἠκούσθησαν τὰ ψηλαφῶντα οὕτως εἰπεῖν βήματά του,
a while there were heard his groping steps, so to say,

ἐπὶ τῆς σκοτεινῆς κλίμακος, οὐδεὶς δὲ ἐσυλλογίσθη νὰ
on the dark   staircase, but no one thought to

φωτίσῃ τὸν ἄθλιον, ὅπως μὴ κατακυλήσῃ τὸν κατήφορον.
light the wretch, lest he should roll down the precipice.

ἐν-νοεῖται: for ἐν-νοέ-εται, 'it is understood,' 'of course.' νοε-
for γνοε-; see above. ἔννοια = 'meaning;' συνεννοούμεθα, 'we

understand one another;' συνεννοοῦμαι, 'I make myself understood' (in conversation).

πανάκεια == 'panacea,' 'sovereign cure:' from πάν(τ)- and ἀκε-, 'cure,' 'soothe' (ἀκέομαι, ἀκοῦμαι), kin to ἀκέων, 'still,' 'silent,' 'calm.' ἤπιος for ἤκιος, 'mild,' 'gentle.'

προσθέτει: it may be useful here to add the principal tenses: προσθέτω (προστίθημι), προσέθηκα or προσέθεσα, προσθέσω.

αὐταρέσκου (αὐτάρεσκο-): from αὐτό-, 'self,' ἀρεσκ-, 'please,' frequentative of ἀρ-, 'fit,' 'suit,' explained above.

βραδέως: adverb of βραδύ-, 'late.' Cases: βραδ-ύς -εῖα -ύ· -ύν -εῖα -ύ· -έος -είας -έος· -εῖ -είᾳ -εῖ· -εῖς -εῖαι -έα· -εῖς -είας -έα· -έων -ειῶν -έων· -έσι -είαις -έσι; kin to Sanscrit mṛdus for mardus, and standing for μράδυς. Hence τὸ βράδυ, 'the evening.' Observe accent, and cf. Italian *sera*, French *soir*, from Latin *sera*, *serum*.

οἱονεῖ = οἱον = 'such,' 'so as' + εἰ = 'if.' Hence οἱονεί = 'as if.'

ἐν-αβρυ-ν-όμενος: from ἀβρό- [ἀβρύ-], 'delicate,' explained above.

ἐπαναλαμβάνων (ἐπ-ανα-λα(μ)β-άν-ων (λαβ-), 'taking up again,' 'resuming.'

εὐθύς (for εὐθύτ): adverb of εὐθύ, 'straight' = 'straightway.' Perhaps from εὐ, 'well' + θεF- θυ-, 'run,' i. e. with a good run.

ἐπίσης, i. e. ἐπ' ἴσης γραμμῆς = 'on a straight line,' 'equally,' 'evenly,' 'also;' cf. our 'even so.'

σταματᾷ (στα-ματ-ά-ει): from στα-ματ-, 'a *stand-ing*,' 'a stop.' Hence σταματ-ά-ω, 'I come to a standstill.'

δύναμι-ς: noun of δύνα-μαι, 'I can,' 'I am able' = 'power,' 'ability.'

ἐπιφωνεῖ (ἐπι-φωνέ-ει), 'cries-in-regard-to' what has been said. The exact force of this word is hard to render in English.

τῇ ἀληθείᾳ: dative used here instead of the more colloquial μὰ τὴν ἀλήθειαν.

μεσημέρι(ν): for μεσημέριον = μεσο + ἡμερ + ιο- (substantival suffix) = 'the midday space,' 'noon.'

φοβ-ε-ρὸ- : adjective by suffix -ε-ρὸ- of root φοβ-, 'fear,' verb φοβέ-ω, 'I frighten,' φοβέ-ομαι, φοβοῦμαι, 'I am afraid.' Hence φοβερὸν, 'fearful ;' cf. τρομερά above.

πυρετὸν : apparently verbal adjective from πυρε- (not found), verbal stem of πῦρ-, *fire*, with which it is kin.

κρεββάτι (κρεββάτιον) : diminutive of κράββατον, 'bed ;' seemingly a foreign word, found in Latin as *grabbatum*.

πρὸ τριῶν ὡρῶν, literally 'before three hours,' i. e. since three hours, three hours ago (and still), or these three hours.

ἐλπίζων (ἐλπίδ?ων) : from ἐλπίδ- (nom. ἐλπίς), 'hope,' kin to Latin *volup-* in *voluptas*, and standing for Ϝελπίδ-, root Ϝέλ-π-, lengthened from Ϝελ-, kin to *volo* and *will*.

μαντευ- : verbal stem of μάντι-, 'a prophet,' kin to μα(ν)θάνω, *men(t)s, mind*, &c. Hence μαντεύω, 'I prophesy,' 'I divine,' 'I guess.'

δυστυχῆ (cf. δυστυχῶς above) : from δυς-, 'ill,' and τύχα-, 'fortune ;' stands for δυστυχῆ[ν], and that for δυστυχέαν, and that for δυστυχέσαν. The stem is δυστυχές-. Cases : δυστυχ-ὴς -ες· ῆ -ἐς· -οῦς (-έος)· -εῖ (-έ-ει)· -εῖς (-έες) -ῆ· -ῶν (-έων)· -έσι (-έσ-σι). The forms in brackets are obsolete for the most part.

ἀπ-έναντι = ἀπὸ + ἐν + ἀν-τὶ, 'from-in-front-of :' compare such compounds as French *devant* = *de ab ante*, Spanish *adelante* = *ab de illo ante*, Italian *innanzi* = *in ante*, &c.

ἄφωνοι : from ἀ- = *un-*, and φωνά-. Hence ἄφωνο-, 'voiceless,' 'unvoiced,' 'dumb.'

ἐρωτηματικὰ : from stem ἐρωτα-, explained above, whence comes ἐρώτημα(τ), 'a question,' ἐρωτηματ-ικό-, 'belonging to a question,' 'interrogatory.'

σημεῖα : plural of σημεῖο-, explained under σημειωτέον above.

αἰσθ-άν-εται : by suffix -σθ-, from stem αι, root ἀϜ-, 'hear,' 'learn,' Sanscrit *av- ár-á-mi*, 'attend,' Latin *au-* in *au-di-o*. Hence verbal stem αἰσθ- lengthened to imperfect stem αἰσθαν-. N.B.—αἰσθάνω is not found, only the intransitive αἰσθάνομαι, ᾐσθόμην, and the aorist subjunctive is formed from imperfect stem in Modern Greek αἰσθανθῶ (contrary to rule). Also in common parlance, past, ἠσθάνθην for ᾐσθόμην.

ἐκολλήθη: from κόλλα-, 'glue,' whence κολλά-ομαι, 'I am glued,' ἐκολλήθην, 'I was glued.'

λάρυγγ-, 'throat;' nominative λάρυγξ-, whence our *larynx*.

πλὴν: a form of πλέον, 'more' = 'but,' like Italian *mai*, Spanish *mas*, from Latin *magis*, 'more.'

ὅπως δή-ποτε, literally 'how now ever,' i. e. however, somehow or other.

δια-λογίζ-εται: the force of διὰ is here distributive = 'backwards and forwards.' Hence διάλογος, 'a conversation,' διαλογίζομαι, 'I say to myself,' 'hold an inward dialogue.'

τολμηρὸ-: from τόλμη (+ ρο-), 'daring,' noun of root τολ- τελ- or τλα-, explained above, by suffix -μη- (-μα-).

ἀσθενεῖς: plural nominative of ἀσθενὲς- (cf. δυστυχὲς-), from ἀ, 'without,' and σθένες-, 'strength.' Hence ἀσθενὴς = 'strengthless,' 'weak,' 'ill,' ἀσθενεῖς = 'sick persons,' 'patients.' σθένος probably for στένος, from στε- στα-, hence = 'standing power,' 'steadfastness.'

μέλλοντες (for μέλροντες), 'thinking to do,' 'about to do;' root μελ- or μερ-, kin to Latin *mora*.

κατα-πί-ωσι, 'drink down,' i. e. swallow.

πικρὸν: root πικ-, 'to sting,' 'prick.' Hence πικ-ρὸ- = 'stinging,' 'bitter.'

τιμὴν: accusative singular of τιμὰ-, 'honour,' literally 'price,' 'payment,' substantive of τι- τι-ν-, 'pay,' 'recompense,' 'fine.'

λυποῦμαι (λυπέ-ομαι): verb from λύπα-, 'grief;' see above.

σκάσω: present σκάζω, 'I burst.' In classical Greek, σκάζω means 'I limp,' but this is from a different root, σκαγ-, corrupted to σκαδ-; whereas σκάζω, 'I burst,' seems to come from an original root σκαδ- (*scad*-), and to be kin to English *shatter*, German *scheitern*. No doubt if we knew all the Greek that was spoken in classical times we should find this word; as it is, we have a bye-form of the same word in σκεδα- (σκεδά-νν-υμι, ἐσκέδασε), kin to *scatter*, which itself is a bye-form of *shatter*.

περαστ-ικ-ά: adjective from verbal adjective περαστὸ- of stem περα-, present περνάω, περνῶ, 'pass.' Hence περαστικό- = 'transient.'

ἀκαταμάχητον, ἀ-κατα-μάχητον: from stem μαχε- of root μαχ-, 'to fight,' whence ἐμαχεσάμην, ἐμάχησα, 'I fought,' μαχητὸ-, 'that may be fought,' καταμαχητὸ-, 'that may be fought down,' 'conquered,' ἀκαταμάχητο-, 'un-down-fight-able,' 'invincible,' kin to Latin *mac-illum*, 'butcher's market,' *mac-tare*, 'to slaughter,' Gothic *meki*, 'a knife.'

ὄρεξιν: for ὄρεγ-σι-ν, substantive of ὀρεγ- (ὀρέγ-ομαι), 'desire,' kin to ὀργή, above.

ἐξ-ορύχ-σῃ: ὀρυχ- = 'dig' (present ὀρύσσω). Hence ἐξορύξῃ, 'dig out.'

μερ-ικ-άς: μερ-ικό-, adjective of μέρες-, 'a part.' Hence = 'partial,' 'some,' 'few.' First used by the philosophic school of the Cyrenaics to distinguish particular pleasures (μερικαὶ ἡδοναί) from pleasure in the abstract.

ἔνευσαν: from νευ-, root νυ-, as in Latin *nuo*, our *no-d* = 'nodded.'

συμφώνου: συν + φωνά-, whence σύμφωνο-, 'with common voice,' 'in agreement,' ἐκ συμφώνου, 'by agreement,' 'in concert.'

αὐτό-ματα: αὐτὸ-, 'self' + μα-, 'desire' (Homer, μεμαώς, perfect participle, 'desiring'). Hence αὐτόματο-, 'self-prompted,' 'spontaneous,' αὐτόματα, 'automata,' 'marionettes.'

ψηλαφῶντα: from ψηλὸ, 'fine,' adjective of ψά-, literally 'rubbed' + ἀφὰ-, 'a touch,' root ἁπ- (ἅπ-τομαι). Hence ψηλαφάω, 'to touch lightly,' 'gingerly,' 'to grope.'

οὕτως εἰπεῖν, 'so to say:' εἰπεῖν, the old aorist infinitive, modern εἰπεῖ, used in the old infinitive sense, for which, in the vernacular, νὰ with subjunctive is substituted. Colloquially, οὕτως εἰπεῖν would be ἔτσι νὰ 'πῶμεν or ποῦμε.

βήματα (Doric βά-ματ-α), 'goings,' 'steps,' root βα-.

I

σκοτεινῆς: adjective from σκότες-, 'darkness.' Hence for σκοτεσ-ινῆς, σκοτεϊνῆς, kin to *shadow*, *shade*.

φωτίσῃ: φωτιζ- from φωτ- (nominative φῶς, 'light').

ἄθλιο-: from ἄθλο-, 'a contest,' 'a struggle.' Hence literally 'a struggler,' 'a wretch.' ἄθλο- ἄεθλο- for ἄ-ϝεθ-λο, of which ά is euphonic and -λο- suffix; root ϝεθ-, kin to Latin *vad-s*, 'a pledge,' 'surety,' German *wet-te*, English *wed*.

κατα-κυλήσῃ: from κυλα-, 'roll,' root κυλ- or κυρ-, whence by reduplication κύκλος for κύκυλος, 'a circle,' Latin *cir-c-us*, German and English *ring* for *hring*. On the nasalization, see above.

κατήφορον: for κατάφορον, a lengthened to η by force of accent, from κατα-φερ-, 'bear down.' Hence κατήφορο-ς, 'a bearing down,' 'a descent,' 'a precipice,' 'a headlong rush' or 'fall.' νὰ κατακυλήσῃ τὸν κατήφορον, 'to roll down headlong.'

EXERCISE XIII.

Πανάκεια διὰ τοὺς ἀσθενεῖς εἶνε ὁ χορός. Ὁ κύριος προφέρει βραδέως τὴν τελευταίαν λέξιν οἰονεῖ ἐναβρινόμενος δι' αὐτήν, καὶ τὴν ἐπαναλαμβάνει ἔτι βραδύτερον. Αὐτάρεσκον μειδίαμα ἀπαντᾷ. Τί τρέχει; τίποτε σπουδαιότερον; Ναὶ μάλιστα· φοβερὸς πυρετός. Ἐσταμάτησε φαίνεται τὸ ὡρολόγι μου. Λέγεις νἀκρύωσε; Δὲν ἠξεύρω· κρυολογοῦν λοιπὸν καὶ τὰ ὡρολόγια; Ὅταν κρυολογήσῃ κανεὶς ματαίως προσπαθεῖ νὰ μειδιάσῃ. Διατί σταματᾷς; Διότι μὲ κατέλειψεν ἡ δύναμις νὰ τελειώσω. Ἐλπίζω ὅμως νὰ μὲ μαντεύσητε. Δὲν θέλει κανεὶς νὰ μὲ μαντεύσῃ τὸν ἄθλιον; Πῶς νὰ σὲ μαντεύσωμεν; Δὲν εἴμεθα μάντεις. Τὰ ἐρωτηματικὰ σημεῖα εἶνε ἄφωνα. Ἡ γλῶσσα μου κολλᾶται ἐν τῷ λάρυγγί μου. Τι διαλογίζεσθε; Διαλογίζομαι πῶς θὰ τελειώσῃ τὸ πρᾶγμα. Θὰ τελειώσῃ ὅπως δήποτε. Πρέπει ὅμως νὰ τελειώσῃ. Οἱ δειλοὶ ἀσθενεῖς μέλλοντες νὰ καταπίωσι πικρὸν ἰατρικὸν κλείουν πολλάκις (often) τοὺς ὀφθαλμούς, καὶ δὲν ἠξεύρετε πῶς λυποῦνται, τοὺς ἔρχεται σᾶς βεβαιόνω νὰ σκάσουν. Ἂς σκάσουν λοιπόν, εὔχομαι νὰ εἶνε περαστικά. Διατί φυσᾷς καὶ ἀερίζεσαι μὲ τὸ μανδύλιόν σου; Διότι αἰσθάνομαι ἀκαταμάχητον ὄρεξιν νὰ ἐξορύξω τοὺς ὀφθαλμοὺς

ὅλου τοῦ κόσμου. Διὰ τοῦτο προςπαθῶν μάτην νὰ προσθέσω
μερικὰς λέξεις, νεύω ὡς αὐτόματον τὴν κεφαλὴν καὶ ἀναχωρῶ.
Μετὰ μικρὸν θὰ ἀκούσητε τὰ ψηλαφῶντα οὕτως εἰπεῖν βήματά μου
ἐπὶ τῆς σκοτεινῆς κλίμακος· οὐδεὶς δὲ θὰ συλλογισθῇ νὰ μὲ φωτίσῃ
τὸν δυστυχῆ καὶ χωρὶς ἄλλο θὰ κατακυλήσω τὸν κατήφορον.

The couple nod in concert, and reply with a self-satisfied smile, Dancing is doubtless a sovereign cure. It is a bitter medicine, however, for timid patients, replied my friend. I always catch cold when I dance. I have been in bed these three days with (ἀπὸ) a fearful fever. My watch has stopped. It seems to have caught cold likewise. I hope it may pass off; but I feel that my tongue has cloven to the roof of my mouth. Well, it must end somehow! Perhaps I shall feel better if I close my eyes, like invalids when they are about to take medicine. It is impossible that I should have the honour of seeing you at my house this evening. You can't think how sorry I am. I'm like to burst. No one can guess my chagrin. I feel as if I had an invincible desire to scratch your eyes out. In vain I try to add a few words. I can only say "Good night!" and "Long life to you." If you hear my feet groping on the dark staircase, and do not think to light me, do not murmur if I fall headlong, nor stand (μηδὲ σταθῇς) like a sign of interrogation, as if you did not know what had happened. Why do you repeat the last word with a self-satisfied smile, as if you luxuriated in it? Because in truth it is so. Why do not you attempt to smile likewise?

ΔΕΚΑΤΟΝ ΤΕΤΑΡΤΟΝ ΜΑΘΗΜΑ.
Fourteenth Lesson.

Ὁ Δημητράκης καὶ ἡ Φρόσω ἔμειναν μόνοι. Σιωπῶσι
   Demetrakes and Phrosy were left alone. They are
δὲ ἀμφότεροι, καίτοι διάφορα αἰσθήματα κυμαίνουσι τὰς
  both silent, although various sentiments agitate their

καρδίας των, κατὰ τὴν φράσιν τῶν τραγικῶν ποιητῶν.
hearts, to use the language of the tragic poets.
Τὰ εἶδές τα! λέγει ἐπὶ τέλους, μὴ δυναμένη πλέον νὰ
You see! says at last, unable longer to
κρατηθῇ, μήτε ξεθυμαινουσα ἀρκούντως διὰ μόνου
restrain herself, nor finding vent sufficiently in mere
τοῦ φυσήματος, ἡ Κυρία Παρδαλοῦ. Τὰ εἶδές τα!
panting, Mrs. Pardalós. You see!
Ὁριστε τώρα; "Οταν σοῦ ἔλεγα ἐγὼ νὰ μὴν πᾶμε...
What d'ye say now? When I told you not to go!..
—Αἴ, ματάκια μου! τί θέλεις νὰ κάμῃ ὁ ἄνθρωπος,
—Eh, my life! (lit. eyes) what would you have the man do,
ἀφ' οὗ ἀρρώστησε ἡ γυναῖκά του;—Αὐτὰ εἶνε διὰ
when his wife has fallen ill? — That's for
νὰ τὰ πιστεύητε σεῖς οἱ ἄνδρες! Ἐμένα, ὅμως,
you men to believe! As for me, however,
δὲν μὲ γελᾷ ἡ Κυρὰ Σουσαμάκενα,
Mrs. Susamákis does not cheat me (lit. laugh at me),
κ'ἔννοιά της. Φαντάζομαι ἐγὼ τὶ θὰ ἔτρεξε
and she needn't think it. I've a pretty shrewd fancy what's up
μεταξύ των. Θὰ τσακώθηκαν πάλι, καθὼς συμβαίνει
between them. They will have quarrelled again, as happens
τακτικὰ μιὰν φορὰν τὴν ἑβδομάδα τοὐλάχιστον, καὶ
regularly once a week at least, and
τὸ τσάκωμά τους ξέσπασε 'ς τὸ κεφάλιμας αὐτὴν τὴν φοράν.
their quarrel has burst on our head(s) this time.
— Σημειωτέον ἐνταῦθα χάριν τῆς περιεργείας
—It is to be noted here for the sake of-the curiosity

τῶν ἡμετέρων ἀναγνωστῶν, ὅτι ἡ Κυρία Παρδαλοῦ ἐμάντευεν
of our readers, that Mrs. Pardalós guessed

ὀρθότατα διὰ τῆς γυναικείας ἐκείνης ὀξυνοίας, ἀφ' ἧς
most correctly with that womanly acumen, from which

μάτην ἀγωνίζονται νὰ κρυβῶσι πολλάκις οἱ ἄνδρες.
in vain men strive to hide themselves often.

Ἡ Κυρία Σουσαμάκη ἐδίωξε τῆς οἰκίας τὰ κομισθέντα
Mrs. Susamákis had driven from the house the (brought

ἐκ τοῦ ζαχαροπλαστείου ἀφθόνως γλυκίσματα, δροσιστικά,
from the confectioner's plentifully) sweetmeats, refreshments,

κ.τ.λ. Ὁ Σουσαμάκης ἔμαθε τοῦτο κατὰ τὴν ἄφιξίν του, καὶ
&c. Susamákis learned this on his arrival, and

ὀργισθεὶς καὶ φρυάξας, ἐβρόντησε κατὰ τῆς Πασιφάης του, ὅσον
enraged and restive, thundered at his Pasiphae, as far

ἐπέτρεπον τοῦτο αἱ τριάκοντα τῆς προικός του χιλιάδες. Ἀλλ'
as permitted (this) his thirty thousands of dowry. But

ἡ Κυρία Σουσαμάκη ἔπαθε τὰ νεῦρά της,
Mrs. Susamákis had a nervous attack (lit. suffered in her nerves),

ἐκτύπησε τοὺς τοίχους διὰ τῶν χειρῶν της, τὸ πάτωμα διὰ
struck the walls with her hands, the floor with

τοῦ ποδὸς αὐτῆς, καὶ τὸν Ὀρέστην διὰ τῆς παντούφλας της,
her foot, and Orestes with her slipper,

καὶ, ἐξαπλωθεῖσα εἰς τὴν κλίνην της, προσεποιήθη τὴν
and, extended in her bed, pretended to have

λειπόθυμον, ἐφ' ὅσην ὥραν ἐνόμισεν ἱκανὴν ὅπως
fainted, till such time as she thought sufficient for

πεισθῇ ὁ σύζυγός της, ὅτι πᾶσα ἑσπερινὴ συναναστροφὴ
persuading her husband, that any evening party

ἦν ἀδύνατος. Τῆς καταιγίδος ταύτης εἴδομεν πρὸ μικροῦ
was impossible. Of this tempest we saw lately

τὸ ἀποτέλεσμα παρὰ τῷ Κυρίῳ Παρδαλῷ. Μόλις
the result at the house of Mr. Pardalós. Scarcely

εἶχε τελειώσῃ τὴν φράσιν αὐτῆς ἡ Κυρία Φρόσω, καὶ
had finished her sentence Mrs. Phrosy, when

νέος κρότος ἁμάξης ἔπαυσε πρὸ τῆς θύρας τῆς
ι fresh noise of a carriage stopped before the door of the

οἰκίας Παρδαλοῦ. Ἦτο ἡ ἅμαξα ἦν μετὰ πολλοῦ κόπου
dwelling of Pardalós. It was the carriage which with much trouble

κατώρθωσε νὰ εὕρῃ ὁ ταλαίπωρος Θοδωρῆς. Δὲν
poor John had succeeded in finding. We

περιγράφομεν τὴν ἀπελπιστικὴν καὶ σπαραξικάρδιον
do not describe the desperate and heartrending

τριῳδίαν μεταξὺ ἁμαξηλάτου ζητοῦντος ἁδρὰν ἀποζημίωσιν
triody between (the) cabman seeking abundant indemnity

ἐπὶ τῷ ματαίῳ κόπῳ, Παρδαλοῦ ἀξιοῦντος νὰ πληρώσῃ
for his vain trouble, Pardalós claiming to pay

μίαν μόνην δραχμὴν, καὶ τοῦ δυστυχοῦς Θοδωρῆ
one single drachm, and the unfortunate John

εὑρισκομένου εἰς δυσχερῆ καὶ δυσέκβολον θέσιν
finding himself in a difficult position from which it was hard to escape

μεταξὺ τοῦ ὠργισμένου κυρίου του καὶ τοῦ ἁμαξηλάτου,
between his enraged master and the cabman,

ὃν αὐτὸς ἐμίσθωσεν. Ἡ σκηνὴ διελύθη ἐπὶ τέλους,
whom he himself had hired. The scene broke up at last,

ἀποζημιωθέντος τοῦ ἁμαξηλάτου. Δὲν κατωρθώσαμεν
with the indemnification of the cabman. We have not succeeded

ὅμως νὰ ἐξακριβώσωμεν τί ἐπλήρωσεν ὁ Κύριος Παρδαλός.
however in accurately determining what Mr. Pardalós paid.

Ἡ Κυρία Παρδαλοῦ ὡρκίσθη νὰ μὴν ὑπάγῃ πλέον ποτὲ
Mrs. Pardalós swore that she would never again

εἰς συναναστροφὴν οἵαν δήποτε.
go to any party whatsoever.

ἔ-μειν-αν: μειν-, aorist stem lengthened from μεν-, 'remain.'

μόνο-ι: from the same root. This vowel change in forming adjectives is very common: e. g. root τεν- ταν-, 'stretch,' τόνο-ς, 'accent,' τον-ή, 'tension;' root τεμ- ταμ-, 'cut,' τομ-ή, 'a cutting;' root γεν-, 'beget,' ἀπό-γονος, 'offspring,' κ.τ.λ.

σιωπῶσι = σιωπά-ουσι: from σιωπά-, 'silence' (nominative σιωπή), which also forms verbal stem.

διάφορα: adjective neuter plural of verb διαφερ-, 'differ.'

αἰσθ-ή-ματ-α: from root αἰσθ-, 'feel,' explained above + connecting vowel η, κ.τ.λ.

κυμαίνουσι (κυμάν?-ουσι): from κῦ-ματ-, 'a wave,' from root κυ-, 'to swell,' the same as *ho-* in *hollow, hole*, variously modified in κοῖ-λο- for κόϜι-λο-, 'hollow,' Latin *cae-lum* for *ca-vi-lum*, 'the vault of heaven,' *cav-us*, 'hollow,' &c.

καρδ-ί-α-ς: for καρδ-ί-αν-ς, formed by suffix ία- from root καρδ-, Latin *cord-*, English *heart*.

τραγικῶν: from τράγο-, 'a goat;' the primitive ballads whence the tragic poems sprang being, according to some, sung at the sacrifice of a goat, according to others, by persons dressed in goat-skins. Hence τραγῳδία, 'a goat-song,' 'tragedy;' Modern Greek diminutive τραγοῦδι, any song, τραγουδέω, τραγουδῶ, 'I sing.' Goats as well as sheep are sacrificed at Easter to this day in Greece.

ποιητῶν, literally 'makers,' 'creators:' from ποιε-, 'make,' explained above.

τὰ εἶδές τα; 'Did you see them?' with popular and pleonastic repetition of pronoun. Observe the accent, and absence of accent on the proclitic and enclitic respectively.

κρατ-η-θῇ, 'hold herself:' passive with middle sense.

ἐθυμαίνουσα: from ξεθυμαιν- for ἐκθυμαιν-, the ε being really an encrusted augment ε from the past tenses ἐξεθύμαινον, ἐξεθύμανα. ἐκθυμαιν- = ἐκ + θυμαιν-, verbal stem from θυμό-, 'wrath,' 'anger,' 'impetuosity,' explained above. Hence ἐκθυμαίνω = 'I anger out,' i. e. find vent, outlet, for anger.

ἀρκούντως: for ἀρκε-όντ-ως, adverb of participial adjective ἀρκουντ-, 'sufficient,' explained above under ἀρκεῖται.

φυσήματος: substantive genitive singular of φυσα-.

ματάκια μου, literally 'my little eyes!' i. e. my life, my darling; cf. the expression 'guard as the apple of mine eye.' Diminutive of μάτι(ν), 'eye,' itself a diminutive = ὀμμάτ-ι-ον of ὄπ-ματ-, from root ὀπ-, kin to *eye*, German *Auge*, explained above.

ἀφ' οὗ = ἀπὸ οὗ, 'from which,' i. e. since.

ἀρρώστησε: aorist 3rd singular of ἀρρωστε-, verb of ἀρρωστο- from ἀ = 'un-' + ρωστό-, verbal adjective of ῥο-, 'be strong.' ῥώμη, 'strength,' ῥωμα-λέ-ο-, 'strong,' κ.τ.λ. Hence the greeting ἔρρωσο, i. e. ἔν-ρωσο, 'be strong,' middle imperative aorist (classical ἔρρωσαι) of verb ἔρρο-. The doubling of ρ is due to lost σ, whence we are led to connect σρο-, as a bye-form, with root σρυ- ρυ-, whence ῥέω, ῥεύω, 'I flow,' ῥύμη, 'impetus,' ῥυ-θ-μό-ς, 'the flow of a verse,' kin to *stream* for *sream*, &c.

σεῖς: for σϝέ-ες, modern plural σϝὲ- for τϝὲ- (σὲ-), stem of σύ (τύ), *thou*, Latin *tu*, &c. Introduced to avoid ambiguity of ὑμεῖς, 'you,' and ἡμεῖς, 'we,' when these words could no longer be distinguished in sound.

ἄνδρες: for ἄνρες (cf. *stream* for *sream*), plural of stem ἀνερ- (nominative ἀνὴρ for ἀνέρς); the ἀ- is euphonic, the root νερ- kin to Sanscrit *nara-s*, 'man,' Latin *Ner-o*, &c. Hence probably ἄνθρωπος for ἄνδρ-ωπος, i. e. man-like; cf. German *Mensch*, i. e. *männisch* ('mannish') from *Mann*. In meaning ἀνὴρ = *vir*, ἄνθρωπος = *homo*.

κυρὰ: shortened from κυρία through κυριά.

Σουσαμάκαινα: feminine of Σουσαμακη-; cf. λέαινα, feminine of λέοντ-, Λάκαινα, feminine of Λάκον-.

φαντάζομαι: verb of φαντὸ-, verbal adjective of φαν-, 'appear,' present φαίνω, aorist passive ἐφάνην, φανῶ. Hence φαντάζομαι = 'I have appearances,' φαντά, 'I fancy;' φάντασμα = 'ghost,' 'apparition,' from root φα-, 'say,' φημὶ, 'I say,' Latin *fa-* in *fa-bu-la, fa-ma,* &c.

τσακώθηκαν: for ἐ-τσακώ-θη-καν, literally 'they have been caught.' 'they have caught together,' 'become entangled (in a quarrel).' τσακον- perhaps for σακκον-, 'bag,' 'catch,' from σάκκο-, 'a bag.'

τακτικὰ: plural neuter = adverb of τακτικὸ-, adjective of verbal adjective τακτὸ-, from root ταγ- or τακ-, whence τάσσω = τάκῳω, 'I command,' 'order.' Hence τακτικὰ, 'orderly,' 'regularly.' Our *tactics* is the same word.

τοὐλάχιστον: contracted from τὸ ἐλάχιστον, i. e. the least, superlative degree of ἐ-λαχύ-, Sanscrit *laghu-*, Latin *levis* for *lĕ(g)-vis* (cf. βραχύ- and *brĕ(g)vis*), English *ligh-t.*

ξέσπασε: for ἐξέσπασε = ἐξ + ἔσπασε, 1st aorist of σπα-, 'break,' originally 'stretch (to bursting).' Hence *spasm,* σπάσμα, σπασμός, kin to *spa-n.*

κεφάλι: diminutive of κεφαλή, 'head.'

ἀναγνωστῶν: genitive plural of ἀναγνώστα- (nominative -ης), from ἀναγνο- (present ἀναγινώσκω = ἀνα-γι-γνώ-σκ-ω), 'I read;' cf. Latin *re-co-gno-sc-o* in same sense, literally 'recognize,' i. e. the meaning of the letters and words.

ὀξυ-νοίας, 'sharp-wit:' nominative ὀξύνοια for ὀξύ-γνοια; ὀξύ- for ὀκ-σ-ύ, from root ἀκ- ὀκ-, kin to Latin *ac-* in *acu-s,* 'needle,' *acer,* 'sharp,' our *edge,* Old High German *egg-ju,* 'I sharpen;' cf. also English *egg on.*

ἀγωνίζονται: from ἀγῶν-, 'struggle,' from root ἀγ-, 'lead [to war].'

κομισθέντα: neuter plural of participle κομισθέντ- of κομιζ-, verbal stem from κομιδά-, 'a bringing,' from κομ-, probably kin to our *home*; see above. Hence κομίζω = 'I convey home.'

ζαχαροπλαστείου: from ζάχαρα- (nominative ζάχαρης), a foreign word, and πλαστ-εῖο- from πλαστό-, verbal adjective of πλα-, 'make' + locative suffix -εῖο-. Hence πλαστεῖον = 'a place where things are made.' ζαχαροπλαστεῖον, 'a sugar manufactory,' 'a confectioner's shop.'

γλυκίσματα: from stem γλυκ-ι-δ- from γλυκ-ύ-, 'sweet,' probably kin to Latin *dulci-s* for *gulci-s*, to avoid two gutturals.

δροσιστικά: adjective of δροσιστό- from δροσιζ- (δροσιδ-) from δρόσο-, probably for Ϝρόσο-, kin to ἔρση for Ϝέρση, 'dew,' Sanscrit *varsh-a-s*, 'rain,' perhaps Latin *ro-s*, 'dew,' Slavonian *rosa*, Lithuanian *rasà*. Hence δροσίζω = 'I bedew,' 'I cool,' 'I refresh,' δροσιστικὰ, 'refreshments,' δροσερὸ-, 'cool.'

ἀφθόνως: adverb of ἄ-φθονο- = 'without grudging' or 'envy.' Hence 'plenteously.' φθόνο-ς probably for φθάνος, kin to φθάνω, 'reach' or 'overtake,' literally 'the overtaker,' personified by the ancient Greeks as 'that which was sure to catch a man,' 'the jealousy,' φθόνος, 'of destiny.'

ἄφιξιν: for ἄφ-ικ-σι-ν, from ἀπὸ + ἰκ-, 'to reach,' present (classical) ἀφικνέομαι, 'I arrive,' 'I reach,' for Ϝικ-, Sanscrit *viç-â-mi*, 'I reach,' 'touch.'

ὀργισθείς = ὀργισ-θέντ-ς: from ὀργίζομαι, from ὀργά-.

φρυάξας: aorist participle nominative masculine singular of φρυαγ- (φρυάζομαι), 'to be restive,' 'neigh' (of a horse). The root is φρυ-, kin to *bray*, the αγ- is suffix.

ἐβρόντησε: from βροντα-, verbal stem from βροντὰ-, 'thunder,' this again a verbal for βρομ-τά- from root βρεμ-, kin (in spite of irregularity as regards initial consonant) to Latin *frem-o*, German *brummen*, Sanscrit *bhram*; perhaps, too, connected, so far as βρε- is concerned, with the foregoing φρυ-.

ἐπέτρεπον = ἐπ' for ἐπὶ + ἔτρεπον: ἐπι-τρέπ-ω = literally 'I turn over [to any one],' 'I allow,' 'permit.' τρεπ- [τρακ-] kin to German *dreh-en*, 'turn.'

ἔπαθε (present πάσχω for πάθ-σκω; cf. γιγνώ-σκω, κ.τ.λ.), 'suffered,' kin to Latin *pat-i-or*, *pat-i-enti-a*, whence our *patience*, &c.

νεῦρα: kin to Latin *nervo-*, where the *r* and *v* are transposed.

ἐκτύπησε: from κτυπα-, from κτύπο-, the Homeric γδοῦπο- in ἐρίγδουπο-, 'land-resounding,' 'the sound of a blow.' Hence κτυπάω, 'I strike,' ἐκτυπήθη μόνος του, 'he was struck or stabbed by himself,' 'committed suicide, or attempted it.'

τοῖχο-: distinguished from τεῖχος, with which it is kin, as the partition from the outer wall of a house, *paries*, not *murus*, in Latin, still less *moenia*, 'the walls of a town:' *Wand* as opposed to *Mauer* in German.

πάτωμα[τ], literally 'that which is trodden:' from πατο-, 'path,' whence πατό-ν-ω (not found), 'I make a path of,' πατέω, 'I tread.' Hence πάτωμα = 'floor,' 'storey,' τὸ ἄνω πάτωμα, 'the upper storey,' τὸ κάτω πάτωμα, 'the lower storey.'

παντοῦφλα: from the French *pantoufle*, 'a slipper.'

ἐξαπλωθεῖσα: from ἐξαπλόνω, literally 'to simplify one's self out,' 'to stretch one's self out,' 'to lie down,' from ἁ-πλό-ο-, 'one-folded,' *sim-ple-c-s*, *simplex*; πλο- is kin to Latin *pli-* in *plica-*, and our *fol-* in *fold*. Hence, too, διπλό-ο-ς (διπλοῦς), 'double,' τριπλοῦς, 'threefold,' τετραπλοῦς, 'fourfold,' κ.τ.λ. ἁ- = σα-, also ὁμ- ἁμ- = σομ- σαμ-, kin to Latin *sim-* in *sim-plex*, *sim-ilis*, our *same*, &c.

λειπόθυμον: from λειπ-, imperfect stem of λιπ-, 'leave,' and θυμό-ς, 'soul,' 'spirit.' Hence λειπόθυμος, 'with failing spirit,' 'faint' (ὁ καὶ ἡ).

πεισθῇ: for πειθ-σ-θῇ, from πειθ- πιθ-, 'to persuade,' kin to *fid-* in *fides*, 'fidelity,' &c.

ἱκανήν: from root Ϝικ-, 'reach.' Hence ἱκανὸ- ἁ- = 'what reaches,' 'is sufficient.'

ἦν: the classical form (active) for the Modern middle ἦτο(ν) in more general use.

καταιγίδος: stem καταιγίδ-, compound of κατὰ and αἰγ-ίδ-, 'a storm' = 'a downright storm,' 'a tempest.' αἰγ- kin to εἰγ- in ἐπ-είγ-ω, 'I urge on,' Sanscrit ég'-á-mi for aig-á-mi, 'I shake,' 'tremble;' perhaps cognate with Latin aeg-er, 'sick,' 'trembling,' 'infirm,' also with αἴγειρος for αἴγ-ερι-ο-ς, 'the aspen,' 'the quivering tree.'

ἀποτέλεσμα: from ἀποτέλεσ-, 'finish off' = 'the finishing off,' 'the result,' 'the issue.'

ἔπαυσε: active used intransitively of παυ-, 'to stay,' kin to pau- in pau-s-a (Latin), 'pause,' also in pau-l-us, pau-c-us, and the English *few*. Cf. Eccles. xii. 3: "The grinders cease because they are few."

σπαραξικάρδ-ι-ο-ν: from σπαρακ- (σπαράκιω, σπαράσσω, ἐσ-πάραξα), 'rend,' from root σπαρ- + suffix -ακ-, found also in σπαίρω [σπάρ?ω], ἀσπαίρω, 'to quiver;' kin to our *spring*, German *springen* intransitive, and *sprengen* transitive + καρδ-, *heart* + adjectival suffix -ιο- + ν.

τριωδ-ί-αν: from τρι-, *three*, and ᾠδά- for ἀοιδά-, 'song,' from root ἀειδ-, 'sing,' for ἀϝειδ-, kin to ὑδ-ω, ὑδ-έ-ω, 'I sing,' ἀηδών [ἀϝηδών], 'the nightingale,' Sanscrit vád-á-mi, 'I speak,' 'I say.'

ἀπελπιστικὴν: from ἀπελπιδ- (ἀπελπίζω), 'despair,' from ἀπὸ + ἐλπίδ-, 'hope.'

ζητοῦντος (ζητ-έ-οντ-ος): from ζητε-, from root ζη + suffix τε- for ιη- = ιᾱ-, Sanscrit ja-, 'to go,' so that ζητέω meant originally, 'I go about.' Compare the more modern γυρεύω from γύρο-, 'a circle,' literally 'I go about in a circle.' Hence 'I seek;' cf. also *chercher*, *cercare*, i.e. Latin *circare*, Albanian *k'erk'umun*, 'seek.'

ἁδρὰν: feminine accusative of ἁδρὸ-, kin (-ρὸ- = suffix) to ἅδην, also ἅδην for σάδ-η-ν. The root is σα-, found in Latin sa-tur, sa-tis, &c., in German *satt*, 'satisfied,' our *sad*.

ἀξιοῦντος = ἀξιό-οντ-ος: from ἀξιο- (ἀξιό-ω, ἀξιόνω), 'count worthy,' from adjective ἄξιο-, i. e. ἄγ-σιο-, literally 'takeable,' 'acceptable.' Hence ἀξιοῦντος = literally 'counting worthy, and so claiming.' Hence, too, ἀξίωμα, 'dignity,' 'office,' ἀξία, 'worth.'

πληρώσῃ: from πληρο-, verbal stem from πλῆρες-, 'full,' explained above. Hence πληρόνω, literally 'I fulfil,' i. e. demands, and thus = 'pay.'

δυσχερῆ: stem δυσχερὲς-, literally 'ill to handle,' 'ill for the hand,' from δυσ-, 'ill,' and χερ- (nominative χείρ, genitive χερός and χειρός), 'hand.'

δυσέκβολον = 'hard to get out of,' 'hard of exit' (ἐκβολή), from ἐκ and βαλ- (ἐκβάλλω), 'put out,' and intransitively 'get out.'

διελύθη: aorist passive of διαλυ-, from διὰ, δϝιὰ, 'apart,' and λυ-, kin to our *loo-* in *loose*. Hence διαλύω, 'loose apart,' 'dissolve,' 'disperse.'

ἐξακριβώσωμεν: ἐξακριβο- from ἐξ, 'out,' ἀκριβὸ-, bye-form of ἀκριβὲσ-, 'exact,' probably for ἀκρυβὲσ-, from ἀ + κρυβ-, 'hide ;' cf. ἀληθές. κρυβ- seems to be a shorter form of καλυβ- (καλύπτω, 'Apocalypse'), kin to *cel-are*, whence *conceal*, -υπ-τ- being extension ; καλ-ιὰ, 'hut,' Old High German *hel-an*, Modern High German *hehl*, *verhehlen*. Hence ἀκριβής = 'unconcealed,' 'clearly discovered,' 'accurate,' in both active and passive sense. Usage has decided that the form ἀκριβὲσ- shall be retained in the original sense, while ἀκριβό- means 'dear' in both senses, e. g. τὸ ψωμὶ εἶνε ἀκριβόν, 'bread is dear,' and ἀκριβή μου μῆτερ, 'my dear mother.'

ὡρκίσθη: from ὀρκιζ-, from ὅρκο-, 'oath.'

Exercise XIV.

Τίνες ἔμειναν μόνοι; Οἱ δύο σύζυγοι. Τί ἔκαμαν; Ἀμφότεροι ἐσιώπων, καίτοι διάφορα αἰσθήματα ἐκύμαινον τὰς καρδίας των, ἤ, ἂν θέλετε, αἱ καρδίαι των ἐκυμαίνοντο ὑπὸ διαφόρων αἰσθημάτων. Ἐπὶ τέλους ἡ Πασιφάη δὲν ἠδύνατο πλέον νὰ κρατηθῇ. Δὲν ἐκθυμάνθην (ξεθυμάνθηκα), λέγει, ἀρκούντως ἀκόμη. Ὁρίστε τῶρα· τί λέγεις; Τί λέγω; ἀπήτησε μειλιχίως ὁ σύζυγός της· ἐγὼ λέγω νὰ μὴν πᾶμε; καὶ πῶς νὰ πᾶμε ἀφ' οὗ ἀρρώστησε τοῦ ἀνθρώπου ἡ γυναίκα του (γυνή του); Σεῖς οἱ ἄνδρες πιστεύετε πολλά. Ἐγὼ ὅμως φαντάζομαι ἀρκούντως καλὰ τί θὰ ἔτρεξε μεταξύ των. Συμβαίνει τακτικὰ μίαν φορὰν τοὐλάχιστον τῆς ἑβδομάδος νὰ τσακωθοῦν, καὶ αὐτὴν τὴν φορὰν φαίνεται πῶς ἡ καταιγὶς ξέσπασε εἰς τὸ κεφάλι μας· τὰ εἶδές τα. Ἡ γυναικεία ὀξύνοια εἶνε βεβαίως γνωστὴ εἰς τοὺς ἀναγνώστας μας. Πολλάκις καὶ αὐτοὶ ἂν ἦνε ἄνδρες προσεπάθησαν ματαίως νὰ κρυβῶσι ἀπὸ τῆς περιεργείας τῶν γυναικῶν. Τί κρίμα νὰ διώξῃ ἡ Κυρία Σουσαμάκη ὅλα τὰ γλυκίσματα καὶ δροσιστικὰ τὰ τόσον ἀφθόνως ἀπὸ τὸ ζαχαροπλαστεῖον κομισθέντα. Δὲν ἔπρεπεν ὅμως νὰ φρυάξῃ καὶ βροντήσῃ ὁ κύριος συζυγός της ἀφ᾽ οὗ ἔμαθε τοῦτο. Τοῦτο δὲν ἐπέτρεπον οὔτε αἱ τριάκοντα τῆς προικός του χιλιάδες οὔτε τὰ καλὰ ἤθη. Ἐπίσης ἡ Σουσαμάκαινα καίτοι ἔπασχε τὰ νεῦρά της δὲν ἔπρεπε νὰ κτυπήσῃ τὸν Ὀρέστην διὰ τῆς παντούφλας της, οὔτε νὰ προσποιηθῇ τὴν λειπόθυμον ἂν δὲν ἦτο τῇ ἀληθείᾳ λειπόθυμος, τὸ ὁποῖον δὲν ἐφαίνετο πιθανὸν (probable) κατὰ τὴν δύναμιν μεθ᾽ ἧς ἐκτύπησε τὸν ἄνδρα της. Ἰδοὺ τὸ ἀποτέλεσμα παρὰ τῷ Κυρίῳ Παρδαλῷ. Ὢ ταλαίπωρε Θοδωρῆ! εὑρίσκεσαι εἰς δυσχερῆ καὶ δυσέκβολον θέσιν. Τὶ ἀπελπιστικὴ καὶ σπαραξικάρδιος σκηνή. Ὁ Παρδαλὸς ἀξιοῖ νὰ πληρώσῃ μίαν μόνον δραχμήν. Ὁ ἁμαξηλάτης ὅμως ζητεῖ ἁδρὰν ἀποζημίωσιν ἐπὶ τῷ ματαίῳ κόπῳ. Ὁ κύριος ἦτο ὀργισμένος, ἀλλὰ τέλος πάντων ἡ σκηνὴ διελύθη, καὶ ἡ Εὐφροσύνη ὡρκίσθη νὰ μὴν ὑπάγῃ πλέον ποτὲ εἰς ἑσπερίδα οἵαν δήποτε.

Why did Euphrosyne swear she would never go again to any evening party whatsoever? We will not describe the scene: it is too (πάρα πολὺ) heartrending and desperate to describe. How terrible was the result of the tempest! The wall was beaten with hands, the floor with feet, and Orestes with a slipper. Moreover, Pasiphae had a nervous attack, and pretended to faint away. But these things were but the beginning of evils. The cabman had to be (ἔπρεπε νὰ) indemnified for his vain trouble. Mr. Pardalós got angry, and Mrs. Pardalós swore a frightful oath. All this happened because Pasiphae had driven away the refreshments so abundantly brought from the confectioner's. What wonder (τί θαῖμα) if Susamákis stormed and raged? The curiosity of our readers will have guessed most correctly that the pair (οἱ σύζυγοι) had quarrelled. This generally happened regularly once or twice a week, at least. Oh, my life! The man's wife is ill. What can he do? She does not cheat me, however, said the lady, so she needn't think it. We are both silent because we have nothing to say, though various sentiments agitate our breasts. No man can find sufficient vent for his anger by merely panting. He must say something, but he need not swear. If he must, it is better that he should remain alone. In vain does Mrs. Susamákis strive to escape the keen-wittedness of Mrs. Pardalós. She fancies accurately enough what must have happened betwixt her and her husband.

PART II.

INTRODUCTION.

The student will by this time have attained so complete an insight into the general structure of the Greek language, that he will have no difficulty in seeing his way through the following conversational sentences.

How to use the Dialogues.

(*a*) First learn a page by heart, committing each column to memory, so far as to be able, when the right-hand column is covered with a sheet of paper, to recall the words by looking at the left.

(*b*) Now write out in an exercise-book the left-hand column from sight; put the "Guide" out of view, and translate on the opposite page from memory.

(*c*) Open the "Guide," and correct carefully any mistakes, down to every accent and breathing.

(*d*) Re-write till there remains no jot or tittle to correct.

(*e*) Practise yourself in the composition of original dialogues (1) by ringing the changes on the column already written out, e. g. :—

Προετοιμάσθη ἡ ἀναχώρησις. Προετοιμάσθησαν τὰ πάντα. Εἶνε ἕτοιμα τὰ πάντα; Μὴ λησμονῆτε τὴν ἀναχώρησιν τῆς ἀμαξοστοιχίας. Ἡ ἀμαξοστυιχία ἀναχωρεῖ. Ἡ ἀμαξοστοιχία φθάνει ἀργά, κ.τ.λ.

(*f*) Afterwards these original exercises may be enlarged to any extent by consulting the classified vocabulary at the end of the book, Part III.

CONVERSATIONS.—ΔΙΑΛΟΓΟΙ.

Δια = 'between two' + λόγο- = 'word,' 'discourse.'

A JOURNEY TO GREECE.—Ταξίδιον εἰς τὴν Ἑλλάδα.

ταξίδιον, diminutive of τάξι-ς = τάγ-σι-ς, literally 'an order,' 'arrangement,' 'mission.' Hence ταξίδιον = 'little mission,' 'trip,' 'journey.'

Προετοιμάσθητε κατὰ πάντα διὰ τὴν ἀναχώρησιν;

Are you all ready to go? (lit. Did you prepare yourself in everything for the departure?).

Τὰ πράγματά σας εἶνε πάντα ἕτοιμα;

Are your things all ready?

Τὰ πάντα εἶνε ἕτοιμα.

Everything is ready.

Μὴ λησμονῆτε ὅτι τὸ γραφεῖον τῶν εἰσιτηρίων κλείεται πέντε λεπτὰ πρὸ τῆς ἀναχωρήσεως τῆς ἁμαξοστοιχίας.

Don't forget that the ticket office closes five minutes before the departure of the train.

Ὄχι εἰς τὴν Ἀγγλίαν!

Not in England!

Ἐκτὸς δὲ τούτου ἔλαβον τὸ εἰσιτήριόν μου προηγουμένως.

And besides, I have taken my ticket beforehand.

Πολὺ καλά· ἀλλὰ τὰ κιβώτιά σας;

Very well. But your boxes?

Ἀνέγνωσα κάπου εἰδοποίησιν, ὅτι πᾶσα ἀποσκευὴ φθάνουσα πολὺ ἀργὰ κρατεῖται ὀπίσω μέχρι τῆς ἀκολούθου ἁμαξοστοιχίας καὶ ὑποβάλλεται εἰς ἔξοδα μετακομίσεως.

I have read somewhere a notice that all luggage arriving too late is kept back till the next train, and is subject to charge for carriage.

Εἰς τὴν Ἀγγλίαν ἐναντίως δὲν μετακομίζεται διόλου ἀλλὰ κρατεῖται εἰς τὸ γραφεῖον τῶν χαμένων πραγμάτων.

In England, on the contrary, it is not forwarded at all, but is kept at the lost luggage office.

Τοῦτο ὅμως προεφυλάχθην καὶ ἐμίσθωσα βαστάζον νὰ κουβαλήσῃ τὰ πράγματά μου εἰς τὸν σταθμόν.

I have provided, however, against this, and have hired a porter to carry my things to the station.

K

Έλαβα θέσιν εἰς τὸ παντοφορεῖον τοῦ σιδηροδρόμου ὥστε δὲν θὰ χρειασθῶ ἅμαξαν.
I have taken a place in the railway omnibus, so I shall not want a cab.

Ἰδοὺ ἐφθάσαμεν εἰς τὸν σταθμόν.
Here we are (arrived) at the station.

Τί πράγματα ἔχετε, κύριε;
What luggage have you, sir?

Ἔχω δύο κιβώτια, ἕνα σάκκον ὁδοιπορικὸν, καὶ μίαν πιλοθήκην διὰ τὴν ἅμαξαν τῆς ἀποσκευῆς.
I have two trunks, a travelling-bag, and a hat-box, for the luggage van.

Ταῦτα θέλω νὰ ἐγγράψω.
These I wish to register.

Τὰ λοιπά μου πράγματα θὰ πάρω μαζύ μου.
My other luggage I will take with me.

Δηλαδὴ ποδοτύλιγμα, βακτηρίαν, τρεῖς τέσσαρας φακέλλους, ὅπλον, κυνάριον, δύο τουρκικὰς καπνοσύριγγας καὶ ἕνα χελώνιον ζωντανόν.
That is to say—a foot-wrapper, a stick, three or four parcels, a gun, a lap-dog, two Turkish pipes, and a live tortoise.

Ὡς πρὸς τὰ ἄλλα ἂς ἦνε· ἀλλὰ διὰ τὸ κυνάρι (τὸ σκυλάκι) πρέπει νὰ ληφθῇ ἰδιαίτερον γραμμάτιον, καὶ αὐτὸ πρέπει νὰ ὑπάγῃ μὲ τὴν ἀποσκευήν.
As for the rest, let them pass; but for the dog a separate ticket must be taken, and he must go in the van.

Τὸ χελώνι ὅμως πρέπει ν' ἀφήσητε ὀπίσω· ζωΰφια δὲν μετακομίζομεν.
As for the tortoise, you must leave that behind: we don't convey vermin!

Ζωΰφια! λοιπὸν τὸ χελώνι τὸ καταριθμεῖς εἰς τὰ ζωΰφια;
Vermin! So you reckon a tortoise among the vermin?

Μάλιστα, ἐφέντη, εἶνε ἔντομον.
Certainly, sir; it's an insect.

Ἔντομον! Βρὲ ἀδελφέ! ποῦ ἐσπούδασας;
An insect! My good fellow, where did you go to school (study)?

Σὲ παραπέμπω εἰς τὸν Ζωολογικὸν Κῆπον καὶ ἐκεῖ θὰ μάθῃς, ἂν ἔχῃς μυαλό 's τὸ κεφάλι, ὅτι τὸ χελώνι εἶνε τετράποδον ἑρπετὸν καὶ ὅτι τὰ ἔντομα εἶνε ὅλα ἑξάποδα.
I refer you to the Zoological Garden(s), and there you will learn, if you have any brains in your head, that the tortoise is a four-footed reptile, and that insects are all six-footed.

Ἰδοὺ ἓν σελίνιον τιμὴ τῆς εἰσόδου εἰς τὸν Ζωολογικὸν Κῆπον, ἐκτὸς τῆς Δευτέρας ὅταν εἶνε μόνον ἑξάπενον.
There's a shilling for you, the price of admission to the Zoological Gardens, except on Mondays, when it is only sixpence.

Ἂν εὐκαιρῆς τὰς Δευτέρας, πᾶγε δύο φορὰς διὰ νὰ φωτισθῆς καλλίτερα.

Ὢ αὐτὸ εἶνε ἄλλο ζήτημα, κύριε! Καὶ τώρα ἐνθυμοῦμαι ὅτι ὁ ξενοδόχος ἐκεῖ πέρα ἔχει βιβλίον μὲ τέτοια θεριὰ μέσα. Ἂς ἦνε λοιπόν. Μάλον τοῦτο αἱ λέξεις τετράποδον καὶ ἑξάποδον ἔχουν ἄλλην σημασίαν εἰς τὴν ἰδικήν μου δουλείαν.

Τόσῳ τὸ καλλίτερον! κύτταξε λοιπὸν τὴν ἰδικήν σου δουλείαν, καὶ ἄφετε εἰς ἐμένα τὰ τετράποδα ἑρπετά.

Τίνα θέσιν ἐλάβετε;

Τρίτης τάξεως.

Διατί ταξιδεύετε τρίτην;

Διότι δὲν ὑπάρχει τετάρτη.

Εἰς τὴν Ἰρλανδίαν ὅμως ὑπάρχει.

Μάλιστα· πολλὰ ἀλλόκοτα πράγματα ὑπάρχουν ἐκεῖ· τέσσαρες τάξεις, καὶ τάξις οὐδεμία· τοὐλάχιστον μεγάλη ἀταξία.

Μήπως καὶ ἐν Ἑλλάδι εὐρίσκεται μεγαλητέρα εὐταξία;

Θὰ ἴδητε.

Take your places, please.

Come, let us get in quick.

Don't go so near the engine.

Let us try to get a seat near the door.

I like to have my back towards the engine, so as to escape the wind and dust.

I hear the third bell. We are going to start.

Ἰδοὺ τὸ σύριγμα!

What a length the train is!

If you have time on Mondays, go twice, that you may be more thoroughly enlightened.

Oh, that alters the question, sir! And, now I come to think of it, the landlord over the way has a book with those kind of creatures in it. I daresay you're right (lit. Let be then). All the same, four-foot and six-foot have another meaning in my business.

All the better! Mind your own business then, and leave the four-footed reptiles to me.

What place have you taken?

Third class.

Why do you travel third?

Because there's no fourth.

There is in Ireland, however.

Yes, indeed; there are many strange things in Ireland. Four classes (orders), and no order—at least, great disorder.

Is there better order to be found in Greece?

You will see.

Λάβετε τὰς θέσεις σας, παρακαλῶ.

Ἐλᾶτε, ἂς εἰσέλθωμεν γρήγορα.

Μὴ πηγαίνητε τόσον πλησίον τῆς μηχανῆς.

Ἂς προπαθήσωμεν νὰ καταλάβωμεν θέσιν παρὰ τὴν θύραν.

Ἀγαπῶ νὰ ἔχω τὰ νῶτα ἐστραμμένα πρὸς τὸ μέρος τῆς μηχανῆς, ὥστε νὰ ἀποφεύγω τὸν ἄνεμον καὶ τὸν κονιορτόν.

Ἀκούω τὸν τρίτον κώδωνα. μέλλομεν ν' ἀναχωρήσωμεν.

That's the whistle?

Τί μῆκος ὅπου ἔχει ἡ ἁμαξοστοιχία!

Do you know whether it stops at Redhill?	Ἠξεύρετε ἂν σταματᾷ εἰς Κοκκινόβουνον;
The time-table says it passes without stopping.	Τὸ δελτίον λέγει ὅτι διαβαίνει χωρὶς νὰ σταθῇ.
Wait! It does not pass at all.	Στάσου'! δὲν διαβαίνει διόλου.
What a pace!	Ὁποῖον τάχος!
We have already come thirty miles.	Διεδράμομεν (διετρέξομεν) ἤδη τριάκοντα μίλια.
Have you had your luggage booked?	Ἐνεγράψατε τὰ πράγματά σας;
Yes; here is the ticket they gave me.	Μάλιστα καὶ ἰδοὺ ἡ ἀπόδειξις ἣν μου ἔδωκαν.
Keep it carefully. You must give it up when you arrive, in order to get your luggage.	Φυλάξατέ το προσεκτικῶς· πρέπει νὰ τὸ παραδώσητε ὅταν φθάσητε, ἵνα παραλάβητε τὰ πράγματά σας.
Ταξιδεύομεν ὀγλήγορα.	We are travelling quickly.
Φοβοῦμαι μὴ ἐξέλθωμεν τῆς τροχιᾶς.	I am afraid we shall run off the rails.
Κλονίζεται φρικτὰ ἡ ἅμαξα.	The carriage shakes frightfully.
Ἡ αἰτία εἶνε ὅτι ἀπέχομεν μακρὰν τῆς μηχανῆς.	The reason is that we are a long way from the engine.
Ἰδοὺ ἔρχεται μία ἁμαξοστοιχία.	Here is a train coming.
Εἶνε τῆς ἐπιστροφῆς.	It is the up (return) train.
Φαίνεται ὅτι εἶνε ἐπὶ τῆς ἡμετέρας ὁδοῦ.	It looks as if it were on our line (way).
Μὴ ταράττησθε. Αἱ ἐπιστρέφουσαι ἁμαξοστοιχίαι πορεύονται πάντοτε ἐπὶ τῆς ἄλλης γραμμῆς.	Do not be alarmed. The up trains always travel on the other line.
Ἰδοὺ ἐφθάσομεν εἰς τὸν πρῶτον σταθμόν.	Here we are at the first station.
Πόσον θὰ μείνωμεν ἐδῶ;	How long shall we stop here?
Ὄχι πλέον τῶν τριῶν λεπτῶν.	Not more than three minutes.
Σωστὰ φθάνει νὰ καύσωμεν τὰ χείλη μας καταπίνοντες ζεστὸν καφέν.	Just time enough to scald our lips with swallowing hot coffee.
Ἰδοὺ πάλιν ἐξεκινήσαμεν.	We are off again.
Εἴμεθα εἰς τὸ σκότος.	We are in the dark.
Εἶνε ὑπόγειον ὄρυγμα.	It's a tunnel.
Where are we now?	Ποῦ εἴμεθα τώρα;
Ὁμοιάζει ὅτι εἴμεθα εἰς τὸν ἀέρα ἀπῃωρημένοι.	It is as though we were hung in mid-air.

We are passing over a viaduct? — Διαβαίνομεν ἐπὶ ὁδαγωγείου ἢ γεφυρωτῆς ὁδοῦ.

Ἐντὸς ὀλίγου θὰ ἤμεθα εἰς τὸ τέρμα. — We shall soon be at the end (terminus).

Τέλος ἰδοὺ ἐπεβιβάσθημεν εἰς τὸ πλοῖον. — Here we are at last, on board ship.

Βρωμᾷ κατράνι τρομερά. — It smells horribly of tar.

Ὑγιεινή ἡ ὀσμή. — The smell is a wholesome one.

Ἴσως· ἀλλὰ αἰσθάνομαι κεφαλαλγίαν καὶ κατέχομαι ὅλος ἀπὸ ῥίγους. — Perhaps; but I feel a headache, and am all of a chill.

Βρὲ ἀδελφέ! τοῦτο δὲν εἶνε κατράνι. εἶνε ναυτία (θαλασσοζάλη). — Bless you! that is not tar. It's sea-sickness.

Ἂς ἀναβῶμεν ἐπὶ τοῦ καταστρώματος· ὁ δροσερὸς ἀὴρ θὰ σὲ ὠφελήσῃ. — Let's go on deck. The fresh air will do you good.

Ἂν ζαλίζεσθε ἐδῶ μεταξὺ τοῦ Δοβρίου καὶ τοῦ Καλαισίου, τί θὰ κάμητε μεταξὺ τῆς Μασσαλίας καὶ τοῦ Πειραιῶς; — If you are sea-sick here, between Dover and Calais, what will you do between Marseilles and the Piræus?

Μάλιστα· "εἰ ἐν τῷ ὑγρῷ ξύλῳ ταῦτα ποιοῦσιν, ἐν τῷ ξηρῷ τί γένηται;" — Yes, indeed: "If they do these things in the green (wet) tree, what shall be done in the dry?"

Μετάφρασον τοῦτο εἰς τὴν καθομιλουμένην. — Translate that into Modern Greek (the spoken language).

Ἂν εἰς τὸ ὑγρὸν ξύλον πράττωσι ταῦτα, τί θέλει γείνει εἰς τὸ ξηρόν;

Ἔτσι πως λέγομεν σήμερον. — That's about what we should say nowadays.

Ἀλλὰ καὶ εἰς τὸ πρωτότυπον πᾶς τις τὸ καταλαμβάνει. — But even in the original, every one understands it.

The wind is in our favour. — Ὁ ἄνεμος εἶνε οὔριος.

Who is that man on the paddle-box? — Τίς εἶνε οὗτος ὁ ἐπὶ τοῦ ἐμβόλου;

It is the captain. He goes up there to give orders. — Εἶνε ὁ πλοίαρχος· ἀναβαίνει ἐκεῖ διὰ νὰ δώσῃ διαταγάς.

The tide is strong. — Ἡ ἀποθαλασσιὰ εἶνε μεγάλη.

I have heard there is no tide (no ebb and flow) in the Mediterranean. — Ἤκουσα πῶς δὲν ἔχει ἄμπωτιν καὶ παλίῤῥοιαν εἰς τὴν Μεσόγειον θάλασσαν.

It is true.
How is it, then, that the Greeks have three words for it?
Their learned men have manufactured them, or at least have adapted them.
And besides this, you know, the Greeks are and always were splendid sailors, and are found in all parts of the world.
More than this, they are tremendous linguists, and manufacture words by the yard.

Σηκόνουν πανία.
Θὰ ἔχομεν ὀγλήγορον διάπλουν.
What a lovely voyage.
Πόσους κόμβους κάμνομεν τὴν ὥραν;
Ἂς ἐρωτήσωμεν τὸν πηδαλιοῦχον.
Παίρνομεν δέκα κόμβους τὴν ὥραν.

Βλέπω τὴν ἀκτήν.
Θὰ φθάσωμεν εἰς ὀλίγον.
Ἰδοὺ ἐφθάσαμεν.
Πότε φεύγει ἡ ἁμαξοστοιχία διὰ τοὺς Παρισίους;
Εἰς τὰς ἐννέα καὶ ἥμισυ (ἐννιάμισο).
Πότε θὰ φθάσωμεν ἐκεῖ;
Δὲν ἠξεύρω ἀκριβῶς.
Περὶ τὰς δύο, νομίζω.
Διεδράμομεν ἤδη τρία χιλιόμετρα.

Σταματῶμεν.
Ἐσταματήσαμεν.
Πόσην ὥραν μένουν ἐδῶ;
Ὁλόκληρον τέταρτον τῆς ὥρας.
Τόσῳ τὸ καλλίτερον· διότι ἀρχίζω νὰ πεινῶ καὶ νὰ διψῶ.
Ἂς προγευματίσωμεν λοιπόν· ἔχομεν καιρόν.

Εἶνε ἀλήθεια.
Πῶς λοιπὸν ἔχουν οἱ Ἕλληνες τρεῖς λέξεις δι' αὐτήν.
Τὰς κατεσκεύασαν οἱ λογιώτατοί των, ἢ τοὐλάχιστον τὰς ἐφήρμοσαν.
Καὶ ἐκτὸς τούτου, ἠξεύρετε ὅτι οἱ Ἕλληνες εἶνε καὶ πάντοτε ἦσαν τρομεροὶ ναῦται καὶ εὑρίσκονται παντοῦ τοῦ κόσμου.
Πρὸς τούτοις εἶνε καὶ τρομεροὶ φιλόλογοι καὶ δημιουργοῦσι τὰς λέξεις κατὰ πῆχυν.

They are hoisting sail.
We shall have a short passage.
Τί χρυσὸ ταξίδι.
How many knots are we making an hour?
Let's ask the steersman.
We are making ten knots an hour.
I see the shore.
We shall soon be there.
Here we are.
When does the train start for Paris?
At half-past nine.
When shall we get there?
I don't know exactly.
I think about two.
We have already come three kilometres.
We are stopping.
We have stopped.
How long do they stop here?
A full quarter of an hour.
All the better, for I am beginning to get hungry and thirsty.
Let us breakfast, then. We have time.

Plenty.	Ἄφθονον.
Ἰδοὺ τέλος πάντων ἐφθάσαμεν ὑγιεῖς καὶ σῶοι, δόξα τῷ Θεῷ, εἰς τοὺς Παρισίους.	Here we are at last, safe and sound, thank God, in Paris.
Τώρα διὰ τὴν Μασσαλίαν.	Now for Marseilles.
Ἀλλὰ ποῦ νὰ περάσωμεν τὴν νύκτα;	But where are we to pass the night?
Εἰς ξενοδοχεῖον, ὑποθέτω.	At a hotel, I suppose.
Εἰμπαρεῖτε νὰ μοὶ συστήσητε καλὸν καὶ εὔθηνόν;	Can you recommend me a good, cheap one?
Μάλιστα, ἀλλὰ μυστικά! διότι, ἀφοῦ ἐνδεχόμενον νὰ τυπωθοῦν τὰ λόγια μου, ὁ κόσμος θὰ ἔλεγε ὅτι ἐδωροδοκήθην διὰ τὴν σύστασιν.	Yes, but in confidence; for, since it is possible my words may be printed, the world would say I had taken a bribe for my recommendation.
Ἐδῶ τοὐλάχιστον εἶνε ξενοδοχεῖον ἔχον ἀρκετὰ καλὴν ὄψιν καὶ πλησίον τοῦ σταθμοῦ τοῦ σιδηροδρόμου.	Here, at all events, is an inn which looks well enough, and is near the railway station.
Ἀλλὰ τί σημαίνει τοῦτο, ἀφ' οὗ φεύγομεν αὔριον ἀπὸ ἄλλου σταθμοῦ εἰς τὸ μεσημβρινὸν μέρος τῆς πόλεως;	What does that matter? We shall have to start to-morrow from another station in the south part of the town.
Ὄχι τώρα πλέον· εἰμποροῦμεν νὰ ἐξακολουθήσωμεν τὸ ταξίδιόν μας χωρὶς ν' ἀλλάξωμεν σταθμόν.	This is no longer the case. We can continue our journey without change of station.
Λοιπὸν ἂς κουδουνίσωμεν ἐδῶ.	Let us ring here, then.
Have you a double-bedded room (to let)?	Ἔχετε δωμάτιον μὲ δύο κρεββάτια (δύο κλίνας) δι' ἐνοίκιον.
I don't know, sir; but I will ask the landlord.	Δὲν ἠξεύρω κύριε, ἀλλὰ θὰ ἐρωτήσω τὸν ξενοδόχον.
Gentlemen, I have one bedroom with two beds.	Κύριοι, ἔχω ἓν δωμάτιον μὲ δύο κλίνας.
On what floor?	Εἰς ποῖον πάτωμα;
On the second.	Εἰς τὸ δεύτερον.
Bring us soap, water, and towels: we want to wash.	Φέρετέ μας νερὸν μὲ σαπούνι καὶ προσόψια· θέλομεν νὰ πλυνθῶμεν.
But what a tiny basin!	Ἀλλὰ τί μικρὸν λεκανίδιον!
It's the custom in France, sir.	Οὕτως συνειθίζεται εἰς τὴν Γαλλίαν κύριε.

And as for the soap, haven't you brought your own?
No; I forgot that this is also the custom in France.
Tell us how often do people wash a day in France?
According to taste, and to necessity. To tell you a tale, however:—
I had a French friend once on a journey in England, and he went to a hotel in London. He ate (had supper), went to bed, got up next morning, and, looking in the glass, cried out, "Oh! I've got the black death! It's all over with me! I'm dying! Fetch me the doctor!"
It was nothing but London smoke, however.
So you see, gentlemen, it may be that the Frenchman washes once (in his own country), with a minute basin, and no soap, and yet is cleaner than the Englishman who bathes and washes three or four times a day.
Meanwhile, the chambermaid will bring you soap, water, and towels directly.
Will you order supper, gentlemen?
At what o'clock is your ordinary? (lit. Do they eat together?).
At eight precisely.
Now while that joker is gone, it's an excellent opportunity to examine the beds.
Oh! I'm turning entomologist, perforce.

Καὶ ὡς πρὸς σαποῦνι, δὲν ἐφέρετε τὸ ἰδικόν σας;
Ὄχι ἐλησμόνησα ὅτι καὶ τοῦτο συνειθίζεται εἰς τὴν Γαλλίαν.
Πέτε μας ποσάκις πλύνονται οἱ ἄνθρωποι εἰς τὴν Γαλλίαν.
Κατὰ τὴν ἀρέσκειαν, καὶ τὴν ἀνάγκην.
Νὰ σᾶς εἴπω παραμύθιον ὅμως:—
Εἶχά ποτε φίλον Γάλλον ταξιδεύοντα εἰς τὴν 'Αγγλίαν' καὶ ἐπῆγε εἰς ξενοδοχεῖον ἐν Λονδίνῳ. Ἔφαγε, ἐπλάγιασε καὶ τὸ ἐπαύριον ἐσηκώθη καὶ κυττάξας εἰς τὸ κάτοπτρον ἐφώναξε, "Φεῦ! ἔχω τὸν 'μαῦρον θάνατον,' πάγω πλιά! τελειόνω! πάρε μου τὸν ἰατρόν!"

Δὲν ἦτον ὅμως τίποτε παρὰ ὁ καπνὸς τοῦ Λονδίνου.
Ὥστε βλέπετε κύριοι ὅτι ἐνδεχόμενον νὰ πλύνηται ὁ Γάλλος εἰς τὴν ἰδικήν του πατρίδα μίαν φορὰν εἰς μικροσκοπικὸν λεκανίδιον, χωρὶς σαπούνι, καὶ νὰ ἦνε καθαρώτερος ἀπὸ τὸν Ἄγγλον ὁ ὁποῖος λούεται καὶ πλύνεται τρὶς ἢ τετράκις τὴν ἡμέραν.
Ἐν τούτοις ἡ ὑπηρέτρια θὰ σᾶς φέρῃ εὐθὺς σαπούνι, νερὸν καὶ προσόψια.
Θέλετε νὰ παραγγείλητε τὸ δεῖπνόν σας κύριοι;
Ποίαν ὥραν συντρώγουν;

Εἰς τὰς ὀκτὼ ἀκριβῶς.
Τῶρα ποῦ ἔφυγε ἐκεῖνος ὁ μασκαρᾶς, ἐξαίρετος ἡ εὐκαιρία νὰ ἐξετάσωμεν τὰς κλίνας.
Φεῦ! γίνομαι κατ' ἀνάγκην ἐντυμολόγος!

Τί πιάνεις· λεπιδόπτερα; πεταλούδαις;
Τίποτε τόσον εὐχάριστον! ἀφανίπτερα καὶ ἡμίπτερα· ψύλλους καὶ κοριούς.
Δὲν πειράζει· θὰ τὰ εὕρητε ταῦτα τὰ ζωΰφια πολὺ καλλίτερα ἀνεπτυγμένα εἰς τὴν Ἑλλάδα.
Μή μου τὰ ἀναφέρετε.
Λοιπὸν ἂς καταβῶμεν εἰς τὸ δεῖπνον καὶ ἂς δειπνήσωμεν καλά, διότι θὰ χάσωμεν αἷμα ἀπόψε.
Πῶς ἐπεράσατε τὴν νύκτα;
Ἀρκετὰ καλὰ ἀναλόγως τῆς συντροφίας.
Τί συντροφία;
Ἰδοὺ παραδείγματος χάριν, πῶς σᾶς φαίνονται ταῦτα;
Ὦ θεέ μου! θὰ τὰ ἐφέρετε μαζύ σας.
Πολὺ πιθανόν· τοὐλάχιστον σᾶς ἀφήσαμεν ἱκανὰ πρὸς ἀνάμνησιν.

Ὦ τοῦτο εἶνε περιττόν, κύριοι. (Κατ' ἰδίαν) ἀλλόκοτοι ἄνθρωποι οἱ Ἄγγλοι, ἀλλὰ τρῶνε (τρώγουνε) καλὰ καὶ πληρώνουν καλά.
Τί εἴπατε;
Εἶπα ὅτι γνωρίζομεν πάντοτε τοὺς Ἄγγλους διὰ τῆς εὐφυΐας των καὶ τῆς ἐξαιρέτου γαλλικῆς προφορᾶς των.
But my friend is a Greek.
We admire the Greeks, too. They were the Frenchmen of antiquity.
But the Greeks of to-day?
They are the friends of the English.
Ἀκούω τὸ κουδοῦνι.

What are you catching? Lepidoptera? Butterflies?
Nothing so pleasant! Aphaniptera and hemiptera: fleas and bugs.
Never mind. You will find these insects much better developed in Greece.
Don't mention it.
Well, let us go down to supper, and get a good one, for we shall lose blood to-night.
How did you pass the night?
Pretty well, considering the company.
What company?
Look there, for example, what do you think of these?
Good heavens! You must have brought them with you.
Very likely. At all events, we have left you enough behind to remember us by.
Oh, that is superfluous. (*Aside*) Strange fellows, these English; but they eat well, and they pay well.
What did you say?
I said, We always know the English by their ready wit and their excellent French pronunciation.

Ἀλλὰ ὁ φίλος μου εἶνε Ἕλλην.
Θαυμάζομεν καὶ τοὺς Ἕλληνας· ἦσαν οἱ Γάλλοι τῆς ἀρχαιότητος.

Ἀλλὰ οἱ τωρινοί;
Αὐτοὶ εἶνε φίλοι τῶν Ἄγγλων.

I hear the bell.

Ἂς περιπατήσωμεν ταχύτερον. — Let's walk quicker.
Εἴμεθα ὅλο πλησίον. — We are quite near.
Ἰδοὺ πάλιν ἐξεκινήσαμεν. — Here we are, off again.
Ἐκοιμήθην φαίνεται· ποῦ εἴμεθα τώρα; — I have been asleep, it seems. Where are we now?
Εἰς τὸ Λούγδουνον. — At Lyons.
Πόσον καιρὸν ἔχομεν ἐδώ; — How much time have we here?
Ὅσον θέλομεν, διότι ἔχομεν τὸ δικαίωμα νὰ διακόψωμεν ἐδὼ τὴν πορείαν μας. — As much as we like; for we have the right of breaking our journey here.
Αὔτη ἡ ἀμαξοστοιχία ὅμως φεύγει πάλιν μετὰ εἴκοσι πέντε λεπτά. — This train, however, starts again in twenty-five minutes.
Ἂς φάγωμεν λοιπὸν καὶ ἂς ἐξακολουθήσωμεν τὴν πορείαν. — Let's dine, then, and continue our journey.
Βαρύνομαι τὰς ἀναβολάς. — I'm tired of delays.
I want to get on. — Θέλω νὰ προχωρήσω.
So do I. — Καὶ ἐγὼ ἐπίσης.
Ἰδοὺ ὁ προτελευταῖος σταθμός. — Here is the last station but one.

Ἔχομεν ἀκόμη μίαν γέφυραν νὰ περάσωμεν. — We've one more bridge to pass.
Ἐντὸς ὀλίγου θὰ ἤμεθα εἰς τὸ τέρμα τῆς ὁδοιπορίας μας. — We shall soon be at our journey's end.
Not so fast! We have four or five days' sail yet. — Ἀγάλια, ἀγάλια! ἔχομεν τεσσάρων πέντε ἡμερῶν πλοῦν ἀκόμη.
Oh, that's only rest after the railway. — Ὤ τοῦτο δὲν εἶνε παρὰ ἀνάπαυσις μετὰ τὸν σιδηρόδρομον.
I trust you may find it so. — Ἂς δώσῃ ὁ Θεὸς νὰ τὸ εὕρητε οὕτως.

It depends on the weather. — Ἐξαρτᾶται τοῦ καιροῦ.
But it's always fine in the Mediterranean. — Ἀλλὰ εἶνε πάντοτε εὐδία εἰς τὴν Μεσόγειον θάλασσαν.
Yes; except when it thunders, lightens, rains, blows, snows, or hails, it is very pleasant weather there (lit. the weather there is very pleasant). — Μάλιστα, ἐκτὸς ὅταν βροντᾷ, ἀστράπτει, βρέχει, φυσᾷ, χιονίζει ἢ χαλαζόνει εἶνε πολὺ εὐάρεστος ὁ καιρὸς ἐκεῖ.
Τί ὥραν ἀναχωρεῖ τὸ ἀτμόπλοιον αὔριον; — At what o'clock does the steamer start to-morrow?
At seven in the morning. — Εἰς τὰς ἑπτὰ τὸ πρωί.

Πόσον καιρὸν θὰ ἤμεθα καθ' ὁδόν;	How long shall we be on the passage?
Τέσσαρας ἢ πέντε ἡμέρας.	Four or five days.
Συμπεριλαμβάνεται ἡ τροφὴ εἰς τὴν πληρωμήν;	Is food included in the fare?
Μάλιστα κύριε, ὥστε, βλέπετε, ἔχομεν πάντα λόγον νὰ σπεύσωμεν.	Yes, sir; so you see we have every reason for despatch.
Ἐβαρύνθην τόσον νὰ περιπατῶ ἀπὸ τὴν πρῶραν εἰς τὴν πρύμνην, δεξιόθεν πρὸς τἀριστερὰ· ν' ἀκούω τὸν κρότον τῶν τροχῶν καὶ τῆς μηχανῆς, καὶ τὰς κραυγὰς τοῦ ναυκλήρου καὶ τῶν ναυτῶν, καὶ νὰ μὴ βλέπω οὐδὲν παρὰ οὐρανὸν καὶ θάλασσαν καὶ τὸν μέλανα καπνὸν τὸν ἐξεμούμενον ὑπὸ τῆς καπνοδόχης.	I am so tired of walking from stem to stern, from starboard to larboard (right to left), of hearing the noise of the wheels and the engines, and the cries of the pilot and the sailors, and of seeing nothing but sky and sea, and the black smoke vomited by the funnel.
Ἰδέτε πρόσω! Τί βλέπετε ἐκεῖ πέραν.	Look ahead! What do you see yonder (over there)?
Βλέπω ὡς ὑπόλευκόν τε νέφος.	I see, as it were, a whitish cloud.
Εἶνε ἡ ἀκτὴ τῆς Ἰταλίας καὶ εἰς δύο ὥρας θὰ φθάσωμεν εἰς τὸν λιμένα τῆς Νεαπόλεως.	That is the coast of Italy; and in two hours we shall reach the harbour of Naples.
Εἶνε Ἡφαίστειον ὄρος ἐκεῖνο;	Is that a volcano?
Μάλιστα εἶνε ὁ Βεσούβιος.	Yes; it is Vesuvius.
Θὰ δυνηθῶμεν νὰ ἐπισκεφθῶμεν τὰ ἀπομεινάρια τοῦ Ἡρακλείου καὶ τῶν Πομπείων;	Shall we be able to visit the remains of Herculaneum and Pompeii?
Ὄχι· διοτι ἔχομεν καραντίναν.	No; because we are in quarantine.
Διατί τοῦτο;	Why is that?
Διότι τὸ πλοῖον μας ἦτο εἰς τὴν Κωνσταντινούπολιν, ὅπου ἐπικρατεῖ ὁ λοιμός.	Because our ship has been at Constantinople, where the plague prevails.
Τί κρίμα!	What a pity!
Κρίμα τῷόντι! ἀλλὰ τί νὰ κάμωμεν;	Pity, indeed! but there's no help for it (lit. what are we to do?).
Θὰ ἴδωμεν κἆτι ἄλλο Ἡφαίστειον ὄρος κατὰ τὸν πλοῦν;	Shall we see any other volcano on our voyage?

Θὰ ἴδωμεν καὶ τὴν Αἴτναν μακρόθεν διαπλεύσαντες τὰ στενὰ τῆς Μεσσήνης.
: We shall see Etna from a distance, when we have passed the Straits of Messina.

The glass is falling; we shall have a storm.
: Τὸ βαρόμετρον καταβάζεται· θὰ λάβωμεν τρικυμίαν.

The wind has suddenly risen.
: Αἴφνης ἠγέρθη ὁ ἄνεμος.

The sky has become covered with clouds.
: Ὁ οὐρανὸς ἐκαλύφθη (ἐσκεπάσθη) ὑπὸ νεφῶν.

It has clouded over.
: Ἐσυννέφιασε.

The sea is rough.
: Ἡ θάλασσα εἶνε τεταραγμένη.

It is growing rough.
: Ταράσσεται.

I feel sea-sick.
: Ναυτιῶ, ζαλίζομαι.

I'm very bad (lit. I suffer dreadfully).
: Ὑποφέρω τρομερά.

Drink a drop of gin.
: Πίε ὀλίγην ζινέβραν.

I would rather lie down in my hammock; perhaps that will relieve me.
: Προτιμῶ νὰ πλαγιάσω εἰς τὴν ἀνεμοκούνιάν μου· ἴσως τοῦτο μὲ ἀνακουφίσῃ.

My head turns round.
: Ἡ κεφαλή μου περιστρέφεται.

Καλημέρα σας· πῶς εὑρίσκεσθε σήμερον;
: Good morning. How do you find yourself to-day?

Κάμποσον καλλίτερα.
: Somewhat better.

Τί ἀκρωτήριον βλέπομεν ἐκεῖ πέρα.
: What headland do we see out there?

Εἶνε ὁ Μαλέας.
: It is Malea.

Λοιπὸν περιπλέομεν τὴν ἀκτὴν τῆς Πελοποννήσου.
: Then we are sailing round the coast of the Morea.

Πότε θὰ φθάσωμεν εἰς τὸν Πειραιᾶ;
: When shall we reach the Piræus?

Αὔριον τὸ πρωΐ, ἐὰν ἔχομεν πρύμον τὸν ἄνεμον.
: To-morrow morning, if we have the wind at our backs.

Ὁ ἄνεμος εἶνε οὔριος.
: The wind is favourable.

Τί θὰ εἰπῇ ἡ σημαία ἡ ὁποία φαίνεται νὰ τινάσσηται ἐπὶ τοῦ ἐρήμου ἐκείνου βράχου;
: What is the meaning of that flag which seems to be brandished about on that desolate rock?

Κρατεῖται ἐν χειρὶ ἐρημίτου (ἀναχωρήτου), ὅστις τρέφεται ἐκ τῶν ἐλεημοσυνῶν τῶν περιηγητῶν.
: It is held in the hand of a hermit, who is supported by the alms of voyagers.

Ἰδοὺ τοῦ ἔβαλον καλάθι εἰς τὴν θάλασσαν τὸ ὁποῖον τὰ κύματα θὰ φέρουν εἰς τὸν αἰγιαλόν.
: Look, they have flung a basket into the sea, which the waves will carry to the shore.

Καλὴν ὄρεξιν, καλόγηρέ μου.	A good appetite to you, Mr. Monk.
Now he is waving his flag, as a sign of gratitude.	Τώρα τινάσσει τὴν σημαίαν του πρὸς ἔνδειξιν εὐγνωμοσύνης.
He gives us his blessing.	Μᾶς δίδει τὴν εὐχήν του.
Τώρα θὰ πλαγιάσω.	Now I shall go to bed.
Θὰ κοιμηθῶ καὶ ἐγώ.	I will go to sleep, too.
Wake up! We are getting close to the harbour.	Ξυπνᾶτε! κοντεύομεν εἰς τὸν λιμένα.
Will they search our trunks at the custom-house?	Θὰ ἐξετάσουν τὰ κιβώτιά μας εἰς τὸ τελωνεῖον;
Of course.	Φυσικῷ τῷ λόγῳ.
Will they ask to see our passports?	Θὰ ζητήσουν νὰ ἴδωσι τὰ διαβατήριά μας;
Not of Englishmen.	Ὄχι τῶν Ἄγγλων.
How do they distinguish Englishmen?	Πῶς διακρίνουν τοὺς Ἄγγλους;
By their ignorance of foreign languages, and by the airs they give themselves.	Διὰ τῆς ἀγνοίας τῶν ξένων γλωσσῶν, καὶ διὰ τῶν καμαρωμάτων των.
Fine advantages!	Καλὰ προτερήματα!
They will tumble all our things about.	Θὰ ἀνατρέψουν ὅλα τὰ πράγματά μας.
Here come the custom-house officers.	Ἰδοὺ ἔρχονται οἱ ὑπάλληλοι τοῦ τελωνείου.
Please to hand me your passports.	Εὐαρεστηθῆτε νὰ μοὶ ἐγχειρίσητε τὰ διαβατήριά σας.
There they are.	Ἰδοὺ αὐτά.
Where do you come from? Where are you going to?	Πόθεν ἔρχεσθε; ποῦ ὑπάγετε;
You ought to have got your passport signed at the Greek embassy.	Ἔπρεπε νὰ ἐπιθεωρηθῇ τὸ διαβατήριόν σας ὑπὸ τῆς Ἑλληνικῆς πρεσβείας.
I went there, but they put me off till the next day, and so I was compelled to leave without the signature.	Ὑπῆγα ἐκεῖ ἀλλὰ μὲ ἀνέβαλον εἰς τὴν ἐπαύριον ὥστε ἠναγκάσθην νὰ ἀναχωρήσω ἄνευ τῆς ἐπιθεωρήσεως.
There are so many formalities to go through, that a man of business has not always time to conform to them.	Εἶνε τόσοι τύποι πρὸς ἐκπλήρωσιν ὥστε ὁ ἔμπορος δὲν εὐκαιρεῖ πάντοτε νὰ συμμορφωθῇ μὲ αὐτούς.

Besides this, your passport is not in regular order; its date has expired a fortnight.

Πλὴν δὲ τούτου τὸ διαβατήριόν σας δὲν εἶνε ἐν καλῇ τάξει· παρῆλθεν ἡ προθεσμία του πρὸ δεκαπενθημερίας.

I will give you a provisional pass, and your proper passports will be returned to you at the police-office.

Θὰ σᾶς δώσω προσωρινὸν διαβατήριον, καὶ τὰ τακτικά σας διαβατήρια θὰ σᾶς ἐπιστραφῶσιν ἐν τῇ ἀστυνομίᾳ.

What red-tapeism!
Τί γραφειοκρατία!

*Ἔχετέ τι νὰ διαδηλώσητε;
Have you anything to declare?

*Ἔχω δύο τρία πράγματα ὑποκείμενα εἰς τελώνιον· θὰ τὰ εὕρητε ἐπάνω εἰς τὸ κιβώτιον.
I have two or three things liable to duty. You will find them at the top of my trunk.

Ὑπάγετε εἰς τὸ γραφεῖον, πληρώσατε εἰς τὸν πράκτορα καὶ λάβετε ἀπόδειξιν.
Go to the office, pay the receiver, and get a receipt.

Ὑμεῖς δὲ ἔχετε τίποτε νὰ διαδηλώσητε, κύριε;
Have you anything to declare, sir?

*Ἔχω σιγάρα.
I have cigars.

Ταῦτα δὲν εἶνε λαθρεμπόριον ἐδῶ, διότι εἶναι εὐθηνώτερα εἰς τὴν Ἑλλάδα ἢ παρὰ ὑμῖν.
These are not contraband here; for they are cheaper in Greece than with you.

Ἰδοὺ ὅμως τρίχαπτα τῶν Βρυξελλῶν.
But here is some Brussels lace.

Δολιεύεσθε τὰ εἰσοδήματα τοῦ κράτους.
You are defrauding the revenue of the State.

Τὸ καθῆκον μου μὲ ἀναγκάζει νὰ κατάσχω τοῦτο τὸ κιβώτιον.
My duty compels me to seize this box.

Ὁ νόμος εἶνε ῥητὸς καὶ πρέπει νὰ ἐπιβλέπωμεν εἰς τὴν ἐκτέλεσίν του.
The law is positive, and we must see to its execution.

Δύνασθε νὰ ἀναφερθῆτε εἰς τὸν διευθυντὴν τοῦ τελωνείου, ἂν θέλητε.
You may appeal to the director of customs, if you please.

Καὶ τοῦτο τί θὰ κοστίσῃ;
And what will this cost?

Περίπου τὴν ἀξίαν τοῦ τριχάπτου.
About the value of the lace.

Λοιπὸν προτιμῶ νὰ πληρώσω ἀμέσως.
Then I had sooner pay at once.

Ποῦ εἶνε ὁ σταθμὸς τοῦ σιδηροδρόμου;
Where is the railway-station?

Close at hand.
When does a train leave for Athens?
In a quarter of an hour.
What is the fare, third class, to Athens?
Forty-five lepta (fourpence).
And first class?
One drachm (eightpence-halfpenny).
I hear the bell.
Take your seat, please. We start directly.
Νὰ ἡ συρίκτρα.
Ἐξεκινήσαμεν.
Τί πλῆθος καμίνων!
Ἔχει, φαίνεται, ὁ Πειραιεὺς πολλὰ ἐργοστάσια.
What is its chief manufacture?
Silk, cloth, and cotton, I believe.

What trees are those?
Olives.
They are very like willows.
And what are those low plants we see growing among them?

Don't you know them? They are vines.
Will there be many grapes this year?
About as usual.
An average crop.
Ἰδοὺ ἐφθάσαμεν.
Ἐστάθημεν (ἐσταματήσαμεν).
Καὶ τὸ ὡρολόγι μου ἐπίσης.
Ἴσως δὲν τὸ ἐκουρδίσατε.

Δὲν δουλεύει.
Πηγαίνει καλὰ τὸ ἰδικόν σας;

Ἐδὼ πλησίον.
Πότε ἀναχωρεῖ ἁμαξοστοιχία διὰ τὴν πόλιν;
Εἰς ἓν τέταρτον τῆς ὥρας.
Τί εἶνε ἡ πληρωμὴ διὰ τὴν τρίτην τάξιν εἰς Ἀθήνας.
Σαράντα πέντε λεπτὰ (τετράπενον).
Καὶ διὰ τὴν πρώτην;
Μία δραχμή.

Ἀκούω τὸν κώδωνα (τὸ κουδοῦνι).
Ἀνάβητε, σᾶς παρακαλῶ· φεύγομεν ἀμέσως.
There's the whistle.
We are off.
What a number of chimneys!
The Piræus has a lot of factories, it seems.
Τί εἶνε ἡ κυριωτέρα του κατασκευή.
Μετάξι, ἐριοῦχον, καὶ βαμβάκι, πιστεύω.

Τί δένδρα (ποῖα δένδρα) εἶνε αὐτά;
Ἐλαῖαι.
Ὁμοιάζουν πολὺ τὰς ἰτέας.
Καὶ τί εἶνε ἐκεῖνα τὰ χαμηλὰ φυτὰ τὰ ὁποῖα βλέπομεν αὐξάνοντα ἀναμεταξύ των;

Δὲν τὰ γνωρίζετε; εἶνε ἄμπελοι.

Θὰ γείνουν πολλὰ σταφύλια ἐφέτος;

Κατὰ τὸ σύνηθες περίπου.
Μεσιανὸν θέρος.
Here we are.
We have stopped.
So has my watch.
Perhaps you haven't wound it up.
It does not go (serve).
Does yours go right?

Πηγαίνει ἐμπρός.	It is fast.
Εἶνε χαλασμένον.	It is out of order (spoilt).
Καθ' ἑκάστην ἡμέραν μένει ὀπίσω ἓν τέταρτον τῆς ὥρας.	It loses a quarter of an hour every day.
Ὁμοιάζει μὲ τὸ ὡρολόγι τοῦ Πλοιάρχου Σουπιᾶ.	It is like Captain Cuttle's watch.
Τοῦ ἰδικοῦ μου ὅμως τὸ μέγα ἐλατήριον ἐθραύσθη ὥστε δὲν δουλεύει διόλου.	But of mine the mainspring is broken, so that it does not go at all.
Νομίζω ὅτε ἡ ἅλυσις ἐκόπη.	I think the chain is snapped.
Θὰ δώσωμεν καὶ τὰ δύο (ἀμφότερα) νὰ διορθωθῶσιν ἅμα εὕρωμεν ξενοδοχεῖον.	We will get both of them put to rights as soon as we have found an inn.
Κάμητέ μοι τὴν χάριν νὰ μοῦ εἴπητε τὸ καλλίτερον ξενοδοχεῖον.	Do me the favour to tell me the best hotel.
Δύνασθε νὰ ὑπάγητε ἐν πάσῃ ἀσφαλείᾳ εἰς τὸ ξενοδοχεῖον τῆς Αἰγύπτου.	You may go with perfect safety to the Egyptian Hotel.
Καλὰ θὰ εἶσθε ἐκεῖ.	You will be comfortable there.
Εἰς ποίαν ὁδὸν εἶνε.	In what street is it?
Εἶνε εἰς τὴν πλατεῖαν τοῦ Πανεπιστημίου.	It is in University Square.
Ἂς πάρωμεν τὸ παντοφορεῖον.	Let us take the omnibus.
Κράξε τὸν ὁδηγόν.	Call to the conductor.
Στάσου ὁδηγέ!	Stop, conductor!
Ἡ ἅμαξα εἶνε γεμάτη.	The carriage (omnibus) is full.
Δὲν ἔχει τόπον.	There is no room.
Ἕνας τόπος μόνον εἶνε ἄδειος.	There is only one place free.
Πρέπει νὰ περιμένωμεν.	We must wait.
Ἰδοὺ ἄλλο παντοφορεῖον.	There's another omnibus.
Ἀλλὰ ὑπάγει πρὸς ἄλλην διεύθυνσιν.	But it is going another way (in another direction).
Ὁδηγέ ποῦ ὑπάγετε;	Where are you going, conductor?
Ὑπάγομεν πρὸς τὴν τράπεζαν.	We are going to the bank.
Ὑπάγετε πρὸς τὸ Πανεπιστήμιον;	Are you going to the University?
Ὅλο πλησίον.	Quite close.
Ἂς ἀναβῶμεν.	Let us get up.
Δὲν εἰμπορῶ νὰ καθήσω.	I can't sit down.
Λάβετε παρακαλῶ, κύριε, τὴν καλωσύνην νὰ τραβιχθῆτε παρέκει.	Have the goodness, sir, please, to move a little further on.

Καθήσατε εἰς ταύτην τὴν γωνίαν. Sit in this corner.
Ὀχούμεθα πολὺ ἀργά. We are driving very slowly.
Ἡ ὁδὸς εἶνε πλήρης ἁμαξῶν. The road is full of vehicles.
Ὅταν βιάζωμαι ποτὲ δὲν ὀχοῦμαι ἐπὶ παντοφορείου. When I am in a hurry, I never ride in an omnibus.
Ποῦ εἴμεθα τώρα; Where are we now?
Εἴμεθα εἰς τὴν ὁδὸν τοῦ Ἑρμοῦ. We are in Hermes Street.
Ὁδηγὲ ἄφες με νὰ ἔβγω (νὰ ἐκβῶ) εἰς ταύτην τὴν γωνίαν. Conductor, set me down (let me get out) at this corner.
Ἄφες με νὰ ἐξέλθω πρῶτος. Let me get out first.
Προσέξατε. Take care.
Βάρδα (guarda) ἐμπρός! (Driver's cry.) Look out in front!

Σταθῆτε παρακαλῶ. Stop, please.
Δότε μοι τὴν χεῖρά σας. Give me your hand.
Μὴ βιάζεσθε. Don't be in a hurry.
Καταλύομεν ἐδῶ. We put up here.
Ἂς ἐμβῶμεν. Τί χάνομεν παρὰ νὰ κακοπεράσωμεν μίαν νύκτα. Let us go in. We only risk passing a bad night.
Εἰμπορεῖ τις ἐδῶ νὰ δειπνήσῃ; Can we have supper here?
Μάλιστα, κύριε. Certainly, sir.
Ἔχετε κενὰ δωμάτια; Have you any spare rooms?
Εἰμποροῦμεν νὰ κοιμηθῶμεν ἐδῶ; Can we sleep here?
Μᾶς δέχεσθε νὰ κοιμηθῶμεν ἐδῶ τὴν νύκτα ταύτην; Will you take us in here (to sleep) for the night?
Δυνάμεθα νὰ καταλύσωμεν ἐδῶ αὐτὴν τὴν νύκτα; Can we put up here for the night?
Λάβετε τὴν καλοσύνην νὰ εἰσέλθητε εἰς τὸ καφενεῖον μίαν στιγμήν. Have the goodness to step into the coffee-room a moment.
Τόσοι ἄνθρωποι ἔφθασαν σήμερον ὥστε δὲν ἠξεύρω ἂν ἔχωμεν δύο δωμάτια διὰ ἐνοίκιον. So many people have arrived to-day, that I do not know whether we have two rooms to let.
Ὕπαγε νὰ ἴδῃς, ἀλλὰ γρήγορα. Go and see; but be quick.
Κύριοι, ἔχω μόνον ἓν δωμάτιον μὲ δύο κλίνας νὰ σᾶς προσφέρω. Gentlemen, I have only one room with two beds to offer you.
Δὲν μοὶ μέλει διὰ τὸ δωμάτιον· ἀρκεῖ μόνον ἡ κλίνη νὰ ἦνε καλή, τὰ σινδόνια στεγνὰ καὶ καθαρὰ καὶ νὰ κοιμᾶται τις ἀνενόχλητος. I don't care about the room, provided the bed is good, the sheets well-aired and clean, and that one can sleep undisturbed.
Θὰ τὸ ἀποφασίσωμεν. We will decide on this.

L

The counterpane is dirty.	Τὸ ἐφάπλωμα εἶναι λερόν.
We want bolsters.	Θέλομεν ὑποπροσκέφαλα.
I cannot sleep when my head is low.	Δὲν εἰμπορῶ νὰ κοιμηθῶ ὅταν ἡ κεφαλή μου κεῖται χαμηλά.
Take off this feather bed, or put it under the mattress.	Βγάλε (ἔκβαλε) τοῦτο τὸ πτυλόστρωμα ἢ βάλε το ὑπὸ τὸ ὑπόστρωμα.
Tell them to make us a good fire.	Εἰπέ νὰ μᾶς ἑτοιμάσουν καλὴν φωτιάν.
It is quite ready. It only wants lighting.	Ὅλο ἑτοίμη εἶνε· θέλει μόνον νὰ τὴν ἀνάψουν.
What a smoke! I am smothered.	Τί καπνός! πνίγομαι.
Let's go down to supper.	Ἂς καταβῶμεν νὰ δειπνήσωμεν.
Bring the bill of fare.	Φέρετε τὸν κατάλογον τῶν φαγητῶν.
Here it is. What soup will you take, gentlemen?	Ἰδού. Τί ῥοφήματα θέλετε κύριοι;
Lentil soup.	Σοῦπα φακιαῖς.
Pea soup.	Σοῦπα πιζέλλια.
Haricot soup.	Σοῦπα κουκιά.
Let us have three dozen oysters, and some red wine.	Δός μαι τρεῖς δωδεκάδας ὀστρέων καὶ λίγο κόκκινο κρασί (ὀλίγον ἐρυθρὸν οἶνον).
The tablecloth is not clean. Put on another.	Τὸ τραπεζομάνδυλον δὲν εἶνε καθαρόν· βάλε ἄλλο.
Have you anything else to give us?	Ἔχετε τίποτες ἄλλο νὰ μᾶς δώσητε.
Read the bill of fare, gentlemen.	Διαβάσατε τὸν κατάλογον, κύριοι.
Leg of mutton, duck pie, beef and cabbage, cold fowl, roast pigeon, and sweets.	Μηρίον προβάτου, πίτταν μὲ πάππιαις, δαμαλάκι μὲ λάχανα, πουλερικὰ κρύα, περιστέρια 'ς τὴν σούβλαν καὶ γλυκίσματα.
Have you any fish quite fresh?	Ἔχεις ὀψάρια πολὺ πρόσφατα;
Lobster, salmon, barbels, soles, octopus, and cuttlefish.	Ἀστακόν, σολομόν, μπαρμπούνια, γλώσσαις, 'χταπόδια (ὀκταπόδια), καὶ σουπιαῖς (σηπίας).
What! do they eat cuttlefish and octopus here?	Τί; τρῶνε (τρώγουνε) καὶ σουπιαῖς καὶ ὀκταπόδια ἐδῶ;
Yes, sir; many like them.	Μάλιστα, κύριε· τὰ ἀγαποῦνε πολλοί.
Why do you eat them?	Διατί τὰ τρώγετε;

Διατί τρώγουσιν οἱ Ἄγγλοι τὸ βιφτέκιον, καὶ οἱ Γάλλοι βατράχους, καὶ οἱ Χινέζοι φωλεάς;
Why do Englishmen eat beefsteak, and Frenchmen frogs, and Chinese birds'-nests?
Διότι τοὺς ἀρέσουν, ὑποθέτω.
Because they like them, I suppose.
Ἰδοὺ ὁ λόγος δι' ὅντινα τρώγομεν ταῖς σουπιαῖς (τὰς σηπίας).
That's the reason we eat cuttle-fish.
Ἀλλὰ διατί σᾶς ἀρέσουν;
But why do you like them?
Περὶ ὀρέξεως οὐδεὶς λόγος.
There's no accounting for tastes.
Ἀλλὰ εἶνε ἆρά γε ὑγιειναί;
But are they wholesome?
Μάλιστα, εἶνε θρεπτικώταται.
Yes; they are very nourishing.
Καὶ πρὸς τούτοις εἶνε συγχωρημέναι τὴν σαρακοστήν (τεσσαρακοστήν).
And besides, they are allowed in Lent.
Ἐγὼ δὲν καταλαμβάνω πῶς νὰ δυνηθῇ κάνεὶς νὰ φάγῃ ποτὲ τέτοια πράγματα.
I don't understand how any one can ever eat such things.
Τὰ ἐδοκιμάσετε ποτέ;
Have you ever tried them?
Ποτέ μου.
Never in my life.
Λοιπὸν τί ἀξίζει ἡ γνώμη σας;
Then what is your opinion worth?
Τίποτε· ἔχετε δίκαιον.
Nothing! You are right.
Ἂς τὰ δοκιμάσωμεν.
Let's try them.
Τὸ ποῖον;
Which?
Ἀμφότερα μαζύ.
Both together.
Καλά, ἀμέσως. Νά τα!
Very well; directly. There they are.

Ποῖον εἶνε τὸ ὀκταπόδιον καὶ ποῖον ἡ σουπιά;
Which is the octopus, and which the cuttlefish?
Τὸ πρὸς τἀριστερὰ εἶνε τὸ 'χταπόδι καὶ τὸ πρὸς τὰ δεξιὰ εἶνε ἡ σουπιά.
The one to the right is the octopus, and the one to the left is the cuttlefish.
Πῶς σᾶς ἀρέσουν;
How do you like them?
Νοστιμεύουν θάλασσαν.
They taste of the sea.
Πολὺ πιθανόν· ἐκεῖ καὶ εὑρίσκονται.
Very likely; that's where they are found.

Σᾶς ἀρέσουν τὰ σπανάκια;
Do you like spinach?
Τί λαχανικὰ ἀγαπᾶτε;
What vegetables will you have?
Πατάταις (γεώμηλα) καὶ λαχανοκράμβην.
Potatoes and cauliflower.

Φέρε μας σολομόν.
Bring us some salmon.
Δύς μας ὀλίγον κρασί (οἶνον).
Give us a little wine.
Τί εἶδος (τί λογῆς) οἴνου;
What sort of wine?

Malmsey [still common in Greece].	Τῆς Μονεμβασίας.
Thera (Santorini).	Τῆς Θήρας (Σαντορίνης).
Red [black].	Κόκκινο, μαῦρο.
White.	Ἄσπρο [probably for ἄσπλο = ἄσπιλο = spotless], λευκόν.
Πῶς τὸν προτιμᾶτε τὸν σολομόν;	How do you prefer the salmon?
Τηγανητὸν μὲ ξύδι καὶ λάδι (ὄξος καὶ ἔλαιον).	Fried with vinegar and oil.
Ἀγαπᾶτε καρύκευμα (σάλτσαν);	Do you like sauce.
Θέλετε νὰ ἑτοιμάσητε τὴν σαλάταν μόνοι σας;	Would you like to make the salad yourselves?
Μάλιστα· δός μοι τὸ ἅλας, τὸ πιπέρι, τὸ σινάπι (τὴν μουστάρδαν), τὸ ἔλαιον καὶ τὸ ὄξος.	Certainly. Give me the salt, the pepper, the mustard, the oil, and the vinegar.
Δός μοι ὀλίγον νέον ἄρτον (ψωμί)· οὗτος (τοῦτο) εἶνε πολὺ παλαιός (-όν).	Give me some new bread: this is very stale.
Πάρε αὐτὰ τὰ πινάκια καὶ δός μας μέσην βοὸς μὲ μανιτάρια.	Take away these plates, and bring us loin of beef with mushrooms.
Have you any game?	Ἔχετε κυνήγιον;
Not yet, sir. The shooting season has not begun.	Ἀκόμη κύριε· ἡ κυνηγετικὴ ἐποχὴ δὲν ἤρχισεν ἀκόμη.
What dessert will you have?	Τί ἐπιδόρπιον θέλετε;
We will have some cheese first, and afterwards some pears.	Τυρίον θέλομεν πρῶτον καὶ ἔπειτα ἀπίδια.
The bill, please.	Τὴν σημείωσιν (τὸν λογαριασμὸν), ἂν ἀγαπᾶτε.
Παιδίον! δύο καφέδες καὶ δύο ποτήρια κονιάκ.	Waiter, two cups of coffee, and two glasses of brandy.
Φέρε μας καὶ σιγάρα πούρα.[1]	Bring us some cigars, too.
Θέλετε κρέμα (ἀνθόγαλα).	Will you have cream?
Ὄχι· θὰ πάρω ἁπλῶς καφέν.	No; I will take coffee alone.
Waiter, give me the *Times*.	Ὑπηρέτα δός μοι τοὺς Καιρούς.
It is being read, sir.	Ἀναγινώσκεται, κύριε.
Well, then, the *Daily News*, or the *Illustrated London News*.	Καλὰ λοιπὸν· τὰ Ἡμερήσια Νέα, ἢ τὰ Εἰκονοφόρα Νέα τοῦ Λονδίνου.

---

[1] σιγάρο, σιγαράκι, is "a cigarette;" σιγάρο πούρο, i.e. puro (Italian), "a pure cigar," viz. tobacco without paper.

They say an insurrection has broken out in Crete.
A false report, perhaps.
So the rumour runs.
I read something of the kind in the *Standard*, but the Greek papers make no mention of it.

Let us go to the club; there we shall find all the papers.
Τί είνε τὰ ἀξιολογώτερα ἀξιοθέατα τῶν Ἀθηνῶν;
Τὰ ἀρχαῖα δηλαδή;
Μάλιστα· καὶ τὰ νεώτερα.
Αἱ κυριώτεραι ἀρχαιότητες εἶνε ὁ Παρθενὼν καὶ τὸ Θησεῖον (ἐκ τῆς ἐποχῆς τοῦ Περικλέους), τὸ Στάδιον, τὸ ῥυάκιον Ἰλισσός, αἱ στῆλαι τοῦ Ὀλυμπίου Διός, ἡ Πύλη τοῦ Ἀδριανοῦ, τὰ μνημεῖα τοῦ Λυσικράτους καὶ τοῦ Φιλοπάππου, τὰ θέατρα τοῦ Διονύσου καὶ τοῦ Ἡρώδου Ἀττικοῦ, τὸ Ἀσκληπεῖον, ὁ ναὸς τῆς Ἀπτέρου Νίκης, τὰ Προπύλαια, ἡ Πινακοθήκη, τὸ Ἐρεχθεῖον καὶ αἱ Καρυάτιδες, ὁ Ἄρειος πάγος, ἡ Πνύξ, τὰ λείψανα τῆς Βουλῆς, καὶ τῆς Ποικίλης Στοᾶς, ὁ Ναὸς τοῦ Αἰόλου ἢ τῶν Ἀνέμων, καὶ ἡ Πύλη τῆς Ἀγορᾶς.

Τὰ ἐπισημότερα νεώτερα οἰκοδομήματα εἶνε τὰ ἑξῆς·
Τὰ Ἀνάκτορα, ἡ Μητρόπολις, τὸ Ἐθνικὸν Πανεπιστήμιον, δύο ὀρφανοτροφεῖα, τὸ Νοσοκομεῖον, τὸ Πτωχοκομεῖον, ἡ Ἐθνικὴ Βιβλιοθήκη, τὸ Βρεφοκομεῖον, τὸ

Λέγεται ὅτι ἐπανάστασις ἐξερράγη εἰς τὴν Κρήτην.
Ψευδὴς φήμη ἴσως.
Ἔτσι λόγος τρέχει.
Ἀνέγνωσα τέτοιόν τι εἰς τὴν Σημαίαν ἀλλὰ αἱ Ἑλληνικαὶ ἐφημερίδες τίποτε δὲν ἀναφέρουν περὶ αὐτοῦ.
Ἂς πᾶμε 'ς τὴν Λέσχην· ἐκεῖ θὰ εὕρωμεν ὅλας τὰς ἐφημερίδας.
What are the principal sights of Athens?
Do you mean the ancient ones?
Yes; and the modern ones too.
The chief antiquities are the Partbenon and Theseum (of the age of Pericles), the Racecourse, the brook Ilissus, the Pillars of Jove, the Gate of Hadrian, the tombs of Lysicrates and Philopappus, the theatres of Dionysus and Herodes Atticus, the Temple of Æsculapius, the Temple of the Wingless Victory, the Propylæa (or Gateway), the Picture Gallery, the Erechtheum with the Caryatides, Mars' Hill, the Pnyx, the remains of the Council Chamber and of the Chequered Porch, the Temple of Æolus or of the Winds, and the Gate of the Market.
The most noteworthy modern public buildings are as follows:
The Palace, the Cathedral, the National University, two Orphanages, the Infirmary, the Almshouse, the National Library, the Infants' Asylum,

Πρότυπον Νηπταγωγεῖον τῆς Φιλεκπαιδευτικῆς Ἑταιρίας, τὸ Ἀρσάκειον ἢ Παρθεναγωγεῖον τῆς αὐτῆς, τὸ Ὀφθαλμοϊατρεῖον, τὸ Λύκειον, τὸ Ἀστεροσκοπεῖον, τὸ νομισματικὸν καὶ ἀρχαιολογικὸν Μουσεῖα, ἡ Ἀκαδημία, τὸ Πολυτεχνεῖον, καὶ τὸ Μέγαρον τῶν Ὀλυμπίων.

the Model Infant School of the Educational Society, the Arsaceum or High School for Girls of the same, the Eye Hospital, the Lyceum, the Observatory, the Numismatic and Archæological Museums, the Academy, the Polytechnic, and the Exhibition Hall.

PART III.

INTRODUCTION.

The Classified Vocabulary is intended both for easy reference on any topic, and also to be applied to the construction of original exercises founded thereon. Now that the student has worked through Parts I. and II., and has rung the changes on the dialogues so as to be thoroughly familiar with the ordinary usages of grammar, and with many phrases and idioms, he will find the greatest advantage in constructing sentences for himself under each heading of the classified vocabulary. The following is a sample :—

Τὰ προάστεια καὶ τὰ περίχωρα εἶνε μέρη τῆς πόλεως. Ὁ δρόμος διαβαίνει τὸ κέντρον τῆς πόλεως. Οἱ πεζοὶ ἵστανται εἰς τὴν διασταύρωσιν τῶν ὁδῶν. Ἡ δίοδος φέρει εἰς τὴν πλατεῖαν.

If the student is at a loss for a word, it is better to think of another expression than to cast about for the missing word. By the time he has worked through the vocabulary, and used his accumulated knowledge to illustrate each succeeding section, he will find himself in a position to express with certainty and ease almost anything he may desire to say.

CLASSIFIED VOCABULARY.

N.B.—vl. signifies "vernacular."

I.

Πόλις.   Town.

μέρη τῆς πόλεως· κοινότης·   *Parts of the town; community,*
                                              or municipality.
ἡ πόλις   The town, the city.
ἡ συνοικία· τὸ τμῆμα   The district; the ward.
τὸ κέντρον τῆς πόλεως   The centre of the town.
τὸ προάστειον   The suburb.
τὰ περίχωρα   The environs.
τὸ τεῖχος   The wall.
ἡ ὁδός, ὁ δρόμος   The way, the road.
ὁ δρομίσκος   The lane.
τὸ τέρμα (τὸ ἄκρον, τὸ τέλος) τῆς ὁδοῦ   The end of the road.
ἡ γωνία   The corner.
ἡ διασταύρωσις τῶν ὁδῶν (τὸ σταυ-   The crossing of the roads (cross-
  ροδρόμιον)   roads).
καθ' ὁδόν   On the way.
ὁδὸς διαβατική, ὁδὸς πολυάνθρωπος   A passable, frequented road.
τὸ γαιόστρωτον, ἡ στρωτὴ ὁδός   The pavement, paved way.
τὸ λιθόστρωτον   The paving-stones.
τὸ πεζοδρόμιον   The footway.
  οἱ πεζοὶ βαδίζουσιν ἐπὶ τοῦ πεζο-   Foot-passengers walk on the
    δρομίου   footway.
ἡ ἀγγελία, ἡ κοινοποίησις, ἡ γνω-   The message, communication, de-
  στοποίησις, ἡ εἰδοποίησις   claration, advertisement.
  τοιχοκολλῶ ἀγγελίαν   I post a notice.
ἡ δίοδος   The passage.
ἡ πλατεῖα   The square.
ἡ ἀγορά   The market-place.
ἡ γέφυρα   The bridge.
  κρεμαστὴ γέφυρα   A suspension bridge.
  διαβαίνω τὴν γέφυραν   I cross the bridge.
ὁ φωτισμός   The lighting.

το φωταέριον (τὸ ἀεριόφως) The gas.
ὁ φανός, τὸ φανάριον The lamp, light.
τὸ οἰκοδόμημα, ἡ οἰκοδομή The building, edifice.
δημοσία οἰκοδομή, δημόσιον οἰκοδόμημα A public building, public edifice.
τὰ ἀνάκτορα, vl. τὸ παλάτι The palace, royal residence.
τὸ μέγαρον The hall.
ἡ δημαρχία, τὸ δημαρχεῖον The mansion-house, mayor's residence.

ἡ κοινότης The community.
ὁ δήμαρχος The mayor.
αἱ ἀρχαί, ἡ ἐξουσία The authorities.
ἡ δημοσία διάταξις Public order.
ἡ ἐθνοφυλακή Constabulary.
τὸ ξενοδοχεῖον. The inn, hotel (eating-house).
τὸ πανδοχεῖον The hotel (on a large scale).
ὁ ξενοδόχος· ἡ ξενοδόχος The host, landlord; hostess, landlady.
ὁ ὑπηρέτης The waiter.
   οἰκία δι' ἐνοίκιον or πρὸς ἐνοικίασιν Houses to let, lodgings to let.
   ἐνοικιάζονται δωμάτια μετ' ἐπίπλων Rooms are let furnished.
   καταλύω εἰς ξενοδοχεῖον I put up at an inn.
   διαμένω, κατοικῶ εἰς ξενοδοχεῖον I stay or live at an hotel.
ἰδιωτικὴ οἰκία Private house.
τὸ καφενεῖον The coffee-house.
τὸ ζαχαροπλαστεῖον The confectioner's.
τὸ καπηλεῖον The shop (stall).
ὁ κάπηλος Small ware dealer, pedlar.
τὸ οἰνοπωλεῖον The wine-shop.
τὸ ξενοδοχεῖον The inn.
   γευματίζω εἰς ξενοδοχεῖον I dine at a restaurant.
τὸ χρηματιστήριον The exchange.
τὸ νομισματοκοπεῖον The mint.
τὸ νοσοκομεῖον The hospital.
τὸ θεραπευτήριον The convalescent home.
τὸ φρενοκομεῖον The asylum.
τὸ ὀρφανοτροφεῖον The orphanage.
ἡ ἐκκλησία The church.

τὸ κωδωνοστάσιον	The belfry.
ὁ κώδων, vl. ἡ καμπάνα	The bell.
ὁ κωδωνοκρούστης	The bell-ringer.
ὁ θόλος	The dome.
ἡ μητρόπολις	The cathedral.
ἡ βιβλιοθήκη	The library.
ὁ στρατών	The barracks.
τὸ ταχυδρομεῖον	The post, post-office.
τὸ γραμματοκιβώτιον	The letter-box.
τὸ γραμματόσημον	The stamp.
τὸ τηλεγραφεῖον	The telegraph-office.
τηλεγραφικὸν σύρμα	Telegraph-wire.
ἡ στήλη	Column, pillar.
ὁ ἀνδριάς	The statue.
ὁ περίπατος	The walk.
τὸ ἀναβρυτήριον	The fountain.
τὸ φρέαρ, τὸ πηγάδιον	The well.
τὸ ὑδραγωγεῖον	The aqueduct.
οἱ σωλῆνες	The pipes.
ἡ ὑδραντλία	The pump.
ὁ νυκτοφύλαξ	The night watchman.
ὁ περίπολος, οἱ περίπολοι	The patrol.

II.

Οἰκία.   House.

μέρη τῆς οἰκίας καὶ κατοικίας.	Parts of the house and home.
ἡ οἰκία· ὁ οἰκίσκος	The house, the cottage.
θέτω τὸν θεμέλιον λίθον	I lay the foundation stone.
οἰκοδομῶ, κτίζω οἰκίαν	I build, erect a house.
καταρρίπτω οἰκίαν	I pull down a house.
κατοικῶ ἔν τινι οἰκίᾳ	I live in a house.
κατοικῶ οἰκίαν τινά	I inhabit a house.
ποῦ κατοικεῖτε;	Where do you live?
ἡ καλύβη	The hut.
οἰκία λιθόκτιστος, πλινθόκτιστος, μαρμαρόκτιστος	A stone house, a brick house, a house of marble.
ξυλίνη οἰκία	A wooden house.
τὰ ἐρείπια	The ruins.
τεῖχος παλαιόν	An old wall.

ἡ οἰκία αὕτη ἀπειλεῖ κατάπτωσιν	This house threatens to fall down.
τὸ οἰκοδόμημα, ἡ οἰκοδομή	The building, the edifice.
ἡ στέγη	The roof.
τὸ ἔδαφος	The floor.
ὁ κέραμος, τὸ κεραμίδιον	The tiling, the tile.
στέγη ἐκ κεράμων, στέγη ἐκ ψευδαργύρου	A roof of tiles, a roof of zinc.
τὸ ἀνεμόμετρον	The weathercock.
τὸ ἀλεξικέραυνον	The lightning conductor.
ἡ ὀροφή	The ceiling.
ἡ ξυλική, ἡ ξυλεία	The woodwork, the laths.
αἱ δοκοί, τὰ δοκάρια	The beams, the planks.
ὁ τοῖχος	The wall.
ὁ στῦλος	The post, pillar.
ἡ θύρα· ἡ πύλη, vl. ἡ ἐξώπορτα	The door; the gate (outer door).
τὸ παράθυρον	The window.
τὸ μέτωπον	The front.
τὸ ἀέτωμα	The wing.
ὁ κώδων	The bell.
ὁ θυρωρός	The door-keeper, porter.
ἐξοχικὴ οἰκία	A country house.
ἡ ἔπαυλις	The villa.
ἡ κλῖμαξ, vl. ἡ σκάλα	The staircase, stairs.
αἱ βαθμίδες, vl. τὰ σκαλιά	Steps, stairs.
τὸ πάτωμα	The storey.
τὸ ἰσόγειον	The ground floor.
πρῶτον, δεύτερον, τρίτον πάτωμα	First, second, third storey (floor).
ἡ ἀποθήκη, ἡ ὀψοθήκη, vl. τὸ κελάρι	The cellar, storehouse.
ὁ θόλος	The dome.
ἡ αὐλή	The courtyard; yard, court.
ὁ ἐξώστης, vl. τὸ μπαλκόνι	The balcony.
ἡ κατοικία	Lodgings; residence.
ἡ κατοικία αὕτη σύγκειται ἐκ πολλῶν δωματίων	These lodgings consist of many apartments.
ἐνοικιάζω	I hire.
τὸ ἐνοίκιον	(Hired) lodgings.
ἡ προθεσμία	The term; notice.
ὁ ἐνοικιαστής	Hirer; lodger.
τὸ ἐνοικιαστήριον	The lodging-house.

ἡ προκαταβολή	The deposit.
ἡ προπληρωμή	Payment in advance.
ὁ οἰκοδεσπότης· ἡ οἰκοδέσποινα	The landlord, landlady; master, mistress, of the house.
ὁ προθάλαμος	The anteroom, vestibule.
τὸ δωμάτιον, ὁ θάλαμος, vl. ἡ κάμαρη	The chamber, room, apartment.
παρακείμενον, γειτονεῦον δωμάτιον	Adjacent, adjoining room.
ὁ γείτων· ἡ γειτόνισσα	The neighbour (male); ditto (female).
ἡ γειτονία	The neighbourhood.
δωμάτιον τοῦ ὕπνου	A bedroom.
τὸ ἑστιατήριον, vl. ἡ τραπεζαρία	The dining-room.
ἡ αἴθουσα	The parlour; drawing-room.
τὸ μαγειρεῖον	The kitchen.
ἡ οὐδός, τὸ κατώφλιον	The threshold.
οὐδέποτε θὰ πατήσω πλέον τὸ κατώφλιόν του	I will never cross his threshold again.
τὸ δάπεδον	The floor.
ἡ στέγη, τὸ σανίδωμα	The roof; the wainscot.
σανιδόνω	I board up, wainscot.
οἱ τοῖχοι	The walls.
ἡ θύρα	The door.
ἡ θύρα τρίζει	The door creaks.
τὰ φύλλα τῆς θύρας, αἱ δικλίδες	The folding doors.
ἡ θύρα δὲν κλείει	The door doesn't shut.
ὁ στροφεύς, ᾧ στρόφιγξ	The door-handle.
κλείσατε τὴν θύραν	Shut the door.
ἡμίκλειστος θύρα	A door ajar.
ἡ κλειδονία, vl. ἡ κλειδαμιά	The lock.
ὁ μοχλός	The bar.
ὁ σύρτης, ὁ μάνδαλος	The bolt.
τὸ κλειδίον	The key.
ἀνοίγω τὴν θύραν	I open the door.
βάλλω τὸν μάνδαλον, μανδαλόνω	I bolt.
ὁ τάπης	The carpet.
τὸ παράθυρον	The window.
τὸ παράθυρον βλέπει πρὸς τὴν αὐλήν, πρὸς τὸν δρόμον	The window looks into the yard, into the street.
προβαίνω εἰς τὸ παράθυρον	I go up to the window.

ἡ ὕαλος τοῦ παραθύρου, vl. τὸ τζάμι	The window-pane.
διπλοῦν παράθυρον	A double window.
τὸ παραθυρόφυλλον, vl. τὸ κανάτι	The window-sill.
αἱ κιγκλίδες, vl. τὰ κάγκελα	The banisters, balustrade.
τὸ παραπέτασμα	The curtain.
ἡ θερμάστρα	The fireplace, stove.
ἡ θέρμανσις	Heating.
ἡ κάμινος	The chimney.
ἡ καπνοδόχη, vl. ἡ καμινάδα	The chimney-pot.
ἡ πυράγρα, vl. ἡ μασιά	The tongs.
τὰ ξύλα	The fuel.
ὁ λιθάνθρακες, οἱ γαιάνθρακες	The coal.
οἱ ἄνθρακες, vl. τὰ κάρβουνα	Charcoal.
τὸ σάρωθρον, ἡ παρασύρα, vl. ἡ σκοῦπα	The broom.

III.

Ἔπιπλα. οἰκιακὰ σκεύη· ἱματισμός· φωτισμός.	FURNITURE. *Household implements; clothing; lighting.*
τὸ ἔπιπλον· τὰ ἔπιπλα, ἡ οἰκοσκευή	Furniture; articles of furniture.
ὁ ἐπιπλοπώλης	The upholsterer.
τὸ συρτάριον, τὸ ἑρμάριον	The drawer.
τὸ γραφεῖον	The office, study.
ἡ βιβλιοθήκη	The library.
ὁ κομμωτήρ	The chest of drawers.
τὸ χρηματοκιβώτιον	The safe.
τὸ τραπέζιον	The table.
τὸ κάθισμα, ἡ καθέκλα	The seat, the chair.
ὁ κλιντήρ, vl. ἡ πολυθρόνα	The armchair.
τὸ ὑποπόδιον, ὁ σκίμπους, τὸ σκαμνίον	The footstool, hassock.
τὸ θρανίον	The ottoman.
τὸ ἀνάκλιντρον, vl. ὁ καναπές	The sofa.
τὸ προσκέφαλον, vl. τὸ μαξιλάρι	The cushion.
τὸ κάτοπτρον, vl. ὁ καθρέπτης	The looking-glass.
κατοπτρίζομαι.	I look in the glass.
ἡ κλίνη, vl. τὸ κρεβάτι	The bed, the couch.
στρώνω τὸ κρεβάτι	I make the bed.

τὸ στρῶμα	The mattress.
στρῶμα ἐλαστικόν	Spring-mattress.
τὸ σινδόνιον	The sheet.
τὸ ἐφάπλωμα, vl. τὸ πάπλωμα	The coverlet, coverlid.
τὸ προσκεφάλαιον, τὸ προσκέφαλον	The pillow.
τὰ σινδόνια	The sheets.
ὁ νιπτήρ	The washing-stand.
ἡ λεκάνη, ὁ λουτήρ	The basin.
ὕδωρ ψυχρόν, χλιαρόν, θερμόν, βραστόν	Cold, lukewarm, warm, boiling water.
τὸ χειρόμακτρον, τὸ προσόψιον	The towel.
τὸ σαπώνιον, vl. τὸ σαπούνι	The soap.
ἡ ὀδοντόκονις	The tooth-powder.
ὁ ψυκτὴρ τῶν ὀδόντων, vl. ἡ βροῦτσα	The tooth-brush.
τὸ κτένιον· κτενίζομαι	The comb; I comb my hair.
τραπέζιον τῆς νυκτός	Night-stool.
τὰ ἐναύσματα, vl. τὰ σπίρτα	Matches, lights.
ὁ λαμπτήρ, ἡ λυχνία, ὁ λύχνος, vl. ἡ λάμπα	The lamp.
ἡ θρυαλλὶς, τὸ ἐλλύχνιον, vl. τὸ φυτύλι	The wick.
τὸ πετρέλαιον	Petroleum.
τὸ ἔλαιον	Oil.
ὁ λυχνοστάτης, τὸ κηροπήγιον, vl. τὸ καντιλιέρι or ὁ καντιλιέρης	The candlestick.
ὁ κηρός, vl. τὸ κερί· τὸ σπερματσέτον	The candle; the spermaceti candle.
τὸ φῶς	The light.
τὸ κανδήλιον	The taper.
ἀνάπτω φῶς	I make a light.
σβύνω	I put out, quench, extinguish.

IV.

Ἱματισμὸς τοῦ ἀνδρός.	MAN'S CLOTHING.
ἐνδύματα· κάλυμμα τῆς κεφαλῆς· ὑπόδεσις· ἀντικείμενα πρὸς χρῆσιν τοῦ ἀνδρός.	Clothes; covering for the head, for the feet; articles for the use of men.
ὁ ἱματισμός, ἡ ἐνδυμασία	Dressing, attire.
ἐνδύματα, φορέματα	Clothes, garments.

ἐνδύω, ἐκδύω	I dress, undress.
εἶνε ὡραῖα ἐνδεδυμένη	She is nicely dressed.
ὁ φράκος vl., ἡ βελάδα vl.	The dress-coat.
τὸ ἐπανωφόριον, τὸ παλτόν	The overcoat, paletot.
παραγγέλλω ἓν ἐπανωφόριον	I order an overcoat.
τὸ κολάρον vl., τὸ φωκῶλον vl.	The collar.
τὸ στῆθος	The chest, breast.
αἱ χειρίδες, vl. τὰ μανίκια	Gloves, mittens.
τὸ ὑπόρραμμα, vl. ἡ φόδρα, ἡ βάτα	The skirt.
τὸ θυλάκιον, vl. ἡ τσέπη	The pocket.
ὁ μανδύας	The cloak, mantle.
τὸ παλτόν	The paletot.
ὁ σουλτοῦκον vl.	The surtout.
ἡ διφθέρα, vl. ἡ γοῦνα	Fur; leather garment.
τὸ περιστήθιον, ἡ περιστηθίς, vl. τὸ γελέκον	The waistcoat.
τὸ ζιπόνι vl.	Under-petticoat.
τὸ κομβίον· ἡ κομβότρυπα	The button; the button-hole.
δύο σειραὶ κομβίων, vl. δυὸ σειραῖς κομβιά	Two rows of buttons.
κομβόνω· ξεκομβόνω vl.	I button; I unbutton.
αἱ περικνημίδες, vl. τὸ πανταλόνι	Trousers.
τὸ ἐσώβρακον	Drawers.
ὁ κοιτωνίτης, vl. ἡ ῥομπατεκάμερα	The dressing-room.
ἡ ὑπόδεσις	Boots and shoes.
τὸ ὑπόδημα	The boot.
τὸ ὑπόδημα, vl. τὸ παποῦτσι	The shoe.
ἡ ἐμβάς, vl. ἡ παντόφλα	The slipper.
παρήγγειλα ἓν ζεῦγος ὑποδημάτων	I ordered a pair of boots.
ὁ ὑποδηματοποιός, vl. ὁ παπουτσῆς	The shoemaker.
βάλλω τὸ ὑπόδημα	I put on the boot.
ἐκβάλλω τὰ ὑποδήματα	I take off my boots.
αὐτὰ τὰ ὑποδήματα μὲ πληγόνουν	These boots pinch me.
τὸ δέρμα	The leather.
τὸ πέδιλον, vl. ἡ σόλα	The sole.
τὸ ὑποπτέρνιον, ἡ πτέρνα, vl. τὸ τακοῦνι	The heel.

γυαλίζω or λουστράρω τὰ παπούτσια vl.	I black or polish the shoes.
ἡ μελαντηρία, τὸ λογχωτόν, vl. ἡ μπογιά	The blacking.
ἡ βούρτσα vl.	The brush.
αἱ πηλοβατίδες, vl. τὰ καλόσια	The galoshes.
ἡ κεφαλή	The head.
τὸ κάλυμμα τῆς κεφαλῆς	The covering of the head.
ὁ πῖλος, vl. τὸ καπέλον	The hat.
τὸ κασκέτον vl.	The cap.
κάτω τὸ καπέλον! vl.	Off with your hat.
μανδύλιον τοῦ λαιμοῦ	Neckerchief.
τὸ σάλιον vl.	The shawl.
τὸ χειρόκτιον	The glove.
τὸ ὡρολόγιον	The clock, watch.
ὁ κύλινδρος, ἡ ἄγκυρα	The cylinder; the escapement.
χρυσοῦν, ἀργυροῦν ὡρολόγιον	A gold, silver watch.
τὸ ὡρολόγιον μου ἐστάθη or ἐσταμάτησε	My watch has stopped.
πηγαίνει μίαν ὥραν ἐμπρός, ὀπίσω	It is an hour fast, slow.
χορδίζω (vl. κουρδίζω) τὸ ὡρολόγιον	I wind up my watch.
τὸ κλειδίον τοῦ ὡρολογίου	The watch-key.
τὸ ἐλατήριον ἔσπασε	The spring is broken.
ὁ δείκτης· ὁ ὡροδείκτης· ὁ λεπτοδείκτης	The hand; the hour-hand; the minute-hand.
ἡ ἅλυσις τοῦ ὡρολογίου	The watch-chain.
τὰ δίοπτρα, vl. τὰ ματογυάλια	The spectacles; glasses.
τὸ χαρτοφυλάκιον	The card-case.
τὸ σημειωματάριον	The note-book.
σημειόνω τι	I make a note of, note.
τὸ βαλάντιον, vl. τὸ πουγγί	The purse.
τὸ ῥαβδίον, vl. τὸ μπαστούνι	The cane, walking-stick.
ἡ καπνοσύριγξ, vl. ἡ πίπα	The tobacco-pipe; pipe.
καπνίζω	I smoke.
ὁ καπνός	Tobacco (*lit.* smoke).
τὸ σιγάρον	The cigar (cigarette).
ὁ ταμβάκος	The snuff.
ἡ ταμβακοθήκη, vl. ἡ ταμβακιέρα	The snuff-box.

V.

Ἱματισμὸς τῆς γυναικός.	WOMAN'S DRESS.
καλλωπισμός· χρυσαφικά· ἀσπρόρουχα (vl.)· ἐργόχειρα γυναικεῖα.	Ornaments; trinkets; linen; female work.
τὸ φόρεμα, vl. τὸ φουστάνι	The dress.
ἡ οὐρά	The train.
τὸ ἐσωφόριον, vl. μεσοφόρεμα	Under garment.
τὸ ἀτημέλητον	The negligé, morning dress.
τὸ στηθόδεσμον, vl. ὁ κορσές	Stays, corset.
τὸ σάλιον	The shawl.
τὸ μανδύλιον	The cloak.
ἡ ζώνη	The sash, girdle.
τὰ τρίχαπτα, vl. ἡ δαντέλλαις	Lace.
τὸ περίζωμι, vl. ἡ ποδιά	The apron.
ἡ σκούφια	The cap.
ὁ πέπλυς	The gown.
ἡ κόμη, τὰ μαλλιά	The hair.
αἱ πλεξίδες	The plaits.
ἡ χωρίστρα	The parting.
τὸ κτένιον· κτενίζομαι	The comb; I comb my hair.
τὰ ἀρώματα, vl. ἡ μυρωδιαῖς	The perfumes; scents.
ὁ μυρεψός	The perfumer.
τὰ χρυσαφικά, τὰ στολίδια	Trinkets, ornaments.
τὸ ψιμύθιον, vl. τὸ φυκιασίδι	Rouge.
τὸ βέλος	The hairpin.
τὰ ἐνώτια, vl. τὰ σκωλαρίκια	The earrings, eardrops.
τὸ μανδύλιον τοῦ λαιμοῦ	The neckerchief.
τὸ ψέλλιον, τὸ βραχιόλιον	The bracelet.
τὸ ἀνεμιστήριον, vl. ἡ βεντάλια	The fan.
τὸ ἀλεξήλιον, vl. τὸ παρασόλι	The parasol.
τὸ ἀλεξιβρόχιον, vl. ἡ ὀμπρέλλα	The umbrella.
ἀνοίγω τὸ ἀλεξήλιον	I put up my umbrella.
κλείω τὸ ἀλεξιβρόχιον or ἀλεξίβροχον	I put down, shut my umbrella.
τὰ ἀσπρόρουχα vl.	The linen; washing.
πλύνω	I wash.
ἡ πλύντρια, ἡ πλύστρα	The washerwoman.
τὸ ὑποχιτώνιον, τὸ ὑποκάμισον	The chemise, shirt.

λινοῦν ὑποκάμισον	A linen shirt.
βαμβάκινον or βαμβακερὸν ὑποκάμισον	A cotton, calico shirt.
τὰ κομβία	The buttons.
ἡ περικνημίς, vl. ἡ κάλτσα	The stockings.
τὰ τσουράπια vl.	The socks.
ὁ καλτσοδέτης vl.	The garter.
τὸ ῥινόμακτρον, τὸ μανδύλιον, τὸ μιξομάνδυλον.	The pocket-handkerchief.
αἱ γυναικεῖαι ἐργασίαι	Female employments.
τὰ ἐργόχειρα	"Work," handiwork.
ῥάπτω· ἡ ῥάπτρια	I sew; the sempstress.
τὸ ὕφασμα, τὸ πανίον	The stuff, the cloth.
ἡ ῥαφή	The seam.
τὸ νύγμα, ἡ βελονιά	The stitch.
τὸ ῥάψιμον	Sewing.
τραπέζιον τοῦ ῥαψίματος	Work-table.
ἡ μηχανὴ ῥαπτικῆς, ἡ ῥαπτομηχανή	The sewing-machine.
ἡ δακτυλήθρα	The thimble.
τὸ ψαλίδιον	The scissors.
ἡ βελόνη· ἡ καρφοβελόνη	The needle; the bodkin.
τὸ νῆμα, ἡ κλωστή	The thread.
τὸ πλεκτόν	Plaiting, knitting.
τὸ βελόνιον (τοῦ πλεξίματος)	Knitting-needle.
ἡ βελονοθήκη	The needle-case.
ἀναρράπτω, συρράπτω, vl. μπαλόνω	I mend, patch.
τὸ κέντημα, τὸ κεντητόν	Embroidery, embroidered work.
κεντῶ	I embroider.
τὸ δεῖγμα	The pattern.
κλώθω	I spin.

VI.

Ἀνθρώπινον σῶμα.	HUMAN BODY.
μέρη τοῦ σώματος· ἰδιότητες· θέσεις.	Parts of the body; qualities; attitudes.
ἡ κεφαλή	The head.
ἡ κόμη· ἡ θρίξ	The hair; locks.
μέλαινα κόμη, vl. μαῦρα μαλλιά	Black hair, black tresses.
κόμη καστανόχρους, vl. καστανὰ μαλλιά	Auburn hair.

ξανθός· πολιός, πολιόθριξ	Yellow-haired, blond; grey-haired.
κόμη λευκή, vl. ἄσπρα μαλλιά	White hair.
κουρεύομαι	I have my hair cut.
ἡ κουρά	Hair-cutting.
ἡ φενάκη, vl. ἡ περούκα	The wig.
ἡ κορυφὴ τῆς κεφαλῆς	The top of the head.
τὸ κρανίον	The skull.
ὁ ἐγκέφαλος, ὁ μυελός	The brain.
ἄνθρωπος χωρὶς μυαλά vl.	A brainless idiot.
τὸ πρόσωπον· ἡ ὄψις	The face; the countenance.
ἔχω ὄψιν	I have the appearance, look as if.
τὸ μέτωπον	The forehead.
μέτωπον ὑψηλόν	A high forehead.
ἔχει ῥυτίδας ἐπὶ τοῦ μετώπου	He has wrinkles in his forehead.
ὁ ὀφθαλμός, vl. τὸ μάτι	The eye.
τὸ ὄμμα, τὸ βλέμμα	The glance, the look.
προσηλώνω τὸ βλέμμα μου ἐπί τινος	I fix my gaze on something.
ἀποστρέφω τοὺς ὀφθαλμούς	I turn away my eyes.
βλέμμα ὀξύ	A sharp, quick eye.
μάρτυς αὐτόπτης	An eye-witness.
ὁ βολβός, ὁ ὀφθαλμός	The apple of the eye.
ἡ κόρη τοῦ ὀφθαλμοῦ	The pupil of the eye.
αἱ ὀφρύες	The eyebrows.
τὰ βλέφαρα	The eyelids.
αἱ βλεφαρίδες	The eyelashes.
ἡ ῥίς	The nose.
ὁμιλεῖ or λαλεῖ διὰ τῆς ῥινός	He speaks through the nose.
ἄγει καὶ φέρει διὰ τῆς ῥινός	He leads by the nose.
ἡ παρειά, vl. τὸ μάγουλον	The cheek; the jowl.
τὸ οὖς, τὰ ὦτα, vl. τὰ αὐτία	The ear, the ears.
ὁ λοβός, τὸ ἐξωτερικὸν οὖς	The lobe, outer ear.
τὸ τύμπανον	The drum of the ear.
τὸ στόμα	The mouth.
τὸ χεῖλος	The lip.
χονδρά, λεπτὰ χείλη	Coarse, thin lips.
ἡ γλῶσσα	The tongue.
τὸ ἄκρον τῆς γλώσσης	The tip of the tongue.

τρέχει εἰς τὴν γλῶσσαν μου	It's on my tongue (of a word).
δάκνω (vl. δαγκάνω) τὴν γλῶσσάν μου	I bite my tongue.
ὁ οὐρανίσκος	The roof of the mouth.
ἡ κιονίς, ὁ γαργαρεών	The uvula.
ὁ φάρυγξ	The gullet.
ἡ σιαγών	The jaw.
μασῶ, μασᾷ	I chew, he chews.
ὁ ὀδούς· οἱ ὀδόντες, τὰ ὀδόντια	The tooth; the teeth.
τὸ οὖλον, τὰ οὖλα	The gum, the gums.
δὲν ἀνοίγει τὸ στόμα του	He does not open his mouth.
ὁ πώγων	The chin.
τὸ γένειον· ἡ γενειάς	The beard; whiskers.
γενειάτης· ἀγένειος	Bearded; beardless.
ὁ μύσταξ, vl. τὸ μουστάκι	The moustache.
ξυρίζομαι	I shave (myself).
ὁ λαιμός	The throat.
ὁ τράχηλος, ὁ αὐχήν	The neck.
ὁ σφόνδυλος	The backbone, vertebra.
ὁ λάρυγξ	The windpipe.
καγχάζω	I hiccup.
ὁ ὦμος, vl. ὁ νῶμος	The shoulder.
ἡ μασχάλη	The armpit.
ὁ βραχίων· ἡ ἀγκάλη	The arm; the embrace.
ἐναγκαλίζομαι, περιπτύσσομαι	I embrace, put my arms round.
ἀσπάζομαι, φιλῶ	I greet, I kiss.
προσφέρω τὸν βραχίονά μου	I offer my arm.
ὁ πῆχυς· ὁ ἀγκών	The forearm; the elbow.
ἡ χείρ (δεξιά, ἀριστερά)	The hand (right, left).
ἔρχομαι εἰς χεῖρας	I come within arms' length, engage, come to blows.
σφίγγω τὴν χεῖρα	I squeeze, press the hand.
τὸ δάκτυλον, ὁ δάκτυλος	The finger.
τὸ ἄκρον τοῦ δακτύλου	The tip of the finger.
δακτυλοδεικτῶ τινα	I point at some one with the finger.
ὁ ἀντίχειρ, ὁ δάκτυλος	The thumb.
ὁ λιχανός, ὁ δείκτης	The fore-finger.
ὁ μέσος	The middle finger.
ὁ παράμεσος	The fourth finger.

ὁ μικρός	The little finger.
ὁ ὄνυξ, τὸ ὀνύχιον	The nail.
ἡ παρωνυχίς	The whitlow.
ἡ πυγμή, ὁ γρόνθος	The fist.
ἡ γρονθιά	The blow with the fist.
ἡ σπιθαμή	The span.
τὰ νῶτα	The back.
στρέφω τὰ νῶτα πρός τινα	I turn my back to any one.
ἡ σφονδυλικὴ στήλη, τὸ ῥαχοκόκκαλον	The vertebral column.
ἡ ὀσφύς	The loin.
ἡ πλευρά	The rib.
τὸ πλευρόν	The side.
τὸ στῆθος	The chest.
ὁ μαστός, vl. τὸ βυζί	The breast.
ὁ κόλπος	The bosom, lap.
ἡ γαστήρ, ἡ κοιλία	The belly.
τὸ ὑπογάστριον	The abdomen.
ἡ κνήμη· τὸ σκέλος	The shank; the leg.
τὸ γόνυ, vl. τὸ γόνατον	The knee.
γονυκλινής	On bended knees.
γονατίζω	I fall on my knees, kneel.
πίπτω εἰς τοὺς πόδας τινός	I fall at any one's feet.
ἡ γαστροκνημία, ἡ κνήμη	The thigh.
τὸ σφυρόν, ὁ ἀστράγαλος	The ankle.
ὁ πούς, vl. τὸ ποδάρι	The foot.
τὸ πέλμα, τὸ πέδιλον	The sole.
οἱ δάκτυλοι, τὰ δάκτυλα	The toes.
βαδίζω ἀκροποδητί	I go on tip-toe.
ἡ πτέρνα	The heel.
τὸ μέλος· τὸ δέρμα	The limb; the skin.
ἡ ἁρμογή· τὸ ἄρθρον, ὁ κόνδυλος	The joint.
τὸ ὀστοῦν, τὸ κόκκαλον· ὀστέϊνος	The bone; bone, of bone.
ὁ μυελός	The marrow.
τὸ κρέας	The flesh.
τὸ νεῦρον· νευρικός· νευρώδης	The nerve; nervous.
ἡ ἴς, αἱ ἴνες	The sinew, sinews.
ὁ μῦς, οἱ μυῶνες	The muscle, the muscles.
ἡ ἰσχὺς τῶν μυώνων	Strength of muscle.
τὸ αἷμα· αἱματηρός, αἱμοσταγής	The blood; bloody, bleeding.

αἱμοβόρος, αἱμοχαρής — Bloodthirsty, sanguinary.
ἡ φλέψ· ἡ ἀρτηρία — The vein; the artery.
ὁ σφυγμός — The pulse.
ἡ καρδία· ἐγκάρδιος — The heart; hearty.
  ἡ καρδία πάλλει — The heart beats.
οἱ παλμοὶ τῆς καρδίας — The throbbings of the heart.
ὁ πνεύμων· οἱ πνεύμονες — The lung; the lungs.
ἡ ἀναπνοή, τὸ ἆσθμα — Inspiration, breathing.
  ἀσθμαίνων — Panting.
  ἀναπνέω — I breathe.
ἡ χάσμη, τὸ χάσμημα — The gape, yawn.
  χασμῶμαι — I gape, I yawn.
ὁ στόμαχος — The stomach.
χωνεύω· ἡ πέψις, ἡ χώνευσις — I digest; digestion.
τὰ ἔντερα, τὰ ἐντόσθια — The bowels, the entrails.
τὸ ἧπαρ· ἡ σπλήν — The liver; the spleen.
ἡ χολη — The gall, bile.
τὸ σίαλον· τὸ φλέγμα — The spittle; phlegm.
τὸ ἀπόχρεμμα, τὸ πτύσμα· πτύω — Expectoration; I spit.
ὁ ἱδρώς· ἱδρόνω — Sweat; I sweat.
ἡ ἐξάτμησις· ἡ διαπνοή, ἡ ἵδρωσις — Transpiration, sweating.
αἱ πόροι· πορώδης — The pores; porous.
ὁ πταρμός· πταρνίζομαι — Sneezing; I sneeze.
τὸ δάκρυον· δακρύων — The tear; weeping.
  κλαίω· χύνω δάκρυα — I cry; I shed tears.
  μετὰ δακρύων εἰς τοὺς ὀφθαλμούς — With tears in his eyes.
ἡ χροιά, τὸ χρῶμα — The colour, complexion.
ἡ ὄψις — The appearance, look.
  ἔχει ὄψιν καλήν — He looks well.
  ἔχει ὄψιν ἠθοποιοῦ — He has the look of an actor (a theatrical air).

ἡ ὠχρότης· ὠχρός — Pallor; pale.
ἡ εὐσωματία, ἡ πολυσαρκία — Stoutness, fatness.
ἡ ἰσχνότης· ἰσχνός — Leanness; lean.
εὐμήκης, ἰσχνός — Lank, thin.
εὐμεγέθης — Large of stature.
ἡ ὡραιότης, τὸ κάλλος· ὡραῖος, εὐειδής, εὔμορφος· καθωραΐζω — Beauty, loveliness; fair, beautiful, lovely; I beautify.
ἡ κομψότης· κομψός· λεπτός — Prettiness; pretty; delicate.
ἡ ἀσχημία· δυσειδής, ἄσχημος — Ugliness; misshapen, ugly.

ἡ δυσμορφία· δύσμορφος	Deformity; deformed.
ἡ ἐπιτηδειότης· ἐπιτήδειος	Cleverness; clever.
ἡ δεξιότης· δεξιός	Dexterity; dexterous.
ἡ εὐκινησία· εὐκίνητος	Nimbleness; nimble.
ἡ βαρύτης· βαρύς	Heaviness; heavy, clumsy.
ἡ ἰσχύς, ἡ ῥώμη· ῥωμαλέος	Strength, vigour; vigorous.
ἡ ἀδυναμία, ἀδύνατος· ἐξασθενῶ	Feebleness; feeble; I grow feeble.
ὁ κόπος, ὁ κάματος	Trouble; toil.
κατάπονος, κατάκοπος, κουρασμένος	Fatigued, toilworn, weary.
καταπονῶ, κουράζω	I wear out, weary.
ὁ ὕπνος· ὑπναλέος	Sleep; sleepy.
νυστάζω	I am sleepy.
κοιμῶμαι· ἀποκοιμῶμαι	I sleep; fall asleep.
ῥογχαλίζω· ὁ ῥογχαλισμός	I snore; snoring.
ἀγρυπνῶ· ἡ ἀγρυπνία	I watch, lie awake; wakefulness.
ἐξυπνῶ, ἡ ἔγερσις	I awake; awaking, rising.
ἀφυπνίζω, ἐξυπνίζω, ἐξυπνῶ	I waken, wake up.
ἡ μιμική, ἡ παντομιμία	Mimicry, pantomime.
ὁ παντόμιμος, ὁ μῖμος	The mimic, pantomimist.
ὁ μορφασμός	The (making a) face.
μορφάζομαι	I make a face.
ἡ στάσις	The posture.
τὸ βάδισμα	Walking, gait.
ὑπάγω, πηγαίνω· τρέχω	I go; I run.
τὸ βῆμα· βαδίζω, βηματίζω	The step; I walk, step.
ἡ θέσις	The position.
ἴσταμαι, στέκω· ὄρθιος	I stand; upright.
κάθημαι· καθήμενος	I sit; sitting.
καθίζω	I sit down.
λάβετε θέσιν, καθήσατε	Take a seat, sit down.
κεῖμαι, vl. κοίτομαι· κείμενος	I lie; lying.
κατακλίνομαι	I recline.

VII.

Ὑγίεια or ὑγεῖα.	HEALTH.
ἀσθένειαι· φάρμακα· σωματικὰ ἐλαττώματα.	*Diseases; medicines; bodily defects.*
ἡ ὑγίεια, ὑγεία· ὑγιής	Health; healthy.
ὑγιεινός· βλαβερός	Wholesome; injurious.

πῶς ἔχετε; πῶς ἔχει ἡ ὑγίεια σας; πῶς εὑρίσκεσθε;	How are you? How is your health? How do you find yourself?
εὐχαριστῶ, πολὺ καλά	Thank you, very well.
ὅλη ἡ οἰκογένειά μου εἶνε ὑγιής	All my family are well.
ἡ ἀδιαθεσία, ἡ κακοδιαθεσία	Indisposition.
εἶμαι ἀδιάθετος, κακοδιάθετος	I am out of sorts, poorly.
δὲν εἶμαι τόσῳ καλά	I am not so very well.
ἡ ἀσθένεια· ἀσθενής, ἄρρωστος	Illness; ill, unwell.
ὁ ἀσθενής	The patient.
φιλάσθενος· καχεκτικός	Weakly, ailing, delicate.
ἀσθενῶ	I am ill.
ἡ κεφαλαλγία, ὁ πονοκέφαλος, ὁ κεφαλόπονος	Headache, pain in the head.
ἡ ὀδονταλγία, ὁ ὀδοντόπονος, ὁ πονόδοντος	Toothache.
ἡ δυσπεψία, ἡ ἀπεψία	Indigestion, bad digestion.
δύσπεπτος	Indigestible, subject to indigestion.
πάσχω δυσπεψίαν	I suffer from indigestion.
ἔχω στομαχόπονον	I have a stomach-ache.
τὸ κρυολόγημα	The cold.
ἐκρυολόγησα, ἐκρύωσα	I have caught cold, taken cold.
ὁ βήξ· βήχω	The cough; I cough.
ἡ συνάγχη· ὁ βράγχος	The cold; hoarseness.
ὁ ῥευματισμός	Rheumatism.
τὸ πρῆσμα, τὸ πρήξιμον	A swelling, swelling.
πρήσκομαι	I swell.
ὁ κατάρρους· αἱ αἱμορροΐδες	The cold in the head; piles.
ὁ ἔμετος, ὁ ἐμετός	Sickness, vomiting.
ἐξεμῶ, vl. ξερνῶ	I am sick, vomit.
οἱ σπασμοί· σπασμωδικός	Spasms; spasmodic.
ἡ ἐπιληψία	Epilepsy, falling sickness.
ἡ ἀποπληξία	Apoplexy.
ὑπὸ ἀποπληξίας προσβάλλομαι	I am stricken with apoplexy.
ἡ παράλυσις, ἡ παραπληξία· παράλυτος	Paralysis, palsy; paralytic.
ὁ πυρετός· πυρετώδης	Fever; feverish.
προσβολὴ πυρετοῦ	An attack of fever.
ἡ ἐρυθρῖτις, vl. ἡ ἵλερη	Scarlet fever, scarlatina.

τὸ ἐμβόλιον· ἐμβολιάζω	Lymph; I inoculate.
ὁ ἐμβολιασμός	Vaccination, inoculation.
ἡ ποδάγρα· ἡ ἀρθρῖτις	Gout; inflammation of the joints.
ἡ φθίσις· φθισικός	Consumption; consumptive.
τὸ ἆσθμα	Asthma.
ἡ φλόγωσις	Inflammation.
ἡ περιπνευμονία	Inflammation of the lungs.
ἡ δυσεντερία	Dysentery.
τὸ μίασμα· ἀσθένεια κολλητική	Miasma; contagious disease.
ἡ ἐπιδημία· ἐπιδημικός	The epidemic; epidemic.
ὁ λοιμός	The plague, pestilence.
ἡ χολέρα· χολερικός	Cholera; liable or leading to cholera.
ἡ ζάλη· ζαλίζομαι	Dizziness; giddiness; I am dizzy, giddy.
ἡ ὑπνοβασία· ὁ ὑπνοβάτης	Somnambulism; the somnambulist.
ἡ ἀναισθησία, ἡ νάρκη· ἀναίσθητος	Insensibility, torpor; insensible.
ὁ πνιγαλίων, ὁ ἐφιάλτης	Oppression, nightmare.
ἡ ληθαργία	Lethargy.
ἡ αἱμοπτυσία· ἡ αἱμορραγία	Blood-spitting; bleeding.
ἡ κυκλοφορία τοῦ αἵματος	The circulation of the blood.
ἡ αἱμόρροια τῆς ῥινός	Bleeding at the nose.
τὸ ἐρυσίπελας, τὸ ἀνεμοπύρωμα	Erysipelas.
τὸ χείμετλον, ἡ χιονίστρα	Chilblains.
ἡ κνῆσις, τὸ ξύσιμον	Itching, the itch.
ἡ ἐξάρθρωσις	Dislocation.
ἡ τομή, τὸ κόψιμον	Cutting, smarting, sharp pain in the bowels.
κόπτομαι	I smart, have a pain in the bowels.
ἡ γάγγραινα	Gangrene.
ἡ πληγή· ἡ οὐλή	The wound; the scar, scab.
ἡ πτῶσις· πίπτω	The fall; I fall.
ὁ χειροῦργος	The surgeon.
ὁ ἰατρός	The doctor.
ἔχει πελατείαν πολυάριθμον	He has a large practice.
ὁ ὀδοντοϊατρός· ὀφθαλμιατρός	The dentist; eye-doctor.
ἡ ὀφθαλμία	Bad eyes, ophthalmia.
ὁ φαρμακοποιός	The druggist.
τὸ φαρμακεῖον	The druggist's shop.

ἡ συνταγή	The prescription.
τὸ φάρμακον· ἡ δόσις	The medicine ; the dose.
τὸ προφυλακτικὸν μέσον	The measure of precaution.
τὸ ἐνδυναμωτικόν	The tonic.
τὸ καταπότιον· ἡ κόνις	The pill ; the powder.
ἡ φλεβοτομία· φλεβοτομῶ	Bleeding ; I bleed (transitive).
ἡ δίαιτα· ἡ μεταχείρισις	The diet ; the treatment.
περιποιοῦμαι ἀσθενῆ	I treat a patient.
νοσηλεύω, νοσοκομῶ	I nurse, tend the sick.
ἐπισκέπτομαι ἀσθενῆ	I visit a patient.
αἰσθάνομαι τὸν σφυγμόν	I feel the pulse.
ἔχετε ὄρεξιν ;	Have you any appetite ?
θὰ τηρήσητε δίαιταν	You will take care what you eat (observe diet).
ὁ πόνος· ἀλγεινός	The pain ; painful.
ἡ ἀνάρρωσις· ἀναλαμβάνω	Recovery ; I recover.
ἡ θεραπεία· θεραπεύω	Cure, curing ; I cure, heal.
ὁ βίος, ἡ ζωή· ζῶ· ζῶν	The life, ditto (vital principle) ; I live ; living.
ζωηρός· ἡ ζωηρότης	Lively ; liveliness, animation, vivacity.
ὁ θάνατος· ἀποθνήσκω· νεκρός	Death ; I die ; dead.
ἡ ἀγωνία, ἡ ψυχομαχία	Death struggle, last struggle.
θνητός· ἡ θνητότης	Mortal ; mortality.
ἀθάνατος· ἡ ἀθανασία	Immortal ; immortality.
ὁ μακαρίτης πατήρ του	His late father (lit. blessed).
ἡ μακαρῖτις βασίλισσα	The late queen.
τὰ σωματικὰ ἐλαττώματα.	Bodily defects.
τυφλός· ἡ τυφλότης, vl. τύφλα	Blind ; blindness.
τυφλὸς ἐκ γενετῆς	Blind from birth.
μονόφθαλμος· παραβλώψ, vl. ἀλήθωρος	One-eyed ; wall-eyed, with a cast in the eye.
ὁ στραβισμός· στραβίζω	Squinting ; I squint.
μύωψ· ἡ μυωπία	Short-sighted ; short-sightedness.
κωφός· ἡ κωφότης	Deaf ; deafness.
ἄλαλος, ἄφωνος, vl. μουγγός	Dumb.
κωφάλαλος	Deaf and dumb.
ψελλός· ψελλίζω	Stammering ; I stammer.
φαλακρός· ἡ φαλάκρα	Bald ; baldness.
χωλός· χωλαίνω· ἡ χωλότης	Lame ; I am lame ; lameness.

ἀνάπηρος· κυφός, κυρτός, vl. καμ-   Maimed; bent, hump-backed.
πούρης
ἀριστερός   Left-handed.
ὁ νάννος· ὁ γίγας   The dwarf; the giant.
τὸ τέρας· τερατώδης   The monster; monstrous.

VIII.

Ψυχή. — SOUL.
αἰσθήσεις· ἐνέργειαι τῆς ψυχῆς· γλῶσσα. — Senses; activities of the mind; language.

ἡ ψυχή — The soul.
αἱ πέντε αἰσθήσεις — The five senses.
ἡ ὅρασις· βλέπω — Sight; I see.
παρατηρῶ, vl. κυττάζω — I observe, look at.
ὁρατός· ἀόρατος — Visible; invisible.
εἶμαι μύωψ. — I am short-sighted.
μύωψ, ἀμβλὺς τὴν ὄψιν — Short-sighted, dim-sighted.
  γνωρίζω αὐτὸν ἐξ ὄψεως — I know him by sight.
ἡ ἀκοή· ἀκούω· ἀνήκουστος — Hearing; I hear; unheard of.
ἀκροάζομαι — I listen.
  ἀκούσατέ με — Hear me.
ἡ ὄσφρησις· ὀσφραίνομαι, μυρί-
ζομαι — Smell; I smell, I scent.
  ὀσφράνθητε or μυρίσθητε αὐτὸ
τὸ ἄνθος — Smell this flower.
  ἔχει ἀποφοράν — It has an odour.
  εὐωδιάζει· βρωμεῖ — It smells nice; it stinks.
ἡ ἁφή· ἅπτομαι, αἰσθάνομαι — Touch; I touch, feel.
ἡ γεῦσις· γεύομαι, δοκιμάζω — Taste; I taste, try.
γλυκύς· ἡ γλυκύτης — Sweet; sweetness.
ὀξύς, vl. ξεινός· ἡ ὀξύτης, vl. ἡ
ξεινάδα — Sour, sharp; acidity.
πικρός· ἡ πικρότης, ἡ πικρία — Bitter; bitterness.
τὸ πνεῦμα· ἡ εὐφυΐα — Wit; wittiness.
εὐφυής, πνωματώδης, vl. ἔξυπνος — Witty, spirited, clever.
ἡ καρδία· ἐγκάρδιος — The heart; cordial.
τὸ λογικόν· λογικός — The reason; reasoning.
ἡ σύνεσις· συνετός, φρόνιμος — The understanding; sensible.
φληναφῶ, φλυαρῶ — I talk rubbish, nonsense.

ἔχω δίκαιον, ἄδικον	I am right, wrong.
ἔχω λόγον, αἰτίαν	I have reason, cause.
ἀπαιτῶ ἱκανοποίησιν	I demand satisfaction.
σωφροσύνη	Prudence, moderation.
εἶνε ἀνοησία	It is folly, nonsense.
ὁ νοῦς· νουνεχής	The mind; intelligent.
καταληπτός· ἀκατάληπτος	Intelligible; unintelligible.
σᾶς παρενόησα	I misunderstood you.
ἡ παρανόησις	The misunderstanding.
ἐννοεῖται!	Of course (It is understood)!
νοῶ, ἐννοῶ, καταλαμβάνω	I understand, I see, I comprehend.
τὸ ἀντιληπτικόν	Power of apprehension.
τοῦτο εἶνε ἀκατανόητον	This is incomprehensible.
ἡ ἱκανότης· ἱκανός· ἀνίκανος	The ability; able; incompetent.
ἡ καλοκαρδία	Humour, vivacity. .
ἡ μεγαλοφυΐα· μεγαλοφυής	Genius; possessed of genius.
εἶνε δύσνους· ἀντιλαμβάνεται δυσκόλως	He is slow of apprehension; understands with difficulty.
ἡ ἰδέα	The idea.
σκέπτομαι, συλλογίζομαι· ἀναλογίζομαι	I consider, reflect; reason.
ὀνειρεύομαι· τὸ ὄνειρον (pl. -ατα)	I dream; the dream.
δὲν ἠξεύρω τί νὰ ὑποθέσω	I don't know what to suppose.
ἡ ἰδέα· ἰδανικός	Idea; ideal.
ἡ ἰδανικότης· τὸ ἰδανικόν	Ideality; the ideal.
οὐδεμίαν ἰδέαν ἔχει περὶ τούτου	He hasn't a notion of this.
ἀναπτύσσω τὰς ἰδέας μου	I develop (or unfold) my ideas.
ἡ γνώμη, ἡ δοξασία	The opinion, view.
εἶμαι τῆς γνώμης ὅτι —	I am of the opinion that —
ἡ συμβουλή· συμβουλεύω	The advice; I advise.
συμβουλεύομαί τινα	I consult some one.
τὸ συμβούλιον	The council.
ἡ ἀναπώλησις, ὁ ἀναλογισμός· ἀναπολῶ, ἀναλογίζομαι	The reconsideration, the reflection; I reconsider, reflect.
ὁ συλλογισμός· συλλογίζομαι	The reflection; I reflect.
ἡ κρίσις· κρίνω	The judgment; I judge.
ὁ δικαστής· δικάζω	The juryman; I try.
ἡ πρόληψις· ἡ δεισιδαιμονία	The prejudice; the superstition.
ἡ ὑπόθεσις· ὑποθέτω	The supposition (also business); I suppose.

εἰκάζω· ἡ εἰκασία	I conjecture; the conjecture.
τὸ συμπέρασμα, τὸ πόρισμα	The inference; the conclusion.
συμπεραίνω	I infer.
ἐκ τούτου ἕπεται ὅτι —	From this it follows that —
ἡ παρατήρησις· θεωρῶ	The remark; I regard.
ὁ παρατηρητής	The observer.
παρατηρῶ	I observe, remark.
ἀξιοσημείωτος	Worth noting, noteworthy.
ἡ διάκρισις	The distinction.
ἡ ἐξαιρετικότης	The exceptionality.
διακρίνω· διακρίνομαι	I distinguish, am distinguished.
ἡ πειθώ· πείθω	Persuasion; I persuade.
πειστικός· καταπείθω	Persuasive; I dissuade.
ἡ βεβαιότης· ἡ ἀσφάλεια	The certainty; the safety.
ἡ βεβαίωσις· βεβαιόνω	The assurance; I assure.
ἡ πεποίθησις	The conviction.
βέβαιος· πεπεισμένος	Sure; persuaded.
ἡ ἀμφιβολία· ἀμφιβάλλω	The doubt; I doubt.
ἀμφίβολος· ἀβέβαιος	Doubtful; uncertain.
μαντεύω· τὸ μάντευμα	I guess; the guess.
ἡ φαντασία· φαντάζομαι	The fancy; I fancy.
φαντασιώδης	Fanciful, fantastic.
ἡ μνήμη, τὸ μνημονικόν	The memory; the reminder, power of memory.
ἀξιομνημόνευτος	Memorable.
ἐξ ἀμνημονεύτων χρόνων	From immemorial times.
ἡ ἀνάμνησις	The remembrance.
ἡ λήθη· λησμονῶ· ἐπιλήσμων	Forgetfulness; I forget; forgetful.
ἡ γνῶσις· ἡ γνωριμία	Knowledge; acquaintance.
βαθεῖαι γνώσεις	Profound knowledge[s].
εἷς γνώριμός μου	An acquaintance of mine.
γνωστός· ἄγνωστος	Known; unknown.
σοφός· λόγιος, πεπαιδευμένος	Wise; learned, cultured.
ἀμαθής	Illiterate, unlearned.
ἡ ὀξύνοια· ἡ ἀγχίνοια	Quickness of wit; presence of mind.
ἀγχίνους	Ready (of resource).
ἡ δεξιότης· δεξιός· ἀδέξιος	Dexterity; dexterous, awkward.
ἡ μωρία, ἡ βλακία, vl. ἡ κουταμάρα	Folly, stupidity.
μωρός, βλάξ, vl. κουτός	A fool, a dullard, a blockhead.
ἡ σοφία· σοφός	Wisdom; wise, clever.

τὸ αἴσθημα· ἡ αἴσθησις	The feeling (thing felt); the (power of) feeling.
αἰσθάνομαι· αἰσθητός, ἐπαισθητός	I feel; sensible, appreciable.
εὐαίσθητος· ἀναίσθητος	Sensitive; insensible, senseless, insensate.
ἡ εὐαισθησία· ἡ ἀναισθησία	Sensitiveness; insensibility.
ἡ διάθεσις	The disposition.
καλῆς, κακῆς διαθέσεως	Of a good, an evil disposition.
ἡ ἐντύπωσις	The impression.
ἡ ἐπιθυμία· ὁ πόθος	The desire; the longing.
ἐπιθυμῶ· ἐπιθυμητός	I wish; desirable.
ἡ θέλησις· θέλω	The will; I will.
ἑκούσιος· ἀκούσιος· ἐθελοντής	Willing; unwilling; a volunteer.
ἀσμένως· μετὰ χαρᾶς	Gladly; with pleasure.
ὁ σκοπός, ἡ πρόθεσις	The object, the purpose.
πρόκειμαι, προτίθεμαι, ἔχω σκοπόν	I am going to, I propose, intend.
ἔχει κακοὺς σκοποὺς	He has evil intentions, means ill.
ἡ ἀπόφασις· ἀποφασίζω	The decision; I decide.
ἡ ἐπιρροή	The influence.
τὸ πάθος, ἡ ὁρμή	The passion, impulse.
ἐμπαθής· ἀπαθής	Passionate; passionless.
ἡ ἀδιαφορία· ἀδιάφορος	Indifference; indifferent.
ὁ ἔρως, ἡ ἀγάπη· ἀγαπῶ	Love, affection; I love, like.
ἀγαπᾷ τὸν περίπατον	He likes walking.
ἐραστής	Lover.
τὸ μῖσος· μισῶ	Hatred; I hate.
μισητός· μοχθηρός	Hateful; villainous.
ἡ τρυφερότης· τρυφερός	Delicacy, luxuriousness; delicate.
ἡ συγκίνησις· συγκινητικός	The emotion; touching, emotional.
συγκινῶ· συγκεκινημένος	I move, touch; moved, touched, affected.
ἡ ἀφοσίωσις· ἀφωσιωμένος	Devotion; devoted.
ἡ κλίσις, ἡ ῥοπή	Inclination, bent, propensity.
εὐδιάθετος, πρόθυμος	In good spirits, well-disposed, eager, ready.
ἡ ἀντιπάθεια, ἡ ἀποστροφή	Dislike, disgust.
ἀντιπαθητικός	Full of dislikes.
ἡ ἀηδία· ἀηδής	Unpleasantness; unpleasant.

σικχαίνομαι, ἀηδιάζω τι	I am disgusted, I loathe a thing.
βδελυκτός· ἀποτρόπαιος	Loathsome, abominable.
ἡ φρίκη· ἡ ἀγανάκτησις	Terror; indignation.
ἀποστρέφομαι	I abhor.
εὐάρεστος· δυσάρεστος	Pleasing; unpleasant.
ἡ εὔνοια· εὐνοῶ	Favour; I favour.
ὁ εὐνοούμενος· ἡ εὐνοουμένη	The favoured one (m. and f.).
ἡ φιλία· φιλικός, φίλιος	Friendship; friendly, kindly.
ὁ φίλος· ἡ φίλη	The friend; dear one.
ἡ ἐξοικείωσις· ἐξοικειοῦμαι	Familiarization; I familiarize myself.
ἡ ἔχθρα· ἐχθρικός	Enmity; hostile, inimical.
ὁ ἐχθρός· πολέμιος	The enemy; foe.
διαλλαγή, ἡ διάλλαξις	The reconcilement, reconciliation.
διαλλάσσομαι	I am reconciled.
ἡ ὑπόληψις· ὑπολήπτομαι	Reputation; I am reputed.
ἄξιος ὑπολήψεως· ἀνεκτίμητος	Worthy of repute; invaluable.
ἡ καταφρόνησις· καταφρονῶ	Contempt; I despise.
τὸ σέβας· σέβομαι	Respect; I respect, reverence.
σεβάσμιος, σεβαστός	Venerable, august.
ἡ περιφρόνησις· περιφρονῶ	The neglect; I neglect.
ὁ θαυμασμός· θαυμάζω	Wonder, admiration; I wonder, admire.
θαυμάσιος, θαυμαστός	Wonderful, marvellous.
ἡ ἔκπληξις· καταπληκτικός	Astonishment; astonishing.
καταπλήττω	I astound.
ἐκπλήττομαι· θαυμάζω	I am surprised; I marvel.
ἔκθαμβυς	Dumbfounded.
ἡ ὀργή· ὀργίλος	Wrath; wrathful.
ὀργίζομαι· ὀξύθυμος	I am angry; quick-tempered.
ἡ ἔξαψις, ἡ παραφορά	The fit of passion, fury.
ἐξάπτομαι, ἀφαρπάζομαι	I fire up, I am carried away.
ἡ λύσσα· ἡ μανία	Frenzy; madness.
λυσσώδης, μανιώδης	Raving, mad.
ὁ κόρος, ὁ χορτασμός	Satiety, surfeit.
ἡ διαφορά, ἡ διένεξις, ἡ φιλονεικία	The difference, feud, quarrel.
ἡ ἔρις· ἡ λογομαχία	Strife; war of words.
φιλονεικῶ· ἐρίζω πρός τινα	I quarrel; I dispute with a man.
φιλόνεικος	Quarrelsome.
ἡ λύπη	Grief.

προξενῶ λύπην	I cause grief.
τοῦτο μὲ ἐλύπησε πολύ	This (has) grieved me much.
λυποῦμαι	I am grieved, sorry.
εἶνε ἀξιολύπητος	He is deserving of pity.
εἶνε λυπηρόν ὅτι —	It is sad that —
ἡ θλίψις· τεθλιμμένος	Affliction; afflicted.
ἡ δυσθυμία, ἡ λύπη· περίλυπος	Heaviness of heart, grief; sorrowful.
ἡ μελαγχολία· μελαγχολικός	The melancholy; melancholy.
ἡ ὑποχονδρία· ὑποχονδριακός	Hypochondriasis; hypochondriac.
ἡ φαιδρότης· φαιδρός	Joyfulness; joyful.
ἡ εὐθυμία· εὔθυμος	Gladness; glad.
εὐθυμῶ, διασκεδάζω	I am gay, I amuse myself.
φαιδρύνω	I gladden.
ἡ χαρά· εὔχαρις, περιχαρής	Joy; merry, jocund.
τὸ θέλγητρον, τὰ θέλγητρα	The charm, the charms.
ἔνθους, ἐνθουσιασμένος	Inspired, carried away.
ἡ ἡδονή· αἱ ἡδοναί	Pleasure; pleasures.
ἡ διασκέδασις	Amusement, diversion.
αἱ διασκεδάσεις	Amusements.
θελκτικός, θελξικάρδιος	Charming, captivating.
καταθέλγω	I charm, captivate.
ὁ γέλως· γελῶ	Laughter; I laugh.
μειδιῶ· τὸ μειδίαμα	I smile; the smile.
γελοῖος· ἡ γελοιότης	Laughable; absurdity.
καταγέλαστον ποιῶ τινα	I make a man ridiculous.
ὁ ἄνθρωπος οὗτος κατήντησε παίγνιον τοῦ κόσμου	This man has become a laughing-stock to the world.
ἐμπαίζω τινά	I make fun of a man, mock him.
σκώπτω, καταγελῶ	I scoff, laugh at.
ἡ ἀστειότης, ὁ ἀστεϊσμός, vl. ὁ χορατᾶς	The fun, the joke, the jest.
ἡ σοβαρότης· σοβαρός	Gravity; grave.
σπουδαίως	Seriously.
ἡ στέρξις, ἡ εὐχαρίστησις	Contentment, pleasure.
εὐχαριστημένος· στέργω	Pleased, contented; I am content.
ἡ δυσαρέσκεια· δυσαρεστῶ	Displeasure; I displease.
ἡ ἀπόλαυσις· ἀπολαύω	Enjoyment; I enjoy.

ἡ προσοχή	Attention.
περιποιητικός· περιποιοῦμαι νοσοκομῶ	Attentive; I attend to. I tend, nurse.
φροντίζω· μεριμνῶ	I provide; I care for.
πολύφροντις· ἄφροντις· ἀμέριμνος	Full of care; thoughtless, free from care.
ἡ προσδοκία· προσδοκῶ, περιμένω	Expectation; I expect, await.
ἡ ἀδημονία	Bewilderment.
ἡ βάσανος· βασανίζω	Torture; I torment.
ἡ ἀνησυχία· ἀνήσυχος	Uneasiness; restless, uneasy.
ἡσυχάζω· καθησυχάζω	I am quiet; I quiet.
ἀνησυχῶ	I am disturbed, restless.
ἡ ἡσυχία· ἥσυχος	Tranquillity; tranquil.
ἡ ἔξαψις· ἐξημμένος	Excitement; excited.
ἡ ἀνάπαυσις· ἐπαναπαύω	Rest; I soothe, lull to rest.
ὁ φόβος· φοβοῦμαι	Fear; I fear.
φοβοῦμαί τινα	I am afraid of any one.
δειλός· περίφοβος· φοβερός	Fearful; timid; dreadful.
ὁ τρόμος· τρομερός	Terror; tremendous.
ἐκφοβῶ, ἐκφοβίζω	I frighten, alarm.
ἡ φρίκη· φρικώδης, φρικαλέος	Fright; frightful, dreadful.
ἡ ἔκπληξις, τὸ ἀπροσδόκητον	Astonishment, the unexpected(ness).
ἡ ἀπελπιστία, ἡ ἀπελπισία· ἀπελπίζομαι	Despair, desperation; I despair.
εἶνε ἀπελπισία	It is a desperate case.
ἄπελπις	Despairing.
ἡ ἐλπίς· ἐλπίζω	Hope; I hope.
εὔελπις	Of good hope, hopeful.
ἡ παρηγορία· παρήγορος	Comfort; comforter.
ἀπαραμύθητος, ἀπαρηγόρητος	Inconsolable, disconsolate.
ἡ γλῶσσα	Language.
ἡ διάλεκτος	The dialect.
ἡ λέξις	The word.
ὁ λόγος	The speech.
λαλῶ, ὁμιλῶ πρός τινα	I talk, speak to any one.
ἡ ἔκφρασις	The expression.
ἐν ἑνὶ λόγω	In a word, in one word.
ἡ συνομιλία· συνομιλῶ	The conversation; I converse.
ἡ συνδιάλεξις· συνδιαλέγομαι	The conference; I confer.

N

φλυαρῶ· ἡ φλυαρία· φλύαρος	I talk nonsense; nonsense; a babbler.
φωνάζω· καλῶ	I call; I summon.
ὀνομάζω· ὀνομάζομαι, καλοῦμαι	I name; I am named, called.
τὸ προσωνύμιον· τὸ ὄνομα· τὸ ἐπώνυμον	The Christian name; the name; the surname.
τὸ ὄργανον· ἡ φωνή	The organ; the voice.
ὁμιλεῖτε δυνατώτερα	Speak louder.
σιγὰ ὁμιλεῖτε	Speak softly.
ἡ σιωπή, ἡ σιγή· σιωπηρός, σιωπηλός	Silence; silent, taciturn.
σιωπῶ	I hold my peace, am silent.
ἡ ἐρώτησις	The question.
ἐρωτῶ περί τινος	I ask about something.
παρακαλῶ περί τινος	I make a request.
προσαγόρευσις	The address.
ὀνομάζω· ἀναγορεύω	I name; I proclaim.
ἐκφωνῶ λόγον	I deliver a speech.
εὔηχος, βραγχαλέα φωνή	A sonorous, a hoarse voice.
ἡ ἐρώτησις· ἡ παράκλησις	The question; the request.
ἱκετεύω· ἐξορκίζω	I beseech; conjure.
ὑμνύω, ὁρκίζομαι	I swear, take an oath.
ἡ ἀναφορά	The reference, mention, appeal.
ἡ ἀπόκρισις, ἡ ἀπάντησις	The answer, reply.
ἀποκρίνομαι, ἀπαντῶ	I answer, reply.
ἐπανέλαβε	He repeated.
διαπραγματεύομαι· ἡ διαπραγμάτευσις	I negotiate; the negotiation.
ἡ διήγησις, ἡ ἀφήγησις	The narrative, the recital.
διηγοῦμαι, ἀφηγοῦμαι	I recount, narrate.
ἡ εὐφράδεια, ἡ εὐγλωττία· εὐφραδής, εὔγλωττος	The eloquence; eloquent.

IX.

Ἀρεταὶ καὶ κακίαι	VIRTUES AND VICES.
προτερήματα καὶ ἐλαττώματα.	*Advantages and defects.*
ἡ ἀρετή· ἐνάρετος	Virtue; virtuous.
ἡ κακία, τὸ ἐλάττωμα	The vice, the defect.

τὸ προτέρημα, τὸ προσόν	The advantage, the attribute, qualification.
τὸ ἐλάττωμα	The defect, drawback.
ἡ ἔλλειψις, τὸ σφάλμα	The want, the fault.
ἡ ἠθική, ἡ ἠθικότης· ἠθικός	Moral (virtue), morality; moral.
τὸ ἀνήθικον, ἡ ἀνηθικότης· ἀνήθικος	The immoral, immorality; immoral.
τὰ ἤθη	Morals.
τὸ καθῆκον, τὸ χρέος	The duty, the obligation.
ἐκτελῶ τὰ καθήκοντά μου	I perform my duties.
ἐκπληρῶ τὸ χρέος μου	I fulfil my obligation.
παραμελῶ τὰ χρέη μου	I neglect my obligations.
τὸ ὑπόδειγμα, ὁ ὑπογραμμός	The pattern, model.
ἡ ἀγαθότης, ἡ καλωσύνη	Goodness, kindness.
τὸ ἀγαθόν· καλός	The good; good.
ἀγαθός	Good.
φιλόφρων· εὐμενής· εὐνοϊκός	Kind; kindly; favourable.
ἡ ἐπιείκεια· ἐπιεικής	Equity; fair, equitable.
ἡ κακία, ἡ μοχθηρία· κακός	Wickedness, depravity; bad.
μοχθηρός, κακεντρεχής	Depraved, villainous.
τὸ κακόν	The evil.
εὔτακτος· ἄτακτος	Orderly; disorderly.
οὐδαμινός, οὐτιδανός	Worthless, good-for-nothing.
ἡ ὁμόνοια· ἡ διχόνοια	Agreement; disagreement.
ἡ εὐεργεσία· ὁ εὐεργέτης	The benefit; the benefactor.
ἡ εὐποιΐα· ἐλεήμων, εὐεργετικός	Beneficence; compassionate, beneficent.
ὁ κακοῦργος· τὸ κακούργημα	The evil-doer; the crime.
ὁ οἶκτος· οἰκτίρμων, συμπαθής, εὔσπλαγχνος	Pity; pitiful, compassionate, merciful.
τὸ ἔλεος· ἀνιλεής· οἰκτρός, ἐλεεινός	Mercy; merciless; piteous, wretched.
ἡ εὐσέβεια· εὐσεβής, θρῆσκος	Piety; pious, religious.
ἡ ἀσέβεια· ἀσεβής	Impiety; impious.
ἡ σκληρότης· σκληρός, σκληρόκαρδος	Severity, harshness; harsh, hard-hearted.
ἡ γενναιοψυχία· γενναιόψυχος	Generosity; generous.
ἡ μεγαλοψυχία· μεγαλόψυχος	Magnanimity; magnanimous.
ἡ φιλοξενία· φιλόξενος	Hospitality; hospitable.
ἡ ἀφιλοξενία· ἀφιλόξενος	Want of hospitality; inhospitable.

ἡ εὐγνωμοσύνη· ἡ χάρις — Gratitude; the favour.
ἀγνώμων, ἀχάριστος — Ungrateful; thankless.
σᾶς εὐγνωμόνω — I am grateful to you.
ἡ ἀχαριστία· ἡ ἀγνωμοσύνη — Thanklessness; ingratitude.
ἡ εἰλικρίνεια· εἰλικρινής — Sincerity; sincere.
ἡ προσποίησις· προσποίητος — Pretence; pretended.
προσποιοῦμαι — I pretend.
ἡ ὑπόκρισις, ἡ ὑποκρισία· ὑποκριτής — Hypocrisy; hypocrite.
τὸ ψεῦδος· ψεύστης — Falsehood, lie; liar.
ἡ ἀλήθεια· ἀληθής — Truth; true.
ὁμιλεῖτε ἀληθῶς; — Are you speaking the truth?
ἡ δολιότης· δόλιος — Craftiness; crafty.
ὁ λάθος· λανθάνομαι, λανθάνω — The mistake; I am mistaken, wrong.

ἡ συκοφαντία, ἡ διαβολή — Slander, calumny.
διαβάλλω, συκοφαντῶ· συκοφάντης — I accuse, slander; a slanderer.
ἡ κατηγορία, ἡ κακολογία· κακολογῶ — Accusation, evil-speaking; I defame.
ἡ ἐχεμυθία· ἐχέμυθος — Taciturnity; taciturn.
ἡ ἀδιακρισία· ἀδιάκριτος — Indiscretion; indiscreet.
ἡ περιεργία, ἡ περιέργεια· περίεργος — Curiosity; curious.
τοῦτο εἶνε περίεργον — This is curious.
ἡ ἁβροφροσύνη· ἁβρόφρων — Delicacy; delicate, tender.
ἡ ἐμπιστοσύνη· ἐμπιστεύομαι — Confidence; I confide.
ὁ ἐμπεπιστευμένος· ἐμπιστευτικός — The confidant; confidential.
ἡ δυσπιστία· δύσπιστος — Distrust; distrustful.
ἡ εὐπιστία· εὔπιστος — Trustfulness, credulity; credulous.
ἡ ἀπιστία· ἄπιστος — Faithlessness, infidelity; incredulous, infidel, faithless.

ἡ πίστις· πιστός — Faith, troth; faithful.
ἡ ὑποψία, ἡ ὑπόνοια — Suspicion, misgiving.
καχύποπτος· ὕποπτος — Distrusted, suspected.
ὑποπτεύομαί τινα — I suspect some one.
ἡ ζηλοτυπία· ζηλότυπος — Jealousy; jealous.
ὁ ἀντίπαλος — The rival, antagonist.
ὁ φθόνος· φθονερός· φθονῶ — Envy; envious; I envy.
δὲν φθονῶ τὴν εὐτυχίαν του — I do not grudge him his luck.
ἡ δεισιδαιμονία· δεισιδαίμων — Superstition; superstitious.
ἡ σεμνότης, ἡ κοσμιότης — Gravity, propriety.

σεμνός, κόσμιος	Grave, proper, decent.
ἡ ἀσχημοσύνη, ἡ ἀπρέπεια	Impropriety, indecency.
ἄσεμνος, ἀσχήμων	Improper, indecent.
ἡ ταπεινοφροσύνη· ταπεινόφρων	Humility; humble.
ἡ ταπείνωσις	Humiliation.
ἡ μικροπρέπεια· ἡ χαμέρπεια	Meanness; grovelling.
μικροπρεπής· χαμερπής	Mean; grovelling.
ἡ ἀξιοπρέπεια· ἀξιοπρεπής	Seemliness; seemly.
τὸ ἀναξιοπρεπές· ἀναξιοπρεπής	Unseemliness; unseemly.
ἡ ἀγανάκτησις	Indignation.
ἡ ἀναισχυντία, ἡ ἀναίδεια	Shamelessness, audacity.
ἀναιδής, ἀναίσχυντος	Audacious, shameless.
ἡ συστολή, ἡ δειλία· δειλός	Embarrassment, timidity; timid.
ἡ τόλμη	Daring.
τολμηρός, ῥιψοκίνδυνος	Bold, rash, daring.
ἡ ἀφοβία	Fearlessness.
ἀτρόμητος, ἄφοβος	Intrepid, fearless.
ἡ θρασύτης· θρασύς	Rashness; rash.
τὸ θάρρος· θαρραλέος	Courage; courageous.
ἐνθαρρύνω· ἡ ἐνθάρρυνσις	I encourage; encouragement.
ἀποθαρρύνω· ἡ ἀποθάρρυνσις	I discourage; discouragement.
ἡ ἀνανδρία· ἄνανδρος	Cowardice; cowardly.
ἡ ἀνδρεία, ἡ γενναιότης	Bravery, valour.
ἀνδρεῖος, γενναῖος	Brave, valorous.
ἡ στερεότης· στερεός	Firmness; firm.
ἡ ἀδυναμία· ἀδύνατος	Powerlessness; powerless, weak.
ἐξασθενῶ, ἐξασθενίζω	I weaken.
ἡ ἰσχύς· ἰσχυρός	Strength; strong.
ἐνισχύω, ἐνδυναμόνω	I strengthen, fortify.
ἡ ἐπιείκεια· ἐπιεικής	Fairness; fair.
ἡ αὐστηρότης· αὐστηρός	Austerity; austere.
ἡ ἀνεκτικότης· ἀνεκτικός	Tolerance; tolerant.
ἀνέχομαι, ὑπομένω, ὑποφέρω	I endure, bear, suffer.
ἀνεκτός· ἀφόρητος, ἀνυπόφορος	Bearable; unendurable, insufferable.
ἡ φιλανθρωπία· φιλάνθρωπος	Philanthropy; benevolent, humane.
ἡ ἀπανθρωπία· ἀπάνθρωπος	Inhumanity; inhuman.
ἡ βαρβαρότης· βάρβαρος	Barbarity; barbarous.
ἡ σκληρότης· σκληρός	Severity; severe.

ἡ ἀγριότης· ἄγριος — Savagery; savage.
ἡ σφοδρότης· σφοδρός — Vehemence; vehement.
ἡ παραβίασις· παραβιαστής — Violation; violator.
παραβιάζω — I violate.
ἡ ὠμότης· ὠμός — Cruelty; cruel,
ἡ πραότης· πρᾶος (πραεῖα, fem.) — Gentleness; gentle.
καταπραΰνω — I soothe, appease.
ἡ λεπτότης· λεπτός — Subtlety; fine, subtle.
ἡ εὐγένεια· εὐγενής — Nobility; noble.
ἡ ἀγένεια — Baseness; low birth.
ἀπολίτευτος, ἀγενής — Impolite, ungentle.
ἡ ἀγροικία· ἄγροικος — Boorishness; boorish.
ἡ βαναυσότης· βάναυσος — Vulgarity; vulgar.
ἔλλειψις ἀγωγῆς, ἀπαιδευσία — Want of breeding; want of education.
ἀπαίδευτος· ἀνάγωγος, κακοαναθρεμμένος — Uneducated; ill-bred.
ἡ ἀγωγή, ἡ ἀνατροφή — Breeding; bringing-up.
ἡ εὐπροσηγορία· εὐπροσήγορος — Affability; affable.
τὸ ἀξιέραστον, τὸ ἀξιαγάπητον — Amiability, lovableness.
ἐράσμιος, ἀξιέραστος, ἀξιαγάπητος — Lovable, amiable.
ἡ κολακεία· κόλαξ — Flattery; a flatterer.
κολακευτικός — Flattering (adj.).
ἡ τιμιότης· τίμιος — Honesty; honest.
χρηστότης· χρηστός — Goodness; good.
ἡ ἀπάτη· ἀπατηλός — Deception; deceptive.
ὁ, ἡ ἀπατεών· ἀπατῶ — The deceiver; I deceive.
ἡ συνείδησις, τὸ συνειδός· εὐσυνείδητος — Conscience, consciousness; conscientious.
εὐσυνειδότως — Conscientiously.
ἡ τύψις τοῦ συνειδότος — The pricking of the conscience.
ἡ συνείδησις μὲ τύπτει — My conscience pricks or smites me.
ἡ μεταμέλεια, ἡ μετάνοια· μετανοῶ τι — Repentance, penitence; I repent of anything.
τὸ διαφέρον· τὸ ἐνδιαφέρον· διαφέρων, ἐνδιαφέρων — The difference; the interest; differing; interesting.
ἡ ἰδιοτέλεια· ἰδιοτελής — Self-interest; interested.
ἐνδιαφέρομαι περί τινος — I am interested in anything.
ἡ φιλαυτία· φίλαυτος — Selfishness; selfish.

ὁ ἐγωῖσμός· ἐγωῖστής	Conceit; conceited.
ὁ ζῆλος	Zeal.
ἡ πλεονεξία· πλεονέκτης	Avarice; avaricious.
ἡ φιλοκέρδεια· φιλοκερδής	Greed; greedy of gain.
ἡ φιλαργυρία· φιλάργυρος	The love of money; money-loving.
ἡ γενναιοδωρία· γενναιόδωρος	Generosity; generous, liberal.
ἡ ἀσωτία· ἄσωτος	Loose-living; loose-lived, "fast."
δαπανῶ, καταναλίσκω, ἐξοδεύω	I spend, I expend, I lay out.
ἡ δαπάνη, τὰ ἔξοδα	Expenditure, outlay, expenses.
ἡ οἰκονομία· οἰκονόμος	Domestic management, saving; a manager, saver.
οἰκονομῶ	I save.
θησαυρίζω	I hoard.
ἡ ἀκρίβεια· ἀκριβής· ἀκριβός	Accuracy; accurate; dear (i.e. "beloved" and expensive).
ἡ ἀθωότης· ἀθῶος	Innocence; innocent.
ἡ καθαρότης· καθαρός	Cleanliness; clean.
ἡ ἐθιμοταξία, ἐθιμοπρεπής	Steadiness; steady, moral.
ἡ εὐπρέπεια· εὐπρεπής	Seemliness; seemly.
ἡ ἀτοπία· ἄτοπος	Absurdity; absurd.
ἡ μετριότης· μέτριος	Moderation; moderate.
ἡ μετρίασις· μετριάζω	Moderation (as a process); I moderate.
ἡ ἀδηφαγία, ἡ γαστριμαργία· ἡ λαιμαργία· ἡ λιχνεία	Greediness, gluttony; gourmandizing; daintiness.
λαίμαργος, ἀδηφάγος· λίχνος	Greedy, gluttonous; dainty.
ὁ φαγᾶς· ὁ λίχνος	The glutton; the gourmand.
τὸ λίχνευμα	The tit-bit, gourmet.
ἡ τρυφή· τρυφηλός	Luxury; luxurious.
ἡ μέθη· μέθυσος	Drunkenness; drunken.
ἡ μέθυσις· μέθυσος, οἰνοβαρής	Getting drunk; drunkard, tipsy man.
ἡ τάξις· ἡ ἀταξία	Order; disorder.
τακτικὸς ἄνθρωπος	An orderly, regular man.
ἄτακτος, ἀκατάστατος	A disorderly, unsteady man.
ἡ καθαριότης· καθαρός	Cleanliness; cleanly.
ἡ ἀκαθαρσία· ἀκάθαρτος	Uncleanness; unclean.
ἡ ῥυπαρότης· ῥυπαρός	Dirtiness; dirty.
ἡ ἀμέλεια· ἀμελής	Negligence; negligent.

ἡ ἐπιμέλεια· ἐπιμελής	Diligence; diligent.
ἡ φιλοπονία· φιλόπονος	Industry; industrious.
ἡ ὀκνηρία· ὀκνηρός	Laziness; lazy.
ἡ δραστηριότης	Activity.
δραστήριος, ἐνεργητικός	Active, energetic.
ἡ ἀργία· ἄεργος· ἀργός	Idleness; idle; slow.
ἡ ἀπραξία· ἡ ἀργία	Inactivity; idleness.
ὁ ζῆλος	Zeal, ardour.
ἡ ζωηρότης· ζωηρός	Liveliness; lively.
ἡ ἀγρυπνία· ἄγρυπνος	Watchfulness; watchful, wakeful.
ἡ προσοχή· προσεκτικός	Attention; attentive.
καθιστῶ τινα προσεκτικόν	I call a man's attention (make him attentive).
ἡ ἀπροσεξία· ἀπρόσεκτος	Inattention; inattentive.
προσέχω εἴς τι	I attend to a thing.
ἡ ἀπόνοια· ἀφῃρημένος	Absent-mindedness; absent-(minded), abstracted.
ἡ διασκέδασις· διασκεδάζω τινα	Diversion; I divert, amuse any one.
ἡ ἀσυνεσία, ἡ ἀπερισκεψία	Want of intelligence, want of caution.
ἀσύνετος, ἀπερίσκεπτος	Senseless, uncircumspect, hasty.
ἡ ἀπροβουλία, ἡ ἀπρονοησία	Want of forethought, improvidence.
ἀπροβούλευτος· προνοητικός	Improvident; provident.
λαμβάνω προνοητικὰ μέσα	I take precautionary measures.
ἡ φρόνησις	Prudence.
φρόνιμος	Prudent.
ἡ σταθερότης, ἡ εὐστάθεια	Steadfastness, stability.
σταθερός, εὐσταθής	Steadfast, stable.
ἡ ἀστασία· ἄστατος	Inconstancy; inconstant.
ἡ καρτερία· καρτερικός	Perseverance; persistent.
ἡ ὑπομονή· ὑπομονητικός	Patience; patient.
ἡ ἀνυπομονησία· ἀνυπόμονος	Impatience; impatient.
ἡ εὐπείθεια· εὐπειθής	Obedience; obedient.
ἡ ἀπείθεια· ἀπειθής	Disobedience; disobedient.
ἡ δυστροπία· δύστροπος	Bad behaviour; unmannerly.
ἡ ἰσχυρογνωμοσύνη· ἰσχυρογνώμων	Obstinacy; obstinate.
ἡ πεισμονή· πεισματώδης	Spite; spiteful.
ἡ ἀκολουθία, ἡ συνέπεια	Consequence, result.

πρὸς πεῖσμά τινος κάμνω τι	I do a thing to spite any one, or in spite of him.
ἀκόλουθος, συνεπής	Consequent, consistent.
ἀνακόλουθος, ἀσυνεπής	Inconsequent, inconsistent.
ἡ ἀνακολουθία, ἡ ἀσυνέπεια	Inconsequence, inconsistency.

X.

Ἀφῃρημένα.	ABSTRACTIONS.
Ἔννοιαι γενικαί· χῶρος· χρώματα κ. τ. λ.	*General notions; space; colours, &c.*
ἡ ὕπαρξις· ὑπάρχω	Existence; I exist.
τὸ ὄν· ἡ οὐσία· οὐσιώδης	Being; essence; essential.
οὐσιωδῶς	Essentially.
τὸ πρᾶγμα	The thing.
ἡ κατάστασις· ἡ θέσις	The condition; the situation.
εἶμαι εἰς κατάστασιν or θέσιν νὰ πράξω τι	I am in a position to do anything.
ἡ πραγματικότης· πραγματικός	Actuality; actual.
ἐπαληθεύω	I verify.
ἡ ὄψις, ἡ ἐμφάνεια· ἀναφαίνομαι	The look, the appearance; I appear, arise.
κατὰ τὰ φαινόμενα	According to appearances.
ἡ ἐμφάνισις, ἡ παρουσία	The appearance, the presence.
χθὲς δὲν ἐφάνη	He was not seen yesterday.
τοῦτο τὸ βιβλίον ἐξεδόθη ἐν Ἀθήναις	This book was published (appeared) in Athens.
φαίνεται	It seems.
ἐὰν ἐγκρίνητε αὐτό	If you approve it.
ἡ πιθανότης· πιθανός	Probability; probable.
παραδεκτός	Acceptable.
ἡ ὁμοιότης· ὅμοιος	Similarity, likeness; like.
ὁμοιάζω	I resemble (seem like, seem likely).
τὸ δυνατόν· δυνατός	The possible; possible (strong).
τὸ ἀδύνατον· ἀδύνατος	The impossible; impossible (weak).
εἶνε ἀδύνατον	It is impossible.
ἡ δύναμις· δύναμαι	Power; I can.
δυνατός, ἰσχυρός	Powerful, strong.
ἀντικείμενον	Object.

ἡ περίπτωσις· ἡ πτῶσις	Case; case (in grammar).
ἡ περίστασις· ἡ εὐκαιρία	The circumstance; the occasion.
τὸ συμβάν, τὸ συμβεβηκός, τὸ σύμβαμα	The event, the occurrence.
συμβαίνει	It happens, occurs.
τί συνέβη;	What has happened?
τὸ δυστύχημα	The misfortune.
ἡ τύχη, ἡ συντυχία	The fortune, the coincidence.
διακυβεύω τι	I hazard, chance a thing.
ὁ κίνδυνος, τὸ κινδύνευμα	The danger, the risk.
διατρέχω κίνδυνον	I run a risk.
ἡ τύχη· τυχαῖος	Fortune, chance; chance (adj.).
κατὰ τύχην	By chance.
ἡ τύχη	Luck.
ἡ εὐτυχία· εὐτυχής	Good luck; happy.
ἡ δυστυχία· δυστυχής	Misfortune; unlucky.
ἡ ἐπιτυχία	Success.
ἡ εὐδαιμονία· εὐδαίμων	Happiness; happy.
ἡ συμφορά	Calamity.
ὁ κίνδυνος· ἐπικίνδυνος	Danger; dangerous.
ἡ ἀνάγκη· ἀναγκαῖος	Necessity; necessary.
ἡ χρεία· χρειάζομαί τι	Need; I need something.
ἡ ἔλλειψις· ἔλλειψίς τινος	Lack; lack of something.
ἔχομεν ἔλλειψιν χρημάτων	We are short of money.
ἡ ἀφθονία· ἄφθονος	Plenty; plentiful.
ἔχω ἀφθονίαν	I have plenty.
ἡ εὐπορία· εὔπορος	Easy circumstances; well off.
ἡ πενία, ἡ πτωχία· πένης, πτωχός	Penury, poverty; needy, poor.
ἡ ἔνδεια· ἐνδεής	Want; in want.
ὁ πλοῦτος· πλούσιος	Wealth; wealthy.
πλουτίζω· πλουτῶ	I enrich; I am rich.
ἡ ἀθλιότης· ἄθλιος	Misery; miserable.
κατήντησεν ἐλεεινός	He has become miserable.
ἡ βοήθεια	Succour.
ὁ ὅρος	The term, limit, condition.
ἡ ποιότης, τὸ ποιόν	Quality.
ἡ ποσότης, τὸ ποσόν	Quantity.
τὸ σύνολον, τὸ ὅλον	The whole, the sum total.
τὸ μέρος· ἡ μερίς	The part; the portion, share.
τὸ κόμμα, ἡ μερίς	The party, side.

τὸ μερίδιον	The particle.
τὸ τεμάχιον	The bit, piece.
τὸ περιεχόμενον· περιέχω	The content(s); I contain.
τὸ σχῆμα· σχηματίζω	The form; I form.
ἡ μορφή· μορφόνω	The shape; I shape.
ἡ ἐπιφάνεια· ἐπιπόλαιος	The surface; superficial.
ἡ ἀρχή, ἡ ἔναρξις	The beginning, commencement.
ἄρχομαι, ἀρχίζω	I begin; commence.
ἀρχάριος	A beginner.
τὸ τέλος· τελειόνω, περατόνω	The end; I end, finish.
τὸ ἄκρον· ἄκρος	The extreme, tip, point, corner; extreme.
τὸ μέσον· ἐν τῷ μέσῳ	The middle; in the midst.
μέτριος	Moderate.
εἶνε μετρίου ἀναστήματος	He is of middle stature.
κατὰ μέσον ὅρον	. On an average, taking the mean.
τὸ κέντρον· κεντρικός	The centre; central.
ἡ περιφέρεια	The circumference.
ἡ συνέχεια, ἡ ἐξακολούθησις	The continuity, connexion, the continuation.
ἐξακολουθῶ	I continue.
ἐξηκολούθησε	He continued.
ἡ ἀκολουθία· ἀκολουθῶ	The consequence; I follow.
ἡ ἐπανάληψις· ἐπαναλαμβάνω	The repetition; I repeat.
τὰ ἤθη· τὸ ἔθιμον	Morals; morality.
ἡ συνήθεια· συνήθης	Habit, custom; usual.
ἡ χρῆσις· μεταχειρίζομαι	The use; I use, employ.
ἡ κατάχρησις· καταχρῶμαι	The abuse; I abuse.
ἡ διαταγή	The order.
δίδω διαταγήν	I give order(s).
ἡ τάξις· τακτικός	Order; regular.
ἔκτακτος	Irregular, disorderly.
τὸ ἀλλόκοτον	Originality.
ἀλλόκοτος, παράξενος	Original, strange, peculiar.
ξένος· ἀλλοδαπός	Strange; foreign.
ἡ ἀλλαγή, ἡ μεταβολή	Change, alteration.
ἀλλάσσω, μεταβάλλω	I change, alter.
ἡ μεταλλαγή	The transformation.
εὐμετάβλητος· ἀμετάβλητος	Changeable; unchangeable.
ἡ διαφορά· διάφορος	Difference; different.

διαφέρω	I differ.
τοῦτο διαφέρει	This differs.
ἡ συμφωνία	The agreement.
συμφώνως πρός —	Agreeably to.
ὁ χωρισμός· χωρίζω	Separation; I separate (trans.).
ἡ ἕνωσις· ἑνόνω, συνενόνω	Union; I unite, I join together.
τὸ ἀμοιβαῖον, ἡ ἀμοιβαιότης	Reciprocity.
ἀμοιβαῖος	Reciprocal.
ἡ κανονικότης· κανονικός	Normality; normal.
ὁ κανών· κανονίζω	The standard; I regulate.
ἡ ἀνωμαλία· ἀνώμαλος	Anomaly; abnormal.
ἡ ἐξαίρεσις· κατ' ἐξαίρεσιν	The exception; as an exception.
τὸ παράδειγμα· παραδειγματικός	The example; exemplary.
παραδείγματος χάριν — π. χ.	For example, for instance.
ἵνα ἀναφέρω ἓν παράδειγμα	To quote an instance.
τὸ δεῖγμα, τὸ ὑπόδειγμα	The sample, the pattern.
ἡ ἀπομίμησις· μιμοῦμαι	The imitation; I imitate.
ἀμίμητος	Inimitable.
τὸ ἀντίγραφον· ἀντιγράφω	The copy; I copy.
ἡ ἐφεύρεσις· ἐφευρίσκω	The invention; I invent.
ἡ τελειότης· τέλειος	The perfection; perfect, complete.
ἡ ἀτέλεια· ἀτελής	Imperfection; imperfect.
τελειοποιῶ	I perfect.
ἡ μετριότης· μέτριος	Moderation; moderate.
ὁ βαθμός	The degree.
εἰς τὸν ὕψιστον or ὑπέρτατον βαθμόν	In the highest degree.
ἡ σύγκρισις· συγκρίνω, παραβάλλω	The comparison; I compare, liken.
παραβλητός· ἀπαράβλητος	Comparable; incomparable.
ἡ σχέσις· σχετικός	Relation; relative.
ἡ ἀναφορά	The reference.
ὁ τρόπος	The manner.
τίνι τρόπῳ;	In what manner?
οἱ τρόποι	The manners.
ἡ ἀρχή· ἀρχικός	The beginning; initial.
τὸ πρωτότυπον· πρωτότυπος	The original; original.
ὁ σκοπός· τὸ σχέδιον	The aim; the plan.
ἐπίτηδες, σκοπίμως	On purpose, intentionally.
ἡ αἰτία, τὸ αἴτιον	The cause, the reason.

προξενῶ τι	I cause anything.
ὁ λόγος, ἡ αἰτία	The ground, reason, cause.
τὸ ἀποτέλεσμα	The result.
τὸ σχέδιόν μου ἐναυάγησε	My plan is shipwrecked.
ἡ πρότασις	The proposal.
ἡ περίστασις, ἡ εὐκαιρία	The circumstance; opportunity.
ἡ δοκιμή	The trial.
ἡ πεῖρα	The attempt, experience.
πεπειραμένος ἄνθρωπος	A tried, experienced man.
ἔμπειρος· πολύπειρος	Experienced; of great experience.
ἡ ἀπόδειξις· ἀποδεικνύω	The proof; I prove.
τὸ μέσον· ὁ σκοπός	The means; the end.
κατορθόνω τὸν σκοπόν μου	I succeed in my object.
ἡ ἀσχολία· ἐνασχολοῦμαι εἴς τι	Employment; I am busy in anything.
ἐνησχολημένος	Engaged, busy.
ἡ ἐργασία· ἐργάζομαι	Business; I work.
ἡ προσπάθεια· προσπαθῶ	The attempt, endeavour; I try.
ἡ ὠφέλεια, τὸ ὄφελος· ὠφέλιμος	The benefit, the gain; beneficial.
ἀνωφελής· ὠφελῶ	Useless; I benefit.
ἡ βλάβη· βλάπτω	The injury; I injure.
ἡ ζημία· ζημιόνω	The damage; I damage.
ἡ ἀποζημίωσις· ἀποζημιῶ	Indemnity; I indemnify: compensation; I compensate.
δὲν ὠφελεῖ οὐδέν	It's no good, avails naught.
ἐπωφελής· ἐπιζήμιος	Advantageous; injurious.
ἐπιβλαβής	Harmful.
τὸ ἐμπόδιον· ἐμποδίζω, κωλύω	The hindrance; I hinder, prevent.
ἡ ἐνόχλησις· ἐνοχλῶ	The annoyance; I annoy.
μήπως σᾶς ἐνοχλῶ;	I hope I don't annoy you.
μήπως σᾶς ἀνησυχίζω;	I trust I don't disturb you.
μὴ ἐνοχλεῖσθε, μὴ ταράττεσθε	Don't disturb yourself, don't be alarmed.
ἡ διακοπή· διακόπτω	The interruption; I interrupt.
αἱ διακοπαί	The holidays.
ἡ ταραχή· ὁ θόρυβος	The disturbance; the noise.
ὁ ἔπαινος· ἐπαινῶ· ἀξιέπαινος	The praise; I praise; praiseworthy.
ἡ φήμη· φημίζομαι	Fame; I am talked about.
περίφημος· φημίζω	Famous; I blaze abroad.

περιώνυμος· ὀνομαστόν — Illustrious; noteworthy.
περιβόητος· διαβόητος — Celebrated; notorious.
ἡ λαμπρότης· λάμπω· λαμπρός — Splendour; I shine; brilliant.
ἡ μεγαλοπρέπεια· μεγαλοπρεπής — Magnificence; magnificent.
ἡ πομπή· πομπώδης — The display; showy, pompous.
ἐξαίρετος, ἐξαίσιος — Exceptional, extraordinary.
ἡ προτίμησις· προτιμῶ — The preference; I prefer.
   τοῦτο εἶνε προτιμότερον —   This is preferable.
ἡ σπανιότης· σπάνιος — Rarity; rare.
ὁ ὁρισμός· ὁρίζω — The definition; I define.
ἡ ἀπόφασις· ἀποφασίζω — The resolution; I resolve.
ἡ ἀνακοίνωσις· κοινοποιῶ — The announcement; I announce.
ἡ προσφορά· προσφέρω — The offer; I offer.
ἡ παραδοχή· παραδέχομαι — The acceptance; I accept.
ἡ ἀποποίησις· ἀποποιοῦμαι — The refusal; I refuse.
τὰ συγχαρητήρια· συγχαίρω — Congratulations; I congratulate.
ἡ ὑποδοχή· ὑποδέχομαι — The undertaking; I undertake.
ἡ ὑπόσχεσις· ὑπισχνοῦμαι, ὑπόσχο- — The promise; I promise, profess.
  μαι, ἐπαγγέλλομαι
ἡ ἄδεια· ἐπιτρέπω — The leave; I allow.
ἡ ἀπαγόρευσις· ἀπαγορεύω — The prohibition; I forbid.
ἡ πρότασις· προτείνω — The proposal; I propose.
ἡ πίεσις· πιέζω — The pressure; I press.
ἡ καταπίεσις· καταπιέζω — The oppression; I oppress.
ἡ ἀπελευθέρωσις· ἀπελευθερόνω — The deliverance; I free.
ἡ ἐλευθερία· ἐλεύθερος — Freedom; free.
ἡ δουλεία· δουλεύω — Slavery; I am a slave.
ὑπηρετῶ — I serve.
ἡ ἰσότης· ἴσος· ἐξισῶ — Equality; equal; I equalize.
ἡ ὑπηρεσία, ἡ ἐκδούλευσις — The service; the obligation.
τὸ κέρδος· κερδαίνω — The gain; I win, gain.
   πορίζομαι τὸν ἄρτον μου —   I earn my bread.
ἡ ζημία· ζημιοῦμαι — The loss; I suffer loss.
ὁ λογαριασμός — The bill, reckoning, account.
   δίδω λόγον· ὑπεύθυνος· εὐθύνη —   I give account; responsible responsibility.

ὁ χῶρος· εὐρύχωρος — Space; spacious.
ἡ ἔκτασις· ἐκτενής, ἐκτεταμένος — Extension; extensive, extended.
τὸ μῆκος· μακρός — Length; long.
ἐπιμηκύνω — I prolong, lengthen.

αὐτὴ ἡ γέφυρα ἔχει μῆκος ἑκατὸν ποδῶν	This bridge is a hundred feet long.
ἡ βραχύτης· βραχύς, κοντός	Shortness; short.
ἡ συντομία· σύντομος	Brevity; short, brief.
ἐπιβραχύνω, συντομεύω	I shorten, abridge.
ἐν συντόμῳ, ἐν ὀλίγοις	In short, in a few words.
τὸ πλάτος· εὐρύνω, πλατύνω	Breadth, width; I broaden, widen.
πλατύς, εὐρύς	Broad, wide.
τὸ βάθος· βαθύς· ἐμβαθύνω	Depth; deep; I deepen.
τὸ ὕψος· ὑψηλός	Height; high.
ὑψώνω· ἡ ὕψωσις	I raise, heighten; the heightening, exaltation, elevation.
τὸ πάχος· παχύς· πυκνός	The thickness; thick; close.
τὸ μέγεθος· μέγας, μεγάλος	The size; great, large.
αὐξάνω· ἡ αὔξησις	I increase (trans. and intrans., grow; increase, growth.
τὸ μεγαλεῖον· ἡ μεγαλειότης	Majesty, prowess; the greatness.
ἡ σμικρότης· μικρός	Littleness; small, little.
κολοσσιαῖος	Colossal.
ἡ στενότης· στενός	Narrowness; narrow.
ἐπαυξάνω· ἡ αὔξησις	I increase, enhance; increase, advancement.
ἐλαττόνω· ἡ ἐλάττωσις	I lessen; decrease.
ὁ ἀριθμός· πολυάριθμος	Number; numerous.
ἄπειρος, ἀπειράριθμος	Boundless, innumerable, countless.
ἀριθμῶ· ἡ ἀρίθμησις	I count; counting, calculation.
ὁ ἀριθμός· ἀριθμολογῶ	The number; I calculate.
ἡ βαρύτης· βαρύς	Gravity; heavy.
τὸ βάρος· ἔχω βάρος	Weight; I have weight, I weigh.
ἡ ἐλαφρότης· ἐλαφρύς	Lightness; light.
ἐλαφρύνω, ἀνακουφίζω	I lighten, relieve.
ἡ δυσκολία· δύσκολον	Difficulty; difficult.
ἡ εὐκολία· εὔκολος	Easiness; easy.
εὐκολύνω	I facilitate.
ἡ κίνησις· κινῶ	Movement; I move.
κινητός, εὐκίνητος	Movable, nimble.
ἀκίνητος	Immovable, motionless.

ἡ ταχύτης	Speed.
ταχύς	Swift.
ἡ βραδύτης· βραδύς	Slowness, sloth; slow.
ἡ διεύθυνσις· ἀπευθύνω, κατευθύνω, διευθύνω	The direction; I direct, level, point (also manage).
ἡ θέσις	The position.
ἡ πόλις κεῖται	The town lies, is situated.
ὁ τόπος· ἡ πλατεῖα	The place; the square.
ἡ ἀπόστασις· ἀπομακρύνω	The distance; I withdraw.
πόσον ἀπέχει — ;	How far is — off?
τὸ χρῶμα· χρωματίζω	The colour; I colour.
βάφω	I dye.
(χρῶμα) ἀνοικτόν· βαθύ	A light, dark (colour).
ὠχρός· κάτωχρος	Pale; pallid.
τὸ χρῶμα τοῦτο κλίνει πρὸς τὸ κυανοῦν	This colour has a bluish tint.
τὸ λευκόν· λευκός· λευκαίνω	White (subst.); white (adj.); I whiten.
ἡ λευκότης· ὑπόλευκος	Whiteness; whitish.
τὸ μέλαν, τὸ μαῦρον· μέλας, μαῦρος	Black (subst.); black (adj.).
ὑπομέλας· μαυρίζω	Blackish; I blacken.
ἡ μελανότης· μελανωπός	Blackness; dark.
τὸ πολιόν, τὸ ψαρόν· πολιός, ψαρός	Grey; grey.
τὸ κυανοῦν· κυανοῦς, κυανόχρους	Blue; blue, bluish.
κυανωπός, ὑπόγλαυκος	Bluish, greyish.
ἰοειδής	Violet.
τὸ πράσινον· πράσινος	Green; green.
πρασινίζω· χλοερός	I make green, grow green; greenish.
τὸ κίτρινον· κίτρινος	Yellow; yellow.
κιτρινίζω· κιτρινωπός	I turn yellow; yellowish.
τὸ ἐρυθρόν, τὸ κόκκινον	Red, crimson.
ἐρυθρός, κόκκινος· πυρρός, κατακόκκινος	Red, crimson; reddish, reddened.
ἡ ἐρυθρότης· ἡ ἐριθρίασις	Redness; reddening.
ἐρυθρωπός· πορφυρόχρους	Red-hued; crimson-coloured.
ῥοδόχρους	Rose-coloured, rosy.
τὸ φαιόν, μελάγχρουν	Brown, brownish colour.
φαιός, μελάγχρους, μελαγχροινός	Brown, blackish, swarthy.

XI.

Σύμπαν.	UNIVERSE.
φαινόμενα· καιρός· ὧραι τοῦ ἔτους.	Phenomena; time; seasons of the year.
τὸ σύμπαν· παγκόσμιος	The universe; universal.
ὁ κόσμος· κοσμικός	The world; secular, worldly.
ἡ φύσις· φυσικός	Nature; natural.
ὁ οὐρανός· οὐράνιος	Heaven; heavenly.
ὁ ἀστήρ· τὸ ἄστρον, ὁ ἀστερισμός	The star; the constellation.
ἡ κίνησις τῶν ἀστέρων	The motion of the stars.
ὁ ἀπλανὴς ἀστήρ	The fixed star.
ὁ πολικὸς ἀστήρ	The polar star.
ὁ διάττων ἀστήρ	The shooting star.
ὁ ἀστερόεις οὐρανός	The starry heavens.
ἐν ὑπαίθρῳ	In the open air.
ὁ πλανήτης· τὸ πλανητικὸν σύστημα	The planet; the planetary system.
ὁ κομήτης· ἡ οὐρά	The comet; the tail.
ὁ γαλαξίας	The milky way.
ἡ ἕως· τὸ βόρειον σέλας	The dawn; the aurora borealis, northern light.
ὁ ἥλιος· τὸ ἡλιακὸν ἔτος	The sun; the solar year.
αἱ ἀκτῖνες τοῦ ἡλίου	The rays of the sun.
ἡ ἔκλειψις τοῦ ἡλίου	The eclipse of the sun.
ὁ ἥλιος ἀνατέλλει	The sun rises.
ἡ ἀνατολὴ τοῦ ἡλίου	Sunrise.
ὁ ἥλιος δύει, βασιλεύει (vl.)	The sun sets.
ἡ δύσις τοῦ ἡλίου	The setting of the sun.
ἡλιοκαής	Sunburnt.
τὸ φῶς· φωτεινός	The light; luminous.
ἡ αἴγλη, ἡ στίλβη· στίλβω	The sparkle; I sparkle.
ἡ λάμψις· λαμπρός	The sheen; bright.
τὸ σκότος· στοτεινός	The darkness; dark.
τὸ λυκόφως	The twilight.
ἡ σκιά· σκιερός	The shade, shadow; shady.
ἡ σελήνη· τὸ σεληνιακὸν ἔτος	The moon; the lunar year.
αἱ τέσσαρες φάσεις τῆς σελήνης	The four quarters of the moon.
ἡ νουμηνία· ἡ πανσέληνος	The new moon; the full moon.
τὸ πρῶτον, τὸ τελευταῖον τέταρτον	The first, the last quarter.

τὸ κλίμα	The clime, climate.
αἱ ἀνατολαί, ἡ ἀνατολή· ἀνατολικός	The east; eastern.
αἱ δυσμαί, ἡ δύσις	The west.
δυτικός, ἑσπέριος	Western.
ὁ νότος, ἡ μεσημβρία	South, midday.
μεσημβρινός	Southern.
ὁ βορρᾶς, ἡ ἄρκτος· βόρειος, ἀρκτικός	The north; northern, arctic.
ὁ βόρειος ἄνεμος	The north wind.
ὁ νότιος ἄνεμος	The south wind.
ὁ ἀνατολικός, δυτικὸς ἄνεμος	The east, west wind.
τὸ φαινόμενον· τὸ μετέωρον	The appearance; the meteor.
ὁ ἀήρ· ἀέριος, ἀέρινος	The air; aerial, airy.
ἀναπνέω δροσερὸν ἀέρα	I breathe cool air.
τὸ ἀερόστατον	The balloon.
ὁ ἀερόλιθος, τὸ ἀστροπελέκι	The aerolith, falling star.
ἡ ἀεραντλία	The air-pump.
τὸ ῥεῦμα ἀέρος	The draught, current of air.
ἡ ἀτμόσφαιρα· ἀτμοσφαιρικός	The atmosphere; atmospheric.
τὸ πῦρ· ἡ φλόξ	The fire; the flame.
ἡ καῦσις	The heat.
ὁ σπινθήρ· σπινθηρίζω	The beam, ray; I radiate.
ὁ καπνός· καπνίζω	Smoke (also tobacco); I smoke.
ὁ ἀτμός· αἱ ἀναθυμιάσεις	Steam; the exhalations.
ἀτμιδώδης· ἡ ἐξάτμισις	Volatile, vaporous, gaseous; evaporation.
ἡ ἀτμομηχανή	The steam-engine.
τὸ ἀτμόπλοιον, ἀτμόπλουν	The steam-boat.
ἡ νεφέλη· τὸ νέφος	The mist; the cloud.
ἡ θύελλα· θυελλώδης	The storm; stormy.
ἡ ἀστραπή· ἀστράπτει	The lightning; it lightens.
ἡ βροντή· βροντᾷ	The thunder; it thunders.
ὁ κεραυνός	The thunderbolt.
ἡ ἶρις, τὸ οὐράνιον τόξον	The rainbow.
ἡ καταιγίς, ἡ τρικυμία	The tempest, the storm (at sea).
ὁ στρόβιλος, ὁ ἀνεμοστρόβιλος	The whirlwind.
ἡ βροχή· βροχερός, ὄμβριος	The rain; rainy, showery.
τὸ πηγαῖον ὕδωρ	Spring water.
τὸ ὕδωρ· ἡ σταγών	The water; the drop.

βρέχει· ὁ ὄμβρος, ἡ ῥαγδαία βροχή	It rains; the shower, the heavy rain.
ἡ χάλαζα· πίπτει χάλαζα	The hail; it hails.
ἡ χιών· χιονίζει	The snow; it snows.
ὁ πάγος· παγετώδης	The frost, ice; frosty, icy.
ἡ πλήμμυρα· πλημμυρῶ	The flood; I flood.
τὸ ψῦχος· ψυχρός	The cold; cold.
ὁ ἄνεμος	The wind.
ἡ δροσιά· δροσερός	The cool; cool.
ἡ θερμότης· ὁ καύσων	Warmth; heat.
ἡ δρόσος· ἡ πάχνη	The dew; the hoar-frost, rime.
ἡ ὑγρασία, ἡ ὑγρότης· ὑγρός	The damp, moisture; moist, damp.
ἡ ξηρασία	Drought.
ξηρός· ξηραίνω	Dry; I dry.
ἡ ὥρα τοῦ ἔτους	The time of the year, season.
τὸ ἔαρ, ἡ ἄνοιξις	The spring.
τὸ θέρος, τὸ καλοκαίριον	The summer.
τὸ φθινόπωρον	The autumn.
ὁ χειμών	The winter.

XII.

Γῆ.

θάλασσα, ποταμός, ὄρος, κ.τ.λ.

Earth.

Sea, river, mountain, &c.

ἡ γῆ· γήϊνος· ἡ γηΐνος σφαῖρα	The earth; terrestrial; the terrestrial globe.
τὸ ἡμισφαίριον	The hemisphere.
ὁ βόρειος (or ἀρκτικὸς) πόλος	The north pole.
ὁ νότιος (or ἀνταρκτικὸς) πόλος	The south pole.
ὁ ἄξων	The axis.
ὁ ἰσημερινός	The equator.
ὁ παράλληλος κύκλος	The parallel, line of latitude.
ὁ μεσημβρινός· ὁ βαθμός	The meridian; the degree.
ὁ τροπικὸς τοῦ καρκίνου, τοῦ αἰγόκερω	The tropic of Cancer, of Capricorn.
ὁ βόρειος πολικὸς κύκλος	The arctic circle.
ὁ νότιος πολικὸς κύκλος	The antarctic circle.
ἡ διακεκαυμένη ζώνη	The torrid zone.
αἱ εὔκρατοι ζῶναι	The temperate zones.

αἱ κατεψυγμέναι ζῶναι	The frigid zones.
ἡ γεωγραφικὴ θέσις τόπου	The geographical position of a place.
τὸ μῆκος· τὸ πλάτος	The length; the breadth.
ἡ περιστροφὴ τῆς γῆς περὶ τὸν ἄξωνά της (περὶ τὸν ἥλιον)	The revolution of the earth on its axis (round the sun).
ἡ γῆ στρέφεται περὶ ἑαυτήν	The earth turns round.
ἡ ἤπειρος	The mainland, continent.
ἡ θάλασσα· ὁ ὠκεανός	The sea; the ocean.
ἡ παλίρροια· ἡ πλημμυρὶς καὶ ἄμπωτις	The tide; the ebb and flow.
ἡ πλημμυρίς· ἡ ἄμπωτις	The flow, high tide; the ebb, low tide.
τὸ κῦμα· ἡ κυματωγή	The wave; the undulation.
ὁ σκόπελος· ἡ ὑφαλός	The rock; the shoal.
ἡ ἀκτή, τὸ παράλιον· ἡ προκυμαία	The shore, the beach; the breakwater.
ὁ κόλπος· ὁ ὅρμος	The gulf; the anchorage, haven.
ὁ πορθμός· ὁ ἰσθμός	The strait; the isthmus, neck of land.
ὁ λιμήν	The harbour.
τὸ ἀκρωτήριον	The promontory, headland.
ἡ χερσόνησος· ἡ νῆσος· τὸ νησίδιον	The peninsula; the island; the islet.
ὁ νησιώτης	The islander.
ἡ λίμνη	The lake.
ὁ ποταμός· ὁ χείμαρρος	The river; the torrent.
ὁ ῥύαξ, τὸ ῥυάκιον· ἡ πηγή, ἡ βρύσις	The brook, the rivulet; the spring, the fountain.
τὸ παραποτάμιον	The tributary.
ὁ πλωτὸς ποταμός	The navigable river.
τὸ στόμιον	The river's mouth, estuary.
ὁ καταρράκτης	The waterfall.
ἡ πλήμμυρα· πλημμυρῶ	The flood; I flood.
ἡ διῶρυξ	The canal, dyke.
τὸ ὄρος· ὀρεινός· βουνώδης	The mountain; mountain(ous), hilly.
ἡ πεδιάς· τὸ ὀροπέδιον	The plain; the table-land.
ἡ δειράς· ἡ ἀκρώρεια	The chain, neck; the peak.
ἡ ὑπώρεια· ἡ κλιτύς	The foot; the slope, side.

ἡ ῥάχις	The ridge.
ὁ λόφος· τὸ λοφίδιον· τὸ ὕψωμα	The hill; the hillock; the height.
ὁ βράχος· ὁ κρημνός	The rock; the precipice.
ἡ κοιλάς	The valley.
τὸ ἡφαίστειον (ὄρος)· ὁ κρατήρ	The volcano; the crater.
ἡ ἔκρηξις· ὁ ῥύαξ	The eruption; the stream (of lava).
τὸ ἄντρον· τὸ σπήλαιον	The cave; the cavern.
ἡ ἔρημος· ἡ ἐρημία	The wilderness; the desert.
ἡ χώρα· ὁ τόπος	The country, region; the place.
τὰ περίχωρα	The neighbourhood, environs.
τὸ ὅριον· ἡ μεθορία χώρα, τὰ σύνορα	The boundary; the borderland, frontier.
ἡ ἄμμος· ἀμμώδης	The sand; sandy.
ὁ κονιορτός, vl. ἡ σκόνη	The dust.
ὁ πηλός· ἡ ἄργιλλος	The mud; the loam, marl.

XIII.

Χρόνος.	Time.
διαίρεσις τοῦ χρόνου· ὀνόματα τῶν μηνῶν καὶ ἡμερῶν· ὥρα· ἡλικία.	Division of time; names of months and days; hour; age.
ὁ χρόνος· ἔχω καιρόν	The time; I have time.
ἡ χρονολογία· χρονολογικός	Chronology; chronological.
ὁ ἀναχρονισμός	The anachronism; confusion of dates.
πρὸ Χριστοῦ (π. Χ.)	B.C.
μετὰ Χριστόν (μ. Χ.)	A.D.
τὸ παρόν, τὸ ἐνεστός	The present (instant).
τὸ παρελθόν· τὸ μέλλον	The past; the future (coming): or ult.; prox.
ἡ περίοδος· περιοδικός	The period; periodical.
ἡ ἐποχή· ὁ αἰών	The era; the age.
ἡ ἑκατονταετηρίς	The century.
τὸ ἔτος· ἐτήσιος· ἡ ἐπετηρίς	The year; yearly; the anniversary.
τρὶς τοῦ ἔτους	Thrice in the year.
ἡ ἑξαμηνία, τὸ ἑξάμηνον	The half-year, six months.
τὸ δίσεκτον (βίσεκτον) ἔτος	The leap-year.
ἡ τριμηνία, τὸ τρίμηνον	The quarter, three months.

τρίμηνος	Three months long.
ὁ μήν· μηνιαῖος	The month; monthly.
ἡ πρώτη, δευτέρα μαΐον	The first, second of May.
ἡ ἑβδομάς· ἑβδομαδιαῖος	The week; weekly.
τὸ ἑβδομαδιαῖον φύλλον	The weekly journal.
ἡ ἡμέρα· ἡμερήσιος	The day; daily.
τὰ ἡμερήσια νέα	The news of the day, "Daily News."
πρὸ ὀκτὼ ἡμερῶν	A week ago.
πρὸ δεκαπέντε ἡμερῶν	A fortnight ago.
ἡμέραν παρ' ἡμέραν	Day by day.
ὁ ἐπιούσιος ἄρτος	The daily bread.
ἀπὸ καιροῦ εἰς καιρόν	From time to time.
ἡ νύξ· τὸ μεσονύκτιον	The night; midnight.
ἡ πρωΐα, τὸ πρωΐ	The morning, the forenoon.
καλὴν ἡμέραν, vl. καλημέρα	Good day.
ἡ μεσημβρία, τὸ μεσημέριον	Midday, noon.
πρὸ μεσημβρία (π. μ.)	Before noon (a.m.).
μετὰ μεσημβρίαν (μ. μ.)	After noon (p.m.).
ἡ ἑσπέρα, τὸ ἑσπέρας	The evening.
ἀπόψε	This evening, to-night.
ἡ ἑσπερίς	The evening party.
σήμερον τὴν πρωΐαν (τὸ πρωΐ)	This morning.
χθές· προχθές	Yesterday; the day before yesterday.
αὔριον· μεθαύριον	To-morrow; the day after to-morrow.
ἡ προτεραία	The day before.
ἡ ἐπιοῦσα, ἡ ὑστεραία, ἡ ἐπαύριον	The following day; the morrow.
ἡ ὥρα· ἐνωρίς	The hour; early.
μία ὥρα καὶ ἡμίσεια	An hour and a half.
τὸ λεπτόν· τὸ δευτερόλεπτον	The minute; the second.
ἡ στιγμή	The moment.
ποία (τί) ὥρα εἶνε ;	What o'clock is it?
δευτέρα (δύο) καὶ τέταρτον	A quarter past two.
τρίτη (τρεῖς) καὶ ἡμίσεια	Half past three.
ἑπτὰ παρὰ τέταρτον	Quarter to seven.
παρὰ δέκα (λεπτά)	Ten minutes to ——.
ἀκριβῶς δέκα	Just ten, ten precisely.
περὶ τὴν δεκάτην ὥραν	About the tenth hour.

εἶνε δωδεκάτη ὥρα, μεσημέριον	It is twelve o'clock, midday.
ἡ ἡλικία	The age.
ποίαν ἡλικίαν ἔχετε;	What age are you?
πόσων ἐτῶν εἶσθε;	How old are you?
εἶμαι εἴκοσιν ἐτῶν	I am twenty (years old).
εἰσέρχεται εἰς τὸ δέκατον ἔνατον ἔτος	He is entering on his nineteenth year.
συνεπλήρωσα τὸ τεσσαρακοστὸν ἔτος	I have completed my fortieth year.
πλησιάζει εἰς τὸ τριακοστὸν ἔτος	He is approaching his thirtieth year.
φαίνεται νεώτερος ἢ ὅσον εἶνε	He looks younger than he is.
ἡ νηπιώτης	Infancy, childhood.
ἡ νεότης· νέος	Youth; young.
ὁ νεανίας· ἡ νεᾶνις	The young man; the young woman.
ἡ νεολαία	The youth (collectively), young people.
ὁ πρεσβύτερος· ὁ νεώτερος	The elder; the younger.
ἡ ἡλικία, ἡ ἐνηλικότης· ἐνήλικος	Age; full age, majority; of age.
ἡ ἀνηλικότης· ἀνήλικος	Minority; a minor, under age.
τὸ γῆρας	Old age.
γέρων, γραῖα	An old man, an old woman.
οἱ ἀρχαῖοι (παλαιοὶ) Ἕλληνες	The ancient (old) Greeks.
ἡ ἀρχαιότης· ἀρχαῖος	Antiquity; ancient.
ἡ ἀρχαιότης· ἀρχαιολόγος, ἀρχαιοδίφης	The antiquity; antiquarian, archæologist.

XIV.

Οἰκογένεια.	FAMILY.
ὀνόματα τῆς συγγενείας· οἰκονομικὴ διάταξις· ὑπηρέται.	Names of relationship; domestic economy; servants.
ἡ οἰκογένεια	The family.
οἰκογενειάρχης	The head of a family.
ὁ ἀρχηγὸς οἰκογενείας	The founder of a family.
καλῆς οἰκογενείας	Of good family.
ἡ συγγένεια· συγγενής	Relationship, kindred; kin, relative.
ὁ βαθμὸς τῆς συγγενείας	The degree of relationship.

οἱ προγόνοι, οἱ προπάτορες	The ancestors, forefathers.
οἱ ἀπόγονοι	The descendants.
ἡ μεταγενεστέρα γενεά	The later generation, posterity.
ὁ πάππος· ἡ μάμμη	The grandfather; the grandmother.
ὁ ἀνήρ· ὁ σύζυγος	The man, the husband.
ἡ γυνή· ἡ σύζυγος	The woman, wife; the consort, the spouse.
νυμφεύω, ὑπανδρεύω	I marry, wed.
νυμφεύομαι, ὑπανδρεύομαι	I am wedded, married; also, I wed (the man—the woman).
ὁ γάμος, τὸ συνοικέσιον	The marriage, the alliance.
οἱ ἀρραβῶνες	The pledges, betrothal.
ἀρραβωνίζομαι, μνηστεύομαι	I am plighted, betrothed.
ὁ μνηστήρ· ἡ μνηστή	The suitor; the *fiancée*.
ὁ γαμβρός· ἡ νύμφη	The bridegroom; the bride.
οἱ μελλόνυμφοι· οἱ νεόνυμφοι	The bridal pair; the newly married couple.
ἡ προίξ· προικίζω	The dowry; I endow.
οἱ γάμοι	The wedding.
τὸ γαμήλιον δῶρον	The wedding presents.
ὁ πατήρ· πατρικός	The father; paternal, fatherly.
ἡ μήτηρ· μητρικός	The mother; maternal, motherly.
ὁ πατρυιός, ὁ μητρυιός	The paternal uncle, maternal uncle.
ὁ πενθερός· ἡ πενθερά	The father-in-law; the mother-in-law.
ὁ γαμβρός	The brother-in-law.
ἡ μητρυιά	The step-mother.
τὸ τέκνον· τὸ παιδίον	The child; the boy.
ἡ παιδικὴ ὄψις	The childlike look.
οἱ δίδυμοι	The twins.
τὸ παιδίον, ὁ παῖς	The little boy, the boy.
ὁ υἱός· ἡ θυγάτηρ	The son; the daughter.
παιδικός· υἱϊκός	Boyish; filial.
παιδαριώδης	Childish.
τὸ κοράσιον	The girl.
ἡ παρθένος· παρθενικός	The maiden; maidenly.
ἡ παρθενία	Maidenhood, virginity.
ὁ γαμβρός· ἡ νύμφη	The bridegroom; the bride.

ὁ πρόγονος· ἡ προγόνη	The ancestor; the ancestress.
ὁ ἔγγονος· ἡ ἐγγόνη	The offspring (male); ditto (female).
ὁ ἀπέγγονος, ὁ δισέγγονος· ἡ ἀπέγγονος, ἡ δισέγγονος	The descendant of the second generation (male); ditto (female).
ὁ ἀδελφός· ἡ ἀδελφή	The brother; the sister.
ἡ ἀδελφότης	The brotherhood, fraternity.
ἡ ἀδελφικότης· ἀδελφικός	Brotherliness; brotherly.
ὁ θεῖος, ἡ θεία	The uncle; the aunt.
ὁ ἀνεψιός· ἡ ἀνεψιά	The nephew; the niece.
ὁ ἐξάδελφος· ἡ ἐξαδέλφη	The cousin; ditto (female).
ἡ γέννησις· γεννῶμαι	The birth; I am born.
τὸ γένος, τὸ φῦλον	The race; the tribe.
ὁ ὀρφανός· ἡ ὀρφανή	The orphan (boy); the orphan (girl).
ὁ κηδεμών· ἡ κηδεμονία	The guardian; the guardianship.
ὁ χῆρος· ἡ χήρα	The widower; the widow.
ἡ χηρεία	Widowhood.
ἡ ἀγαμία· ὁ ἄγαμος	The unmarried state; the single man.
ὁ κληρονόμος· ἡ κληρονόμος	The heir; the heiress.
ἡ κληρονομία· ὁ κληροδότης	The inheritance; the bequeather.
ἡ διαθήκη	The will, testament.
ἡ διαδοχή, οἱ διάδοχοι	The succession; the successors.
οἱ οἰκονομικὴ διάταξις, τὰ οἰκονομικά	Household management; domestic matters.
ἡ οἰκονόμος, ἡ ταμία	The housekeeper; stewardess.
ἡ ὑπηρετεία, οἱ ὑπηρέται	The service, the servants.
ὑπηρετῶ· ἡ ὑπηρεσία	I serve; service.
ὁ μισθός	The wages.
ὁ ὑπηρέτης· ἡ ὑπηρέτις, ἡ ὑπηρέτρια	The servant; the maid, the maid-servant.
ἡ θαλαμηπόλος, ὁ θεράπων	The chambermaid, the attendant.
ὁ ἁμαξηλάτης	The coachman.
ὁ μάγειρος· ἡ μαγείρισσα	The cook (male); ditto (female).
ἡ παιδοκόμος	The nurse.
ἡ θαλαμηπόλος, ἡ θεράπαινα	The housemaid.

XV.

Κοινωνία. — Society.

εἴδη κυβερνήσεων· τίτλοι καὶ ἀξιώματα· διοίκησις, κ.τ.λ.	Forms of government; titles and offices; administration, &c.
ἡ κοινωνία.	Society.
τὸ ἔθνος· ἡ ἐθνικότης, ἡ ἐθνότης	The nation; the nationality.
ἐθνικός· ὁ ἰθαγενής, ὁ αὐτόχθων	National; the native, aboriginal.
ὁ ξένος· ξένος, ἀλλοδαπός· ἡ ἀλλοδαπή	The foreigner, stranger; the foreign country.
ὁ λαός· ὁ ὄχλος	The people; the populace, mob.
ὁ πληθυσμός· πολυάνθρωπος	The population; populous.
ἡ δημοτικότης· δημοτικός	Popularity; popular.
ἡ πατρίς· ὁ πατριώτης, ὁ φιλόπατρις	The (native) country, fatherland; the countryman, patriot.
ἡ φιλοπατρία· πατριωτικός	Patriotism; patriotic.
ὁ συμπατριώτης, ὁ πατριώτης, ὁ ὁμογενής	The fellow-countryman, the man of the same race.
ὁ κυριάρχης· ἡ κυριαρχία	The sovereign; sovereignty.
ὁ ἐπικυριάρχης· ἡ ἐπικυριαρχία	The feudal lord; feudal lordship.
ὁ ὑπήκοος· ὁ πολίτης	The subject; the citizen.
ὁ δοῦλος· ἡ δουλεία	The slave; slavery.
τὸ πολίτευμα	The constitution.
ἡ μοναρχία· ὁ μονάρχης	The monarchy; the monarch.
μοναρχικός	Monarchic.
ἡ ἀπόλυτος μοναρχία	The absolute monarchy.
ἡ συνταγματικὴ μοναρχία	The constitutional monarchy.
ἡ ἐθνικὴ συνέλευσις, ἡ ἐθνοσυνέλευσις	The national assembly.
ἡ νομοθετικὴ βουλή	The legislative council.
ἡ γερουσία	The senate.
ἡ βουλή	The parliament.
ὁ πρόεδρος· ἡ προεδρεία	The president; presidency.
συγκαλῶ· διαλύω	I summon; dissolve.
ὁ βουλευτής	The member of parliament.
ἐκλέγω· ἡ ἐκλογή· ὁ ἐκλογεύς	I elect; the election; the elector.
ἡ δημοκρατία	The democracy, republic.
ὁ δημοκρατικός· δημοκρατικός	The democrat; republican.
ἡ ἀριστοκρατία· ὁ ἀριστοκράτης	Aristocracy; the aristocrat.
ἡ συντηρητικὴ μερίς	The conservative party.

φιλελεύθερος· ριζοσπαστικός	Liberal; radical.
ἡ αὐτοκρατορία· ὁ αὐτοκράτωρ	The empire; the emperor.
ἡ αὐτοκράτειρα· αὐτοκρατορικός	The empress; imperial.
τὸ βασίλειον· ὁ βασιλεύς	The kingdom; the king.
ἡ βασίλισσα· βασιλικός	The queen; kingly, regal.
βασιλεύω· ἡ βασιλεία	I reign; the reign, rule.
ὁ ἀντιβασιλεύς	The viceroy.
ὁ διάδοχος τοῦ θρόνου	The successor to the throne.
ἡ ἀνάβασις εἰς τὸν θρόνον	The ascent of the throne.
ὁ διάδοχος· ἡ διαδοχή	The successor; the succession.
ὁ προκάτοχος	The regent.
τὸ στέμμα· τὸ σκῆπτρον	The crown; the sceptre.
ἡ Μεγαλειότης· μεγαλεῖος	Majesty; majestic.
Μεγαλειότατε !	Your Majesty.
ὁ ἐκλέκτωρ· ὁ δούξ· ἡ δούκισσα	The elector; the duke; the duchess.
ὁ μέγας δούξ· ὁ ἀρχιδούξ	The grand-duke; the arch-duke.
ὁ ἡγεμών, ὁ πρίγκηψ	The prince.
ἡ ἡγεμονία· ἡ ἡγεμονίς, ἡ πριγκίπισσα	The princedom, principality; the princess.
ὁ ἡγεμονικὸς οἶκος	The princely house.
ὁ κόμης· ἡ κόμησσα· ἡ κομητία	The count; the countess; the county.
ὁ βαρῶνος· ἡ βαρώνη, ἡ βαρωνίς	The baron; the baroness the barony.
ὁ ἱππότης· ἱππoτικός	The knight; knightly.
ἡ αὐλή· αὐλικός	The court; courtly.
κυρία τῆς αὐλῆς or τῆς τιμῆς	Lady in waiting, maid of honour.
ὁ αὐλάρχης	The master of the court.
οἱ εὐπατρίδαι, οἱ εὐγενεῖς	The nobles, the lords.
εὐπατρίδης, εὐγενής	Noble, well-born.
ἡ διπλωματία· ὁ διπλωμάτης	Diplomacy; the diplomatist.
διπλωματικός	Diplomatic.
ἡ πρεσβεία· ὁ πρεσβευτής	The embassy; the ambassador.
οἱ πρέσβεις	The legates, delegates.
ὁ ἐπιτετραμμένος, ὁ ἀντιπρόσωπος	The *chargé d'affaires*, the representative.
ὁ γραμματεὺς πρεσβείας	The secretary to the embassy.
ὁ τίτλος· τὸ ἀξίωμα	The title; the office.
ὁ ὑπάλληλος	The clerk, subordinate.

ἡ διοίκησις· διοικῶ	Administration; I administer.
αἱ διοικητικαὶ ἀρχαί	The administrative powers.
τὸ ὑπουργεῖον· ὁ ὑπουργός	The ministry; the minister.
τὸ συμβούλιον	The cabinet (council).
ἡ ἐπαρχία· ἐπαρχιακός	The province; provincial.
ὁ ἐπαρχιώτης	The provincial.
ὁ νομός· ὁ δῆμος	The district; the township.
ἡ πρωτεύουσα· ἡ καθέδρα	The capital; the seat of government.
ἡ κωμόπολις· τὸ χωρίον, ἡ κώμη	The town; the village, the hamlet.
ὁ χωρίτης, χωρικός	The countryman; country (adj.).
ἡ ἀστυνομία· ὁ ἀστυνόμος	The police; the police inspector.
ὁ ὑπαστυνόμος· ὁ κλητήρ	The policeman; constable.
ὁ χωροφύλαξ	The *gendarme;* country policeman.

XVI.

Στρατός.	Army.
ὁ στρατός	The army.
ὁ στρατιώτης	The soldier.
ὁ ἐθελοντής· ὁ μισθωτὸς στρατιώτης	The volunteer; the mercenary.
ἡ στρατολογία· ὁ νεοσύλλεκτος	The enlistment; the recruit.
ἡ φρουρά· ὁ φρουρός	The garrison; the man on garrison duty.
ἡ ἐθνοφυλακή	The militia.
ὁ ἀπόμαχος	The old soldier, retired soldier.
τὸ ἱππικόν· ὁ ἱππεύς	The cavalry; the horse-soldier.
τὸ πεζικόν· ὁ πεζός	The infantry; the foot-soldier.
ὁ εὔζωνος	Rifleman, sharpshooter.
τὸ πυροβολικόν· ὁ πυροβολητής	The artillery; the artilleryman.
τὸ μηχανικόν (σῶμα)	The engineers.
ὁ ἀξιωματικὸς τοῦ πυροβολικοῦ	The artillery officer.
στρατιωτικὸν σῶμα	A body (corps), force of soldiers.
ἡ μεραρχία	The division.
τὸ σύνταγμα	The regiment.
τὸ τάγμα	The batallion.
ὁ λόχος	The company.
τὸ ἐπιτελεῖον	The regimental staff.

τὸ γενικὸν ἐπιτελεῖον	The general staff.
ὁ ὑπασπιστής	The adjutant.
ἡ σημαία	The standard.

στρατιωτικοὶ βαθμοί.	MILITARY GRADES
οἱ στρατηγοί.	*The generals.*
ὁ στρατάρχης, ὁ ἀρχιστράτηγος	The commander, commander-in-chief.
ὁ στρατηγός	The general.
ὁ ἀντιστράτηγος	The lieutenant-general.
ὁ μοίραρχος	The general of division.
ὁ ὑπομοίραρχος	The lieutenant-major.
ἐπιτελεῖς, ἀνώτεροι ἀξιωματικοί.	*Staff-officers, higher officers.*
ὁ συνταγματάρχης	The colonel.
ὁ ἀντισυνταγμάρχης	The lieutenant-colonel.
ὁ ταγματάρχης	The major (of infantry).
ὁ ἵππαρχος	Ditto (of cavalry), the commander of cavalry.
κατώτεροι ἀξιωματικοί.	*Lower rank officers.*
ὁ λοχαγός	The captain.
ὁ ἴλαρχος	The captain of the horse.
ὁ ὑπολοχαγός	The lieutenant.
ὁ ἀνθυπολοχαγός	The vice-lieutenant, second lieutenant.
ὑπαξιωματικοί.	*Non-commissioned officers.*
ὁ ἀνθυπασπιστής	The ensign.
ὁ ἐπιλοχίας	The corporal.
ὁ λοχίας	The vice-corporal.
ὁ δεκανεύς	The sergeant.
ὁ ὑποδεκανεύς	The lance-corporal.
ὁ ἁπλοῦς στρατιώτης	The common soldier, private.

XVII.

Θέατρον.	THEATRE.
τὸ θέατρον· θεατρικός	The theatre; theatrical.
ἡ σκηνή· σκηνικός	The scene; scenic.
ἡ αὐλαία, τὸ κατάβλημα	The curtain.
ἡ σκηνογραφία	The scenery.

ἡ ἱματοθήκη	The wardrobe, dress.
ἡ ὀρχήστρα	The orchestra.
ἡ πλατεῖα	The pit.
τὰ θεωρεῖα	The boxes.
θεωρεῖον τῆς πρώτης, δευτέρας σειρᾶς	Box in the first, second row.
τὸ ἀμφιθέατρον	The dress-circle (amphitheatre).
τὸ ὑπερῷον	The gallery.
τὸ εἰσιτήριον	The ticket.
ἡ δραματικὴ τέχνη	The dramatic art.
ἡ παράστασις	The representation.
ἡ εὐεργετικὴ παράστασις	The benefit.
ἡ δοκιμή	The rehearsal.
ἡ τραγῳδία· τραγικός	The tragedy; tragic.
ὁ ἠθοποιός· ἡ ἠθοποιός	The actor; the actress.
τὸ δρᾶμα· δραματικός	The drama; dramatic.
τὸ μελόδραμα	The melodrama.
ἡ πρᾶξις· τὸ διάλειμμα	The act; the interlude.
ἡ σκηνή	The scene.
ὁ διευθυντής	The manager.
ὁ θίασος	The company.
τὸ πρόσωπον	The character (mask); *dramatis persona*.
αἱ χειροκροτήσεις· χειροκροτῶ, ἐπικροτῶ	The applause; I applaud, I clap.
συρίζω	I hiss.
τὸ νευροσπαστικὸν θέατρον	The marionette theatre.
ὁ σχοινοβάτης	The rope-dancer.
ὁ θαυματοποιός	The conjuror.
ὁ ταχυδακτυλουργός	The prestidigitateur.
τὸ ἱπποδρόμιον	The circus.

XVIII.

Ταξείδιον.	JOURNEY.
ἅμαξα· ὁδός· ταχυδρομεῖον· σιδηρόδρομος	*Carriage; road; post; railway.*
τὸ ταξείδιον, ἡ περιήγησις	The journey, voyage.
ὁ περιηγητής	The traveller.
ἡ ἀναχώρησις· ἡ ἐπάνοδος	The departure; the return.

ἡ διαμονή· ἡ ἄφιξις	The stay; the arrival.
ἡ περιοδεία· ἡ πεζοπορία	The tour; the walking tour.
ὁ πεζοπόρος	The pedestrian.
ὁ πεζός	The walker.
τὸ διαβατήριον	The passport.
ὁ ὁδηγός· ὁδηγῶ	The guide; I guide.
ὁ ξεναγός	The cicerone.
ἀναχωρῶ διὰ τοῦ ταχυδρομείου	I leave by post.
τὸ ταχυδρομεῖον	The post (office).
ὁ διευθυντὴς τοῦ ταχυδρομείου	The postmaster.
ὁ ἄγγαρος, ὁ ἡμεροδρόμος	The messenger, courier.
ὁ γραμματοκομιστής	The letter-carrier, postman.
ἡ ἅμαξα	The carriage.
ὁ ἁμαξηλάτης ἡνιοχεῖ	The coachman drives.
ὁ ἁμαξηλάτης· ὁ ἡνίοχος	The driver; the charioteer.
ἡ φορτηγὸς ἅμαξα, τὸ κάρρον	The waggon, the cart.
δίτροχον, τετράτροχον κάρρον	A two-wheeled, four-wheeled cart.
ἡ χειράμαξα	The velocipede.
τὸ λεωφορεῖον· τὸ ἕλκηθρον	The omnibus; the sledge.
τὰ σκεύη· τὸ κιβώτιον	The luggage; the box.
ἡ ὁδός, ὁ δρύμος· ἡ λεωφόρος	The way, the road; the high road.
ὁ σιδηρόδρομος	The railroad.
ἀναχωρῶ διὰ τοῦ σιδηροδρόμου	I leave by rail.
ὁ σιδηροδρομικὸς σταθμός	The railway station.
ὁ ἱπποσιδηρόδρομος	The tramway.
ὁ σταθμός	The station.
ἡ ἀτμομηχανή	The steam-engine.
ἡ λέβης· ὁ θερμαντήρ	The boiler; the stove.
ἡ ἀτμάμαξα	The locomotive.
τὸ εἰσιτήριον	The ticket.
ἡ ἀπόδειξις (τῶν σκευῶν, τῶν πραγμάτων)	The ticket (for luggage, baggage, &c.).
τὸ εἰσιτήριον πρώτης, δευτέρας θέσεως	First, second class ticket.
ἡ ἁμαξοστοιχία	The train.
ἡ ἁμαξοστοιχία ἀναχωρεῖ, φθάνει	The train starts, arrives.
ἡ φορτηγὸς ἁμαξοστοιχία	The luggage train.
ἡ ἔκτακτος ἁμαξοστοιχία	The special, extra train.
ἡ ἁμαξοστοιχία ἐπιβατῶν	The passenger train.
ἡ ταχεῖα ἁμαξοστοιχία	The fast train.

ἡ κατ' εὐθεῖαν ἁμαξοστοιχία	The express train.
ἡ σύγκρουσις δύο ἁμαξοστοιχιῶν	The collision of two trains.
τὸ προσωπικὸν τῶν ὑπαλλήλων σιδηροδρόμου	The *personnel* of the railway officials.
ὁ διευθυντής	The manager.
ἡ διεύθυνσις	The management.
ὁ σταθμάρχης	The station-master.
ὁ ἁμαξοστοιχιάρχης	The guard.
ὁ μηχανικός	The engineer, driver.
ὁ ὑπάλληλος σιδηροδρόμου	The railway clerk.
ὁ ὁδηγός	The conductor.
ὁ σταθμοφύλαξ	The inspector.
τὸ δρομολόγιον	The time-table.
τὸ τηλεγραφικὸν σύρμα	The telegraph wire.
τὸ τηλεγραφεῖον	The telegraph office.
ὁ ὑποβρύχιος τηλέγραφος	The submarine telegraph.
τὸ τηλεγράφημα	The telegram.

XIX.

Τροφή.	Food.
ἐδέσματα καὶ ποτά· ἐπιτραπέζια σκεύη· μαγειρικὰ σκεύη.	*Eatables and drinkables; table requisites; kitchen articles.*
ἡ τροφή	Food.
τρέφω· θρεπτικός	I nourish; nourishing.
τὸ πρόγευμα· προγευματίζω	Breakfast; I breakfast.
τὸ γεῦμα· γευματίζω	Dinner; I dine.
τρέφομαι ἔκ τινος	I live on anything.
τὸ δειλινόν, τὸ πρόδειπνον· προδειπνῶ	The evening meal; I take an evening meal.
τὸ δεῖπνον· δειπνῶ	Supper; I sup.
τρώγω· ἐδώδιμος	I eat; eatable.
πίνω· πόσιμος	I drink; drinkable.
ὁ τρώκτης· ὁ πότης	The eater; the drinker.
λαίμαργος· ἡ λαιμαργία· ὁ φαγᾶς	The glutton; gluttony; the guzzler.
ὁ λίχνος· ἡ λιχνεία	The gourmand; daintiness.
τὸ λίχνευμα	The dainty, tit-bit.
πεινῶ· πειναλέος	I am hungry; hungry.

ἡ ὄρεξις· ὀρεκτικός — Appetite; appetizing.
διψῶ· ἡ δίψα — I am thirsty; thirst.
τὸ συμπόσιον — The banquet.
ὁ συμποσιάρχης — The chairman of a banquet.
οἱ συνδαιτυμόνες· οἱ ξένοι — The guests.
ὁ ξενοδόχος — The host.
αἱ τροφαί, τὰ τρόφιμα — The victuals, the provisions.
τὸ φαγητόν· τὸ ἀγαπητὸν φαγητόν — The viands; the favourite dish.
ὁ ζωμός, vl. ἡ σούπα — The soup, the broth.
τὸ κρέας· τὸ βραστόν (κρέας) — The meat; boiled meat.
βραστὸν βιδέλιον — Boiled veal.
τὸ ψητόν· τὸ πάχος — Roast; the fat.
τὸ βωδινόν· τὸ βιδέλιον — Beef; veal.
οἱ νεφροί, τὰ νεφρά — Kidneys.
τὸ πρόβειον· τὸ ψητὸν πρόβειον — Mutton; roast mutton.
τὸ χοιρινόν· τὸ χοιρομήριον — Pork; ham.
ἡ καπνιστὴ γλῶσσα — Smoked tongue.
τὰ πλευρίον, vl. ἡ κοτελέττα — Chop, cutlet.
ἰνδιάνος (ψητὸς) — Roast turkey.
ὀρνίθιον ψητόν — Roast fowl.
τὸ μέρος· ἡ μερίς — The piece; the help.
τὸ ἄρτυμα, vl. ἡ σάλτσα — The sauce.
τὸ παραγεμιστόν — The stuffing.
τὸ ψάριον — The fish.
τὰ λάχανα — The vegetables.
τὰ γεώμηλα, vl. ἡ πατάταις — The potatoes.
τὰ γαλάκτια, γαλακτερικά — Puddings.
τὸ σφουγγάτον — The omelette.
τὸ ὠόν, τὸ αὐγάν — The egg.
ὁ ἄρτος, τὸ ψωμίον· τὸ ψωμάκιον — The bread; the roll.
ἡ κόρα, vl. ἡ ψίχα — The crust; the crumb.
τὸ γλύκισμα — The sweetmeat, confectionery.
τὸ ζαχαρωτόν — The ice (sugar).
ἡ μελιτοῦττα, ἡ μελόπηττα — The honey cake.
τὸ γλυκύεφθον, vl. ἡ κομπόστα — Jam, preserve.
τὰ ἐπιδόρπια, τὰ τραγήματα — Dessert, fruit.
τὸ βούτυρον — The butter.
τὸ βουτυρωμένον ψωμίον — The bread and butter.
τὸ λίπος — The dripping.
τὸ τυρίον — The cheese.

P

τὸ ἅλας· ἁλατίζω	The salt; I salt.
τὸ πιπέριον	The pepper.
τὸ σινάπιον, vl. ἡ μουστάρδα	The mustard.
τὸ ὄξος, τὸ ξύδιον	The vinegar.
τὸ ἔλαιον, vl. τὸ λάδι	The oil.
τὸ κιννάμωμον, vl. ἡ καννέλλα	The cinnamon.
τὸ καρυόφυλλον, vl. τὸ γαρόφαλλον	The clove.
ἡ ζάκχαρις, τὸ ζάκχαρον	The sugar.
τὸ ὕδωρ, vl. τὸ νερόν	The water.
ὁ ζῦθος, vl. ἡ μπίρα	The beer.
ὁ βαυαρικὸς ζῦθος	Bavarian beer.
ὁ οἶνος, vl. τὸ κρασί	The wine.
ὁ οἶνος τοῦ Ῥήνου	Rhine wine.
ὁ γαλλικὸς οἶνος	French wine.
ὁ καμπανίτης	Champagne.
τὸ γάλα· τὸ ἀνθόγαλα, vl. τὸ καϊμάκι	The milk; the cream.
τὸ ὀξύγαλα, vl. τὸ γιαοῦρτι	Buttermilk.
τὰ πνευματώδη ποτά	Spirituous liquors.
τὸ οἰνόπνευμα	Spirits of wine.
τὸ ῥακίον, ἡ ῥακή	Brandy.
τὸ ῥώμιον	Rum.
ἡ λεμονάς, ἡ λεμονάδα	Lemonade.
ἡ σοκολάτα	Chocolate.
ὁ καφές	Coffee.
καφὲς χωρὶς γάλα(κτος)	Coffee without milk.
τὸ τέϊον, vl. τὸ τσάϊ	Tea.
τὰ ἐπιτραπέζια σκεύη	Table requisites.
ἑτοιμάζω· στρώνω· σηκόνω	I prepare; lay, cover; take away.
τὸ τραπέζιον εἶνε ἕτοιμον	The table is laid
καθίζω εἰς τὸ τραπέζιον	I sit down to table.
τὸ τραπεζομάνδυλον	The table-cloth.
τὸ χειρόμακτρον, vl. ἡ πετσέτα	The napkin.
ἡ πορσελλάνη	The china.
τὸ τρυβλίον, τὸ πιάτον	The dish.
τὸ κοχλιάριον, τὸ κουτάλιον	The spoon.
τὸ μαχαίριον	The knife.
τὸ πηρούνιον	The fork.
τὸ φιάλιον, vl. τὸ φλυτζάνι	The cup.
τὸ ποτήριον	The glass.

ἡ φιάλη	The bottle.
τὸ κανάτιον	The pot.
τὸ μαγειρεῖον	The kitchen.
ὁ μάγειρος· ἡ μαγείρισσα	The cook.
ἡ ὀψοθήκη, ὁ ἐδεσματοθήκη	The cupboard.
τὸ ὀψοφυλάκιον, τὸ ταμεῖον	The store-room; larder.
τὰ μαγειρικὰ σκεύη	The kitchen utensils.
ἡ χύτρα, τὸ χαλκεῖον, vl. τὸ τσουκάλι, ὁ τέντζερης	The pitcher, the brazen vessel.
ὁ λέβης, vl. τὸ καζάνιον	The cauldron, the boiler.
τὸ τηγάνιον	The frying-pan.
ἡ ἐσχάρα, vl. ἡ σκάρα	The hearth.
ὁ ὀβελός	The spit.
τὸ στραγγιστήριον	The strainer.
τὸ κνῆστρον, ὁ τρίπτης	The grater.
τὸ ἰγδίον, vl. τὸ γουδί	The mortar.
ὁ δοίδυξ, vl. τὸ γουδοχέρι	The pestle.
ἡ χώνη, τὸ χωνίον	The funnel.
τὸ κόσκινον· κοσκινίζω	The sieve.
τὸ ζωμήρυστρον, τὸ ἐξαφριστήριον	The skimming-ladle.
τὸ κοχλιάριον, τὸ κουτάλιον	The spoon.
ἡ σπαθίς, τὸ τάρακτρον	The whisk.
τὸ κρεατοσάνιδον	The chopping-board.
ἡ μηχανὴ τοῦ καφέ	The coffee-pot.
ὁ μύλος τοῦ καφέ	The coffee-mill.
τὸ καρβουνιστῆρι vl.	The coal-box.
ὁ κάδος	The tub.
ἡ κάρδοπος, τὸ ξυλοπίνακον, vl. ἡ γαβάθα	The wooden plate.
τὸ καλάθιον	The basket.
ἡ ἀποθήκη	The cellar.
ὁ πίθος, τὸ πιθάριον, vl. τὸ κιοῦπι	The cask, the keg.
τὸ βιτίον, vl. τὸ βουτσί, τὸ βαρέλλι	The barrel.
ἡ στρόφιγξ, vl. ἡ κάνουλα	The tap.
τὸ πῶμα, vl. τὸ στούμπωμα	The bung.
ὁ φελλός	The cork.
ὁ ἐκπωμαστήρ	The corkscrew.

PART IV.

The Accidence.

By accidence we mean the changes which words undergo in order to show their relation to other words in a sentence.

Such changes are called inflections, and affect both nouns and verbs.

The noun is the *name* of a thing (*nomen*); the verb is the word which says of a *thing* what it *does*. It is the *action-word*.

Besides these there are a number of a words called *particles*, not subject to inflection, but useful to define, qualify, or restrict the meaning of other words.

The parts of speech may therefore be divided into—
 1. Inflected, (α) Nouns and (β) Verbs;
 2. Uninflected, Particles.

Nouns.

The inflections of nouns are called case-endings.

In the singular they are as follows:—

(1) If we want to say a thing does or is so and so (nominative case) the ending is either ς, ν, or nothing: the second in neuters, the last in some feminines and neuters.

(2) If the thing is the object of an action (objective or accusative case) the ending is ν, α[ν] (masculine, feminine, and neuter) or nothing (neuter).

(3) If we want to express the relation *of* or *from* (genitive or possessive case) the ending is υ (shortened from σιο) or ος, masculine (sometimes feminine) and neuter, or ς, feminine; in a few (chiefly modern) masculines nothing.

(4) If we want to express the relation *to, at, on,* or *by* (dative, locative, or instrumental case) by a mere ending, that ending is -ι, but the relation is more usually expressed in Modern Greek by a preposition with an objective or other case. See *Prepositions*.

(5) If the thing be addressed, the stem itself is used without inflection, except that ο is modified to ε. This is called the vocative case.

In the plural nouns are inflected as follows :—

Nom. and Voc., masc. and fem.	ι or ες.
Objective, masc. and fem. .	νς becoming after ο, α, and a consonant υς, ς, and ας respectively.
Nom., Obj., and Voc., neuter .	α.
Genitive in all genders . .	ων.
Dative in all genders . .	ις or σι.

In this short scheme we have given a summary and rationale of the whole of Greek declension. There are no exceptions, and all seeming irregularities arise from the way in which these case-endings are combined with the stem of the word to which they are added.

The simplest division of all nouns is that into nouns with—

    1. Consonantal stems, and stems in ι and υ;
    2. Vowel stems in α (η) and ο.

NOUNS WITH CONSONANTAL OR QUASI-CONSONANTAL STEMS.

Here the endings ς, α[ν], for ν, ος, ι, and ες, ας, ων, σι (masc. and fem.), or —, ος, ι, and α, ων, σι (neut.) are simply added on to the stem; but be it observed—

(1) That as ρς cannot end a word, ηρς and ερς become ηρ, the ε being lengthened for the sake of compensation; similarly ορς becomes ωρ, κ.τ.λ. For like reasons ηνς and ενς become ην, ονς and ωνς become ων, as do also οντς and ωντς, while εντς becomes εις.

(2) δ, θ, and τ fall away before ς, σ, and at the end of a word; ν falls away *before* σ, as ς *after* ν; e.g. πρᾶγμα[τ], πράγμα[τ]σιν, νεᾶνι[δ]ς, νεάνι[δ]σιν, ποιμήν for ποιμένς, ποιμέ[ν]σι, κ.τ.λ.

(3) γ, κ, χ all combine with ς, σ to form ξ, while β, π, φ combine with ς, σ to form ψ.

(4) σ falls out between two vowels, εο, εἴ, εα, έων contract to ου, ει, η, and ῶν respectively, σσ is avoided, and the neuter stem ες is written in substantive nouns as ος in the nominative only; e.g. τέλος, τέλεος shortened to τέλους for τέλεσος, τέλει for τέλεσι, τέλη for τέλεσα, τελῶν for τελέσων, τέλεσι for τέλεσσι, ἀληθής for ἀληθέσς (neut. ἀληθές). A few do not contract in the genitive plural, as ἀνθέων, ὀρέων.

(5) υ between two vowels (= F) falls out, and if short is modified before a vowel to ε; e.g. βαθύ, βαθέος, βαθέων, contracting before ε, ι, and ας, βαθεῖ, βαθεῖ; βαθέες, βαθεῖς; βαθέας, βαθεῖς.

In a few words it is long, and suffers neither modification nor contraction, e.g. ἰχθύς, 'a fish,' ἰχθύος, ἰχθύι, but swallows up α in accusative plural, ἰχθύας, ἰχθῦς.

Stems in ι, or υ unaccented, also in ευ (εϜ), lengthen the ο of ος, and form their cases as follows: ιν and εα, εως, ει; εις, εις and εας, εων, εσι, and εὖσιν for έϜσιν.

Πειραιεύς, the harbour of that name, for obvious phonetic reasons, contracts as follows: Πειραιᾶ for έα, ῶς for έως, εῖ for έει. In all these cases various ancient dialects present forms more strictly regular.

Stems in υ and ι, though they present the general features of consonantal stems, are in strictness vowel stems, and, save in the case of ευ = εϜ, form their objective in ν, not in α; e.g. βοῦ-ν, ναῦ-ν, πόλι-ν. Unaccented stems in δ have an optional objective in ν for δν; e.g. πολύπουν or -ποδα, εὔελπιν or εὐέλπιδα.

(6) If the word be a monosyllable, the endings ός, ί, ῶν, σί are (thus) accented, except πάντων, πᾶσι, 'all,' παίδων, 'boys,' φώτων, 'lights,' τίνος, τίνι, τίνων, τίσι, interrogative, ὄντος, ὄντι,

ὄντων, οὖσι. Here, however, the apparent monosyllabic stem has been contracted from a dissyllabic one, e. g. φωτ- for φαοτ-, οντ- for ἐοντ-, or, in the case of τίνος, κ.τ.λ., the accent is a mark of distinction: τινὸς = 'some one's,' τίνος, 'whose?'

(7) Stems in ηρ and ων are circumflexed in the oblique cases: κλητήρ, -ῆρος; ἀγών, -ῶνος.

Some stems in ερ (nominative ηρ = ερς) throw back their accent in the vocative, and drop the ε in the genitive and dative; e. g. πατήρ, πάτερ, πατρὸς, πατρί; ἀνήρ, ἀνδρὸς (for ἀνρός), κ.τ.λ. Objective πατέρα, not πάτρα; but ἄνδρα, not ἀνέρα. The reason being apparently that the originally euphonic and parasitic δ has so glued together the ν and the ρ, that they cannot again be parted. Of μήτηρ and θυγάτηρ, declined generally like πατήρ, the vocatives are respectively μῆτερ and θύγατερ, (observe accent). All these words, as well as ἀστερ- (ἀστήρ) 'a star,' form the dative plural in ράσι or ρασι, for ἐρσι or ερσι.

(8) The following apparent irregularities should be noted:—

Ἄρης (Mars), stem and vocative Ἄρες, accusative Ἄρην or Ἄρη [Ἄρεα, Ἄρεσα], Ἄρεος or -ως, Ἄρει.

γάλα, stem γάλακτ-.

γόνυ (stem), γόνατος, γόνατι for γόνϝατος, γόνϝατι; also δόρυ, δόρατος, κ.τ.λ.

γυνή (stem γυναικ-), vocative γύναι [γύναικ], γυναῖκα -ός -ί.

Ζεὺς for Διεύς, Ζεῦ, Δία, Διός, Διΐ.

θρίξ, stem τριχ-, to avoid two aspirates.

κύων, 'dog' (stem κυον-), contracts to κύν-, κύνα, κυνός, κ.τ.λ.

μάρτυς for μάρτυρ-ς, also μάρτυρ, which is stem.

νὺξ for νύκτ-ς (Gothic *Naht-s*), νύκτα, νυκτός, κ.τ.λ.

οὖς for αὔατ, αὔτ, ὠτ, ὠτός, ὠτί; ὦτα, ὤτων, ὠσίν, κ.τ.λ.

ὕδωρ for ὕδαρτ, ὕδατος for ὕδαρτος, κ.τ.λ.

NOUNS WITH VOWEL STEMS.

These may be divided roughly into α-stems and ο-stems (the υ and ι-stems being for purposes of declension semi-consonantal).

I. A-stems.

1. These are preponderatingly feminine. The feminine endings are —, —, ν, ς, ι (subscript), ι, ι, ς, ων, ις. Wherever the stem ends in ία or ρα these endings require to be simply added on, and the declension is complete.

In other cases the vowel α is modified (by a preference of the Ionic dialect) to η before ς and ι, e. g. τράπεζα, τραπέζης, δόξα, δόξης, κ.τ.λ.; not however in the popular speech. The genitive άων in all these words necessarily contracts to ῶν, though even this is sometimes ignored in the vernacular.

The genitive and dative singular of these words, if oxytone, are circumflexed, σκιᾶς, σκιᾷ.

A large majority of stems whose vowel is preceded by any consonant except σ and the double consonants ξ and ζ, adopt the vowel η for α throughout the singular. This makes no difference in the plural; e. g. τιμή, στήλη, φιάλη, ψυχή, plural τιμαί, τιμάς, τιμῶν, τιμαῖς, κ.τ.λ.

2. Masculines in α and η have the ending ς, —, ν, ο (= ου when combined with α), ι, and in the plural are identical with feminines. The vocative is always the stem vowel, viz. α (not η), e. g. νεανίας, genitive νεανίου, vocative νεανία; στρατιώτης, genitive στρατιώτου, vocative στρατιῶτα; but here be it observed that all masculines in τη, likewise all compounds of μετρη-, πωλη-, ἀρχη-, have the α short, and consequently where admissible circumflex the foregoing vowel, e. g. στρατιῶτα, βιβλιοπῶλα, κ.τ.λ.

3. A number of masculines in α, signifying an agent, and a few others, with most proper names of this form, as well as many in η in the vernacular, simplify this declension by merely leaving the stem bare in the genitive and vocative, e.g. τοῦ ψηθήρα, τοῦ βορρᾶ, τοῦ φαγᾶ, τοῦ Θωμᾶ, τοῦ Μανόλη, ὦ Μανόλη, κ.τ.λ.

4. If ε precedes η (α) in the stem, εα becomes ῆ, and ε is swallowed up in all other cases, causing circumflexion of last syllable, e. g. χρυσέα, χρυσῆ, χρυσέη, χρυσῇ, κ.τ.λ.

II. O-stems.

Chiefly masculine and neuter, with some feminines.

The case-endings are (practically) ς, — (with ο modified to ε), ν, υ, ͺ, ι, υς, ων (absorbing ο but without accent), ις for the masculine and feminine; ν, υ, ͺ, α absorbing ο, ων, ις for the neuter.

If the ο of the stem is preceded by ε or ο, contraction takes place, οο and εο becoming ου, while in the other cases ε and ο are simply swallowed up. With monosyllables the circumflex marks this process, but not otherwise except the ε or ο has the accent, e.g. τοῦ πλόου, τοῦ πλοῦ, τὸ ὀστέον, τὸ ὀστοῦν, but ὁ περίπλους, τοῦ περίπλου.

ὁ χρυσοῦς is really for ὁ χρυσέος, although ὁ χρύσεος is the uncontracted form actually found in ancient Greek.

A few stems in ο seem to have lost an σ, and to have been originally consonantal; such are the classical feminines ἡ ἠχὼ, ἡ αἰδὼς, which decline οῖ, ὼ, οῦς, οῖ, and the proper names Κλειὼ, Σαπφὼ, Λητώ. Like these are the modern proper names ἡ Χίω, genitive τῆς Χίως, accusative τὴν Χίω(ν), ἡ Μαριγώ, κ.τ.λ.

A few nouns are heteroclite or of mixed declension, e.g. τὸ ὄνειρον, 'the dream,' plural τὰ ὀνείρατα, τὸ γράψιμον and its analogues, plural τὰ γραψίματα. Also the accusatives of proper names in γένες, κράτες, μῆδες, φάνες, τέλες, which form their accusative in ην instead of in εα, η.

This doubtless arises from false analogy, the nominative -ης suggesting η instead of ες as the stem-ending.

METAPLASTIC NOUNS.

In the vernacular a number of accusatives like πατέρα(ν), λαμπάδα(ν), suggest a fresh stem πατέρα-, λαμπάδα-. Hence we get such nominatives as ὁ πατέρας, ὁ ἄνδρας, ἡ λαμπάδα, ἡ νύκτα, for πατήρ, ἀνήρ, λαμπά(δ)ς, νύξ. Such forms frequently preserve the old genitive, as τῆς νυκτός, τοῦ ἀνδρός.

A number of nouns in a and η, chiefly circumflexed on the stem-vowel, form their plurals from the stems αδ and ηδ in the vernacular; also a few paroxytones like μάννα, 'mother,' χάχας, 'laugher,' χάσκας, 'gaper,' παπατρέχας, 'rambler.' The masculine forms do not draw forward the accent in the genitive plural, e. g. χάχαδων, παπατρέχαδων.

Foreign vowel stems follow the analogy of those in a, e. g. ὁ καφὲς, τοῦ καφί, plural οἱ καφέδες; ἡ μαϊμοῦ, 'the monkey,' τῆς μαϊμοῦς, αἱ μαϊμοῦδες; but if paroxytones, as ὁ κόντες, 'the count,' the plural is -ηδες, κ.τ.λ.

Other curious mixtures difficult to classify are: ὁ κόρακας for κόραξ, ὦ κόρακε, τὸν κόρακα(ν), τοῦ κοράκου, οἱ κοράκοι, τοὺς κοράκους, τῶν κοράκων, κ.τ.λ.; but these belong wholly to the vernacular.

The vernacular also writes αις for αι and ᾶς, accusative feminine plural, ες or αις for ᾶς, masculine accusative plural, and ἡ for αἱ, feminine plural of the article.

Other instances of metaplasm and heteroclite declension in the vernacular are: τοῦ πραγμάτου for πράγματος, πράξι, πράξις for πράξις, πράξεως, παχεῖ or παχεῖ for παχεῖς, plural nominative masculine of παχύ-, 'fat,' κ.τ.λ.

GENDERS OF NOUNS.

1. Masculines:—

(a) All stems in ευ.

(b) All substantives in ντ (except those in ουντ), and most in ην, ηρ, ωρ, ωτ, π; but ἡ φρὴν, ἡ χὴν, and, of course, ἡ μήτηρ and ἡ θυγάτηρ, τὸ φῶς, 'the light,' τὸ οὖς, 'the ear.'

2. Feminines:—

(a) The few whose nominatives are ὠς and ώ.

(b) Most in δ; but παιδ-, 'boy,' 'girl,' λογάδ-, 'picked man or woman,' φυγάδ-, 'fugitive,' σποράδ-, 'scattered,' ἔπηλυδ-, 'immigrant,' νέηλυδ-, 'new comer,' are common.

(c) All in ι and τητ, and most in ιτ.

Of those in o, nominative ος, the great majority are masculine.

Of those in a and η, all are feminine but a few whose nominatives take ς.

3. Neuters:—

(*a*) All in o whose nominative is ον.

(*b*) All in αρ, ατ, and one in ιτ—τὸ μέλι, 'the honey,' genitive μέλιτος.

Of Adjectives in Particular.

1. Of three endings, masculine, feminine, and neuter (τρικατάληκτα ἐπίθετα):—

(*a*) ο-ς, η, ο-ν or ο-ς, α, ο-ν, i.e. α in case of vowel or ρ preceding (but ὀγδόη, 'eighth'). These are the commonest kind; a few in εο contract, e.g. χρυσοῦς, χρυσῆ, χρυσοῦν.

(*b*) ὐ-ς, εῖα, ύ, all oxytone, but ἥμισυ-ς, ἡμίσεια, ἥμισυ, next commonest.

(*c*) ἰεντ-ς, ἰεντ-σα, ἰεντ, becoming ἰεις, ἰεσσα, ἰεν according to phonetic law.

(*d*) ὁεντ-ς, κ.τ.λ., similarly formed.

(*e*) Two, viz. μέλαν- and τάλαν-, thus declined: μέλας, μέλαινα, μέλαν, 'black,' μέλανα, μέλαιναν, μέλαν, where μέλαινα = μέλανϳα.

(*f*) All participles, whether imperfect passive (-μενο-), perfect passive (-μένο-), imperfect active (-οντ-), aorist passive (-έντ-), 1st aorist active (-αντ-), perfect (-ότ-, -υῖα, -ότ-), nominative ώς, υῖα, ός (for ότς, υῖα, ότ).

2. Of two terminations, δικατάληκτα (masculine or feminine, and neuter).

(*a*) All whose stem is ες, nominative ης, ες.

(*b*) All in ον, nominative ων, ον.

(*c*) All in ι, nominative ις, ι.

(*d*) Most compounds and derivatives from compound verbs, except those which are oxytone. Also βάρβαρο-, ἥσυχο-, ἥμερο-. The vernacular ignores this class, using the feminines ἡ ἥσυχη, κ.τ.λ., in disregard of the accentual laws.

3. Adjectives of one ending (μονοκατάληκτα) are simply such as are masculine and feminine, and have no neuter, e. g. ὁ, ἡ ἄπαις, 'childless,' and a few which are practically substantives in apposition, as ὁ γέρων, 'the old man,' ἡ ἐθελοντής, 'the volunteer.'

ADJECTIVES OF MIXED DECLENSION.

These are μέγας for μέγαλς, 'great,' of which the singular nominative and accusative masculine and neuter are formed as though from μέγαλ-, dropping the λ according to phonetic laws, and the rest of the cases from the stem μεγάλο-, and πολύς, κ.τ.λ., in which the same cases are formed from stem πολύ-, the rest from stem πολλό- ή-, for πολιό- ή-. The Ionic dialect declines πολλό- πολλή- throughout, and the vernacular μεγάλο- η- throughout.

COMPARISON OF ADJECTIVES.

1. The regular way of comparing adjectives is by adding—

τερο τέρα τερο, comparative.

τατο τάτη τατο to the stem of the masculine and neuter.

e. g.   λεπτό-   λεπτότερο- | σαφὲς   σαφέστερο-
       —   λεπτότατο- | —   σαφέστατο-

If the preceding syllable is short the o-stem is lengthened, e. g. σοφώτερο-, κ.τ.λ., not σοφότερο-.

2. Stems in εντ *change* to ες, and stems in ον *take* ες before adding the comparative endings, e. g. χαρίεντ-, χαριέστερο-, εὐδαίμον-, εὐδαιμονέστερο-.

3. As alternatives to τερο-, τατο-, the endings ιον-, ιστο- are added to a few adjectives, while in other cases the stem of the positive is changed. Hence arise the following seeming irregularities: αἰσχρό-, 'base,' αἴσχιστο-; ἄσμενο-, 'glad,' ἀσμενέστερο-; κακό-, 'bad,' χειρότερο-, χείρον-, κάκιστο- and χείριστο-; καλό-, καλλίον- (neuter κάλλιον) or καλήτερο-, κάλλιστο-; μέγαλ-, μείζον- for μέγιον-, also μεγαλήτερο-, μέγιστο-; ὀλίγο-, ἐλάσσον- for ἐλάχιον- from ἐλαχύ-, ἐλάχιστος, also ὀλιγώτερο-, ὀλίγιστο-;

πολύ-, πλεῖον- or πλειότερο-, πλεῖστο-, also περισσότερο- ; τάχιστο- as superlative of ταχύ- ; ὕψιστο- of ὑψηλό-.

Note too ἁπλοῦ-ς, ἁπλούστερο-ς, ἀγχίνου-ς, ἀγχινούστερος, as though the stem were ουσ.

4. The following comparatives of adverbs and prepositions are noticeable :—

πλησίον, 'near' πλησιέστερος, -τατος.
ἀπό, 'from' ('far') ἀπώτερος, 'further,' -ατος, 'furthest.'
πρό, 'before' πρότερος, 'earlier,' πρῶτος, 'first,' πρώτιστος, 'first of all,' *quasi* "firstest."
ἐξ, ἐκ, 'out' ἔσχατος for ἐκ-σ-ατος, 'uttermost,' 'last.'
ὑπέρ, 'over' ὑπέρτερος, 'superior,' ὑπέρτατος, 'supreme.'

In ordinary parlance the comparative with the article = superlative, the superlative itself = 'very,' e. g. ὁ καλήτερος, 'the best man,' κάλλιστος ἄνθρωπος, 'a very good man.'

Substantive Pronouns.

1. Personal pronouns :

I	ἐγώ, μὲ (ἐμὲ, ἐμένα), μοῦ (ἐμοῦ), μοὶ (ἐμοί).
Thou	σὺ (ἐσὺ), σε (ἐσὲ, σένα, ἐσένα), σοῦ, σοί.
He	αὐτός, αὐτὸν (τὸν), αὐτοῦ (τοῦ), αὐτῷ (τῷ).
She	—ή —ήν —ήν —ῆς —ῆς —ῇ —ῇ
It	—ὸ —ὸ- —ὸ like masculine.
We	ἡμεῖς, ἡμᾶς (μᾶς), ἡμῶν (μᾶς), ἡμῖν (μᾶς).
You	ὑμεῖς (ἐσεῖς, σεῖς), ὑμῶν (σᾶς), ὑμῖν (σᾶς).
They	αὐτοί, αὐτοὺς (τοὺς), αὐτῶν (τῶν), αὐτοῖς (τοῖς).
Fem.	—αὶ —ὰς —ὰς — —αῖς, κ.τ.λ.
Neut.	—ὰ —ὰ —ὰ and the rest as the masculine.

(*a*) The shorter forms are the less emphatic, and when written after the words governing them lose their accent, e. g. τοῦ ἔδωκά το, or τὸ ἔδωκά του, 'I gave it him.

(*b*) The nominatives are not expressed with verbs, save for emphasis.

2. Reflective pronouns :—

I myself, (ἐγὼ) αὐτὸς or -ή, κ.τ.λ.
Of myself, ἐμαυτοῦ, -ῆς, κ.τ.λ., and so on.
Ourselves, (ἡμεῖς) αὐτοί, ἡμῶν αὐτῶν, κ.τ.λ.
Thyself, σεαυτοῦ, κ.τ.λ.; yourselves (ὑμεῖς) αὐτοί, κ.τ.λ.
Himself, αὐτὸς, of himself, ἑαυτοῦ, κ.τ.λ.; herself, αὐτή, ἑαυτῆς, κ.τ.λ.

But the Greeks also say in the objective—τὸν ἑαυτόν μου, τὸν ἑαυτόν σου, κ.τ.λ., and sometimes τὸν ἴδιον ἑαυτόν μου, κ.τ.λ., lit. 'the own self of me;' also in the nominative, ἐγὼ ὁ ἴδιος, 'I myself.'

3. Reciprocal pronoun :—

ἀλλήλους, -ας, ἄ, κ.τ.λ.

The Article. Adjectival Pronouns.

1. The definite article ὁ, ἡ, τὸ, plural οἱ, αἱ, τὰ, is declined in other cases as from the stems τὸ-, τὴ-, τό-. As indefinite articles, τις, τι, or εἷς, μία, ἕν, the numeral 'one,' are used.

N.B.—Masculine and neuter stem = ἕν, feminine = μία.

2. 'My,' &c., is expressed by ὁ — μου, κ.τ.λ.; 'mine' or 'my own' by ὁ ἰδικός μου, κ.τ.λ., and so on of the other pronouns.

Demonstrative Pronouns.

3. 'This,' 'that,' when not over emphatic, is αὐτὸς -ή -ό, always combined with the article, thus, ὁ ἄνθρωπος αὐτὸς or αὐτὸς ὁ ἄνθρωπος, 'this man,' whereas ὁ αὐτὸς ἄνθρωπος means 'the same man.' But as ὁ ἄνθρωπος αὐτὸς may mean also 'the man himself,' the less ambiguous and more emphatic pronoun οὗτος αὕτη (observe accent) τοῦτο is used in preference. This being really a compound of several stems is given at length :—

SINGULAR.			PLURAL.		
οὗτος	αὕτη	τοῦτο	οὗτοι	αὗται	ταῦτα
τοῦτον	ταύτην	τοῦτο	τούτους	ταύτας	ταῦτα
τούτου	ταύτης	τούτου		τούτων	
τούτῳ	ταύτῃ	τούτῳ	τούτοις	ταύταις	τούτοις

Here, too, the article must accompany the substantive.

ἐκεῖνος '-η ˆ-ο, 'that, yonder,' is declined quite regularly, except that the neuter nominative and accusative drop ν. The use of the article is the same as with οὗτος.

τοσοῦτο-, 'so great,' and τοιοῦτο-, 'such,' follow the declension of οὗτος, κ.τ.λ., except that the initial τ of ταύτην, κ.τ.λ., is never inserted.

ἄλλος, ἄλλη, ἄλλο, 'other,' is as regular as αὐτό-. Observe that all these pronominal words drop ν in the neuter accusative and nominative.

An old demonstrative compounded of the article + δε is used in certain cases, e. g. μέχρι τοῦδε, 'hitherto.'

The article with μέν and δέ (not written in one word), ὁ μέν — ὁ δέ, κ.τ.λ., means 'the one' — 'the other.' Also ὁ δέ alone means 'and he' or 'but he.'

Indefinite and Interrogatory Pronouns.

These are: τιν-, nominative τὶς, τὶ, indefinite, losing accent when enclitic, e. g. ἄνθρωπός τις εἶχε δύο υἱούς, 'a certain man had two sons;' and τίς; τί; interrogatory. ποῖο-; ποία-; originally = 'of what kind?' but now = τίς; τί; ὁ δεῖνα or ὁ δεῖνας (heteroclite), τὸν δεῖνα, τοῦ δεῖνος, τῷ δεῖνι, and ὁ τάδε or ὁ τάδες, τὸν τάδε, τοῦ τάδε (dative not found).

The following distich was for some time the motto of a Greek satirical journal in Athens called τὸ Φῶς, 'the Light,' appended to a caricature of the fallen and standing Prime Ministers, one of whom was represented head downwards, and the other in his natural position :—

> Καὶ ὁ δεῖνας καὶ ὁ τάδες
> Εἶνε ὅλοι μασκαράδες.

Mr. This and Mr. That
Each and all are Messrs. Flat.

To which in one of the comic papers the prompt rejoinder appeared:—

> Καὶ ὁ Συντάκτης τοῦ Φωτός
> Μασκαρᾶς εἶνε καὶ αὐτός.
>
> And the Editor of Light
> Is as flat as any, quite.

Relative Pronouns.

The commonest relative pronoun is ὁ ὁποῖος, ἡ ὁποία, τὸ ὁποῖον. Occasionally the more classical ὅς, ἥ, ὅ, or the compounds ὅσπερ, ἥπερ, ὅπερ are used: περ is a mere indeclinable particle, in force equivalent originally to 'very' or 'same.' For the rest ὅς, κ.τ.λ., is declined quite regularly, as is also τις in composition, e. g. ὅντινα, ἥντινα, ὅ,τι, οὕτινος, ἧστινος, κ.τ.λ., but οὕπερ, ἧσπερ, κ.τ.λ. Finally the indeclinable ὅπου or ποῦ is used in the vernacular as a relative for all cases and genders. Compare the German *wo* in the South.

Correlative Pronouns.

Such are πότερος, 'which of two?' 'whether of two?' neuter πότερον = 'whether;' ὁ ἕτερος, 'one of two;' ὁπότερος, 'which of two' (relative); πόσος, 'how great,' 'how many;' ὅσος, 'as great as;' τόσος or τοσοῦτος, 'so great,' 'so many;' ποῖος, ὁποῖος, 'of what kind;' τοιοῦτος or τέτοιος (accent invariably on έ), 'such;' οἷος, ὁποῖος, 'such as.'

The Numerals.

As some of these are subject to inflection, they are given in this place.

CARDINALS.

1 εἷς (for ἕν-ς), μία, ἕν (fem. gen. and dat. μιᾶς, μιᾷ).
2 δύο or δύω.
3 τρεῖς, τρία (gen. τριῶν).
4 τέσσαρες, τέσσαρα.
5 πέντε.
6 ἕξ, vl. ἕξι.
7 ἑπτά.

A GUIDE TO MODERN GREEK.   225

8 ὀκτώ.
9 ἐννέα.
10 δέκα.
11 ἕνδεκα.
12 δώδεκα.
13 δεκατρεῖς -ία.
14 δεκατέσσαρες -α, κ.τ.λ.
20 εἴκοσι.
21 εἴκοσι καὶ εἷς or εἴκοσιν εἷς, κ.τ.λ.
30 τριάκοντα (τριάντα).
40 τεσσαράκοντα (σαράντα).
50 πεντήκοντα (πενῆντα).
60 ἑξήκοντα (ἑξῆντα).
70 ἑβδομήκοντα (ἑβδομῆντα).
80 ὀγδοήκοντα (ὀγδῶντα or ὀγδοῆντα).
100 ἑκατόν.
101 ἑκατὸν (καὶ) εἷς, κ.τ.λ.
103 ἑκατὸν τρεῖς, κ.τ.λ.
200 διακόσιοι (declined).
300 τριακόσιοι.
400 τετρακόσιοι.
500 πεντακόσιοι.

600 ἑξακόσιοι.
700 ἑπτακόσιοι.
800 ὀκτακόσιοι.
900 ἐν(νε)ακόσιοι.
1000 χίλιοι.
2000 δισχίλιοι or δύο χιλιάδες (in apposition), and so on, adding χίλιοι to τρὶς, τετράκις, πεντάκις, ἑξάκις, ἑπτάκις, κ.τ.λ., meaning 'thrice,' &c., to χίλιοι, or combining the first ten numerals with χιλιάδες.
10,000 δεκακισχίλιοι or μύριοι (classical). N.B.—μυρίοι means 'countless' (note accent).
20,000 εἴκοσι χιλιάδες or δισμύριοι.
1,000,000 ἓν ἑκατομμύριον = 100 × 10,000.
A billion, δισεκατομμύριον.
1883 χίλια ὀκτακόσια ὀγδοήκοντα τρία.

ORDINALS.

1st πρῶτος '-η -ον.
2nd δεύτερος '-α -ον.
3rd τρίτος, κ.τ.λ.
4th τέταρτος, κ.τ.λ.
5th πέμπτος.
7th ἕβδομος.
9th ἔνατος.
10th δέκατος.
11th ἑνδέκατος.
12th δωδέκατος.
13th δέκατος τρίτος, κ.τ.λ.

20th εἰκοστός.
21st εἰκοστὸς πρῶτος.
30th τριακοστός.
40th τεσσαρακοστός (σαρακοστός), κ.τ.λ.
100th ἑκατοστός, κ.τ.λ., the ending -στὸς being added to the stem; e.g. 'in the 1883rd year,' ἐν ἔτει χιλιοστῷ ὀκτακοσιοστῷ ὀγδοηκοστῷ τρίτῳ.

Fractions are expressed by the neuter of the ordinals: δεύτερον (or ἥμισυ) = $\frac{1}{2}$, δύο τρίτα = $\frac{2}{3}$, κ.τ.λ.

The Verb.

The verb consists of a root (or stem) combined with personal affixes or endings.

Verbs are divided into Active and Passive. Most have both an active and passive form. Those that have only a passive form are for the most part active in sense, having lost in the process of usage their originally passive meaning.

Verbs are further distinguished as to tense or time.

The two main tense divisions are—

1. Imperfect tenses, or those denoting a continued action.
2. Aorist tenses, or those denoting an instantaneous action.

The future tense in Modern Greek is expressed by combinations or adaptations of these other two.

Verbs are further subject to changes of mood according to whether the action is represented as actual, or conditional, or commanded. These moods are called respectively, indicative, subjunctive, and imperative.

For the imperfect there is sometimes, but not always, a separate stem, called the imperfect stem.

The aorist stem is in such cases the root of the verb.

Given the imperfect stem, the present imperfect tense in the indicative mood in all its persons may be formed at once by adding on the following affixes :—

	ACTIVE.				PASSIVE.		
	1	2	3		1	2	3
Sing.	ω	εις	ει	Sing.	ομαι	εσαι	εται
Pl.	ομεν	ετε	ουσι (ουν)	Pl.	ομεθα	εσθε	ονται

A slight vowel change transforms these endings into the appropriate ones for the subjunctive mood of the imperfect tenses.

N.B.—There is no distinction of past and present in the subjunctive mood.

	ACTIVE.				PASSIVE.		
Sing.	ω	ῃς	ῃ	Sing.	ωμαι	ησαι	ηται
Pl.	ωμεν	ητε	ωσι (ουν)	Pl.	ωμεθα	ησθε	ωνται

The past tenses take a prefix ἐ, called the augment, which with ε combines to form εἰ or ἠ, with ι, εἰ, and with α, ἠ.

To form the past imperfect indicative the prefix ε is placed before the stem (or root), and the following are the endings:—

	ACTIVE.				PASSIVE.		
Sing.	ον (vl. α)	ες	ε	Sing.	ὀμην	εσο	ετο
Pl.	ομεν	ετε	ον (αν)	Pl.	ὀμεθα	εσθε	οντο

The aorist is formed in two ways. In case the imperfect stem is lengthened from the root, the aorist reverts to the root, and with that exception forms its persons (in the active) precisely as the imperfect past, e.g. φεύγω, root φυγ-, present imperfect ἔφευγον, aorist ἔφυγον. This is called the 2nd or *strong* aorist.

In case the imperfect stem is the simple root, the letter σ is interposed between stem and personal endings, or the syllable lengthened in cases where for the sake of euphony the σ is suppressed, and the endings are as follow in the active: while in the passive the 1st aorist interposes θ, the 2nd aorist nothing, and the endings are as follows:—

	ACTIVE.				PASSIVE.		
Sing.	α	ας	ε	Sing.	ην	ης	η
Pl.	αμεν	ατε	αν	Pl.	ημεν	ητε	ησαν

Examples: βάλλω, 'I put' or 'throw,' ἔβαλλον, 'I was throwing,' ἔβαλον, 'I threw,' ἐβάλην, 'I was thrown;' λύω, 'I loose,' ἔλυον, ἔλυσα, ἐλύθην.

In the subjunctive mood, the same stems (without the ἐ) are used as in the indicative, while the personal endings are as follows:—

ACTIVE.	PASSIVE.
Same as for the imperfect.	Ditto, circumflexed throughout.
λύσω, βάλω, κ.τ.λ.	λυθῶ, βαλῶ, κ.τ.λ.

N.B.—The vernacular is fond of forming the indicative passive aorist by adding to the aorist stem, whether 1st or 2nd, the endings of the 1st aorist active, preceded by the letters ηκ, e. g. ἐβάληκα, ἐβλήθηκα, for ἐβάλην, ἐβλήθην, κ.τ.λ.

The future tense is expressed either by the subjunctive mood preceded by the particle θὰ, or by the verb θέλω, 'I will,' &c., followed by the

INFINITIVE.

This is formed of the stem + the ending ει(ν), passive -εσθαι, in the aorist ῆ(ναι), e. g. θὰ λύω, 'I will loose' (as a habit); θὰ λύσω, 'I will loose' (on some special occasion); passive θὰ λυθῶ, κ.τ.λ. θέλω βάλλει(ν), 'I shall put' (habitually); θέλω βάλει(ν), 'I shall put' (once for all); θέλω βάλλεσθαι, θέλω βαλῆ. N.B.—'I *will* put' is θέλω νὰ βάλω, κ.τ.λ.

The infinitive is properly the old locative case of a noun. It is still used as an indeclinable substantive with the article, but in this case the old classical form is employed, i. e. the ν is never dropped in imperfect and 2nd aorist, and for the 1st aorist αι is used instead of ει, while the ειν of the 2nd aorist active is always circumflexed, e. g. τὸ βάλλειν, τὸ βαλεῖν, τὸ λύσαι, τὸ λυθῆναι, κ.τ.λ.

The modern form of the infinitive aorist is also used with ἔχω, 'I have,' to form a compound perfect and pluperfect, e. g. ἔχω λύσει, 'I have loosed;' ἔχω βάλει, 'I have put;' εἶχον (for ἐεχον) λύσει, βάλει, κ.τ.λ., 'I had,' &c. Another way of forming the perfect and pluperfect is ἔχω + the perfect passive participle in -μένο- η, e. g. ἔχω (λε)λυμένας τὰς σπονδάς, 'I have broken the treaty.' The doubling of the first syllable is optional.

IMPERATIVE MOOD, OR MOOD OF COMMANDING.

To the imperfect stem the following endings are added, in the active :—

ε[ς] ('thou') and occasionally ἔτω ('he').

ετε ('ye') very rarely ἔτωσαν or ὄντων ('they').

and in the passive :—

εσο (ου)   έσθω.
εσθε   έσθωσαν or έσθων.

As a rule a wish regarding all other persons but the second is expressed by ἄς followed by the subjunctive, e.g. ἄς λύσω, ἄς λύσῃ, ἄς λύσουν.

ἄς is short for ἄφες, 2nd aorist imperative of ἀφ-ε-, imperfect ἀφίημι, 'let,' 'permit.'

To the 1st aorist stem the following endings are added:—

ACTIVE.

ε   or ον   άτω.
ετε or ατε   άντων.

PASSIVE.

ου or ητι or ηθι (the latter if no aspirate precedes)   ήτω.
ητε   ήτωσαν or έντων.

N.B.—(1) To form the 2nd aorist imperative the endings of the imperfect are added to 2nd aorist stem: whereas in the passive the endings are alike for 1st and 2nd aorist. (2) ου requires the *active* stem, e.g. γράψου, not γράφθου.

The foregoing supplies the key to all the most ordinary forms of the verb except the participles; but before we speak of these it may be well to mention a few classical forms not in common use, but cropping up in occasional phrases, such are:—

THE CLASSICAL FUTURE.

This is simply the same as the present imperfect + the insertion of σ between stem and personal ending in the active, and θησ between stem and personal ending in the passive, e.g. λύσω, λυθήσομαι, κ.τ.λ.

THE MIDDLE AORIST.

Middle means halfway between passive and active. Those passive verbs which have an active meaning may form (not must) their aorists as follows: To the 1st aorist stems are added the following personal endings:—

άμην   αμεθα
ω for ασο   ασθε
ατο   αντο

and to the 2nd aorist stem the endings of the imperfect past passive.

A future middle is also sometimes formed, which is identical with the passive except that σ is substituted for θησ.

THE PERFECT ACTIVE.

This is formed by doubling the first consonant and inserting ε, e. g. λελ for λ, γεγ for γ, κ.τ.λ., and if the root end in a vowel or a liquid inserting κ, aspirating a mute or medial, and leaving an aspirate intact, and then adding the endings of the 1st aorist, save that the 3rd person plural ends in αντι instead of αν, e. g. λελύκασι from λυ-, γεγράφασι from γραφ-, κ.τ.λ.

A perfect passive formed by adding to the reduplicated stem the endings μαι, σαι, ται; μεθα, θε (after vowels σθε), and (where possible) νται, is found in such isolated phrases as τετέλεσται, 'it is finished,' from root τελεσ-.

N.B.—σ and sometimes λ are dropped in reduplication, e. g. ἐστέρημαι for σεστέρημαι, εἴλημμαι for λέλημμαι. Observe, too, β, π, φ are assimilated to μ, e. g. γέγραμμαι for γέγραφμαι, also, spirants[1] become tenues before τ, e. g. γέγραπται for γέγραφται.

THE PARTICIPLES.

The imperfect participle active is formed by adding to the imperfect stem the syllable οντ, which becomes with the signs of case and gender, ων [οντ-ς], ουσα [οντ-σα], and ον[τ], in masculine, feminine, and neuter respectively, and is declined according to the scheme for nouns given above. The 2nd aorist is made by adding the same endings on to the 2nd aorist stem.

The 1st aorist participle active is formed by adding to the corresponding stem the endings ας, ασα, αν [αντ-ς, αντ-σα, αντ], κ.τ.λ.

The perfect passive participle is formed by adding to the root (of which the reduplication is optional) the endings μένο-ς, μέν-η, μένο-ν, κ.τ.λ. Observe the accent, invariably on the ε.

---

[1] The term "spirant" includes all consonants but tenues and liquids, according to Modern Greek phonetics.

The imperfect participle passive is made by adding to the imperfect stem the endings όμενος, ομένη, όμενον, κ.τ.λ.

The passive participle aorist is made by adding the suffix ἐντ + generic endings = είς [εντς], εῖσα [εντ-σα], ἐν[τ], to the 1st or 2nd aorist stems.

Besides these there are occasionally found a future active and passive participle formed by adding on the imperfect endings to the future stems given above in the account of the classical tense, e.g. λύ-σ-ων, λυ-θησ-όμενος, κ.τ.λ.; and also an

ACTIVE PERFECT PARTICIPLE,

formed by adding to the reduplicated root the suffix ότ- for masculine and neuter, and υῖα- for the feminine, thus producing ώς [οτ-ς], υῖα, ός [οτ], respectively. Observe the accent, which is always on the suffix save in the feminine genitive plural, which is circumflexed according to rule.

CONTRACT VERBS.

Where the verbal root ends in a, ε, or ο, contraction arises with those personal endings which begin with a vowel. In forming these contractions it has only to be remembered that—

αο, άω, έω, όω, and άου contract to		ω, ῶ.
εο, οο, οε, έου, όου	,,	ου, οῦ respectively.
αε, αη, άει, αῃ	,,	α, ᾳ.
εε, έει	,,	ει, εῖ.
όει	,,	οῖ.
έη, έῃ	,,	ῃ, ῇ.

But for the most part verbs in ο insert ν in Modern Greek before a vowel, and thus contraction is avoided, e.g. διορθόνει for διορθόει, διορθοῖ, 'he corrects.'

Keeping the above contractions in view, the student will be able to write out correctly the paradigm of any contract verb.

Apparent exceptions in the mouths of the common people, e.g. ἐτιμούμουν or ἐτιμούμην for ἐτιμώμην, arise from the tendency to assimilate all contract verbs to a common scheme, and as the vowels a and ε (and even o) were probably in origin variants of one indeterminate vowel sound, there is some justification for the process.

As a rule verbs in a, ε, and o lengthen these vowels to η and ω respectively in forming the aorist, e.g. τιμάω, τιμῶ, 'I honour,' ἐτίμησα, θὰ τιμήσω; ζητέω -ῶ, 'I seek,' ἐζήτησα, θὰ ζητήσω; διορθώνω, 'I correct,' διώρθωσα or ἐδιόρθωσα, κ.τ.λ.

Apparent exceptions, such as γελάω, γελάσω, 'laugh,' ἀρκέω, ἀρκέσω, 'suffice,' διψάω, διψάσω, 'thirst,' πεινάω, πεινάσω, 'hunger,' σπάω, σπάσω, 'break,' καλέω, καλέσω, 'call,' ἐξεμέω, 'vomit,' τελέω, 'finish,' αἰνέω, 'praise,' κ.τ.λ., reveal in their passive forms, e.g. διψασμένος, ἠρκέσθην, τετελεσμένος, κ.τ.λ., that they have lost an σ after the root-vowel a or ε, so that they do not properly come under the rule. Such other exceptions as occur (and they are very rare) are probably due to false analogy.

Such is the general scheme of conjugation, and to it there are no exceptions. Given the imperfect and aorist stem of a verb, the whole conjugation is known. Some verbs have both 2nd and 1st aorists, and some only 1st or 2nd. As a rule, when the imperfect stem and the root of the verb are identical, the 1st aorist is used, when the imperfect is a secondary formation, the 2nd.

In forming the 1st aorist it must be remembered that:—

(1) β, π, φ combine with σ to form ψ
γ, κ, χ   „   „   „   ξ
while δ, θ, τ are lost before   .   σ

(2) that λ, μ, ν, ρ absorb the following σ, the preceding vowel being lengthened by way of compensation; e.g. ἔμεινα for ἔμενσα, ἔστειλα for ἔστελσα, ἐπῆρε for ἐπάρσε, κ.τ.λ.

To form the imperfect stem either the simple root is retained, as in γράφω, λύω, τιμάω, ζητέω, ἀγαπάω, τήκω, νήφω, νηστεύω, κ.τ.λ., or it is increased in various ways:—

1. By the frequentative affix σκ, accompanied sometimes with reduplication, or by reduplication alone, in which case the reduplicated vowel is not ε as in the perfect, but ι; e. g. γιγνώσκω, 'I know,' from γνο-, γίγνομαι for γιγένομαι from γεν-, 'become,' χάσκω, 'I gape,' from root χα-, θνήσκω or θναίσκω for θάνσκω from θαν-, 'die,' μιμνήσκω, 'I remind,' from root μνα-, and so forth.

2. By adding τ after a labial, as θάπ-τω, 'I bury,' τύπ-τω, 'I strike.'

3. By adding ι consonantal, which becomes absorbed, producing a change in the final consonant of the root, δι becoming ζ, while γ, κ, χ + ι = σσ (or ττ); γνωρίζω, 'I know,' for γνωρίδιω, πράσσω for πράκιω, διατάσσω for διατάγιω, κ.τ.λ.

4. By the affix αν often accompanied by nasalization of the root, e. g. λαμβάνω, 'I take,' from λαβ-, μανθάνω, 'I learn,' from μαθ-, λανθάνω, 'I hide,' from λαθ- ; or by suffix αν + ι consonantal = αιν, as παθαίνω, 'I suffer,' from παθ- ; or by ν alone, as φέρνω from φερ-, accompanied sometimes with change of vowel, as γέρνω from γυρ-, (ἐ)παίρνω from ἐπαρ-. This ν is occasionally inserted between the last consonant and the final vowel, especially a, of a root, e. g. περνάω, 'I pass,' aorist ἐπέρασα.

5. The root-vowel is strengthened, e. g. υ becomes ευ, as φυγ-, 'flee,' φεύγω, 'I flee,' ἔφυγον, 'I fled.'

The following is a list of so-called Irregular Verbs. In some cases the irregularity is produced by a striving for regularity led by false analogy.

αἰσθάνομαι, aor. ᾐσθάνθην, 'feel.'
ἁμαρτάνω, ἡμάρτησα and ἥμαρτον, 'sin.'
ἀναλίσκω, ἠνάλωσα, 'spend.'
ἀνοίγω, ἤνοιξα and ἀνέῳξα, 'open.'
ἀποθνήσκω, ἀπέθανον, θὰ ἀποθάνω, 'die.'
ἀπολλύω, ἀπώλεσα ; pf. p. ἀπολωλώς -υῖα -ός, 'lose.'

ἀρέσκω, ἤρεσα, θὰ ἀρέσω, 'please.'
αὐξάνω, ηὔξησα, θὰ αὐξήσω, 'grow.'
ἀφ-ικνέομαι, θὰ ἀφιχθῶ, ἀφίχθην and ἀφικόμην; p. p. ἀφιγμένος, 'arrive.'
ἀφίνω, ἄφησα and ἀφῆκα; imperat. ἄφες, ἀφήσατε and ἄφετε; p. p. ἀφειμένος, 'leave,' 'let go.'
βαίνω (chiefly found in compounds), ἔβην, ἔβης, ἔβη, κ.τ.λ.; imp. βὰ, βῆτε, 'go;' aor. pass. παρεβάθη, 'it was transgressed;' f. θὰ βῶ. For ἔβην the vernacular uses ἔβηκα, κ.τ.λ.
βάλλω, root βαλ and βλα, θὰ βάλω, ἔβαλον or ἔβαλα, ἐβλήθην, βεβλημένος, 'cast,' 'put,' 'put on.'
βαρύνω, θὰ βαρύνω, ἐβάρυνα, θὰ βαρυνθῶ, ἐβαρύνθην, 'weary,' 'burden.'
βλέπω, aor. from root ἰδ- [ϜΙΔ], εἶδον or -α, ἴδε and ἰδέ, also ἰδές, ἰδών, θὰ ἴδω, 'see.' In compounds regular, as κατέβλεψεν, 'he looked down,' ἀνέβλεψα, 'I looked up.'
βόσκω, aor. from stem βοσκε-, 'feed,' θὰ βοσκήσω, κ.τ.λ.
βούλομαι, 'I will,' 'intend,' θὰ βουληθῶ, ἐ—, also ἠβουλήθην, as if from ἐβουλε-.
βρέχω, pass. aor. ἐβράχην, θὰ βραχῶ, κ.τ.λ., 'rain.'
γηράσκω, ἐγήρασα, κ.τ.λ., 'grow old.'
γίνομαι (γίγνομαι), θὰ γείνω, ἔγεινα or ἐγενόμην, γενόμενος; pf. γέγονα; pf. p. γεγονώς, 'become.'
γινώσκω (γιγνώσκω), θὰ γνώσω, ἔγνωσα and ἔγνων, ἔγνως, ἔγνω, ἔγνωμεν, ἔγνωτε, ἔγνωσαν; imp. γνῶθι, γνῶσον or γνῶσε; aor. p. γνώσας and γνούς (γνοντ-), 'know.' Chiefly in compounds, e. g. ἀνάγνωθι, 'read,' 'recognize.'
δεικνύω, the aor., &c., from δεικ-; p. p. p. δεδειγμένος, 'show.'
δέρνω, δέρω or δαίρω, θὰ δείρω, ἔδειρα; p. θὰ δαρῶ, θὰ δαρθῶ, ἐδάρην or ἐδάρθην, 'flog,' 'flay.' Hence δέρ-μα, 'skin.'
δέχομαι, ἐδέχθην, θὰ δεχθῶ; p. p. δεδεγμένος; aor. m. also found, ἐδεξάμην; p. δεχθεὶς and δεξάμενος, 'receive.'
διδάσκω, the aor. from διδαχ-, 'teach.'
διδράσκω (in comp.) (root δρα-), ἀπέδρασα, ἀπέδρασας, ἀπέδρασεν,

also ἀπέδρας, ἀπέδρα (cf. γνω-); part. ἀποδρὰς, ἀποδρᾶσα, 'run away.'

δίδω, θὰ δώσω, ἔδωσα and ἔδωκα, θὰ δοθῶ, ἐδόθην; p. p. p. δεδομένος, 'give.'

δύνα-μαι -σαι -ται -μεθα -σθε -νται (a throughout); subj. δύνωμαι, δύνησαι, δύνηται, δυνώμεθα, δύνησθε, δύνωνται, or like the indicative; inf. δύνασθαι; p. δυνάμενος; imp. ἐδυνάμην and ἠδυνάμην (cf. βούλομαι), κ.τ.λ (with a throughout); θὰ δυνηθῶ, ἠδυνήθην, 'can,' 'am able.'

ἐγείρω; imp. ἤγειρον; aor. ἤγειρα, θὰ ἐγερθῶ, ἠγέρθην, 'raise,' 'wake,' 'rise,' 'awaken;' p. p. p. ἐγηγερμένος.

εἶμαι (εἰμί), εἶσαι, εἶνε (ἐστί), εἴμεθα (ἐσμὲν), εἶσθε, εἶνε (εἰσί); subj. ἦμαι (ᾦ), ἦσαι (ᾖς), ἦνε (ᾖ), ἤμεθα (ὦμεν), ἦσθε, ἦνε (ὦσι); imp. ἔσο, ἔστω, ἔστωσαν; inf. εἶσθαι (εἶναι); p. ὢν (ὀντ-), 'be.' No aorists, for which ἔγεινα, θὰ γείνω, κ.τ.λ, are used.

ἐκπλήττω; 1st aor. act. from πληγ-; 2nd aor. pass. from πλαγ-, 'astonish.'

ἐμποδίζω, 'hinder,' takes no augment.

ἔρχομαι, 'come' (ἐλθ-); fut. p. ἐλευσόμενος for ἐλυθσόμενος.

εὑρίσκω (εὑρ-, augment optional), 'find.'

εὔχομαι (εὐχη-), 'wish.'

ἔχω (σχ- σχε-), ἔσχον, θὰ σχεθῶ, ἐσχέθην, 'have.'

ζάω, ζῶ, ζῇς, ζῇ, ζῶμεν, ζῆτε, ζῶσι, 'live,' ἔζησα.

ἠξεύρω, 'know,' μαθ-.

θάπτω, 'bury' (ταφ-, pass.); p. p. p. τεθαμμένος.

θέλω, ἐθέλω (θελε- ἐθελε-), 'will.'

θέτω (class. τίθημι) (θε-), ἔθηκα, θὰ θέσω (mid. comp. προτίθεμαι, 'I propose,' 'set before myself'); θὰ τεθῶ, ἐτέθην; part. imp. τιθεὶς; aor. θείς, 'place.'

ἱστάω, ἱστῶ (in comp. chiefly), also σταίνω, στήνω, στέκω; root στα- (class. ἵστημι), 'set,' 'stand,' ἵσταμαι, 'I stand;' ἔστησα, 'I set' (trans.); ἔστην, 'I stood,' also ἐστάθην, in passive sense ἐστήθην; p. ἱστάμενος, στάς.

κάθημαι (= κατά + ἧμαι), 'sit,' ἐκαθήμην, ἐκάθησα, κάθησε, θὰ καθήσω. The chief irregularity here is that the aorists are active in form with intransitive sense.

καίω (καϝ- καυ-), θὰ καύσω, ἔκαυσα, θὰ καῶ, ἐκάην, 'burn.'

καλέω (κλα- κλε-), ἐκλήθην, κεκλημένος, 'call.'

κάμνω (καμ-), 'do.'

κεῖμαι, κ.τ.λ, subj., ditto. Endings added to stem without any intervening vowel. Past impf. ἐκείμην, ἐκεῖσο, κ.τ.λ.; no aor., 'lie.'

κερδαίνω (κερδίζω) (κερδε-), 'gain.'

κερνάω (κεράννυμι), θὰ κεράσω, κ.τ.λ., 'mix.'

κλαίω (κλαϝ-), cf. καίω, 'weep.'

κλέπτω (κλεπ- κλαπ-), 'steal,' ἐκλάπην, θὰ κλαπῶ.

κορέννυμι, not used, but θὰ κορέσω, ἐκόρεσα, 'satiate.'

κόπτω (κοπ- or κοβ-), 'cut.'

κρεμάω, κρεμνάω, κρέμαμαι (cf. δύναμαι); θὰ κρεμάσω, θὰ κρεμασθῶ, κ.τ.λ., 'hang.'

λαγχάνω (λαχ-), 'fall in with,' 'obtain by lot.'

λανθάνω (λαθ-), θὰ λανθασθῶ, 'hide,' 'escape,' in passive 'am mistaken.'

λούω (λου- and λουσ-), θὰ λουσθῶ, λουσμένος or λελουμένος, 'wash.'

μανθάνω (μαθ-), 'learn.'

μάχομαι (only in imperfect), 'fight.' For other tenses, πολεμε-.

μέλλω, 'intend,' 'be about to' (only in impf.); past ἤμελλον and ἔμελλον.

μιγνύω (μιγ-), 'mix,' ἔμιξα, ἐμίγην, ἐμίχθην.

οἶδα (ϝιδ- ϝοιδ-), 'I know.' Chiefly in phrases, τίς οἶδε; 'who knows?' Κύριος οἶδε, 'Lord knows;' οὐκ οἶδα for δὲν ἠξεύρω, 'I don't know.' Cf. our own archaism, *I wot not*.

μιμνήσκω (in comp.) (μνα- μνησ-), ἔμνησα, ἐμνήσθην, 'remind,' 'remember.'

οἰκτείρω, ᾤκτειρον, ᾤκτειρα, 'pity.'

ὀμνύω (ὀμο-), ὤμοσα, θὰ ὀμόσω, 'swear.'

πάσχω (for πάθ-σκω) or παθαίνω (παθ-), 'suffer.'
πείθω, πείθομαι, 'persuade,' 'obey;' ἔπεισα, ἐπείσθην; πέπεισμαι, 'I am persuaded;' πέποιθα, 'I trust.'
πηγαίνω and ὑπάγω (παγ- ὑπαγ-), 'go;' ἐπήγα, θὰ πάγω. The η in ἐπῆγα or ὑπῆγα is the result of the augment in the aorist (or imperfect) of the simple verb ἦγον, ἦγα from ἀγ-.
πίνω (πι-), 'drink;' ἔπιον and ἤπια.
πίπτω (πεσ- for πετ-), 'fall.'
πλέω or πλεύω (πλευ-, πλεϝ-), 'sail.'
πνέω, πνεύω (πνευ- πνεϝ-), ἐπνεύσθην, 'breathe.'
ῥέω, ῥεύω (σρευ- σρεϝ-), ἔῤῥευσα for ἔσρευσα, 'flow.'
ῥηγνύω (ῥήγνυμι), ῥήγνυμαι (cf. δύναμαι), κ.τ.λ (ῥηγ- ῥαγ for ϝραγ-), hence ἐῤῥάγην, κ.τ.λ., 'break.'
ῥώννυμι, obs. except in ἔρρωσο, ἔρρωσθε, 'be strong!' 'hail!' 'farewell!'
σβύνω (σβυ- σβε-), 'quench;' ἔσβεσα and ἔσβυσα, ἐσβέσθην, ἐσβεσμένος.
σέβομαι (σεβα[δ]-), ἐσεβάσθην, 'honour,' 'revere.'
σήπομαι (σαπε-), 'rot;' ἐσάπησα, ἐσαπήθην.
τήκω (τηκ- and τακ-), 'melt;' ἔτηξα, ἐτάκην.
τρέμω, ἔτρεμον, 'tremble.' No aor. Place supplied by ἔτρεσα (classical), ἐτρόμαξα (modern).
τρέπω (τρεπ- and τραπ-), 'turn;' ἔτρεψα, ἐτράπην, τετραμμένος.
τρέφω (θρεπ- and τραφ-, cf. τριχ-, nom. θρίξ), 'feed;' ἔθρεψα, ἐτράφην, τεθρεμμένος or τεθραμμένος. Cf. also θάπτω.
τρέχω (τρεχ- and δραμ-), 'run;' ἔτρεξα and ἔδραμον.
τρώγω (class. ἐσθίω) (φαγ-), 'eat.'
τυγχάνω (τυχ-), 'chance.'
ὑπισχνέομαι or ὑπόσχομαι, ὑπεσχέθην (cf. ἔχω), 'promise.'
φαίνομαι, 'seem,' 'appear' (for φάνομαι), ἐφάνην.
φέρω, φέρνω, 'bring;' imp. ἔφερον; aor. ἔφερα. In a few compounds the stem ἐνεγκ- or ἐνεκ- is used for aor. ἤνεγκα or ον, ἐνεχθῶ, ἠνέχθην, κ.τ.λ.
φεύγω (φυγ-), 'fly,' 'flee,' 'depart.'

φθείρω (φθαρ-), ἔφθειρα, ἐφθάρην, ἐφθαρμένος, 'spoil,' 'corrupt.' In comp.

χαίρω (χαρ-), θὰ χαρῶ, ἐχάρην, 'rejoice,' 'be glad.' Impf. active, aorists passive in form, but intransitive in sense.

χορταίνω (χορτά-), 'satiate.'

χέω (χυ-, χευ-, χεϝ-), χύνω, except in comp., ἔχυσα, κεχυμένος, κ.τ.λ., 'pour.'

On Derivation and Composition.

Closely allied to the subject of Greek accidence is that of the formation of words.

There are two principal ways by which words are built up in Greek, first, by addition of suffixes and prefixes by themselves unmeaning, and secondly, by the compounding of two or more words. The first may be called an inflexional, the second an agglutinative process, or they may be distinguished as the processes of derivation and composition.

DERIVATION BY AFFIX OR PREFIX.

The principal prefixes are:—

a(ν)- = English *un*, e.g. γραπτό-, 'written,' ἄγραπτο-, 'unwritten;' ὑποφερτό-, 'bearable,' ἀνυπόφερτο-, 'unbearable.' Observe change of accent, which is typical.

εὐ-, 'well,' 'easily,' &c., e.g. καταληπτό-, 'comprehensible,' εὐκατάληπτο-, 'easy of comprehension.'

δυσ-, 'ill,' 'hard,' &c., e.g. ἀναβατό-, 'accessible,' 'that may be ascended,' δυσανάβατο-, 'hard to ascend.'

All these prefixes may be compounded with the *essential part* less the formative vowel of a substantive, and form, by the addition of a new formative vowel, an altogether fresh word, e.g. from μορφ-ά-, 'shape,' take α and add ο; the stem μορφο- thus obtained, which has no independent existence, may then be combined, thus: ἄμορφο-, 'shapeless,' δύσμορφο-, 'misshapen,' εὔμορφο-, 'shapely,' 'fair.' Or again, from τύχ-α- (η-), 'fortune,' we derive ἀτυχέσ-, 'luckless,' δυστυχέσ-, 'unlucky,' εὐτυχέσ-, 'lucky.' Such forms should not mislead us to suppose there is any such word as τυχέσ-, μορφό-. This principle is of very wide application, e.g. ἐκβαλ- is a verb root meaning 'to put out,' 'to extricate oneself or others.' There is no such word as ἔκβολο-, 'extricable,' though there is a noun ἐκβολή, 'issue,' 'exit,' but there is the adjective δυσέκβολο-, 'inextricable,' and this form is typical of many others. In this place it is convenient to observe that the change from a or ε to o is very common in forming noun stems from verbal roots, thus: βαλ- becomes βολ-, φερ- φορ-, and similarly many others. Besides ἀ-, εὐ-, and δυσ-, the chief prefixes are prepositions, but as these are independent words, we shall consider them under the head of "Composition." Besides these, we have the merely euphonic ὀ-, ἀ-, as ὀ-λίγος for λίγο-ς, 'small,' 'few;' ἀστάχιον for στάχιον, 'an ear of corn.'

Suffixes.

-μὀ-, masculine = '-ing,' e.g. παλ-, 'pal-pitate,' παλμό-ς, 'palpitation,' 'throb;' also adjectival, e.g. θερ-, 'heat,' θερμό-, 'heated,' 'warm.'

-μὀν-, masculine = '-er,' e.g. ἡγε-, 'lead,' ἡγεμών [όν-ς], 'leader.'

-μον-, masculine, e.g. τλα- τλη-, 'bear,' τλήμων, 'enduring,' 'suffering.'

-μεν-, masculine, '-er;' ποι- (ποε- παε-), 'feed,' ποιμήν [-ένς], 'shepherd.'

-ματ-, neuter, effect of action, e.g. πρακ-, 'do,' πρᾶγμα[τ], 'deed,' 'thing done.'

-μή-, feminine, e.g. γραμ-μή for γραφ-μή, 'a line.'

-τερ-, chiefly in relations, e.g. πα-τήρ, 'father,' μήτηρ, 'mother.'

-τηρ- = '-er;' κλη-τήρ, 'caller,' 'summoner,' 'policeman,' σω-τήρ, 'saviour.'

-τορ- = '-er;' ῥή-τωρ, 'speaker,' 'orator.' Of this, τυρ in μάρ-τυρ is a variant.

-τη = '-er;' πολί-της, 'citizen;' also -τή, e. g. κρι-τής, 'judge.'
-τρια- and τειρα, feminine form of above, as ποιή-τρια, 'poetess,' ὑπηρέ-τρια, 'maid servant.'
-τρίδ- = '-ster,' '-stress;' αὐλη-τρίς, 'flute-player' (female).
-τρο-, -τρό-, neuter = instrument or object of action, e. g. ἄρο-τρο-ν, 'plough,' λου-τρόν, 'bath.'
-θρο-, bye-form of above; ἄρ-θρον, 'ar-ticle,' 'joint,' 'fitting,' from ἀρ-, 'fit.'
-θλη, feminine form of above, e. g. γενέθλη from γενε (γεν-), 'birth,' 'generation.'
-σύνη = '-ness,' feminine, e. g. εὐρφοσύνη = εὐφρον-σύνη, 'gladness.'
-τητ- = '-th,' feminine, e. g. νεό-της [τς], 'youth.'
-ία, -ιᾰ, and ία, ιᾰ = '-th,' feminine, e. g. μαν-, 'rave' (μαίνομαι), μανία, 'madness;' ἀληθὲσ-, 'true,' ἀλήθεια [ἀλήθε(σ)ια], 'truth;' ἀμαθὲσ-, 'unlearned,' ἀμάθεια, 'ignorance;' στρατ-ὸ, 'force,' στρατιὰ, 'army;' σκότ-ες-, 'dark' (subst.) σκοτία, 'darkness.'
ιο-ν, neuter, 'place of,' e. g. Μοῦσα, 'Muse,' μουσεῖον, 'place of Muses' (μουσέ-ι-ον, μουσῆϊον); μνήμη, 'memory,' μνημεῖον, 'place of remembrance,' 'tomb,' 'monument;' Ionic, μνημῆϊον.
-ὼν, masculine, 'abode of;' δένδρ-ε-ο-, δένδρ-ο-, 'tree,' δενδρὼν, δενδρεών, 'plantation.'
-ίδ- = '-ess' ⎫ Sign of female ⎧ Γερμαν-ό-ς, 'German,' Γερ-
           ⎬ agency or   ⎨ μανίδ-, 'German lady.'
-άδ- = '-ess' ⎭ quality.   ⎩ λάμπ-, 'shine,' λαμπάδ-, 'candle.'
-αινα-, 'wife of;' Κώστας, 'Constant,' Κώσταινα, 'Mrs. Constant.'
-ίνα-, 'wife of;' Νικολ-ῆ-ς, Νικολ-ίνα.
ἀρης, ἀριο-ς = 'er;' περίβολ-ο-, 'garden,' περιβολάρης, 'gardener.'
ᾶ-ς, 'dealer in' or 'agent;' φαγ-, 'eat,' φαγᾶ-ς, 'a glutton;' μύλων-, 'mill' (μύλο-ς), μυλωνᾶ-ς, 'miller.'
-ήλα-, -ύλα- = '-ness;' μαῦρ-ο, 'black,' μαυρήλα, 'blackness.'
-οῦ, feminine of ᾶ-ς; βούτυρ-ο-, 'butter,' βουτυρ-οῦ, 'butterwoman.'

-ούρα-, the Latin -*ura*, our -*ure*; σκότ-ος, σκοτούρα, '(black) care;' κλει-, κλει-σ-ούρα, 'an enclosure' (the σ is that of the aorist).

-ουριά-, 'haunt of;' κλέφτ-η-ς (κλέπτης), 'robber,' κλεφτουριά, 'den of robbers.'

-σία- for τ-ία; ἀνόη-τ-ο-, 'senseless,' ἀνοη-σ-ία, 'senselessness.'

-λη- = 'iness;' ὀ-μίχ-λη, 'mist(iness),' νεφέ-λη (νέφες-), 'cloud(iness).'

-ρα-, 'place where,' 'thing by which;' ἕδ-ρα [σέδ-ρα], 'seat.'

-ρο-, neuter, 'thing done;' δῶ-ρον, 'a gift.'

-ον- (-εν-, -ην-); εἰκ-ών, 'like-ness,' 'picture.'

-ανο-, -όνη-, 'instrument;' (ϝ)ὄργ-ανον, 'tool' (root ϝεργ-, 'work), ἀγχ-όνη, 'strangling,' δρέπανον and δρεπάνη, 'sickle' (δρεπ-, 'reap').

-νο- = '-ful,' '-ness;' ὕπ-νος [σύπ-νος], 'sleep,' σκοτεινόν for σκοτεισνόν, 'dark,' σεμνόν for σεβνόν, 'worshipful.'

-νι- = '-ness,' feminine; σπά-νις, 'scantness.'

-τι- = '-er' masculine, '-ing' feminine, also -σι-; μάν-τις, 'warner,' 'prophet,' φύσις, 'growing,' 'nature.'

-τυ- (rare); ἄσ-τυ, ϝάσ-τυ, 'dwelling-place,' 'city.'

-ες- (nominative ος), neuter; γέν-ος, 'kin-dred.'

-πουλο-, -πούλα, 'son,' 'daughter;' Χρηστό-πουλος, 'son of Chrestos,' βοσκο-πούλα, 'shepherd girl.'

-ίδη-, feminine -ιδ-, 'son;' Λασκαρίδης, 'son of Lascar.'

-ιμο-ν, genitive ίματος, action of a verb; γέλα-, 'laugh,' γελά-σιμον, 'laughter.'

-ω, -ώ, ending of some female proper names, e.g. Ἀγγελικώ, Χρύσω, Ἀργυρώ.

-ιο- (ι), -ίο- (ί), -άρι(ο), -άκι-, -άφι-, -ύφι- (neuter), -άκη-ς, ούλη-ς (masculine), -ούλα, -ίτσα, -ούδα (feminine), are all diminutive endings. Sometimes several are combined, e.g. παιδί, παιδάρι-, παιδαράκι for παιδαρ(ι)άκι, 'a very little boy,' κομμάτι, κομματάκι, 'a little piece.' By substituting α for ι, the diminutive is changed to an augmentative, e.g. κομμάτα,

R

'a big piece,' Θεοφιλᾶ-ς, 'big Theophilus.' So, above, φαγ-ᾶ-ς is 'a big eater.'

ADJECTIVE ENDINGS.

Such are:—

-σιο- (old genitive ending, τοῦ = τόσιο), e. g. δίπλα, adverb, 'doubly,' διπλάσιο-, 'two-fold.'

-κό- : πατρ-ι-κό-, 'father-ly,' καρδια-κό-, 'of the heart,' θηλυ-κό-, 'female,' φυσι-κό-, 'natural.'

-μο- : ὠφελ-, 'profit,' ὠφέλιμο-, 'profitable.'

-υ-λο- and -ύλο- : στώμ-υλο-, 'talkative' (στομα(τ) = 'mouth').

-ί-λο- : ὀργ-ί-λο-, 'wrathful.'

-η-λό- : σιωπ-η-λό-, 'silent,' χαμ-η-λό, 'mean,' 'lowly' (χαμαὶ, 'on the ground,' old locative).

-ινο- : ξύλ-ινο-, 'wood-en.'

-ιο- : Ἀθηναῖο- (Ἀθηνά-ϊο-), 'Athenian.'

-ρό- : λυπη-ρό, 'grievous.'

-εντ- (-ϝεντ-) : πτερό-εντ-, 'winged,' μαυρομαλλοῦσσα for μαυρομαλλό-εντ-σα, 'black-haired.'

-τὸ-, verbal adjective : γραπ-τὸ- for γραφ-τό-, 'written,' or 'writeable.'

-τέο-, 'what should be :' τί πρακ-τέο-ν; 'what('s) to be done?'

To these must be added the participial endings given above in connexion with the verb, and the simplest noun stems, affixes, substantive and adjective, -α-, -η-, -σ-, -υ-, -εσ-, κ.τ.λ., with which the student has already been made familiar.

COMPOUND WORDS.

In the composition of words there is no language more prolific than the Greek, whether Ancient or Modern.

The rules of compounding words are very simple.

The chief points requiring attention are—(1) the accent, (2) the part played by the vowel o, (3) the creation by composition of new stems.

(1) As to the accent, the rule is, that in compound words it

goes as far back as possible, quite irrespective of its original place in the final word.

(2) The simplest case of composition is where the stem of the first word ends in o, and the final word begins with a consonant and suffers no change, e. g. παλαιὸ-ν κάστρον, 'an old fortress,' becomes παλαιόκαστρον ('Oldfort'), often the name of a place; ξυνὸ-ν, 'sour,' γάλα, 'milk,' ξυνόγαλα, 'butter-milk.' If the last word begins with a vowel, the o of the preceding stem is absorbed, e. g. ξυλάνθρωπος for ξυλο-άνθρωπος, 'woodenman,' 'blockhead.' If the stem of the first word ends in a consonant, or an a or η, o is either inserted or substituted, e. g. θαλασσόνερον, 'sea-water,' from θάλασσα and νερόν. The diminutive suffix ιο also becomes o in compounds, e. g. κρασοπότηρον, 'wine-cup,' for κρασιοπότηρον, and that even as respects the latter half of the compound, as μολυβοκόνδυλον, 'leadpencil,' from μολυβι(ον) and κονδύλι(ον).

(3) A number of new stems, for the most part verbals in o, arise by the process of composition; and here observe the stem which denotes the agent has (if possible) the accent, o. g. ἀνθρωποκτόνος, 'a man-slayer' (but ἀνθρωπόκτονος, 'slain by man'), λογογράφος, 'a writer of words,' θεολόγος, 'a talker about God,' λειπόθυμος (λειπ- θυμό-), literally, 'leaving life,' i. e. fainting. N.B.—There are no such independent words as κτόνο-ς, 'slayer,' γράφο-ς, 'writer,' λεῖπο-ς, 'leaver.'

Words ending in -ι- cannot stand as the last word of a compound, but are replaced by the more abstract -ία, e. g. λειποταξία, 'leaving the ranks,' not λειπόταξις; παλιγ-γενεσία, 'new-birth,' 'regeneration,' not παλιγγένεσις or παλιγγέννησις. Words like "Parthenogenesis" for "Parthenogenesia," used as terms of science, are barbarous in the last degree. This applies also to compounds with the particles ἀ, εὐ, δυς, as ἀταξία, εὐταξία, δυστυχία, not ἄταξις, εὔταξις, δυστύχη.

PREPOSITIONS IN COMPOSITION.

ἀπὸ, παρὰ, ἀντὶ, ἐπὶ, ἀνὰ, διὰ, μετὰ, lose their final vowel in composition before another vowel; not so περὶ, ἀμφί, e. g. ἐπώνυμος (ὀνόματ, dialectically ὀνύματ), 'named after,' but περιώνυμος, 'famous.'

In the case of verbals in -τὸ- compounded with a preposition, only usage can teach the student where to place the accent, but probably the explanation of the irregularity is that where the compound verbal is taken straight from the verb, e. g. ἀναβατός from ἀναβα-, the accent maintains its natural place; where, however, the verbal is first formed a simple word, and then compounded with the preposition, the accent is thrown back, e. g. θετόν, 'a thing placed,' ἐπί-θετον, 'an adjective.'

Particles or Uninflected Words.

These may be subdivided into adverbs, conjunctions, and prepositions.

Adverbs.

The greater number of these are themselves inflexions of adjectives, and are interesting as revealing to us old case-endings otherwise lost to the language.

Any adjective can be changed to an adverb, either by the ending -ως (for -ωτ), an old instrumental termination, or by using the neuter objective, singular or plural. The plural is used chiefly in the superlative degree of adjectives, the singular sometimes in the comparative, ως in the positive; e. g. from καλὸ-, κακὸ-, 'good,' 'bad,' καλῶς, 'well,' κάλλιον, 'better,' κάλλιστα, 'in the best way,' 'best;' κακῶς, 'ill,' κακώτερον or χεῖρον, 'in a worse way,' χείριστα or κάκιστα, 'in the worst way.' But in familiar phrases, such as πολὺ καλά, 'very well,' εἶμαι καλά, 'I am well,' the neuter plural is preferred.

A considerable number of adverbs are also formed by the following old case-endings:—

-θεν or -θε, ablative = 'from,' e. g. αὐτό-θεν, 'thence,' πό-θεν; 'whence?' ὅθεν, 'whence,' 'wherefore,' ἐκεῖ-θεν, 'thence,' μακρό-θεν, 'from afar,' κ.τ.λ.

-σε, 'to a place,' as ἐκεῖ-σε, 'thither.'
-δε, 'to' or 'at,' as ὧ-δε, 'hither,' ἔνθα-δε, 'hither,' 'here.'
ι dative or locative, e. g. οἴκοι (οἰκο-ι), 'at home,' χαμαί (χαμά-ι), 'on the ground.'
-υ, also locative, e. g. αὐτοῦ, 'there,' 'here,' χάμου, vernacular for χαμαί.
-θι, also locative, e. g. ἀλλαχ-όθι, 'elsewhere.'

The following is a list of the principal adverbs of time and place:—

ADVERBS OF PLACE.

ποῦ; where? whither?
που, somewhere.
ὅπου, where.
πόθεν; whence?
ὅθεν, ὁπόθεν, whence.
ἐνταῦθα, ἐδῶ, ὧδε, here, hither.
αὐτοῦ, there.
ἐκεῖ, there, yonder.
ἐκεῖσε, thither.
ἐκεῖθεν, thence.
ἐντεῦθεν, thence.
τῇδε κἀκεῖσε, hither and thither.
ἐδῶ καὶ ἐκεῖ, here and there.
ἀλλαχοῦ, ἀλλοῦ ἀλλαχόθι, elsewhere, elsewhither.
ἄλλοθεν, elsewhence.
πανταχοῦ, παντοῦ, everywhere.
ἐνιαχοῦ, κἄπου, somewhere.
ἑκατέρωθεν, from or on either side.
ἀμφοτέρωθεν, from or on both sides.
δεξιόθεν, on the right.
ἀριστερόθεν, on the left.
κύκλῳ, τριγύρῳ, round about.
πέριξ, around.
ὑποκάτω, beneath.
κάτω, below.

κάτωθεν, from below.
ἄνωθεν, from above.
δεξιὰ, to the right.
ἀριστερὰ, to the left.
ὁμοῦ, together.
προσωτέρω, further on.
ἐπάνω, above.
ἄνω, above.
πλησίον, ἐγγὺς, near.
ἐντὸς, within.
ἔσωθεν, ἔνδοθεν, from within.
ἐκτὸς, ἔξω, without. ἐκτὸς τοῦ ὅτι, νὰ, κ.τ.λ., except that, &c.
ἔξωθεν, from without.
ὀπίσω, back, backwards.
κατόπιν, behind, afterwards.
ὄπισθεν, from behind.
ἐμπρὸς, before, forwards.
ἔμπροσθεν, from before.
οὐδαμοῦ, nowhere.
μακρὰν, far.
ἐνώπιον, in the presence of, before.
ἀπέναντι, opposite.
πέραν, πέρα, beyond. ἐκεῖ πέρα, over yonder.
περαιτέρω, further.

ADVERBS OF TIME.

πότε, when.
ποτέ, ever.
σήμερον, to-day.
αὔριον, to-morrow.
πρωΐ, early.
μεθαύριον, the day after to-morrow.
χθές, ἐχθές, yesterday.
προχθές, the day before yesterday.
ἄλλοτε, formerly, at another time.
πρίν, πρότερον, sooner, before.
τότε, then.
ἔπειτα, εἶτα, then, afterwards.
τέλος, at last.
πάντοτε, ἀείποτε, ἀεὶ, always.
αἰωνίως, eternally.
εἰσαεί, ἐσαεί, for ever.
νεωστί, lately.
ἐσχάτως, lately.
ἤδη, already, now.
πλέον, henceforth, more.
ἔτι, εἰσέτι, ἀκόμη, still, yet, besides.
ἀμέσως, εὐθύς, straightway, directly.
ἀργά, late.
βραδύτερον, later.
ἔκτοτε, since then.
νῦν, τώρα, now.

ἐνίοτε, κάποτε, sometimes.
πολλάκις, often.
συνεχῶς, συχνάκις, continuously, frequently.
οὐδέποτε, never.
μόλις, scarcely, hardly.
σχεδόν, almost.
αἴφνης, suddenly.
ἔξαφνα, ἐξαίφνης, ἀφνιδίως, suddenly.
ὅσον οὔπω, very soon (lit. just not yet).
ἐφέτος, this year.
τοῦ χρόνου, next year.
πέρυσι, last year.
ἀνέκαθεν, from earliest times.
ἀπόψε, this evening.
ἐψές, yesterday evening.
νυχθημερὸν, day and night.
αὐθημερὸν, on the same day.
ἐνωρίς, early.
συγχρόνως, at the same time.
ταυτοχρόνως, simultaneously.
ἐνταυτῷ, σύναμα, συνάμα, at once.
βαθμηδὸν, by degrees.
ἅμα, along with, at the same time.
λοιπόν, therefore.

Many of these adverbs serve also as conjunctions, and others as prepositions; indeed, no very definite line of demarcation can be drawn between these various particles, but as conjunctions proper the following should be noted:—

καί, and, also, even.
καί — καί, both — and.
τε — καί, both — and, e. g. μικροί τε καὶ μεγάλοι, both small and great

ὄχι μόνον — ἀλλὰ καί, not only — but also.
οὐ μόνον — ἀλλὰ καί, not only — but also.
καὶ — δέ, but — also.

οὔτε — οὔτε (with indic.), neither — nor.
μήτε — μήτε (with subj. and imper.), neither — nor.
οὐδέ, μηδέ, not even.
ἤ, or ; ἤ — ἤ, either — or.
εἴτε — εἴτε, ἐάν τε — ἐάν τε, whether — or.
μέν, indeed, 'tis true. } Never first in a sentence.
δέ, but.
ὁτὲ μέν — ὁτὲ δέ, at one time — at another.
καίτοι, εἰ καί, ἐὰν καί, μ' ὅλον ὅτι, although.
καίπερ, although.
ὅμως, however.
μ' ὅλον τοῦτο, μ' ὅλα ταῦτα, nevertheless.
εἰ δὲ μή, else. εἰ μή, unless.
ὁσάκις, as often as.
ἐνῷ, while.
ἐνόσῳ, as long as.
πρίν, πρὶν ἤ, πρὶν νά, before (followed by subjunctive).

ἕως οὗ, ἕως ὅτου, until.
μέχρις οὗ, ἄχρις οὗ, until.
ἀφοῦ, since.
ἐάν, ἄν, εἰ, if.
ἄν, πότερον, whether.
ὅτι, that (with indic.).
νά, that (with subj.).
ἄρα, so, then.
ἑπομένως, accordingly.
ὥστε, so that.
ὥστε νά, so as to.
δηλαδή, that is to say.
τουτέστι, that is.
ἤτοι, ἤγουν, that is.
ἐπειδή, since.
διότι, because.
ὅσῳ — τόσῳ, ὅσον — τόσον, the — the, as in "the more the merrier."
μᾶλλον, rather, more.
ἵνα, διὰ νά, ὅπως, in order that.
ὡς, ὅπως, as, so as, just as.
ὅσῳ καὶ ἄν, however much.
ὡς ἐάν, ὡσάν, σάν, ὡσεί, as if.

PREPOSITIONS.

In the vernacular all prepositions, in as far as they are used at all, may be construed with the accusative case ; but educated people, following (partly) classical usage, employ them as follows :—

With the Objective (Accusative) alone.

εἰς, 'in,' 'into,' 'at.'
μέ, 'with.'

ἀνά, 'over,' 'up,' 'in,' 'by ; as ἀνὰ σειράν, 'in a series.'
χωρίς, 'without.'

With Genitive alone.

ἀντὶ, 'instead of,' 'for.'	πρὶν, πρὸ, 'before.'
ἄνευ, 'without.'	ἐκ, ἐξ (before vowels), 'out of,' 'from.'
ἐκτὸς, ἔξω, 'beyond,' 'without.'	

With Dative alone.

ἐν, 'in' (never *into*).	σὺν (not common), 'with.'

With Genitive and Accusative.

κατὰ, Gen., 'against,' e. g. κατὰ τοῦ ἀνθρώπου, 'against the man.'
    Acc., 'according to,' 'by,' 'in,' e. g. κατὰ μέρος, 'in part.'

μετὰ, Gen., 'with,' e. g. μετὰ πολλῶν ἀνθρώπων, 'with many men.'
    Acc., 'after,' e. g. μετὰ πολλὰς ἡμέρας, 'after many days.'

ὑπὲρ, Gen., 'for the sake of,' e. g. ὑπὲρ ἐμοῦ, 'on my behalf.'
    Acc., 'over,' e. g. ὑπὲρ τὴν πόλιν, 'over the town.'

ὑπὸ, Gen., 'by,' e. g. ὑπ' ἐμοῦ, 'by me.'
    Acc., 'under,' e. g. ὑπ' ἐμὲ, 'under me.'

ἀπὸ, 'from,' Acc. or Gen. without distinction of meaning, but colloquially with former.

διὰ, Gen., 'with,' 'by means of,' e. g. διὰ τούτου, 'by this means.'
    Acc., 'on account of,' 'for,' e. g. διὰ τοῦτο, 'on this account.'

περὶ, Gen., 'about,' 'concerning,' e. g. περὶ ἐμοῦ ὁμιλοῦσιν, 'they are talking about me.'
    Acc., 'round,' 'near,' e. g. περὶ ἐμὲ ἵστανται, 'they are standing round me.'

With Genitive, Dative, and Accusative.

ἐπὶ, Gen., 'in the time of,' 'upon,' 'on,' e. g. ἐπ' ἐμοῦ, 'in my time,' ἐπὶ τῆς τραπέζης, 'on the table.'
    Acc., 'on to,' 'up to,' e. g. ἐπὶ τὸ τεῖχος ἦλθε, 'he came up to the wall.'

ἐπί, Dat., 'on account of,' 'over,' e.g. ἐπὶ τῇ δυστυχίᾳ μου ὀδύρομαι, 'I wail over,' or 'bewail my misfortune.'

πρός, Gen., 'for the sake of,' e.g. πρὸς θεοῦ! 'for God's sake!'
Acc., 'to,' 'towards,' e.g. πρὸς αὐτὸν ἦλθον, 'I came to him.'
Dat., 'in addition to,' 'besides,' e.g. πρὸς τούτοις, 'more than this.'

παρά, Gen., 'from (the part of),' e.g. παρὰ τοῦ ὑπουργοῦ, 'from the minister.'
Dat., 'with,' 'among,' e.g. παρὰ τοῖς Ἄγγλοις, 'among Englishmen.'
Acc., 'along,' 'by the side of,' 'all but,' 'short of,' e.g. παρὰ τὸν ποταμόν, 'alongside the river;' τρεῖς παρὰ τέταρτον, 'three all but a quarter,' i.e. 2.45; παρ' ὀλίγον ἐφονεύθη, 'he was all but killed.'

Syntax.

The syntax of Modern Greek is on the whole so like the English that a few remarks will suffice.

On Concord.

With regard to number the rules are the same as in English. With regard to person, the first person takes precedence of the second, and the second of the third, where there is more than one subject of the sentence: ἐγὼ καὶ σὺ ἤλθομεν μαζύ, 'you and I came together;' σὺ καὶ αὐτὸς ἤλθετε μαζύ, 'you and he came together.' With regard to gender the masculine takes precedence of other genders in the case of animate, and the neuter in case of inanimate subjects, e.g. ὁ πατὴρ καὶ ἡ μήτηρ του φαίνονται νέοι, 'his father and mother seem young;' οἱ κῆποι, αἱ κοιλάδες καὶ τὰ δάση εἶνε τὸ ἔαρ χλοερά, 'the gardens, the valleys, and the woods are green in springtime.'

The Article.

The definite article is commonly used with proper names, but frequently left out after prepositions before names of places and countries, as ἡ Ἑλλὰς εἶνε ἐλευθέρα, 'Greece is free,' but πηγαίνω εἰς Ἑλλάδα, 'I go to Greece.' It is also used where we should omit it, with all abstract nouns, as ἡ ἀλήθεια, 'Truth,' ἡ φύσις, 'Nature;' not, however, with prepositions or their equivalent case-endings, e. g. φύσει, κατὰ φύσιν. It is commonly omitted where we should use it, before a substantive which is a predicate, e. g. ἡ Ἑλλὰς εἶνε πατρὶς τῶν Ἑλλήνων, 'Greece is the country of the Greeks.' In other similar cases, however, the usage of the two languages coincides, e. g. ἡ νὺξ ἡμέρα ἔγεινε or ἐγένετο, 'the night became day.'

By means of the article, as in English, adverbs can be used as adjectives, as οἱ τότε ἄνθρωποι, 'the men of that time.' Cf. "the above words."

The article is often used alone, some substantive being understood, as τὸ κατ' ἐμέ, 'as regards me;' τὰ τοῦ κόσμου, 'the affairs of the world;' τὴν σήμερον (ἡμέραν), 'the present (day).'

Infinitives with the article (also the subjunctive with νὰ) are used as substantives not subject to inflexion, e. g. τὸ γράφειν or τὸ νὰ γράφωμεν, 'to write,' 'writing,' genitive τοῦ γράφειν, κ.τ.λ.

If it is desired to place the adjective after the substantive, the article must be repeated, e. g. ὁ ἄνθρωπος ὁ καλὸς or ὁ καλὸς ἄνθρωπος, 'the good man,' not ὁ ἄνθρωπος καλός or καλὸς ὁ ἄνθρωπος, either of which would mean 'the man *is* good.

The article admits of almost any number of words being inserted between it and the substantive, e. g. τὰ κομισθέντα ἐκ τοῦ ζαχαροπλαστείου ἀφθόνως γλυκίσματα, 'the sweetmeats plentifully brought from the confectioner's.' In this respect the construction of Modern Greek closely resembles German.

The article is invariably used with the possessive pronouns, except the substantive is either a predicate, or so indefinite that in English it would require the indefinite article, e. g. ὁ ἰδικός μου φίλος or ὁ φίλος μου, 'my friend,' but αὐτὸς εἶνε φίλος μου, 'he is my friend,' φίλος μου τὸ εἶπε, 'a friend of mine said it.'

THE CASES.

THE ACCUSATIVE.

The use of this case is somewhat more extensive than in English. Many verbs which in English would require a preposition (especially intransitives and passives) are in Greek construed with an accusative, e. g. ἐντρέπομαι ἐμαυτόν, 'I am ashamed of myself,' ἐπιτρέπομαι τὸ πρᾶγμα, 'I am entrusted (with) the matter.'

The accusative is also used to mark time both *at* which and *during* which, though for the former the genitive and dative are also employed, e. g. τὴν νύκτα and νυκτός, 'by night,' τὸ θέρος, 'in summer,' ἔζησεν ἑκατὸν ἔτη, 'he lived a hundred years,' τὴν (also τῇ) ἐπαύριον, 'on the following day (ἡμέραν -ᾳ).

The double accusative is as common as in English, as σᾶς ζητῶ συγγνώμην, 'I ask you (your) pardon.'

The predicative accusative is idiomatic, as ἔλαβε τοῦτο δῶρον, 'he got this as a gift' (also δωρεάν). N.B.—'He got this gift' would be ἔλαβε τοῦτο τὸ δῶρον, as explained above.

Another use of the accusative is what is called in ancient Greek Grammars *par excellence* the Greek accusative, or accusative of respect. It is quite common in colloquial Modern Greek, e. g. ἔπαθε τὰ νεῦρά της, 'she suffered (in) her nerves.'

THE GENITIVE.

The general use of this case is so exactly like the English possessive or its equivalent, objective + 'of,' that we need only remark on its employment with comparatives, e. g. μεγαλήτερος ἐμοῦ (for ἢ or παρὰ ἐγώ), 'greater *than* I.' Cf. Latin ablative and Semitic *min*, 'from.'

In a few cases, "from," rather than "of," would be the natural preposition in English. Παρὰ, followed by the nominative, is also used for "than." One usage, however, is decidedly peculiar, e.g. ποτέ μου, 'never (or ever) in my life,' literally 'my ever;' μόνος μου, 'I by myself;' ἐκτυπήθη μόνος του, literally 'he was smitten alone of himself,' i.e. he committed suicide, or stabbed himself.

A few verbs which take the genitive where we might expect the objective, are generally easy to translate by words which even in English suggest the genitive relation, and in nearly all these cases the use of the objective is optional, e.g. ἀπολαύω καλῆς ὑγείας, 'I am in the enjoyment of good health;' δράττομαι τῆς εὐκαιρίας, 'I avail myself of the opportunity.'

THE DATIVE.

This case is rarely used in conversation. The objective either alone or with a preposition, εἰς, πρὸς, διὰ, κ.τ.λ., may be used instead, or in some cases the genitive; but the dative is admissible in verbs of giving, belonging, telling, pleasing, displeasing, fitting, meeting, &c., and after adjectives implying gratitude, ingratitude, plainness, obscurity, indifference, pleasure, pain, likeness, unlikeness, advantage, disadvantage, &c. The dative is also used to express time when (see above), and in a few phrases indicating manner or instrumentality, e.g. τῷ ὄντι, 'in very deed,' 'really,' τίνι τρόπῳ, 'in what way,' λόγῳ καὶ ἔργῳ, 'in word and deed,' παρρησίᾳ, 'with boldness,' 'openly,' παντὶ σθένει, 'with might and main,' τοῖς ἑκατόν, 'per cent.,' πράγματι, 'in fact,' μεγάλῃ τῇ φωνῇ, 'with a loud voice,' literally 'with the voice loud,' χάριτι Θεοῦ, 'by the grace of God,' κ.τ.λ.

THE VERB.

The only really common tenses of the verb are the present imperfect, past imperfect, aorist, and future (aorist and imperfect). Their meanings are best understood from illustration:—
γράφω, 'I write,' or 'am writing.'
ἔγραφον, 'I was writing,' 'began to write,' 'used to write.'

ἔγραψα, 'I wrote (on a certain occasion).'
θὰ γράφω, 'I will write,' 'practise writing,' 'be an author.'
θὰ γράψω, 'I will write (a letter or a book).'
γράψον (ε), 'write (e.g. this letter).'
γράφε, 'begin to write,' 'be writing,' 'be a writer,' 'choose writing for an occupation.'
μὴ γράψῃς, 'do not write (hereafter).'
μὴ γράφῃς, 'stop writing,' or 'refrain from writing now.'

N.B.—The aorist tense indicative stands also for perfect and pluperfect. In cases where misunderstanding might arise, the compound tenses, ἔχω γράψει, εἶχον γράψει, may be used.

THE SUBJUNCTIVE MOOD, AND USE OF PARTICLES.

The subjunctive mood is used after the conjunctions and particles, θὰ, νὰ, ἵνα, διὰ νὰ, ὅπως, ὅστις, εἴθε νὰ, ἴσως, ἅμα, κ.τ.λ., whenever future time is in view, e.g. ἴσως ἔλθω, 'perhaps I shall come,' ὅταν ἔλθω, 'when I come,' but ὅταν ἦλθον, 'when I came.'

θὰ with the imperfect indicative has a conditional meaning, like the Ancient Greek particle ἄν, e.g. θὰ ἤμην, 'I should be' = classical ἤμην ἄν or ἦν ἄν; but θὰ with the aorist indicative has quite another sense, e.g. θὰ ἔφυγε, 'he *must have* gone away,' 'he has probably gone away.'

πρὶν or πρὶν νὰ is followed by the subjunctive, even when past time is in view, e.g. ἔγραψα πρὶν ἔλθῃ (not ἦλθε), 'I wrote before he came.' This usage is contrary to what one might expect, and deserves to be noted.

νὰ is used with the indicative somewhat like θὰ, e.g. εἴθε νὰ ἤμουν, 'would that I were;' and, on the other hand, with the aorist, λέγεις νὰ ἔβρεξε, 'should you say that it had rained?'

THE PARTICIPLE.

The only usage of the participle which differs materially from the English is its frequent combination with the definite article, where we should use the verb with the demonstrative followed by the relative pronoun, e.g. οἱ πράξαντες, 'those who did,' τὰ πραχθέντα, 'the (things) done,' ὁ ἐρχόμενος, 'the comer,' 'he that comes,' &c.

The participle alone is frequently used where we should employ a preposition with the participle or gerundive in *-ing*, or some equivalent construction, e.g. προγευματίζων διαβάζει, 'he reads (while) breakfasting,' or 'at breakfast;' ἰδὼν ἀνέκραξε, 'he exclaimed (on) seeing;' καταναλίσκει παίζων τὸν χρόνον, 'he wastes his time (in) playing; φαίνεται λησμονήσας, 'he seems to have (having) forgotten.' When the subject of the participle is not that of the sentence, the former is put in the so-called absolute genitive, e.g. φθάσαντος αὐτοῦ ἔφυγον, 'on his arrival I left.'

The Negative Particles.

δὲν is used with indicatives, e.g. δὲν ἦλθε, 'he came not.'

οὐχί, ὄχι, with nouns, adjectives, and participles used adjectivally, e.g. ὄχι αὐτός! 'not he!' ὄχι ὡς ἡττηθεὶς ἀλλὰ ὡς νικήσας, 'not as worsted, but as having conquered.'

μὴ with subjunctives and participles, as μὴ νομίσῃς, 'that you may not think;' μὴ δυνάμενος, 'not being able.'

ὄχι, οὐχί, also = 'No!' in answer to a question.

Interrogation.

A question may be indicated in speaking by the simple tone of the voice, and requires no change in the order of the words. In writing, the sign (; = ?) is always placed at the end. Besides this, the following interrogatory particles are in use:—

(*a*) ἆρά γε, where it is uncertain whether the answer "Yes" or "No" is expected, as ἆρά γέ με ἐνθυμεῖται ἔτι; 'Does he yet remember me?' (perhaps "Yes," perhaps "No").

(*b*) μήπως, where the answer "No" is half expected, as μήπως μὲ γνωρίζεις; 'Do you (really) know me?'

(*c*) When the answer "No" is confidently expected, the

particles τοίγαρ or τοιγαροῦν, also μηγαρή (μὴ γὰρ ᾖ), are sometimes used, e. g. τοίγαρ τᾶσπρο των πληγόνει; 'Surely their white hue does not wound?'

Indirect Questions.

In these the same interrogatory pronouns and particles are used as in the direct questions, the indicative mood is kept, except after μήπως (μὴ), which is followed where fear or doubt is expressed by the subjunctive. As a rule, if the first or principal clause of the sentence is in the past tense, the dependent clause is also in the past, but the present is sometimes retained, e. g. μὲ ἐρωτᾷ πόθεν ἔρχομαι, 'He asked me whence I came;' μὲ ἠρώτησε πόθεν ἠρχόμην (also ἔρχομαι), 'He asked me whence I came;' πρόσεχε μήπως πέσῃς, 'Take heed, lest you fall;' ἐρωτῶ ἂν ἤκουσας περὶ τούτου, 'I ask whether you have heard of this.'

APPENDIX.

It has been thought well to add in the form of an Appendix the following specimens of letters received from Greek correspondents. As actual and authentic examples they will possess in the eyes of the student more value than the artificial products to be found in "Guides to Polite Letter-Writing." It is needless to add that all particulars which might lead to identification have been carefully suppressed.

Ἀθήναις, 7/19 Φεβρουαρίου, 1881.[1]

Φίλτατε Κύριε,

Πολλάκις διενοήθην νὰ σᾶς γράψω ὀλίγας γραμμὰς, διότι οὐδαμῶς ἐπεθύμουν οὕτω ἀποτόμως νὰ διακόψω πᾶσαν μετὰ τῶν ἐν Ἀγγλίᾳ φίλων μου σχέσιν, ἀλλὰ δυστυχῶς ἡ διεύθυνσις τῆς κατοικίας σας, ἥν ἀναχωροῦντες ἐντεῦθεν μοὶ ἀφήκατε, ἀπώλετο· ἐγὼ δὲ τότε ἀπετάθην πρὸς τὴν ἐν Λιβερπούλῃ Κυρίαν —— ἥτις τῷ ὄντι μοὶ ἔπεμψε τὴν διεύθυνσίν σας, ἀλλὰ τόσῳ δυσανάγνωστον ὥστε ἤμην βεβαιότατος ὅτι καὶ μηχανικῶς ἂν ἀντέγραφα αὐτὴν, ἡ ἐπιστολή μου δὲν θὰ σᾶς εὕρισκεν. Τούτου ἕνεκα ἐπὶ τῶν τὴν παρελθοῦσαν ἑβδομάδα ἀποσταλεισῶν ὑμῖν ἐφημερίδων προσέθεσα τὸ near London καὶ Κύριος πλέον οἶδεν ἂν μὴ αἵ τε ἐφημερίδες καὶ ἡ παροῦσα μου ἀπολεσθῶσιν.

Ἐγκαίρως περιῆλθεν εἰς χεῖράς μου ἡ ὑμετέρα διατριβὴ "ἡ Ἀναγεννωμένη Ἑλλὰς," ἥν ἀπλήστως ἀνέγνωσα. Μόλον ὅτι δὲ τὸ περιεχόμενον προώρισται μᾶλλον πρὸς φωτισμὸν τῶν μὴ τὴν Ἑλλάδα εἰδότων Ἄγγλων καὶ τῶν διαστροφέων τῆς ἀληθείας, διὰ τῆς δημοσιεύσεως ἔν τινι ἐνταῦθα ἐφημερίδι μεταφράσεως ἂν οὐχὶ τοῦ ὅλου, μέρους τοὐλάχιστον τῆς διατριβῆς σας ἐπεθύμουν νὰ καταστήσω γνωστὸν τὸ ὄνομά σας εἰς τὸ πολὺ ἑλληνικὸν κοινὸν, ἀλλὰ δυστυχῶς γνωρίζω ὅτι αἱ δυνάμεις μου πολὺ ὑστεροῦσι τοῦ ἔργου τούτου καὶ μετὰ λύπης μου ἐγκατέλειψα τὴν ἰδέαν ταύτην. Πλὴν δὲν ἔλειψα νὰ μεταδώσω εἰς πάντας τοὺς φίλους μου καὶ γνωρίσαντας ὑμᾶς ἐνταῦθα τὸ περιεχόμενον τῆς διατριβῆς σας, οἵτινες πάντες ηὐχαριστήθησαν καὶ μετ' ἐμοῦ ὡς Ἕλληνες εὐγνωμονοῦσιν ὑμῖν διὰ τὸ ἐπίκαιρον τῆς δημοσιεύσεως.

Ὡς πρὸς τὰ πολιτικά μας τοῦτο μόνον λέγω ὅτι εὑρισκόμεθα μεταξὺ σφύρας καὶ ἄκμωνος, ὑπερεπιθυμοῦντες μὲν ἀφ' ἑνὸς νὰ προσδράμωμεν πρὸς βοήθειαν τῶν δουλευόντων ἀδελφῶν μας, φοβού-

---

[1] It is usual in Greece to date letters according to both old and new style.

ATHENS, 7/19 *February*, 1881.

DEAR SIR,

Many a time have I had it in my mind to write you a few lines, since I by no means wished so suddenly to drop all connexion with my friends in England, but unfortunately your address, which you left me when you went away from here, got lost; and I then applied to Miss —— in Liverpool, who actually sent me your address, but in so illegible a form that I was quite certain, if I were even to copy it mechanically, that my letter would not find you.

For this reason I added on the newspapers sent last week the words, "near London," and heaven only knows whether both the newspapers and my present letter will be lost.

Your essay on "Græcia Rediviva" has duly come to hand, and I have eagerly read it. Although its contents are rather intended for the enlightenment of Englishmen who do not know Greece, and of perverters of the truth, yet, by the publication in some paper here of a translation—if not of the whole, at least of a portion of your treatise—I should like to make your name known to the general Greek public; but unfortunately I am aware that my powers fall far short of the requirements of the task, and, to my chagrin, I relinquished the idea. I have not failed, however, to communicate to all my friends who have known you here the contents of your treatise, and they were all delighted, and, with myself, are grateful as Greeks for the timeliness of the publication.

As to our politics, I can only say this: that we find ourselves betwixt the hammer and the anvil, longing above everything, on the one hand, to rush to the rescue of our brethren still in

μενοι δ' ἀφ' ἑτέρου μὴ προσκρούσωμεν εἰς τὰς ἰδέας φίλης τινὸς δυνάμεως. Αἱ προετοιμασίαι μας πρὸς πόλεμον εἶνε εἴπερ ποτὲ πλήρεις, δὲν ὑπάρχει δὲ οἰκογένεια ἥτις νὰ μὴν ἔχῃ ἓν ἢ πλειότερα ἄτομα κατατεταγμένα εἰς τὸν στρατόν.

Εἷς τῶν ἀδελφῶν μου ὑπηρετεῖ ὡς ἱππεύς, ἐγὼ δὲ ὑπάγομαι εἰς τοὺς ἐθνοφρουρούς. Γνωρίζοντες τοὺς Τούρκους κάλλιον τῶν εὐρωπαίων δημοσιογράφων, οἵτινες ἀριθμοὺς μόνον λογαριάζουν, καὶ ἐρειδόμενοι εἰς τὴν ἰσχὺν τοῦ ἑλληνισμοῦ, ἂν θέλετε δὲ καὶ εἰς τὰ συμφέροντα τῶν λοιπῶν φυλῶν τῆς Ἀνατολῆς ἔχομεν ἀκράδαντον πεποίθησιν ὅτι μετὰ λυσσώδη πάλην ἡ νίκη ἐπὶ τέλους ἔσται ὑπὲρ ἡμῶν.

Πλὴν δυστυχῶς ὁ πόλεμος ἢ ἡ εἰρήνη δὲν ἐξαρτᾶται, φαίνεται, ἀπὸ ἡμᾶς, ἀλλὰ ἀπὸ τὰς Μεγάλας Δυνάμεις. Μεγάλας! Ὅταν εἰρωνείαν ἐκφράζει ἡ λέξις ὑπὸ ἠθικὴν ἔποψιν.

Ἀκριβῶς ἀπὸ τῆς ἐντεῦθεν ἀναχωρήσεώς σας ἐργάζομαι παρά τινι ἀγγλικῷ γραφείῳ ὡς παρατηρεῖτε ἐπὶ τῆς ἐπικεφαλίδος. Πρὸς δὲ ἔδωκα εἰς γάμον μίαν τῶν ἀδελφῶν μου, ἥτις ἤδη ἀπέκτησε καὶ θυγάτριον.

Εὐελπιστῶν ὅτι τόσῳ ὑμεῖς ὡς καὶ ἡ σεβαστή μοι σύζυγός σας μετὰ τῆς λοιπῆς οἰκογενείας ἀπολαύετε ἄκρας ὑγείας καὶ ὅτι συντόμως θὰ ἀξιωθῶ ἐπιστολῆς σας,

Διατελῶ,

ὑμέτερος φίλος,

Π. Σ.

Υ.Γ. [ὕστερα γραμμένον].—Ἔγραψα ἑλληνιστὶ πρὸς πλειοτέραν ὑμῶν εὐχαρίστησιν. Ἂν δὲν ἀπατῶμαι μοὶ εἴχετε ὑποσχεθῆ μίαν φωτογραφίαν σας. Θέλετε λοιπὸν νὰ τὰς ἀνταλλάξωμεν;

Ἀθήναις, τῇ 8/20 Μαρτίου, 1881.

Φίλτατε Κύριε,

Ἐγκαίρως περιῆλθεν εἰς χεῖράς μου ἡ ἀπὸ εἰκοστῆς ὀγδόης λήξαντος φιλική σας, ἐξ ἧς ἀσμένως εἶδον ὅτι ἤδη

slavery; yet fearing, on the other, lest we run counter to the views of some friendly power. Our preparations for war are complete, if ever preparations were. There is not a family which has not one or more individuals enrolled in the army. One of my brothers is serving in the cavalry, and I am enlisting in the national guards. Knowing the Turks better than European journalists, who only reckon numbers, and relying on the strength of Hellenism, and, if you will, also on the interests of the other races of the East, we have an unshaken conviction that after a furious struggle, victory will at length be on our side.

But unhappily the question of war or peace does not depend, it seems, on us, but on the Great Powers. Great! What an irony does the word express from a moral point of view.

From the very day of your departure hence I have been employed in an English office, as you observe from the heading [of my letter]. Besides this, I have given one of my sisters in marriage, who has now also got a little daughter.

Hoping that both you and your honoured wife, with the rest of your family, are enjoying the best of health, and that I shall soon be favoured with a letter from you,

I remain,
Your friend,
P. S.

P.S.—I have written in Greek for your greater satisfaction. If I am not mistaken, you promised me your photograph. What do you say to an exchange?

ATHENS, 8/20 *March*, 1881.

MY DEAR SIR,

Your kind letter of the 28th of last month has duly come to hand, and I was very glad to see from it that you

ἀπολαύετε ἄκρας ὑγιείας τόσον ὑμεῖς ὅσον καὶ ἡ λοιπὴ οἰκογένειά σας.

Εὐχαριστῶ ὑμῖν εἰλικρινῶς διὰ τὰς φιλοφρονήσεις σας διὰ τὴν θέσιν μου, καὶ τὰς εὐχάς σας ἐπὶ τῷ γάμῳ τῆς ἀδελφῆς μου, κ.τ.λ. Τὴν ἀδελφήν μου δὲν νομίζω ὅτι τὴν εἴδατε κατὰ τὴν ἐνταῦθα διαμονήν σας, καθότι κατὰ τὸν καιρὸν ἐκεῖνον ἔμενεν ὡς διδάσκαλος ἔν τινι κλάδῳ τοῦ Ἀρσακείου Παρθεναγωγείου ἐν Κερκύρᾳ. Ὁ σύζυγός της ἐμπορεύεται ἔλαια, τὸ προϊὸν τῆς νήσου, τὸ δὲ θυγάτριόν των ὠνομάσθη ἐπ᾽ ἐσχάτων Εἰρήνη.

Μετ᾽ ἀγαλλιάσεως ἔλαβα τὴν φωτογραφίαν σας, ἥτις εἶνε τῇ ἀληθείᾳ μᾶλλον ἢ ἐπιτυχημένη. Κατὰ τὴν ὑπόσχεσίν μου καὶ ἀφ᾽ οὗ τὸ θέλετε, ἤδη σᾶς εἰσωκλείω τὴν ἐμήν.

Τὴν παρελθοῦσαν ἑβδομάδα τυχαίως παρετήρησα ἐν τῇ ἐφημερίδι "Νέαι Ἰδέαι" διάφορόν[2] τι ἀφορῶν τὴν ὑμετέραν διατριβήν, ἀλλὰ τόσῳ στεβλωμένον, ὥστε αὐθωρεὶ συνέταξα ἕτερον διάφορον πρὸς καταχώρισιν ἐν τῷ "Τηλεγράφῳ." Ὁ δὲ Συντάκτης τούτου μετά τινας πληροφορίας μου περὶ τῆς διατριβῆς καὶ τοῦ συγγραφέως αὐτῆς εἶχε τὴν καλωσύνην νὰ μοὶ ζητήσῃ τὸ φυλλάδιον ἵνα καταχωρίζῃ κατ᾽ ὀλίγον μετάφρασιν αὐτοῦ. Τοῦτο μὲ κατευχαρίστησεν ὡς πληροῦν τὸν πόθον ὑμῶν τε καὶ ἐμοῦ, καὶ ἀσμένως τῷ παρεχώρησα αὐτό.

Τὸ διάφορόν μου βλέπετε σημειωμένον ἐν τῷ φύλλῳ τῆς Πέμπτης δι᾽ ἐρυθροῦ μολύβδου, πάντα δὲ τὰ λοιπὰ προέρχονται ἐκ τῆς Συντάξεως τοῦ "Τηλεγράφου." Ἡ ἐξακολούθησις τῆς μεταφράσεως θὰ γένηται καὶ τὴν ἑβδομάδα ταύτην, ἐγκαίρως δὲ θέλω σᾶς πέμψει τὰ ἀντίτυπα.

Ἐπειδὴ πολὺ πιθανὸν νὰ μὴ μοὶ ἐπιστραφῇ τὸ φυλλάδιόν σας ἐκ τοῦ "Τηλεγράφου" κατὰ τὸ ἐνταῦθα ἔθιμον, σᾶς παρακαλῶ νὰ μοὶ πέμψητε ἓν ἕτερον πρὸς ἐνθύμησιν.

Παρεκάλεσα καὶ τὸν Συντάκτην τῆς "Παλιγγενεσίας" νὰ καταχωρήσῃ σχετικόν τι διάφορον, ἀλλὰ μέχρι τοῦδε δὲν τὸ ἔκαμεν.

Τὰ πολιτικά μας λίαν ἀμφίβολα, ἐν τούτοις ἐπικρατεῖ πρὸς τὸ

---

[2] διάφορον, literally "a various," i.e. one of the paragraphs usually

yourself are now enjoying the best of health, as well as the rest of your family.

I thank you sincerely for you good wishes in regard to my situation, and your congratulations on my sister's marriage, &c. I do not think that you saw my sister during your stay here, inasmuch as at that time she was staying as teacher in a branch of the Arsakeion (Girls' High School) in Corcyra. Her husband deals in oil, the produce of the island; and their little daughter finally has been named Irene.

I was delighted to get your photograph, which is indeed more than successful. According to my promise, and since you wish it, I herewith enclose you my own.

Last week I observed by chance in the newspaper, *New Ideas*, a paragraph referring to your treatise, but so perverted that I the very same hour drew up another paragraph for insertion in the *Telegraph*. The editor of the latter, after some information from me concerning the treatise and its author, had the goodness to ask me for the pamphlet, that he might insert, by instalments, a translation of it. This pleased me exceedingly, as it meets the wishes both of you and myself, and I gladly let him have it.

My paragraph you see marked in Thursday's paper with red lead, but all the rest proceeds from the editorial office of the *Telegraph*. The continuation of the translation will be made this week also, and I will duly send you the copies.

Since it is very likely that your pamphlet may not be returned to me from the *Telegraph*, according to the custom here, I beg you to send me another as a remembrancer.

I begged the editor of the *Renaissance* also to insert a similar paragraph, but hitherto he has not done so.

Our politics are very uncertain. Meanwhile, for the present,

---

found in newspapers under the heading "various" or "jottings."

παρὸν ἄκρα ἡσυχία. Ὁ πρωθυπουργός μας, ἐναντίον τοῦ κοινοῦ φρονήματος, εἶνε λίαν χλιαρὸς, μόλον ὅτι εἰς τὸ παρελθὸν δὲν ἐκολακεύετο ὀνομαζόμενος ἄνθρωπος τοῦ πυρὸς καὶ τοῦ σιδήρου.

Ἡ μήτηρ μου σᾶς προσφέρει τοὺς σεβασμούς της, λίαν δὲ εὐχαριστήθη μὲ τὴν φωτογραφίαν σας.

Προσφέρετε παρακαλῶ τὰς προσρήσεις μου πρὸς τὴν σεβαστήν μοι κυρίαν σας, δέξασθε δὲ τοὺς ἀσπασμοὺς τοῦ ὅλως ὑμετέρου φίλου σας,

Π. Σ.

ἐν Λονδίνῳ, τῇ 6/18 Ἰαν., 1881.

Αἰδεσιμώτατε Κύριε,

Μυρίας πέμπω ὑμῖν εὐχαριστίας διὰ τὸ ὑμέτερον φυλλάδιον ὅπερ εὐηρεστήθητε νὰ μοὶ πέμψητε. Ἀνέγνων αὐτὸ μετὰ προσοχῆς καὶ ἐχάρην ἰδὼν ὅτι ὑψοῦτε φωνὴν ὑπὲρ τοῦ δικαίου, ὑπερασπίζοντες τὸ ἔθνος τὸ ἑλληνικὸν ὅπερ πολλοί, φίλοι τοῦ σκότους καὶ τοῦ ψεύδους, προπηλακίζουσι καὶ ὑβρίζουσι. Καὶ τοὺς μὲν τοιούτους ἡμεῖς περιφρονοῦμεν, τοὺς δὲ μετὰ παρρησίας κηρύσσοντας τὰ ἡμέτερα δίκαια ἀγαπῶμεν καὶ οὐδέποτε παυόμεθα εὐγνωμονοῦντες αὐτοῖς.

Τὸ ὑμέτερον ὄνομα μοὶ ἦτο γνωστὸν πρὸ πολλοῦ ἐκ τοῦ καλοῦ ὑμῶν ἐγχειριδίου περὶ τῆς καθ᾽ ἡμᾶς Ἑλληνικῆς· καὶ ἤδη χαίρω πολὺ λαμβάνων ἀφορμὴν νὰ ἐπιστείλω ὑμῖν τὰ ὀλίγα ταῦτα.

Ἀσπάζομαι ὑμᾶς, καί εἰμι

ὅλως ὑμέτερος,

Κ. Λ.

Υ.Γ.—Ἐὰν νομίζητε ὅτι δύναμαί ποτε νὰ φανῶ ὑμῖν χρήσιμος εἴς τι, θὰ μὲ εὕρητε πάντοτε πρόθυμον.

Λονδίνῳ, Ἰανουαρίου 14ῃ, 1881.

Ἀξιότιμε Κύριε,

Παρακαλῶ δέξασθε τὰς εἰλικρινεῖς εὐχαριστίας μου διὰ τὸ φυλλάδιον ὅπερ φιλοφρόνως ἐπέμψατέ μοι. Ἀνέγνων αὐτὸ

the utmost tranquillity prevails. Our Prime Minister, in opposition to the general sentiment, is very lukewarm, although in the past he might be called, without flattery, a man of fire and sword.

My mother presents her compliments to you. She was very much pleased with your photograph.

Please remember me most kindly to your good lady, and accept the salutations of yours very truly,

P. S.

LONDON, 6/18 *January*, 1881.

REV. SIR,

I send you very many thanks for your pamphlet, which you were pleased to send me. I read it with attention, and rejoiced to see that you raise your voice on behalf of justice, defending the Greek nation, which many, friends of darkness and falsehood, revile and insult. Such men, indeed, we despise; but those who boldly vindicate our rights we love, and never cease feeling grateful towards them.

Your name was already long known to me from your excellent handbook on Modern Greek; and now I am very glad to have occasion to write you these few words.

I salute you, and am,

Yours truly,

K. L.

P.S.—If you think I can ever show myself of use to you in anything, you will find me always willing.

LONDON, *January* 14, 1881.

DEAR SIR,

Please accept my sincere thanks for the pamphlet which you kindly sent me. I read it with great interest, and

μετὰ μεγάλου διαφέροντος καὶ ὡς Ἕλλην εὐγνωμονῶ ὑμῖν δι' ὅσα τόσον ἀληθῶς καὶ τόσον ἐντόνως ἐγράψατε ὑπὲρ τοῦ ἡμετέρου ἔθνους πρὸς φωτισμὸν ἐκείνων τῶν ὑμετέρων συμπατριωτῶν οἵτινεςχρείαν ἔχουσι φωτισμοῦ περὶ τῆς ἀληθοῦς καταστάσεως τῆς Ἑλλάδος.

Εἰπέτε μοι παρακαλῶ ποῦ δύναμαι ν' ἀγοράσω τρία ἢ τέσσαρα ἀντίτυπα τοῦ περὶ οὗ ὁ λόγος φυλλαδίου ὅπως διανείμω αὐτὰ μεταξὺ φίλων Ἄγγλων.

Ἐπευχόμενος ὑμῖν τὸ νέον ἔτος αἴσιον καὶ εὐτυχὲς, διατελῶ μετὰ πάσης ὑπολήψεως,

Ὅλως ὑμέτερος,

Π. Σ. Α.

Υ.Γ.—Θὰ ἦτο καλὸν νὰ σταλῇ ἓν ἀντίτυπον πρὸς τὸν ἐν Τεργέστῃ ἐκδότην τῆς " Κλειοῦς."

---

9 21 Ἰαν., 1881.

Αἰδεσιμώτατε Κύριε,

Ἔλαβον τὴν ὑμετέραν ἐπιστολὴν καὶ χαίρω ὅτι θέλετε νὰ λάβητε τὴν γνωριμίαν μου.

Ἐπειδὴ δὲ καὶ ἐγὼ τοῦτ' αὐτὸ ἐπιθυμῶ, μεγίστην θὰ αἰσθανθῶ τέρψιν νὰ σᾶς ἴδω καὶ σφίγξω τὴν χεῖρά σας. Λυποῦμαι ὅμως πολὺ ὅτι τὰς καθημερινὰς εἶμαι ἀπησχολημένος εἰς τὰ μαθήματα μέχρι τῆς ἑβδόμης μ.μ. [μετὰ μεσημβρίαν] καὶ ἐπειδὴ εἶμαι μόνος λαμβάνω τὸ δεῖπνόν μου ἔξω καὶ ἐπιστρέφω ἀργὰ εἰς τὴν οἰκίαν μου. Μόνον τὰς κυριακὰς δύναμαι νὰ μείνω κατ' οἶκον, ἀλλὰ φοβοῦμαι ἡ ἡμέρα αὕτη θὰ ἦναι ἴσως ὅλως ἀκατάλληλος εἰς ὑμᾶς. Διὰ νὰ σᾶς ἀπαλλάξω τοῦ κόπου, ἂν θέλητε ἐγὼ νὰ ἔλθω νὰ σᾶς ἴδω ἑσπέραν τινὰ περὶ τὰς ὀκτὼ ἢ κυριακήν τινα μετὰ μεσημβρίαν ἢ τὴν ἑσπέραν· ἀλλ' ἐὰν ὑμεῖς προτιμᾶτε νὰ ἔλθητε παρ' ἐμὲ, ἀρκεῖ μόνον νά μοι γράψητε καὶ θά με εὕρητε κατ' οἶκον ὁποιανδήποτε κυριακὴν καὶ ἂν ἐγκρίνητε.

Τὸν Κύριον ὃν ὀνομάζετε δὲν τὸν γνωρίζω. Ἴσως ὁ συνάδελφός μου —— τὸν εἰξεύρει. Ἐγὼ εἶμαι Μικρασιανὸς ἐκ τῆς Κυζίκου, ἔκαμα ὅμως τὰς σπουδάς μου ἐν Ἀθήναις καὶ ἐν Κωνσταντινουπόλει·

as a Greek I am grateful to you for all that you have written, no less truly than earnestly, on behalf of our nation, for the enlightenment of those among your countrymen who need enlightenment in regard to the real condition of Greece.

Please tell me where I can buy three or four copies of the pamphlet in question, that I may distribute them among English friends.

Wishing you a happy and prosperous New Year, I remain, with all esteem,

Yours very truly,
P. S. A.

P.S.—It would be well that a copy should be sent to the editor of the *Clio*, in Trieste.

9/21 *Jan.*, 1881.

REV. SIR,

I received your letter, and am glad that you wish to make my acquaintance.

Since I also wish the same, I shall feel the greatest pleasure in seeing you, and in clasping your hand. I regret, however, much that on the weekdays I am engaged with lessons until seven p.m., and, as I am single, I take my supper away from home, and return late to my lodgings. Only on Sundays can I remain at home, but I fear this day will be altogether unsuitable to you. To relieve you of trouble, if you choose, let me come to see you some evening about eight, or some Sunday afternoon or evening; or, if you prefer to come to me, it is enough if you simply write to me, and you will find me at home on any Sunday that you may fix.

The gentleman you name I do not know. Perhaps my colleague —— is acquainted with him. I am from Asia Minor—from Cyzicus—but I have studied in Athens and Con-

τοῦτο δὲ εἶνε τὸ δέκατον ἔτος ἀφ' ὅτου ἦλθον εἰς Λονδῖνον. Καὶ ταῦτα ἐπὶ τοῦ παρόντος, πλείονα δὲ ὅταν, σὺν θεῷ, συναντηθῶμεν.

Ἀσπάζομαι ὑμᾶς, καὶ διατελῶ,

ὅλως ὑμέτερος,

Κ. Λ.

Υ.Γ.—Ἀπὸ τῆς 26 τοῦ μηνὸς τούτου θὰ μεταβαίνω κατὰ πᾶσαν Τετάρτην εἰς ―――― χάριν μαθημάτων καὶ νομίζω ὅτι τὸ μέρος τοῦτο δὲν ἀπέχει πολὺ τοῦ τόπου τῆς κατοικίας σας. Πρὸς τὸ παρὸν δὲν δύναμαι νὰ σᾶς εἴπω ποίαν ὥραν ἀκριβῶς θὰ τελειόνῃ τὸ μάθημα· ἴσως περὶ τὰς πέντε ἢ ἕξ μ.μ.

28 Μαρτίου, 1882.

Αἰδέσιμε φίλε,

Μόλις σήμερον περιῆλθεν εἰς χεῖράς μου τὸ ὑμέτερον ταχυδρομικὸν δελτάριον, διότι πρὸ πολλῶν μηνῶν μετεκομίσθην εἰς ἄλλην συνοικίαν. Εὐχαριστῶ ὑμῖν διὰ τὴν πρόσκλησιν καὶ μετὰ πολλῆς προθυμίας θὰ ἠρχόμην παρ' ὑμᾶς, ἂν μικρά τις ἀδιαθεσία δὲν μὲ ἐκώλυεν· Ἐλπίζω ὅταν ἀναλάβω νὰ ἔλθω νὰ προσφέρω ὑμῖν τε καὶ τῇ ὑμετέρᾳ κυρίᾳ τὰ σεβάσματά μου.

Περὶ τοῦ Κυρίου Η. οὐδὲν δύναμαι νὰ εἴπω διότι δὲν εἰξεύρω ποῦ κατοικεῖ.

Ἀσπάζομαι ὑμᾶς, καὶ διατελῶ,

ὅλως ὑμέτερος,

Λ. Γ.

12 Φεβ., 1881.

Αἰδέσιμε Κύριε,

Πέμπω ὑμῖν διὰ τοῦ ταχυδρομείου δύο Ἑβραϊκὰς ἐφημερίδας, ἃς σήμερον ἐκ Κωνσταντινουπόλεως ἔλαβον καὶ ἀσπάζομαι ὑμᾶς.

Μετὰ σεβασμοῦ,

ὅλως ὑμέτερος,

Μ. Ν.

stantinople; and this is the third year since I came to London. So much for the present, and more when (D.V.) we meet.

I salute you, and remain,

Yours very truly,

K. L.

P.S.—Beginning with the 26th of this month, I shall be travelling every Wednesday to —— on account of lessons, and I believe this neighbourhood is not very far from the place of your residence. At present I cannot tell you precisely at what hour the lesson will finish—perhaps about five or six p.m.

---

28 *March*, 1882.

REV. AND DEAR SIR,

Your post-card has only just come to hand to-day, on account of my having moved into another neighbourhood many months ago. I thank you for the invitation, and would have come to your house with much pleasure, had not a slight indisposition prevented me. I hope, when I recover, to come and present my respects to you and your wife.

As to Mr. E. I can say nothing, as I do not know where he lives.

With kindest regards, I remain,

Yours truly,

L. G.

---

12 *Feb.*, 1881.

REV. SIR,

I send you by post two Hebrew newspapers, which I received to-day from Constantinople.

With kind regards,

Yours truly,

M. N.

Τρίτη Ἑσπέρας.

Αἰδέσιμε Κύριε,
  Ἔλαβον τὸ ταχυδρομικὸν ὑμῶν δελτίον καὶ μετὰ πολλῆς χαρᾶς θὰ ἔλθω νὰ σᾶς ἴδω. Ἀλλὰ φοβοῦμαι θὰ σᾶς ἦναι πολὺς κόπος νὰ μὲ ἀνταμώσητε εἰς τὸν σταθμόν, καθ' ὅσον μάλιστα δὲν ἠδυνήθην νὰ ἐξακριβώσω καλὰ τὰ τοῦ σιδηροδρόμου. Νομίζω ὅμως ὅτι εἰς τὰς ἓξ μ.μ. θὰ τελειώσω τὸ μάθημα καὶ θὰ ἔλθω μὲ τὴν πρώτην ἁμαξοστοιχίαν. Ἴσως θὰ ἦναι τὸ καλλίτερον νὰ ἔλθω κατ' εὐθεῖαν εἰς τὴν οἰκίαν σας. Ἐρωτῶν θὰ εὕρω αὐτὴν εὐκόλως.

          Ὅλως ὑμέτερος,
             Λ. Γ.

Αἰδεσιμώτατε Κύριε,
  Παρακαλῶ ὑμᾶς πέμψατέ μου διὰ τοῦ ταχυδρομείου τὰς δύο Ἱσπανο-εβραϊκὰς ἐφημερίδας ἃς εἶχον στείλει ὑμῖν πρό τινος καιροῦ· διότι θέλω νὰ τὰς δώσω εἰς φίλον εἰς τὸν ὁποῖον τὰς ὑπεσχέθην.
   Ἀσπάζομαι ὑμᾶς καὶ εἶμαι,
        ὅλως ὑμέτερος,
            Μ. Ν.

           Δευτέρα.

Αἰδεσιμώτατε Κύριε,
  Σήμερον ἐπιστρέψας ἐκ Παρισίων εὗρον τὸ ὑμέτερον ταχυδρομικὸν δελτίον καὶ εὐχαριστῶ ὑμῖν διὰ τὴν πρόσκλησιν· λυποῦμαι ὅμως σφόδρα ὅτι δὲν θὰ δυνηθῶ νὰ ἔλθω καὶ παρακαλῶ νά μοι παράσχητε συγγνώμην.
   Ἀσπάζομαι ὑμᾶς ἐκ ψυχῆς καὶ διατελῶ,
        ὅλως ὑμέτερος,
            Ν. Λ.

Tuesday Evening.

Rev. Sir,
  I have received your post-card, and with much pleasure shall come to see you. But I fear it will be a great deal of trouble to you to meet me at the station, especially as I have not been able to make out the trains clearly. I think, however, that at six p.m. I shall have finished my lesson, and I will come by the first train afterwards. Perhaps it will be best that I should come straight to your house. By asking, I shall easily find it.

           Yours truly,
             L. G.

Rev. Sir,
  Please send me by post the two Spanish-Hebrew newspapers which I sent to you some time ago; for I want to give them to a friend to whom I had promised them.
    With kind regards, I am,
           Yours truly,
             M. N.

Monday.

Rev. Sir,
  To-day, on my return from Paris, I found your post-card, and thank you for the invitation. I regret, however, exceedingly that I shall not be able to come, and beg that you will excuse me.

With kindest and most cordial regards,
       I remain,
          Yours truly,
            N. L.

Δωμάτια Ἀριθ. 95, 96.

Φίλτατε Κύριε ———,

Χθὲς ἑσπέρας ἔφθασα ἐνταῦθα μετὰ τῆς ἀδελφῆς μου καὶ τοῦ γαμβροῦ μου· θὰ μείνωμεν καὶ αὔριον καὶ ἀναχωροῦμεν τὴν ἐπομένην, ἴσως ἔλθωμεν σημερὸν μ.μ. καὶ σᾶς ἴδωμεν ἀλλὰ αὔριον τὸ γεῦμά μας πέρνομεν εἰς τὸ Ξενοδοχεῖόν μας εἰς τὸ τραπέζι τὴν 5 μ.μ. Εἴμεθα ὅλοι καλὰ καὶ τὸ αὐτὸ εὔχομαι δι' ὑμᾶς καὶ τὴν οἰκογένειάν σας. Προσφέρετε τὰς προσρήσεις ὅλων μας εἰς τὴν Κυρίαν σας.

Σᾶς δὲ ἀσπαζόμεθα,

Π. Β., Δ. Β.

Κύριε Μ———,

Εὑρίσκομαι ἐνταῦθα πρὸ εἴκοσιν ἡμερῶν καὶ δὲν ἀπεφάσισα πότε θ' ἀναχωρήσω.

Κατὰ τὴν ἔλνσίν μου ἐσκόπευον νὰ ἔλθω καὶ σᾶς ἴδω πλὴν εἰδοποιήθην ἐγκαίρως ὅτι ἀπουσιάζατε.[3] Ἅμα εὐκαιρήσω σκοπεύω νὰ ἔλθω νὰ περάσω ὀλίγας ἡμέρας εἰς Λονδῖνον πρὸ τῆς ἀναχωρήσεώς μου καὶ τότε θὰ ἔλθω νὰ σᾶς ἴδω· θέλω ὅμως σᾶς γράψει πρὸ μιᾶς ἡμέρας, μήπως καὶ λείψητε πάλιν. Ἐλπίζων ἡ παροῦσά μου νὰ σᾶς εὕρῃ τόσον ὑμᾶς καθὼς καὶ ὅλην σας τὴν οἰκογένειαν ἀπολαύοντας ὑγείας,

Σᾶς φιλικοασπάζομαι,

Π. Β.

---

[3] In colloquial Modern Greek, the vowel α is used as an alternative of In this instance it has the advantage of marking the tense. ἀπουσιάζετε, present.

Rooms Nos. 95, 96.

DEAR MR. ———,

Yesterday evening I arrived here with my sister and brother-in-law. We shall remain over to-morrow, and leave the following day. Perhaps we shall come this afternoon to see you, but to-morrow we take dinner at our hotel, at the *table d'hôte* at 5 p.m. We are all well, and I hope you and your family are the same. Give my kind remembrances to your wife.

Yours truly,

P. B. and D. B.

DEAR M———,

I have been here for three weeks (20 days), and have not made up my mind when I shall leave.

On my arrival I intended to come and see you, but learned in time that you were away from home. As soon as I have an opportunity I intend to come and pass a few days in London before my departure, and I will come and see you. I will write, however, a day beforehand, lest you should be away again. Hoping that this letter of mine may find you and all your family in good health,

I am, with kindest regards,

P. B.

ϵ in the 2nd person singular and plural of the imperfect past active. the more classically correct form, would not be distinguishable from the

LONDON:
PRINTED BY GILBERT AND RIVINGTON, LIMITED,
ST. JOHN'S SQUARE.

A CATALOGUE OF IMPORTANT WORKS,

PUBLISHED BY

TRÜBNER & CO.

57 AND 59 LUDGATE HILL.

ABEL.—LINGUISTIC ESSAYS. By Carl Abel. CONTENTS: Language as the Expression of National Modes of Thought—The Conception of Love in some Ancient and Modern Languages—The English Verbs of Command—The Discrimination of Synonyms—Philological Methods—The Connection between Dictionary and Grammar—The Possibility of a Common Literary Language for the Slav Nations—Coptic Intensification—The Origin of Language—The Order and Position of Words in the Latin Sentence. Post 8vo, pp. xii. and 282, cloth. 1882. 9s.

ABEL.—SLAVIC AND LATIN. Ilchester Lectures on Comparative Lexicography. Delivered at the Taylor Institution, Oxford. **By Carl Abel, Ph.D.** Post 8vo, pp. vi.-124, cloth. 1883. 5s.

ABRAHAMS.—A MANUAL OF SCRIPTURE HISTORY FOR USE IN JEWISH SCHOOLS AND FAMILIES. By L. B. Abrahams, B.A., Principal Assistant Master, Jews' Free School. With Map and Appendices. Third Edition. Crown 8vo, pp. viii. and 152, cloth. 1883. 1s. 6d.

AGASSIZ.—AN ESSAY ON CLASSIFICATION. By Louis Agassiz. 8vo, pp. vii. and 381, cloth. 1859. 12s.

AHLWARDT.—THE DIVANS OF THE SIX ANCIENT ARABIC POETS, ENNĀBIGA, 'ANTARA, THARAFA, ZUHAIR, 'ALQUAMA, and IMRUULQUAIS; chiefly according to the MSS. of Paris, Gotha, and Leyden, and the Collection of their Fragments, with a List of the various Readings of the Text. Edited by W. Ahlwardt, Professor of Oriental Languages at the University of Greifswald. Demy 8vo, pp. xxx. and 340, sewed. 1870. 12s.

AHN.—PRACTICAL GRAMMAR OF THE GERMAN LANGUAGE. By Dr. F. Ahn. A New Edition. By Dr. Dawson Turner, and Prof. F. L. Weinmann. Crown 8vo, pp. cxii. and 430, cloth. 1878. 3s. 6d.

AHN.—NEW, PRACTICAL, AND EASY METHOD OF LEARNING THE GERMAN LANGUAGE. By Dr. F. Ahn. First and Second Course. Bound in 1 vol. 12mo, pp. 86 and 120, cloth. 1866. 3s.

AHN.—KEY to Ditto. 12mo, pp. 40, sewed. 8d.

AHN.—MANUAL OF GERMAN AND ENGLISH CONVERSATIONS, or Vade Mecum for English Travellers. 12mo, pp. x. and 137, cloth. 1875. 1s. 6d.

AHN.—New, Practical, and Easy Method of Learning the French Language. By Dr. F. Ahn. First Course and Second Course. 12mo, cloth. Each 1s. 6d. The Two Courses in 1 vol. 12mo, pp. 114 and 170, cloth. 1865. 3s.

AHN.—New, Practical, and Easy Method of Learning the French Language. Third Course, containing a French Reader, with Notes and Vocabulary. By H. W. Ehrlich. 12mo, pp. viii. and 125, cloth. 1866. 1s. 6d.

AHN.—Manual of French and English Conversations, for the use of Schools and Travellers. By Dr. F. Ahn. 12mo, pp. viii. and 200, cloth. 1862. 2s. 6d.

AHN.—New, Practical, and Easy Method of Learning the Italian Language. By Dr. F. Ahn. First and Second Course. 12mo, pp. 198, cloth. 1872. 3s. 6d.

AHN.—New, Practical, and Easy Method of Learning the Dutch Language, being a complete Grammar, with Selections. By Dr. F. Ahn. 12mo, pp. viii. and 166, cloth. 1862. 3s. 6d.

AHN.—Ahn's Course. Latin Grammar for Beginners. By W. Ihne, Ph.D. 12mo, pp. vi. and 184, cloth. 1864. 3s.

ALABASTER.—The Wheel of the Law: Buddhism illustrated from Siamese Sources by the Modern Buddhist, a Life of Buddha, and an Account of the Phra Bat. By Henry Alabaster, Esq., Interpreter of Her Majesty's Consulate-General in Siam. Demy 8vo, pp. lviii. and 324, cloth. 1871. 14s.

ALI.—The Proposed Political, Legal, and Social Reforms in the Ottoman Empire and other Mohammedan States. By Moulaví Cherágh Ali, H.H. the Nizam's Civil Service. Demy 8vo, pp. liv. and 184, cloth. 1883. 8s.

ALLAN-FRASER.—Christianity and Churchism. By Patrick Allan-Fraser. Second (revised and enlarged) Edition. Crown 8vo, pp. 52, cloth. 1884. 1s.

ALLEN.—The Colour Sense. See English and Foreign Philosophical Library, Vol. X.

ALLIBONE.—A Critical Dictionary of English Literature and British and American Authors (Living and Deceased). From the Earliest Accounts to the latter half of the 19th century. Containing over 46,000 Articles (Authors), with 40 Indexes of subjects. By S. A. Allibone. In 3 vols. royal 8vo, cloth. £5, 8s.

ALTHAUS.—The Spas of Europe. By Julius Althaus, M.D. 8vo, pp. 516, cloth. 1862. 7s. 6d.

AMATEUR MECHANIC'S WORKSHOP (The). A Treatise containing Plain and Concise Directions for the Manipulation of Wood and Metals; including Casting, Forging, Brazing, Soldering, and Carpentry. By the Author of "The Lathe and its Uses." Sixth Edition. Demy 8vo, pp. vi. and 148, with Two Full-Page Illustrations, on toned paper and numerous Woodcuts, cloth. 1880. 6s.

AMATEUR MECHANICAL SOCIETY.—Journal of the Amateur Mechanical Society. 8vo. Vol. i. pp. 344 cloth. 1871-72. 12s. Vol. ii. pp. vi. and 290, cloth. 1873-77. 12s. Vol. iii. pp. iv. and 246, cloth. 1878-79. 12s. 6d.

AMERICAN Almanac and Treasury of Facts, Statistical, Financial, and Political. Edited by Ainsworth R. Spofford, Librarian of Congress. Crown 8vo, cloth. Published yearly. 1878-1884. 7s. 6d. each.

AMERY.—Notes on Forestry. By C. F. Amery, Deputy Conservator N. W. Provinces, India. Crown 8vo, pp. viii. and 120, cloth. 1875. 5s.

AMBERLEY.—An Analysis of Religious Belief. By Viscount Amberley. 2 vols. demy 8vo, pp. xvi. and 496 and 512, cloth. 1876. 30s.

AMONGST MACHINES. A Description of Various Mechanical Appliances used in the Manufacture of Wood, Metal, and other Substances. A Book for Boys, copiously Illustrated. By the Author of "The Young Mechanic." Second Edition. Imperial 16mo, pp. viii. and 336, cloth. 1878. 7s. 6d.

ANDERSON.—PRACTICAL MERCANTILE CORRESPONDENCE. A Collection of Modern Letters of Business, with Notes, Critical and Explanatory, and an Appendix, containing a Dictionary of Commercial Technicalities, pro forma Invoices, Account Sales, Bills of Lading, and Bills of Exchange; also an Explanation of the German Chain Rule. 24th Edition, revised and enlarged. By William Anderson. 12mo, pp. 288, cloth. 5s.

ANDERSON and TUGMAN.—MERCANTILE CORRESPONDENCE, containing a Collection of Commercial Letters in Portuguese and English, with their translation on opposite pages, for the use of Business Men and of Students in either of the Languages, treating in modern style of the system of Business in the principal Commercial Cities of the World. Accompanied by pro forma Accounts, Sales, Invoices, Bills of Lading, Drafts, &c. With an Introduction and copious Notes. By William Anderson and James E. Tugman. 12mo, pp. xi. and 193, cloth. 1867. 6s.

APEL.—PROSE SPECIMENS FOR TRANSLATION INTO GERMAN, with copious Vocabularies and Explanations. By H. Apel. 12mo, pp. viii. and 246, cloth. 1862. 4s. 6d.

APPLETON (Dr.)—LIFE AND LITERARY RELICS. See English and Foreign Philosophical Library, Vol. XIII.

ARAGO.—LES ARISTOCRATIES. A Comedy in Verse. By Etienne Arago. Edited, with English Notes and Notice on Etienne Arago, by the Rev. E. P. H. Brette, B.D., Head Master of the French School, Christ's Hospital, Examiner in the University of London. Fcap. 8vo, pp. 244, cloth. 1868. 4s.

ARMITAGE.—LECTURES ON PAINTING: Delivered to the Students of the Royal Academy. By Edward Armitage, R.A. Crown 8vo, pp. 256, with 29 Illustrations, cloth. 1883. 7s. 6d.

ARNOLD.—INDIAN IDYLLS. From the Sanskrit of the Mahâbhârata. By Edwin Arnold, C.S.I., &c. Crown 8vo, pp. xii. and 282, cloth. 1883. 7s. 6d.

ARNOLD.—PEARLS OF THE FAITH; or, Islam's Rosary: being the Ninety-nine beautiful names of Allah. With Comments in Verse from various Oriental sources as made by an Indian Mussulman. By Edwin Arnold, C.S.I., &c. Third Edition. Crown 8vo, pp. xvi. and 320, cloth. 1884. 7s. 6d.

ARNOLD.—THE LIGHT OF ASIA; or, THE GREAT RENUNCIATION (Mahâbhinishkramana). Being the Life and Teaching of Gautama, Prince of India, and Founder of Buddhism (as told in verse by an Indian Buddhist). By Edwin Arnold, M.A., &c. Twenty-fifth Edition. Crown 8vo, pp. xvi. and 240, limp parchment. 1885. 3s. 6d. Library Edition. 1883. 7s. 6d. Illustrated Edition. Small 4to, pp. xx.-196, cloth. 1884. 21s.

ARNOLD.—THE SECRET OF DEATH: Being a Version, in a popular and novel form, of the Katha Upanishad, from the Sanskrit. With some Collected Poems. By Edwin Arnold, M.A., &c. Third Edition. Crown 8vo. pp. viii.-406, cloth. 1885. 7s. 6d.

ARNOLD.—THE SONG CELESTIAL; or, BHAGAVAD-GITÂ (from the Mahâbhârata). Being a Discourse between Arjuna, Prince of India, and the Supreme Being under the form of Krishna. Translated from the Sanskrit Text. By Edwin Arnold, M.A. Second Edition, crown 8vo, pp. 192, cloth. 1885. 5s.

ARNOLD.—THE ILIAD AND ODYSSEY OF INDIA. By Edwin Arnold, M.A., F.R.G.S., &c., &c. Fcap. 8vo, pp. 24, sewed. 1s.

ARNOLD.—A SIMPLE TRANSLITERAL GRAMMAR OF THE TURKISH LANGUAGE. Compiled from Various Sources. With Dialogues and Vocabulary. By Edwin Arnold, M.A., C.S.I., F.R.G.S. Post 8vo, pp. 80, cloth. 1877. 2s. 6d.

ARNOLD.—INDIAN POETRY. See Trübner's Oriental Series.

ARTHUR.—THE COPARCENERS: Being the Adventures of two Heiresses. By F. Arthur. Crown 8vo, pp. iv.-312, cloth. 1885. 10s. 6d.

ARTOM.—SERMONS. By the Rev. B. Artom, Chief Rabbi of the Spanish and Portuguese Congregations of England. First Series. Second Edition. Crown 8vo, pp. viii. and 314, cloth. 1876. 6s.

4   A Catalogue of Important Works,

ASIATIC SOCIETY OF BENGAL. List of Publications on application.

ASIATIC SOCIETY.—Journal of the Royal Asiatic Society of Great Britain and Ireland, from the Commencement to 1863. First Series, complete in 20 Vols. 8vo, with many Plates. £10, or in parts from 4s. to 6s. each.

ASIATIC SOCIETY.—Journal of the Royal Asiatic Society of Great Britain and Ireland. New Series. 8vo. Stitched in wrapper. 1864-84.
Vol. I., 2 Parts, pp. iv. and 490, 16s.—Vol. II., 2 Parts, pp. 522, 16s.—Vol. III., 2 Parts, pp. 516, with Photograph, 22s.—Vol. IV., 2 Parts, pp. 521, 16s.—Vol. V., 2 Parts, pp. 463, with 10 full-page and folding Plates, 18s. 6d.—Vol. VI., Part 1, pp. 212, with 2 Plates and a Map, 8s. —Vol. VI. Part 2, pp. 272, with Plate and Map, 8s.—Vol. VII., Part 1, pp. 194, with a Plate. 8s.—Vol. VII., Part 2, pp. 204, with 7 Plates and a Map, 8s.—Vol. VIII., Part 1, pp. 156, with 3 Plates and a Plan, 8s.—Vol. VIII., Part 2, pp. 152, 8s.—Vol. IX., Part 1, pp. 154, with a Plate, 8s.—Vol. IX., Part 2, pp. 292, with 3 Plates, 10s. 6d.—Vol. X., Part 1, pp. 156, with 2 Plates and a Map, 8s.—Vol. X., Part 2, pp. 146, 6s.—Vol. X., Part 3, pp. 204, 8s.—Vol. XI., Part 1, pp. 128, 5s.—Vol. XI., Part 2, pp. 158, with 2 Plates, 7s. 6d.—Vol. XI., Part 3, pp. 250, 8s.—Vol. XII., Part 1, pp. 152, 5s.—Vol. XII., Part 2, pp. 182, with 2 Plates and Map, 6s.— Vol. XII., Part 3, pp. 100, 4s.—Vol. XII., Part 4, pp. x., 152., cxx. 16, 8s.—Vol. XIII., Part 1, pp. 120, 5s.—Vol. XIII., Part 2, pp. 170, with a Map, 8s.—Vol. XIII., Part 3, pp. 178, with a Table, 7s. 6d.—Vol. XIII., Part 4, pp. 282, with a Plate and Table, 10s. 6d.—Vol. XIV., Part 1, pp. 124, with a Table and 2 Plates, 5s.—Vol. XIV., Part 2, pp. 164, with 1 Table, 7s. 6d.—Vol. XIV., Part 3, pp. 206, with 6 Plates, 8s.—Vol. XIV., Part 4, pp. 492, with 1 Plate, 14s.—Vol. XV., Part 1, pp. 136, 6s. ; Part 2, pp. 158, with 3 Tables, 5s. : Part 3, pp. 192, 6s. ; Part 4, pp. 140, 5s.—Vol. XVI., Part 1, pp. 138, with 2 Plates, 7s. Part 2, pp. 184, with 1 Plate, 9s. Part 3, July 1884, pp. 74-clx., 10s. 6d. Part 4, pp. 132, 8s.—Vol. XVII., Part 1, pp. 144, with 6 Plates, 10s. 6d. Part 2, pp. 194, with a Map, 9s.

ASPLET.—The Complete French Course. Part II. Containing all the Rules of French Syntax, &c., &c. By Georges C. Asplet, French Master, Frome. Fcap. 8vo, pp. xx. and 276, cloth. 1880. 2s. 6d.

ASTON.—A Short Grammar of the Japanese Spoken Language. By W. G. Aston, M.A. Third Edition. Crown 8vo, pp. 96, cloth. 1873. 12s.

ASTON.—A Grammar of the Japanese Written Language. By W. G. Aston, M.A., Assistant Japanese Secretary H.B.M.'s Legation, Yedo, Japan. Second Edition. 8vo, pp. 306, cloth. 1877. 28s.

ASTONISHED AT AMERICA. Being Cursory Deductions, &c., &c. By Zigzag. Fcap. 8vo, pp. xvi.-108, boards. 1880. 1s.

AUCTORES SANSCRITI.
Vol. I. The Jaiminīya-Nyāya-Mālā-Vistara. Edited for the Sanskrit Text Society, under the supervision of Theodor Goldstücker. Large 4to, pp. 582, cloth. £3, 13s. 6d.
Vol. II. The Institutes of Gautama. Edited, with an Index of Words, by A. F. Stenzler, Ph.D., Prof. of Oriental Languages in the University of Breslau. 8vo, pp. iv. and 78, cloth. 1876. 4s. 6d. Stitched, 3s. 6d.
Vol. III. Vaitāna Sutra: The Ritual of the Atharva Veda. Edited, with Critical Notes and Indices, by Dr. R. Garbe. 8vo, pp. viii. and 120, sewed. 1878. 5s.
Vols. IV. and V.—Vardhamana's Ganaratnamahodadhi, with the Author's Commentary. Edited, with Critical Notes and Indices, by Julius Eggeling, Ph.D. 8vo. Part I., pp. xii. and 240, wrapper. 1879. 6s. Part II., pp. 240, wrapper. 1881. 6s.

AUGIER.—Diane. A Drama in Verse. By Émile Augier. Edited with English Notes and Notice on Augier. By T. Karcher, LL.B., of the Royal Military Academy and the University of London. 12mo, pp. xiii. and 146, cloth. 1867. 2s. 6d.

AUSTIN.—A Practical Treatise on the Preparation, Combination, and Application of Calcareous and Hydraulic Limes and Cements. To which is added many useful Recipes for various Scientific, Mercantile, and Domestic Purposes. By James G. Austin, Architect. 12mo, pp. 192, cloth. 1862. 5s.

AUSTRALIA.—The publications of the various Australian Government Lists on application.

AUSTRALIA.—The Year Book of Australia for 1885. Published under the auspices of the Governments of the Australian Colonies. Demy 8vo, pp. 774; with 6 Large Maps; boards. 5s.

AXON.—THE MECHANIC'S FRIEND. A Collection of Receipts and Practical Suggestions relating to Aquaria, Bronzing, Cements, Drawing, Dyes, Electricity, Gilding, Glass-working, &c. Numerous Woodcuts. Edited by W. E. A. Axon, M.R.S.L., F.S.S. Crown 8vo, pp. xii. and 339, cloth. 1875. 4s. 6d.

BABA.—An Elementary Grammar of the Japanese Language, with Easy Progressive Exercises. By Tatui Baba. Crown 8vo, pp. xiv. and 92, cloth. 1873. 5s.

BACON.—THE LIFE AND TIMES OF FRANCIS BACON. Extracted from the Edition of his Occasional Writings by James Spedding. 2 vols. post 8vo, pp. xx., 710, and xiv., 708, cloth. 1878. 21s.

BADEN-POWELL.—PROTECTION AND BAD TIMES, with Special Reference to the Political Economy of English Colonisation. By George Baden-Powell, M.A., F.R.A.S., F.S.S., Author of "New Homes for the Old Country," &c., &c. 8vo, pp. xii.-376, cloth. 1879. 6s. 6d.

BADER.—THE NATURAL AND MORBID CHANGES OF THE HUMAN EYE, AND THEIR TREATMENT. By C. Bader. Medium 8vo, pp. viii. and 506, cloth. 1868. 16s.

BADER.—PLATES ILLUSTRATING THE NATURAL AND MORBID CHANGES OF THE HUMAN EYE. By C. Bader. Six chromo-lithographic Plates, each containing the figures of six Eyes, and four lithographed Plates, with figures of Instruments. With an Explanatory Text of 32 pages. Medium 8vo, in a portfolio. 21s. Price for Text and Atlas taken together, £1, 12s.

BADLEY.—INDIAN MISSIONARY RECORD AND MEMORIAL VOLUME. By the Rev. B. H. Badley, of the American Methodist Mission. 8vo, pp. xii. and 280, cloth. 1876. 10s. 6d.

BALFOUR.—WAIFS AND STRAYS FROM THE FAR EAST; being a Series of Disconnected Essays on Matters relating to China. By Frederick Henry Balfour. Demy 8vo, pp. 224, cloth. 1876. 10s. 6d.

BALFOUR.—THE DIVINE CLASSIC OF NAN-HUA; being the Works of Chuang Tsze, Taoist Philosopher. With an Excursus, and Copious Annotations in English and Chinese. By F. H. Balfour. 8vo, pp. xlviii. and 426, cloth. 1881. 14s.

BALFOUR.—TAOIST TEXTS, Ethical, Political, and Speculative. By F. H. BALFOUR, Editor of the *North-China Herald*. Imp. 8vo, pp. vi.-118, cloth. 10s. 6d.

BALL.—THE DIAMONDS, COAL, AND GOLD OF INDIA; their Mode of Occurrence and Distribution. By V. Ball, M.A., F.G.S., of the Geological Survey of India. Fcap. 8vo, pp. viii. and 136, cloth. 1881. 5s.

BALL.—A MANUAL OF THE GEOLOGY OF INDIA. Part III. Economic Geology. By V. Ball, M.A., F.G.S. Royal 8vo, pp. xx. and 640, with 6 Maps and 10 Plates, cloth. 1881. 10s.

BALLAD SOCIETY—Subscriptions, small paper, one guinea; large paper, two guineas per annum. List of publications on application.

BALLANTYNE.—ELEMENTS OF HINDI AND BRAJ BHAKHA GRAMMAR. Compiled for the use of the East India College at Haileybury. By James R. Ballantyne. Second Edition. Crown 8vo, pp. 38, cloth. 1868. 5s.

BALLANTYNE.—FIRST LESSONS IN SANSKRIT GRAMMAR; together with an Introduction to the Hitopadeśa. Fourth Edition. By James R. Ballantyne, LL.D., Librarian of the India Office. 8vo, pp. viii. and 110, cloth. 1884. 3s. 6d.

BALLANTYNE.—THE SANKHYA APHORISMS OF KAPILA. See Trübner's Oriental Series.

BARANOWSKI.—VADE MECUM DE LA LANGUE FRANÇAISE, rédigé d'après les Dictionnaires classiques avec les Exemples de Bonnes Locutions que donne l'Académie Française, ou qu'on trouve dans les ouvrages des plus célèbres auteurs. Par J. J. Baranowski, avec l'approbation de M. E. Littré, Sénateur, &c. Second Edition. 32mo, pp. 224. 1883. Cloth, 2s. 6d.

BARANOWSKI.—ANGLO-POLISH LEXICON. By J. J. Baranowski, formerly Under-Secretary to the Bank of Poland, in Warsaw. Fcap. 8vo, pp. viii. and 492, cloth. 1883. 6s.

BARANOWSKI.—SLOWNIK POLSKO-ANGIELSKI. (Polish-English Lexicon.) By J. J. Baranowski. Fcap. 8vo, pp. iv.-402, cloth. 1884. 6s. 6d.

BARENTS' RELICS.—Recovered in the summer of 1876 by Charles L. W. Gardiner, Esq., and presented to the Dutch Government. Described and explained by J. K. J. de Jonge, Deputy Royal Architect at the Hague. Published by command of His Excellency, W. F. Van F.R.P. Taelman Kip, Minister of Marine. Translated, with a Preface, by S. R. Van Campen. With a Map, Illustrations, and a fac-simile of the Scroll. 8vo, pp. 70, cloth. 1877. 5s.

BARRIÈRE and CAPENDU.—LES FAUX BONSHOMMES, a Comedy. By Théodore Barrière and Ernest Capendu. Edited, with English Notes and Notice on Barrière, by Professor Ch. Cassal, LL.D., of University College, London. 12mo, pp. xvi. and 304, cloth. 1868. 4s.

BARTH.—THE RELIGIONS OF INDIA. See Trübner's Oriental Series.

BARTLETT.—DICTIONARY OF AMERICANISMS. A Glossary of Words and Phrases colloquially used in the United States. By John Russell Bartlett. Fourth Edition, considerably enlarged and improved. 8vo, pp. xlvi. and 814, cloth. 1877. 20s.

BATTYE.—WHAT IS VITAL FORCE? or, a Short and Comprehensive Sketch, including Vital Physics, Animal Morphology, and Epidemics; to which is added an Appendix upon Geology, IS THE DENTRITAL THEORY OF GEOLOGY TENABLE? By Richard Fawcett Battye. 8vo, pp. iv. and 336, cloth. 1877. 7s. 6d.

BAZLEY.—NOTES ON THE EPICYCLODIAL CUTTING FRAME of Messrs. Holtzapffel & Co. With special reference to its Compensation Adjustment, and with numerous Illustrations of its Capabilities. By Thomas Sebastian Bazley, M.A. 8vo, pp. xvi. and 192, cloth. Illustrated. 1872. 10s. 6d.

BAZLEY.—THE STARS IN THEIR COURSES: A Twofold Series of Maps, with a Catalogue, showing how to identify, at any time of the year, all stars down to the 5.6 magnitude, inclusive of Heis, which are clearly visible in English latitudes. By T. S. Bazley, M.A., Author of "Notes on the Epicycloidal Cutting Frame." Atlas folio, pp. 46 and 24, Folding Plates, cloth. 1878. 15s.

BEAL.—A CATENA OF BUDDHIST SCRIPTURES FROM THE CHINESE. By S. Beal, B.A., Trinity College, Cambridge; a Chaplain in Her Majesty's Fleet, &c. 8vo, pp. xiv. and 436, cloth. 1871. 15s.

BEAL.—THE ROMANTIC LEGEND OF SAKYA BUDDHA. From the Chinese-Sanskrit. By the Rev. Samuel Beal. Crown 8vo, pp. 408, cloth. 1875. 12s.

BEAL.—DHAMMAPADA. See Trübner's Oriental Series.

BEAL.—BUDDHIST LITERATURE IN CHINA: Abstract of Four Lectures, Delivered by Samuel Beal, B.A., Professor of Chinese at University College, London. Demy 8vo, pp. xx. and 186, cloth. 1882. 10s. 6d.

BEAL.—SI-YU-KI. Buddhist Records of the Western World. See Trübner's Oriental Series.

BEAMES.—OUTLINES OF INDIAN PHILOLOGY. With a Map showing the Distribution of Indian Languages. By John Beames, M.R.A.S., B.C.S., &c. Second enlarged and revised Edition. Crown 8vo, pp. viii. and 96, cloth. 1868. 5s.

BEAMES.—A COMPARATIVE GRAMMAR OF THE MODERN ARYAN LANGUAGES OF INDIA, to wit, Hindi, Panjabi, Sindhi, Gujarati, Marathi, Oriya, and Bengali. By John Beames, B.C.S., M.R.A.S., &c., &c. Demy 8vo. Vol. I. On Sounds. Pp. xvi. and 360, cloth. 1872. 16s.—Vol. II. The Noun and the Pronoun. Pp. xii. and 348, cloth. 1875. 16s.—Vol. III. The Verb. Pp. xii. and 316, cloth. 1879. 16s.

BELLEW.—FROM THE INDUS TO THE TIGRIS. A Narrative of a Journey through Balochistan, Afghanistan, Khorassan, and Iran in 1872; together with a Synoptical Grammar and Vocabulary of the Brahoe Language, and a Record of the Meteorological Observations on the March from the Indus to the Tigris. By Henry Walter Bellew, C.S.I., Surgeon, B.S.C. 8vo, pp. viii. and 496, cloth. 1874. 14s.

BELLEW.—KASHMIR AND KASHGHAR; a Narrative of the Journey of the Embassy to Kashghar in 1873-74. By H. W. Bellew, C.S.I. Demy 8vo, pp. xxxii. and 420, cloth. 1875. 16s.

BELLEW.—THE RACES OF AFGHANISTAN. Being a Brief Account of the Principal Nations Inhabiting that Country. By Surgeon-Major H. W. Bellew, C.S.I., late on Special Political Duty at Kabul. 8vo, pp. 124, cloth. 1880. 7s. 6d.

BELLOWS.—ENGLISH OUTLINE VOCABULARY for the use of Students of the Chinese, Japanese, and other Languages. Arranged by John Bellows. With Notes on the Writing of Chinese with Roman Letters, by Professor Summers, King's College, London. Crown 8vo, pp. vi. and 368, cloth. 1867. 6s.

BELLOWS.—OUTLINE DICTIONARY FOR THE USE OF MISSIONARIES, EXPLORERS, AND STUDENTS OF LANGUAGE. By Max Müller, M.A., Taylorian Professor in the University of Oxford. With an Introduction on the proper use of the ordinary English Alphabet in transcribing Foreign Languages. The Vocabulary compiled by John Bellows. Crown 8vo, pp. xxxi. and 368, limp morocco. 1867. 7s. 6d.

BELLOWS.—TOUS LES VERBES. Conjugations of all the Verbs in the French and English Languages. By John Bellows. Revised by Professor Beljame, B.A., LL.B., of the University of Paris, and Official Interpreter to the Imperial Court, and George B. Strickland, late Assistant French Master, Royal Naval School, London. Also a New Table of Equivalent Values of French and English Money, Weights, and Measures. 32mo, 76 Tables, sewed. 1867. 1s.

BELLOWS.—FRENCH AND ENGLISH DICTIONARY FOR THE POCKET. By John Bellows. Containing the French-English and English-French divisions on the same page; conjugating all the verbs; distinguishing the genders by different types; giving numerous aids to pronunciation; indicating the *liaison* or *non-liaison* of terminal consonants; and translating units of weight, measure, and value, by a series of tables differing entirely from any hitherto published. The new edition, which is but six ounces in weight, has been remodelled, and contains many thousands of additional words and renderings. Miniature maps of France, the British Isles, Paris, and London, are added to the Geographical Section. Second Edition. 32mo, pp. 608, roan tuck, or persian without tuck. 1877. 10s. 6d.; morocco tuck, 12s. 6d.

BENEDIX.—DER VETTER. Comedy in Three Acts. By Roderich Benedix. With Grammatical and Explanatory Notes by F. Weinmann, German Master at the Royal Institution School, Liverpool, and G. Zimmermann, Teacher of Modern Languages. 12mo, pp. 128, cloth. 1863. 2s. 6d.

BENFEY.—A PRACTICAL GRAMMAR OF THE SANSKRIT LANGUAGE, for the use of Early Students. By Theodor Benfey, Professor of Sanskrit in the University of Göttingen. Second, revised, and enlarged Edition. Royal 8vo, pp. viii. and 296, cloth. 1868. 10s. 6d.

BENTHAM.—THEORY OF LEGISLATION. By Jeremy Bentham. Translated from the French of Etienne Dumont by R. Hildreth. Fourth Edition. Post 8vo, pp. xv. and 472, cloth. 1882. 7s. 6d.

BETTS.—*See* VALDES.

BEVERIDGE.—THE DISTRICT OF BAKARGANJ. Its History and Statistics. By H. Beveridge, B.C.S., Magistrate and Collector of Bakarganj. 8vo, pp. xx. and 460, cloth. 1876. 21s.

BHANDARKAR.—EARLY HISTORY OF THE DEKKAN DOWN TO THE MAHOMEDAN CONQUEST. By Ramkrishna Gopal Bhandarkar, M.A., Hon. M.R.A.S., Professor of Oriental Languages, Dekkan College. Written for the *Bombay Gazette*. Royal 8vo, pp. 128, wrapper. 1884. 5s.

BICKNELL.—*See* HAFIZ.

BIERBAUM.—HISTORY OF THE ENGLISH LANGUAGE AND LITERATURE.—By F. J. Bierbaum, Ph.D. Crown 8vo, pp. viii. and 270, cloth. 1883. 3s.

BIGANDET.—THE LIFE OF GAUDAMA. See Trübner's Oriental Series.

BILLINGS.—The Principles of Ventilation and Heating, and their Practical Application. By John S. Billings, M.D., LL.D. (Edinb.), Surgeon U.S. Army. Demy 8vo, pp. x. and 216, cloth. 1884. 15s.

BIRCH.—Fasti Monastici Aevi Saxonici; or, An Alphabetical List of the Heads of Religious Houses in England previous to the Norman Conquest, to which is prefixed a Chronological Catalogue of Contemporary Foundations. By Walter de Gray Birch. 8vo, pp. vii. and 114, cloth. 1873. 5s.

BIRD.—Physiological Essays. Drink Craving, Differences in Men, Idiosyncrasy, and the Origin of Disease. By Robert Bird, M.D. Demy 8vo, pp. 246, cloth. 1870. 7s. 6d.

BIZYENOS.—ΑΤΘΙΔΕΣ ΑΥΡΑΙ. Poems. By George M. Bizyenos. With Frontispiece Etched by Prof. A. Legros. Royal 8vo, pp. viii.-312, printed on hand-made paper, and richly bound. 1883. £1, 11s. 6d.

BLACK.—Young Japan, Yokohama and Yedo. A Narrative of the Settlement and the City, from the Signing of the Treaties in 1858 to the Close of 1879; with a Glance at the Progress of Japan during a Period of Twenty-one Years. By J. R. Black, formerly Editor of the "Japan Herald," &c. 2 vols. demy 8vo, pp. xviii. and 418; xiv. and 522, cloth. 1881. £2, 2s.

BLACKET.—Researches into the Lost Histories of America; or, The Zodiac shown to be an Old Terrestrial Map, in which the Atlantic Isle is delineated; so that Light can be thrown upon the Obscure Histories of the Earthworks and Ruined Cities of America. By W. S. Blacket. Illustrated by numerous Engravings. 8vo, pp. 336, cloth. 1883. 10s. 6d.

BLADES.—Shakspere and Typography. Being an Attempt to show Shakspere's Personal Connection with, and Technical Knowledge of, the Art of Printing; also Remarks upon some common Typographical Errors, with especial reference to the Text of Shakspere. By William Blades. 8vo, pp. viii. and 78, with an Illustration, cloth. 1872. 3s.

BLADES.—The Biography and Typography of William Caxton, England's First Printer. By W. Blades. Founded upon the Author's "Life and Typography of William Caxton." Brought up to the Present Date. Elegantly and appropriately printed in demy 8vo, on hand-made paper, imitation old bevelled binding. 1877. £1, 1s. Cheap Edition. Crown 8vo, cloth. 1881. 5s.

BLADES.—The Enemies of Books. By William Blades, Typograph. Crown 8vo, pp. xvi. and 112, parchment wrapper. 1880.

BLADES.—An Account of the German Morality Play entitled Depositio Cornuti Typographici, as Performed in the Seventeenth and Eighteenth Centuries. With a Rhythmical Translation of the German Version of 1648. By William Blades (Typographer). To which is added a Literal Reprint of the unique Original Version, written in Plaat Deutsch by Paul de Wise, and printed in 1621. Small 4to, pp. xii.-144, with facsimile Illustrations, in an appropriate binding. 1885. 7s. 6d.

BLAKEY.—Memoirs of Dr. Robert Blakey, Professor of Logic and Metaphysics, Queen's College, Belfast. Edited by the Rev. Henry Miller. Crown 8vo, pp. xii. and 252, cloth. 1879. 5s.

BLEEK.—Reynard the Fox in South Africa; or, Hottentot Fables and Tales, chiefly Translated from Original Manuscripts in the Library of His Excellency Sir George Grey, K.C.B. By W. H. I. Bleek, Ph.D. Post 8vo, pp. xxvi. and 94, cloth. 1864. 3s. 6d.

BLEEK.—A Brief Account of Bushman Folk Lore, and other Texts. By W. H. I. Bleek, Ph.D. Folio, pp. 21, paper. 2s. 6d.

BLUMHARDT.—See Charitabali.

BOEHMER.—See Valdes, and Spanish Reformers.

BOJESEN.—A Guide to the Danish Language. Designed for English Students. By Mrs. Maria Bojesen. 12mo, pp. 250, cloth. 1863. 5s.

BOLIA.—THE GERMAN CALIGRAPHIST: **Copies for** German Handwriting. By C. Bolia. Oblong 4to, sewed. 1s.

BOOLE.—MESSAGE OF PSYCHIC SCIENCE TO MOTHERS AND NURSES. By Mary Boole. Crown 8vo, pp. xiv. and 266, cloth. 1883. 5s.

BOTTRELL.—STORIES AND **FOLK-LORE OF** WEST CORNWALL. By William Bottrell. With Illustrations by **Joseph Blight.** Third Series. 8vo, pp. viii. and 200, cloth. 1884. 6s.

BOY ENGINEERS.—See under LUKIN.

BOYD.—NÁGÁNANDA; or, the Joy of the Snake World. A Buddhist Drama in Five Acts. Translated into English Prose, with Explanatory Notes, from the Sanskrit of Sá-Harsha-Deva. By Palmer Boyd, B.A., Cambridge. With an Introduction by Professor Cowell. Crown 8vo, pp. xvi. and 100, cloth. 1872. 4s. 6d.

BRADSHAW.—DICTIONARY OF BATHING PLACES AND CLIMATIC HEALTH RESORTS. Much Revised and Considerably Enlarged. With a Map in Eleven Colours. Third Edition. Crown 8vo, pp. lxxviii. and 364, cloth. 1884. 2s. 6d.

BRENTANO.—ON THE HISTORY **AND DEVELOPMENT OF GILDS, AND THE** ORIGIN OF TRADE-UNIONS. By Lujo **Brentano**, of Aschaffenburg, Bavaria, Doctor Juris Utriusque et Philosophiæ. **1. The** Origin of Gilds. 2. Religious (or Social) Gilds. 3. Town-Gilds or Gild-Merchants. 4. Craft-Gilds. 5. Trade-Unions. 8vo, pp. xvi. and 136, cloth. 1870. 3s. 6d.

BRETSCHNEIDER.—EARLY EUROPEAN RESEARCHES INTO THE FLORA OF CHINA. By E. Bretschneider, M.D., Physician of the Russian Legation at Peking. Demy 8vo, pp. iv. and 194, sewed. 1881. 7s. 6d.

BRETSCHNEIDER.—BOTANICON SINICUM. Notes on Chinese Botany, from Native and Western Sources. By E. Bretschneider, M.D. Crown 8vo, pp. 228, wrapper. 1882. 10s. 6d.

BRETTE.—FRENCH EXAMINATION PAPERS SET AT THE UNIVERSITY OF LONDON FROM 1839 TO 1871. Arranged and edited by the Rev. P. H. Ernest Brette, B.D. Crown 8vo, pp. viii. and 278, cloth. 3s. 6d.; interleaved, 4s. 6d.

BRITISH MUSEUM.—LIST OF PUBLICATIONS OF THE TRUSTEES OF THE BRITISH MUSEUM, on application.

BROWN.—THE DERVISHES; OR, ORIENTAL SPIRITUALISM. By John P. Brown, Secretary and Dragoman of the Legation of the United States of America at Constantinople. Crown 8vo, pp. viii. and 416, cloth, with 24 Illustrations. 1868. **14s.**

BROWN.—SANSKRIT PROSODY AND NUMERICAL SYMBOLS EXPLAINED. By Charles Philip Brown, M.R.A.S., Author of a Telugu Dictionary, Grammar, &c., Professor of Telugu in the University of London. 8vo, pp. viii. and 56, cloth. 1869. 3s. 6d.

BROWNE.—HOW TO USE THE OPHTHALMOSCOPE; being Elementary Instruction in Ophthalmoscopy. Arranged for the use of Students. By Edgar A. Browne, Surgeon to the Liverpool Eye and Ear Infirmary, &c. Second Edition. Crown 8vo, pp. xi. and 108, with 35 Figures, cloth. 1883. 3s. 6d.

BROWNE.—A BÁNGÁLÍ PRIMER, in Roman Character. By J. F. Browne, B.C.S. Crown 8vo, pp. 32, cloth. 1881. 2s.

BROWNE.—A HINDI PRIMER IN ROMAN CHARACTER. By J. F. Browne, B.C.S. Crown 8vo, pp. 36, cloth. 1882. 2s. 6d.

BROWNE.—AN URIYÁ PRIMER IN ROMAN CHARACTER. By J. F. Browne, B.C.S. Crown 8vo, pp. 32, cloth. 1882. 2s. 6d.

BROWNING SOCIETY'S PAPERS.—Demy 8vo, wrappers. 1881-84. Part I., pp. 116. 10s. Bibliography of Robert Browning from 1833-81. Part II., pp. 142. 10s. Part III., pp. 168. 10s. Part IV., pp. 148. 10s. Part V., pp. . 10s.

BROWNING'S POEMS, ILLUSTRATIONS TO. 4to, boards. Parts I. and II. 10s. each.

BRUNNOW.—See SCHEFFEL.

BRUNTON.—MAP OF JAPAN. See under JAPAN.

BUDGE.—ARCHAIC CLASSICS. Assyrian Texts; being Extracts from the Annals of Shalmaneser II., Sennacherib, and Assur-Bani-Pal. With Philological Notes. By Ernest A. Budge, B.A., M.R.A.S., Assyrian Exhibitioner, Christ's College, Cambridge. Small 4to, pp. viii. and 44, cloth. 1880. 7s. 6d.

BUDGE.—HISTORY OF ESARHADDON. See Trübner's Oriental Series.

BUNYAN.—SCENES FROM THE PILGRIM'S PROGRESS. By. R. B. Rutter. 4to, pp. 142, boards, leather back. 1882. 5s.

BURGESS :—
  ARCHÆOLOGICAL SURVEY OF WESTERN INDIA :—
   REPORT OF THE FIRST SEASON'S OPERATIONS IN THE BELGÂM AND KALADI DISTRICTS. January to May 1874. By James Burgess, F.R.G.S. With 56 Photographs and Lithographic Plates. Royal 4to, pp. viii. and 45; half bound. 1875. £2, 2s.
   REPORT ON THE ANTIQUITIES OF KÂTHIÂWÂD AND KACHH, being the result of the Second Season's Operations of the Archæological Survey of Western India, 1874-75. By James Burgess, F.R.G.S. Royal 4to, pp. x. and 242, with 74 Plates; half bound. 1876. £3, 3s.
   REPORT ON THE ANTIQUITIES IN THE BIDAR AND AURANGABAD DISTRICTS, in the Territories of His Highness the Nizam of Haiderabad, being the result of the Third Season's Operations of the Archæological Survey of Western India, 1875-76. By James Burgess, F.R.G.S., M.R.A.S., Archæological Surveyor and Reporter to Government, Western India. Royal 4to, pp. viii. and 138, with 63 Photographic Plates; half bound. 1878. £2, 2s.
   REPORT ON THE BUDDHIST CAVE TEMPLES AND THEIR INSCRIPTIONS; containing Views, Plans, Sections, and Elevation of Façades of Cave Temples; Drawings of Architectural and Mythological Sculptures; Facsimiles of Inscriptions, &c.; with Descriptive and Explanatory Text, and Translations of Inscriptions, &c., &c. By James Burgess, LL.D., F.R.G.S., &c. Royal 4to, pp. x. and 140, with 86 Plates and Woodcuts; half-bound.
   REPORT ON ELURA CAVE TEMPLES, AND THE BRAHMANICAL AND JAINA CAVES IN WESTERN INDIA. By James Burgess, LL.D., F.R.G.S., &c. Royal 4to, pp. viii. and 90, with 66 Plates and Woodcuts; half-bound.
   } 2 Vols. 1883. £6, 6s.

BURMA.—THE BRITISH BURMA GAZETTEER. Compiled by Major H. R. Spearman, under the direction of the Government of India. 2 vols. 8vo, pp. 764 and 878, with 11 Photographs, cloth. 1880. £2, 10s.

BURMA.—HISTORY OF. See Trübner's Oriental Series, page 70.

BURNE.—SHROPSHIRE FOLK-LORE. A Sheaf of Gleanings. Edited by Charlotte S. Burne, from the Collections of Georgina F. Jackson. Demy 8vo. Part I., pp. xvi.-176, wrapper. 1883. 7s. 6d. Part II., pp. 192, wrapper. 1885. 7s. 6d.

BURNELL.—ELEMENTS OF SOUTH INDIAN PALÆOGRAPHY, from the Fourth to the Seventeenth Century A.D., being an Introduction to the Study of South Indian Inscriptions and MSS. By A. C. Burnell. Second enlarged and improved Edition. 4to, pp. xiv. and 148, Map and 35 Plates, cloth. 1878. £2, 12s. 6d.

BURNELL.—A CLASSIFIED INDEX TO THE SANSKRIT MSS. IN THE PALACE AT TANJORE. Prepared for the Madras Government. By A. C. Burnell, Ph.D., &c., &c. 4to, stiff wrapper. Part I., pp. iv.-80, Vedic and Technical Literature. Part II., pp. iv.-80, Philosophy and Law. Part III., Drama, Epics, Purânas, and Zantras; Indices. 1879. 10s. each.

BURTON.—Handbook for Overland Expeditions; being an English Edition of the "Prairie Traveller," a Handbook for Overland Expeditions. With Illustrations and Itineraries of the Principal Routes between the Mississippi and the Pacific, and a Map. By Captain R. B. Marcy (now General and Chief of the Staff, Army of the Potomac). Edited, with Notes, by Captain Richard F. Burton. Crown 8vo, pp. 270, numerous Woodcuts, Itineraries, and Map, cloth. 1863. 6s. 6d.

BUTLER.—Erewhon; or, Over the Range. By Samuel Butler. Seventh Edition. Crown 8vo, pp. xii. and 244, cloth. 1884. 5s.

BUTLER.—The Fair Haven. A Work in Defence of the Miraculous Element in Our Lord's Ministry upon Earth, both as against Rationalistic Impugners and certain Orthodox Defenders. By the late John Pickard Owen. With a Memoir of the Author by William Bickersteth Owen. By Samuel Butler. Second Edition. Demy 8vo, pp. x. and 248, cloth. 1873. 7s. 6d.

BUTLER.—Life and Habit. By Samuel Butler. Second Edition. Crown 8vo, pp. x. and 308, cloth. 1878. 7s. 6d.

BUTLER.—Gavottes, Minuets, Fogues, and other short pieces for the Piano. By Samuel Butler, Author of "Erewhon," "Life and Habit," &c. (Op. I. mus.), and Henry Festing Jones (Op. I.)

BUTLER.—Evolution, Old and New; or, The Theories of Buffon, Dr. Erasmus Darwin, and Lamarck, as compared with that of Mr. Charles Darwin. By Samuel Butler. Second Edition, with an Appendix and Index. Crown 8vo, pp. xii. and 430, cloth. 1882. 10s. 6d.

BUTLER.—Unconscious Memory: A Comparison between the Theory of Dr. Ewald Hering, Professor of Physiology at the University of Prague, and the "Philosophy of the Unconscious" of Dr. Edward von Hartmann. With Translations from these Authors, and Preliminary Chapters bearing on "Life and Habit," "Evolution, New and Old," and Mr. Charles Darwin's edition of Dr. Krause's "Erasmus Darwin." By Samuel Butler. Crown 8vo, pp. viii. and 288, cloth. 1880. 7s. 6d.

BUTLER.—Alps and Sanctuaries of Piedmont and the Canton Ticino. Profusely Illustrated by Charles Gogin, H. F. Jones, and the Author. By Samuel Butler. Foolscap 4to, pp. viii. and 376, cloth. 1882. 21s.

BUTLER.—Selections from his Previous Works, with Remarks on Mr. G. J. Romanes' recent work, "Mental Evolution in Animals," and "A Psalm of Montreal." By Samuel Butler. Crown 8vo, pp. viii. and 326, cloth. 1884. 7s. 6d.

BUTLER.—The Spanish Teacher and Colloquial Phrase-Book. An Easy and Agreeable Method of acquiring a Speaking Knowledge of the Spanish Language. By Francis Butler. Fcap. 8vo, pp. xviii. and 240, half-roan. 2s. 6d.

BUTLER.—Hungarian Poems and Fables for English Readers. Selected and Translated by E. D. Butler, of the British Museum; with Illustrations by A. G. Butler. Foolscap, pp. vi. and 88, limp cloth. 1877. 2s.

BUTLER.—The Legend of the Wondrous Hunt. By John Arany. With a few Miscellaneous Pieces and Folk-Songs. Translated from the Magyar by E. D. Butler, F.R.G.S. Crown 8vo, pp. viii. and 70. Limp cloth. 2s. 6d.

CAITHNESS.—Lectures on Popular and Scientific Subjects. By the Earl of Caithness, F.R.S. Delivered at various times and places. Second enlarged Edition. Crown 8vo, pp. 174, cloth. 1879. 2s. 6d.

CALCUTTA REVIEW.—Selections from Nos. I.-XXXVII. 5s. each.

CALDER.—The Coming Era. By A. Calder, Officer of the Legion of Honour, and Author of "The Man of the Future." 8vo, pp. 422, cloth. 1879. 10s. 6d.

CALDWELL.—A Comparative Grammar of the Dravidian or South Indian Family of Languages. By the Rev. R. Caldwell, LL.D. A second, corrected, and enlarged Edition. Demy 8vo, pp. 804, cloth. 1875. 28s.

CALENDARS OF STATE PAPERS. List on application.

CALL.—Reverberations. Revised. With a chapter from My Autobiography. By W. M. W. Call, M.A., Cambridge, Author of "Lyra Hellenica" and "Golden Histories." Crown 8vo, pp. viii. and 200, cloth. 1875. 4s. 6d.

CALLAWAY.—Nursery Tales, Traditions, and Histories of the Zulus. In their own words, with a Translation into English, and Notes. By the Rev. Canon Callaway, M.D. Vol. I., 8vo, pp. xiv. and 378, cloth. 1868. 16s.

CALLAWAY.—The Religious System of the Amazulu.

Part I.—Unkulunkulu; or, The Tradition of Creation as existing among the Amazulu and other Tribes of South Africa, in their own words, with a Translation into English, and Notes. By the Rev. Canon Callaway, M.D. 8vo, pp. 128, sewed. 1868. 4s.

Part II.—Amatongo; or, Ancestor-Worship as existing among the Amazulu, in their own words, with a Translation into English, and Notes. By the Rev. Canon Callaway, M.D. 8vo, pp. 127, sewed. 1869. 4s.

Part III.—Izinyanga Zokubula; or, Divination, as existing among the Amazulu, in their own words, with a Translation into English, and Notes. By the Rev. Canon Callaway, M.D. 8vo, pp. 150, sewed. 1870. 4s.

Part IV.—On Medical Magic and Witchcraft. 8vo, pp. 40, sewed, 1s. 6d.

CAMBRIDGE PHILOLOGICAL SOCIETY (Transactions). Vol. I., from 1872-1880. 8vo, pp. xvi.-420, wrapper. 1881. 15s. Vol. II., for 1881 and 1882. 8vo, pp. viii.-286, wrapper. 1883. 12s.

CAMERINI.—L'Eco Italiano; a Practical Guide to Italian Conversation. By E. Camerini. With a Vocabulary. 12mo, pp. 98, cloth. 1860. 4s. 6d.

CAMPBELL.—The Gospel of the World's Divine Order. By Douglas Campbell. New Edition. Revised. Crown 8vo, pp. viii. and 364, cloth. 1877. 4s. 6d.

CANADA.—A Guide Book to the Dominion of Canada. Containing Information for intending Settlers, with many Illustrations and Map. Published under the Direction of the Government of Canada. Demy 8vo, pp. xiv.-138, thick paper, sewed. 1885. 6d.

CANDID Examination of Theism. By Physicus. Post 8vo, pp. xviii. and 198, cloth. 1878. 7s. 6d.

CANTICUM CANTICORUM, reproduced in facsimile, from the Scriverius copy in the British Museum. With an Historical and Bibliographical Introduction by I. Ph. Berjeau. Folio, pp. 36, with 16 Tables of Illustrations, vellum. 1860. £2, 2s.

CAREY.—The Past, the Present, and the Future. By H. C. Carey. Second Edition. 8vo, pp. 474, cloth. 1856. 10s. 6d.

CARLETTI.—History of the Conquest of Tunis. Translated by J. T. Carletti. Crown 8vo, pp. 40, cloth. 1883. 2s. 6d.

CARNEGY.—Notes on the Land Tenures and Revenue Assessments of Upper India. By P. Carnegy. Crown 8vo, pp. viii. and 136, and forms, cloth. 1874. 6s.

CATHERINE II., Memoirs of the Empress. Written by herself. With a Preface by A. Herzen. Trans. from the French. 12mo, pp. xvi. and 352, bds. 1859. 7s. 6d.

CATLIN.—O-Kee-Pa. A Religious Ceremony; and other Customs of the Mandans. By George Catlin. With 13 coloured Illustrations. Small 4to, pp. vi. and 52, cloth. 1867. 14s.

CATLIN.—The Lifted and Subsided Rocks of America, with their Influence on the Oceanic, Atmospheric, and Land Currents, and the Distribution of Races. By George Catlin. With 2 Maps. Cr. 8vo, pp. xii. and 238, cloth. 1870. 6s. 6d.

CATLIN.—Shut your Mouth and Save your Life. By George Catlin, Author of "Notes of Travels amongst the North American Indians," &c., &c. With 29 Illustrations from Drawings by the Author. Eighth Edition, considerably enlarged. Crown 8vo, pp. 106, cloth. 1882. 2s. 6d.

CAXTON.—The Biography and Typography of. See Blades.

CAXTON CELEBRATION, 1877.—Catalogue of the Loan Collection of Antiquities, Curiosities, and Appliances Connected with the Art of Printing. Edited by G. Bullen, F.S.A. Post 8vo, pp. xx. and 472, cloth, 3s. 6d.

CAZELLES.—Outline of the Evolution-Philosophy. By Dr. W. E. Cazelles. Translated from the French by the Rev. O. B. Frothingham. Crown 8vo, pp. 156, cloth. 1875. 3s. 6d.

CESNOLA.—Salaminia (Cyprus). The History, Treasures, and Antiquities of Salamis in the Island of Cyprus. By A. Palma di Cesnola, F.S.A., &c. With an Introduction by S. Birch, Esq., D.C.L., LL.D., Keeper of the Egyptian and Oriental Antiquities in the British Museum. Royal 8vo, pp. xlviii. and 325, with upwards of 700 Illustrations and Map of Ancient Cyprus, cloth. 1882. 31s. 6d.

CHALMERS.—Structure of Chinese Characters, under 300 Primary Forms after the Shwoh-wan, 100 A.D., and the Phonetic Shwoh-wan, 1833. By J. Chalmers, M.A., LL.D., A.B. Demy 8vo, pp. x. and 200, with two plates, limp cloth. 1882. 12s. 6d.

CHAMBERLAIN.—The Classical Poetry of the Japanese. By Basil Hall Chamberlain, Author of "Yeigo Henkaku, Ichiran." Post 8vo, pp. xii. and 228, cloth. 1880. 7s. 6d.

CHAPMAN.—Chloroform and other Anæsthetics: Their History and Use during Childbirth. By John Chapman, M.D. 8vo, pp. 51, sewed. 1859. 1s.

CHAPMAN.—Diarrhœa and Cholera: Their Nature, Origin, and Treatment through the Agency of the Nervous System. By John Chapman, M.D., M.R.C.P., M.R.C.S. 8vo, pp. xix. and 248, cloth. 7s. 6d.

CHAPMAN.—Medical Charity: its Abuses, and how to Remedy them. By John Chapman, M.D. 8vo, pp. viii. and 108, cloth. 1874. 2s. 6d.

CHAPMAN.—Sea-Sickness, and how to Prevent it. An Explanation of its Nature and Successful Treatment, through the Agency of the Nervous System, by means of the Spinal Ice Bag; with an Introduction on the General Principles of Neuro-Therapeutics. By John Chapman, M.D., M.R.C.P., M.R.C.S. Second Edition. 8vo, pp. viii. and 112, cloth. 1868. 3s.

CHAPTERS on Christian Catholicity. By a Clergyman. 8vo, pp. 282, cloth. 1878. 5s.

CHARITABALI (The), or, Instructive Biography. By Isvarachandra Vidyasagara. With a Vocabulary of all the Words occurring in the Text. By J. F. Blumhardt, Bengal Lecturer at the University College, London; and Teacher of Bengali for the Cambridge University. 12mo, pp. 174, cloth. 1884. 5s. The Vocabulary only, 2s. 6d.

CHARNOCK.—A Glossary of the Essex Dialect. By Richard Stephen Charnock, Ph.D., F.S.A. Fcap., pp. xii. and 64, cloth. 1880. 3s. 6d.

CHARNOCK.—Prœnomina; or, The Etymology of the Principal Christian Names of Great Britain and Ireland. By R. S. Charnock, Ph.D., F.S.A. Crown 8vo, pp. xvi. and 128, cloth. 1882. 6s.

CHATTERJEE. See Phillips.

CHATTOPADHYAYA.—The Yátrás; or, The Popular Dramas of Bengal. By N. Chattopadhyaya. Post 8vo, pp. 50, wrapper. 1882. 2s.

CHAUCER SOCIETY.—Subscription, two guineas per annum. List of Publications on application.

CHILDERS.—A Pali-English Dictionary, with Sanskrit Equivalents, and with numerous Quotations, Extracts, and References. Compiled by Robert Cæsar Childers, late of the Ceylon Civil Service. Imperial 8vo, double columns, pp. 648, cloth. 1875. £3, 3s.

CHILDERS.—The Mahaparinibbanasutta of the Sutta Pitaka. The Pali Text. Edited by the late Professor R. C. Childers. 8vo, pp. 72, limp cloth. 1878. 5s.

CHINTAMON.—A COMMENTARY ON THE TEXT OF THE BHAGAVAD-GITÁ; or, The Discourse between Khrishna and Arjuna of Divine Matters. A Sanskrit Philosophical Poem. With a few Introductory Papers. By Hurrychund Chintamon, Political Agent to H. H. the Guicowar Mulhar Rao Maharajah of Baroda. Post 8vo, pp. 118, cloth. 1874. 6s.

CHRONICLES AND MEMORIALS OF GREAT BRITAIN AND IRELAND DURING THE MIDDLE AGES. List on application.

CLARK.—MEGHADUTA, THE CLOUD MESSENGER. Poem of Kalidasa. Translated by the late Rev. T. Clark, M.A. Fcap. 8vo, pp. 64, wrapper. 1882. 1s.

CLARK.—A FORECAST OF THE RELIGION OF THE FUTURE. Being Short Essays on some important Questions in Religious Philosophy. By W. W. Clark. Post 8vo, pp. xii. and 238, cloth. 1879. 3s. 6d.

CLARKE.—TEN GREAT RELIGIONS: An Essay in Comparative Theology. By James Freeman Clarke. Demy 8vo, pp. x. and 528, cloth. 1871. 15s.

CLARKE.—TEN GREAT RELIGIONS. Part II., A Comparison of all Religions. By J. F. Clarke. Demy 8vo, pp. xxviii.-414, cloth. 1883. 10s. 6d.

CLARKE.—THE EARLY HISTORY OF THE MEDITERRANEAN POPULATIONS, &c., in their Migrations and Settlements. Illustrated from Autonomous Coins, Gems, Inscriptions, &c. By Hyde Clarke. 8vo, pp. 80, cloth. 1882. 5s.

CLAUSEWITZ.—ON WAR. By General Carl von Clausewitz. Translated by Colonel J. J. Graham, from the third German Edition. Three volumes complete in one. Fcap 4to, double columns, pp. xx. and 564, with Portrait of the author, cloth. 1873. 10s. 6d.

CLEMENT AND HUTTON.—ARTISTS OF THE NINETEENTH CENTURY AND THEIR WORKS. A Handbook containing Two Thousand and Fifty Biographical Sketches. By Clara Erskine Clement and Lawrence Hutton. Third, Revised Edition. 2 vols. crown 8vo. pp. 844, cloth. 1885. 21s.

COKE.—CREEDS OF THE DAY: or, Collated Opinions of Reputable Thinkers. By Henry Coke. In Three Series of Letters. 2 vols. Demy 8vo, pp. 302-324, cloth. 1883. 21s.

COLEBROOKE.—THE LIFE AND MISCELLANEOUS ESSAYS OF HENRY THOMAS COLEBROOKE. The Biography by his Son, Sir T. E. Colebrooke, Bart., M.P. 3 vols. Vol. I. The Life. Demy 8vo, pp. xii. and 492, with Portrait and Map, cloth. 1873. 14s. Vols. II. and III. The Essays. A new Edition, with Notes by E. B. Cowell, Professor of Sanskrit in the University of Cambridge. Demy 8vo, pp. xvi. and 544, and x. and 520, cloth. 1873. 28s.

COLENSO.—NATAL SERMONS. A Series of Discourses Preached in the Cathedral Church of St Peter's, Maritzburg. By the Right Rev. John William Colenso, D.D., Bishop of Natal. 8vo, pp. viii. and 373, cloth. 1866. 7s. 6d. The Second Series. Crown 8vo, cloth. 1868. 5s.

COLLINS.—A GRAMMAR AND LEXICON OF THE HEBREW LANGUAGE, Entitled Sefer Hassoham. By Rabbi Moseh Ben Yitshak, of England. Edited from a MS. in the Bodleian Library of Oxford, and collated with a MS. in the Imperial Library of St. Petersburg, with Additions and Corrections, by G. W. Collins, M.A. Demy 4to, pp. 112, wrapper. 1882. 7s. 6d.

COLYMBIA.—Crown 8vo, pp. 260, cloth. 1873. 5s.

"The book is amusing as well as clever."—*Athenæum.* "Many exceedingly humorous passages."—*Public Opinion.* "Deserves to be read."—*Scotsman.* "Neatly done."—*Graphic.* "Very amusing."—*Examiner.*

COMTE.—THE CATECHISM OF POSITIVE RELIGION: Translated from the French of Auguste Comte. By Richard Congreve. Second Edition. Revised and Corrected, and conformed to the Second French Edition of 1874. Crown 8vo, pp. 316, cloth. 1883. 2s. 6d.

COMTE.—THE EIGHT CIRCULARS OF AUGUSTE COMTE. Translated from the French, under the auspices of R. Congreve. Fcap. 8vo, pp. iv. and 90, cloth. 1882. 1s. 6d.

COMTE.—Preliminary Discourse on the Positive Spirit. Prefixed to the "Traité Philosophique d'Astronomie Populaire." By M. Auguste Comte. Translated by W. M. W. Call, M.A., Camb. Crown 8vo, pp. 154, cloth. 1883. 2s. 6d.

COMTE.—The Positive Philosophy of Auguste Comte. Translated and condensed by Harriet Martineau. 2 vols. Second Edition. 8vo, cloth. Vol. I., pp. xxiv. and 400; Vol. II., pp. xiv. and 468. 1875. 25s.

CONGREVE.—The Roman Empire of the West. Four Lectures delivered at the Philosophical Institution, Edinburgh, February 1855, by Richard Congreve, M.A. 8vo, pp. 176, cloth. 1855. 4s.

CONGREVE.—Elizabeth of England. Two Lectures delivered at the Philosophical Institution, Edinburgh, January 1862. By Richard Congreve. 18mo, pp. 114, sewed. 1862. 2s. 6d.

CONTOPOULOS.—A Lexicon of Modern Greek-English and English Modern Greek. By N. Contopoulos. Part I. Modern Greek-English. Part II. English Modern Greek. 8vo, pp. 460 and 582, cloth. 1877. 27s.

CONWAY.—The Sacred Anthology: A Book of Ethnical Scriptures. Collected and Edited by Moncure D. Conway. Fifth Edition. Demy 8vo, pp. viii. and 480, cloth. 1876. 12s.

CONWAY.—Idols and Ideals. With an Essay on Christianity. By Moncure D. Conway, M.A., Author of "The Eastern Pilgrimage," &c. Crown 8vo, pp. 352, cloth. 1877. 4s.

CONWAY.—Emerson at Home and Abroad. See English and Foreign Philosophical Library.

CONWAY.—Travels in South Kensington. By M. D. Conway. Illustrated. 8vo, pp. 234, cloth. 1882. 12s.
  Contents.—The South Kensington Museum—Decorative Art and Architecture in England—Bedford Park.

COOMARA SWAMY.—The Dathavansa; or, The History of the Tooth Relic of Gotama Buddha, in Pali verse. Edited, with an English Translation, by Mutu Coomara Swamy, F.R.A.S. Demy 8vo, pp. 174, cloth. 1874. 10s. 6d. English Translation. With Notes. pp. 100. 6s.

COOMARA SWAMY.—Sutta Nipata; or, Dialogues and Discourses of Gotama Buddha (2500 years old). Translated from the original Pali. With Notes and Introduction. By Mutu Coomara Swamy, F.R.A.S. Crown 8vo, pp. xxxvi. and 160, cloth. 1874. 6s.

COPARCENERS (The): Being the Adventures of Two Heiresses. See "Arthur."

CORNELIA. A Novel. Post 8vo, pp. 250, boards. 1863. 1s. 6d.

COTTA.—Geology and History. A Popular Exposition of all that is known of the Earth and its Inhabitants in Pre-historic Times. By Bernhard Von Cotta, Professor of Geology at the Academy of Mining, Freiberg, in Saxony. 12mo, pp. iv. and 84, cloth. 1865. 2s.

COUSIN.—The Philosophy of Kant. Lectures by Victor Cousin. Translated from the French. To which is added a Biographical and Critical Sketch of Kant's Life and Writings. By A. G. Henderson. Large post 8vo, pp. xciv. and 194, cloth. 1864. 6s.

COUSIN.—Elements of Psychology: included in a Critical Examination of Locke's Essay on the Human Understanding, and in additional pieces. Translated from the French of Victor Cousin, with an Introduction and Notes. By Caleb S. Henry, D.D. Fourth improved Edition, revised according to the Author's last corrections. Crown 8vo, pp. 568, cloth. 1871. 8s.

COWELL.—A Short Introduction to the Ordinary Prakrit of the Sanskrit Dramas. With a List of Common Irregular Prâkrit Words. By E. B. Cowell, Professor of Sanskrit in the University of Cambridge, and Hon. LL.D. of the University of Edinburgh. Crown 8vo, pp. 40, limp cloth. 1875. 3s. 6d.

COWELL.—PRAKRITA-PRAKASA; or, The Prakrit Grammar of Vararuchi, with the Commentary (Manorama) of Bhamaha; the first complete Edition of the Original Text, with various Readings from a collection of Six MSS. in the Bodleian Library at Oxford, and the Libraries of the Royal Asiatic Society and the East India House; with Copious Notes, an English Translation, and Index of Prakrit Words, to which is prefixed an Easy Introduction to Prakrit Grammar. By Edward Byles Cowell, of Magdalen Hall, Oxford, Professor of Sanskrit at Cambridge. New Edition, with New Preface, Additions, and Corrections. Second Issue. 8vo, pp. xxxi. and 204, cloth. 1868. 14s.

COWELL.—THE SARVADARSANA SAMGRAHA. See Trübner's Oriental Series.

COWLEY.—POEMS. By Percy Tunnicliff Cowley. Demy 8vo, pp. 104, cloth. 1881. 5s.

CRAIG.—THE IRISH LAND LABOUR QUESTION, Illustrated in the History of Ralahine and Co-operative Farming. By E. T. Craig. Crown 8vo, pp. xii. and 202, cloth. 1882. 2s. 6d. Wrappers, 2s.

CRANBROOK.—CREDIBILIA; or, Discourses on Questions of Christian Faith. By the Rev. James Cranbrook, Edinburgh. Reissue. Post 8vo, pp. iv. and 190, cloth. 1868. 3s. 6d.

CRANBROOK.—THE FOUNDERS OF CHRISTIANITY; or, Discourses upon the Origin of the Christian Religion. By the Rev. James Cranbrook, Edinburgh. Post 8vo, pp. xii. and 324. 1868. 6s.

CRAVEN.—THE POPULAR DICTIONARY IN ENGLISH AND HINDUSTANI, AND HINDUSTANI AND ENGLISH. With a Number of Useful Tables. Compiled by the Rev. T. Craven, M.A. 18mo, pp. 430, cloth. 1881. 3s. 6d.

CRAWFORD.—RECOLLECTIONS OF TRAVEL IN NEW ZEALAND AND AUSTRALIA. By James Coutts Crawford, F.G.S., Resident Magistrate, Wellington, &c., &c. With Maps and Illustrations. 8vo, pp. xvi. and 468, cloth. 1880. 18s.

CROSLAND.—APPARITIONS; An Essay explanatory of Old Facts and a New Theory. To which are added Sketches and Adventures. By Newton Crosland. Crown 8vo, pp. viii. and 166, cloth. 1873. 2s. 6d.

CROSLAND.—PITH: ESSAYS AND SKETCHES GRAVE AND GAY, with some Verses and Illustrations. By Newton Crosland. Crown 8vo, pp. 310, cloth. 1881. 5s.

CROSLAND.—THE NEW PRINCIPIA; or, The Astronomy of the Future. An Essay Explanatory of a Rational System of the Universe. By N. Crosland, Author of "Pith," &c. Foolscap 8vo, pp. 88, cloth limp elegant, gilt edges. 1884. 2s. 6d.

CROSS.—HESPERIDES. The Occupations, Relaxations, and Aspirations of a Life. By Launcelot Cross, Author of "Characteristics of Leigh Hunt," "Brandon Tower," "Business," &c. Demy 8vo, pp. iv.-486, cloth. 1883. 10s. 6d.

CSOMA DE KÖRÖS.—LIFE OF. See Trübner's Oriental Series.

CUMMINS.—A GRAMMAR OF THE OLD FRIESIC LANGUAGE. By A. H. Cummins, A.M. Crown 8vo, pp. x. and 76, cloth. 1881. 3s. 6d.

CUNNINGHAM.—THE ANCIENT GEOGRAPHY OF INDIA. I. The Buddhist Period, including the Campaigns of Alexander and the Travels of Hwen-Thsang. By Alexander Cunningham, Major-General, Royal Engineers (Bengal Retired). With 13 Maps. 8vo, pp. xx. and 590, cloth. 1870. £1, 8s.

CUNNINGHAM.—THE STUPA OF BHARHUT: A Buddhist Monument ornamented with numerous Sculptures illustrative of Buddhist Legend and History in the Third Century B.C. By Alexander Cunningham, C.S.I., C.I.E., Maj.-Gen., R.E. (B.R.), Dir.-Gen. Archæol. Survey of India. Royal 8vo, pp. viii. and 144, with 57 Plates, cloth. 1879. £3, 3s.

CUNNINGHAM.—ARCHÆOLOGICAL SURVEY OF INDIA. Reports from 1862-80. By A. Cunningham, C.S.I., C.I.E., Major-General, R.E. (Bengal Retired), Director-General, Archæological Survey of India. With numerous Plates, cloth, Vols. I.-XI. 10s. each. (Except Vols. VII., VIII., and IX., and also Vols. XII. to XVIII., which are 12s. each.)

CUSHMAN.—CHARLOTTE CUSHMAN: Her Letters and Memories of her Life. Edited by her friend, Emma Stebbins. Square 8vo, pp. viii. and 308, cloth. With Portrait and Illustrations. 1879. 12s. 6d.

CUST.—LANGUAGES OF THE EAST INDIES. See Trübner's Oriental Series.

CUST.—LINGUISTIC AND ORIENTAL ESSAYS. See Trübner's Oriental Series.

CUST.—LANGUAGES OF AFRICA. See Trübner's Oriental Series.

CUST.—PICTURES OF INDIAN LIFE, Sketched with the Pen from 1852 to 1881. By R. N. Cust, late I.C.S., Hon. Sec. Royal Asiatic Society. Crown 8vo, pp. x. and 346, cloth. With Maps. 1881. 7s. 6d.

CUST.—THE SHRINES OF LOURDES, ZARAGOSSA, THE HOLY STAIRS AT ROME, THE HOLY HOUSE OF LORETTO AND NAZARETH, AND ST. ANN AT JERUSALEM. By R. N. Cust, Member of Committees of the Church Missionary Society, and British and Foreign Bible Society. With Four Autotypes from Photographs obtained on the spot. Fcap. 8vo, pp. iv. and 63, stiff wrappers. 1885. 2s.

DANA.—A TEXT-BOOK OF GEOLOGY, designed for Schools and Academies. By James D. Dana, LL.D., Professor of Geology, &c., at Yale College. Illustrated. Crown 8vo, pp. vi. and 354, cloth. 1876. 10s.

DANA.—MANUAL OF GEOLOGY, treating of the Principles of the Science, with special Reference to American Geological History; for the use of Colleges, Academies, and Schools of Science. By James D. Dana, LL.D. Illustrated by a Chart of the World, and over One Thousand Figures. 8vo, pp. xvi. and 800, and Chart, cl. 21s.

DANA.—THE GEOLOGICAL STORY BRIEFLY TOLD. An Introduction to Geology for the General Reader and for Beginners in the Science. By J. D. Dana, LL.D. Illustrated. 12mo, pp. xii. and 264, cloth. 7s. 6d.

DANA.—A SYSTEM OF MINERALOGY. Descriptive Mineralogy, comprising the most Recent Discoveries. By J. D. Dana, aided by G. J. Brush. Fifth Edition, re-written and enlarged, and illustrated with upwards of 600 Woodcuts, with three Appendixes and Corrections. Royal 8vo, pp. xlviii. and 892, cloth. £2, 2s.

DANA.—A TEXT BOOK OF MINERALOGY. With an Extended Treatise on Crystallography and Physical Mineralogy. By E. S. Dana, on the Plan and with the Co-operation of Professor J. D. Dana. Third Edition, revised. Over 800 Woodcuts and 1 Coloured Plate. 8vo, pp. viii. and 486, cloth. 1879. 18s.

DANA.—MANUAL OF MINERALOGY AND LITHOLOGY; Containing the Elements of the Science of Minerals and Rocks, for the Use of the Practical Mineralogist and Geologist, and for Instruction in Schools and Colleges. By J. D. Dana. Fourth Edition, rearranged and rewritten. Illustrated by numerous Woodcuts. Crown 8vo, pp. viii. and 474, cloth. 1882. 7s. 6d.

DARWIN.—CHARLES DARWIN: A Paper contributed to the Transactions of the Shropshire Archæological Society. By Edward Woodall. With Portrait and Illustrations. Post 8vo, pp. iv.-64, cloth. 1884. 3s. 6d.

DATES AND DATA RELATING TO RELIGIOUS ANTHROPOLOGY AND BIBLICAL ARCHÆOLOGY. (Primæval Period.) 8vo, pp. viii. and 106, cloth. 1876. 5s.

DAVIDS.—BUDDHIST BIRTH STORIES. See Trübner's Oriental Series.

DAVIES.—HINDU PHILOSOPHY. 2 vols. See Trübner's Oriental Series.

DAVIS.—NARRATIVE OF THE NORTH POLAR EXPEDITION, U.S. SHIP *Polaris*, Captain Charles Francis Hall Commanding. Edited under the direction of the Hon. G. M. Robeson, Secretary of the Navy, by Rear-Admiral C. H. Davis, U.S.N. Third Edition. With numerous Steel and Wood Engravings, Photolithographs, and Maps. 4to, pp. 696, cloth. 1881. £1, 8s.

DAY.—THE PREHISTORIC USE OF IRON AND STEEL; with Observations on certain matter ancillary thereto. By St. John V. Day, C.E., F.R.S.E., &c. 8vo, pp. xxiv. and 278, cloth. 1877. 12s.

DE FLANDRE.—MONOGRAMS OF THREE OR MORE LETTERS, DESIGNED AND DRAWN ON STONE. By C. De Flandre, F.S.A. Scot., Edinburgh. With Indices, showing the place and style or period of every Monogram, and of each individual Letter. 4to, 42 Plates, cloth. 1880. Large paper, £7, 7s.; small paper, £3, 3s.

B

DELBRUCK.—INTRODUCTION TO THE STUDY OF LANGUAGE: A Critical Survey of the History and Methods of Comparative Philology of the Indo-European Languages. By B. Delbrück. Authorised Translation, with a Preface by the Author. 8vo, pp. 156, cloth. 1882. 5s. Sewed, 4s.

DELEPIERRE.—HISTOIRE LITTERAIRE DES FOUS. Par Octave Delepierre. Crown 8vo, pp. 184, cloth. 1860. 5s.

DELEPIERRE.—MACARONEANA ANDRA; overum Nouveaux Mélanges de Litterature Macaronique. Par Octave Delepierre. Small 4to, pp. 180, printed by Whittingham, and handsomely bound in the Roxburghe style. 1862. 10s. 6d.

DELEPIERRE.—ANALYSE DES TRAVAUX DE LA SOCIETE DES PHILOBIBLON DE LONDRES. Par Octave Delepierre. Small 4to, pp. viii. and 134, bound in the Roxburghe style. 1862. 10s. 6d.

DELEPIERRE.—REVUE ANALYTIQUE DES OUVRAGES ÉCRITS EN CENTONS, depuis les Temps Anciens, jusqu'au xixième Siècle. Par un Bibliophile Belge. Small 4to, pp. 508, stiff covers. 1868. £1, 10s.

DELEPIERRE.—TABLEAU DE LA LITTÉRATURE DU CENTON, CHÉZ LES ANCIENS ET CHEZ LES MODERNES. Par Octave Delepierre. 2 vols, small 4to, pp. 324 and 318. Paper cover. 1875. £1, 1s.

DELEPIERRE.—L'ENFER: Essai Philosophique et Historique sur les Légendes de la Vie Future. Par Octave Delepierre. Crown 8vo, pp. 160, paper wrapper. 1876. 6s. Only 250 copies printed.

DENNYS.—A HANDBOOK OF THE CANTON VERNACULAR OF THE CHINESE LANGUAGE. Being a Series of Introductory Lessons for Domestic and Business Purposes. By N. B. Dennys, M.R.A.S., &c. Royal 8vo, pp. iv. and 228, cloth. 1874. 30s.

DENNYS.—A HANDBOOK OF MALAY COLLOQUIAL, as spoken in Singapore, being a Series of Introductory Lessons for Domestic and Business Purposes. By N. B. Dennys, Ph.D., F.R.G.S., M.R.A.S. Impl. 8vo, pp. vi. and 204, cloth. 1878. 21s.

DENNYS.—THE FOLK-LORE OF CHINA, AND ITS AFFINITIES WITH THAT OF THE ARYAN AND SEMITIC RACES. By N. B. Dennys, Ph.D., F.R.G.S., M.R.A.S. 8vo, pp. 166, cloth. 1876. 10s. 6d.

DE VALDES.—See VALDES.

DE VINNE.—THE INVENTION OF PRINTING: A Collection of Texts and Opinions. Description of Early Prints and Playing Cards, the Block-Books of the Fifteenth Century, the Legend of Lourens Janszoon Coster of Haarlem, and the Works of John Gutenberg and his Associates. Illustrated with Fac-similes of Early Types and Woodcuts. By Theo. L. De Vinne. Second Edition. In royal 8vo, elegantly printed, and bound in cloth, with embossed portraits, and a multitude of Fac-similes and Illustrations. 1877. £1 1s.

DICKSON.—WHO WAS SCOTLAND'S FIRST PRINTER? Ane Compendious and breue Tractate, in Commendation of Androw Myllar. Compylit be Robert Dickson, F.S.A. Scot. Fcap. 8vo, pp. 24, parchment wrapper. 1881. 1s.

DOBSON.—MONOGRAPH OF THE ASIATIC CHIROPTERA, and Catalogue of the Species of Bats in the Collection of the Indian Museum, Calcutta. By G. E. Dobson, M.A., M.B., F.LS., &c. 8vo, pp. viii. and 228, cloth. 1876. 12s.

D'ORSEY.—A PRACTICAL GRAMMAR OF PORTUGUESE AND ENGLISH, exhibiting in a Series of Exercises, in Double Translation, the Idiomatic Structure of both Languages, as now written and spoken. Adapted to Ollendorff's System by the Rev. Alexander J. D. D'Orsey, of Corpus Christi College, Cambridge, and Lecturer on Public Reading and Speaking at King's College, London. Third Edition. 12mo, pp. viii. and 298, cloth. 1868. 7s.

DOUGLAS.—CHINESE-ENGLISH DICTIONARY OF THE VERNACULAR OR SPOKEN LANGUAGE OF AMOY, with the principal variations of the Chang-Chew and Chin-Chew Dialects. By the Rev. Carstairs Douglas, M.A., LL.D., Glasg., Missionary of the Presbyterian Church in England. High quarto, double columns, pp. 632, cloth. 1873. £3, 3s.

DOUGLAS.—CHINESE LANGUAGE AND LITERATURE. Two Lectures delivered at the Royal Institution, by R. K. Douglas, of the British Museum, and Professor of Chinese at King's College. Crown 8vo, pp. 118, cloth. 1875. 5s.

DOUGLAS.—THE LIFE OF JENGHIZ KHAN. Translated from the Chinese. With an Introduction. By Robert K. Douglas, of the British Museum, and Professor of Chinese at King's College. Crown 8vo, pp. xxxvi. and 106, cloth. 1877. 5s.

DOUGLAS.—POEMS: Lyrical and Dramatic. By Evelyn Douglas. Foolscap 8vo, pp. 256, cloth. 1885. 5s.

DOUGLAS.—THE QUEEN OF THE HID ISLE: An Allegory of Life and Art. And LOVE'S PERVERSITY; or, Eros and Anteros. A Drama. By Evelyn Douglas. Fcap. 8vo, pp. viii.-258, cloth. 1885. 5s.

DOWSON.—DICTIONARY OF HINDU MYTHOLOGY, &c. See Trübner's Oriental Series.

DOWSON.—A GRAMMAR OF THE URDÛ OR HINDÛSTÂNÎ LANGUAGE. By John Dowson, M.R.A.S., Professor of Hindûstânî, Staff College, Sandhurst. Crown 8vo, pp. xvi. and 264, with 8 Plates, cloth. 1872. 10s. 6d.

DOWSON.—A HINDÛSTÂNÎ EXERCISE BOOK; containing a Series of Passages and Extracts adapted for Translation into Hindûstânî. By John Dowson, M.R.A.S., Professor of Hindûstânî, Staff College, Sandhurst. Crown 8vo, pp. 100, limp cloth. 1872. 2s. 6d.

DUKA.—THE LIFE AND TRAVELS OF ALEXANDER CSOMA DE KÖRÖS: A Biography, compiled chiefly from hitherto Unpublished Data; With a Brief Notice of each of his Published Works and Essays, as well as of his still Extant Manuscripts. By Theodore Duka, Doctor of Medicine; Fellow of the Royal College of Surgeons of England; Surgeon-Major, Her Majesty's Bengal Medical Service, Retired; Knight of the Order of the Iron Crown; Corresponding Member of the Academy of Sciences of Hungary. Post 8vo, with Portrait, pp. xii.-234, cloth. 1885. 9s.

DUSAR.—A GRAMMAR OF THE GERMAN LANGUAGE; with Exercises. By P. Friedrich Dusar, First German Master in the Military Department of Cheltenham College. Second Edition. Crown 8vo, pp. viii. and 208, cloth. 1879. 4s. 6d.

DUSAR.—A GRAMMATICAL COURSE OF THE GERMAN LANGUAGE. By P. Friedrich Dusar. Third Edition. Crown 8vo, pp. x. and 134, cloth. 1883. 3s. 6d.

DYMOCK.—THE VEGETABLE MATERIA MEDICA OF WESTERN INDIA. By W. Dymock, Surgeon-Major Bombay Army, &c. &c. To be completed in four parts. 8vo, Part I., pp. 160; Part II., pp. 168; wrappers, 4s. each.

EARLY ENGLISH TEXT SOCIETY.—Subscription, one guinea per annum. *Extra Series.* Subscriptions—Small paper, one guinea; large paper, two guineas, per annum. List of publications on application.

EASTWICK.—KHIRAD AFROZ (the Illuminator of the Understanding). By Maulaví Hafízu'd-dín. A New Edition of the Hindûstânî Text, carefully revised, with Notes, Critical and Explanatory. By Edward B. Eastwick, F.R.S., M.R.A.S., &c. Imperial 8vo, pp. xiv. and 319, cloth. Reissue, 1867. 18s.

EASTWICK.—THE GULISTAN. See Trübner's Oriental Series.

EBERS.—THE EMPEROR. A Romance. By Georg Ebers. Translated from the German by Clara Bell. In two volumes, 16mo, pp. iv. 319 and 322, cloth. 1881. 7s. 6d. Paper, 5s.

EBERS.—A QUESTION: The Idyl of a Picture by his friend, Alma Tadema. Related by Georg Ebers. From the German, by Mary J. Safford. 16mo, pp. 125, with Frontispiece, cloth. 1881. 4s. Paper, 2s. 6d.

EBERS.—SERAPIS. A Romance. By Georg Ebers. From the German by Clara Bell. 16mo, pp. iv.-388, cloth. 1885. 4s. Paper, 2s. 6d.

ECHO (DEUTSCHES). THE GERMAN ECHO. A Faithful Mirror of German Conversation. By Ludwig Wolfram. With a Vocabulary. By Henry P. Skelton. Post 8vo, pp. 130 and 70, cloth. 1863. 3s.

ECHO FRANÇAIS. A PRACTICAL GUIDE TO CONVERSATION. By Fr. de la Fruston. With a complete Vocabulary. By Anthony Maw Border. Post 8vo, pp. 120 and 72, cloth. 1860. 3s.

ECO ITALIANO (L'). A PRACTICAL GUIDE TO ITALIAN CONVERSATION. By Eugene Camerini. With a complete Vocabulary. By Henry P. Skelton. Post 8vo, pp. vi., 128, and 98, cloth. 1860. 4s. 6d.

ECO DE MADRID. THE ECHO OF MADRID. A Practical Guide to Spanish Conversation. By J. E. Hartzenbusch and Henry Lemming. With a complete Vocabulary, containing copious Explanatory Remarks. By Henry Lemming. Post 8vo, pp. xii., 144, and 83, cloth. 1860. 5s.

ECKSTEIN.—PRUSIAS: A Romance of Ancient Rome under the Republic. By Ernst Eckstein. From the German by Clara Bell. Two vols. 16mo, pp. 356 and 336, cloth. 1884. 7s. 6d.; paper, 5s.

ECKSTEIN.—QUINTUS CLAUDIUS. A Romance of Imperial Rome. By Ernst Eckstein. From the German by Clara Bell. Two vols. 16mo, pp. 314 and 304, cloth. 1884. 7s. 6d.; paper, 5s.

EDDA SÆMUNDAR HINNS FRODA. The Edda of Sæmund the Learned. Translated from the Old Norse, by Benjamin Thorpe. Complete in 1 vol. fcap. 8vo, pp. viii. and 152, and pp. viii. and 170, cloth. 1866. 7s. 6d.

EDGREN.—SANSKRIT GRAMMAR. See Trübner's Collection.

EDKINS.—CHINA'S PLACE IN PHILOLOGY. An attempt to show that the Languages of Europe and Asia have a common origin. By the Rev. Joseph Edkins. Crown 8vo, pp. xxiii. and 403, cloth. 1871. 10s. 6d.

EDKINS.—INTRODUCTION TO THE STUDY OF THE CHINESE CHARACTERS. By J. Edkins, D.D., Peking, China. Royal 8vo, pp. 340, paper boards. 1876. 18s.

EDKINS.—RELIGION IN CHINA. See English and Foreign Philosophical Library, Vol. VIII., or Trübner's Oriental Series.

EDKINS.—CHINESE BUDDHISM. See Trübner's Oriental Series.

EDMONDS.—GREEK LAYS, IDYLLS, LEGENDS, &c. A Selection from Recent and Contemporary Poets. Translated by E. M. Edmonds. With Introduction and Notes. Crown 8vo, pp. xiv. and 264, cloth. 1885. 6s. 6d.

EDMUNDSON.—MILTON AND VONDEL: a Curiosity of Literature. By George Edmundson, M.A., Late Fellow and Tutor of Brasenose College, Oxford, Vicar of Northolt, Middlesex. Crown 8vo, pp.   , cloth.

EDWARDS.—MEMOIRS OF LIBRARIES, together with a Practical Handbook of Library Economy. By Edward Edwards. Numerous Illustrations. 2 vols. royal 8vo, cloth. Vol. i. pp. xxviii. and 841; Vol. ii. pp. xxxvi. and 1104. 1859. £2, 8s.
DITTO, large paper, imperial 8vo, cloth. £4, 4s.

EDWARDS.—CHAPTERS OF THE BIOGRAPHICAL HISTORY OF THE FRENCH ACADEMY. 1629-1863. With an Appendix relating to the Unpublished Chronicle "Liber de Hyda." By Edward Edwards. 8vo, pp. 180, cloth. 1864. 6s.
DITTO, large paper, royal 8vo. 10s. 6d.

EDWARDS.—LIBRARIES AND FOUNDERS OF LIBRARIES. By Edward Edwards. 8vo, pp. xix. and 506, cloth. 1865. 18s.
DITTO, large paper, imperial 8vo, cloth. £1, 10s.

EDWARDS.—FREE TOWN LIBRARIES, their Formation, Management, and History in Britain, France, Germany, and America. Together with Brief Notices of Book Collectors, and of the respective Places of Deposit of their Surviving Collections. By Edward Edwards. 8vo, pp. xvi. and 634, cloth. 1869. 21s.

EDWARDS.—LIVES OF THE FOUNDERS OF THE BRITISH MUSEUM, with Notices of its Chief Augmentors and other Benefactors. 1570-1870. By Edward Edwards. With Illustrations and Plans. 2 vols. 8vo, pp. xii. and 780, cloth. 1870. 30s.

EDWARDES.—See ENGLISH AND FOREIGN PHILOSOPHICAL LIBRARY, Vol. XVII.

EGER.—TECHNOLOGICAL DICTIONARY IN THE ENGLISH AND GERMAN LANGUAGES. Edited by Gustav Eger, Professor of the Polytechnic School of Darmstadt, and Sworn Translator of the Grand Ducal Ministerial Departments. Technically Revised and Enlarged by Otto Brandes, Chemist. Two vols., royal 8vo, pp. viii. and 712, and pp. viii. and 970, cloth. 1884. £1, 7s.

EGER AND GRIME.—An Early English Romance. Edited from Bishop Percy's Folio Manuscripts, about 1650 A.D. By J. W. Hales, M.A., Fellow of Christ's College, Cambridge, and F. J. Furnivall, M.A., of Trinity Hall, Cambridge. 4to, large paper, half bound, Roxburghe style, pp. 64. 1867. 10s. 6d.

EGERTON.—SUSSEX FOLK AND SUSSEX WAYS. Stray Studies in the Wealden Formation of Human Nature. By the Rev. J. Coker Egerton, M.A., Rector of Burwash. Crown 8vo, pp. 140, cloth. 1884. 2s.

EGGELING.—See AUCTORES SANSKRITI, Vols. IV. and V.

EGYPT EXPLORATION FUND :—
THE STORE-CITY OF PITHOM, and the Route of the Exodus. By Edouard Naville. 4to, pp. viii. and 32, with Thirteen Plates and Two Maps, boards. 1885. 25s.

EGYPTIAN GENERAL STAFF PUBLICATIONS :—
GENERAL REPORT ON THE PROVINCE OF KORDOFAN. Submitted to General C. P. Stone, Chief of the General Staff Egyptian Army. By Major H. G. Prout, Commanding Expedition of Reconnaissance. Made at El-Obeiyad (Kordofan), March 12th, 1876. Royal 8vo, pp. 232, stitched, with 6 Maps. 1877. 10s. 6d.
PROVINCES OF THE EQUATOR: Summary of Letters and Reports of the Governor-General. Part 1. 1874. Royal 8vo, pp. viii. and 90, stitched, with Map. 1877. 5s.
REPORT ON THE SEIZURE BY THE ABYSSINIANS of the Geological and Mineralogical Reconnaissance Expedition attached to the General Staff of the Egyptian Army. By L. H. Mitchell, Chief of the Expedition. Containing an Account of the subsequent Treatment of the Prisoners and Final Release of the Commander. Royal 8vo, pp. xii. and 126, stitched, with a Map. 1878. 7s. 6d.

EGYPTIAN CALENDAR for the year 1295 A.H. (1878 A.D.) : Corresponding with the years 1594, 1595 of the Koptic Era. 8vo, pp. 98, sewed. 1878. 2s. 6d.

EHRLICH.—FRENCH READER : With Notes and Vocabulary. By H. W. Ehrlich. 12mo, pp. viii. and 125, limp cloth. 1877. 1s. 6d.

EITEL.—BUDDHISM : Its Historical, Theoretical, and Popular Aspects. In Three Lectures. By E. J. Eitel, M.A., Ph.D. Third Revised Edition. Demy 8vo, pp. x.-146. 1884. 5s.

EITEL.—FENG-SHUI ; or, The Rudiments of Natural Science in China. By E. J. Eitel, M.A., Ph.D. Royal 8vo, pp. vi. and 84, sewed. 1873. 6s.

EITEL.—HANDBOOK FOR THE STUDENT OF CHINESE BUDDHISM. By the Rev. E. J. Eitel, of the London Missionary Society. Crown 8vo, pp. viii. and 224, cloth. 1870. 18s.

ELLIOT.—MEMOIRS ON THE HISTORY, FOLK-LORE, AND DISTRIBUTION OF THE RACES OF THE NORTH-WESTERN PROVINCES OF INDIA. By the late Sir Henry M. Elliot, K.C.B. Edited, revised, and rearranged by John Beames, M.R.A.S., &c., &c. In 2 vols. demy 8vo, pp. xx., 370, and 396, with 3 large coloured folding Maps, cloth. 1869. £1 16s.

ELLIOT.—THE HISTORY OF INDIA, as told by its own Historians. The Muhammadan Period. Edited from the Posthumous Papers of the late Sir H. M. Elliot, K.C.B., East India Company's Bengal Civil Service. Revised and continued by Professor John Dowson, M.R.A.S., Staff College, Sandhurst. 8vo. Vol. I.—Vol. II., pp. x. and 580, cloth. Vol. III., pp. xii. and 627, cloth. 24s.—Vol. IV., pp. xii. and 564, cloth. 1872. 21s.—Vol. V., pp. x. and 576, cloth. 1873. 21s.—Vol. VI., pp. viii. 574, cloth. 21s.—Vol. VII., pp. viii.-574. 1877. 21s. Vol. VIII., pp. xxxii.-444. With Biographical, Geographical, and General Index. 1877. 24s. Complete sets, £8, 8s. Vols. I. and II. not sold separately.

ELLIS.—ETRUSCAN NUMERALS. By Robert Ellis, B.D., late Fellow of St. John's College, Cambridge. 8vo, pp. 52, sewed. 1876. 2s. 6d.

ELY.—FRENCH AND GERMAN SOCIALISM IN MODERN TIMES. By R. T. Ely, Ph.D., Associate Professor of Political Economy in the Johns Hopkins University, Baltimore ; and Lecturer on Political Economy in Cornell University, Ithaca, N. Y. Crown 8vo, pp. viii.-274, cloth. 1884. 3s. 6d.

EMERSON AT HOME AND ABROAD. See English and Foreign Philosophical Library, Vol. XIX.

EMERSON.—INDIAN MYTHS ; or, Legends, Traditions, and Symbols of the Aborigines of America, compared with those of other Countries, including Hindostan, Egypt, Persia, Assyria, and China. By Ellen Russell Emerson. Illustrated. Post 8vo, pp. viii.-678, cloth. 1884. £1, 1s.

ENGLISH DIALECT SOCIETY.—Subscription, 10s. 6d. per annum. List of publications on application.

ENGLISH AND FOREIGN PHILOSOPHICAL LIBRARY (THE).
Post 8vo, cloth, uniformly bound.

I. to III.—A HISTORY OF MATERIALISM, and Criticism of its present Importance. By Professor F. A. Lange. Authorised Translation from the German by Ernest C. Thomas. In three volumes. Vol. I. Second Edition. pp. 350. 1878. 10s. 6d.—Vol. II., pp. viii. and 398. 1880. 10s. 6d. —Vol. III., pp. viii. and 376. 1881. 10s. 6d.

IV.—NATURAL LAW: an Essay in Ethics. By Edith Simcox. Second Edition. Pp. 366. 1878. 10s. 6d.

V. and VI.—THE CREED OF CHRISTENDOM; its Foundations contrasted with Superstructure. By W. R. Greg. Eighth Edition, with a New Introduction. In two volumes, pp. cxiv.-154 and vi.-282. 1883. 15s.

VII.—OUTLINES OF THE HISTORY OF RELIGION TO THE SPREAD OF THE UNIVERSAL RELIGIONS. By Prof. C. P. Tiele. Translated from the Dutch by J. Estlin Carpenter, M.A., with the author's assistance. Third Edition. Pp. xx. and 250. 1884. 7s. 6d.

VIII.—RELIGION IN CHINA; containing a brief Account of the Three Religions of the Chinese; with Observations on the Prospects of Christian Conversion amongst that People. By Joseph Edkins, D.D., Peking. Third Edition. Pp. xvi. and 260. 1884. 7s. 6d.

IX.—A CANDID EXAMINATION OF THEISM. By Physicus. Pp. 216. 1878. 7s. 6d.

X.—THE COLOUR-SENSE; its Origin and Development; an Essay in Comparative Psychology. By Grant Allen, B.A., author of "Physiological Æsthetics." Pp. xii. and 282. 1879. 10s. 6d.

XI.—THE PHILOSOPHY OF MUSIC; being the substance of a Course of Lectures delivered at the Royal Institution of Great Britain in February and March 1877. By William Pole, F.R.S., F.R.S.E., Mus. Doc., Oxon. Pp. 336. 1879. 10s. 6d.

XII.—CONTRIBUTIONS TO THE HISTORY OF THE DEVELOPMENT OF THE HUMAN RACE: Lectures and Dissertations, by Lazarus Geiger. Translated from the German by D. Asher, Ph.D. Pp. x. and 156. 1880. 6s.

XIII.—DR. APPLETON: his Life and Literary Relics. By J. H. Appleton, M.A., and A. H. Sayce, M.A. Pp. 350. 1881. 10s. 6d.

XIV.—EDGAR QUINET: His Early Life and Writings. By Richard Heath. With Portraits, Illustrations, and an Autograph Letter. Pp. xxiii. and 370. 1881. 12s. 6d.

XV.—THE ESSENCE OF CHRISTIANITY. By Ludwig Feuerbach. Translated from the German by Marian Evans, translator of Strauss's "Life of Jesus." Second Edition. Pp. xx. and 340. 1881. 7s. 6d.

XVI.—AUGUSTE COMTE AND POSITIVISM. By the late John Stuart Mill, M.P. Third Edition. Pp. 200. 1882. 3s. 6d.

XVII.—ESSAYS AND DIALOGUES OF GIACOMO LEOPARDI. Translated by Charles Edwardes. With Biographical Sketch. Pp. xliv. and 216. 1882. 7s. 6d.

XVIII.—RELIGION AND PHILOSOPHY IN GERMANY: A Fragment. By Heinrich Heine. Translated by J. Snodgrass. Pp. xii. and 178, cloth. 1882. 6s.

XIX.—EMERSON AT HOME AND ABROAD. By M. D. Conway. Pp. viii. and 310. With Portrait. 1883. 10s. 6d.

XX.—ENIGMAS OF LIFE. By W. R. Greg. Fifteenth Edition, with a Postscript. CONTENTS: Realisable Ideals—Malthus Notwithstanding—Non-Survival of the Fittest—Limits and Directions of Human Development—The Significance of Life—De Profundis—Elsewhere—Appendix. Pp. xx. and 314, cloth. 1883. 10s. 6d.

ENGLISH AND FOREIGN PHILOSOPHICAL LIBRARY—*continued.*

XXI.—ETHIC DEMONSTRATED IN GEOMETRICAL ORDER AND DIVIDED INTO FIVE PARTS, which treat (1) Of God, (2) Of the Nature and Origin of the Mind, (3) Of the Origin and Nature of the Affects, (4) Of Human Bondage, or of the Strength of the Affects, (5) Of the Power of the Intellect, or of Human Liberty. By Benedict de Spinoza. Translated from the Latin by William Hale White. Pp. 328. 1883. 10s. 6d.

XXII.—THE WORLD AS WILL AND IDEA. By Arthur Schopenhauer. Translated from the German by R. B. Haldane, M.A., and John Kemp, M.A. 3 vols. Vol. I., pp. xxxii.-532. 1883. 18s.

XXV. to XXVII.—THE PHILOSOPHY OF THE UNCONSCIOUS. By Eduard Von Hartmann. Speculative Results, according to the Inductive Method of Physical Science. Authorised Translation, by William C. Coupland, M.A. 3 vols. pp. xxxii.-372; vi.-368; viii.-360. 1884. 31s. 6d.

XXVIII. to XXX.—THE GUIDE OF THE PERPLEXED OF MAIMONIDES. Translated from the Original Text and Annotated by M. Friedlander, Ph.D. 3 vols., pp.

Extra Series.

I. and II.—LESSING : His Life and Writings. By James Sime, M.A. Second Edition. 2 vols., pp. xxii. and 328, and xvi. and 358, with portraits. 1879. 21s.

III. and VI.—AN ACCOUNT OF THE POLYNESIAN RACE: its Origin and Migrations, and the Ancient History of the Hawaiian People to the Times of Kamehameha I. By Abraham Fornander, Circuit Judge of the Island of Maui, H.I. Vol. I., pp. xvi. and 248. 1877. 7s. 6d. Vol. II., pp. viii. and 400, cloth. 1880. 10s. 6d.

IV. and V.—ORIENTAL RELIGIONS, and their Relation to Universal Religion—India. By Samuel Johnson. In 2 vols., pp. viii. and 408; viii. and 402. 1879. 21s.

VI.—AN ACCOUNT OF THE POLYNESIAN RACE. By A. Fornander. Vol. II., pp. viii. and 400, cloth. 1880. 10s. 6d.

ER SIE ES.—FACSIMILE OF A MANUSCRIPT supposed to have been found in an Egyptian Tomb by the English soldiers last year. Royal 8vo, in ragged canvas covers, with string binding, with dilapidated edges (? just as discovered). 1884. 6s. 6d.

EYTON.—DOMESDAY STUDIES : AN ANALYSIS AND DIGEST OF THE STAFFORDSHIRE SURVEY. Treating of the Method of Domesday in its Relation to Staffordshire, &c. By the Rev. R. W. Eyton. 4to, pp. vii. and 135, cloth. 1881. £1, 1s.

FABER.—THE MIND OF MENCIUS. See Trübner's Oriental Series.

FALKE.—ART IN THE HOUSE. Historical, Critical, and Æsthetical Studies on the Decoration and Furnishing of the Dwelling. By J. von Falke, Vice-Director of the Austrian Museum of Art and Industry at Vienna. Translated from the German. Edited, with Notes, by C. C. Perkins, M.A. Royal 8vo, pp. xxx. 356, cloth. With Coloured Frontispiece, 60 Plates, and over 150 Illustrations. 1878. £3.

FARLEY.—EGYPT, CYPRUS, AND ASIATIC TURKEY. By J. L. Farley, author of "The Resources of Turkey," &c. 8vo, pp. xvi. and 270, cloth gilt. 1878. 10s. 6d.

FAUSBOLL.—See JATAKA.

FEATHERMAN.—THE SOCIAL HISTORY OF THE RACES OF MANKIND. By A. Featherman. Demy 8vo, cloth. Vol. I. THE NIGRITIANS. Pp. xxvi. and 800. 1885. £1, 11s. 6d. Vol. V. THE ARAMÆANS. Pp. xvii. and 664. 1881. £1, 1s.

FENTON.—EARLY HEBREW LIFE: a Study in Sociology. By John Fenton. 8vo, pp. xxiv. and 102, cloth. 1880. 5s.

FERGUSSON.—ARCHÆOLOGY IN INDIA. With especial reference to the works of Babu Rajendralala Mitra. By James Fergusson, C.I.E., F.R.S., D.C.L., LL.D., V.-P.R.A.S., &c. Demy 8vo, pp. 116, with Illustrations, sewed. 1884. 5s.

FERGUSSON.—THE TEMPLE OF DIANA AT EPHESUS. With Especial Reference to Mr. Wood's Discoveries of its Remains. By James Fergusson, C.I.E., D.C.L., LL.D., F.R.S., &c. From the Transactions of the Royal Institute of British Architects. Demy 4to, pp. 24, with Plan, cloth. 1883. 5s.

FERGUSSON AND BURGESS.—THE CAVE TEMPLES OF INDIA. By James Fergusson, D.C.L., F.R.S., and James Burgess, F.R.G.S. Impl. 8vo, pp. xx. and 536, with 98 Plates, half bound. 1880. £2, 2s.

FERGUSSON.—CHINESE RESEARCHES. First Part. Chinese Chronology and Cycles. By Thomas Fergusson, Member of the North China Branch of the Royal Asiatic Society. Crown 8vo, pp. viii. and 274, sewed. 1881. 10s. 6d.

FEUERBACH.—THE ESSENCE OF CHRISTIANITY. See English and Foreign Philosophical Library, vol. XV.

FICHTE.—J. G. FICHTE'S POPULAR WORKS: The Nature of the Scholar—The Vocation of Man—The Doctrine of Religion. With a Memoir by William Smith, LL.D. Demy 8vo, pp. viii. and 564, cloth. 1873. 15s.

FICHTE.—CHARACTERISTICS OF THE PRESENT AGE. By J. G. Fichte. Translated from the German by W. Smith. Post 8vo, pp. xi. and 271, cloth. 1847. 6s.

FICHTE.—MEMOIR OF JOHANN GOTTLIEB FICHTE. By William Smith. Second Edition. Post 8vo, pp. 168, cloth. 1848. 4s.

FICHTE.—ON THE NATURE OF THE SCHOLAR, AND ITS MANIFESTATIONS. By Johann Gottlieb Fichte. Translated from the German by William Smith. Second Edition. Post 8vo, pp. vii. and 131, cloth. 1848. 3s.

FICHTE.—NEW EXPOSITION OF THE SCIENCE OF KNOWLEDGE. By J. G. Fichte. Translated from the German by A. E. Kroeger. 8vo, pp. vi. and 182, cloth. 1869. 6s.

FIELD.—OUTLINES OF AN INTERNATIONAL CODE. By David Dudley Field. Second Edition. Royal 8vo, pp. iii. and 712, sheep. 1876. £2, 2s.

FIGANIERE.—ELVA: A STORY OF THE DARK AGES. By Viscount de Figanière, G.C. St. Anne, &c. Crown 8vo, pp. viii. and 194, cloth. 1878. 5s.

FINN.—PERSIAN FOR TRAVELLERS. By Alexander Finn, F.R.G.S., &c., H.B.M. Consul at Resht. Oblong 32mo, pp. xxii.-232, cloth. 1884. 5s.

FISKE.—THE UNSEEN WORLD, and other Essays. By John Fiske, M.A., LL.B. Crown 8vo, pp. 350. 1876. 10s.

FISKE.—MYTHS AND MYTH-MAKERS; Old Tales and Superstitions, interpreted by Comparative Mythology. By John Fiske, M.A., LL.B., Assistant Librarian, and late Lecturer on Philosophy at Harvard University. Crown 8vo, pp. 260, cloth. 1873. 10s.

FITZGERALD.—AUSTRALIAN ORCHIDS. By R. D. Fitzgerald, F.L.S. Folio.—Part I. 7 Plates.—Part II. 10 Plates.—Part III. 10 Plates.—Part IV. 10 Plates.—Part V. 10 Plates.—Part VI. 10 Plates. Each Part, Coloured 21s.; Plain, 10s. 6d. —Part VII. 10 Plates. Vol. II., Part I. 10 Plates. Each, Coloured, 25s.

FITZGERALD.—AN ESSAY ON THE PHILOSOPHY OF SELF-CONSCIOUSNESS. Comprising an Analysis of Reason and the Rationale of Love. By P. F. Fitzgerald. Demy 8vo, pp. xvi. and 196, cloth. 1882. 5s.

FORJETT.—EXTERNAL EVIDENCES OF CHRISTIANITY. By E. H. Forjett. 8vo, pp. 114, cloth. 1874. 2s. 6d.

FORNANDER.—THE POLYNESIAN RACE. See English and Foreign Philosophical Library, Extra Series, Vols. III. and VI.

FORSTER.—POLITICAL PRESENTMENTS.—By William Forster, Agent-General for New South Wales. Crown 8vo, pp. 122, cloth. 1878. 4s. 6d.

FOULKES.—THE DAYA BHAGA, the Law of Inheritance of the Sarasvati Vilasa. The Original Sanskrit Text, with Translation by the Rev. Thos. Foulkes, F.L.S., M.R.A.S., F.R.G.S., Fellow of the University of Madras, &c. Demy 8vo, pp. xxvi. and 194-162, cloth. 1881. 10s. 6d.

FOX.—MEMORIAL EDITION OF COLLECTED WORKS, by W. J. Fox. 12 vols. 8vo, cloth. £3.

FRANKLYN.—Outlines of Military Law, and the Laws of Evidence. By H. B. Franklyn, LL.B. Crown 16mo, pp. viii. and 152, cloth. 1874. 3s. 6d.

FREEMAN.—Lectures to American Audiences. By E. A. Freeman, D.C.L., LL.D., Honorary Fellow of Trinity College, Oxford. I. The English People in its Three Homes. II. The Practical Bearings of General European History. Post 8vo. pp. viii.-454, cloth. 1883. 8s. 6d.

FRIEDRICH.—Progressive German Reader, with Copious Notes to the First Part. By P. Friedrich. Crown 8vo, pp. 166, cloth. 1868. 4s. 6d.

FRIEDRICH.—A Grammatical Course of the German Language. See under Dusar.

FRIEDRICH.—A Grammar of the German Language, with Exercises. See under Dusar.

FRIEDERICI.—Bibliotheca Orientalis, or a Complete List of Books, Papers, Serials, and Essays, published in England and the Colonies, Germany and France, on the History, Geography, Religions, Antiquities, Literature, and Languages of the East. Compiled by Charles Friederici. 8vo, boards. 1876, 2s. 6d. 1877, 3s. 1878, 3s. 6d. 1879, 3s. 1880, 3s. 1881, 3s. 1882, 3s. 1883, 3s. 6d.

FRŒMBLING.—Graduated German Reader. Consisting of a Selection from the most Popular Writers, arranged progressively; with a complete Vocabulary for the first part. By Friedrich Otto Frœmbling. Eighth Edition. 12mo, pp. viii. and 306, cloth. 1883. 3s. 6d.

FRŒMBLING.—Graduated Exercises for Translation into German. Consisting of Extracts from the best English Authors, arranged progressively; with an Appendix, containing Idiomatic Notes. By Friedrich Otto Frœmbling, Ph.D., Principal German Master at the City of London School. Crown 8vo, pp. xiv. and 322, cloth. With Notes, pp. 66. 1867. 4s. 6d. Without Notes, 4s.

FROUDE.—The Book of Job. By J. A. Froude, M.A., late Fellow of Exeter College, Oxford. Reprinted from the *Westminster Review*. 8vo, pp. 38, cloth. 1s.

FRUSTON.—Echo Français. A Practical Guide to French Conversation. By F. de la Fruston. With a Vocabulary. 12mo, pp. vi. and 192, cloth. 3s.

FRYER.—The Khyeng People of the Sandoway District, Arakan. By G. E. Fryer, Major, M.S.C., Deputy Commissioner, Sandoway. With 2 Plates. 8vo, pp. 44, cloth. 1875. 3s. 6d.

FRYER.—Páli Studies. No. I. Analysis, and Páli Text of the Subodhálankara, or Easy Rhetoric, by Sangharakkhita Thera. 8vo, pp. 35, cloth. 1875. 3s. 6d.

FURNIVALL.—Education in Early England. Some Notes used as forewords to a Collection of Treatises on "Manners and Meals in Olden Times," for the Early English Text Society. By Frederick J. Furnivall, M.A. 8vo, pp. 4 and lxxiv., sewed. 1867. 1s.

GALDOS.—Trafalgar: A Tale. By B. Perez Galdos. From the Spanish by Clara Bell. 16mo, pp. 256, cloth. 1884. 4s. Paper, 2s. 6d.

GALDOS.—Marianela. By B. Perez Galdos. From the Spanish, by Clara Bell. 16mo, pp. 264, cloth. 1883. 4s. Paper, 2s. 6d.

GALDOS.—Gloria: A Novel. By B. Perez Galdos. From the Spanish, by Clara Bell. Two volumes, 16mo, pp. vi. and 318, iv. and 362, cloth. 1883. 7s. 6d. Paper, 5s.

GALLOWAY.—A Treatise on Fuel. Scientific and Practical. By Robert Galloway, M.R.I.A., F.C.S., &c. With Illustrations. Post 8vo, pp. x. and 136, cloth. 1880. 6s.

GALLOWAY.—Education: Scientific and Technical; or, How the Inductive Sciences are Taught, and How they Ought to be Taught. By Robert Galloway, M.R.I.A., F.C.S. 8vo, pp. xvi. and 462, cloth. 1881. 10s. 6d.

GAMBLE.—A Manual of Indian Timbers: An Account of the Structure, Growth, Distribution, and Qualities of Indian Woods. By J. C. Gamble, M.A., F.L.S. 8vo, pp. xxx. and 522, with a Map, cloth. 1881. 10s.

GARBE.—See AUCTORES SANSKRITI, Vol. III.

GARFIELD.—THE LIFE AND PUBLIC SERVICE OF JAMES A. GARFIELD, Twentieth President of the United States. A Biographical Sketch. By Captain F. H. Mason, late of the 42d Regiment, U.S.A. With a Preface by Bret Harte. Crown 8vo, pp. vi. and 134, cloth. With Portrait. 1881. 2s. 6d.

GARRETT.—A CLASSICAL DICTIONARY OF INDIA: Illustrative of the Mythology, Philosophy, Literature, Antiquities, Arts, Manners, Customs, &c., of the Hindus. By John Garrett, Director of Public Instruction in Mysore. 8vo, pp. x. and 794, cloth. With Supplement, pp. 160. 1871 and 1873. £1, 16s.

GAUTAMA.—THE INSTITUTES OF. See AUCTORES SANSKRITI, Vol. II.

GAZETTEER OF THE CENTRAL PROVINCES OF INDIA. Edited by Charles Grant, Secretary to the Chief Commissioner of the Central Provinces. Second Edition. With a very large folding Map of the Central Provinces of India. Demy 8vo, pp. clvii. and 582, cloth. 1870. £1, 4s.

GEIGER.—A PEEP AT MEXICO; Narrative of a Journey across the Republic from the Pacific to the Gulf, in December 1873 and January 1874. By J. L. Geiger, F.R.G.S. Demy 8vo, pp. 368, with Maps and 45 Original Photographs. Cloth, 24s.

GEIGER.—CONTRIBUTIONS TO THE HISTORY OF THE DEVELOPMENT OF THE HUMAN RACE: Lectures and Dissertations, by Lazarus Geiger. Translated from the Second German Edition, by David Asher, Ph.D. Post 8vo, pp. x.–156, cloth. 1880. 6s.

GELDART.—FAITH AND FREEDOM. Fourteen Sermons. By E. M. Geldart, M.A. Crown 8vo, pp. vi. and 168, cloth. 1881. 4s. 6d.

GELDART.—A GUIDE TO MODERN GREEK. By E. M. Geldart, M.A. Post 8vo, pp. xii. and 274, cloth. 1883. 7s. 6d. Key, pp. 28, cloth. 1883. 2s. 6d.

GELDART.—GREEK GRAMMAR. See Trübner's Collection.

GEOLOGICAL MAGAZINE (THE); OR, MONTHLY JOURNAL OF GEOLOGY. With which is incorporated "The Geologist." Edited by Henry Woodward, LL.D., F.R.S., F.G.S., &c., of the British Museum. Assisted by Professor John Morris, M.A., F.G.S., &c., and Robert Etheridge, F.R.S., L. & E., F.G.S.; &c., of the Museum of Practical Geology. 8vo, cloth. 1866 to 1884. 20s. each.

GHOSE.—THE MODERN HISTORY OF THE INDIAN CHIEFS, RAJAS, ZAMINDARS, &c. By Loke Nath Ghose. 2 vols. post 8vo, pp. xii. and 218, and xviii. and 612, cloth. 1883. 21s.

GILES.—CHINESE SKETCHES.—By Herbert A. Giles, of H.B.M.'s China Consular Service. 8vo, pp. 204, cloth. 1875. 10s. 6d.

GILES.—A DICTIONARY OF COLLOQUIAL IDIOMS IN THE MANDARIN DIALECT. By Herbert A. Giles. 4to, pp. 65, half bound. 1873. 28s.

GILES.—SYNOPTICAL STUDIES IN CHINESE CHARACTER. By Herbert A. Giles. 8vo, pp. 118, half bound. 1874. 15s.

GILES.—CHINESE WITHOUT A TEACHER. Being a Collection of Easy and Useful Sentences in the Mandarin Dialect. With a Vocabulary. By Herbert A. Giles. 12mo, pp. 60, half bound. 1872. 5s.

GILES.—THE SAN TZU CHING; or, Three Character Classic; and the Ch'Jen Tsu Wen; or, Thousand Character Essay. Metrically Translated by Herbert A. Giles. 12mo, pp. 28, half bound. 1873. 2s. 6d.

GLASS.—ADVANCE THOUGHT. By Charles E. Glass. Crown 8vo, pp. xxxvi. and 188, cloth. 1876. 6s.

GOETHE'S FAUST.—See SCOONES and WYSARD.

GOETHE'S MINOR POEMS.—See SELSS.

GOLDSTÜCKER.—A DICTIONARY, SANSKRIT AND ENGLISH, extended and improved from the Second Edition of the Dictionary of Professor H. H. Wilson, with his sanction and concurrence. Together with a Supplement, Grammatical Appendices, and an Index, serving as a Sanskrit-English Vocabulary. By Theodore Goldstücker. Parts I. to VI. 4to, pp. 400. 1856-63. 6s. each.

GOLDSTÜCKER.—See AUCTORES SANSKRITI, Vol. I.

GOOROO SIMPLE. Strange Surprising Adventures of the Venerable G. S. and his Five Disciples, Noodle, Doodle, Wiseacre, Zany, and Foozle; adorned with Fifty Illustrations, drawn on wood, by Alfred Crowquill. A companion Volume to "Münchhausen" and "Owlglass," based upon the famous Tamul tale of the Gooroo Paramartan, and exhibiting, in the form of a skilfully-constructed consecutive narrative, some of the finest specimens of Eastern wit and humour. Elegantly printed on tinted paper, in crown 8vo, pp. 223, richly gilt ornamental cover, gilt edges. 1861. 10s. 6d.

GORKOM.—HANDBOOK OF CINCHONA CULTURE. By K. W. Van Gorkom, formerly Director of the Government Cinchona Plantations in Java. Translated by B. D. Jackson, Secretary of the Linnæan Society of London. With a Coloured Illustration. Imperial 8vo, pp. xii. and 292, cloth. 1882. £2.

GOUGH.—The SARVA-DARSANA-SAMGRAHA. See Trübner's Oriental Series.

GOUGH.—PHILOSOPHY OF THE UPANISHADS. See Trübner's Oriental Series.

GOVER.—THE FOLK-SONGS OF SOUTHERN INDIA. By C. E. Gover, Madras. Contents: Canarese Songs; Badaga Songs; Coorg Songs; **Tamil** Songs; The Cural; Malayalam Songs; Telugu Songs. 8vo, pp. xxviii. and 300, cloth. 1872. 10s. 6d.

GRAY.—DARWINIANA: Essays and Reviews pertaining to Darwinism. By Asa Gray. Crown 8vo, pp. xii. and 396, cloth. 1877. 10s.

GRAY.—NATURAL SCIENCE AND RELIGION: Two Lectures Delivered to the Theological School of Yale College. By Asa Gray. Crown 8vo, pp. 112, cloth. 1880. 5s.

GREEN.—SHAKESPEARE AND THE EMBLEM-WRITERS: An Exposition of their Similarities of Thought and Expression. Preceded by a View of the Emblem-Book Literature down to A.D. 1616. By Henry Green, M.A. In one volume, pp. xvi. 572, profusely illustrated with Woodcuts and Photolith. Plates, elegantly bound in cloth gilt. 1870. Large medium 8vo, £1, 11s. 6d.; large imperial 8vo, £2, 12s. 6d.

GREEN.—ANDREA ALCIATI, and his Books of Emblems: A Biographical and Bibliographical Study. By Henry Green, M.A. With Ornamental Title, Portraits, and other Illustrations. Dedicated to Sir William Stirling-Maxwell, Bart., Rector of the University of Edinburgh. Only 250 copies printed. Demy 8vo, pp. 360, handsomely bound. 1872. £1, 1s.

GREENE.—A NEW METHOD OF LEARNING TO READ, WRITE, AND SPEAK THE FRENCH LANGUAGE; or, First Lessons in French (Introductory to Ollendorff's Larger Grammar). By G. W. Greene, Instructor in Modern Languages in Brown University. Third Edition, enlarged and rewritten. Fcap. 8vo, pp. 248, cloth. 1869. 3s. 6d.

GREENE.—THE HEBREW MIGRATION FROM EGYPT. By J. Baker Greene, LL.B., M.B., Trin. Coll., Dub. Second Edition. Demy 8vo, pp. xii. and 440, cloth. 1882. 10s. 6d.

GREG.—TRUTH VERSUS EDIFICATION. By W. R. Greg. Fcap. 8vo, pp. 32, cloth. 1869. 1s.

GREG.—WHY ARE WOMEN REDUNDANT? By W. R. Greg. Fcap. 8vo, pp. 40, cloth. 1869. 1s.

GREG.—LITERARY AND SOCIAL JUDGMENTS. By W. R. Greg. Fourth Edition, considerably enlarged. 2 vols. crown 8vo, pp. 310 and 288, cloth. 1877. 15s.

GREG.—Mistaken Aims and Attainable Ideals of the Artisan Class. By W. R. Greg. Crown 8vo, pp. vi. and 332, cloth. 1876. 10s. 6d.

GREG.—Enigmas of Life. By W. R. Greg. Fifteenth Edition, with a postscript. Contents: Realisable Ideals. Malthus Notwithstanding. Non-Survival of the Fittest. Limits and Directions of Human Development. The Significance of Life. De Profundis. Elsewhere. Appendix. Post 8vo, pp. xxii. and 314, cloth. 1883. 10s. 6d.

GREG.—Political Problems for our Age and Country. By W. R. Greg. Contents: I. Constitutional and Autocratic Statesmanship. II. England's Future Attitude and Mission. III. Disposal of the Criminal Classes. IV. Recent Change in the Character of English Crime. V. The Intrinsic Vice of Trade-Unions. VI. Industrial and Co-operative Partnerships. VII. The Economic Problem. VIII. Political Consistency. IX. The Parliamentary Career. X. The Price we pay for Self-government. XI. Vestryism. XII. Direct v. Indirect Taxation. XIII. The New Régime, and how to meet it. Demy 8vo, pp. 342, cloth. 1870. 10s. 6d.

GREG.—The Great Duel: Its True Meaning and Issues. By W. R. Greg. Crown 8vo, pp. 96, cloth. 1871. 2s. 6d.

GREG.—The Creed of Christendom. See English and Foreign Philosophical Library, Vols. V. and VI.

GREG.—Rocks Ahead; or, The Warnings of Cassandra. By W. R. Greg. Second Edition, with a Reply to Objectors. Crown 8vo, pp. xliv. and 236, cloth. 1874. 9s.

GREG.—Miscellaneous Essays. By W. R. Greg. First Series. Crown 8vo, pp. iv.–268, cloth. 1881. 7s. 6d.
   Contents:—Rocks Ahead and Harbours of Refuge. Foreign Policy of Great Britain. The Echo of the Antipodes. A Grave Perplexity before us. Obligations of the Soil. The Right Use of a Surplus. The Great Twin Brothers: Louis Napoleon and Benjamin Disraeli. Is the Popular Judgment in Politics more Just than that of the Higher Orders? Harriet Martineau. Verify your Compass. The Prophetic Element in the Gospels. Mr. Frederick Harrison on the Future Life. Can Truths be Apprehended which could not have been Discovered?

GREG.—Miscellaneous Essays. By W. R. Greg. Second Series. Pp. 294. 1884. 7s. 6d.
   Contents:—France since 1848. France in January 1852. England as it is. Sir R. Peel's Character and Policy. Employment of our Asiatic Forces in European Wars.

GRIFFIN.—The Rajas of the Punjab. Being the History of the Principal States in the Punjab, and their Political Relations with the British Government. By Lepel H. Griffin, Bengal Civil Service, Acting Secretary to the Government of the Punjab, Author of "The Punjab Chiefs," &c. Second Edition. Royal 8vo, pp. xvi. and 630, cloth. 1873. £1, 1s.

GRIFFIN.—The World under Glass. By Frederick Griffin, Author of "The Destiny of Man," "The Storm King," and other Poems. Fcap. 8vo, pp. 204, cloth gilt. 1879. 3s. 6d.

GRIFFIN.—The Destiny of Man, The Storm King, and other Poems. By F. Griffin. Second Edition. Fcap. 8vo, pp. vii.–104, cloth. 1883. 2s. 6d.

GRIFFIS.—The Mikado's Empire. Book I. History of Japan, from 660 B.C. to 1872 A.D.—Book II. Personal Experiences, Observations, and Studies in Japan, 1870–1874. By W. E. Griffis, A.M. Second Edition. 8vo, pp. 626, cloth. Illustrated. 1883. 20s.

GRIFFIS.—Japanese Fairy World. Stories from the Wonder-Lore of Japan. By W. E. Griffis. Square 16mo, pp. viii. and 304, with 12 Plates. 1880. 7s. 6d.

GRIFFITH.—The Birth of the War God. See Trübner's Oriental Series.

GRIFFITH.—YUSUF AND ZULAIKHA. See Trübner's Oriental Series.

GRIFFITH.—SCENES FROM THE RAMAYANA, MEGHADUTA, &c. Translated by Ralph T. H. Griffith, M.A., Principal of the Benares College. Second Edition. Crown 8vo, pp. xviii. and 244, cloth. 1870. 6s.

CONTENTS.—Preface—Ayodhya—Ravan Doomed—The Birth of Rama—The Heir-Apparent—Manthara's Guile—Dasaratha's Oath—The Step-mother—Mother and Son—The Triumph of Love—Farewell ?—The Hermit's Son—The Trial of Truth—The Forest—The Rape of Sita—Rama's Despair—The Messenger Cloud—Khumbakarna—The Suppliant Dove—True Glory—Feed the Poor—The Wise Scholar.

GRIFFITH.—THE RÁMÁYAN OF VÁLMÍKI. Translated into English Verse. By Ralph T. H. Griffith, M.A., Principal of the Benares College. Vol. I., containing Books I. and II., demy 8vo, pp. xxxii. and 440, cloth. 1870. —Vol. II., containing Book II., with additional Notes and Index of Names. Demy 8vo, pp. 504, cloth. 1871. —Vol. III., demy 8vo, pp. 390, cloth. 1872. —Vol. IV., demy 8vo, pp. viii. and 432, cloth. 1873. —Vol. V., demy 8vo, pp. viii. and 360, cloth. 1875. The complete work, 5 vols. £7, 7s.

GROTE.—REVIEW of the Work of Mr. John Stuart Mill entitled "Examination of Sir William Hamilton's Philosophy." By George Grote, Author of the "History of Ancient Greece," "Plato, and the other Companions of Socrates," &c. 12mo, pp. 112, cloth. 1868. 3s. 6d.

GROUT.—ZULU-LAND; or, Life among the Zulu-Kafirs of Natal and Zulu-Land, South Africa. By the Rev. Lewis Grout. Crown 8vo, pp. 352, cloth. With Map and Illustrations. 7s. 6d.

GROWSE.—MATHURA : A District Memoir. By F. S. Growse, B.C.S., M.A., Oxon, C.I.E., Fellow of the Calcutta University. Second edition, illustrated, revised, and enlarged, 4to, pp. xxiv. and 520, boards. 1880. 42s.

GUBERNATIS.—ZOOLOGICAL MYTHOLOGY ; or, The Legends of Animals. By Angelo de Gubernatis, Professor of Sanskrit and Comparative Literature in the Instituto di Studii Superori e di Perfezionamento at Florence, &c. 2 vols. 8vo, pp. xxvi. and 432, and vii. and 442, cloth. 1872. £1, 8s.

This work is an important contribution to the study of the comparative mythology of the Indo-Germanic nations. The author introduces the denizens of the air, earth, and water in the various characters assigned to them in the myths and legends of all civilised nations, and traces the migration of the mythological ideas from the times of the early Aryans to those of the Greeks, Romans, and Teutons.

GULSHAN I. RAZ: THE MYSTIC ROSE GARDEN OF SA'D UD DIN MAHMUD SHABISTARI. The Persian Text, with an English Translation and Notes, chiefly from the Commentary of Muhammed Bin Yahya Lahiji. By E. H. Whinfield, M.A., Barrister-at-Law, late of H.M.B.C.S. 4to, pp. xvi., 94, 60, cloth. 1880. 10s. 6d.

GUMPACH.—TREATY RIGHTS OF THE FOREIGN MERCHANT, and the Transit System in China. By Johannes von Gumpach. 8vo, pp. xviii. and 421, sewed. 10s. 6d.

HAAS.—CATALOGUE OF SANSKRIT AND PALI BOOKS IN THE BRITISH MUSEUM. By Dr. Ernst Haas. Printed by permission of the Trustees of the British Museum. 4to, pp. viii. and 188, paper boards. 1876. 21s.

HAFIZ OF SHIRAZ.—SELECTIONS FROM HIS POEMS. Translated from the Persian by Hermann Bicknell. With Preface by A. S. Bicknell. Demy 4to, pp. xx. and 384, printed on fine stout plate-paper, with appropriate Oriental Bordering in gold and colour, and Illustrations by J. R. Herbert, R.A. 1875. £2, 2s.

HAFIZ.—See Trübner's Oriental Series.

HAGEN.—NORICA ; or, Tales from the Olden Time. Translated from the German of August Hagen. Fcap. 8vo, pp. xiv. and 374. 1850. 5s.

HAGGARD.—CETYWAYO AND HIS WHITE NEIGHBOURS ; or, Remarks on Recent Events in Zululand, Natal, and the Transvaal. By H. R. Haggard. Crown 8vo, pp. xvi. and 294, cloth. 1882. 7s. 6d.

HAGGARD.—See "The Vazir of Lankuran."

HAHN.—Tsuni-||Goam, the Supreme Being of the Khoi-Khoi. By Theophilus Hahn, Ph.D., Custodian of the Grey Collection, Cape Town, &c., &c. Post 8vo, pp. xiv. and 154. 1882. 7s. 6d.

HALDANE.—See Schopenhauer, or English and Foreign Philosophical Library, vol. xxii.

HALDEMAN.—Pennsylvania Dutch: A Dialect of South Germany with an Infusion of English. By S. S. Haldeman, A.M., Professor of Comparative Philology in the University of Pennsylvania, Philadelphia. 8vo, pp. viii. and 70, cloth. 1872. 3s. 6d.

HALL.—On English Adjectives in -Able, with Special Reference to Reliable. By FitzEdward Hall, C.E., M.A., Hon. D.C.L. Oxon; formerly Professor of Sanskrit Language and Literature, and of Indian Jurisprudence in King's College, London. Crown 8vo, pp. viii. and 238, cloth. 1877. 7s. 6d.

HALL.—Modern English. By FitzEdward Hall, M.A., Hon. D.C.L. Oxon. Crown 8vo, pp. xvi. and 394, cloth. 1873. 10s. 6d.

HALL.—Sun and Earth as Great Forces in Chemistry. By T. W. Hall, M.D., L.R.C.S.E. Crown 8vo, pp. xii. and 220, cloth. 1874. 3s.

HALL.—The Pedigree of the Devil. By F. T. Hall, F.R.A.S. With Seven Autotype Illustrations from Designs by the Author. Demy 8vo, pp. xvi. and 256, cloth. 1883. 7s. 6d.

HALL.—Arctic Expedition. See Nourse.

HALLOCK.—The Sportsman's Gazetteer and General Guide. The Game Animals, Birds, and Fishes of North America: their Habits and various methods of Capture, &c., &c. With a Directory to the principal Game Resorts of the Country. By Charles Hallock. New Edition. Crown 8vo, cloth. Maps and Portrait. 1883. 15s.

HAM.—The Maid of Corinth. A Drama in Four Acts. By J. Panton Ham. Crown 8vo, pp. 65, sewed. 2s. 6d.

HARLEY.—The Simplification of English Spelling, specially adapted to the Rising Generation. An Easy Way of Saving Time in Writing, Printing, and Reading. By Dr. George Harley, F.R.S., F.C.S. 8vo, pp. 128, cloth. 1877. 2s. 6d.

HARRISON.—Woman's Handiwork in Modern Homes. By Constance Cary Harrison. With numerous Illustrations and Five Coloured Plates, from designs by Samuel Colman, Rosina Emmet, George Gibson, and others. 8vo, pp. xii. and 242, cloth. 1881. 10s.

HARTMANN.—See English and Foreign Philosophical Library, vol. XXV.

HARTZENBUSCH and LEMMING.—Eco de Madrid. A Practical Guide to Spanish Conversation. By J. E. Hartzenbusch and H. Lemming. Second Edition. Post 8vo, pp. 250, cloth. 1870. 5s.

HASE.—Miracle Plays and Sacred Dramas: An Historical Survey. By Dr. Karl Hase. Translated from the German by A. W. Jackson, and Edited by the Rev. W. W. Jackson, Fellow of Exeter College, Oxford. Crown 8vo, pp. 288. 1880. 9s.

HAUG.—Glossary and Index of the Pahlavi Texts of the Book of Arda Viraf, the Tale of Gosht—J. Fryano, the Hadokht Nask, and to some extracts from the Dinkard and Nirangistan; prepared from Destur Hoshangji Jamaspji Asa's Glossary to the Arda Viraf Namak, and from the Original Texts, with Notes on Pahlavi Grammar by E. W. West, Ph.D. Revised by M. Haug, Ph.D., &c. Published by order of the Bombay Government. 8vo, pp. viii. and 352, sewed. 1874. 25s.

HAUG.—THE SACRED LANGUAGE, &c., OF THE PARSIS. See Trübner's Oriental Series.

HAUPT.—THE LONDON ARBITRAGEUR; or, The English Money Market, in connection with Foreign Bourses. A Collection of Notes and Formulæ for the Arbitration of Bills, Stocks, Shares, Bullion, and Coins, with all the Important Foreign Countries. By Ottomar Haupt. Crown 8vo, pp. viii. and 196, cloth. 1870. 7s. 6d.

HAWKEN.—UPA-SASTRĀ: Comments, Linguistic, Doctrinal, on Sacred and Mythic Literature. By J. D. Hawken. Crown 8vo, pp. viii. and 288, cloth. 1877. 7s. 6d.

HAZEN.—THE SCHOOL AND THE ARMY IN GERMANY AND FRANCE, with a Diary of Siege Life at Versailles. By Brevet Major-General W. B. Hazen, U.S.A., Col. 6th Infantry. 8vo, pp. 408, cloth. 1872. 10s. 6d.

HEATH.—EDGAR QUINET. See English and Foreign Philosophical Library, Vol. XIV.

HEATON—AUSTRALIAN DICTIONARY OF DATES AND MEN OF THE TIME. Containing the History of Australasia from 1542 to May 1879. By I. H. Heaton. Royal 8vo, pp. iv. and 554, cloth. 15s.

HEBREW LITERATURE SOCIETY.

HECHLER.—THE JERUSALEM BISHOPRIC DOCUMENTS. With Translations, chiefly derived from "Das Evangelische Bisthum in Jerusalem," Geschichtliche Darlegung mit Urkunden. Berlin, 1842. Published by Command of His Majesty Frederick William IV., King of Prussia. Arranged and Supplemented by the Rev. Prof. William H. Hechler, British Chaplain at Stockholm. 8vo, pp. 212, with Maps, Portrait, and Illustrations, cloth. 1883. 10s. 6d.

HECKER.—THE EPIDEMICS OF THE MIDDLE AGES. Translated by G. B. Babington, M.D., F.R.S. Third Edition, completed by the Author's Treatise on Child-Pilgrimages. By J. F. C. Hecker. 8vo, pp. 384, cloth. 1859. 9s. 6d.

CONTENTS.—The Black Death—The Dancing Mania—The Sweating Sickness—Child Pilgrimages.

HEDLEY.—MASTERPIECES OF GERMAN POETRY. Translated in the Measure of the Originals, by F. H. Hedley. With Illustrations by Louis Wanke. Crown 8vo, pp. viii. and 120, cloth. 1876. 6s.

HEINE.—RELIGION AND PHILOSOPHY IN GERMANY. See English and Foreign Philosophical Library, Vol. XVIII.

HEINE.—WIT, WISDOM, AND PATHOS from the Prose of Heinrich Heine. With a few pieces from the "Book of Songs." Selected and Translated by J. Snodgrass. With Portrait. Crown 8vo, pp. xx. and 340, cloth. 1879. 7s. 6d.

HEINE.—PICTURES OF TRAVEL. Translated from the German of Henry Heine, by Charles G. Leland. 7th Revised Edition. Crown 8vo, pp. 472, with Portrait, cloth. 1873. 7s. 6d.

HEINE.—HEINE'S BOOK OF SONGS. Translated by Charles G. Leland. Fcap. 8vo, pp. xiv. and 240, cloth, gilt edges. 1874. 7s. 6d.

HEITZMANN.—MICROSCOPICAL MORPHOLOGY OF THE ANIMAL BODY IN HEALTH AND DISEASE. By C. Heitzmann, M.D. Royal 8vo, pp. xx.-850, cloth. 1884. 31s. 6d.

HENDRIK.—MEMOIRS OF HANS HENDRIK, THE ARCTIC TRAVELLER; serving under Kane, Hayes, Hall, and Nares, 1853-76. Written by Himself. Translated from the Eskimo Language, by Dr. Henry Rink. Edited by Prof. Dr. G. Stephens, F.S.A. Crown 8vo, pp. 100, Map, cloth. 1878. 3s. 6d.

HENNELL.—PRESENT RELIGION: As a Faith owning Fellowship with Thought. Vol. I. Part I. By Sara S. Hennell. Crown 8vo, pp. 570, cloth. 1865. 7s. 6d.

HENNELL.—COMPARATIVISM; An Introduction to the Second Part of "Present Religion," explaining the Principle by which Religion appears still to be set in Necessary Antagonism to Positivism. By Sara S. Hennell. 8vo, pp. 160, cloth. 1869. 3s.

HENNELL.—COMPARATIVE ETHICS—I. Section I. Moral Standpoint. Present Religion, Vol. III. By Sara S. Hennell. 8vo, pp. 66, wrapper. 1882. 2s.

HENNELL.—COMPARATIVE ETHICS—I. Sections II. and III. Moral Principle in Regard to Sexhood. Present Religion, Vol. III. By S. Hennell. Crown 8vo, pp. 92, wrapper. 1884. 2s.

HENNELL.—PRESENT RELIGION: As a Faith owning Fellowship with Thought. Part II. First Division. Intellectual Effect: shown as a Principle of Metaphysical Comparativism. By Sara S. Hennell. Crown 8vo, pp. 618, cloth. 1873. 7s. 6d.

HENNELL.—PRESENT RELIGION, Vol. III. Part II. Second Division. The Effect of Present Religion on its Practical Side. By S. S. Hennell. Crown 8vo, pp. 68, paper covers. 1882. 2s.

HENNELL.—COMPARATIVISM shown as Furnishing a Religious Basis to Morality. (Present Religion. Vol. III. Part II. Second Division: Practical Effect.) By Sara S. Hennell. Crown 8vo, pp. 220, stitched in wrapper. 1878. 3s. 6d.

HENNELL.—COMPARATIVE ETHICS. II. Sections I. and II. Moral Principle in regard to Brotherhood. (Present Religion, Vol. III.) By Sara S. Hennell. Crown 8vo, pp. 52, wrapper. 1884. 2s.

HENNELL.—THOUGHTS IN AID OF FAITH. Gathered chiefly from recent Works in Theology and Philosophy. By Sara S. Hennell. Post 8vo, pp. 428, cloth. 1860. 6s.

HENWOOD.—THE METALLIFEROUS DEPOSITS OF CORNWALL AND DEVON; with Appendices on Subterranean Temperature; the Electricity of Rocks and Veins: the Quantities of Water in the Cornish Mines; and Mining Statistics. (Vol. V. of the Transactions of the Royal Geographical Society of Cornwall.) By William Jory Henwood, F.R.S., F.G.S. 8vo, pp. x. and 515; with 113 Tables, and 12 Plates, half bound. £2, 2s.

HENWOOD.—OBSERVATIONS ON METALLIFEROUS DEPOSITS, AND ON SUBTERRANEAN TEMPERATURE. (Vol. VIII. of the Transactions of the Royal Geological Society of Cornwall.) By William Jory Henwood, F.R.S., F.G.S., President of the Royal Institution of Cornwall. In 2 Parts. 8vo, pp. xxx., vii. and 916; with 38 Tables, 31 Engravings on Wood, and 6 Plates. £1, 16s.

HEPBURN.—A JAPANESE AND ENGLISH DICTIONARY. With an English and Japanese Index. By J. C. Hepburn, M.D., LL.D. Second Edition. Imperial 8vo, pp. xxxii., 632, and 201, cloth. £8, 8s.

HEPBURN.—JAPANESE-ENGLISH AND ENGLISH-JAPANESE DICTIONARY. By J. C. Hepburn, M.D., LL.D. Abridged by the Author. Square fcap., pp. vi. and 536, cloth. 1873. 18s.

HERNISZ.—A GUIDE TO CONVERSATION IN THE ENGLISH AND CHINESE LANGUAGES, for the Use of Americans and Chinese in California and elsewhere. By Stanislas Hernisz. Square 8vo, pp. 274, sewed. 1855. 10s. 6d.

HERSHON.—TALMUDIC MISCELLANY. See Trübner's Oriental Series.

HERZEN.—DU DÉVELOPPEMENT DES IDÉES RÉVOLUTIONNAIRES EN RUSSIE. Par Alexander Herzen. 12mo, pp. xxiii. and 144, sewed. 1853. 2s. 6d.

HERZEN.—A separate list of A. Herzen's works in Russian may be had on application.

HILL.—THE HISTORY OF THE REFORM MOVEMENT in the Dental Profession in Great Britain during the last twenty years. By Alfred Hill, Licentiate in Dental Surgery, &c. Crown 8vo, pp. xvi. and 400, cloth. 1877. 10s. 6d.

HILLEBRAND.—FRANCE AND THE FRENCH IN THE SECOND HALF OF THE NINETEENTH CENTURY. By Karl Hillebrand. Translated from the Third German Edition. Post 8vo, pp. xx. and 262, cloth. 1881. 10s. 6d.

HINDOO MYTHOLOGY POPULARLY TREATED. Being an Epitomised Description of the various Heathen Deities illustrated on the Silver Swami Tea Service presented, as a memento of his visit to India, to H.R.H. the Prince of Wales, K.G., G.C.S.I., by His Highness the Gaekwar of Baroda. Small 4to, pp. 42, limp cloth. 1875. 3s. 6d.

HITTELL.—THE COMMERCE AND INDUSTRIES OF THE PACIFIC COAST OF NORTH AMERICA. By J. S. Hittell, **Author of** "The Resources of California." 4to, pp. 820. 1882. £1, 10s.

HODGSON.—ACADEMY LECTURES. **By** J. E. Hodgson, R.A., Librarian and Professor of Painting to the Royal Academy. Cr. 8vo, pp. viii. and 312, cloth. 1884. 7s. 6d.

HODGSON.—ESSAYS ON THE LANGUAGES, LITERATURE, AND RELIGION OF NEPÁL AND TIBET. Together with further Papers on the Geography, Ethnology, and Commerce of those Countries. By B. H. Hodgson, late British Minister at the Court of Nepál. Royal 8vo, cloth, pp. xii. and 276. 1874. 14s.

HODGSON.—ESSAYS ON INDIAN SUBJECTS. See Trübner's Oriental **Series.**

HODGSON.—THE EDUCATION OF GIRLS; AND THE EMPLOYMENT OF WOMEN OF THE UPPER CLASSES EDUCATIONALLY CONSIDERED. Two Lectures. By W. B. Hodgson, LL.D. Second Edition. Cr. 8vo, pp. xvi. and 114, cloth. 1869. 3s. 6d.

HODGSON.—TURGOT: His Life, Times, and Opinions. Two Lectures. By W. B. Hodgson, LL.D. Crown 8vo, pp. vi. and 83, sewed. 1870. 2s.

HOERNLE.—A COMPARATIVE GRAMMAR OF THE GAUDIAN LANGUAGES, with **Special** Reference to the Eastern Hindi. Accompanied by a Language Map, and a **Table** of Alphabets. By A. F. Rudolf Hoernle. Demy 8vo, pp. 474, cloth. 1880. 18s.

HOLBEIN SOCIETY.—Subscription, one guinea per annum. List of publications on application.

HOLMES-FORBES.—THE SCIENCE OF BEAUTY. An Analytical Inquiry into the Laws of Æsthetics. By Avary W. Holmes-Forbes, of Lincoln's Inn, Barrister-at-Law. Post 8vo, cloth, pp. vi. and 200. 1881. 6s.

HOLST.—THE CONSTITUTIONAL AND POLITICAL HISTORY OF THE UNITED STATES. By Dr. H. von Holst. Translated by J. J. Lalor and A. B. Mason. Royal 8vo. Vol. I. 1750-1833. State Sovereignty and Slavery. Pp. xvi. and 506. 1876. 18s.—Vol. II. 1828-1846. Jackson's Administration—Annexation of Texas. Pp. 720. 1879. £1, 2s.—Vol. III. 1846-1850. Annexation of Texas—Compromise of 1850. Pp. x. and 598. 1881. 18s.

HOLYOAKE.—TRAVELS IN SEARCH OF A SETTLER'S GUIDE-BOOK OF AMERICA AND CANADA. By George Jacob Holyoake, Author of "The History of Co-operation in England." Post 8vo, pp. 148, wrapper. 1884. 2s. 6d.

HOLYOAKE.—THE HISTORY OF CO-OPERATION IN ENGLAND: its Literature and its Advocates. By G. J. Holyoake. Vol. I. The Pioneer Period, 1812-44. Crown 8vo, pp. xii. and 420, cloth. 1875. 4s.—Vol. II. The Constructive Period, 1845-78. Crown 8vo, pp. x. and 504, **cloth.** 1878. 8s.

HOLYOAKE.—THE TRIAL OF THEISM ACCUSED OF OBSTRUCTING SECULAR LIFE. By G. J. Holyoake. Crown 8vo, pp. xvi. and 256, cloth. 1877. 2s. 6d.

HOLYOAKE.—REASONING FROM **FACTS**: A Method **of** Everyday Logic. By **G. J.** Holyoake. Fcap., pp. xii. and 94, wrapper. 1877. **1s.** 6d.

HOLYOAKE.—SELF-HELP BY THE PEOPLE. Thirty-three Years of Co-operation in Rochdale. In Two Parts. Part I., 1844-1857; Part II., 1857-1877. By G. J. Holyoake. **Ninth** Edition. Crown 8vo, pp. 174, cloth. 1883. 2s. 6d.

HOPKINS.—ELEMENTARY GRAMMAR OF THE TURKISH LANGUAGE. With a few Easy Exercises. By F. L. Hopkins, M.A., Fellow and Tutor of Trinity Hall, Cambridge. **Crown** 8vo, pp. 48, cloth. 1877. 3s. 6d.

HORDER.—A SELECTION FROM "THE BOOK OF PRAISE FOR CHILDREN," as Edited by W. Garrett Horder. For the Use of Jewish Children. Fcap. 8vo, pp. 80, cloth. 1883. 1s. 6d.

HOSMER.—THE PEOPLE AND POLITICS; or, The Structure of States and the Significance and Relation of Political Forms. By G. W. Hosmer, M.D. Demy 8vo, pp. viii. and 310, cloth. 1883. 15s.

HOWELLS.—A LITTLE GIRL AMONG THE OLD MASTERS. With Introduction and Comment. By W. D. Howells. Oblong crown 8vo, cloth, pp. 66, with 54 plates. 1884. 10s.

HOWELLS.—Dr. Breen's Practice: A Novel. By W. D. Howells. English Copyright Edition. Crown 8vo, pp. 272, cloth. 1882. 6s.

HOWSE.—A Grammar of the Cree Language. With which is combined an Analysis of the Chippeway Dialect. By Joseph Howse, F.R.G.S. 8vo, pp. xx. and 324, cloth. 1865. 7s. 6d.

HULME.—Mathematical Drawing Instruments, and How to Use Them. By F. Edward Hulme, F.L.S., F.S.A., Art-Master of Marlborough College, Author of "Principles of Ornamental Art," &c. With Illustrations. Second Edition. Imperial 16mo, pp. xvi. and 152, cloth. 1881. 3s. 6d.

HUMBERT.—On "Tenant Right." By C. F. Humbert. 8vo, pp. 20, sewed. 1875. 1s.

HUMBOLDT.—The Sphere and Duties of Government. Translated from the German of Baron Wilhelm Von Humboldt by Joseph Coulthard, jun. Post 8vo, pp. xv. and 203, cloth. 1854. 5s.

HUMBOLDT.—Letters of William Von Humboldt to a Female Friend. A complete Edition. Translated from the Second German Edition by Catherine M. A. Couper, with a Biographical Notice of the Writer. 2 vols. crown 8vo, pp. xxviii. and 592, cloth. 1867. 10s.

HUNT.—The Religion of the Heart. A Manual of Faith and Duty. By Leigh Hunt. Fcap. 8vo, pp. xxiv. and 259, cloth. 2s. 6d.

HUNT.—Chemical and Geological Essays. By Professor T. Sterry Hunt. Second Edition. 8vo, pp. xxii. and 448, cloth. 1879. 12s.

HUNTER.—A Comparative Dictionary of the Non-Aryan Languages of India and High Asia. With a Dissertation, Political and Linguistic, on the Aboriginal Races. By W. W. Hunter, B.A., M.R.A.S., Hon. Fel. Ethnol. Soc., Author of the "Annals of Rural Bengal," of H.M.'s Civil Service. Being a Lexicon of 144 Languages, illustrating Turanian Speech. Compiled from the Hodgson Lists, Government Archives, and Original MSS., arranged with Prefaces and Indices in English, French, German, Russian, and Latin. Large 4to, toned paper, pp. 230, cloth. 1869. 42s.

HUNTER.—The Indian Musalmans. By W. W. Hunter, B.A., LL.D., Director-General of Statistics to the Government of India, &c., Author of the "Annals of Rural Bengal," &c. Third Edition. 8vo, pp. 219, cloth. 1876. 10s. 6d.

HUNTER.—Famine Aspects of Bengal Districts. A System of Famine Warnings. By W. W. Hunter, B.A., LL.D. Crown 8vo, pp. 216, cloth. 1874. 7s. 6d.

HUNTER.—A Statistical Account of Bengal. By W. W. Hunter, B.A., LL.D., Director-General of Statistics to the Government of India, &c. In 20 vols. 8vo, half morocco. 1877. £5.

HUNTER.—Catalogue of Sanskrit Manuscripts (Buddhist). Collected in Nepal by B. H. Hodgson, late Resident at the Court of Nepal. Compiled from Lists in Calcutta, France, and England, by W. W. Hunter, C.I.E., LL.D. 8vo, pp. 28, paper. 1880. 2s.

HUNTER.—The Imperial Gazetteer of India. By W. W. Hunter, C.I.E., LL.D., Director-General of Statistics to the Government of India. In Nine Volumes. 8vo, pp. xxxiii. and 544, 539, 567, xix. and 716, 509, 513, 555, 537, and xii. and 478, half morocco. With Maps. 1881.

HUNTER.—The Indian Empire: Its History, People, and Products. By W. W. Hunter, C.I.E., LL.D. Post 8vo, pp. 568, with Map, cloth. 1882. 16s.

HUNTER.—An Account of the British Settlement of Aden, in Arabia. Compiled by Capt. F. M. Hunter, Assistant Political Resident, Aden. 8vo, pp. xii. and 232, half bound. 1877. 7s. 6d.

HUNTER.—A Statistical Account of Assam. By W. W. Hunter, B.A., LL.D., C.I.E., Director-General of Statistics to the Government of India, &c. 2 vols. 8vo, pp. 420 and 490, with 2 Maps, half morocco. 1879. 10s.

HUNTER.—A BRIEF HISTORY OF THE INDIAN PEOPLE. By W. W. Hunter, C.I.E., LL.D. Fourth Edition. Crown 8vo, pp. 222, cloth. With Map. 1884. 3s. 6d.

HURST.—HISTORY OF RATIONALISM: embracing a Survey of the Present State of Protestant Theology. By the Rev. John F. Hurst, A.M. With Appendix of Literature. Revised and enlarged from the Third American Edition. Crown 8vo, pp. xvii. and 525, cloth. 1867. 10s. 6d.

HYETT.—PROMPT REMEDIES FOR ACCIDENTS AND POISONS: Adapted to the use of the Inexperienced till Medical aid arrives. By W. H. Hyett, F.R.S. A Broadsheet, to hang up in Country Schools or Vestries, Workshops, Offices of Factories, Mines and Docks, on board Yachts, in Railway Stations, remote Shooting Quarters, Highland Manses, and Private Houses, wherever the Doctor lives at a distance. Sold for the benefit of the Gloucester Eye Institution. In sheets, 21½ by 17¼ inches, 2s. 6d.; mounted, 3s. 6d.

HYMANS.—PUPIL *Versus* TEACHER. Letters from a Teacher to a Teacher. Fcap. 8vo, pp. 92, cloth. 1875. 2s.

IHNE.—A LATIN GRAMMAR FOR BEGINNERS. By W. H. Ihne, late Principal of Carlton Terrace School, Liverpool. Crown 8vo, pp. vi. and 184, cloth. 1864. 3s.

IKHWÁNU-S SAFÁ; or, Brothers of Purity. Translated from the Hindustani by Professor John Dowson, M.R.A.S., Staff College, Sandhurst. Crown 8vo, pp. viii. and 156, cloth. 1869. 7s.

INDIA.—ARCHÆOLOGICAL SURVEY OF WESTERN INDIA. See Burgess.

INDIA.—PUBLICATIONS OF THE ARCHÆOLOGICAL SURVEY OF INDIA. A separate list on application.

INDIA.—PUBLICATIONS OF THE GEOGRAPHICAL DEPARTMENT OF THE INDIA OFFICE, LONDON. A separate list, also list of all the Government Maps, on application.

INDIA.—PUBLICATIONS OF THE GEOLOGICAL SURVEY OF INDIA. A separate list on application.

INDIA OFFICE PUBLICATIONS :—
Aden, Statistical Account of. 5s.
Assam, do. do. Vols. I. and II. 5s. each.
Baden Powell, Land Revenues, &c., in India. 12s.
    Do. Jurisprudence for Forest Officers. 12s.
Beal's Buddhist Tripitaka. 4s.
Bengal, Statistical Account of. Vols. I. to XX. 100s. per set.
    Do. do. do. Vols. VI. to XX. 5s. each.
Bombay Code. 21s.
Bombay Gazetteer. Vol. II., 14s. Vol. VIII., 9s. Vol. XIII. (2 parts), 16s. Vol. XV. (2 parts), 16s.
    Do. do. Vols. III. to VII., and X., XI., XII., XIV., XVI. 8s. each.
    Do. do. Vols. XXI., XXII., and XXIII. 9s. each.
Burgess' Archæological Survey of Western India. Vols. I. and III. 42s. each.
    Do. do. do. Vol. II. 63s.
    Do. do. do. Vols. IV. and V. 126s.
Burma (British) Gazetteer. 2 vols. 50s.
Catalogue of Manuscripts and Maps of Surveys. 12s.
Chambers' Meteorology (Bombay) and Atlas. 30s.
Cole's Agra and Muttra. 70s.
Cook's Gums and Resins. 5s.
Corpus Inscriptionem Indicarum. Vol. I. 32s.
Cunningham's Archæological Survey. Vols. I. to XVIII. 10s. and 12s. each.
    Do. Stupa of Bharut. 63s.
Egerton's Catalogue of Indian Arms. 2s. 6d.
Ferguson and Burgess, Cave Temples of India. 42s.
    Do. Tree and Serpent Worship. 105s.
Finance and Revenue Accounts of the Government of India for 1883-4. 2s. 6d.
Gamble, Manual of Indian Timbers. 10s.
Hunter's Imperial Gazetteer. 9 vols.

36   *A Catalogue of Important Works,*

INDIA OFFICE PUBLICATIONS—*continued.*
    Indian Education Commission, Report of the. 12s. Appendices. 10 vols. 10s.
    Jaschke's Tibetan-English Dictionary. 30s.
    King. Chinchona-Planting. 1s.
    Kurz. Forest Flora of British Burma. Vols. I. and II. 15s. each.
    Liotard's Materials for Paper. 2s. 6d.
    Liotard's Silk in India. Part I. 2s.
    Loth. Catalogue of Arabic MSS. 10s. 6d.
    Markham's Tibet. 21s.
        Do.   Memoir of Indian Surveys. 10s. 6d.
        Do.   Abstract of Reports of Surveys. 1s. 6d.
    Mitra (Rajendralala), Buddha Gaya. 60s.
    Moir, Torrent Regions of the Alps. 1s.
    Mueller. Select Plants for Extra-Tropical Countries. 8s.
    Mysore and Coorg Gazetteer. Vols. I. and II. 10s. each.
        Do.   do.   Vol. III. 5s.
    N. W. P. Gazetteer. Vols. I. and II. 10s. each.
        Do.   do.   Vols. III. to XI., XIII., and XIV. 12s. each.
    Oudh   do.   Vols. I. to III. 10s. each.
    People of India, The. Vols. I. to VIII. 45s. each.
    Raverty's Notes on Afghanistan and Baluchistan. Sections I. and II. 2s. Section III. 5s. Section IV. 3s.
    Rajputana Gazetteer. 3 vols. 15s.
    Saunders' Mountains and River Basins of India. 3s.
    Sewell's Amaravati Tope. 3s.
    Smyth's (Brough) Gold Mining in Wynaad. 1s.
    Taylor. Indian Marine Surveys. 2s. 6d.
    Trigonometrical Survey, Synopsis of Great. Vols. I. to VI. 10s. 6d. each.
    Trumpp's Adi Granth. 52s. 6d.
    Waring. Pharmacopœia of India, The. 6s.
    Watson's Cotton Gins. Boards, 10s. 6d. Paper, 10s.
        Do.   Rhea Fibre. 2s. 6d.
        Do.   Tobacco. 5s.
    Wilson. Madras Army. Vols. I. and II. 21s.

INDIAN GAZETTEERS.—See GAZETTEER, and INDIA OFFICE PUBLICATIONS.

INGLEBY.—See SHAKESPEARE.

INMAN.—NAUTICAL TABLES. Designed for the use of British Seamen. By the Rev. James Inman, D.D., late Professor at the Royal Naval College, Portsmouth. Demy 8vo, pp. xvi. and 410, cloth. 1877. 15s.

INMAN.—HISTORY OF THE ENGLISH ALPHABET: A Paper read before the Liverpool Literary and Philosophical Society. By T. Inman, M.D. 8vo, pp. 36, sewed. 1872. 1s.

IN SEARCH OF TRUTH. Conversations on the Bible and Popular Theology, for Young People. By A. M. Y. Crown 8vo, pp. x. and 138, cloth. 1875. 2s. 6d.

INTERNATIONAL NUMISMATA ORIENTALIA (THE).—Royal 4to, in paper wrapper. Part I. Ancient Indian Weights. By E. Thomas, F.R.S. Pp. 84, with a Plate and Map of the India of Manu. 9s. 6d.—Part II. Coins of the Urtukí Turkumáns. By Stanley Lane Poole, Corpus Christi College, Oxford. Pp. 44, with 6 Plates. 9s.—Part III. The Coinage of Lydia and Persia, from the Earliest Times to the Fall of the Dynasty of the Achæmenidæ. By Barclay V. Head, Assistant-Keeper of Coins, British Museum. Pp. viii.-56, with 3 Autotype Plates. 10s. 6d.—Part IV. The Coins of the Tuluni Dynasty. By Edward Thomas Rogers. Pp. iv.-22, and 1 Plate. 5s.—Part V. The Parthian Coinage. By Percy Gardner, M.A. Pp. iv.-66, and 8 Autotype Plates. 18s.—Part VI. The Ancient Coins and Measures of Ceylon. By T. W. Rhys Davids. Pp. iv. and 60, and 1 Plate. 10s.—Vol. I., containing the first six parts, as specified above. Royal 4to, half bound. £3, 13s. 6d.

INTERNATIONAL NUMISMATA—*continued.*

Vol. II. COINS OF THE JEWS. Being a History of the Jewish Coinage and Money in the Old and New Testaments. By Frederick W. Madden, M.R.A.S., Member of the Numismatic Society of London, Secretary of the Brighton College, &c., &c. With 279 woodcuts and a plate of alphabets. Royal 4to, pp. xii. and 330, sewed. 1881. £2.

Vol. III. Part I. THE COINS OF ARAKAN, OF PEGU, AND OF BURMA. By Lieut.-General Sir Arthur Phayre, C.B., K.C.S.I., G.C.M.G., late Commissioner of British Burma. Also contains the Indian Balhara, and the Arabian Intercourse with India in the Ninth and following Centuries. By Edward Thomas, F.R.S. Royal 4to, pp. viii. and 48, with Five Autotype Illustrations, wrapper. 1882. 8s. 6d.

Part II. THE COINS OF SOUTHERN INDIA. By Sir W. Elliot. Royal 4to.

JACKSON.—ETHNOLOGY AND PHRENOLOGY AS AN AID TO THE HISTORIAN. By the late J. W. Jackson. Second Edition. With a Memoir of the Author, by his Wife. Crown 8vo, pp. xx. and 324, cloth. 1875. 4s. 6d.

JACKSON.—THE SHROPSHIRE WORD-BOOK. A Glossary of Archaic and Provincial Words, &c., used in the County. By Georgina F. Jackson. Crown 8vo, pp. civ. and 524, cloth. 1881. 31s. 6d.

JACOB.—HINDU PANTHEISM. See Trübner's Oriental Series.

JAGIELSKI.—ON MARIENBAD SPA, and the Diseases Curable by its Waters and Baths. By A. V. Jagielski, M.D., Berlin. Second Edition. Crown 8vo, pp. viii. and 186. With Map. Cloth. 1874. 5s.

JAMISON.—THE LIFE AND TIMES OF BERTRAND DU GUESCLIN. A History of the Fourteenth Century. By D. F. Jamison, of South Carolina. Portrait. 2 vols. 8vo, pp. xvi., 287, and viii., 314, cloth. 1864. £1, 1s.

JAPAN.—MAP OF NIPPON (Japan): Compiled from Native Maps, and the Notes of most recent Travellers. By R. Henry Brunton, M.I.C.E., F.R.G.S., 1880. Size, 5 feet by 4 feet, 20 miles to the inch. In 4 Sheets, £1, 1s.; Roller, varnished. £1, 11s. 6d.; Folded, in Case, £1, 5s. 6d.

JASCHKE.—A TIBETAN-ENGLISH DICTIONARY. With special reference to the Prevailing Dialects. To which is added an English-Tibetan Vocabulary. By H. A. Jäschke, late Moravian Missionary at Kyèlang, British Lahoul. Imperial 8vo, pp. xxiv.-672, cloth. 1881. £1, 10s.

JASCHKE.—TIBETAN GRAMMAR. By H. A. Jäschke. Crown 8vo, pp. viii.-104, cloth. 1883. 5s.

JATAKA (THE), together with its COMMENTARY: being tales of the Anterior Birth of Gotama Buddha. Now first published in Pali, by V. Fausböll. Text. 8vo. Vol. I., pp. viii. and 512, cloth. 1877. 28s.—Vol. II., pp. 452, cloth. 1879, 28s.—Vol. III., pp. viii. and 544, cloth. 1883. 28s. (For Translation see Trübner's Oriental Series, "Buddhist Birth Stories.")

JENKINS.—A PALADIN OF FINANCE: Contemporary Manners. By E. Jenkins, Author of "Ginx's Baby." Crown 8vo, pp. iv. and 392, cloth. 1882. 7s. 6d.

JENKINS.—VEST-POCKET LEXICON. An English Dictionary of all except familiar Words, including the principal Scientific and Technical Terms, and Foreign Moneys, Weights and Measures; omitting what everybody knows, and containing what everybody wants to know and cannot readily find. By Jabez Jenkins. 64mo, pp. 564, cloth. 1879. 1s. 6d.

JOHNSON.—ORIENTAL RELIGIONS. India. See English and Foreign Philosophical Library, Extra Series, Vols. IV. and V.

JOHNSON.—ORIENTAL RELIGIONS AND THEIR RELATION TO UNIVERSAL RELIGION. Persia. By Samuel Johnson. With an Introduction by O. B. Frothingham. Demy 8vo, pp. xliv. and 784, cloth. 1885. 18s.

JOLLY.—See NARADÍYA.

JOMINI.—THE ART OF WAR. By Baron de Jomini, General and Aide-de-Camp to the Emperor of Russia. A New Edition, with Appendices and Maps. Translated from the French. By Captain G. H. Mendell, and Captain W. O. Craighill. Crown 8vo, pp. 410, cloth. 1879. 9s.

JOSEPH.—RELIGION, NATURAL AND REVEALED. A Series of Progressive Lessons for Jewish Youth. By N. S. Joseph. Crown 8vo, pp. xii.-296, cloth. 1879. 3s.

JUVENALIS SATIRÆ. With a Literal English Prose Translation and Notes. By J. D. Lewis, M.A., Trin. Coll. Camb. Second Edition. Two vols. 8vo, pp. xii. and 230 and 400, cloth. 1882. 12s.

KARCHER.—QUESTIONNAIRE FRANÇAIS. Questions on French Grammar, Idiomatic Difficulties, and Military Expressions. By Theodore Karcher, LL.B. Fourth Edition, greatly enlarged. Crown 8vo, pp. 224, cloth. 1879. 4s. 6d. Interleaved with writing paper, 5s. 6d.

KARDEC.—THE SPIRIT'S BOOK. Containing the Principles of Spiritist Doctrine on the Immortality of the Soul, &c., &c., according to the Teachings of Spirits of High Degree, transmitted through various mediums, collected and set in order by Allen Kardec. Translated from the 120th thousand by Anna Blackwell. Crown 8vo, pp. 512, cloth. 1875. 7s. 6d.

KARDEC.—THE MEDIUM'S BOOK; or, Guide for Mediums and for Evocations. Containing the Theoretic Teachings of Spirits concerning all kinds of Manifestations, the Means of Communication with the Invisible World, the Development of Medianimity, &c., &c. By Allen Kardec. Translated by Anna Blackwell. Crown 8vo, pp. 456, cloth. 1876. 7s. 6d.

KARDEC.—HEAVEN AND HELL; or, the Divine Justice Vindicated in the Plurality of Existences. By Allen Kardec. Translated by Anna Blackwell. Crown 8vo, pp. viii. and 448, cloth. 1878. 7s. 6d.

KEMP. See SCHOPENHAUER.

KENDRICK.—GREEK OLLENDORFF. A Progressive Exhibition of the Principles of the Greek Grammar. By Asahel C. Kendrick. 8vo, pp. 371, cloth. 1870. 9s.

KERMODE.—NATAL: Its Early History, Rise, Progress, and Future Prospects as a Field for Emigration. By W. Kermode, of Natal. Crown 8vo, pp. xii. and 228, with Map, cloth. 1883. 3s. 6d.

KEYS OF THE CREEDS (THE). Third Revised Edition. Crown 8vo, pp. 210, cloth. 1876. 5s.

KINAHAN.—VALLEYS AND THEIR RELATION TO FISSURES, FRACTURES, AND FAULTS. By G. H. Kinahan, M.R.I.A., F.R.G.S.I., &c. Dedicated by permission to his Grace the Duke of Argyll. Crown 8vo, pp. 256, cloth, illustrated. 7s. 6d.

KING'S STRATAGEM (The); OR, THE PEARL OF POLAND; A Tragedy in Five Acts. By Stella. Second Edition. Crown 8vo, pp. 94, cloth. 1874. 2s. 6d.

KINGSTON.—THE UNITY OF CREATION. A Contribution to the Solution of the Religious Question. By F. H. Kingston. Crown 8vo, pp. viii. and 152, cloth. 1874. 5s.

KISTNER.—BUDDHA AND HIS DOCTRINES. A Bibliographical Essay. By Otto Kistner. 4to, pp. iv. and 32, sewed. 1869. 2s. 6d.

KNOX.—ON A MEXICAN MUSTANG. See under SWEET.

KLEMM.—MUSCLE BEATING; or, Active and Passive Home Gymnastics, for Healthy and Unhealthy People. By C. Klemm. With Illustrations. 8vo, pp. 60, wrapper. 1878. 1s.

KOHL.—TRAVELS IN CANADA AND THROUGH THE STATES OF NEW YORK AND PENNSYLVANIA. By J. G. Kohl. Translated by Mrs. Percy Sinnett. Revised by the Author. Two vols. post 8vo, pp. xiv. and 794, cloth. 1861. £1, 1s.

KRAPF.—DICTIONARY OF THE SUAHILI LANGUAGE. Compiled by the Rev. Dr. L. Krapf, missionary of the Church Missionary Society in East Africa. With an Appendix, containing an outline of a Suahili Grammar. Medium 8vo, pp. xl. and 434, cloth. 1882. 30s.

KRAUS.—CARLSBAD AND ITS NATURAL HEALING AGENTS, from the Physiological and Therapeutical Point of View. By J. Kraus, M.D. With Notes Introductory by the Rev. J. T. Walters, M.A. Second Edition. Revised and enlarged. Crown 8vo, pp. 104, cloth. 1880. 5s.

KROEGER.—THE MINNESINGER OF GERMANY. By A. E. Kroeger. Fcap. 8vo, pp. 290, cloth. 1873. 7s.

KURZ.—FOREST FLORA OF BRITISH BURMA. By S. Kurz, Curator of the Herbarium, Royal Botanical Gardens, Calcutta. 2 vols. crown 8vo, pp. xxx., 550, and 614, cloth. 1877. 30s.

LACERDA'S JOURNEY TO CAZEMBE in 1798. Translated and Annotated by Captain R. F. Burton, F.R.G.S. Also Journey of the Pombeiros, &c. Demy 8vo, pp. viii. and 272. With Map, cloth. 1873. 7s. 6d.

LANARI.—COLLECTION OF ITALIAN AND ENGLISH DIALOGUES. By A. Lanari. Fcap. 8vo, pp. viii. and 200, cloth. 1874. 3s. 6d.

LAND.—THE PRINCIPLES OF HEBREW GRAMMAR. By J. P. N. Land, Professor of Logic and Metaphysics in the University of Leyden. Translated from the Dutch, by Reginald Lane Poole, Balliol College, Oxford. Part I. Sounds. Part II. Words. With Large Additions by the Author, and a new Preface. Crown 8vo, pp. xx. and 220, cloth. 1876. 7s. 6d.

LANE.—THE KORAN. See Trübner's Oriental Series.

LANGE.—A HISTORY OF MATERIALISM. See English and Foreign Philosophical Library, Vols. I. to III.

LANGE.—GERMANIA. A German Reading-book Arranged Progressively. By F. K. W. Lange, Ph.D. Part I. Anthology of German Prose and Poetry, with Vocabulary and Biographical Notes. 8vo, pp. xvi. and 216, cloth, 1881, 3s. 6d. Part II. Essays on German History and Institutions, with Notes. 8vo, pp. 124, cloth. 1881. 3s. 6d. Parts I. and II. together. 5s. 6d.

LANGE.—GERMAN PROSE WRITING. Comprising English Passages for Translation into German. Selected from Examination Papers of the University of London, the College of Preceptors, London, and the Royal Military Academy, Woolwich, arranged progressively, with Notes and Theoretical as well as Practical Treatises on themes for the writing of Essays. By F. K. W. Lange, Ph.D., Assistant German Master, Royal Academy, Woolwich; Examiner, Royal College of Preceptors London. Crown 8vo, pp. viii. and 176, cloth. 1881. 4s.

LANGE.—GERMAN GRAMMAR PRACTICE. By F. K. W. Lange, Ph.D. Crown 8vo, pp. viii. and 64, cloth. 1882. 1s. 6d.

LANGE.—COLLOQUIAL GERMAN GRAMMAR. With Special Reference to the Anglo-Saxon Element in the English Language. By F. K. W. Lange, Ph.D., &c. Crown 8vo, pp. xxxii. and 380, cloth. 1882. 4s. 6d.

LANMAN.—A SANSKRIT READER. With Vocabulary and Notes. By Charles Rockwell Lanman, Professor of Sanskrit in Harvard College. Part I. Imperial 8vo, pp. xx. and 294, cloth. 1884. 10s. 6d.

LARSEN.—DANISH-ENGLISH DICTIONARY. By A. Larsen. Crown 8vo, pp. viii. and 646, cloth. 1884. 7s. 6d.

LASCARIDES.—A Comprehensive Phraseological English-Ancient and Modern Greek Lexicon. Founded upon a manuscript of G. P. Lascarides, and Compiled by L. Myriantheus, Ph.D. 2 vols. 18mo, pp. xi. and 1338, cloth. 1882. £1, 10s.

LATHE (The) and its Uses; or, Instruction in the Art of Turning Wood and Metal, including a description of the most modern appliances for the Ornamentation of Plain and Curved Surfaces, &c. Sixth Edition. With additional Chapters and Index. Illustrated. 8vo, pp. iv. and 316, cloth. 1883. 10s. 6d.

LE-BRUN.—Materials for Translating from English into French; being a short Essay on Translation, followed by a Graduated Selection in Prose and Verse. By L. Le-Brun. Seventh Edition. Revised and corrected by Henri Van Laun. Post 8vo, pp. xii. and 204, cloth. 1882. 4s. 6d.

LEE.—Illustrations of the Physiology of Religion. In Sections adapted for the use of Schools. Part I. By Henry Lee, F.R.C.S., formerly Professor of Surgery, Royal College of Surgeons, &c. Crown 8vo, pp. viii. and 108, cloth. 1880. 3s. 6d.

LEES.—A Practical Guide to Health, and to the Home Treatment of the Common Ailments of Life: With a Section on Cases of Emergency, and Hints to Mothers on Nursing, &c. By F. Arnold Lees, F.L.S. Crown 8vo, pp. 334, stiff covers. 1874. 3s.

LEGGE.—The Chinese Classics. With a Translation, Critical and Exegetical, Notes, Prolegomena, and copious Indexes. By James Legge, D.D., of the London Missionary Society. In 7 vols. Royal 8vo. Vols. I.-V. in Eight Parts, published, cloth. £2, 2s. each Part.

LEGGE.—The Chinese Classics, translated into English. With Preliminary Essays and Explanatory Notes. Popular Edition. Reproduced for General Readers from the Author's work, containing the Original Text. By James Legge, D.D. Crown 8vo. Vol. I. The Life and Teachings of Confucius. Third Edition. Pp. vi. and 338, cloth. 1872. 10s. 6d.—Vol. II. The Works of Mencius. Pp. x. and 402, cloth, 12s.—Vol. III. The She-King; or, The Book of Poetry. Pp. vi. and 432, cloth. 1876. 12s.

LEGGE.—Confucianism in Relation to Christianity. A Paper read before the Missionary Conference in Shanghai, on May 11th, 1877. By Rev. James Legge, D.D., LL.D., &c. 8vo, pp. 12, sewed. 1877. 1s. 6d.

LEGGE.—A Letter to Professor Max Müller, chiefly on the Translation into English of the Chinese Terms *Ti* and *Shang Ti*. By James Legge, Professor of the Chinese Language and Literature in the University of Oxford. Crown 8vo, pp. 30, sewed. 1880. 1s.

LEIGH.—The Religion of the World. By H. Stone Leigh. 12mo, pp. xii. and 66, cloth. 1869. 2s. 6d.

LEIGH.—The Story of Philosophy. By Aston Leigh. Post 8vo, pp. xii. and 210, cloth. 1881. 6s.

LEÏLA-HANOUM.—A Tragedy in the Imperial Harem at Constantinople. By Leïla-Hanoum. Translated from the French, with Notes by General R. E. Colston. 16mo, pp. viii. and 300, cloth. 1883. 4s. Paper, 2s. 6d.

LELAND.—The Breitmann Ballads. The only authorised Edition. Complete in 1 vol., including Nineteen Ballads, illustrating his Travels in Europe (never before printed), with Comments by Fritz Schwackenhammer. By Charles G. Leland. Crown 8vo, pp. xxviii. and 292, cloth. 1872. 6s.

LELAND.—The Music Lesson of Confucius, and other Poems. By Charles G. Leland. Fcap. 8vo, pp. viii. and 168, cloth. 1871. 3s. 6d.

LELAND.—Gaudeamus. Humorous Poems translated from the German of Joseph Victor Scheffel and others. By Charles G. Leland. 16mo, pp. 176, cloth. 1872. 3s. 6d.

LELAND.—THE EGYPTIAN SKETCH-BOOK. By C. G. Leland. Crown 8vo, pp. viii. and 316, cloth. 1873. 7s. 6d.

LELAND.—THE ENGLISH GIPSIES AND THEIR LANGUAGE. By Charles G. Leland. Second Edition. Crown 8vo, pp. xvi. and 260, cloth. 1874. 7s. 6d.

LELAND.—FU-SANG; OR, THE DISCOVERY OF AMERICA by Chinese Buddhist Priests in the Fifth Century. By Charles G. Leland. Crown 8vo, pp. 232, cloth. 1875. 7s. 6d.

LELAND.—PIDGIN-ENGLISH SING-SONG; or, Songs and Stories in the China-English Dialect. With a Vocabulary. By Charles G. Leland. Crown 8vo, pp. viii. and 140, cloth. 1876. 5s.

LELAND.—THE GYPSIES. By C. G. Leland. Crown 8vo, pp. 372, cloth. **1882.** 10s. 6d.

LEOPARDI.—See English and Foreign Philosophical Library, Vol. XVII.

LEO.—FOUR CHAPTERS OF NORTH'S PLUTARCH, Containing the Lives of Caius Marcius, Coriolanus, Julius Cæsar, Marcus Antonius, and Marcus Brutus, as Sources to Shakespeare's Tragedies; Coriolanus, Julius Cæsar, and Antony and Cleopatra; and partly to Hamlet and Timon of Athens. Photolithographed in the size of the Edition of 1595. With Preface, Notes comparing the Text of the Editions of 1579, 1595, 1603, and 1612; and Reference Notes to the Text of the Tragedies of Shakespeare. Edited by Professor F. A. Leo, Ph.D., Vice-President of the New Shakespeare Society; Member of the Directory of the German Shakespeare Society; and Lecturer at the Academy of Modern Philology at Berlin. Folio, pp. 22, 130 of facsimiles, half-morocco. Library Edition (limited to 250 copies), £1, 11s. 6d.; Amateur Edition (50 copies on a superior large hand-made paper), £3, 3s.

LEO.—SHAKESPEARE-NOTES. By F. A. Leo. Demy 8vo, pp. viii. and 120, cloth. 1885. 6s.

LEONOWENS.—LIFE AND TRAVEL IN INDIA: Being Recollections of a Journey before the Days of Railroads. By Anna Harriette Leonowens, Author of "The English Governess at the Siamese Court," and "The Romance of the Harem." 8vo, pp. 326, cloth, Illustrated. 1885. 10s. 6d.

LERMONTOFF.—THE DEMON. By Michael Lermontoff. Translated from the Russian by A. Condie Stephen. Crown 8vo, pp. 88, cloth. 1881. 2s. 6d.

LESLEY.—MAN'S ORIGIN AND DESTINY. Sketched from the Platform of the Physical Sciences. By. J. P. Lesley, Member of the National Academy of the United States, Professor of Geology, University of Pennsylvania. Second (Revised and considerably Enlarged) Edition, crown 8vo, pp. viii. and 142, cloth. 1881. 7s. 6d.

LESSING.—LETTERS ON BIBLIOLATRY. By Gotthold Ephraim Lessing. Translated from the German by the late H. H. Bernard, Ph.D. 8vo, pp. 184, cloth. 1862. 5s.

LESSING.—See English and Foreign Philosophical Library, Extra Series, Vols. I. and II.

LETTERS ON THE WAR BETWEEN GERMANY AND FRANCE. By Mommsen, Strauss, Max Müller, and Carlyle. Second Edition. Crown 8vo, pp. 120, cloth. 1871. 2s. 6d.

LEWES.—PROBLEMS OF LIFE AND MIND. By George Henry Lewes. First Series: The Foundations of a Creed. Vol. I., demy 8vo. Fourth edition, pp. 488, cloth. 1884. 12s.—Vol. II., demy 8vo, pp. 552, cloth. 1875. 16s.

LEWES.—PROBLEMS OF LIFE AND MIND. By George Henry Lewes. Second Series. THE PHYSICAL BASIS OF MIND. 8vo, with Illustrations, pp. 508, cloth. 1877. 16s. Contents.—The Nature of Life; The Nervous Mechanism; Animal Automatism; The Reflex Theory.

LEWES.—PROBLEMS OF LIFE AND MIND. By George Henry Lewes. Third Series. Problem the First—The Study of Psychology: Its Object, Scope, and Method. Demy 8vo, pp. 200, cloth. 1879. 7s. 6d.

LEWES.—Problems of Life and Mind. By George Henry Lewes. Third Series. Problem the Second—Mind as a Function of the Organism. Problem the Third—The Sphere of Sense and Logic of Feeling. Problem the Fourth—The Sphere of Intellect and Logic of Signs. Demy 8vo, pp. x. and 500, cloth. 1879. 15s.

LEWIS.—See Juvenal and Pliny.

LIBRARIANS, Transactions and Proceedings of the Conference of, held in London, October 1877. Edited by Edward B. Nicholson and Henry R. Tedder. Imperial 8vo, pp. 276, cloth. 1878. £1, 8s.

LIBRARY ASSOCIATION OF THE UNITED KINGDOM, Transactions and Proceedings of the Annual Meetings of the. Imperial 8vo, cloth. First, held at Oxford, October 1, 2, 3, 1878. Edited by the Secretaries, Henry R. Tedder, Librarian of the Athenæum Club, and Ernest C. Thomas, late Librarian of the Oxford Union Society. Pp. viii. and 192. 1879. £1, 8s.—Second, held at Manchester, September 23, 24, and 25, 1879. Edited by H. R. Tedder and E. C. Thomas. Pp. x. and 184. 1880. £1, 1s.—Third, held at Edinburgh, October 5, 6, and 7, 1880. Edited by E. C. Thomas and C. Welsh. Pp. x. and 202. 1881. £1, 1s.—Fourth and Fifth, held in London, September 1881, and at Cambridge, September 1882. Edited by E. C. Thomas. Pp. x.-258. 1885. 28s.

LIEBER.—The Life and Letters of Francis Lieber. Edited by T. S. Perry. 8vo, pp. iv. and 440, cloth, with Portrait. 1882. 14s.

LITTLE FRENCH READER (The). Extracted from "The Modern French Reader." Third Edition. Crown 8vo, pp. 112, cloth. 1884. 2s.

LLOYD and Newton.—Prussia's Representative Man. By F. Lloyd of the Universities of Halle and Athens, and W. Newton, F.R.G.S. Crown 8vo, pp. 648, cloth. 1875. 10s. 6d.

LOBSCHEID.—Chinese and English Dictionary, arranged according to the Radicals. By W. Lobscheid. 1 vol. imperial 8vo, pp. 600, cloth. £2, 8s.

LOBSCHEID.—English and Chinese Dictionary, with the Punti and Mandarin Pronunciation. By W. Lobscheid. Four Parts. Folio, pp. viii. and 2016, boards. £8, 8s.

LONG.—Eastern Proverbs. See Trübner's Oriental Series.

LOVETT.—The Life and Struggles of William Lovett in his pursuit of Bread, Knowledge, and Freedom; with some short account of the different Associations he belonged to, and of the Opinions he entertained. 8vo, pp. vi. and 474, cloth. 1876. 5s.

LOVELY.—Where to go for Help: Being a Companion for Quick and Easy Reference of Police Stations, Fire-Engine Stations, Fire-Escape Stations, &c., &c., of London and the Suburbs. Compiled by W. Lovely, R.N. Third Edition. 18mo, pp. 16, sewed. 1882. 3d.

LOWELL.—The Biglow Papers. By James Russell Lowell. Edited by Thomas Hughes, Q.C. A Reprint of the Authorised Edition of 1859, together with the Second Series of 1862. First and Second Series in 1 vol. Fcap., pp. lxviii.-140 and lxiv.-190, cloth. 1880. 2s. 6d.

LUCAS.—The Children's Pentateuch: With the Haphtarahs or Portions from the Prophets. Arranged for Jewish Children. By Mrs. Henry Lucas. Crown 8vo, pp. viii. and 570, cloth. 1878. 5s.

LUDEWIG.—The Literature of American Aboriginal Languages. By Hermann E. Ludewig. With Additions and Corrections by Professor Wm. W. Turner. Edited by Nicolas Trübner. 8vo, pp. xxiv. and 258, cloth. 1858. 10s. 6d.

LUKIN.—The Boy Engineers: What they did, and how they did it. By the Rev. L. J. Lukin, Author of "The Young Mechanic," &c. A Book for Boys; 30 Engravings. Imperial 16mo, pp. viii. and 344, cloth. 1877. 7s. 6d.

LUX E TENEBRIS; or, The Testimony of Consciousness. A Theoretic Essay. Crown 8vo, pp. 376, with Diagram, cloth. 1874. 10s. 6d.

MACCORMAC.—THE CONVERSATION OF A SOUL WITH GOD: A Theodicy. By Henry MacCormac, M.D. 16mo, pp. xvi. and 144, cloth. 1877. 3s. 6d.

MACHIAVELLI.—THE HISTORICAL, POLITICAL, AND DIPLOMATIC WRITINGS OF NICCOLO MACHIAVELLI. Translated from the Italian by C. E. Detmold. With Portraits. 4 vols. 8vo, cloth, pp. xli., 420, 464, 488, and 472. 1882. £3, 3s.

MACKENZIE.—HISTORY OF THE RELATIONS OF THE GOVERNMENT WITH THE HILL TRIBES OF THE NORTH-EAST FRONTIER OF BENGAL. By Alexander Mackenzie, of the Bengal Civil Service; Secretary to the Government of India in the Home Department, and formerly Secretary to the Government of Bengal. Royal 8vo, pp. xviii. and 586, cloth, with Map. 1884. 16s.

MADDEN.—COINS OF THE JEWS. Being a History of the Jewish Coinage and Money in the Old and New Testaments. By Frederick W. Madden, M.R.A.S. Member of the Numismatic Society of London, Secretary of the Brighton College, &c., &c. With 279 Woodcuts and a Plate of Alphabets. Royal 4to, pp. xii. and 330, cloth. 1881. £2, 2s.

MADELUNG.—THE CAUSES AND OPERATIVE TREATMENT OF DUPUYTREN'S FINGER CONTRACTION. By Dr. Otto W. Madelung, Lecturer of Surgery at the University, and Assistant Surgeon at the University Hospital, Bonn. 8vo, pp. 24, sewed. 1876. 1s.

MAHAPARINIBBANASUTTA.—See CHILDERS.

MAHA-VIRA-CHARITA; or, The Adventures of the Great Hero Rama. An Indian Drama in Seven Acts. Translated into English Prose from the Sanskrit of Bhavabhūti. By John Pickford, M.A. Crown 8vo, cloth. 5s.

MAIMONIDES.—THE GUIDE OF THE PERPLEXED OF MAIMONIDES. See English and Foreign Philosophical Library.

MALLESON.—ESSAYS AND LECTURES ON INDIAN HISTORICAL SUBJECTS. By Colonel G. B. Malleson, C.S.I. Second Issue. Crown 8vo, pp. 348, cloth. 1876. 5s.

MAN.—ON THE ABORIGINAL INHABITANTS OF THE ANDAMAN ISLANDS. By Edward Horace Man, Assistant Superintendent, Andaman and Nicobar Islands, F.R.G.S., M.R.A.S., M.A.I. With Report of Researches into the Language of the South Andaman Islands. By A. J. Ellis, F.R.S., F.S.A. Reprinted from "The Journal of the Anthropological Institute of Great Britain and Ireland." Demy 8vo, pp. xxviii.-298, with Map and 8 Plates, cloth. 1885. 10s. 6d.

MANDLEY.—WOMAN OUTSIDE CHRISTENDOM. An Exposition of the Influence exerted by Christianity on the Social Position and Happiness of Women. By J. G. Mandley. Crown 8vo, pp. viii. and 160, cloth. 1880. 5s.

MANIPULUS VOCABULORUM. A Rhyming Dictionary of the English Language. By Peter Levins (1570). Edited, with an Alphabetical Index, by Henry B. Wheatley. 8vo, pp. xvi. and 370, cloth. 1867. 14s.

MANŒUVRES.—A RETROSPECT OF THE AUTUMN MANŒUVRES, 1871. With 5 Plans. By a Recluse. 8vo, pp. xii. and 133, cloth. 1872. 5s.

MARIETTE-BEY.—THE MONUMENTS OF UPPER EGYPT: a translation of the "Itinéraire de la Haute Egypte" of Auguste Mariette-Bey. Translated by Alphonse Mariette. Crown 8vo, pp. xvi. and 262, cloth. 1877. 7s. 6d.

MARKHAM.—QUICHUA GRAMMAR AND DICTIONARY. Contributions towards a Grammar and Dictionary of Quichua, the Language of the Yncas of Peru. Collected by Clements R. Markham, F.S.A. Crown 8vo, pp. 223, cloth. £1, 11s. 6d.

MARKHAM.—OLLANTA: A Drama in the Quichua Language. Text, Translation, and Introduction. By Clements R. Markham, C.B. Crown 8vo, pp. 128, cloth. 1871. 7s. 6d.

MARKHAM.—A MEMOIR OF THE LADY ANA DE OSORIO, Countess of Chincon, and Vice-Queen of Peru, A.D. 1629-39. With a Plea for the correct spelling of the Chinchona Genus. By Clements R. Markham, C.B., Member of the Imperial Academy Naturæ Curiosorum, with the Cognomen of Chinchon. Small 4to, pp. xii. and 100. With 2 Coloured Plates, Map, and Illustrations. Handsomely bound. 1874. 28s.

MARKHAM.—A MEMOIR ON THE INDIAN SURVEYS. By Clements R. Markham, C.B., F.R.S., &c., &c. Published by Order of H. M. Secretary of State for India in Council. Illustrated with Maps. Second Edition. Imperial 8vo, pp. xxx. and 481, boards. 1878. 10s. 6d.

MARKHAM.—NARRATIVES OF THE MISSION OF GEORGE BOGLE TO TIBET, and of the Journey of Thomas Manning to Lhasa. Edited with Notes, an Introduction, and Lives of Mr. Bogle and Mr. Manning. By Clements R. Markham, C.B., F.R.S. Second Edition. 8vo, pp. clxv. and 362, cloth. With Maps and Illustrations. 1879. 21s.

MARKS.—SERMONS. Preached on various occasions at the West London Synagogue of British Jews. By the Rev. Professor Marks, Minister of the Congregation. Published at the request of the Council. Second Series, demy 8vo, pp. viii.-310, cloth. 1885. 7s. 6d. Third Series, demy 8vo, pp. iv.-284, cloth. 1885. 7s. 6d.

MARMONTEL.—BELISAIRE. Par Marmontel. Nouvelle Edition. 12mo, pp. xii. and 123, cloth. 1867. 2s. 6d.

MARSDEN.—NUMISMATA ORIENTALIA ILLUSTRATA. THE PLATES OF THE ORIENTAL COINS, ANCIENT AND MODERN, of the Collection of the late William Marsden, F.R.S., &c. &c. Engraved from Drawings made under his Directions. 4to, 57 Plates, cloth. 31s. 6d.

MARTIN AND TRÜBNER.—THE CURRENT GOLD AND SILVER COINS OF ALL COUNTRIES, their Weight and Fineness, and their Intrinsic Value in English Money, with Facsimiles of the Coins. By Leopold C. Martin, of Her Majesty's Stationery Office, and Charles Trübner. In 1 vol. medium 8vo, 141 Plates, printed in Gold and Silver, and representing about 1000 Coins, with 160 pages of Text, handsomely bound in embossed cloth, richly gilt, with Emblematical Designs on the Cover, and gilt edges. 1863. £2, 2s.

MARTIN.—THE CHINESE; THEIR EDUCATION, PHILOSOPHY, AND LETTERS. By W. A. P. Martin, D.D., LL.D., President of the Tungwen College, Pekin. 8vo, pp. 320, cloth. 1881. 7s. 6d.

MARTINEAU.—ESSAYS, PHILOSOPHICAL AND THEOLOGICAL. By James Martineau. 2 vols. crown 8vo, pp. iv. and 414—x. and 430, cloth. 1875. £1, 4s.

MARTINEAU.—LETTERS FROM IRELAND. By Harriet Martineau. Reprinted from the *Daily News*. Post 8vo, pp. viii. and 220, cloth. 1852. 6s. 6d.

MASON.—BURMA: ITS PEOPLE AND PRODUCTIONS; or, Notes on the Fauna, Flora, and Minerals of Tenasserim, Pegu and Burma. By the Rev. F. Mason, D.D., M.R.A.S., Corresponding Member of the American Oriental Society, of the Boston Society of Natural History, and of the Lyceum of Natural History, New York. Vol. I. GEOLOGY, MINERALOGY AND ZOOLOGY. Vol. II. BOTANY. Rewritten and Enlarged by W. Theobald, late Deputy-Superintendent Geological Survey of India. Two Vols., royal 8vo, pp. xxvi. and 560; xvi. and 788 and xxxvi., cloth. 1884. £3.

MATHEWS.—ABRAHAM IBN EZRA'S COMMENTARY ON THE CANTICLES AFTER THE FIRST RECENSION. Edited from the MSS., with a translation, by H. J. Mathews, B.A., Exeter College, Oxford. Crown 8vo, pp. x., 34, and 24, limp cloth. 1874. 2s. 6d.

MATERIA MEDICA, PHYSIOLOGICAL AND APPLIED. Vol. I. Contents:—Aconitum, by R. E. Dudgeon, M.D.; Crotalus, by J. W. Hayward, M.D.; Digitalis, by F. Black, M.D.; Kali Bichromicum, by J. J. Drysdale, M.D.; Nux Vomica, by F. Black, M.D.; Plumbum, by F. Black, M.D. Demy 8vo, pp. xxiv.-726, cloth. 1884. 15s.

MAXWELL.—A MANUAL OF THE MALAY LANGUAGE. By W. E. Maxwell, of the Inner Temple, Barrister-at-Law; Assistant Resident, Perak, Malay Peninsula. With an Introductory Sketch of the Sanskrit Element in Malay. Crown 8vo, pp. viii. and 182, cloth. 1882. 7s. 6d.

MAY.—A BIBLIOGRAPHY OF ELECTRICITY AND MAGNETISM. 1860 to 1883. With Special Reference to Electro-Technics. Compiled by G. May. With an Index by O. Salle, Ph.D. Crown 8vo, pp. viii.-204, cloth. 1884. 5s.

MAYER.—ON THE ART OF POTTERY: with a History of its Rise and Progress in Liverpool. By Joseph Mayer, F.S.A., F.R.S.N.A., &c. 8vo, pp. 100, boards. 1873. 5s.

MAYERS.—TREATIES BETWEEN THE EMPIRE OF CHINA AND FOREIGN POWERS, together with Regulations for the conduct of Foreign Trade, &c. Edited by W. F. Mayers, Chinese Secretary to H.B.M.'s Legation at Peking. 8vo, pp. 246, cloth. 1877. 25s.

MAYERS.—THE CHINESE GOVERNMENT: a Manual of Chinese Titles, categorically arranged and explained, with an Appendix. By Wm. Fred. Mayers, Chinese Secretary to H.B.M.'s Legation at Peking, &c., &c. Royal 8vo, pp. viii. and 160, cloth. 1878. 30s.

M'CRINDLE.—ANCIENT INDIA, AS DESCRIBED BY MEGASTHENES AND ARRIAN; being a translation of the fragments of the Indika of Megasthenes collected by Dr. Schwanbeck, and of the first part of the Indika of Arrian. By J. W. M'Crindle, M.A., Principal of the Government College, Patna, &c. With Introduction, Notes, and Map of Ancient India. Post 8vo, pp. xi. and 224, cloth. 1877. 7s. 6d.

M'CRINDLE.—THE COMMERCE AND NAVIGATION OF THE ERYTHRÆAN SEA. Being a Translation of the Periplus Maris Erythræi, by an Anonymous Writer, and of Arrian's Account of the Voyage of Nearkhos, from the Mouth of the Indus to the Head of the Persian Gulf. With Introduction, Commentary, Notes, and Index. By J. W. M'Crindle, M.A., Edinburgh, &c. Post 8vo, pp. iv. and 238, cloth. 1879. 7s. 6d.

M'CRINDLE.—Ancient India as Described by Ktesias the Knidian; being a Translation of the Abridgment of his "Indika" by Photios, and of the Fragments of that Work preserved in other Writers. With Introduction, Notes, and Index. By J. W. M'Crindle, M.A., M.R.S.A. 8vo, pp. viii. and 104, cloth. 1882. 6s.

MECHANIC (THE YOUNG). A Book for Boys, containing Directions for the use of all kinds of Tools, and for the construction of Steam Engines and Mechanical Models, including the Art of Turning in Wood and Metal. Fifth Edition. Imperial 16mo, pp. iv. and 346, and 70 Engravings, cloth. 1878. 6s.

MECHANIC'S WORKSHOP (AMATEUR). A Treatise containing Plain and Concise Directions for the Manipulation of Wood and Metals, including Casting, Forging, Brazing, Soldering, and Carpentry. By the Author of "The Lathe and its Uses." Sixth Edition. Demy 8vo, pp. iv. and 148. Illustrated, cloth. 1880. 6s.

MEDITATIONS ON DEATH AND ETERNITY. Translated from the German by Frederica Rowan. Published by Her Majesty's gracious permission. 8vo, pp. 386, cloth. 1862. 10s. 6d.

DITTO. Smaller Edition, crown 8vo, printed on toned paper, pp. 352, cloth. 1884. 6s.

MEDITATIONS ON LIFE AND ITS RELIGIOUS DUTIES. Translated from the German by Frederica Rowan. Dedicated to H.R.H. Princess Louis of Hesse. Published by Her Majesty's gracious permission. Being the Companion Volume to "Meditations on Death and Eternity." 8vo, pp. vi. and 370, cloth. 1863. 10s. 6d.

DITTO. Smaller Edition, crown 8vo, printed on toned paper, pp. 338. 1863. 6s.

MEDLICOTT.—A MANUAL OF THE GEOLOGY OF INDIA, chiefly compiled from the observations of the Geological Survey. By H. B. Medlicott, M.A., Superintendent, Geological Survey of India, and W. T. Blanford, A.R.S.M., F.R.S., Deputy Superintendent. Published by order of the Government of India. 2 vols. 8vo, pp. xviii.-lxxx.-818. with 21 Plates and large coloured Map mounted in case, uniform, cloth. 1879. 16s. (For Part III. see BALL.)

MEGHA-DUTA (THE). (Cloud-Messenger.) By Kālidāsa. Translated from the Sanskrit into English Verse by the late H. H. Wilson, M.A., F.R.S. The Vocabulary by Francis Johnson. New Edition. 4to, pp. xi. and 180, cloth. 10s. 6d.

MEREDYTH.—ARCA, A REPERTOIRE OF ORIGINAL POEMS, Sacred and Secular. By F. Meredyth, M.A., Canon of Limerick Cathedral. Crown 8vo, pp. 124, cloth. 1875. 5s.

METCALFE.—THE ENGLISHMAN AND THE SCANDINAVIAN. By Frederick Metcalfe, M.A., Fellow of Lincoln College, Oxford; Translator of "Gallus" and "Charicles;" and Author of "The Oxonian in Iceland." Post 8vo, pp. 512, cloth. 1880. 18s.

MICHEL.—LES ÉCOSSAIS EN FRANCE, LES FRANÇAIS EN ÉCOSSE Par Francisque Michel, Correspondant de l'Institut de France, &c. In 2 vols. 8vo, pp. vii., 547, and 551, rich blue cloth, with emblematical designs. With upwards of 100 Coats of Arms, and other Illustrations. Price, £1, 12s.—Also a Large-Paper Edition (limited to 100 Copies), printed on Thick Paper. 2 vols. 4to, half morocco, with 3 additional Steel Engravings. 1862. £3, 3s.

MICKIEWICZ.—KONRAD WALLENROD. An Historical Poem. By A. Mickiewicz. Translated from the Polish into English Verse by Miss M. Biggs. 18mo, pp. xvi. and 100, cloth. 1882. 2s. 6d.

MILL.—AUGUSTE COMTE AND POSITIVISM. By the late John Stuart Mill, M.P. Third Edition. 8vo, pp. 200, cloth. 1882. 3s. 6d.

MILLHOUSE.—MANUAL OF ITALIAN CONVERSATION. For the Use of Schools. By John Millhouse. 18mo, pp. 126, cloth. 1866. 2s.

MILLHOUSE.—NEW ENGLISH AND ITALIAN PRONOUNCING AND EXPLANATORY DICTIONARY. By John Millhouse. Vol. I. English-Italian. Vol. II. Italian-English. Fourth Edition. 2 vols. square 8vo, pp. 654 and 740, cloth. 1867. 12s.

MILNE.—NOTES ON CRYSTALLOGRAPHY AND CRYSTALLO-PHYSICS. Being the Substance of Lectures delivered at Yedo during the years 1876-1877. By John Milne, F.G.S. 8vo, pp. viii. and 70, cloth. 1879. 3s.

MILTON AND VONDEL.—See EDMUNDSON.

MINOCHCHERJI.—PAHLAVI, GUJARATI, AND ENGLISH DICTIONARY. By Jamashji Dastur Minochcherji. Vol. I., with Photograph of Author. 8vo, pp. clxxii. and 168, cloth. 1877. 14s.

MITRA.—BUDDHA GAYA: The Hermitage of Sākya Muni. By Rajendralala Mitra, LL.D., C.I.E., &c. 4to, pp. xvi. and 258, with 51 Plates, cloth. 1879. £3.

MOCATTA.—MORAL BIBLICAL GLEANINGS AND PRACTICAL TEACHINGS, Illustrated by Biographical Sketches Drawn from the Sacred Volume. By J. L. Mocatta. 8vo, pp. viii. and 446, cloth. 1872. 7s.

MODERN FRENCH READER (THE). Prose. Junior Course. Tenth Edition. Edited by Ch. Cassal, LL.D., and Théodore Karcher, LL.B. Crown 8vo, pp. xiv. and 224, cloth. 1884. 2s. 6d.

SENIOR COURSE. Third Edition. Crown 8vo, pp. xiv. and 418, cloth. 1880. 4s.

MODERN FRENCH READER.—A GLOSSARY of Idioms, Gallicisms, and other Difficulties contained in the Senior Course of the Modern French Reader; with Short Notices of the most important French Writers and Historical or Literary Characters, and hints as to the works to be read or studied. By Charles Cassal, LL.D., &c. Crown 8vo, pp. viii. and 104, cloth. 1881. 2s. 6d.

MODERN FRENCH READER.—SENIOR COURSE AND GLOSSARY combined. 6s.

MORELET.—TRAVELS IN CENTRAL AMERICA, including Accounts of some Regions unexplored since the Conquest. From the French of A. Morelet, by Mrs. M. F. Squier. Edited by E. G. Squier. 8vo, pp. 430, cloth. 1871. 8s. 6d.

MORFILL.—SIMPLIFIED POLISH GRAMMAR. See Trübner's Collection.

MORFIT.—A Practical Treatise on the Manufacture of Soaps. By Campbell Morfit, M.D., F.C.S., formerly Professor of Applied Chemistry in the University of Maryland. With Illustrations. Demy 8vo, pp. xii. and 270, cloth. 1871. £2, 12s. 6d.

MORFIT.—A Practical Treatise on Pure Fertilizers, and the Chemical Conversion of Rock Guanos, Marlstones, Coprolites, and the Crude Phosphates of Lime and Alumina generally into various valuable Products. By Campbell Morfit, M.D., F.C.S., formerly Professor of Applied Chemistry in the University of Maryland. With 28 Plates. 8vo, pp. xvi. and 547, cloth. 1873. £4, 4s.

MORRIS.—A Descriptive and Historical Account of the Godavery District, in the Presidency of Madras. By Henry Morris, formerly of the Madras Civil Service, author of "A History of India, for use in Schools," and other works. With a Map. 8vo, pp. xii. and 390, cloth. 1878. 12s.

MOSENTHAL.—Ostriches and Ostrich Farming. By J. de Mosenthal, late Member of the Legistive Council of the Cape of Good Hope, &c., and James E. Harting, F.L.S., F.Z.S., Member of the British Ornithologist's Union, &c. Second Edition. With 8 full-page illustrations and 20 woodcuts. Royal 8vo, pp. xxiv. and 246, cloth. 1879. 10s. 6d.

MOTLEY.—John Lothrop Motley; a Memoir. By Oliver Wendell Holmes. English Copyright Edition. Crown 8vo, pp. xii. and 275, cloth. 1878. 6s.

MUELLER.—The Organic Constituents of Plants and Vegetable Substances, and their Chemical Analysis. By Dr. G. C. Wittstein. Authorised Translation from the German Original, enlarged with numerous Additions, by Baron Ferd. von Mueller, K.C.M.G., M. & Ph. D., F.R.S. Crown 8vo, pp. xviii. and 332, wrapper. 1880. 14s.

MUELLER.—Select Extra-Tropical Plants readily eligible for Industrial Culture or Naturalisation. With Indications of their Native Countries and some of their Uses. By F. Von Mueller, K.C.M.G., M.D., Ph.D., F.R.S. 8vo, pp. x., 394, cloth. 1880. 8s.

MUHAMMED.—The Life of Muhammed. Based on Muhammed Ibn Ishak. By Abd El Malik Ibn Hisham. Edited by Dr. Ferdinand Wüstenfeld. One volume containing the Arabic Text. 8vo, pp. 1026, sewed. £1, 1s. Another volume, containing Introduction, Notes, and Index in German. 8vo, pp. lxxii. and 266, sewed. 7s. 6d. Each part sold separately.

MUIR.—Extracts from the Coran. In the Original, with English rendering. Compiled by Sir William Muir, K.C.S.I., LL.D., Author of "The Life of Mahomet." Second Edition. Crown 8vo, pp. viii. and 64, cloth. 1885. 2s. 6d.

MUIR.—Original Sanskrit Texts, on the Origin and History of the People of India, their Religion and Institutions. Collected, Translated, and Illustrated by John Muir, D.C.L., LL.D., Ph.D., &c. &c.

Vol. I. Mythical and Legendary Accounts of the Origin of Caste, with an Inquiry into its existence in the Vedic Age. Second Edition, rewritten and greatly enlarged. 8vo, pp. xx. and 532, cloth. 1868. £1, 1s.

Vol. II. The Trans-Himalayan Origin of the Hindus, and their Affinity with the Western Branches of the Aryan Race. Second Edition, revised, with Additions. 8vo, pp. xxxii. and 512, cloth. 1871. £1, 1s.

Vol. III. The Vedas: Opinions of their Authors, and of later Indian Writers, on their Origin, Inspiration, and Authority. Second Edition, revised and enlarged. 8vo, pp. xxxii. and 312, cloth. 1868. 16s.

Vol. IV. Comparison of the Vedic with the later representation of the principal Indian Deities. **Second** Edition, revised. 8vo, pp. xvi. and 524, cloth. 1873. £1, 1s.

MUIR.—ORIGINAL SANSKRIT TEXTS—*continued.*
  Vol. V. Contributions to a Knowledge of the Cosmogony, Mythology, Religious Ideas, Life and Manners of the Indians in the Vedic Age. Third Edition. 8vo, pp. xvi. and 492, cloth. 1884. £1, 1s.

MUIR.—TRANSLATIONS FROM THE SANSKRIT. See Trübner's Oriental Series.

MULHALL.—HANDBOOK OF THE RIVER PLATE, Comprising the Argentine Republic, Uruguay, and Paraguay. With Six Maps. By M. G. and E. T. Mulhall, Proprietors and Editors of the Buenos Ayres *Standard.* Fifth Edition (Ninth Thousand), crown 8vo, pp. x. and 732, cloth. 1885. 7s. 6d.

MÜLLER.—OUTLINE DICTIONARY, for the Use of Missionaries, Explorers, and Students of Language. With an Introduction on the proper Use of the Ordinary English Alphabet in transcribing Foreign Languages. By F. Max Müller, M.A. The Vocabulary compiled by John Bellows. 12mo, pp. 368, morocco. 1867. 7s. 6d.

MÜLLER.—LECTURE ON BUDDHIST NIHILISM. By F. Max Müller, M.A. Fcap. 8vo, sewed. 1869. 1s.

MÜLLER.—THE SACRED HYMNS OF THE BRAHMINS, as preserved to us in the oldest collection of religious poetry, the Rig-Veda-Sanhita. Translated and explained, by F. Max Müller, M.A., Fellow of All Souls' College, Professor of Comparative Philology at Oxford, Foreign Member of the Institute of France, &c., &c. Vol. 1. Hymns to the Maruts or the Storm-Gods. 8vo, pp. clii. and 264, cloth. 1869. 12s. 6d.

MÜLLER.—THE HYMNS OF THE RIG-VEDA, in the Samhita and Pada Texts. Reprinted from the Editio Princeps. By F. Max Müller, M.A., &c. Second Edition, with the two Texts on Parallel Pages. In two vols. 8vo, pp. 1704, sewed. £1, 12s.

MÜLLER.—A SHORT HISTORY OF THE BOURBONS. From the Earliest Period down to the Present Time. By R. M. Müller, Ph.D., Modern Master at Forest School, Walthamstow, and Author of "Parallèle entre 'Jules César,' par Shakespeare, et 'Le Mort de César,' par Voltaire," &c. Fcap. 8vo, pp. 30, wrapper. 1882. 1s.

MÜLLER.—ANCIENT INSCRIPTIONS IN CEYLON. By Dr. Edward Müller. 2 Vols. Text, crown 8vo, pp. 220, cloth, and Plates, oblong folio, cloth. 1883. 21s.

MÜLLER.—PALI GRAMMAR. See Trübner's Collection.

MULLEY.—GERMAN GEMS IN AN ENGLISH SETTING. Translated by Jane Mulley. Fcap., pp. xii. and 180, cloth. 1877. 3s. 6d.

NÁGÁNANDA; OR, THE JOY OF THE SNAKE WORLD. A Buddhist Drama in Five Acts. Translated into English Prose, with Explanatory Notes, from the Sanskrit of Sri-Harsha-Deva, by Palmer Boyd, B.A. With an Introduction by Professor Cowell. Crown 8vo, pp. xvi. and 100, cloth. 1872. 4s. 6d.

NAPIER.—FOLK LORE; or, Superstitious Beliefs in the West of Scotland within this Century. With an Appendix, showing the probable relation of the modern Festivals of Christmas, May Day, St. John's Day, and Hallowe'en, to ancient Sun and Fire Worship. By James Napier, F.R.S.E., &c. Crown 8vo, pp. vii. and 190, cloth. 1878. 4s.

NARADIYA DHARMA-SASTRA; OR, THE INSTITUTES OF NARADA. Translated, for the first time, from the unpublished Sanskrit original. By Dr. Julius Jolly, University, Wurzburg. With a Preface, Notes, chiefly critical, an Index of Quotations from Narada in the principal Indian Digests, and a general Index. Crown 8vo, pp. xxxv. and 144, cloth. 1876. 10s. 6d.

NAVILLE.—PITHOM. See Egypt Exploration Fund.

NEVILL.—HAND LIST OF MOLLUSCA IN THE INDIAN MUSEUM, CALCUTTA. By Geoffrey Nevill, C.M.Z.S., &c., First Assistant to the Superintendent of the Indian Museum. Part I. Gastropoda, Pulmonata, and Prosobranchia-Neurobranchia. 8vo, pp. xvi. and 338, cloth. 1878. 15s.

NEWMAN.—THE ODES OF HORACE. Translated into Unrhymed Metres, with Introduction and Notes. By F. W. Newman. Second Edition. Post 8vo, pp. xxi. and 247, cloth. 1876. 4s.

NEWMAN.—THEISM, DOCTRINAL AND PRACTICAL; or, Didactic Religious Utterances. By F. W. Newman. 4to, pp. 184, cloth. 1858. 4s. 6d.

NEWMAN.—HOMERIC TRANSLATION IN THEORY AND PRACTICE. A Reply to Matthew Arnold. By F. W. Newman. Crown 8vo, pp. 104, stiff covers. 1861. 2s. 6d.

NEWMAN.—HIAWATHA: Rendered into Latin. With Abridgment. By F. W. Newman. 12mo, pp. vii. and 110, sewed. 1862. 2s. 6d.

NEWMAN.—A HISTORY OF THE HEBREW MONARCHY from the Administration of Samuel to the Babylonish Captivity. By F. W. Newman. Third Edition. Crown 8vo, pp. x. and 354, cloth. 1865. 8s. 6d.

NEWMAN.—PHASES OF FAITH; or, Passages from the History of my Creed. By F. W. Newman. New Edition; with Reply to Professor Henry Rogers, Author of the "Eclipse of Faith." Crown 8vo, pp. viii. and 212, cloth. 1881. 3s. 6d.

NEWMAN.—A HANDBOOK OF MODERN ARABIC, consisting of a Practical Grammar, with numerous Examples, Dialogues, and Newspaper Extracts, in European Type. By F. W. Newman. Post 8vo, pp. xx. and 192, cloth. 1866. 6s.

NEWMAN.—TRANSLATIONS OF ENGLISH POETRY INTO LATIN VERSE. Designed as Part of a New Method of Instructing in Latin. By F. W. Newman. Crown 8vo, pp. xiv. and 202, cloth. 1868. 6s.

NEWMAN.—THE SOUL: Her Sorrows and her Aspirations. An Essay towards the Natural History of the Soul, as the True Basis of Theology. By F. W. Newman. Tenth Edition. Post 8vo, pp. xii. and 162, cloth. 1882. 3s. 6d.

NEWMAN.—THE TEXT OF THE IGUVINE INSCRIPTIONS. With Interlinear Latin Translation and Notes. By F. W. Newman. 8vo, pp. 56, sewed. 1868. 2s.

NEWMAN.—MISCELLANIES; chiefly Addresses, Academical and Historical. By F. W. Newman. 8vo, pp. iv. and 356, cloth. 1869. 7s. 6d.

NEWMAN.—THE ILIAD OF HOMER, faithfully translated into Unrhymed English Metre, by F. W. Newman. Royal 8vo, pp. xvi. and 384, cloth. 1871. 10s. 6d.

NEWMAN.—A DICTIONARY OF MODERN ARABIC. 1. Anglo-Arabic Dictionary. 2. Anglo-Arabic Vocabulary. 3. Arabo-English Dictionary. By F. W. Newman. In 2 vols. crown 8vo, pp. xvi. and 376-464, cloth. 1871. £1, 1s.

NEWMAN.—HEBREW THEISM. By F. W. Newman. Royal 8vo, pp. viii. and 172. Stiff wrappers. 1874. 4s. 6d.

NEWMAN.—THE MORAL INFLUENCE OF LAW. A Lecture by F. W. Newman, May 20, 1860. Crown 8vo, pp. 16, sewed. 3d.

NEWMAN.—RELIGION NOT HISTORY. By F. W. Newman. Foolscap, pp. 58, paper wrapper. 1877. 1s.

NEWMAN.—MORNING PRAYERS IN THE HOUSEHOLD OF A BELIEVER IN GOD. By F. W. Newman. Second Edition. Crown 8vo, pp. 80, limp cloth. 1882. 1s. 6d.

NEWMAN.—REORGANIZATION OF ENGLISH INSTITUTIONS. A Lecture by Emeritus Professor F. W. Newman. Delivered in the Manchester Athenæum, October 15, 1875. Crown 8vo, pp. 28, sewed. 1880. 6d.

NEWMAN.—WHAT IS CHRISTIANITY WITHOUT CHRIST? By F. W. Newman, Emeritus Professor of University College, London. 8vo, pp. 28, stitched in wrapper. 1881. 1s.

NEWMAN.—LIBYAN VOCABULARY. An Essay towards Reproducing the Ancient Numidian Language out of Four Modern Languages. By F. W. Newman. Crown 8vo, pp. vi. and 204, cloth. 1882. 10s. 6d.

NEWMAN.—A CHRISTIAN COMMONWEALTH. By F. W. Newman. Crown 8vo, pp. 60, cloth. 1883. 1s.

NEWMAN.—CHRISTIANITY IN ITS CRADLE. By F. W. Newman, once Fellow of Balliol College, Oxford, now Emeritus Professor of University College, London. Crown 8vo, pp. iv. and 132, cloth. 1884. 2s.

NEWMAN.—Comments on the Text of Æschylus. By F. W. Newman, Honorary Fellow of Worcester College, Oxford, and formerly Fellow of Balliol College. Demy 8vo, pp. xii. and 144, cloth. 1884. 5s.

NEWMAN.—Rebilius Cruso: Robinson Crusoe in Latin. A Book to Lighten Tedium to a Learner. By F. W. Newman, Emeritus Professor of Latin in University College, London; Honorary Fellow of Worcester College, Oxford. Post 8vo, pp. xii. and 110, cloth. 1884. 5s.

NEW SOUTH WALES, Publications of the Government of. List on application.

NEW SOUTH WALES.—Journal and Proceedings of the Royal Society of Published annually. Price 10s. 6d. List of Contents on application.

NEWTON.—Patent Law and Practice: showing the mode of obtaining and opposing Grants, Disclaimers, Confirmations, and Extensions of Patents. With a Chapter on Patent Agents. By A. V. Newton. Enlarged Edition. Crown 8vo, pp. xii. and 104, cloth. 1879. 2s. 6d.

NEWTON.—An Analysis of the Patent and Copyright Laws: Including the various Acts relating to the Protection of Inventions, Designs, Trade Marks; Literary and Musical Compositions, Dramatic Performances; Engravings, Sculpture, Paintings, Drawings, and Photographs. By A. Newton, author of "Patent Law and Practice." Demy 8vo, pp. viii. and 70, cloth. 1884. 3s. 6d.

NEW ZEALAND INSTITUTE PUBLICATIONS:—
 I. Transactions and Proceedings of the New Zealand Institute. Demy 8vo, stitched. Vols. I. to XVI., 1868 to 1883. £1, 1s. each.
 II. An Index to the Transactions and Proceedings of the New Zealand Institute. Vols. I. to VIII. Edited and Published under the Authority of the Board of Governors of the Institute. By James Hector, C.M.G., M.D., F.R.S. Demy, 8vo, 44 pp., stitched. 1877. 2s. 6d.

NEW ZEALAND.—Geological Survey. List of Publications on application.

NOIRIT.—A French Course in Ten Lessons. By Jules Noirit, B.A. Lessons I.-IV. Crown 8vo, pp. xiv. and 80, sewed. 1870. 1s. 6d.

NOIRIT.—French Grammatical Questions for the use of Gentlemen preparing for the Army, Civil Service, Oxford Examinations, &c., &c. By Jules Noirit. Crown 8vo, pp. 62, cloth. 1870. 1s. Interleaved, 1s. 6d.

NOURSE.—Narrative of the Second Arctic Expedition made by Charles F. Hall. His Voyage to Repulse Bay; Sledge Journeys to the Straits of Fury and Hecla, and to King William's Land, and Residence among the Eskimos during the years 1864-69. Edited under the orders of the Hon. Secretary of the Navy, by Prof. J. E. Nourse, U.S.N. 4to, pp. l. and 644, cloth. With maps, heliotypes, steel and wood engravings. 1880. £1, 8s.

NUGENT'S Improved French and English and English and French Pocket Dictionary. Par Smith. 24mo, pp. 489 and 320, cloth. 1873. 3s.

NUTT.—Two Treatises on Verbs containing Feeble and Double Letters. By R. Jehuda Hayug of Fez. Translated into Hebrew from the original Arabic by R. Moses Gikatilia of Cordova, with the Treatise on Punctuation by the same author, translated by Aben Ezra. Edited from Bodleian MSS., with an English translation, by J. W. Nutt, M.A. Demy 8vo, pp. 312, sewed. 1870. 5s.

NUMISMATA ORIENTALIA ILLUSTRATA. See Marsden, and International.

NUTT.—A Sketch of Samaritan History, Dogma, and Literature. An Introduction to "Fragments of a Samaritan Targum." By J. W. Nutt, M.A., &c., &c. Demy 8vo, pp. 180, cloth. 1874. 5s.

OEHLENSCHLÄGER.—Axel and Valborg: a Tragedy, in Five Acts, and other Poems. Translated from the Danish of Adam Oehlenschläger by Pierce Butler, M.A., late Rector of Ulcombe, Kent. Edited by Professor Palmer, M.A., of St. John's Coll., Camb. With a Memoir of the Translator. Fcap. 8vo, pp. xii. and 164, cloth. 1874. 5s.

OERA LINDA BOOK (The).—From a Manuscript of the 13th Century, with the permission of the proprietor, C. Over de Linden of the Helder. The Original Frisian Text as verified by Dr. J. O. Ottema, accompanied by an English Version of Dr. Ottema's Dutch Translation. By W. R. Sandbach. 8vo, pp. xxv. and 254, cloth. 1876. 5s.

OGAREFF.—Essai sur la Situation Russe. Lettres à un Anglais. Par N. Ogareff. 12mo, pp. 150, sewed. 1862. 3s.

OLCOTT.—A Buddhist Catechism, according to the Canon of the Southern Church. By Colonel H. S. Olcott, President of the Theosophical Society. 24mo, pp. 32. 1s.

OLCOTT.—The Yoga Philosophy: Being the Text of Patanjali, with Bhojarajah's Commentary. A Reprint of the English Translation of the above, by the late Dr. Ballantyne and Govind Shastri Deva; to which are added Extracts from Various Authors. With an Introduction by Colonel H. S. Olcott, President of the Theosophical Society. The whole Edited by Tukaram Tatia, F.T.S. Crown 8vo, pp. xvi.-294, wrapper. 1882. 7s. 6d.

OLLENDORFF.—Metodo para aprender a Leer, escribir y hablar el Inglés segun el sistema de Ollendorff. Por Ramon Palenzuela y Juan de la Carreño. 8vo, pp. xlvi. and 460, cloth. 1873. 7s. 6d.
Key to Ditto. Crown 8vo, pp. 112, **cloth**. 1873. **4s.**

OLLENDORFF.—Metodo para aprender a Leer, escribir y hablar el Frances, segun el verdadero sistema de Ollendorff; ordenado en lecciones progresivas, consistiendo de ejercicios orales y escritos; enriquecido de la pronunciacion figurada como se estila en la conversacion; y de un Apéndice abrazando las reglas de la sintáxis, la formacion de los verbos regulares, y la conjugacion de los irregulares. Por Teodoro Simonné, Professor de Lenguas. Crown 8vo, pp. 342, cloth. 1873. 6s.
Key to Ditto. Crown 8vo, pp. 80, cloth. 1873. 3s. 6d.

OPPERT.—On the Classification of Languages: A Contribution to Comparative Philology. By Dr. Gustav Oppert, Ph.D., Professor of Sanskrit, Presidency College, Madras. 8vo, paper, pp. viii. and 146. 1883. 7s. 6d.

OPPERT.—Lists of Sanskrit Manuscripts in Private Libraries of Southern India, Compiled, Arranged, and Indexed by Gustav Oppert, Ph.D., Professor of Sanskrit, Presidency College, Madras. Vol. I. 8vo, pp. vii. and 620, cloth. 1883. £1, 1s.

OPPERT.—On the Weapons, Army Organisation, and Political Maxims of the Ancient Hindus; with special reference to Gunpowder and Firearms. By Dr. Gustav Oppert, Ph.D., Professor of Sanskrit, Presidency College, Madras. 8vo, paper, pp. vi. and 162. 1883. 7s. 6d.

ORIENTAL SERIES.—See Trübner's Oriental Series.

ORIENTAL Text Society's Publications. **A list may be had** on application.

ORIENTAL CONGRESS.—Report of the Proceedings of the Second International Congress of Orientalists held in London, 1874. Royal 8vo, pp. viii. and 68, sewed. 1874. 5s.

ORIENTALISTS.—Transactions of the Second Session of the International Congress of Orientalists. Held in London in September 1874. Edited by Robert K. Douglas, Hon. Sec. 8vo, pp. viii. and 456, cloth. 1876. 21s.

OTTÉ.—How to Learn Danish (Dano-Norwegian): a Manual for Students of Danish based on the Ollendorffian system of teaching languages, and adapted for self-instruction. By E. C. Otté. Second Edition. Crown 8vo, pp. xx. and 338, cloth. 1884. **7s. 6d.**
Key to above. Crown 8vo, pp. 84, cloth. 3s.

OTTÉ.—Simplified Danish and Swedish Grammars. See Trübner's Collection.

OVERBECK.—Catholic Orthodoxy and Anglo-Catholicism. A Word about the Intercommunion between the English and Orthodox Churches. By J. J. Overbeck, D.D. 8vo, pp. viii. and 200, cloth. 1866. 5s.

OVERBECK.—Bonn Conference. By J. J. Overbeck, D.D. Crown 8vo, pp. **48**, sewed. 1876. **1s.**

OVERBECK.—A Plain View of the Claims of the Orthodox Catholic Church as Opposed to all other Christian Denominations. By J. J. Overbeck, D.D. Crown 8vo, pp. iv. and 138, wrapper. 1881. 2s. 6d.

OWEN.—Footfalls on the Boundary of Another World. With Narrative Illustrations. By R. D. Owen. An enlarged English Copyright Edition. Post 8vo, pp. xx. and 392, cloth. 1875. 7s. 6d.

OWEN.—The Debatable Land between this World and the Next. With Illustrative Narrations. By Robert Dale Owen. Second Edition. Crown 8vo, pp. 456, cloth. 1874. 7s. 6d.

OWEN.—Threading my Way: Twenty-Seven Years of Autobiography. By R. D. Owen. Crown 8vo, pp. 344, cloth. 1874. 7s. 6d.

OXLEY.—Egypt: And the Wonders of the Land of the Pharaohs. By William Oxley, author of "The Philosophy of Spirit." Illustrated by a New Version of the Bhagavat-Gita, an Episode of the Mahabharat, one of the Epic Poems of Ancient India. Crown 8vo, pp. viii.-328, cloth. 1884. 7s. 6d.

OYSTER (The): Where, How, and When to Find, Breed, Cook, and Eat It. Second Edition, with a New Chapter, "The Oyster-Seeker in London." 12mo, pp. viii. and 106, boards. 1863. 1s.

PALESTINE.—Memoirs of the Survey of Western Palestine. Edited by W. Besant, M.A., and E. H. Palmer, M.A., under the Direction of the Committee of the Palestine Exploration Fund. Complete in seven volumes. Demy 4to, cloth, with a Portfolio of Plans, and large scale Map. Second Issue. Price Twenty Guineas.

PALMER.—A Concise English-Persian Dictionary; together with a simplified Grammar of the Persian Language. By the late E. H. Palmer, M.A., Lord Almoner's Reader, and Professor of Arabic, Cambridge, &c. Completed and Edited, from the MS. left imperfect at his death, by G. Le Strange. Royal 16mo, pp. 606, cloth. 1883. 10s. 6d.

PALMER.—A Concise Persian-English Dictionary. By E. H. Palmer, M.A., of the Middle Temple, Barrister-at-Law, Lord Almoner's Reader, and Professor of Arabic, and Fellow of St. John's College in the University of Cambridge. Second Edition. Royal 16mo, pp. 726, cloth. 1884. 10s. 6d.

PALMER.—The Song of the Reed, and other Pieces. By E. H. Palmer, M.A., Cambridge. Crown 8vo, pp. 208, cloth. 1876. 5s.

PALMER.—Hindustani, Arabic, and Persian Grammar. See Trübner's Collection.

PALMER.—The Patriarch and the Tsar. Translated from the Russ by William Palmer, M.A. Demy 8vo, cloth. Vol. I. The Replies of the Humble Nicon. Pp. xl. and 674. 1871. 12s.—Vol. II. Testimonies concerning the Patriarch Nicon, the Tsar, and the Boyars. Pp. lxxviii. and 554. 1873. 12s.—Vol. III. History of the Condemnation of the Patriarch Nicon. Pp. lxvi. and 558. 1873. 12s.—Vols. IV., V., and VI. Services of the Patriarch Nicon to the Church and State of his Country, &c. Pp. lxxviii. and 1 to 660; xiv.-661-1028, and 1 to 254; xxvi.-1029-1656, and 1-72. 1876. 36s.

PARKER.—Theodore Parker's Celebrated Discourse on Matters Pertaining to Religion. People's Edition. Cr. 8vo, pp. 351. 1872. Stitched, 1s. 6d.; cl., 2s.

PARKER.—Theodore Parker. A Biography. By O. B. Frothingham. Crown 8vo, pp. viii. and 588, cloth, with Portrait. 1876. 12s.

PARKER.—The Collected Works of Theodore Parker, Minister of the Twenty-eighth Congregational Society at Boston, U.S. Containing his Theological, Polemical, and Critical Writings; Sermons, Speeches, and Addresses; and Literary Miscellanies. In 14 vols. 8vo, cloth. 6s. each.

    Vol. I. Discourse on Matters Pertaining to Religion. Preface by the Editor, and Portrait of Parker from a medallion by Saulini. Pp. 380.
    Vol. II. Ten Sermons and Prayers. Pp. 360.
    Vol. III. Discourses of Theology. Pp. 318.
    Vol. IV. Discourses on Politics. Pp. 312.

PARKER.—COLLECTED WORKS—*continued.*
    Vol. V. Discourses of Slavery. I. Pp. 336.
    Vol. VI. Discourses of Slavery. II. Pp. 323.
    Vol. VII. Discourses of Social Science. Pp. 296.
    Vol. VIII. Miscellaneous Discourses. Pp. 230.
    Vol. IX. Critical Writings. I. Pp. 292.
    Vol. X. Critical Writings. II. Pp. 308.
    Vol. XI. Sermons of Theism, Atheism, and Popular Theology. Pp. 257.
    Vol. XII. Autobiographical and Miscellaneous Pieces. Pp. 356.
    Vol. XIII. Historic Americans. Pp. 236.
    Vol. XIV. Lessons from the World of Matter and the World of Man. Pp. 352.

PARKER.—MALAGASY GRAMMAR. See Trübner's Collection.

PARRY.—A SHORT CHAPTER ON LETTER-CHANGE, with Examples. Being chiefly an attempt to reduce in a simple manner the principal classical and cognate words to their primitive meanings. By J. Parry, B.A., formerly Scholar of Corpus Christi College, Cambridge. Fcap. 8vo, pp. 16, wrapper. 1884. 1s.

PATERSON.—NOTES ON MILITARY SURVEYING AND RECONNAISSANCE. By Lieut.-Colonel William Paterson. Sixth Edition. With 16 Plates. Demy 8vo, pp. xii. and 146, cloth. 1882. 7s. 6d.

PATERSON.—TOPOGRAPHICAL EXAMINATION PAPERS. By Lieut.-Col. W. Paterson. 8vo, pp. 32, with 4 Plates. Boards. 1882. 2s.

PATERSON.—TREATISE ON MILITARY DRAWING. With a Course of Progressive Plates. By Captain W. Paterson, Professor of Military Drawing at the Royal Military College, Sandhurst. Oblong 4to, pp. xii. and 31, cloth. 1862. £1, 1s.

PATERSON.—THE OROMETER FOR HILL MEASURING, combining Scales of Distances, Protractor, Clinometer, Scale of Horizontal Equivalents, Scale of Shade, and Table of Gradients. By Captain William Paterson. On cardboard. 1s.

PATERSON.—CENTRAL AMERICA. By W. Paterson, the Merchant Statesman. From a MS. in the British Museum, 1701. With a Map. Edited by S. Bannister, M.A. 8vo, pp. 70, sewed. 1857. 2s. 6d.

PATON.—A HISTORY OF THE EGYPTIAN REVOLUTION, from the Period of the Mamelukes to the Death of Mohammed Ali; from Arab and European Memoirs, Oral Tradition, and Local Research. By A. A. Paton. Second Edition. 2 vols. demy 8vo, pp. xii. and 395, viii. and 446, cloth. 1870. 7s. 6d.

PATON.—HENRY BEYLE (otherwise DE STENDAHL). A Critical and Biographical Study, aided by Original Documents and Unpublished Letters from the Private Papers of the Family of Beyle. By A. A. Paton. Crown 8vo, pp. 340, cloth. 1874. 7s. 6d.

PATTON.—THE DEATH OF DEATH; or, A Study of God's Holiness in Connection with the Existence of Evil, in so far as Intelligent and Responsible Beings are Concerned. By an Orthodox Layman (John M. Patton). Revised Edition, crown 8vo, pp. xvi. and 252, cloth. 1881. 6s.

PAULI.—SIMON DE MONTFORT, EARL OF LEICESTER, the Creator of the House of Commons. By Reinhold Pauli. Translated by Una M. Goodwin. With Introduction by Harriet Martineau. Crown 8vo, pp. xvi. and 340, cloth. 1876. 6s.

PETTENKOFER.—THE RELATION OF THE AIR TO THE CLOTHES WE WEAR, THE HOUSE WE LIVE IN, AND THE SOIL WE DWELL ON. Three Popular Lectures delivered before the Albert Society at Dresden. By Dr. Max Von Pettenkofer, Professor of Hygiene at the University of Munich, &c. Abridged and Translated by Augustus Hess, M.D., M.R.C.P., London, &c. Cr. 8vo, pp. viii. and 96, limp cl. 1873. 2s. 6d.

PETRUCCELLI.—PRELIMINAIRES DE LA QUESTION ROMAINE DE M. ED. ABOUT. Par F. Petruccelli de la Gattina. 8vo, pp. xv. and 364, cloth. 1860. 7s. 6d.

PEZZI.—ARYAN PHILOLOGY, according to the most recent researches (Glottologia Aria Recentissima). Remarks Historical and Critical. By Domenico Pezzi. Translated by E. S. Roberts, M.A. Crown 8vo, pp. xvi. and 200, cloth. 1879. 6s.

PHAYRE.—A History of Burma. See Trübner's Oriental Series.

PHAYRE.—The Coins of Arakan, of Pegu, and of Burma. By Sir Arthur Phayre, C.B., K.C.S.I., G.C.M.G., late Commissioner of British Burma. Royal 4to, pp. viii.-48, with Autotype Illustrative Plates. Wrapper. 1882. 8s. 6d.

PHILLIPS.—The Doctrine of Addai, the Apostle, now first edited in a complete form in the Original Syriac, with English Translation and Notes. By George Phillips, D.D., President of Queen's College, Cambridge. 8vo, pp. xv. and 52 and 53, cloth. 1876. 7s. 6d.

PHILLIPS.—Kopal-Kundala: A Tale of Bengali Life. Translated from the Bengali of Bunkim Chandra Chatterjee. By H. A. D. Phillips, Bengal Civil Service. Crown 8vo, pp. xxx.-208, cloth. 1885. 6s.

PHILOLOGICAL SOCIETY, Transactions of, published irregularly. List of publications on application.

PHILOSOPHY (The) of Inspiration and Revelation. By a Layman. With a preliminary notice of an Essay by the present Lord Bishop of Winchester, contained in a volume entitled "Aids to Faith." 8vo, pp. 20, sewed. 1875. 6d.

PICCIOTTO.—Sketches of Anglo-Jewish History. By James Picciotto. Demy 8vo, pp. xi. and 420, cloth. 1875. 12s.

PIESSE.—Chemistry in the Brewing-Room: being the substance of a Course of Lessons to Practical Brewers. With Tables of Alcohol, Extract, and Original Gravity. By Charles H. Piesse, F.C.S., Public Analyst. Fcap., pp. viii. and 62, cloth. 1877. 5s.

PIRY.—Le Saint Edit, Étude de Litterature Chinoise. Préparée par A. Théophile Piry, du Service des Douanes Maritimes de Chine. 4to, pp. xx. and 320, cloth. 1879. 21s.

PLAYFAIR.—The Cities and Towns of China. A Geographical Dictionary. By G. M. H. Playfair, of Her Majesty's Consular Service in China. 8vo, pp. 506, cloth. 1879. £1, 5s.

PLINY.—The Letters of Pliny the Younger. Translated by J. D. Lewis, M.A., Trinity College, Cambridge. Post 8vo, pp. vii. and 390, cloth. 1879. 5s.

PLUMPTRE.—King's College Lectures on Elocution; on the Physiology and Culture of Voice and Speech and the Expression of the Emotions by Language, Countenance, and Gesture. To which is added a Special Lecture on the Causes and Cure of the Impediments of Speech. Being the substance of the Introductory Course of Lectures annually delivered by Charles John Plumptre, Lecturer on Public Reading and Speaking at King's College, London, in the Evening Classes Department. Dedicated by permission to H.R.H. the Prince of Wales. Fourth, greatly Enlarged Illustrated, Edition. Post 8vo, pp. xviii. and 494, cloth. 1883. 15s.

PLUMPTRE.—General Sketch of the History of Pantheism. By C. E. Plumptre. Vol. I., from the Earliest Times to the Age of Spinoza; Vol. II., from the Age of Spinoza to the Commencement of the 19th Century. 2 vols. demy 8vo, pp. viii. and 395; iv. and 348, cloth. 1881. 18s.

POLE.—The Philosophy of Music. See English and Foreign Philosophical Library. Vol. XI.

PONSARD.—Charlotte Corday. A Tragedy. By F. Ponsard. Edited, with English Notes and Notice on Ponsard, by Professor C. Cassal, LL.D. 12mo, pp. xi. and 133, cloth. 1867. 2s. 6d.

PONSARD.—L'Honneur et L'Argent. A Comedy. By François Ponsard. Edited, with English Notes and Memoir of Ponsard, by Professor C. Cassal, LL.D. Fcap. 8vo, pp. xvi. and 172, cloth. 1869. 3s. 6d.

POOLE.—An Index to Periodical Literature. By W. F. Poole, LL.D., Librarian of the Chicago Public Library. Third Edition, brought down to January 1882. Royal 8vo, pp. xxviii. and 1442, cloth. 1883. £3, 13s. 6d. Wrappers, £3, 10s.

PRACTICAL GUIDES :—
  France, Belgium, Holland, and the Rhine. 1s.—Italian Lakes. 1s.—Wintering Places of the South. 2s.—Switzerland, Savoy, and North Italy. 2s. 6d.—General Continental Guide. 5s.—Geneva. 1s.—Paris. 1s.—Bernese Oberland. 1s.—Italy. 4s.

PRATT.—A Grammar and Dictionary of the Samoan Language. By Rev. George Pratt, Forty Years a Missionary of the London Missionary Society in Samoa. Second Edition. Edited by Rev. S. J. Whitmee, F.R.G.S. Crown 8vo, pp. viii. and 380, cloth. 1878. 18s.

PRINSEP.—Record of Services of the Honourable East India Company's Civil Servants in the Madras Presidency, from 1741 to 1858. Compiled and Edited from Records in the possession of the Secretary of State for India. By C. C. Prinsep, late Superintendent of Records, India Office. Post 8vo, pp. xxxvi.-164, cloth. 1885. 10s. 6d.

PSYCHICAL RESEARCH, Proceedings of the Society for. Published irregularly. Post 8vo, cloth. Vol. I., pp. 338. 1884. 10s. Vol. II., pp. 356. 1884. 10s.

PURITZ.—Code-Book of Gymnastic Exercises. By Ludwig Puritz. Translated by O. Knofe and J. W. Macqueen. Illustrated. 32mo, pp. xxiv.-292, boards. 1883. 1s. 6d.

QUINET.—Edgar Quinet. See English and Foreign Philosophical Library, Vol. XIV.

RAM RAZ.—Essay on the Architecture of the Hindus. By Ram Raz, Native Judge and Magistrate of Bangalore, Corr. Mem. R.A.S. With 48 Plates. 4to, pp. xiv. and 64, sewed. 1834. £2, 2s.

RAMSAY.—Tabular List of all the Australian Birds at present known to the Author, showing the distribution of the species. By E. P. Ramsay, F.L.S., &c., Curator of the Australian Museum, Sydney. 8vo, pp. 36, and Map ; boards 1878. 5s.

RASK.—Grammar of the Anglo-Saxon Tongue, from the Danish of Erasmus Rask. By Benjamin Thorpe. Third Edition, corrected and improved, with Plate. Post 8vo, pp. vi. and 192, cloth. 1879. 5s. 6d.

RASK.—A Short Tractate on the Longevity ascribed to the Patriarchs in the Book of Genesis, and its relation to the Hebrew Chronology ; the Flood, the Exodus of the Israelites, the Site of Eden, &c. From the Danish of the late Professor Rask, with his manuscript corrections, and large additions from his autograph, now for the first time printed. With a Map of Paradise and the circumjacent Lands. Crown 8vo, pp. 134, cloth. 1863. 2s. 6d.

RAVENSTEIN.—The Russians on the Amur ; its Discovery, Conquest, and Colonization, with a Description of the Country, its Inhabitants, Productions, and Commercial Capabilities, and Personal Accounts of Russian Travellers. By E. G. Ravenstein, F.R.G.S. With 4 tinted Lithographs and 3 Maps. 8vo, pp. 500, cloth. 1861. 15s.

RAVENSTEIN AND HULLEY.—The Gymnasium and its Fittings. By E. G. Ravenstein and John Hulley. With 14 Plates of Illustrations. 8vo, pp. 32, sewed. 1867. 2s. 6d.

RAVERTY.—Notes on Afghanistan and Part of Baluchistan, Geographical, Ethnographical, and Historical, extracted from the Writings of little known Afghan, and Tajyik Historians, &c., &c., and from Personal Observation. By Major H. G. Raverty, Bombay Native Infantry (Retired). Foolscap folio. Sections I. and II., pp. 98, wrapper. 1880. 2s. Section III., pp. vi. and 218. 1881. 5s. Section IV. 1884. 3s.

READE.—The Martyrdom of Man. By Winwood Reade. Eighth Edition. Crown 8vo, pp. viii. and 544, cloth. 1884. 7s. 6d.

RECORD OFFICE.—A Separate Catalogue of the Official Publications of the Public Record Office, on sale by Trübner & Co., may be had on application.

RECORDS OF THE HEART. By Stella, Author of "Sappho," "The King's Stratagem," &c. Second English Edition. Crown 8vo, pp. xvi. and 188, with six steel-plate engravings, cloth. 1881. 3s. 6d.

REDHOUSE.—THE MESNEVI. See Trübner's Oriental Series.

REDHOUSE.—SIMPLIFIED OTTOMAN-TURKISH GRAMMAR. See Trübner's Collection.

REDHOUSE.—THE TURKISH VADE-MECUM OF OTTOMAN COLLOQUIAL LANGUAGE: Containing a Concise Ottoman Grammar; a Carefully Selected Vocabulary Alphabetically Arranged, in two Parts, English and Turkish, and Turkish and English; Also a few Familiar Dialogues and Naval and Military Terms. The whole in English Characters, the Pronunciation being fully indicated. By J. W. Redhouse, M.R.A.S. Third Edition. 32mo, pp. viii. and 372, cloth. 1882. 6s.

REDHOUSE.—ON THE HISTORY, SYSTEM, AND VARIETIES OF TURKISH POETRY Illustrated by Selections in the Original and in English Paraphrase, with a Notice of the Islamic Doctrine of the Immortality of Woman's Soul in the Future State. By J. W. Redhouse, Esq., M.R.A.S. 8vo, pp. 62, cloth, 2s. 6d.; wrapper, 1s. 6d. 1879.

REEMELIN.—A CRITICAL REVIEW OF AMERICAN POLITICS. By C. Reemelin, of Cincinnati, Ohio. Demy 8vo, pp. xxiv. and 630, cloth. 1881. 14s.

RELIGION IN EUROPE HISTORICALLY CONSIDERED: An Essay in Verse. By the Author of "The Thames." Fcap. 8vo, pp. iv. and 152, cloth. 1883. 2s. 6d.

RENAN.—PHILOSOPHICAL DIALOGUES AND FRAGMENTS. From the French of Ernest Renan. Translated, with the sanction of the Author, by Ras Bihari Mukharji. Post 8vo, pp. xxxii. and 182, cloth. 1883. 7s. 6d.

RENAN.—AN ESSAY ON THE AGE AND ANTIQUITY OF THE BOOK OF NABATHÆAN AGRICULTURE. To which is added an Inaugural Lecture on the Position of the Shemitic Nations in the History of Civilisation. By Ernest Renan. Crown 8vo, pp. xvi. and 148, cloth. 1862. 3s. 6d.

RENAN.—THE LIFE OF JESUS. By Ernest Renan. Authorised English Translation. Crown 8vo, pp. xii. and 312, cloth. 2s. 6d.; sewed, 1s. 6d.

REPORT OF A GENERAL CONFERENCE OF LIBERAL THINKERS, for the discussion of matters pertaining to the religious needs of our time, and the methods of meeting them. Held June 13th and 14th, 1878, at South Place Chapel, Finsbury, London. 8vo, pp. 77, sewed. 1878. 1s.

RHODES.—UNIVERSAL CURVE TABLES FOR FACILITATING THE LAYING OUT OF CIRCULAR ARCS ON THE GROUND FOR RAILWAYS, CANALS, &c. Together with Table of Tangential Angles and Multiples. By Alexander Rhodes, C.E. Oblong 18mo, band, pp. ix. and 104, roan. 1881. 5s.

RHYS.—LECTURES ON WELSH PHILOLOGY. By John Rhys, M.A., Professor of Celtic at Oxford, Honorary Fellow of Jesus College, &c., &c. Second Edition, Revised and Enlarged. Crown 8vo, pp. xiv. and 467, cloth. 1879. 15s.

RICE.—MYSORE AND COORG. A Gazetteer compiled for the Government of India. By Lewis Rice, Director of Public Instruction, Mysore and Coorg. Vol. I. Mysore in General. With 2 Coloured Maps. Vol. II. Mysore, by Districts. With 10 Coloured Maps. Vol. III. Coorg. With a Map. 3 vols. royal 8vo, pp. xii. 670 and xvi.; 544 and xxii.; and 427 and xxvii., cloth. 1878. 25s.

RICE.—MYSORE INSCRIPTIONS. Translated for the Government by Lewis Rice. 8vo, pp. xcii. and 336-xxx., with a Frontispiece and Map, boards. 1879. 30s.

RIDLEY.—KÁMILARÓI, AND OTHER AUSTRALIAN LANGUAGES. By the Rev. William Ridley, B.A. Second Edition, revised and enlarged by the author; with comparative Tables of Words from twenty Australian Languages, and Songs, Traditions, Laws, and Customs of the Australian Race. Small 4to, pp. vi. and 172, cloth. 1877. 10s. 6d.

RIG-VEDA-SANHITA. A Collection of Ancient Hindu Hymns. Constituting the 1st to the 8th Ashtakas, or Books of the Rig-Veda; the oldest authority for the Religious and Social Institutions of the Hindus. Translated from the Original Sanskrit. By the late H. H. Wilson, M.A., F.R.S., &c., &c.
  Vol. I. 8vo, pp. lii. and 348, cloth. 21s.
  Vol. II. 8vo, pp. xxx. and 346, cloth. 1854. 21s.
  Vol. III. 8vo, pp. xxiv. and 525, cloth. 1857. 21s.
  Vol. IV. Edited by E. B. Cowell, M.A. 8vo, pp. 214, cloth. 1866. 14s.
  Vols. V. and VI. in the Press.

RILEY.—MEDIÆVAL CHRONICLES OF THE CITY OF LONDON. Chronicles of the Mayors and Sheriffs of London, and the Events which happened in their Days, from the Year A.D. 1188 to A.D. 1274. Translated from the original Latin of the "Liber de Antiquis Legibus" (published by the Camden Society), in the possession of the Corporation of the City of London; attributed to Arnold Fitz-Thedmar, Alderman of London in the Reign of Henry III.—Chronicles of London, and of the Marvels therein, between the Years 44 Henry III., A.D. 1260, and 17 Edward III., A.D. 1343. Translated from the original Anglo-Norman of the "Croniques de London," preserved in the Cottonian Collection (Cleopatra A. iv.) in the British Museum. Translated, with copious Notes and Appendices, by Henry Thomas Riley, M.A., Clare Hall, Cambridge, Barrister-at-Law. 4to, pp. xii. and 319, cloth. 1863. 12s.

RIOLA.—HOW TO LEARN RUSSIAN: a Manual for Students of Russian, based upon the Ollendorffian System of Teaching Languages, and adapted for Self-Instruction. By Henry Riola, Teacher of the Russian Language. With a Preface by W.R.S. Ralston, M.A. Second Edition. Crown 8vo, pp. 576, cloth. 1883. 12s.
  KEY to the above. Crown 8vo, pp. 126, cloth. 1878. 5s.

RIOLA.—A GRADUATED RUSSIAN READER, with a Vocabulary of all the Russian Words contained in it. By Henry Riola, Author of "How to Learn Russian." Crown 8vo, pp. viii. and 314, cloth. 1879. 10s. 6d.

RIPLEY.—SACRED RHETORIC; or, Composition and Delivery of Sermons. By Henry I. Ripley. 12mo, pp. 234, cloth. 1858. 2s. 6d.

ROCHE.—A FRENCH GRAMMAR, for the use of English Students, adopted for the Public Schools by the Imperial Council of Public Instruction. By A. Roche. Crown 8vo, pp. xii. and 176, cloth. 1869. 3s.

ROCHE.—PROSE AND POETRY. Select Pieces from the best English Authors, for Reading, Composition, and Translation. By A. Roche. Second Edition. Fcap. 8vo, pp. viii. and 226, cloth. 1872. 2s. 6d.

ROCKHILL.—UDANAVARGA. See Trübner's Oriental Series.

ROCKHILL.—THE LIFE OF THE BUDDHA. See Trübner's Oriental Series.

RODD.—THE BIRDS OF CORNWALL AND THE SCILLY ISLANDS. By the late Edward Hearle Rodd. Edited, with an Introduction, Appendix, and Memoir, by J. E. Harting. 8vo, pp. lvi. and 320, with Portrait and Map, cloth. 1880. 14s.

ROGERS.—THE WAVERLEY DICTIONARY: An Alphabetical Arrangement of all the Characters in Sir Walter Scott's Waverley Novels, with a Descriptive Analysis of each Character, and Illustrative Selections from the Text. By May Rogers. 12mo, pp. 358, cloth. 1879. 10s.

ROSING.—ENGLISH-DANISH DICTIONARY. By S. Rosing. Crown 8vo, pp. x. and 722, cloth. 8s. 6d.

ROSS.—ALPHABETICAL MANUAL OF BLOWPIPE ANALYSIS; showing all known Methods, Old and New. By Lieut.-Colonel W. A. Ross, late R.A., Member of the German Chemical Society (Author of "Pyrology, or Fire Chemistry"). Crown 8vo, pp. xii. and 148, cloth. 1880. 5s.

ROSS.—PYROLOGY, OR FIRE CHEMISTRY; a Science interesting to the General Philosopher, and an Art of infinite importance to the Chemist, Metallurgist, Engineer, &c., &c. By W. A. Ross, lately a Major in the Royal Artillery. Small 4to, pp. xxviii. and 346, cloth. 1875. 36s.

ROSS.—CELEBRITIES OF THE YORKSHIRE WOLDS. By Frederick Ross, Fellow of the Royal Historical Society. 12mo, pp. 202, cloth. 1878. 4s.

ROSS.—THE EARLY HISTORY OF LAND HOLDING AMONG THE GERMANS. By Denman W. Ross, Ph.D. 8vo, pp. viii. and 274, cloth. 1883. 12s.

ROSS.—COREAN PRIMER: being Lessons in Corean on all Ordinary Subjects. Transliterated on the principles of the "Mandarin Primer," by the same author. By Rev. John Ross, Newchwang. 8vo, pp. 90, wrapper. 1877. 10s.

ROSS.—HONOUR OR SHAME? By R. S. Ross. 8vo, pp. 183. 1878. Cloth. 3s. 6d.; paper, 2s. 6d.

ROSS.—REMOVAL OF THE INDIAN TROOPS TO MALTA. By R. S. Ross. 8vo, pp. 77, paper. 1878. 1s. 6d.

ROSS.—THE MONK OF ST. GALL. A Dramatic Adaptation of Scheffel's "Ekkehard." By R. S. Ross. Crown 8vo, pp. xlii. and 218. 1879. 5s.

ROSS.—ARIADNE IN NAXOS. By R. S. Ross. Square 16mo, pp. 200, cloth. 1882. 5s.

ROTH.—THE ANIMAL PARASITES OF THE SUGAR CANE. By H. Ling Roth, late Hon. Sec. to the Mackay Planters' Association. Demy 8vo, pp. 16, wrapper. 1885. 1s.

ROTH.—NOTES ON CONTINENTAL IRRIGATION. By H. L. Roth. Demy 8vo, pp. 40, with 8 Plates, cloth. 1882. 5s.

ROUGH NOTES OF JOURNEYS made in the years 1868-1873 in Syria, down the Tigris, India, Kashmir, Ceylon, Japan, Mongolia, Siberia, the United States, the Sandwich Islands, and Australasia. Demy 8vo, pp. 624, cloth. 1875. 14s.

ROUSTAING.—THE FOUR GOSPELS EXPLAINED BY THEIR WRITERS. With an Appendix on the Ten Commandments. Edited by J. B. Roustaing. Translated by W. E. Kirby. 3 vols. crown 8vo, pp. 440-456-304, cloth. 1881. 15s.

ROUTLEDGE.—ENGLISH RULE AND NATIVE OPINION IN INDIA. From Notes taken in 1870-74. By James Routledge. 8vo, pp. x. and 338, cloth. 1878. 10s. 6d.

ROWE.—AN ENGLISHMAN'S VIEWS ON QUESTIONS OF THE DAY IN VICTORIA. By C. J. Rowe, M.A. Crown 8vo, pp. 122, cloth. 1882. 4s.

ROWLEY.—ORNITHOLOGICAL MISCELLANY. By George Dawson Rowley, M.A., F.Z.S. Vol. I. Part 1, 15s.—Part 2, 20s.—Part 3, 15s.—Part 4, 20s.
Vol. II. Part 5, 20s.—Part 6, 20s.—Part 7, 10s. 6d.—Part 8, 10s. 6d.—Part 9, 10s. 6d.—Part 10, 10s. 6d.
Vol. III. Part 11, 10s. 6d.—Part 12, 10s. 6d.—Part 13, 10s. 6d.—Part 14, 20s.

ROYAL SOCIETY OF LONDON (THE).—CATALOGUE OF SCIENTIFIC PAPERS (1800-1863), Compiled and Published by the Royal Society of London. Demy 4to, cloth, per vol. £1; in half-morocco, £1, 8s. Vol. I. (1867), A to Cluzel. pp. lxxix. and 960; Vol. II. (1868), Coakley—Graydon. pp. iv. and 1012; Vol. III. (1869), Greatheed—Leze. pp. v. and 1002; Vol. IV. (1870), L'Héritier de Brutille—Pozzetti. pp. iv. and 1006; Vol. V. (1871), Praag—Tizzani. pp. iv. and 1000; Vol. VI. (1872), Tkalec—Zylius, Anonymous and Additions. pp. xi. and 763. Continuation of above (1864-1873); Vol. VII. (1877), A to Hyrtl. pp. xxxi. and 1047; Vol. VIII. (1879), Ibañez—Zwicky. pp. 1310. A List of the Publications of the Royal Society (Separate Papers from the Philosophical Transactions), on application.

RUNDALL.—A SHORT AND EASY WAY TO WRITE ENGLISH AS SPOKEN. Méthode Rapide et Facile d'Ecrire le Français comme on le Parle. Kurze und Leichte Weise Deutsch zu Schreiben wie man es Spricht. By J. B. Rundall, Certificated Member of the London Shorthand Writers' Association. 6d. each.

RUSSELL.—THE WAVE OF TRANSLATION IN THE OCEANS OF WATER, AIR, AND ETHER. By John Scott Russell, M.A., F.R.S.S. L. and E. Demy 8vo, pp. 318, with 10 Diagrams, cloth. 1885. 12s. 6d.

RUTHERFORD.—THE AUTOBIOGRAPHY OF MARK RUTHERFORD, Dissenting Minister. Edited by his friend, Reuben Shapcott. Crown 8vo, pp. xii. and 180, boards. 1881. 5s.

RUTHERFORD.—MARK RUTHERFORD'S DELIVERANCE: Being the Second Part of his Autobiography. Edited by his friend, Reuben Shapcott. Crown 8vo, pp. viii. and 210, boards. 1885. 5s.

RUTTER.—See BUNYAN.

SÂMAVIDHÂNABRÂHMANA (THE) (being the Third Brâhmana) of the Sâma Veda. Edited, together with the Commentary of Sâyana, an English Translation, Introduction, and Index of Words, by A. C. Burnell. Vol. I. Text and Commentary, with Introduction. Demy 8vo, pp. xxxviii. and 104, cloth. 1873. 12s. 6d.

SAMUELSON.—HISTORY OF DRINK. A Review, Social, Scientific, and Political. By James Samuelson, of the Middle Temple, Barrister-at-Law. Second Edition. 8vo, pp. xxviii. and 288, cloth. 1880. 6s.

SAND.—MOLIÈRE. A Drama in Prose. By George Sand. Edited, with Notes, by Th. Karcher, LL.B. 12mo, pp. xx. and 170, cloth. 1868. 3s. 6d.

SARTORIUS.—MEXICO. Landscapes and Popular Sketches. By C. Sartorius. Edited by Dr. Gaspey. With Engravings, from Sketches by M. Rugendas. 4to, pp. vi. and 202, cloth gilt. 1859. 18s.

SATOW.—AN ENGLISH JAPANESE DICTIONARY OF THE SPOKEN LANGUAGE. By Ernest Mason Satow, Japanese Secretary to H.M. Legation at Yedo, and Ishibashi Masakata of the Imperial Japanese Foreign Office. Second Edition. Imperial 32mo, pp. xv. and 416, cloth. 1879. 12s. 6d.

SAVAGE.—THE MORALS OF EVOLUTION. By M. J. Savage, Author of "The Religion of Evolution," &c. Crown 8vo, pp. 192, cloth. 1880. 5s.

SAVAGE.—BELIEF IN GOD; an Examination of some Fundamental Theistic Problems. By M. J. Savage. To which is added an Address on the Intellectual Basis of Faith. By W. H. Savage. 8vo, pp. 176, cloth. 1881. 5s.

SAVAGE.—BELIEFS ABOUT MAN. By M. J. Savage. Crown 8vo, pp. 130, cloth. 1882. 5s.

SAYCE.—AN ASSYRIAN GRAMMAR for Comparative Purposes. By A. H. Sayce, M.A., Fellow and Tutor of Queen's College, Oxford. Crown 8vo, pp. xvi. and 188, cloth. 1885.

SAYCE.—THE PRINCIPLES OF COMPARATIVE PHILOLOGY. By A. H. Sayce, M.A. Third, Revised, and Enlarged Edition. Crown 8vo, pp. xlviii.–422, cloth. 1885. 10s. 6d.

SCHAIBLE.—AN ESSAY ON THE SYSTEMATIC TRAINING OF THE BODY. By C. H. Schaible, M.D., &c., &c. A Memorial Essay, Published on the occasion of the first Centenary Festival of Frederick L. Jahn, with an Etching by H. Herkomer. Crown 8vo, pp. xviii. and 124, cloth. 1878. 5s.

SCHEFFEL.—MOUNTAIN PSALMS. By J. V. von Scheffel. Translated by Mrs. F. Brunnow. Fcap., pp. 62, with 6 Plates after designs by A. Von Werner. Parchment. 1882. 3s. 6d.

SCHILLER.—THE BRIDE OF MESSINA. Translated from the German of Schiller in English Verse. By Emily Allfrey. Crown 8vo, pp. viii. and 110, cloth. 1876. 2s.

SCHLAGINTWEIT.—BUDDHISM IN TIBET: Illustrated by Literary Documents and Objects of Religious Worship. By Emil Schlagintweit, LL.D. With a folio Atlas of 20 Plates, and 20 Tables of Native Print in the Text. Roy. 8vo, pp. xxiv. and 404. 1863. £2, 2s.

SCHLAU, SCHLAUER, AM SCHLÄUESTEN.—Facsimile of a Manuscript supposed to have been found in an Egyptian Tomb by the English Soldiers. Royal 8vo, in ragged canvas covers, with string binding, and dilapidated edges (? just as discovered). 1884. 6s.

SCHLEICHER.—A COMPENDIUM OF THE COMPARATIVE GRAMMAR OF THE INDO-EUROPEAN, SANSKRIT, GREEK, AND LATIN LANGUAGES. By August Schleicher. Translated from the Third German Edition, by Herbert Bendall, B.A., Chr. Coll., Camb. 8vo. Part I., Phonology. Pp. 184, cloth. 1874. 7s. 6d. Part II., Morphology. Pp. viii. and 104, cloth. 1877. 6s.

SCHOPENHAUER.—THE WORLD AS WILL AND IDEA. By Arthur Schopenhauer. Translated from the German by R. B. HALDANE, M.A., and J. KEMP, M.A. Vol. I., containing Four Books. Post 8vo, pp. xxxii.–532, cloth. 1883. 18s.

SCHULTZ.—UNIVERSAL DOLLAR TABLES (Complete United States). Covering all Exchanges between the United States and Great Britain, France, Belgium, Switzerland, Italy, Spain, and Germany. By C. W. H. Schultz. 8vo, cloth. 1874. 15s.

SCHULTZ.—UNIVERSAL INTEREST AND GENERAL PERCENTAGE TABLES. On the Decimal System. With a Treatise on the Currency of the World, and numerous examples for Self-Instruction. By C. W. H. Schultz. 8vo, cloth. 1874. 10s. 6d.

SCHULTZ.—ENGLISH GERMAN EXCHANGE TABLES. By C. W. H. Schultz. With a Treatise on the Currency of the World. 8vo, boards. 1874. 5s.

SCHWENDLER.—INSTRUCTIONS FOR TESTING TELEGRAPH LINES, and the Technical Arrangements in Offices. Written on behalf of the Government of India, under the Orders of the Director-General of Telegraphs in India. By Louis Schwendler. Vol. I., demy 8vo, pp. 248, cloth. 1878. 12s. Vol. II., demy 8vo, pp. xi. and 268, cloth. 1880. 9s.

SCOONES.—FAUST. A Tragedy. By Goethe. Translated into English Verse, by William Dalton Scoones. Fcap., pp. vi. and 230, cloth. 1879. 5s.

SCOTT.—THE ENGLISH LIFE OF JESUS. By Thomas Scott. Crown 8vo, pp. xxviii. and 350, cloth. 1879. 2s. 6d.

SCOTUS.—A NOTE ON MR. GLADSTONE'S "The Peace to Come." By Scotus. 8vo, pp. 106. 1878. Cloth, 2s. 6d.; paper wrapper, 1s. 6d.

SELL.—THE FAITH OF ISLAM. By the Rev. E. Sell, Fellow of the University of Madras. Demy 8vo, pp. xiv. and 270, cloth. 1881. 6s. 6d.

SELL.—IHN-I-TAJWID; OR, ART OF READING THE QURAN. By the Rev. E. Sell, B.D. 8vo, pp. 48, wrappers. 1882. 2s. 6d.

SELSS.—GOETHE'S MINOR POEMS. Selected, Annotated, and Rearranged. By Albert M. Selss, Ph.D. Crown 8vo, pp. xxxi. and 152, cloth. 1875. 3s. 6d.

SERMONS NEVER PREACHED. By Philip Phosphor. Crown 8vo, pp. vi. and 124, cloth. 1878. 2s. 6d.

SEWELL.—REPORT ON THE AMARAVATI TOPE, and Excavations on its Site in 1877. By Robert Sewell, of the Madras C.S., &c. With four plates. Royal 4to, pp. 70, boards. 1880. 3s.

SEYPPEL.—SHARP, SHARPER, SHARPEST: A Humorous Tale of Old Egypt. Penned down and Depicted in the Year 1315 A.C. By C. M. Seyppel, Court Painter and Poet Laureate of His Majesty King Rhampsinit III., and done into the English tongue by Two Mummies of the Old Dynasty. Memphis, 35, Mummies Arcade. (Ring three times). Imperial 8vo, pp. 42, in ragged canvas cover, with dilapidated edges, and string binding (? just as discovered), price 6s.

SHADWELL.—POLITICAL ECONOMY FOR THE PEOPLE. By J. L. Shadwell, Author of "A System of Political Economy." Fcap., pp. vi. and 154, limp cloth. 1880. 1s. 6d.

SHAKESPEARE.—A NEW STUDY OF SHAKESPEARE: An Inquiry into the connection of the Plays and Poems, with the origins of the Classical Drama, and with the Platonic Philosophy, through the Mysteries. Demy 8vo, pp. xii. and 372, with Photograph of the Stratford Bust, cloth. 1884. 10s. 6d.

SHAKESPEARE'S CENTURIE OF PRAYSE; being Materials for a History of Opinion on Shakespeare and his Works, culled from Writers of the First Century after his Rise. By C. M. Ingleby. Medium 8vo, pp. xx. and 384. Stiff cover. 1874. £1, 1s. Large paper, fcap. 4to, boards. £2, 2s.

SHAKESPEARE.—HERMENEUTICS; OR, THE STILL LION. Being an Essay towards the Restoration of Shakespeare's Text. By C. M. Ingleby, M.A., LL.D., of Trinity College, Cambridge. Small 4to, pp. 168, boards. 1875. 6s.

SHAKESPEARE.—THE MAN AND THE BOOK. By C. M. Ingleby, M.A., LL.D. Small 4to. Part I., pp. 172, boards. 1877. 6s.

SHAKESPEARE.—OCCASIONAL PAPERS ON SHAKESPEARE; being the Second Part of "Shakespeare: the Man and the Book." By C. M. Ingleby, M.A., LL.D., V.P.R.S.L. Small 4to, pp. x. and 194, paper boards. 1881. 6s.

SHAKESPEARE'S BONES.—The Proposal to Disinter them, considered in relation to their possible bearing on his Portraiture: Illustrated by instances of Visits of the Living to the Dead. By C. M. Ingleby, LL.D., V.P.R.S.L. Fcap. 4to, pp. viii. and 48, boards. 1883. 1s. 6d.

SHAKESPEARE.—A New Variorum Edition of Shakespeare. Edited by Horace Howard Furness. Royal 8vo. Vol. I. Romeo and Juliet. Pp. xxiii. and 480, cloth. 1871. 18s.—Vol. II. Macbeth. Pp. xix. and 492. 1873. 18s.—Vols. III. and IV. Hamlet. 2 vols. pp. xx. and 474 and 430. 1877. 36s.—Vol. V. King Lear. Pp. vi. and 504. 1880. 18s.

SHAKESPEARE.—Concordance to Shakespeare's Poems. By Mrs. H. H. Furness. Royal 8vo, cloth. 18s.

SHAKESPEARE-Notes. By F. A. Leo. Demy 8vo, pp. viii. and 120, cloth. 1885. 6s.

SHAKSPERE SOCIETY (The New).—Subscription, One Guinea per annum. List of Publications on application.

SHERRING.—The Sacred City of the Hindus. An Account of Benares in Ancient and Modern Times. By the Rev. M. A. Sherring, M.A., LL.D.; and Prefaced with an Introduction by FitzEdward Hall, D.C.L. With Illustrations. 8vo, pp. xxxvi. and 388, cloth. 21s.

SHERRING.—Hindu Tribes and Castes; together with an Account of the Mohamedan Tribes of the North-West Frontier and of the Aboriginal Tribes of the Central Provinces. By the Rev. M. A. Sherring, M.A., LL.B., Lond., &c. 4to. Vol. II. Pp. lxviii. and 376, cloth. 1879. £2, 8s.—Vol. III., with Index of 3 vols. Pp. xii. and 336, cloth. 1881. 32s.

SHERRING.—The Hindoo Pilgrims. By Rev. M. A. Sherring, M.A., LL.D. Crown 8vo, pp. 126, cloth. 1878. 5s.

SHIELDS.—The Final Philosophy; or, System of Perfectible Knowledge issuing from the Harmony of Science and Religion. By Charles W. Shields, D.D., Professor in Princeton College. Royal 8vo, pp. viii. and 610, cloth. 1878. 18s.

SIBREE.—The Great African Island. Chapters on Madagascar. A Popular Account of Recent Researches in the Physical Geography, Geology, and Exploration of the Country, and its Natural History and Botany; and in the Origin and Divisions, Customs and Language, Superstitions, Folk-lore, and Religious Beliefs and Practices of the Different Tribes. Together with Illustrations of Scripture and Early Church History from Native Habits and Missionary Experience. By the Rev. James Sibree, jun., F.R.G.S., Author of "Madagascar and its People," &c. 8vo, pp. xii. and 272, with Physical and Ethnological Maps and Four Illustrations, cloth. 1879. 12s.

SIBREE.—Poems: including "Fancy," "A Resting Place," &c. By John Sibree, M.A., London. Crown 8vo, pp. iv. and 134, cloth. 1884. 4s.

SIMCOX.—Episodes in the Lives of Men, Women, and Lovers. By Edith Simcox. Crown 8vo, pp. 312, cloth. 1882. 7s. 6d.

SIMCOX.—Natural Law. See English and Foreign Philosophical Library, Vol. IV.

SIME.—Lessing. See English and Foreign Philosophical Library, Extra Series, Vols. I. and II.

SIMPSON-BAIKIE.—The Dramatic Unities in the Present Day. By E. Simpson-Baikie. Third Edition. Fcap. 8vo, pp. iv. and 108, cloth. 1878. 2s. 6d.

SIMPSON-BAIKIE.—The International Dictionary for Naturalists and Sportsmen in English, French, and German. By Edwin Simpson-Baikie. 8vo, pp. iv. and 284, cloth. 1880. 15s.

SINCLAIR.—The Messenger: A Poem. By Thomas Sinclair, M.A. Foolscap 8vo, pp. 174, cloth. 1875. 5s.

SINCLAIR.—Loves's Trilogy: A Poem. By Thomas Sinclair, M.A. Crown 8vo, pp. 150, cloth. 1876. 5s.

SINCLAIR.—The Mount: Speech from its English Heights. By Thomas Sinclair, M.A. Crown 8vo, pp. viii. and 302, cloth. 1877. 10s.

SINCLAIR.—Goddess Fortune: A Novel. By Thomas Sinclair, M.A. Three vols., post 8vo, pp. viii. 302, 302, 274, cloth. 1884. 31s. 6d.

SINCLAIR.—Quest: A Collection of Essays. By Thomas Sinclair, M.A. Crown 8vo, pp. 184, cloth. 1885. 2s. 6d.

SINGER.—Hungarian Grammar. See Trübner's Collection.

SINNETT.—The Occult World. By A. P. Sinnett. Fourth Edition. With an Appendix of 20 pages, on the subject of Mr. Kiddle's Charge of Plagiarism. 8vo, pp. xx. and 206, cloth. 1884. 3s. 6d.

SMITH.—THE DIVINE GOVERNMENT. By S. Smith, **M.D.** Fifth Edition. Crown 8vo, pp. xii. and 276, cloth. 1866. 6s.

SMITH.—THE RECENT DEPRESSION OF TRADE. Its Nature, its Causes, and the Remedies which have been suggested for it. By Walter E. Smith, B.A., New College. Being the Oxford Cobden Prize Essay for 1879. Crown 8vo, pp. vi. and 108, cloth. 1880. 3s.

SMYTH.—THE ABORIGINES OF VICTORIA. With Notes relating to the Habits of the Natives of other Parts of Australia and Tasmania. Compiled from various sources for the Government of Victoria. By R. Brough Smyth, F.L.S., F.G.S., &c., &c. 2 vols. royal 8vo, pp. lxxii.-484 and vi.-456, Maps, Plates, and Woodcuts, cloth. 1878. £3, 3s.

SNOW—A THEOLOGICO-POLITICAL TREATISE. By G. D. Snow. Crown 8vo, pp. 180, cloth. 1874. 4s. 6d.

SOLLING.—DIUTISKA : An Historical and Critical Survey of the Literature of Germany, from the Earliest Period to the Death of Goethe. By Gustav Solling. 8vo, pp. xviii. and 368. 1863. 10s. 6d.

SOLLING.—SELECT PASSAGES FROM THE WORKS OF SHAKESPEARE. Translated and Collected. German and English. By G. Solling. 12mo, pp. 155, cloth. 1866. 3s. 6d.

SOLLING.—MACBETH. Rendered into Metrical German (with English Text adjoined). By Gustav Solling. Crown 8vo, pp. 160, wrapper. 1878. 3s. 6d.

SONGS OF THE SEMITIC IN ENGLISH VERSE. By G. E. W. Crown 8vo, pp. iv. and 134, cloth. 1877. 5s.

SOUTHALL.—THE EPOCH OF THE MAMMOTH AND THE APPARITION OF MAN UPON EARTH. By James C. Southall, A.M., LL.D. Crown 8vo, pp. xii. and 430, cloth. Illustrated. 1878. 10s. 6d.

SPANISH REFORMERS OF TWO CENTURIES FROM 1520 ; Their Lives and Writing, according to the late Benjamin B. Wiffen's Plan, and with the Use of His Materials. Described by E. Boehmer, D.D., Ph.D. Vol. I. With B. B. Wiffen's Narrative of the Incidents attendant upon the Republication of Reformistas Antiguos Españoles, and with a Memoir of B. B. Wiffen. By Isaline Wiffen. Royal 8vo, pp. xvi. and 216, cloth. 1874. 12s. 6d. Roxburghe, 15s.—Vol. II. Royal 8vo, pp. xii.-374, cloth. 1883. 18s.

SPEDDING.—THE LIFE AND TIMES OF FRANCIS BACON. Extracted from the Edition of his Occasional Writings, by James Spedding. 2 vols. post 8vo, pp. xx.-710 and xiv.-708, cloth. 1878. 21s.

SPIERS.—THE SCHOOL SYSTEM OF THE TALMUD. By the Rev. B. Spiers. 8vo, pp. 48, cloth. 1882. 2s. 6d.

SPINOZA.—BENEDICT DE SPINOZA : his Life, Correspondence, and Ethics. By R. Willis, M.D. 8vo, pp. xliv. and 648, cloth. 1870. 21s.

SPINOZA.—ETHIC DEMONSTRATED IN GEOMETRICAL ORDER AND DIVIDED INTO FIVE PARTS, which treat—I. Of God ; II. Of the Nature and Origin of the Mind ; III. Of the Origin and Nature of the Affects ; IV. Of Human Bondage, or of the Strength of the Affects ; V. Of the Power of the Intellect, or of Human Liberty. By Benedict de Spinoza. Translated from the Latin by W. Hale White. Post 8vo, pp. 328, cloth. 1883. 10s. 6d.

SPIRITUAL EVOLUTION, AN ESSAY ON, considered in its bearing upon Modern Spiritualism, Science, and Religion. By J. P. B. Crown 8vo, pp. 156, cloth. 1879. 3s.

SPRUNER.—DR. KARL VON SPRUNER'S HISTORICO-GEOGRAPHICAL HAND-ATLAS, containing 26 Coloured Maps. Obl. cloth. 1861. 15s.

SQUIER.—HONDURAS ; Descriptive, Historical, and Statistical. By E. G. Squier, M.A., F.S.A. Cr. 8vo, pp. viii. and 278, cloth. 1870. 3s. 6d.

STATIONERY OFFICE.—PUBLICATIONS OF HER MAJESTY'S STATIONERY OFFICE. List on application.

STEDMAN.—OXFORD : Its Social and Intellectual Life. With Remarks and Hints on Expenses, the Examinations, &c. By Algernon M. M. Stedman, B.A., Wadham College, Oxford. Crown 8vo, pp. xvi. and 309, cloth. 1878. 7s. 6d.
STEELE.—AN EASTERN LOVE STORY. Kusa Játakaya : A Buddhistic Legendary Poem, with other Stories. By Th. Steele. Cr. 8vo, pp. xii. and 260, cl. 1871. 6s.
STENT.—THE JADE CHAPLET. In Twenty-four Beads. A Collection of Songs, Ballads, &c. (from the Chinese). By G. C. Stent, M.N.C.B.R.A.S. Post 8vo, pp. viii. and 168, cloth. 1874. 5s.
STENZLER.—See AUCTORES SANSKRITI, Vol. II.
STOCK.—ATTEMPTS AT TRUTH. By St. George Stock. Crown 8vo, pp. vi. and 248, cloth. 1882. 5s.
STOKES.—GOIDELICA—Old and Early-Middle Irish Glosses: Prose and Verse. Edited by Whitley Stokes. 2d Edition. Med. 8vo, pp. 192, cloth. 1872. 18s.
STOKES.—BEUNANS MERIASEK. The Life of Saint Meriasek, Bishop and Confessor. A Cornish Drama. Edited, with a Translation and Notes, by Whitley Stokes. Med. 8vo, pp. xvi. and 280, and Facsimile, cloth. 1872. 15s.
STOKES.—TOGAIL TROY, THE DESTRUCTION OF TROY. Transcribed from the Facsimile of the Book of Leinster, and Translated, with a Glossarial Index of the Rarer Words, by Whitley Stokes. Crown 8vo, pp. xvi. and 188, paper boards. 1882. 18s.
STOKES.—THREE MIDDLE-IRISH HOMILIES ON THE LIVES OF SAINTS—PATRICK, BRIGIT, AND COLUMBA. Edited by Whitley Stokes. Crown 8vo, pp. xii. and 140, paper boards. 1882. 10s. 6d.
STONE.—CHRISTIANITY BEFORE CHRIST ; or, Prototypes of our Faith and Culture. By Charles J. Stone, F.R.S.L., F.R.Hist.S., Author of "Cradle-Land of Arts and Creeds." Crown 8vo, pp. , cloth.
STRANGE.—THE BIBLE ; is it "The Word of God"? By Thomas Lumisden Strange. Demy 8vo, pp. xii. and 384, cloth. 1871. 7s.
STRANGE.—THE SPEAKER'S COMMENTARY. Reviewed by T. L. Strange. Cr. 8vo, pp. viii. and 159, cloth. 1871. 2s. 6d.
STRANGE.—THE DEVELOPMENT OF CREATION ON THE EARTH. By T. L. Strange. Demy 8vo, pp. xii. and 110, cloth. 1874. 2s. 6d.
STRANGE.—THE LEGENDS OF THE OLD TESTAMENT. By T. L. Strange. Demy 8vo, pp. xii. and 244, cloth. 1874. 5s.
STRANGE.—THE SOURCES AND DEVELOPMENT OF CHRISTIANITY. By Thomas Lumisden Strange. Demy 8vo, pp. xx. and 256, cloth. 1875. 5s.
STRANGE.—WHAT IS CHRISTIANITY? An Historical Sketch. Illustrated with a Chart. By T. L. Strange. Foolscap 8vo, pp. 72, cloth. 1880. 2s. 6d.
STRANGE.—CONTRIBUTIONS TO A SERIES OF CONTROVERSIAL WRITINGS, issued by the late Mr. Thomas Scott, of Upper Norwood. By Thomas Lumisden Strange. Fcap. 8vo, pp. viii. and 312, cloth. 1881. 2s. 6d.
STRANGFORD.—ORIGINAL LETTERS AND PAPERS OF THE LATE VISCOUNT STRANGFORD UPON PHILOLOGICAL AND KINDRED SUBJECTS. Edited by Viscountess Strangford. Post 8vo, pp. xxii. and 284, cloth. 1878. 12s. 6d.
STRATMANN.—THE TRAGICALL HISTORIE OF HAMLET, PRINCE OF DENMARKE. By William Shakespeare. Edited according to the first printed Copies, with the various Readings and Critical Notes. By F. H. Stratmann. 8vo, pp. vi. and 120, sewed. 3s. 6d.
STRATMANN.—A DICTIONARY OF THE OLD ENGLISH LANGUAGE. Compiled from Writings of the Twelfth, Thirteenth, Fourteenth, and Fifteenth Centuries. By F. H. Stratmann. Third Edition. 4to, pp. x. and 662, sewed. 1878. 30s.
STUDIES OF MAN. By a Japanese. Crown 8vo, pp. 124, cloth. 1874. 2s. 6d.
SUMNER.—WHAT SOCIAL CLASSES OWE TO EACH OTHER. By W. G. Sumner, Professor of Political and Social Science in Yale College. 18mo, pp. 170, cloth. 1884. 3s. 6d.
SUYEMATZ.—GENJI MONOGATARI. The Most Celebrated of the Classical Japanese Romances. Translated by K. Suyematz. Crown 8vo, pp. xvi. and 254, cloth. 1882. 7s. 6d.

SWEET.—SPELLING REFORM AND ENGLISH LITERATURE. By Henry Sweet, M.A. 8vo, pp. 8, wrapper. 1884. 2d.

SWEET.—HISTORY OF ENGLISH SOUNDS, from the Earliest Period, including an Investigation of the General Laws of Sound Change, and full Word Lists. By Henry Sweet. Demy 8vo, pp. iv.-164, cloth. 1874. 4s. 6d.

SWEET.—ON A MEXICAN MUSTANG THROUGH TEXAS FROM THE GULF TO THE RIO GRANDE. By Alex. E. Sweet and J. Armoy Knox, Editors of "Texas Siftings." English Copyright Edition. Demy 8vo, pp. 672. Illustrated, cloth. 1883. 10s.

SYED AHMAD.—A SERIES OF ESSAYS ON THE LIFE OF MOHAMMED, and Subjects subsidiary thereto. By Syed Ahmad Khan Bahadur, C.S.I. 8vo, pp. 532, with 4 Tables, 2 Maps, and Plate, cloth. 1870. 30s.

TALBOT.—ANALYSIS OF THE ORGANISATION OF THE PRUSSIAN ARMY. By Lieutenant Gerald F. Talbot, 2d Prussian Dragoon Guards. Royal 8vo, pp. 78, cloth. 1871. 3s.

TAYLER.—A RETROSPECT OF THE RELIGIOUS LIFE OF ENGLAND; or, Church, Puritanism, and Free Inquiry. By J. J. Tayler, B.A. Second Edition. Reissued, with an Introductory Chapter on Recent Development, by James Martineau, LL.D., D.D. Post 8vo, pp. 380, cloth. 1876. 7s. 6d.

TAYLOR.—PRINCE DEUKALION: A Lyrical Drama. By Bayard Taylor. Small 4to, pp. 172. Handsomely bound in white vellum. 1878. 12s.

TECHNOLOGICAL DICTIONARY of the Terms employed in the Arts and Sciences; Architecture; Civil Engineering; Mechanics; Machine-Making; Shipbuilding and Navigation; Metallurgy; Artillery; Mathematics; Physics; Chemistry; Mineralogy, &c. With a Preface by Dr. K. Karmarsch. Second Edition. 3 vols.
    Vol. I. German-English-French. 8vo, pp. 646. 12s.
    Vol. II. English-German-French. 8vo, pp. 666. 12s.
    Vol. III. French-German-English. 8vo, pp. 618. 12s.

TECHNOLOGICAL DICTIONARY.—A POCKET DICTIONARY OF TECHNICAL TERMS USED IN ARTS AND MANUFACTURES. English-German-French, Deutsch-Englisch-Französisch, Français-Allemand-Anglais. Abridged from the above Technological Dictionary by Rumpf, Mothes, and Unverzagt. With the addition of Commercial Terms. 3 vols. sq. 12mo, cloth, 12s.

TEMPLE.—THE LEGENDS OF THE PUNJAB. By Captain R. C. Temple, Bengal Staff Corps, F.G.S., &c. Vol. I., 8vo, pp. xviii.-546, cloth. 1884. £1, 6s.

THÉÂTRE FRANÇAIS MODERNE.—A Selection of Modern French Plays. Edited by the Rev. P. H. E. Brette, B.D., C. Cassal, LL.D., and Th. Karcher, LL.B.

    First Series, in 1 vol. crown 8vo, cloth, 6s., containing—

CHARLOTTE CORDAY. A Tragedy. By F. Ponsard. Edited, with English Notes and Notice on Ponsard, by Professor C. Cassal, LL.D. Pp. xii. and 134. Separately, 2s. 6d.

DIANE. A Drama in Verse. By Emile Augier. Edited, with English Notes and Notice on Augier, by Th. Karcher, LL.B. Pp. xiv. and 145. Separately, 2s. 6d.

LE VOYAGE À DIEPPE, A Comedy in Prose. By Wafflard and Fulgence. Edited, with English Notes, by the Rev. P. H. E. Brette, B.D. Pp. 104. Separately, 2s. 6d.

    Second Series, crown 8vo, cloth, 6s., containing—

MOLIÈRE. A Drama in Prose. By George Sand. Edited, with English Notes and Notice of George Sand, by Th. Karcher, LL.B. Fcap. 8vo, pp. xx. and 170, cloth. Separately, 3s. 6d.

LES ARISTOCRATIES. A Comedy in Verse. By Etienne Arago. Edited, with English Notes and Notice of Etienne Arago, by the Rev. P. H. E. Brette, B.D. 2d Edition. Fcap. 8vo, pp. xiv. and 236, cloth. Separately, 4s.

THEATRE FRANÇAIS MODERNE—*continued*.
  Third Series, **crown 8vo**, cloth, 6s., containing—

LES FAUX BONSHOMMES. A Comedy. By Théodore Barrière and Ernest Capendu. Edited, with **English Notes** and Notice on Barrière, by Professor C. Cassal, LL.D. Fcap. 8vo, pp. xvi. and 304. 1868. Separately, 4s.

L'HONNEUR ET L'ARGENT. A Comedy. By François Ponsard. Edited, with English Notes and Memoir of Ponsard, by Professor C. Cassal, LL.D. 2d Edition. Fcap. 8vo, pp. xvi. and 171, cloth. 1869. Separately, 3s. 6d.

THEISM.—A CANDID EXAMINATION OF THEISM. By Physicus. Post 8vo, pp. xviii. and 198, cloth. **1878.** 7s. 6d.

THEOBALD.—SELECTIONS FROM THE POETS; or, Passages Illustrating Peculiarities of their **Style,** Pathos, or Wit. By W. Theobald, M.R.A.S., late Deputy-Superintendent Geological Survey of India. With Notes, Historical, Explanatory, and Glossarial, for the Use of Young Readers. **Demy 8vo,** pp. xii. and 208, cloth. 1885. 5s.

THEOSOPHY AND THE HIGHER LIFE; or, Spiritual Dynamics and the Divine and Miraculous **Man.** By G. W., M.D., Edinburgh, President of the British Theosophical Society. 12mo, pp. iv. and 138, cloth. 1880. 3s.

THOM.—ST. PAUL'S EPISTLES TO THE CORINTHIANS. An Attempt to convey their Spirit and Significance. By the Rev. J. H. Thom. 8vo, **pp.** xii. and 408, cloth. 1851. 5s.

THOMAS.—EARLY SASSANIAN INSCRIPTIONS, SEALS, AND COINS, illustrating the Early History of the Sassanian Dynasty, containing Proclamations of Ardeshir Babek, Sapor I., and his Successors. With a Critical Examination and Explanation of the celebrated Inscription in the Hájíábad Cave, demonstrating that Sapor, the Conqueror of Valerian, was a professing Christian. By Edward Thomas. Illustrated. 8vo, pp. 148, cloth. 7s. 6d.

THOMAS.—THE CHRONICLES OF THE PATHAN KINGS OF DEHLI. Illustrated by Coins, Inscriptions, and other Antiquarian Remains. By E. Thomas, F.R.A.S. With Plates and Cuts. Demy 8vo, pp. xxiv. and 467, cloth. 1871. 28s.

THOMAS.—THE REVENUE RESOURCES OF THE MUGHAL EMPIRE IN INDIA, from A.D. 1593 to A.D. 1707. A Supplement to "The Chronicles of the Pathán Kings of Delhi." By E. Thomas, F.R.S. 8vo, pp. 60, cloth. 3s. 6d.

THOMAS.—SASSANIAN COINS. Communicated to the Numismatic Society of London. By E. Thomas, F.R.S. Two Parts, 12mo, pp. 43, 3 Plates and a Cut, sewed. 5s.

THOMAS.—JAINISM; OR, THE EARLY FAITH OF ASOKA. With Illustrations of the Ancient Religions of the East, from the Pantheon of the Indo-Scythians. To which is added a Notice on Bactrian Coins and Indian Dates. By Edward Thomas, F.R.S. 8vo, pp. viii.-24 and 82. With two Autotype Plates and Woodcuts. 1877. 7s. 6d.

THOMAS.—THE THEORY AND PRACTICE OF CREOLE GRAMMAR. By J. J. Thomas. 8vo, pp. viii. and 135, boards. 12s.

THOMAS.—RECORDS OF THE GUPTA DYNASTY. Illustrated by Inscriptions, Written History, Local Tradition, and Coins. To which is added a Chapter on the Arabs in Sind. By Edward Thomas, F.R.S. Folio, with a Plate, pp. iv. and 64, cloth. 14s.

THOMAS.—THE INDIAN BALHARA, and the Arabian Intercourse with India in the Ninth and following Centuries. By Edward Thomas, F.R.S. (Contained in International Numismata Orientalia. Vol. III., Part I. Coins of Arakan.) Royal 4to, pp. viii.-48, wrappers. 1882. 8s. 6d.

THOMAS.—BOYHOOD LAYS. By William Henry Thomas. 18mo, pp. iv. and 74, cloth. 1877. 2s. 6d.

THOMPSON.—DIALOGUES, RUSSIAN AND ENGLISH. Compiled by A. R. Thompson, sometime Lecturer of the English Language in the University of St. Vladimir, Kieff. Crown 8vo, pp. iv. and 132, cloth. 1882. 5s.

E

THOMSON.—EVOLUTION AND INVOLUTION. By George Thomson, Author of "The World of Being," &c. Crown 8vo, pp. viii. and 206, cloth. 1880. 5s.

THORBURN.—BANNÚ; OR, OUR AFGHAN FRONTIER. By S. S. Thorburn, F.C.S., Settlement Officer of the Bannú District. 8vo, pp. x. and 480, cloth. 1876. 18s.

THORPE.—DIPLOMATARIUM ANGLICUM ÆVI SAXONICI. A Collection of English Charters, from the reign of King Æthelberht of Kent, A.D. DCV., to that of William the Conqueror. Containing: I. Miscellaneous Charters. II. Wills. III. Guilds. IV. Manumissions and Acquittances. With a Translation of the Anglo-Saxon. By the late Benjamin Thorpe, Member of the Royal Academy of Sciences at Munich, and of the Society of Netherlandish Literature at Leyden. 8vo, pp. xlii. and 682, cloth. 1865. £1, 1s.

THOUGHTS ON LOGIC; or, the S.N.I.X. Propositional Theory. Crown 8vo, pp. iv. and 76, cloth. 1877. 2s. 6d.

THOUGHTS ON THEISM, with Suggestions towards a Public Religious Service in Harmony with Modern Science and Philosophy. Ninth Thousand. Revised and Enlarged. 8vo, pp. 74, sewed. 1882. 1s.

THURSTON.—FRICTION AND LUBRICATION. Determinations of the Laws and Co-efficients of Friction by new Methods and with new Apparatus. By Robert H. Thurston, A.M., C.E., &c. Crown 8vo, pp. xvi. and 212, cloth. 1879. 6s. 6d.

TIELE.—See English and Foreign Philosophical Library, Vol. VII. and Trübner's Oriental Series.

TOLHAUSEN.—A SYNOPSIS OF THE PATENT LAWS OF VARIOUS COUNTRIES. By A. Tolhausen, Ph.D. Third Edition. 12mo, pp. 62, sewed. 1870. 1s. 6d.

TONSBERG.—NORWAY. Illustrated Handbook for Travellers. Edited by Charles Tönsberg. With 134 Engravings on Wood, 17 Maps, and Supplement. Crown 8vo, pp. lxx., 482, and 32, cloth. 1875. 18s.

TOPOGRAPHICAL WORKS.—A LIST OF THE VARIOUS WORKS PREPARED AT THE TOPOGRAPHICAL AND STATISTICAL DEPARTMENT OF THE WAR OFFICE may be had on application.

TORCEANU.—ROUMANIAN GRAMMAR. See Trübner's Collection.

TORRENS.—EMPIRE IN ASIA: How we came by it. A Book of Confessions. By W. M. Torrens, M.P. Med. 8vo, pp. 426, cloth. 1872. 14s.

TOSCANI.—ITALIAN CONVERSATIONAL COURSE. A New Method of Teaching the Italian Language, both Theoretically and Practically. By Giovanni Toscani, Professor of the Italian Language and Literature in Queen's Coll., London, &c. Fourth Edition. 12mo, pp. xiv. and 300, cloth. 1872. 5s.

TOSCANI.—ITALIAN READING COURSE. By G. Toscani. Fcap. 8vo, pp. xii. and 160. With table. Cloth. 1875. 4s. 6d.

TOULON.—ITS ADVANTAGES AS A WINTER RESIDENCE FOR INVALIDS AND OTHERS. By an English Resident. The proceeds of this pamphlet to be devoted to the English Church at Toulon. Crown 8vo, pp. 8, sewed. 1873. 6d.

TRADLEG.—A SON OF BELIAL. Autobiographical Sketches. By Nitram Tradleg, University of Bosphorus. Crown 8vo, pp. viii.–260, cloth. 1882. 5s.

TRIMEN.—SOUTH-AFRICAN BUTTERFLIES; a Monograph of the Extra-Tropical Species. By Roland Trimen, F.L.S., F.Z.S., M.E.S., Curator of the South African Museum, Cape Town. Royal 8vo. [*In preparation.*]

TRÜBNER'S AMERICAN, EUROPEAN, AND ORIENTAL LITERARY RECORD. A Register of the most Important Works published in America, India, China, and the British Colonies. With Occasional Notes on German, Dutch, Danish, French, Italian, Spanish, Portuguese, and Russian Literature. The object of the Publishers in issuing this publication is to give a full and particular account of every publication of importance issued in America and the East. Small 4to, 6d. per number. Subscription, 5s. per volume.

TRÜBNER.—Trübner's Bibliographical Guide to American Literature: A Classed List of Books published in the United States of America, from 1817 to 1857. With Bibliographical Introduction, Notes, and Alphabetical Index. Compiled and Edited by Nicolas Trübner. In 1 vol. 8vo, half bound, pp. 750. 1859. 18s.

TRÜBNER'S Catalogue of Dictionaries and Grammars of the Principal Languages and Dialects of the World. Considerably Enlarged and Revised, with an Alphabetical Index. A Guide for Students and Booksellers. Second Edition, 8vo, pp. viii. and 170, cloth. 1882. 5s.

TRÜBNER'S Collection of Simplified Grammars of the Principal Asiatic and European Languages. Edited by Reinhold Rost, LL.D., Ph.D. Crown 8vo, cloth, uniformly bound.

    I.—Hindustani, Persian, and Arabic. By E. H. Palmer, M.A. Second Edition. Pp. 112. 1885. 5s.
    II.—Hungarian. By I. Singer. Pp. vi. and 88. 1882. **4s. 6d.**
    III.—Basque. By W. Van Eys. Pp. xii. and 52. 1883. 3s. 6d.
    IV.—Malagasy. By G. W. Parker. Pp. 66, with Plate. **1883.** 5s.
    V.—Modern Greek. By E. M. Geldart, M.A. Pp. 68. 1883. 2s. 6d.
    VI.—Roumanian. By R. Torceanu. Pp. viii. and 72. 1883. 5s.
    VII.—Tibetan Grammar. By H. A. Jaschke. Pp. viii.-104. 1883. 5s.
    VIII.—Danish. By E. C. Otté. Pp. viii. and 66. 1884. 2s. 6d.
    IX.—Turkish. By J. W. Redhouse, M.R.A.S. Pp. xii. and 204. 1884. 10s. 6d.
    X.—Swedish. By E. C. Otté. Pp. xii.-70. 1884. 2s. 6d.
    XI.—Polish. By W. R. Morfill, M.A. Pp. viii.-64. 1884. 3s. 6d.
    XII.—Pali. By E. Müller. Pp. xvi.-144. 1884. 7s. 6d.
    XIII.—Sanskrit. By H. Edgren. Pp. xii.-178. 1885. 10s. 6d.

TRÜBNER'S ORIENTAL SERIES :—

    Post 8vo, cloth, uniformly bound.

Essays on the Sacred Language, Writings, and Religion of the Parsis. By Martin Haug, Ph.D., late Professor of Sanskrit and Comparative Philology at the University of Munich. Third Edition. Edited and Enlarged by E. W. West, Ph.D. To which is also added, A Biographical Memoir of the late Dr. Haug. By Professor E. P. Evans. Pp. xlviii. and 428. 1884. 16s.

Texts from the Buddhist Canon, commonly known as Dhammapada. With Accompanying Narratives. Translated from the Chinese by S. Beal, B.A., Trinity College, Cambridge, Professor of Chinese, University College, London. Pp. viii. and 176. 1878. 7s. 6d.

The History of Indian Literature. By Albrecht Weber. Translated from the German by J. Mann, M.A., and Dr. T. Zachariae, with the Author's sanction and assistance. 2d Edition. Pp. 368. 1882. 10s. 6d.

A Sketch of the Modern Languages of the East Indies. Accompanied by Two Language Maps, Classified List of Languages and Dialects, and a List of Authorities for each Language. By Robert Cust, late of H.M.I.C.S., and Hon. Librarian of R.A.S. Pp. xii. and 198. 1878. 12s.

The Birth of the War-God: A Poem. By Kálidásá. Translated from the Sanskrit into English Verse, by Ralph T. H. Griffiths, M.A., Principal of Benares College. Second Edition. Pp. xii. and 116. 1879. 5s.

A Classical Dictionary of Hindu Mythology and History, Geography and Literature. By John Dowson, M.R.A.S., late Professor in the Staff College. Pp. 432. 1879. 16s.

Metrical Translations from Sanskrit Writers; with an Introduction, many Prose Versions, and Parallel Passages from Classical Authors. By J. Muir, C.I.E., D.C.L., &c. Pp. xliv.-376. 1879. 14s.

Modern India and the Indians: being a Series of Impressions, Notes, and Essays. By Monier Williams, D.C.L., Hon. LL.D. of the University of Calcutta, Boden Professor of Sanskrit in the University of Oxford. Third Edition, revised and augmented by considerable additions. With Illustrations and Map, pp. vii. and 368. 1879. 14s.

TRÜBNER'S ORIENTAL SERIES—*continued.*

THE LIFE OR LEGEND OF GAUDAMA, the Buddha of the Burmese. With Annotations, the Ways to Neibban, and Notice on the Phongyies, or Burmese Monks. By the Right Rev. P. Bigandet, Bishop of Ramatha, Vicar Apostolic of Ava and Pegu. Third Edition. 2 vols. Pp. xx.-368 and viii.-326. 1880. 21s.

MISCELLANEOUS ESSAYS, relating to Indian Subjects. By B. H. Hodgson, late British Minister at Nepal. 2 vols., pp. viii.-408, and viii.-348. 1880. 28s.

SELECTIONS FROM THE KORAN. By Edward William Lane, Author of an "Arabic-English Lexicon," &c. A New Edition, Revised, with an Introduction. By Stanley Lane Poole. Pp. cxii. and 174. 1879. 9s.

CHINESE BUDDHISM. A Volume of Sketches, Historical and Critical. By J. Edkins, D.D., Author of "China's Place in Philology," "Religion in China," &c., &c. Pp. lvi. and 454. 1880. 18s.

THE GULISTAN; OR, ROSE GARDEN OF SHEKH MUSHLIU'D-DIN SADI OF SHIRAZ. Translated for the first time into Prose and Verse, with Preface and a Life of the Author, from the Atish Kadah, by E. B. Eastwick, F.R.S., M.R.A.S. 2d Edition. Pp. xxvi. and 244. 1880. 10s. 6d.

A TALMUDIC MISCELLANY; or, One Thousand and One Extracts from the Talmud, the Midrashim, and the Kabbalah. Compiled and Translated by P. J. Hershon. With a Preface by Rev. F. W. Farrar, D.D., F.R.S., Chaplain in Ordinary to Her Majesty, and Canon of Westminster. With Notes and Copious Indexes. Pp. xxviii. and 362. 1880. 14s.

THE HISTORY OF ESARHADDON (Son of Sennacherib), King of Assyria, B.C. 681-668. Translated from the Cuneiform Inscriptions upon Cylinders and Tablets in the British Museum Collection. Together with Original Texts, a Grammatical Analysis of each word, Explanations of the Ideographs by Extracts from the Bi-Lingual Syllabaries, and List of Eponyms, &c. By E. A. Budge, B.A., M.R.A.S., Assyrian Exhibitioner, Christ's College, Cambridge. Post 8vo, pp. xii. and 164, cloth. 1880. 10s. 6d.

BUDDHIST BIRTH STORIES; or, Jātaka Tales. The oldest Collection of Folk-Lore extant: being the Jātakatthavannanā, for the first time edited in the original Pali, by V. Fausböll, and translated by T. W. Rhys Davids. Translation. Vol. I. Pp. cxvi. and 348. 1880. 18s.

THE CLASSICAL POETRY OF THE JAPANESE. By Basil Chamberlain, Author of "Yeigio Henkaku, Ichiran." Pp. xii. and 228. 1880. 7s. 6d.

LINGUISTIC AND ORIENTAL ESSAYS. Written from the year 1846-1878. By R. Cust, Author of "The Modern Languages of the East Indies." Pp. xii. and 484. 1880. 18s.

INDIAN POETRY. Containing a New Edition of "The Indian Song of Songs," from the Sanskrit of the Gita Govinda of Jayadeva; Two Books from "The Iliad of India" (Mahábhárata); "Proverbial Wisdom" from the Shlokas of the Hitopadésa, and other Oriental Poems. By Edwin Arnold, C.S.I., &c. Third Edition. Pp. viii. and 270. 1884. 7s. 6d.

THE RELIGIONS OF INDIA. By A. Barth. Authorised Translation by Rev. J. Wood. Pp. xx. and 310. 1881. 16s.

HINDŪ PHILOSOPHY. The Sānkhya Kārikā of Iswara Krishna. An Exposition of the System of Kapila. With an Appendix on the Nyaya and Vaiseshika Systems. By John Davies, M.A., M.R.A.S. Pp. vi. and 151. 1881. 6s.

TRÜBNER'S ORIENTAL SERIES—*continued*.

A MANUAL OF HINDU PANTHEISM. The Vedantasāra. Translated with Copious Annotations. By Major G. A. Jacob, Bombay Staff Corps, Inspector of Army Schools. With a Preface by E. B. Cowell, M.A., Professor of Sanskrit in the University of Cambridge. Pp. x. and 130. 1881. 6s.

THE MESNEVÍ (usually known as the Mesneviyi Sherif, or Holy Mesneví) of Mevlānā (Our Lord) Jelālu-'d-Dīn Muhammed, Er-Rūmī. Book the First. Together with some Account of the Life and Acts of the Author, of his Ancestors, and of his Descendants. Illustrated by a selection of Characteristic Anecdotes as collected by their Historian Mevlānā Shemsu-'d-Dīn Ahmed, El Eflākī El Arifī. Translated, and the Poetry Versified by James W. Redhouse, M.R.A.S., &c. Pp. xvi. and 136, vi. and 290. 1881. £1, 1s.

EASTERN PROVERBS AND EMBLEMS ILLUSTRATING OLD TRUTHS. By the Rev. J. Long, Member of the Bengal Asiatic Society, F.R.G.S. Pp. xv. and 280. 1881. 6s.

THE QUATRAINS OF OMAR KHAYYÁM. A New Translation. By E. H. Whinfield, late of H.M. Bengal Civil Service. Pp. 96. 1881. 5s.

THE QUATRAINS OF OMAR KHAYYÁM. The Persian Text, with an English Verse Translation. By E. H. Whinfield. Pp. xxxii.-335. 1883. 10s. 6d.

THE MIND OF MENCIUS; or, Political Economy Founded upon Moral Philosophy. A Systematic Digest of the Doctrines of the Chinese Philosopher Mencius. The Original Text Classified and Translated, with Comments, by the Rev. E. Faber, Rhenish Mission Society. Translated from the German, with Additional Notes, by the Rev. A. B. Hutchinson, Church Mission, Hong Kong. Author in Chinese of "Primer Old Testament History," &c., &c. Pp. xvi. and 294. 1882. 10s. 6d.

YÚSUF AND ZULAIKHA. A Poem by Jami. Translated from the Persian into English Verse. By R. T. H. Griffith. Pp. xiv. and 304. 1882. 8s. 6d.

TSUNI-‖ GOAM: The Supreme Being of the Khoi-Khoi. By Theophilus Hahn, Ph.D., Custodian of the Grey Collection, Cape Town, Corresponding Member of the Geographical Society, Dresden; Corresponding Member of the Anthropological Society, Vienna, &c., &c. Pp. xii. and 154. 1882. 7s. 6d.

A COMPREHENSIVE COMMENTARY TO THE QURAN. To which is prefixed Sale's Preliminary Discourse, with Additional Notes and Emendations. Together with a Complete Index to the Text, Preliminary Discourse, and Notes. By Rev. E. M. Wherry, M.A., Lodiana. Vol. I. Pp. xii. and 392. 1882. 12s. 6d. Vol. II. Pp. xi. and 408. 1884. 12s. 6d.

HINDU PHILOSOPHY. THE BHAGAVAD GÎTÂ; or, The Sacred Lay. A Sanskrit Philosophical Lay. Translated, with Notes, by John Davies, M.A. Pp. vi. and 208. 1882. 8s. 6d.

THE SARVA-DARSANA-SAMGRAHA; or, Review of the Different Systems of Hindu Philosophy. By Madhava Acharya. Translated by E. B. Cowell, M.A., Cambridge, and A. E. Gough, M.A., Calcutta. Pp. xii. and 282. 1882. 10s. 6d.

TIBETAN TALES. Derived from Indian Sources. Translated from the Tibetan of the Kay-Gyur. By F. Anton von Schiefner. Done into English from the German, with an Introduction. By W. R. S. Ralston, M.A. Pp. lxvi. and 368. 1882. 14s.

LINGUISTIC ESSAYS. By Carl Abel, Ph.D. Pp. viii. and 265. 1882. 9s.

THE INDIAN EMPIRE: Its History, People, and Products. By W. W. Hunter, C.I.E., LL.D. Pp. 568. 1882. 16s.

HISTORY OF THE EGYPTIAN RELIGION. By Dr. C. P. Tiele, Leiden. Translated by J. Ballingal. Pp. xxiv. and 230. 1882. 7s. 6d.

TRÜBNER'S ORIENTAL SERIES—*continued.*

The Philosophy of the Upanishads. By A. E. Gough, M.A., Calcutta. Pp. xxiv.-268. 1882. 9s.

Udanavarga. A Collection of Verses from the Buddhist Canon. Compiled by Dharmatrâta. Being the Northern Buddhist Version of Dhammapada. Translated from the Tibetan of Bkah-hgyur, with Notes, and Extracts from the Commentary of Pradjnavarman, by W. Woodville Rockhill. Pp. 240. 1883. 9s.

A History of Burma, including Burma Proper, Pegu, Taungu, Tenasserim, and Arakan. From the Earliest Time to the End of the First War with British India. By Lieut.-General Sir Arthur P. Phayre, G.C.M.G., K.C.S.I., and C.B. Pp. xii.-312. 1883. 14s.

A Sketch of the Modern Languages of Africa. Accompanied by a Language-Map. By R. N. Cust, Author of "Modern Languages of the East Indies," &c. 2 vols., pp. xvi. and 566, with Thirty-one Autotype Portraits. 1883. 25s.

Religion in China; containing a brief Account of the Three Religions of the Chinese; with Observations on the Prospects of Christian Conversion amongst that People. By Joseph Edkins, D.D., Peking. Third Edition. Pp. xvi. and 260. 1884. 7s. 6d.

Outlines of the History of Religion to the Spread of the Universal Religions. By Prof. C. P. Tiele. Translated from the Dutch by J. Estlin Carpenter, M.A., with the Author's assistance. Third Edition. Pp. xx. and 250. 1884. 7s. 6d.

Si-Yu-Ki. Buddhist Records of the Western World. Translated from the Chinese of Hiuen Tsiang (A.D. 629). By Samuel Beal, Professor of Chinese, University College, London. 2 vols., with a specially prepared Map. Pp. cviii.-242 and viii.-370. 1884. 24s. Dedicated by permission to H.R.H. the Prince of Wales.

The Life of the Buddha, and the Early History of his Order. Derived from Tibetan Works in the Bkah-Hgyur and the Bstan-Hgyur, followed by Notices on the Early History of Tibet and Khoten. By W. W. Rockhill. Pp. xii. and 274. 1884. 10s. 6d.

The Sankhya Aphorisms of Kapila. With Illustrative Extracts from the Commentaries. Translated and Edited by J. R. Ballantyne, LL.D., late Principal of Benares College. Third Edition, now entirely Re-Edited by Fitzedward Hall. Pp. viii. and 464. 1885. 16s.

The Ordinances of Manu. Translated from the Sanskrit. With an Introduction by the late A. C. Burnell, Ph.D., C.I.E. Completed and Edited by Edward W. Hopkins, Ph.D., of Columbia College, New York. Pp. xliv. and 400. 1884. 12s.

The Life and Works of Alexander Csoma De Körös between 1819 and 1842. With a Short Notice of all his Published and Unpublished Works and Essays. From Original and for the most part Unpublished Documents. By T. Duka, M.D., F.R.C.S. (Eng.), Surgeon-Major H.M.'s Bengal Medical Service, Retired, &c. Pp. xii.-234, cloth. 1885. 9s.

TURNER.—The English Language. A Concise History of the English Language, with a Glossary showing the Derivation and Pronunciation of the English Words. By Roger Turner. In German and English on opposite pages. 18mo, pp. viii.-80, sewed. 1884. 1s. 6d.

UNGER.—A Short Cut to Reading: The Child's First Book of Lessons. Part I. By W. H. Unger. Fourth Edition. Cr. 8vo, pp. 32, cloth. 1873. 5d.

Sequel to Part I. and Part II. Fourth Edition. Cr. 8vo, pp. 64, cloth. 1873. 6d. Parts I. and II. Third Edition. Demy 8vo, pp. 76, cloth. 1873. 1s. 6d. In folio sheets. Pp. 44. Sets A to D, 10d. each; set E, 8d. 1873. Complete, 4s.

UNGER.—W. H. Unger's Continuous Supplementary Writing Models, designed to impart not only a good business hand, but correctness in transcribing. Oblong 8vo, pp. 40, stiff covers. 1874. 6d.

UNGER.—THE STUDENT'S BLUE BOOK: Being Selections from Official Correspondence, Reports, &c.; for Exercises in Reading and Copying Manuscripts, Writing, Orthography, Punctuation, Dictation, Précis, Indexing, and Digesting, and Tabulating Accounts and Returns. Compiled by W. H. Unger. Folio, pp. 100, paper. 1875. 2s.

UNGER.—TWO HUNDRED TESTS IN ENGLISH ORTHOGRAPHY, or Word Dictations. Compiled by W. H. Unger. Foolscap, pp. viii. and 200, cloth. 1877. 1s. 6d. plain, 2s. 6d. interleaved.

UNGER.—THE SCRIPT PRIMER: By which one of the remaining difficulties of Children is entirely removed in the first stages, and, as a consequence, a considerable saving of time will be effected. In Two Parts. By W. H. Unger. Part I. 12mo, pp. xvi. and 44, cloth. 5d. Part II., pp. 59, cloth. 5d.

UNGER.—PRELIMINARY WORD DICTATIONS ON THE RULES FOR SPELLING. By W. H. Unger. 18mo, pp. 44, cloth. 4d.

URICOECHEA.—MAPOTECA COLOMBIANA: Catalogo de Todos los Mapas, Planos, Vistas, &c., relativos a la América-Española, Brasil, e Islas adyacentes. Arreglada cronologicamente i precedida de una introduccion sobre la historia cartografica de América. Por el Doctor Ezequiel Uricoechea, de Bogóta, Nueva Granada. 8vo, pp. 232, cloth. 1860. 6s.

URQUHART.—ELECTRO-MOTORS. A Treatise on the Means and Apparatus employed in the Transmission of Electrical Energy and its Conversion into Motive-power. For the Use of Engineers and Others. By J. W. Urquhart, Electrician. Crown 8vo, cloth, pp. xii. and 178, illustrated. 1882. 7s. 6d.

VAITANA SUTRA.—See AUCTORES SANSKRITI, Vol. III.

VALDES.—LIVES OF THE TWIN BROTHERS, JUÁN AND ALFONSO DE VALDÉS. By E. Boehmer, D.D. Translated by J. T. Betts. Crown 8vo, pp. 32, wrappers. 1882. 1s.

VALDES.—SEVENTEEN OPUSCULES. By Juán de Valdés. Translated from the Spanish and Italian, and edited by John T. Betts. Crown 8vo, pp. xii. and 188, cloth. 1882. 6s.

VALDES.—JUÁN DE VALDÉS' COMMENTARY UPON THE GOSPEL OF ST. MATTHEW. With Professor Boehmer's "Lives of Juán and Alfonso de Valdés." Now for the first time translated from the Spanish, and never before published in English. By John T. Betts. Post 8vo, pp. xii. and 512-30, cloth. 1882. 7s. 6d.

VALDES.—SPIRITUAL MILK; or, Christian Instruction for Children. By Juán de Valdés. Translated from the Italian, edited and published by John T. Betts. With Lives of the twin brothers, Juán and Alfonso de Valdés. By E. Boehmer, D.D. Fcap. 8vo, pp. 60, wrappers. 1882. 2s.

VALDES.—SPIRITUAL MILK. Octaglot. The Italian original, with translations into Spanish, Latin, Polish, German, English, French, and Engadin. With a Critical and Historical Introduction by Edward Boehmer, the Editor of "Spanish Reformers." 4to, pp. 88, wrappers. 1884. 6s.

VALDES.—THREE OPUSCULES; an Extract from Valdés' Seventeen Opuscules. By Juán de Valdés. Translated, edited, and published by John T. Betts. Fcap. 8vo, pp. 58, wrappers. 1881. 1s. 6d.

VALDES.—JUÁN DE VALDÉS' COMMENTARY UPON OUR LORD'S SERMON ON THE MOUNT. Translated and edited by J. T. Betts. With Lives of Juán and Alfonso de Valdés. By E. Boehmer, D.D. Crown 8vo, pp. 112, boards. 1882. 2s. 6d.

VALDES.—JUÁN DE VALDÉS' COMMENTARY UPON THE EPISTLE TO THE ROMANS. Edited by J. T. Betts. Crown 8vo, pp. xxxii. and 296, cloth. 1883. 6s.

VALDES.—JUÁN DE VALDÉS' COMMENTARY UPON ST. PAUL'S FIRST EPISTLE TO THE CHURCH AT CORINTH. Translated and edited by J. T. Betts. With Lives of Juán and Alphonso de Valdés. By E. Boehmer. Crown 8vo, pp. 390, cloth. 1883. 6s.

VAN CAMPEN.—THE DUTCH IN THE ARCTIC SEAS. By Samuel Richard Van Campen, author of "Holland's Silver Feast." 8vo. Vol. I. A Dutch Arctic Expedition and Route. Third Edition. Pp. xxxvii. and 263, cloth. 1877. 10s. 6d. Vol. II. *in preparation.*

VAN DE WEYER.—CHOIX D'OPUSCULES PHILOSOPHIQUES, HISTORIQUES, POLITIQUES ET LITTÉRAIRES de Sylvain Van de Weyer, Précédés d'Avant propos de l'Editeur. Roxburghe style. Crown 8vo. PREMIÈRE SÉRIE. Pp. 374. 1863. 10s. 6d.—DEUXIÈME SÉRIE. Pp. 502. 1869. 12s.—TROISIÈME SÉRIE. Pp. 391. 1875. 10s. 6d.—QUATRIÈME SÉRIE. Pp. 366. 1876. 10s. 6d.

VAN EYS.—BASQUE GRAMMAR. See Trübner's Collection.

VAN LAUN.—GRAMMAR OF THE FRENCH LANGUAGE. By H. Van Laun. Parts I. and II. Accidence and Syntax. 13th Edition. Cr. 8vo, pp. 151 and 120, cloth. 1874. 4s. Part III. Exercises. 11th Edition. Cr. 8vo, pp. xii. and 285, cloth. 1873. 3s. 6d.

VAN LAUN.—LEÇONS GRADUÉES DE TRADUCTION ET DE LECTURE; or, Graduated Lessons in Translation and Reading, with Biographical Sketches, Annotations on History, Geography, Synonyms and Style, and a Dictionary of Words and Idioms. By Henri Van Laun. 4th Edition. 12mo, pp. viii. and 400, cloth. 1868. 5s.

VAN PRAAGH.—LESSONS FOR THE INSTRUCTION OF DEAF AND DUMB CHILDREN, in Speaking, Lip-reading, Reading, and Writing. By W. Van Praagh, Director of the School and Training College for Teachers of the Association for the Oral Instruction of the Deaf and Dumb, Officier d'Academie, France. Fcap. 8vo, Part I., pp. 52, cloth. 1884. 2s. 6d. Part II., pp. 62, cloth. 1s. 6d.

VARDHAMANA'S GANARATNAMAHODADHI. See AUCTORES SANSKRITI, Vol. IV.

VAZIR OF LANKURAN: A Persian Play. A Text-Book of Modern Colloquial Persian. Edited, with Grammatical Introduction, Translation, Notes, and Vocabulary, by W. H. Haggard, late of H.M. Legation in Teheran, and G. le Strange. Crown 8vo, pp. 230, cloth. 1882. 10s. 6d.

VELASQUEZ AND SIMONNÉ'S NEW METHOD TO READ, WRITE, AND SPEAK THE SPANISH LANGUAGE. Adapted to Ollendorff's System. Post 8vo, pp. 558, cloth. 1882. 6s.
    KEY. Post 8vo, pp. 174, cloth. 4s.

VELASQUEZ.—A DICTIONARY OF THE SPANISH AND ENGLISH LANGUAGES. For the Use of Young Learners and Travellers. By M. Velasquez de la Cadena. In Two Parts. I. Spanish-English. II. English-Spanish. Crown 8vo, pp. viii. and 846, cloth. 1883. 7s. 6d.

VELASQUEZ.—A PRONOUNCING DICTIONARY OF THE SPANISH AND ENGLISH LANGUAGES. Composed from the Dictionaries of the Spanish Academy, Terreos, and Salvá, and Webster, Worcester, and Walker. Two Parts in one thick volume. By M. Velasquez de la Cadena. Roy. 8vo, pp. 1280, cloth. 1873. £1, 4s.

VELASQUEZ.—NEW SPANISH READER: Passages from the most approved authors, in Prose and Verse. Arranged in progressive order. With Vocabulary. By M. Velasquez de la Cadena. Post 8vo, pp. 352, cloth. 1866. 6s.

VELASQUEZ.—AN EASY INTRODUCTION TO SPANISH CONVERSATION, containing all that is necessary to make a rapid progress in it. Particularly designed for persons who have little time to study, or are their own instructors. By M. Velasquez de la Cadena. 12mo, pp. 150, cloth. 1863. 2s. 6d.

VERSES AND VERSELETS. By a Lover of Nature. Foolscap 8vo, pp. viii. and 88, cloth. 1876. 2s. 6d.

VICTORIA GOVERNMENT.—PUBLICATIONS OF THE GOVERNMENT OF VICTORIA. *List in preparation.*

VOGEL.—ON BEER. A Statistical Sketch. By M. Vogel. Fcap. 8vo, pp. xii. and 76, cloth limp. 1874. 2s.

WAFFLARD and FULGENCE.—LE VOYAGE À DIEPPE. A Comedy in Prose. By Wafflard and Fulgence. Edited, with Notes, by the Rev. P. H. E. Brette, B.D. Cr. 8vo, pp. 104, cloth. 1867. 2s. 6d.

WAKE.—The Evolution of Morality. Being a History of the Development of Moral Culture. By C. Stanilaud Wake. 2 vols. crown 8vo, pp. xvi.-506 and xii.-474, cloth. 1878. 21s.

WALLACE.—On Miracles and Modern Spiritualism ; Three Essays. By Alfred Russel Wallace, Author of "The Malay Archipelago," "The Geographical Distribution of Animals," &c., &c. Second Edition, crown 8vo, pp. viii. and 236, cloth. 1881. 5s.

WANKLYN and CHAPMAN.—Water Analysis. A Practical Treatise on the Examination of Potable Water. By J. A. Wanklyn, and E. T. Chapman. Sixth Edition. Entirely rewritten. By J. A. Wanklyn, M.R.C.S. Crown 8vo, pp. 192, cloth. 1884. 5s.

WANKLYN.—Milk Analysis ; a Practical Treatise on the Examination of Milk and its Derivatives, Cream, Butter, and Cheese. By J. A. Wanklyn, M.R.C.S., &c. Crown 8vo, pp. viii. and 72, cloth. 1874. 5s.

WANKLYN.—Tea, Coffee, and Cocoa. A Practical Treatise on the Analysis of Tea, Coffee, Cocoa, Chocolate, Maté (Paraguay Tea), &c. By J. A. Wanklyn, M.R.C.S., &c. Crown 8vo, pp. viii. and 60, cloth. 1874. 5s.

WAR OFFICE.—A List of the various Military Manuals and other Works published under the superintendence of the War Office may be had on application.

WARD.—Ice : A Lecture delivered before the Keswick Literary Society, and published by request. To which is appended a Geological Dream on Skiddaw. By J. Clifton Ward, F.G.S. 8vo, pp. 28, sewed. 1870. 1s.

WARD.—Elementary Natural Philosophy ; being a Course of Nine Lectures, specially adapted for the use of Schools and Junior Students. By J. Clifton Ward, F.G.S. Fcap. 8vo, pp. viii. and 216, with 154 Illustrations, cloth. 1871. 3s. 6d.

WARD.—Elementary Geology : A Course of Nine Lectures, for the use of Schools and Junior Students. By J. Clifton Ward, F.G.S. Fcap. 8vo, pp. 292, with 120 Illustrations, cloth. 1872. 4s. 6d.

WATSON.—Index to the Native and Scientific Names of Indian and other Eastern Economic Plants and Products, originally prepared under the authority of the Secretary of State for India in Council. By John Forbes Watson, M.D. Imp. 8vo, pp. 650, cloth. 1868. £1, 11s. 6d.

WATSON.—Spanish and Portuguese South America during the Colonial Period. By R. G. Watson. 2 vols. post 8vo, pp. xvi.-308, viii.-320, cloth. 1884. 21s.

WEBER.—The History of Indian Literature. By Albrecht Weber. Translated from the Second German Edition, by J. Mann, M.A., and T. Zacharaiae, Ph.D., with the sanction of the Author. Second Edition, post 8vo, pp. xxiv. and 360, cloth. 1882. 10s. 6d.

WEDGWOOD.—The Principles of Geometrical Demonstration, reduced from the Original Conception of Space and Form. By H. Wedgwood, M.A. 12mo, pp. 48, cloth. 1844. 2s.

WEDGWOOD.—On the Development of the Understanding. By H. Wedgwood, A.M. 12mo, pp. 133, cloth. 1848. 3s.

WEDGWOOD.—The Geometry of the Three First Books of Euclid. By Direct Proof from Definitions Alone. By H. Wedgwood, M.A. 12mo, pp. 104, cloth. 1856. 3s.

WEDGWOOD.—On the Origin of Language. By H. Wedgwood, M.A. 12mo, pp. 165, cloth. 1866. 3s. 6d.

WEDGWOOD.—A Dictionary of English Etymology. By H. Wedgwood. Third Edition, revised and enlarged. With Introduction on the Origin of Language. 8vo, pp. lxxii. and 746, cloth. 1878. £1, 1s.

WEDGWOOD.—Contested Etymologies in the Dictionary of the Rev. W. W. Skeat. By H. Wedgwood. Crown 8vo, pp. viii. and 194, cloth. 1882. 5s.

WEISBACH.—THEORETICAL MECHANICS: A Manual of the Mechanics of Engineering and of the Construction of Machines; with an Introduction to the Calculus. Designed as a Text-book for Technical Schools and Colleges, and for the use of Engineers, Architects, &c. By Julius Weisbach, Ph.D., Oberbergrath, and Professor at the Royal Mining Academy at Freiberg, &c. Translated from the German by Eckley B. Coxe, A.M., Mining Engineer. Demy 8vo, with 902 woodcuts, pp. 1112, cloth. 1877. 31s. 6d.

WELLER.—AN IMPROVED DICTIONARY; English and French, and French and English. By E. Weller. Royal 8vo, pp. 384 and 340, cloth. 1864. 7s. 6d.

WEST and BUHLER.—A DIGEST OF THE HINDU LAW OF INHERITANCE, PARTITION, AND ADOPTION; embodying the Replies of the Sástris in the Courts of the Bombay Presidency, with Introductions and Notes. By Raymond West and J. G. Bühler. Third Edition. Demy 8vo, pp. 1450, sewed. 1884. £1, 16s.

WETHERELL.—THE MANUFACTURE OF VINEGAR, its Theory and Practice; with especial reference to the Quick Process. By C. M. Wetherell, Ph.D., M.D. 8vo, pp. 30, cloth. 7s. 6d.

WHEELDON.—ANGLING RESORTS NEAR LONDON: The Thames and the Lea. By J. P. Wheeldon, Piscatorial Correspondent to "Bell's Life." Crown 8vo, pp. viii. and 218. 1878. Paper, 1s. 6d.

WHEELER.—THE HISTORY OF INDIA FROM THE EARLIEST AGES. By J. Talboys Wheeler. Demy 8vo, cloth. Vol. I. containing the Vedic Period and the Mahá Bhárata. With Map. Pp. lxxv. and 576, cl. 1867, o. p. Vol. II. The Ramayana, and the Brahmanic Period. Pp. lxxxviii. and 680, with 2 Maps, cl. 21s. Vol. III. Hindu, Buddhist, Brahmanical Revival. Pp. xxiv.-500. With 2 Maps, 8vo, cl. 1874. 18s. This volume may be had as a complete work with the following title, "History of India; Hindu, Buddhist, and Brahmanical." Vol IV. Part I. Mussulman Rule. Pp. xxxii.-320. 1876. 14s. Vol. IV. Part II. completing the History of India down to the time of the Moghul Empire. Pp. xxviii. and 280. 1881. 12s.

WHEELER.—EARLY RECORDS OF BRITISH INDIA; A History of the English Settlements in India, as told in the Government Records, the works of old Travellers, and other Contemporary Documents, from the earliest period down to the rise of British Power in India. By J. Talboys Wheeler, late Assistant Secretary to the Government of India in the Foreign Department. Royal 8vo, pp. xxxii. and 392, cloth. 1878. 15s.

WHEELER.—THE FOREIGNER IN CHINA. By L. N. Wheeler, D.D. With Introduction by Professor W. C. Sawyer, Ph.D. 8vo, pp. 268, cloth. 1881. 6s. 6d.

WHERRY.—A COMPREHENSIVE COMMENTARY TO THE QURAN. To which is prefixed Sale's Preliminary Discourse, with additional Notes and Emendations. Together with a complete Index to the Text, Preliminary Discourse, and Notes. By Rev. E. M. Wherry M.A., Lodiana. 3 vols. post 8vo, cloth. Vol. I. Pp. xii. and 392 1882. 12s. 6d. Vol. II. Pp. vi. and 408. 1884. 12s. 6d.

WHINFIELD.—QUATRAINS OF OMAR KHAYYAM. See Trübner's Oriental Series.

WHINFIELD.—See GULSHAN I. RAZ.

WHIST.—SHORT RULES FOR MODERN WHIST, Extracted from the "Quarterly Review" of January 1871. Printed on a Card, folded to fit the Pocket. 1878. 6d.

WHITE.—SPINOZA. See English and Foreign Philosophical Library.

WHITNEY.—LANGUAGE AND THE STUDY OF LANGUAGE; Twelve Lectures on the Principles of Linguistic Science. By W. D. Whitney. Fourth Edition, augmented by an Analysis. Crown 8vo, pp. xii. and 504, cloth. 1884. 10s. 6d.

WHITNEY.—LANGUAGE AND ITS STUDY, with especial reference to the Indo-European Family of Languages. Seven Lectures by W. D. Whitney, Instructor in Modern Languages in Yale College. Edited with Introduction, Notes, Tables, &c., and an Index, by the Rev. R. Morris, M.A., LL.D. Second Edition. Crown 8vo, pp. xxii. and 318, cloth. 1880. 5s.

WHITNEY.—Oriental and Linguistic Studies. By W. D. Whitney. First Series. Crown 8vo, pp. x. and 420, cloth. 1874. 12s. Second Series. Crown 8vo, pp. xii. and 434. With chart, cloth. 1874. 12s.

WHITNEY.—A SANSKRIT GRAMMAR, including both the Classical Language and the older Dialects of Veda and Brahmana. By William Dwight Whitney, Professor of Sanskrit and Comparative Philology in Yale College, Newhaven, &c., &c. 8vo, pp. xxiv. and 486. 1879. Stitched in wrapper, 10s. 6d; cloth, 12s.

WHITWELL.—IRON SMELTER'S POCKET ANALYSIS BOOK. By Thomas Whitwell, Member of the Institution of Mechanical Engineers, &c. Oblong 12mo, pp. 152, roan. 1877. 5s.

WILKINSON.—THE SAINT'S TRAVEL TO THE LAND OF CANAAN. Wherein are discovered Seventeen False Rests short of the Spiritual Coming of Christ in the Saints, with a Brief Discovery of what the Coming of Christ in the Spirit is. By R. Wilkinson. Printed 1648; reprinted 1874. Fcap. 8vo, pp. 208, cloth. 1s. 6d.

WILLIAMS.—A SYLLABIC DICTIONARY OF THE CHINESE LANGUAGE; arranged according to the Wu-Fang Yuen Yin, with the pronunciation of the Characters as heard in Pekin, Canton, Amoy, and Shanghai. By S. Wells Williams, LL.D. 4to, pp. 1336. 1874. £5, 5s.

WILLIAMS.—MODERN INDIA AND THE INDIANS. See Trübner's Oriental Series.

WILSON.—WORKS OF THE LATE HORACE HAYMAN WILSON, M.A., F.R.S., &c.

 Vols. I. and II. Essays and Lectures chiefly on the Religion of the Hindus, by the late H. H. Wilson, M.A., F.R.S., &c. Collected and Edited by Dr. Reinhold Rost. 2 vols. demy 8vo, pp. xiii. and 399, vi. and 416, cloth. 21s.

 Vols. III., IV., and V. Essays Analytical, Critical, and Philological, on Subjects connected with Sanskrit Literature. Collected and Edited by Dr. Reinhold Rost. 3 vols. demy 8vo, pp. 408, 406, and 390, cloth. 36s.

 Vols. VI., VII., VIII., IX., and X. (2 parts). Vishnu Puráná, a System of Hindu Mythology and Tradition. Translated from the original Sanskrit, and Illustrated by Notes derived chiefly from other Puránás. By the late H. H. Wilson. Edited by FitzEdward Hall, M.A., D.C.L., Oxon. Vols. I. to V. (2 parts). Demy 8vo, pp. cxl. and 200, 344, 346, 362, and 268, cloth. £3, 4s. 6d.

 Vols. XI. and XII. Select Specimens of the Theatre of the Hindus. Translated from the original Sanskrit. By the late H. H. Wilson, M.A., F.R.S. Third corrected Edition. 2 vols. demy 8vo, pp. lxxi. and 384, iv. and 418, cloth. 21s.

WILSON.—THOUGHTS ON SCIENCE, THEOLOGY, AND ETHICS. By John Wilson, M.A., Trinity College, Dublin. Crown 8vo, pp. 280, cloth. 1885. 3s. 6d.

WISE.—COMMENTARY ON THE HINDU SYSTEM OF MEDICINE. By T. A. Wise, M.D. 8vo, pp. xx. and 432, cloth. 1845. 7s. 6d.

WISE.—REVIEW OF THE HISTORY OF MEDICINE. By Thomas A. Wise. 2 vols. demy 8vo, cloth. Vol. I., pp. xcviii. and 397. Vol. II., pp. 574. 10s.

WISE.—HISTORY OF PAGANISM IN CALEDONIA. By T. A. Wise, M.D., &c. Demy 4to, pp. xxviii.-272, cloth, with numerous Illustrations. 1884. 15s.

WITHERS.—THE ENGLISH LANGUAGE AS PRONOUNCED. By G. Withers. Royal 8vo, pp. 84, sewed. 1874. 1s.

WOOD.—CHRONOS. Mother Earth's Biography. A Romance of the New School. By Wallace Wood, M.D. Crown 8vo, pp. xvi. and 334, with Illustration, cloth. 1873. 6s.

WOMEN.—THE RIGHTS OF WOMEN. A Comparison of the Relative Legal Status of the Sexes in the Chief Countries of Western Civilisation. Crown 8vo, pp. 104, cloth. 1875. 2s. 6d.

WRIGHT.—FEUDAL MANUALS OF ENGLISH HISTORY, a series of Popular Sketches of our National History compiled at different periods, from the Thirteenth Century to the Fifteenth, for the use of the Feudal Gentry and Nobility. Now first edited from the Original Manuscripts. By Thomas Wright, M.A., F.S.A., &c. Small 4to, pp. xxix. and 184, cloth. 1872. 15s.

WRIGHT.—THE HOMES OF OTHER DAYS. A History of Domestic Manners and Sentiments during the Middle Ages. By Thomas Wright, M.A., F.S.A. With Illustrations from the Illuminations in Contemporary Manuscripts and other Sources. Drawn and Engraved by F. W. Fairholt, F.S.A. Medium 8vo, 350 Woodcuts, pp. xv. and 512, cloth. 1871. 21s.

WRIGHT.—ANGLO-SAXON AND OLD ENGLISH VOCABULARIES. By Thomas Wright, M.A., F.S.A., Hon. M.R.S.L. Second Edition, Edited and Collated by Richard Paul Wulcker. 2 vols. demy 8vo, pp. xx.-408, and iv.-486, cloth. 1884. 28s. Illustrating the Condition and Manners of our Forefathers, as well as the History of the forms of Elementary Education, and of the Languages Spoken in this Island from the Tenth Century to the Fifteenth.

WRIGHT.—THE CELT, THE ROMAN, AND THE SAXON; a History of the Early Inhabitants of Britain down to the Conversion of the Anglo-Saxons to Christianity. Illustrated by the Ancient Remains brought to light by Recent Research. By Thomas Wright, M.A., F.S.A., &c., &c. Third Corrected and Enlarged Edition. Cr. 8vo, pp. xiv. and 562. With nearly 300 Engravings. Cloth. 1875. 14s.

WRIGHT.—THE BOOK OF KALILAH AND DIMNAH. Translated from Arabic into Syriac. Edited by W. Wright, LL.D., Professor of Arabic in the University of Cambridge. Demy 8vo, pp. lxxxii.-408, cloth. 1884. 21s.

WRIGHT.—MENTAL TRAVELS IN IMAGINED LANDS. By H. Wright. Crown 8vo, pp. 184, cloth. 1878. 5s.

WYLD.—CLAIRVOYANCE; or, the Auto-Noetic Action of the Mind. By George Wyld, M.D. Edin. 8vo, pp. 32, wrapper. 1883. 1s.

WYSARD.—THE INTELLECTUAL AND MORAL PROBLEM OF GOETHE'S FAUST. By A. Wysard. Parts I. and II. Fcap. 8vo, pp. 80, limp parchment wrapper. 1883. 2s. 6d.

YOUNG MECHANIC (THE).—See MECHANIC.

ZELLER.—STRAUSS AND RENAN. An Essay by E. Zeller. Translated from the German. Post 8vo, pp. 110, cloth. 1866. 2s. 6d.

PERIODICALS

PUBLISHED AND SOLD BY TRÜBNER & CO.

AMATEUR MECHANICAL SOCIETY'S JOURNAL.—Irregular.

ANTANANARIVO ANNUAL AND MADAGASCAR MAGAZINE.—Irregular.

ANTHROPOLOGICAL INSTITUTE OF GREAT BRITAIN AND IRELAND (JOURNAL OF).—Quarterly, 5s.

ARCHITECT (AMERICAN) AND BUILDING NEWS.—Contains General Architectural News, Articles on Interior Decoration, Sanitary Engineering, Construction, Building Materials, &c., &c. Four full-page Illustrations accompany each Number. Weekly. Annual Subscription, £1, 11s. 6d. Post free.

ASIATIC SOCIETY (ROYAL) OF GREAT BRITAIN AND IRELAND (JOURNAL OF).—Irregular.

BIBLICAL ARCHÆOLOGICAL SOCIETY (Transactions of).—Irregular.
BIBLIOTHECA SACRA.—Quarterly, 3s. 6d. Annual Subscription, 14s. Post free.
BRITISH ARCHÆOLOGICAL ASSOCIATION (Journal of).—Quarterly, 8s.
BRITISH CHESS MAGAZINE.—Monthly, 8d.
BRITISH HOMŒOPATHIC SOCIETY (Annals of).—Half-yearly, 2s. 6d.
BROWNING SOCIETY'S PAPERS.—Irregular.
CALCUTTA REVIEW.—Quarterly, 8s. 6d. Annual Subscription, 34s. Post free.
CAMBRIDGE PHILOLOGICAL SOCIETY (Proceedings of).—Irregular.
ENGLISHWOMAN'S REVIEW.—Social and Industrial Questions. Monthly, 6d.
GEOLOGICAL MAGAZINE, or Monthly Journal of Geology, 1s. 6d. Annual Subscription, 18s. Post free.
GLASGOW, GEOLOGICAL SOCIETY OF (Transactions of).—Irregular.
INDEX MEDICUS.—A Monthly Classified Record of the Current Medical Literature of the World. Annual Subscription, 50s. Post free.
INDIAN ANTIQUARY.—A Journal of Oriental Research in Archæology, History, Literature, Languages, Philosophy, Religion, Folklore, &c. Annual Subscription, £2. Post free.
INDIAN EVANGELICAL REVIEW.—Annual Subscription, 10s.
LIBRARY JOURNAL.—Official Organ of the Library Associations of America and of the United Kingdom. Monthly, 2s. Annual Subscription, 20s. Post free.
MANCHESTER QUARTERLY.—1s. 6d.
MATHEMATICS (American Journal of).—Quarterly, 7s. 6d. Annual Subscription, 24s. Post free.
ORIENTALIST (The).—Monthly. Annual Subscription, 12s.
ORTHODOX CATHOLIC REVIEW.—Irregular.
PHILOLOGICAL SOCIETY (Transactions and Proceedings of).—Irregular.
PSYCHICAL RESEARCH (SOCIETY OF).—Proceedings.
PUBLISHERS' WEEKLY.—The American Book-Trade Journal. Annual Subscription, 18s. Post free.
PUNJAB NOTES AND QUERIES.—Monthly. Annual Subscription, 10s.
REVUE COLONIALE INTERNATIONALE.—Monthly. Annual Subscription, 25s. Post free.
SCIENTIFIC AMERICAN.—Weekly. Annual subscription, 18s. Post free.
SUPPLEMENT to ditto.—Weekly. Annual subscription, 24s. Post free.
SCIENCE AND ARTS (American Journal of).—Monthly, 2s. 6d. Annual Subscription, 30s.
SPECULATIVE PHILOSOPHY (Journal of).—Quarterly, 4s. Annual Subscription, 16s. Post free, 17s.
SUNDAY REVIEW.—Organ of the Sunday Society for Opening Museums and Art Galleries on Sunday.—Quarterly, 1s. Annual Subscription, 4s. 6d. Post free.
TRÜBNER'S American, European, and Oriental Literary Record.—A Register of the most Important Works Published in America, India, China, and the British Colonies. With occasional Notes on German, Dutch, Danish, French, Italian, Spanish, Portuguese, and Russian Literature. Subscription for 12 Numbers, 5s. Post free.
TRÜBNER & CO.'S Monthly List of New and Forthcoming Works, Official and other Authorised Publications, and New American Books. Post free.
WESTMINSTER REVIEW.—Quarterly, 6s. Annual Subscription, 22s. Post free.
WOMAN'S Suffrage Journal.—Monthly, 1d.

TRÜBNER & CO.'S CATALOGUES.

Any of the following Catalogues sent per Post on receipt of Stamps.

Africa, Works Relating to the Modern Languages of. 1d.
Agricultural Works. 2d.
Arabic, Persian, and Turkish Books, printed in the East. 1s.
Assyria and Assyriology. 1s.
Bibliotheca Hispano-Americana. 1s. 6d.
Brazil, Ancient and Modern Books relating to. 2s. 6d.
British Museum, Publications of Trustees of the. 1d.
Dictionaries and Grammars of Principal Languages and Dialects of the World. 5s.
Educational Works. 1d.
Egypt and Egyptology. 1s.
Guide Books. 1d.
Important Works, published by Trübner & Co. 2d.
Linguistic and Oriental Publications. 2d.
Medical, Surgical, Chemical, and Dental Publications. 2d.
Modern German Books. 2d.
Monthly List of New Publications. 1d.
Pali, Prakrit, and Buddhist Literature. 1s.
Portuguese Language, Ancient and Modern Books in the. 6d.
Sanskrit Books. 2s. 6d.
Scientific Works. 2d.
Semitic, Iranian, and Tatar Races. 1s.

TRÜBNER'S
COLLECTION OF SIMPLIFIED GRAMMARS
OF THE
PRINCIPAL ASIATIC AND EUROPEAN LANGUAGES.

Edited by REINHOLD ROST, LL.D., Ph.D.

The object of this Series is to provide the learner with a concise but practical Introduction to the various Languages, and at the same time to furnish Students of Comparative Philology with a clear and comprehensive view of their structure. The attempt to adapt the somewhat cumbrous grammatical system of the Greek and Latin to every other tongue has introduced a great deal of unnecessary difficulty into the study of Languages. Instead of analysing existing locutions and endeavouring to discover the principles which regulate them, writers of grammars have for the most part constructed a framework of rules on the old lines, and tried to make the language of which they were treating fit into it. Where this proves impossible, the difficulty is met by lists of exceptions and irregular forms, thus burdening the pupil's mind with a mass of details of which he can make no practical use.

In these Grammars the subject is viewed from a different standpoint; the structure of each language is carefully examined, and the principles which underlie it are carefully explained; while apparent discrepancies and so-called irregularities are shown to be only natural euphonic and other changes. All technical terms are excluded unless their meaning and application is self-evident; no arbitrary rules are admitted; the old classification into declensions, conjugations, &c., and even the usual *paradigms* and tables, are omitted. Thus reduced to the simplest principles, the Accidence and Syntax can be thoroughly comprehended by the student on one perusal, and a few hours' diligent study will enable him to analyse any sentence in the language.

Now Ready.

Crown 8vo, cloth, uniformly bound.

I.—**Hindustani, Persian, and Arabic.** By the late E. H. Palmer, M.A. Second Edition. Pp. 112. 5s.

II.—**Hungarian.** By I. Singer, of Buda-Pesth. Pp. vi. and 88. 4s. 6d.

For continuation see next page.

Trübner's Simplified Grammars—continued.

III.—**Basque.** By W. VAN EYS. Pp. xii. and 52. 3s. 6d.
IV.—**Malagasy.** By G. W. PARKER. Pp. 66. 5s.
V.—**Modern Greek.** By E. M. GELDART, M.A. Pp. 68. 2s. 6d.
VI.—**Roumanian.** By M. TORCEANU. Pp. viii. and 72. 5s.
VII.—**Tibetan.** By H. A. JÄSCHKE. Pp. viii. and 104. 5s.
VIII.—**Danish.** By E. C. OTTÉ. Pp. viii. and 66. 2s. 6d.
IX.—**Turkish.** By J. W. REDHOUSE, M.R.A.S. Pp. xii. and 204. 10s. 6d.
X.—**Swedish.** By Miss E. C. OTTÉ. Pp. xii. and 70. 2s. 6d.
XI.—**Polish.** By W. R. MORFILL, M.A. Pp. viii. and 64. 3s. 6d.
XII.—**Pali.** By E. MÜLLER, Ph.D. Pp. xvi.-144. 7s. 6d.
XIII.—**Sanskrit.** By H. EDGREN. Pp. xii.-178. 10s. 6d.

The following are in preparation:—

SIMPLIFIED GRAMMARS OF

Albanian, by WASSA PASHA, Prince of the Lebanon.
Assyrian, by Prof. SAYCE.
Bengali, by J. F. BLUMHARDT, of the British Museum.
Burmese, by Dr. E. FORCHAMMER.
Cymric and Gaelic, by H. JENNER, of the British Museum.
Egyptian, by Dr. BIRCH.
Finnic, by Prof. OTTO DONNER, of Helsingfors.
Hebrew, by Dr. GINSBURG.
Icelandic, by Dr. WIMMER, Copenhagen.
Lettish, by Dr. M. I. A. VÖLKEL.
Lithuanian, by Dr. M. I. A. VÖLKEL.
Malay, by W. E. MAXWELL, of the Inner Temple, Barrister-at-Law.
Portuguese, by WALTER DE GRAY BIRCH.
Prakrit, by HJALMAR EDGREN, Lund, Sweden.
Russian, Bohemian, Bulgarian and Serbian, by W. R. MORFILL, of Oxford.
Sinhalese, by Dr. EDWARD MÜLLER.

Arrangements are being made with competent Scholars for the early preparation of Grammars of **German, Dutch, Italian, Chinese, Japanese,** *and* **Siamese.**

LONDON: TRÜBNER & CO., LUDGATE HILL.